I0892666

PASSAGES

TEXT AND TRANSFORMATION IN THE PARASHA

PASSAGES

TEXT AND TRANSFORMATION IN THE PARASHA

Rabbi Michael Hattin

URIM PUBLICATIONS
Jerusalem • New York

Passages: Text and Transformation in the Parasha

by Michael Hattin

Copyright © 2012 by Michael Hattin

All rights reserved
No part of this book may be used
or reproduced in any manner whatsoever without
written permission from the copyright owner,
except in the case of brief quotations
embodied in reviews and articles.

Typesetting by Ariel Walden

Printed in Israel

First Edition

ISBN: 978-965-524-119-8

Urim Publications, P.O. Box 52287, Jerusalem 91521 Israel

Lambda Publishers Inc.
527 Empire Blvd., Brooklyn, New York 11225 U.S.A.
Tel: 718-972-5449 Fax: 718-972-6307

mh@ejudaica.com

www.UrimPublications.com

Contents

Introduction

THE TORAH is the most studied book in human history. It has been intensively studied and commented upon for thousands of years. It seems doubtful at this point that anything new could be added to the accumulated material. At the same time, the Torah encourages each one of us, in every generation and in every place, to study it and then study it again, indicating that something of value can yet be extracted, something of significance and inspiration that speaks to *us*. The voluminous exegesis composed without interruption, from ancient times until the present, is the best indicator that every age must find its own particular meaning in the Torah's eternal text.

What of our age? We live in a time of endless amounts of information that are accessible immediately. But the awesome potential inherent in such a reality comes at a price. Our instantaneous need for answers breeds impatience and the glut of knowledge fosters superficiality. On our modern communication highways, passing and shallow familiarity has taken the place of enduring and profound connection. The implications for Torah learning are immense: For many people, the measured, deliberate and methodical study of a text and then its equally diligent review in the hopes of extracting additional insight, are no longer values.

This book is a modest attempt to introduce some of the medieval luminaries of biblical interpretation via a careful literary reading of the text. While most have heard of Rashi, fewer are familiar with any of his actual comments. And some have not heard of Ibn Ezra, Ramban, or Seforno at all. Those that have heard of them have generally not studied them as part of a process of detailed textual study. But to appreciate the medievals or the *Rishonim* as they are known (literally "the first ones"), demands such study. Unlike modern exegetes that aim for comprehensive treatments of the subject, the medievals offer us only glimpses. And unlike contemporary commentaries that can be appreciated as independent compositions, the interpretations of the medievals are bound up with the original text. But in their brief remarks, usually presented as local comments to individual verses, the medievals extend to us an unrivalled invitation: to consider, to reflect, to engage and to continue the study. The work of these commentaries, who are often in veiled conversation with each other and with the vast corpus of earlier Rabbinic literature that inspired them, forms the foundation for all subsequent exegesis of the Torah text, up until the present day.

I will not present a systematic study of their methodologies or those of other interpreters who were their contemporaries, whose combined labors spanned some five-hundred years. Nor will I attempt to provide any sort of comprehensive anthology of their comments on a given passage. Instead, we will meet the *Rishonim* through the study of the text itself, via an attentive reading that will naturally introduce them. To study the text thoroughly is to anticipate many of their questions and to more fully appreciate their solutions. A student who immediately consults Rashi or Ramban after a cursory reading of the verse has failed to adequately understand either one of them or the subtleties of the verse itself. While the methodologies of the *Rishonim* will not be explored explicitly in this book, the careful reader will detect certain trends concerning their approaches as he or she covers the material.

While this is a book and books are *read*, the Torah encourages us to engage in *study*. The difference between the two is not only a function of cognitive intensity but of relational context as well. Reading is typically a solitary pursuit that takes place at home or in the library, but study in our text tradition takes place with others. In the classroom or the Beit Midrash, we actively engage others in the enterprise, exchanging ideas, challenging interpretations and arriving at a more complex and nuanced understanding as a result. I have benefited immensely from fruitful exploration with my students and peers, whether at the Pardes Institute in Jerusalem where I have been privileged to teach for the last decade or else at the Golf Manor Synagogue in Cincinnati where some of these ideas first began to germinate. My advice to my readers is therefore to follow up their reading with *study*.

All of the translations, whether of the biblical text or the commentaries, are my own. As any translator knows, sometimes exactitude must be sacrificed for the sake of readability. Any shortcomings in the translation are therefore mine alone. While this book can be read as an independent work, I recommend that it be read in conjunction with the *Parasha*. Each article in the book, however, is self-contained. I have made no assumptions about the reader's prior familiarity with the primary material.

I would like to take this opportunity to thank all of those who have assisted me in this undertaking, a project that took much longer than anticipated. The following pages detail their kindness and generosity. Much of this material was originally composed as a series of online articles for the Virtual Beit Midrash of Yeshivat Har Etzion. This innovative institution, where I was privileged to study for a number of years, has benevolently allowed me the opportunity to rework and publish the original articles in book format. A special thanks is extended to Jerrold Rapaport who graciously offered to read the manuscript and offered many helpful and insightful comments.

I would especially like to thank my dear wife Rivka and wonderful children Elchanan, Akiva, Hillel, Leeba and Miriam. All of them provided constant inspiration and support. I also commend my siblings Lisa and Allan Garman, Adrienne, Simone and Alan for their encouragement. This book is dedicated to my dear parents Bernard and Cecille Hattin who taught me one of life's most precious lessons: "דרך ארץ קדמה לתורה".

—Michael Hattin
Alon Shevut
Kislev 5772, December 2011
mh.passages@gmail.com

ספר זה מוקדש באהבה רבה
לעילוי נשמת אבינו מורנו
ראובן אביי בן מרדכי ולאה פריש ז"ל
ולכבוד הורינו היקרים שיחיו
שרה בת אליעזר ופינקל פריש
הרב יום טוב משה בן חיים וזלאטא הרצוג
הדסה בת הרב אברהם ורבקה הרצוג

מאת בניהם
לאה ואברהם חיים הרצוג

This sefer is dedicated in loving memory
to our dear father
Dr. Rudolf A. Frisch, ob"m
And with great honor
to our dear parents
Mrs. Susana Frisch
Rabbi Jerome and Hadassah Herzog

By their children
Leah and Rabbi Avram Herzog
All of them have fostered in us love of all wisdom,
dedication to learning, and true *Yir'at Shamayim*.

The author gratefully acknowledges
the following people, whose initial backing
for this project was instrumental:

Drs. David and Ann Alden

Deanna Basofin

Charles Benis

Dr. Michael and Carol Dean

Edwin and Judith Epstein
in honor of their children and grandchildren

Marvin and Lois Epstein

Melvin Gallant in honor of Barbara Gallant

Mark and Faith Goldstein
in memory of dear parents Arnold and Arlene Sachs

Dr. Leonard and Marilyn Horwitz and family

Jeff and Malkah Karas in memory of Harvey Karas

Steve and Sarah Levy

Dr. Ned and Esti Mehlman
in memory of Chaim ben Nachman Mehlman

Dr. Sidney and Miriam Peerless עליהם השלום

Steve and Beatrice Rosedale and family

Dr. Bruce and BG Younger

BREISHEET

The Creation of Man and Woman

Genesis 1:1-6:8

PARASHAT BREISHEET introduces God the creator. Summoning substance from nothingness and imposing order where chaos had reigned, God imbues His creation with direction, meaning and purpose. During a climactic process that lasts for seven days, primal energy is transformed into amorphous substance and then given more distinct shape. Inexorably, lifeless water and inert earth yield vegetation, primitive life, more complex creatures and finally, man. The penultimate sixth day describes the formation of land animals and then humanity:

> The Lord said: "Let the earth bring forth living creatures after their kind, animals and creeping things and wild beasts of the earth after their kind," and it was so. The Lord fashioned (ויעש) the wild beasts of the earth after their kind, and the animals after their kind, and the things that creep upon the earth after their kind, and the Lord saw that it was good. The Lord said: "Let us make man (אדם) in our image after our likeness, and they will have dominion over the fish of the sea, the birds of the sky, the animals and all of the earth, and over all things that creep upon the earth." The Lord created (ויברא) the man (האדם) in His image, in the image of the Lord He created him, male and female He created them. The Lord blessed them and said to them: "Be fruitful and multiply and fill the earth and rule over it; exercise dominion over the fish of the sea, the birds of heaven and over all life that crawls upon the earth." . . . The Lord saw all that He had fashioned and behold, it was very good; it was evening and it was morning, the sixth day. (*Breisheet* 1:24–31)

It is useful to contrast the terseness that characterizes the formation of the other creatures with the lavish lexicon that describes the fashioning of man. All of the other creatures are formed by a single, curt divine fiat that is then concretized with action: "The Lord *said*: 'Let the earth bring forth living creatures after their kind . . .' and it was so. The Lord *fashioned* the beasts of the earth after their kind . . . and the Lord saw that it was good" (1:24–25). The creation of man, on the other hand, is introduced with a unique expression of divine deliberation that is unparalleled in the entire account: "The Lord said: 'Let us make man in our image after our likeness . . .'" (1:26). Humanity emerges not as the result of an irresistible divine utterance, but rather as the consequence of God's involvement and care.

Furthermore, rather than being the product of fashioning or עשייה, man is the product of creation or בריאה. The Hebrew root ברא that signifies creation typically describes a particular exploit of which only God is capable: the bringing forth of substance from oblivion. Thus, the Torah begins its account of creation *ex nihilo* with בראשית ברא א־להים, "In the beginning of the Lord's creation . . ." Similarly, the enormous sea monsters fashioned on the fifth day (1:21) are described as having been "created" by God (ויברא א־להים את התנינם) because their creation points to His unparalleled capabilities (commentary of the Ramban, 13th century, Spain). The threefold use of the term "ברא" in the short context of man's formation must therefore signify the divine conferral of absolute uniqueness: Man is a creature unlike any other, endowed with unrivaled potential and fashioned in "the Lord's image." Lastly, it is only after the creation of man that the entire enterprise of the six days is characterized as "*very* good," while at the completion of every other stage of creation, the text states only that "it was good." The implication is clear: The creation of humanity is the culminating act without which the universe is incomplete.

Notwithstanding all of the above nuances that emerge from a careful reading, the *mechanism* of this creation of man – its various steps and stages – is shrouded in utter mystery. Only the broadest possible outline, enough to trace the essential attributes of the first humans and no more, is here recorded. Male and female make their appearance contemporaneously, in a lyrical verse emphasizing their equal claim to the divine image. Together they stand to receive God's blessing and instruction, and to secure the imprimatur of "God saw all that He had done and behold, it was very good."

Our account of the creation closes with the blessing and the sanctity with which God infused the Shabbat (2:1–3). On that final day, God ceased from His creative work in order to demonstrate His utter mastery, for only an omnipotent being transcending the cosmos could arrest the overwhelming forces that He had marshaled to fashion it. In the end, each precious component of the grand scheme of creation was positioned in its proper place, the motion of every individual particle was in perfect synchrony with all of the others, and a harmonious structure framed the whole. If approached as a divine biography, this first creation account portrays God as sovereign over His pristine and flawless universe, forever.

The Second Account

There is a second account of creation that is preserved in Parashat Breisheet, a lengthier story that concerns the fashioning of the first man from the dust of the earth, his naming of all of the other animals, the subsequent preparation of Chava as his companion, and the fabled garden of delights into which God then invites them. "The listener assumes that this is a different account," avers Rashi (11th century, France) in remarks later echoed by his grandson the Rashbam (12th century, France), "but it is nothing more than the expansion of the first narrative" (commentary to 2:8). This time, however, the story ends less favorably, for the first humans are soon tempted by the stealthy serpent to abrogate God's command and to eat of the redolent but forbidden fruit of the tree of knowledge. In consequence, God banishes them from idyllic Eden so that they must henceforth eke out their sustenance from the obstinate earth until they succumb to the mortality that God sternly decrees for them. According to this second account,

> God Lord fashioned the man (האדם) out of dust from the earth, and breathed into his nostrils the breath of life, and the man became a living creature . . . God Lord said: "It is not good for the man to be alone, I will fashion a compatible mate to

help him..." The man named all of the animals and all of the birds of the sky and all of the beasts of the field, but did not find among them any that were compatible. God Lord caused a very deep sleep to fall upon the man and he slept; He took one of his ribs and closed up the flesh in its place. God Lord built the rib that He had taken from the man into a woman and brought her to the man. The man said: "This time it is bone from my bones and flesh from my flesh; this one shall be called woman (אשה) for she was fashioned from man (איש)." A man shall therefore leave his father and his mother, and shall cleave to his wife and become one flesh . . . (*Breisheet* 2:19–24)

There are numerous differences between this account and the one narrated by the Torah in chapter 1. First of all, the four-letter name of God is now employed in conjunction with every mention of the creator. Secondly, this narration of man's creation is much more detailed. We learn, for instance, that the first human was fashioned from the dust of the earth, the אדמה from which his name *Adam* was derived. We are also informed that although he was corporeally complete in every respect, man remained inanimate until the breath of life was blown into his nostrils. But the most glaring distinctions between the two accounts concern the creation of the first woman. Here, her creation is temporally far removed from that of her mate, occurring only after a naming exercise that encompasses all of the creatures on the planet! Her formation is not a freestanding creative act by God but rather consists of the removal and refashioning of the first man's rib.

Let us interpret the data according to Rashi, who harmonizes the two narratives by suggesting that the Torah employs a progression from the general to the specific. The first account is a schematic outline of the creation, acquainting us with some of its basic contours. All existence is brought into being by the deliberate will of the creator, and all creatures are organized hierarchically, with humanity at the apex. This humanity, composed of male and female, is the recipient of God's blessing as well as of His charge. The more detailed second account explores the relationship between the male and female in greater depth, and indicates that her fashioning was precipitated by the male's dawning awareness of his aloneness. Though he searched valiantly among the other creatures, calling them by name in the hopes of locating a compatible mate, none of them could fill the existential void. Therefore the woman, unlike the females of other species, was fashioned from the man's very body, intimating an organic cohesiveness that made them unique.

Primary vs. Secondary

But there are more ominous implications to this reading. If the woman is formed out of the rib of the man, then he precedes her in time as well as in divine intention. Man is the primary being while she is secondary, fashioned from his bone and flesh. This generative rib is hardly a vital organ; it is in fact removed with no adverse side effects, further highlighting the female's inferior status. The overall hierarchy of creation in which humanity occupies the most exalted position is therefore mirrored by a further hierarchy within humanity itself.

This unsympathetic approach is adopted by Rabbi David Kimchi (13th century, Provence, known by the acronym "Radak"):

> . . . The human differs from all other creatures that were initially created as male and female. The first human, however, was male. This is a reflection of his

> advantage over the female, whom he rules and whom he can command, for she is like one of his limbs. This is unlike all the other species in which the male enjoys no such preference . . . Since the man is the essence of creation having been created first, and the woman is subsidiary having been fashioned from his substance, he therefore possesses greater abilities than the female in all respects, whether physical or intellectual. (commentary to 2:18)

In the more progressive formulation of Rabbi Ovadiah Seforno (16th century, Italy), the female is only slightly less exalted than the male, but superior he must be. He would otherwise not be entitled to appoint her as his agent to fulfill his needs. The kernel of these views is preserved in the Midrash, which states that "Shemuel says: God took one of the man's ribs from among the others" (Breisheet Rabbah, Parasha 17:6). In the more intriguing but less flattering Talmudic formulation (TB *Berachot* 61a, *Eiruvin* 18b), the opinion is expressed that the removal of the "rib" actually refers to the tailbone of the man! Clearly then, by understanding that the woman is fashioned from the man's rib or some other minor part of his anatomy, Radak's conclusions are not only conceptually warranted but also inevitable.

The critical word in the text around which the above analysis pivots is the infamous "rib": "God Lord caused a very deep sleep to fall upon the man and he slept; He took one of his ribs and closed up the flesh in its place. God Lord built the rib that He had taken from the man into a woman and brought her to the man." In the original Hebrew, the word for "rib" is "צלע." Thus, "He took one of his צלעות and closed up the flesh in its place. God Lord built the צלע that He had taken from the man into a woman and brought her to the man." That צלע unequivocally means "rib" is, however, by no means certain. Of the forty usages of the term in the Tanakh, only two of them mean "rib" in the narrow anatomical sense, and these two are the very subjects of our verses! The vast majority of the other usages of the term pertain to the world of architecture:

> You shall fashion the boards of the Tabernacle out of acacia wood lengthwise. You shall make twenty boards for the southern direction . . . as for the second side (צלע) of the Tabernacle on the north, also twenty boards . . . you shall make five bars of acacia wood for the boards of one side (צלע) of the Tabernacle . . . and for the second side (צלע). (*Shemot* 26:15–27)

The word צלע is therefore more precisely rendered as "side," from which is derived the cognate meaning of "rib," since the ribs define the symmetrical halves of the upper body. In fact, the acacia boards of the Mishkan, repeating elements arrayed in a row on either side, perfectly parallel the structure of the rib cage. This alternative meaning of צלע is borne out by the verb form of the word which occurs in the account of Jacob's nocturnal struggle with the mysterious "man" (*Breisheet* 32:25–33). Jacob emerged from the contest victorious but suffering from a dislocated hip. As dawn broke, Jacob passed the place that he called Penuel, still nursing his injury and limping: "The sun was rising when he passed Penuel, and he was limping (צולע) upon his thigh." Here, the verb צולע is clearly associated with "side" (and not rib), since to limp is to place all of one's weight on one side of the body.

Revisiting the Text

Having established that צלע can be confidently rendered as "side," we can now reassess the meaning of our narrative:

> God Lord caused a very deep sleep to fall upon the man and he slept; He took one of his *sides* and closed up the flesh in its place. God Lord built the *side* that He had taken from the man into a woman and brought her to the man. The man said: "This time it is bone from my bones and flesh from my flesh; this one shall be called women (אשה) for she was fashioned from man (איש) . . ." (2:21–23)

According to this reading, the first woman was not fashioned from the first man's rib at all but rather from his "side." Or, to adopt the striking imagery of the opposing view recorded in the Midrash and Talmud: "דו פרצופין נברא האדם" – "the man was initially created as a two-faced creature" (TB *Berachot* 61a). In other words, the first human being was not exclusively male, but rather a composite being made up of a male and female that were fused to each other at the back! The act of "creating" the female did not consist of fashioning a woman from Adam's rib but rather of separating a binary being possessing both male and female aspects into two discrete and independent entities.

This novel approach does not represent an interpretive flight of fancy but is actually grounded in the text itself. Rabbi Avraham Ibn Ezra (12th century, Spain) alerts us to the provocative language of the first creation narrative that supports the reading:

> The Lord said: "Let us make *man* in our image after our likeness, and *they* will have dominion over the fish of the sea, the birds of the sky, the animals and all of the earth, and over all things that creep upon the earth." The Lord created the man in His image, in the image of the Lord He created *him*, male and female He created *them*. The Lord blessed them and said to them: "Be fruitful and multiply and fill the earth and rule over it . . ." (1:26–28)

As Ibn Ezra explains in his characteristically concise manner, the oscillation between the description of the human in the singular ("let us make *man*"/"in the image of God He created *him*") versus the plural ("*they* will have dominion"/"male and female He created *them*") alludes to the twinned state of the first human being and to the process of separation that is only spelled out later in chapter 2 (commentary to 1:26, end). Therefore, the original human being was a single creature made up of male and female components. These two components that together constitute this dual creature are fashioned simultaneously by God and remain joined together during the bestowal of the blessing and the charge. Only later are the two equal halves divided from each other in order to form freestanding male and female human beings. In other words, there is no implied hierarchy between the male and female, there is no temporal gap in the act of their creation and there is no special measure of divine regard accorded to a man formed first and thus deemed primary in the scheme of things. Instead, the Torah introduces us to a precious human being, a male/female creature that is formed and fashioned to be the crown of creation, beloved of the creator and guided by His word, complete in every respect and lacking only the individuality and sharply defined gender that corporeal discreteness confers. This alternative view of the Ibn Ezra, directly deriving from the Midrashic interpretation that "the initial human being was a two-faced creature" was adopted earlier by Rashi (comments to

2:21) and later by R. Moshe ben Nachman (Ramban, 13th century, Spain – comments to 2:18). It is also the more supported view in the Talmud.

Adam or Earthling? Alone or Together?

The name of this initial human being is "Adam," but aside from the first time that the name appears ("let us make man [*Adam*]"), it is always preceded by the definite article ("the"). Only towards the end of the Parasha does it decisively become the proper name of the first man (4:25, et al.). The use of the definite article indicates that a proper name is *not* being used, any more than one would say "the Abraham" or "the Sarah." How then to understand the first time that the word *Adam* occurs, absent the preceding definite article? Translating the critical phrase as "Let us make man" only returns us to the reading of Radak and Seforno that ascribes primacy to the male, but Rashi, Ibn Ezra and Ramban negated that interpretation by suggesting that the initial human being was not exclusively a man at all!

Knowledge of a simple rule of grammar obviates the difficulty. When a noun or an idea is introduced for the first time, the definite article cannot be employed, since its use would imply prior familiarity with the thing. When one describes his new blue cap to his friend, he introduces the thing by saying "I bought *a* new blue cap." Only after this initial introduction can he go on to describe its features by employing the definite article: "*the* new blue cap has a visor and an elastic strap." Introducing the blue cap for the first time by saying "I bought *the* new blue cap" is unintelligible if his friend knows nothing of the blue cap to begin with. In similar fashion, when the vessels of the Tabernacle are described in the latter half of Sefer Shemot (chapter 25), the first mention of each vessel is always without the definite article ("make an ark . . . a table . . . a menorah") while all subsequent usages incorporate it ("place the testimony in the ark . . . the showbread on the table . . . the lights upon the menorah").

Bearing in mind the second narrative indicating that the human being was fashioned out of the dust of the earth or אדמה, it is now possible to more precisely render this oft-quoted phrase. "נעשה אדם" ought to be translated as "let us make an *earthling*" and all subsequent uses of the term which employ the definite article ought to be translated as "*the* earthling":

> The Lord said: "Let us make *an earthling* in our image after our likeness, and they will have dominion over the fish of the sea, the birds of the sky, the animals and all of the earth, and over all things that creep upon the earth." The Lord created *the earthling* in His image, in the image of the Lord He created him, male and female He created them. (*Breisheet* 1:26–27).

The term "earthling" is, of course, genderless, just as the first human being was not exclusively male or female but rather both.

Having established the literary validity of the reading, we must now ask the succeeding question: What might be the deeper meaning of this interpretation? Why would God so curiously fashion the first human being? Rephrasing the question more contextually, we might ask: If the first human being was in fact a two-faced creature, from the outset composed of a complete male and complete female joined at the back, in what way could this earthling have been "alone?" After all, the impetus for the act of separation was aloneness: "God Lord said: 'It is not good for the earthling to be alone, I will fashion a compatible mate to help him'" (2:18). Where is there aloneness when two human beings are so close that they actually share the same body? What greater togetherness could there be than the same blood coursing through their veins and the same flesh and bone holding them in inextricable embrace?

In the course of the Talmudic discussion on this topic, a query is raised which at first glance appears to be either casuistic or else tongue-in-cheek but actually is terribly profound: "According to the one who says that the first human being was a two-faced creature joined at the back, which one walked first, the male or the female?" (TB *Berachot* 61a). With this question, the Talmud alerts us to an untenable feature of the initial state, notwithstanding all of its intimacy. When two human beings are joined at the back, of necessity one leads and the other is forced to follow. When two human beings are joined at the back, they can never look in the same direction. When two human beings are joined at the back, they are not the paradigm of unity but actually the loneliest creatures in the cosmos. The Talmud thus casts the awesome tension of the human male/female relationship in sharp relief. A man and a woman may join in legal union, may agree to economic partnership, may even share with each other the very warmth of their bodies, but if they are not looking in the same direction, if their goals remain disparate, if one leads and the other follows against his or her will, then true togetherness will always elude them. Only by looking eye to eye, walking side by side and focusing on the same destination will they truly merit to become man and woman, איש ואשה, one flesh. This is the profound lesson of "דו פרצופין נברא האדם".

FOR FURTHER STUDY:

(1) The Talmudic discussion concerning the formation of the woman is quite extensive (TB *Berachot* 61a, *Eiruvin* 18b). While both views are expressed – face versus tailbone – it is mainly the latter that is on the defensive, as the Talmud adduces various proof-texts to support the "two-faced" reading. The medieval commentaries effectively temper the Talmudic debate, since the difference between a rib and a side is less pronounced than the difference between the face and the tailbone!

NOACH

The Tower of Bavel

Genesis 6:9-11:32

THE SERENITY of Eden is short-lived. Soon enough, Adam and Chava abrogate God's simple and forthright command and are banished from the lush and fertile garden. Kayin, their firstborn, filled with jealous rage over God's rejection of his offering of the fruits of mediocrity, murders his own brother Hevel and is himself then driven into exile east of Eden. Enosh, Adam's grandson, presides over humanity's first flirtation with corrosive idolatry. By the conclusion of last week's Parasha, the stage is set for the cleansing floodwaters to wash away the stain of man's insufferable crimes. Only righteous Noach and his family are preserved. Enjoined by compassionate God to build a colossal ark, he obediently completes the protracted project, as all terrestrial species under the heavens begin to anxiously gather at its titanic portal. With the approach of the black storm clouds, the passengers – human and non-human – board. As Noach slowly closes the hatch and God seals it tight, the old man casts one final, plaintive glance towards the verdant landscape. For the denizens of the dank and dusky craft, there will be no turning back.

For just over a year, the floodwaters cover the earth, obliterating all evidence of man's wrongdoing. The ark, tossed by colossal swells, bobs up and down uncertainly, its sturdy timbers – Noach's cautious handiwork – groaning but holding firm. Finally, with an alarming rasp that sends the creatures scrambling for cover, the ark touches down upon the rocky slopes of Mount Ararat. Time now passes interminably, but it will be a few more months before it is possible to disembark. At last, with dazzling sunlight streaming down through an opening in the dense cloud cover, Noach flings open the hatch and breathes deeply. Creatures of every sort tentatively descend to the black and sweet-smelling earth, lingering only briefly in the shadow of the ark's massive eaves before bounding away to replenish the decimated planet.

Noach offers sacrifices of thanksgiving and God accepts, solemnly pledging never to again bring floodwaters upon the earth to obliterate all life. As the leaden storm clouds dissipate, a rainbow, and with it, the promise of God's renewed covenant, brightens the heavens.

The Building of the Tower

Leaving the ark behind him but still reeling from the tragedy of the flood, Noach turns to cultivating the fruit of the vine. Drunk with the numbing juice of its bounty, he brings disgrace upon himself, thus casting his life's final centuries (!) in ignominy. His three sons and their wives beget children, and those children more still, as humanity begins to restore the world. Families give rise to clans, clans merge to become tribes, and as the Parasha draws toward its conclusion, the first outlines of nascent nations emerge. Before relating the genealogical list that culminates with Avram, the Torah turns its attention to the fertile valley of Shinar (Sumer), the cradle of civilization. Here, in a terse passage constituting nine verses, unfolds one of the most inexplicable events in all of the Tanakh, the building of the tower of Bavel:

> All of the land was one language and united in one cause. When they had traveled from the east, they found a valley in the land of Shinar and settled there. Each one of them said to his fellow: "Come, let us make bricks and temper them with fire," so that the bricks became as stone and the clay was used as mortar. They said: "Come, let us build ourselves a city and a tower that reaches to the heavens. Let us make a name for ourselves, lest we be scattered upon the face of the whole earth." God came down to see the city and the tower that the mortals had built. God said: "Behold, they are one nation and have one language, and this is what they have begun to do. Now, shall nothing that they attempt be withheld from them? Let us then descend and confuse their language, so that a person will no longer comprehend the language of his neighbor!" God scattered them from there upon the face of the whole earth, and they ceased to build the city. Therefore, the name of that place was Bavel, for there God confused (בלל) the language of them all, and from there God scattered them upon the face of the whole earth. (*Breisheet* 11:1–9)

The above episode has generated much discussion among the classical commentaries as well as among modern secular scholars of the Bible. The latter tended to view the incident as a late literary invention, a fanciful explanation for the existence of a polyglot humanity that was cleverly anchored in historical reality by referring to the ancient Mesopotamian stepped pyramidal structure known as the ziggurat. These colossal mud brick shrines, their ruins offering mute testimony to humanity's early attempts to ascend heavenward, once dotted the valley between the great rivers of the Euphrates and the Tigris, the site of the ancient empires of Sumer and Akkad, Assyria and Babylon. For many of these modern thinkers our passage is a fairytale, possessing little didactic value.

The classical commentaries, in contrast, were much less concerned with the factual backdrop to the story and much more interested in its message. For them, the important questions to be asked did not focus upon the extraneous historical details of the story, but rather upon its thematic content: What were the people's intentions in erecting the tower? Why was God upset with their endeavor? How did the confusing of their language constitute an appropriate response to their act of indiscretion? These sorts of questions address the kernel rather than the husk and to them must be added what is perhaps the most consequential query of all: If the brotherhood of mankind is one of the Torah's touchstones, then why did merciful God so blatantly undermine humanity's first and most bold attempt at achieving that noble objective?

The Interpretation of Rashi

We will begin by considering Rashi's explanation, itself based upon Rabbinic traditions preserved in the Talmud and Midrash. Rashi suggests that the unity of purpose that characterized the building of the city and tower actually had menacing implications:

> The "united cause" indicates that they gathered with unified counsel, saying: "It is not acceptable that He has taken the heavens for Himself. Let us ascend to the firmament and wage war against him!" Alternatively, the "united cause" means that they arrayed themselves against the one God of the universe... [When the text states that "God came down to see the city and the tower that the children of Adam had built"], whose children would we have expected to have built it, the offspring of donkeys or camels?! Rather, it refers to the builders as the children of that first man Adam, who denied God's beneficence when he blamed Him for his own transgression. [After partaking of the fruit of the tree of knowledge] he said: "The woman that *You* gave to me brought me the fruit of the tree and I ate it." Similarly, these people denied God's kindness in saving them from the flood, and instead rebelled against Him . . . (commentary to 11:1, 5)

For Rashi, the work of the tower builders was nothing less than an attempt to unseat God from His heavenly throne, to rebel against His rule and to reject His laws. When the builders speak of erecting the tower in order to "make a name for ourselves" (*Breisheet* 11:4) they imply that they intend to take God's place in the scheme of things by usurping His authority. In simpler terms, Rashi understands their intentions as idolatrous, the concrete conclusion to antediluvian man's first questioning of God's absoluteness. In the colorful language of the Midrash (Breisheet Rabbah 38:6), the builders said: "Let us make a tower, place an idolatrous image at its summit, and put a sword in the idol's hand, so that it appears to be attacking Him!" The awesome power of a united humanity is here subverted to construct an edifice that will proclaim the ascent of man and the downfall of God.

Thematically, Rashi's comments go far in explaining God's displeasure, but they fail to persuasively address the nature of His reaction. Other than fulfilling a strictly punitive function, how does the imposition of language barriers that result in dispersion constitute fitting retribution for the iniquity of idolatry? Perhaps for Rashi the scattering of a united humanity is meant to suggest a kind of nemesis. Did they not brazenly attempt to shatter the axiom of God's absolute oneness by championing polytheism and the belief in many quarrelling gods? Should they not now suffer the fate that they wished to impose upon Him, by experiencing the divisiveness engendered by multiple languages?

More problematic for Rashi is that the explanation that he advances falls short in addressing the tower builders' own words. After all, they indicate that their intent is not primarily to "make a name for themselves," but rather to avoid the eventuality of being scattered: "Come, let us build ourselves a city and a tower that reaches to the heavens. Let us make a name for ourselves, *lest we be scattered upon the face of the whole earth*" (11:4). It is the fear of dispersion, the unity that precedes it and the disunity that follows, which underscores the entire account.

The View of Ibn Ezra

Rabbi Avraham Ibn Ezra advances a very different explanation to the passage, obliquely rejecting Rashi's reading (as he often does) in his opening remarks (commentary to 11:3–7):

> The builders of the tower were not so foolish as to believe that they could really ascend to heaven . . . the text itself indicates that their desire and objective was to build a great city to dwell in, and to erect a high tower to serve as a glorious

> sign marking the city's position for those who traveled outside of it, such as the shepherds. Of course the tower would also immortalize their own name as long as it would stand. This is the meaning of "Let us make a name for ourselves" . . . do not be astonished by [their expression of building a tower] "that reaches to the heavens" for this is simply hyperbolic, just as Moshe himself described the cities of the Canaanites as "greatly fortified up to the heavens." (*Devarim* 1:28)
>
> These builders did not want to separate from each other, but God decreed otherwise... [God confused their beliefs and their languages] because religious differences create jealousy and hatred, as do differences of tongue . . . some say that God caused them to forget their single language, but I maintain that after they were scattered, Nimrod ruled over Bavel and then other kings arose. After many years, that generation died out and their language was forgotten. God dispersed them and this was beneficial for them, as the verse states: "fill the earth" . . . (*Breisheet* 1:18)

For Ibn Ezra, our section's failure to explicitly mention idolatry is because the episode has nothing to do with the Torah's polemic against paganism. Elsewhere, the Torah roundly condemns this most insidious of human inventions, but not here. The objective of the tower builders was not to wage war against God but simply to avoid being separated! In their great city, they peacefully dwelt together as one and the purpose of the soaring spire rising in their midst was to mark their location forever. From far and wide, people would see the tower and gather to its base, thus ensuring that their concord would never be undone.

God descends to see the work of man and He is displeased. Recognizing that the key to their continued success is their unity, God sows dissension by confusing their tongues. But, says Ibn Ezra, Rashi's unforgettable depiction of maddening confusion, of "this one asking for a brick and that one bringing mortar instead, and the disgruntled bricklayer then smashing his fellow's skull" (commentary to *Breisheet* 11:7), is nothing more than a Midrashic flourish. In fact, says Ibn Ezra, God scatters a monoglot humanity to different regions and climes. It is this geographic dispersion that ultimately gives rise to the development of different languages, and not, as Rashi would have it, the other way around.

The Curse of "Unity"

Ibn Ezra's interpretation admirably addresses the text. It provides a sound rationale for the valley dwellers' ambition to build the tower, explains the significance of the recurring "dispersion" refrain, and even succeeds in cohesively linking God's retribution to the people's transgression. Humanity erred in choosing unity, God corrects by imposing divergence. The people desired to be together in language and purpose, God insists that they be divided. The glaring difficulty with Ibn Ezra's explanation is that it seems to negate one of Judaism's most revolutionary and treasured ideals: the fellowship of humankind! After all, was not the Torah the very first document in human history to proclaim that all human beings, regardless of their race, ethnicity, or religion, were the descendents of the same mother and father, and imbued by their creator with the divine image? Was not the most noble vision of the "world's end" the one that was foreseen by the prophets of Israel, who proclaimed an ideal future of human harmony, universal peace among peoples, and a full rapprochement with God? Why then would God disrupt the work of the tower, history's earliest expression of brotherhood and concord, by "confusing the tongue" of its builders? Why would He introduce to the world distinctions of language and then religion, fiery sparks of contention that, as Ibn Ezra noted above, have ignited terrible conflagrations of hatred that have incinerated innumerable human lives?

Ibn Ezra concludes that "God dispersed them and this was beneficial for them, as the verse states: 'fill the earth,'" but in keeping with his characteristic terseness, he fails to elaborate. The meaning of these words, however, provides us with the clue for deciphering the enigmatic episode of the tower of Bavel. It seems that there are, in fact, two possible paradigms of human unity. In the first, all members of the group live in the same location, speak the same language, subscribe to the same principles and are practically uniform in every respect. Those that stray even slightly from the unifying parameters to become non-conformists are shunned and excluded, so that the "purity" of the congregation is preserved. The advantage of such an arrangement is that it fosters teamwork, concern for the collective, and a readiness to sublimate individual goals for the service of the whole. Its glaring disadvantage, however, is that on the personal level this paradigm tends to breed mediocrity, as well as a diffusion of responsibility whenever group goals are engaged. Since individual goals and accomplishments are anathema to the homogeneity of the group, people soon learn to not try too hard. In more extreme expressions of this social collectivist paradigm, individuality is utterly crushed under the weight of intolerance and tyranny.

Rejecting Totalitarianism

The massive building projects that have always typified totalitarian regimes, whether ancient or modern, are all quite similar in program and in form to the "tower that reaches to the heavens." The awesome expenditures of human effort and capital used to realize these grandiose schemes have been matched only by a corresponding indifference to the value of individual human life and to its inviolability. In radical forms of totalitarianism, such as communism or Nazism, the individual is meaningless and his personal creativity is a crime. Value of the person is calculated solely according to collective needs and national goals. Obviously, under such a regime, the state-sponsored service of God, the gods or even the lack of gods, is going to be superficial, manipulative, and harsh. Extrapolating the paradigm to the global dimension, a humanity that raises up the tower of Bavel may achieve the elusive goal of unity, but only at the unacceptably high cost of sacrificing every attribute that makes a person or a nation unique.

God, therefore, scatters the people and disrupts their plans. While geographic, linguistic and cultural differences are frequently responsible for fostering intolerance, they can also provide us with the hope of one day achieving understanding, acceptance, and appreciation of the other. This is of course the other unity paradigm, in which human diversity is respected even while collective objectives are engaged. In the Torah's vision, every person and every nation has a special role to play in the unfolding saga of human history, and each one is called upon to forge their unique relationship with God. We may not surrender our individual identities or national cultures in the name of an overwhelming unity which cannot save.

That does not mean, of course, that there are no standards or absolutes. In fact, it is precisely in Parashat Noach that the so-called "Seven Noachide Principles" are introduced, no doubt in anticipation of the tower of Bavel episode. While Judaism regards these fundamental moral and religious laws as obligatory upon all people and all civilizations, it does not demand that all people serve God or help men with the same mind-numbing uniformity. In the same way, our Torah requires of its adherents to keep the 613 commandments, but within that framework, allowance is made for a relatively broad spectrum of religious expression. Diversity must not be confused with moral relativism, and respect for differences confounded by the unfiltered acceptance of every form of evil under the sun. The messianic vision of the end of days, the ideal of universal peace and brotherhood, nowhere implies the erasing of national characteristics or individual goals but only the revolutionary recognition that pluralism and human diversity must go hand in hand with observance of God's laws.

The forty-odd centuries of human history that have elapsed since the episode of the tower have confirmed Ibn Ezra's thesis. Nations and peoples have been divided by language, culture and religion and have waged many unnecessary and destructive wars as a result. But during all that time, the Torah's ideal of fellowship has preserved the hope of better days. We look forward to an age in which religious and national differences will no longer serve as impediments to the worship of the one, true God, an age in which cultural diversity will be appreciated as an expression of God's purpose in fashioning the human species. Let us not forget that the tenth chapter of Breisheet, namely the genealogical table that introduces the tower of Bavel episode, lists the descendents of Noach's three sons, "each in his land according to his language" (10:5). All together, there are about seventy names that are enumerated, each one associated with a different geographical location and language. While it may be surmised that the primary purpose of the passage is to provide foreshadowing for the story of the tower and the dispersion that follows, it must also indicate that the diversity of humanity is bound up with the Torah's objectives. After all, these verses describe the divided state of affairs without any negative value judgments, hardly to be expected if the thrust of the tower account was to regard the scattering of humanity as a divine punishment. At the tower of Bavel, we learned that true human unity is not achieved through the erasing of borders and the adoption of a pervasive universal culture, but rather through a respect and love for contrasts, and by the recognition that humanity and its service of God can only be enriched by diversity.

FOR FURTHER STUDY:

(1) The messianic vision of Yeshayahu best expresses the ideal of nations that come together to fulfill God's laws but nevertheless maintain their unique cultural identities:

> It will be at the end of days that the mountain of the house of God will be established upon the highest peak and raised up over the hills, and all of the nations will stream to it. Many peoples will go and say: "Let us go up to the mountain of God and to the house of the Lord of Ya'acov and He will teach us His ways and we will follow in His paths, for out of Zion shall go forth teaching and the word of God from Jerusalem." (*Yeshayahu* 2:2–3)

In this connection, also see *Yeshayahu* 66:18–24 and *Zechariah* 14:16–21.

LECH LECHA

Avram the Smasher of Idols

Genesis 12:1-17:27

PARASHAT LECH Lecha introduces us to one of the greatest odysseys of faith in our tradition. With Adam and Chava an ancient memory and the story of Noach's deliverance from the flood now faded, the Torah invites us to embark upon the next phase of human history. "There are ten generations from Adam to Noach and ten generations from Noach to Avraham" declare the Sages in the Mishna, Tractate *Avot* 5:2, echoing the formulaic genealogies listed at the ends of Parashat Breisheet and Parashat Noach respectively. While each of these ten-generation periods constitutes a self-contained epoch of human development, both nevertheless point to the same overall progress: The pristine work of creation begins to yield before human civilizations that steadily advance socially, culturally and technologically, even as they stagnate morally. Avraham's entry onto the stage, against the backdrop of mighty idolatrous empires ascendant, now redirects that progress in a most unexpected fashion:

> Get thee out of thy land and thy birthplace and thy father's home, to the land that I will show you. I will make you a great nation and I will bless you, and I will make your name great and you shall be a blessing. I shall bless those that bless you and curse the one who curses you, and all of the nations of the earth shall be blessed on your account. (*Breisheet* 12:1–3)

The Context of God's Pronouncement

So startling is this divine pronouncement and so unanticipated that our only recourse is to ponder the events that spark it, as recorded at the end of Parashat Noach. But that passage provides us with few helpful clues to explain the sudden divine interest in our protagonist Avram:

> Terach had lived for seventy years when he begat Avram, Nachor and Haran. These are the descendents of Terach: Terach begat Avram, Nachor and Haran, and Haran begat Lot. Haran died during his father Terach's lifetime, in the land of his birth in Ur Kasdim. Avram and Nachor took wives for themselves. Avram's wife was named Sarai, and Nachor's wife was named Milka, the daughter of Haran who was the father of Milka and Yiska. Sarai was barren and had no children . . . (*Breisheet* 11:26–30)

Who are Avram and Sarai and why does God choose them and their descendents to be the vehicle for His revelation in the world? The textual details concerning the early lives of Avram and Sarai are far too scant to convincingly construct a meaningful profile. We are told nothing of their upbringing and family life, their significant interactions with others or their relationship with God. The biographical details concerning Avram's marriage to Sarai certainly foreshadow later events but seem unrelated to the journey about to unfold. Only their birthplace is spelled out: Ur, a prosperous and culturally advanced city state located on the lower reaches of the Euphrates River, close to where it drains into the Persian Gulf. It should be noted that according to many modern scholars, the city of Ur had, by the time of Avram, passed its golden age as a commercial and cultural center. Not a small number of migrants had already ventured forth beyond its stalwart mud brick walls in search of a better life elsewhere.

> Terach took Avram his son, his grandson Lot the son of Haran, and his daughter-in-law Sarai who was Avram's wife. They left with them from Ur Kasdim to journey to the land of Canaan, but having reached Charan they remained there. Terach lived to be two hundred and five, and died in Charan. (11:31–32)

No consequential facts seem to emerge from these final verses of Parashat Noach. The circumstances surrounding the trek from Ur to Canaan are cryptically concealed. It is true that the route of the journey can be reliably retraced, with the small clan no doubt traveling northwest along the settled length of the Euphrates River, in effect traversing the lower eastern arc of the geographical area known as the Fertile Crescent and leaving behind in their wake every major center of civilization in Mesopotamia. The initial causes for the move, though, remain obscured. Adding to the mystery, the expedition comes to an abrupt end in Charan and there Terach perishes, far from his destination.

Thus does the Torah introduce us to Avraham, the patriarch of our people. It is an introduction both brief as well as enigmatic. Noach, in contrast, had been presented with much more consequential detail, even as the relevant passage was more concise than our own: "These are the generations of Noach. Noach was a righteous man, without blemish in his generations. Noach walked with God" (6:9). The fact that Noach was singled out to fulfill God's purpose, to be saved from the flood and to save all life with him, is immediately comprehensible in the light of such an introduction. But the spartan sketch of Avraham which precedes his odyssey, grounded in names and places and not much else, seems insufficient to justify the lavish and loving attention that God bestows upon him as our Parasha opens.

The Ramban casts our query in sharp relief:

> This section of the Torah has not adequately explained the issue. Why should God tell Avraham "leave your land and I will extend to you the greatest good that has ever been" without first indicating to us that Avraham was a servant of God or a perfectly righteous individual? Or the text should state a reason for God's injunction to Avraham to leave his land, namely that he will achieve closeness to God in the new location. The convention of the Torah is to state "walk before Me, hearken to My voice and I will reward you" as we find by David and Shelomo. This in fact is the pattern throughout the Torah. "If you will follow My statutes . . . then I will provide the rains in their due season" (*VaYikra* 26:3), "if you will surely hearken to My voice . . . then God will elevate you above all of the other nations of the earth" (*Devarim* 28:1). Concerning Yitzchak, it states "on account of Avraham My servant (*Breisheet* 26:24)." But to promise Avraham such

reward solely on account of his leaving his land makes no sense! (commentary to *Breisheet* 12:3)

Avram's Early Life

Following the lead of the Ramban, we must search for an account of Avraham's beginnings. Only by exploring the events of Avraham's childhood, youth and maturation into adulthood shall we be able to appreciate why he is rightly regarded as the founder of our people. But how shall we conduct such a search? The text of the Torah is silent on this topic. Perhaps by reading between the lines, by carefully considering the significance of the meager details that are recorded in the Torah, we will be able to reconstruct the omitted material. Let us begin by reading the passage more closely:

> Terach had lived for seventy years when he begat Avram, Nachor and Haran. These are the descendents of Terach: Terach begat Avram, Nachor and Haran; and Haran begat Lot. Haran died during his father Terach's lifetime, in the land of his birth in Ur Kasdim. Avram and Nachor took wives for themselves. Avram's wife was named Sarai, and Nachor's wife was named Milka, the daughter of Haran who was the father of Milka and Yiska. Sarai was barren and had no children.
>
> Terach took Avram his son, his grandson Lot the son of Haran, and his daughter-in-law Sarai who was Avram's wife. They left with them from Ur Kasdim to journey to the land of Canaan, but having reached Charan they remained there. Terach lived to be two hundred and five, and died in Charan. (11:26–32)

Clearly, the focus of these verses is not Avram at all, but rather his father Terach. It is Terach's life that is here summarized. His fatherhood is recorded, the untimely death of one of his children is recounted, and the marriage of his other sons is outlined. It is Terach who initiates the journey to Canaan, and it is Terach's death in Charan that concludes the passage. In almost all respects, the structure of this passage is no different than that of any of the other genealogies that punctuate the narratives of Sefer Breisheet. They too speak of so-and-so becoming a father to so-and-so at such-and-such an age, and later begetting more sons and daughters. There are, however, two details that are unconventional and these perhaps are the key to advancing our investigation.

First of all, only in the account of Terach's life are place names mentioned. The birthplace of none of the other descendents of Noach (or of Adam for that matter) engages the Torah's attention. Where they were born or lived or from whence they commenced their journeys is apparently inconsequential. Only in our passage do we learn that the family of Avram hailed from the city of Ur and left that place to travel westward to Canaan, eventually arriving in Charan.

Secondly, of all of the ten generations mentioned at the end of Parashat Noach, only in the case of Terach is his death recorded. In contrast, concerning his forebears the Torah relates events according to an unchanging formula:

> These are the generations of Shem. Shem was a hundred years old when he begat Arpachshad, two years after the flood. Shem lived for five hundred years after the birth of Arpachshad, and begat sons and daughters.
>
> Arpachshad lived thirty-five years and begat Shelach. Arpachshad lived for four hundred and three years after the birth of Shelach, and begat sons and daughters . . . (11:10–13)

The Midrashic Account

To further probe the significance of these details, we direct our attention to the Midrash Aggadah. This vast corpus of homiletic literature, preserved in various collections, was for the most part committed to writing between the 5th and 11th centuries CE. It should be noted, however, that the Midrash is the repository for an immense amount of much earlier traditions and explanations of the text. Some of these traditions were transmitted orally down through the generations until it became necessary, due to the unfavorable exigencies of the time, to record them in written form. Some of these traditions, in fact, are so ancient they were understood by later commentaries to constitute authentic truths handed down to Moshe at Sinai. Of course, the Midrash often employs fanciful, fantastic and sometimes forced language to explicate a biblical passage, but the careful reader must move beyond literalism to uncover the deeper import of the matter. Let us carefully consider what is probably one of the most celebrated stories in the entire corpus and attempt to extract its essence, a profound matter related through a whimsical tale that even a child could appreciate. While, technically speaking, the Midrash is often inspired by local questions raised by the text (i.e., How did Haran die in his father's presence? What is the meaning of the place name "Ur?" etc.), it often conveys greater truths:

> R. Chiyya the grandson of R. Adda of Jaffa explained: Terach was a manufacturer of idols. He once went away somewhere and left Avram to sell them in his stead. A man came and wished to buy one. "How old are you?" Avram asked him. "Fifty or sixty" was the reply. "Woe to such a man!" exclaimed Avram, "You are sixty years old and yet would worship a day-old object?!" The man became ashamed and left.
>
> On another occasion, a woman came with a plate full of fine flour and requested: "Take this and offer it to them." Avram took a stick in his hand and smashed all of the idols and then put the stick in the hands of the largest. When his father returned, he demanded "Who did this to them?" Avram responded, "I cannot conceal it from you. A woman came with a plate full of fine flour and requested me to offer it to them. One of them exclaimed 'I must eat first!' while another exclaimed 'I must eat first!' Thereupon, the largest arose, took the stick and broke the others." "Why do you make sport of me," Terach cried out, "have they any knowledge?" Avram retorted, "If only your ears would listen to what your mouth is saying!"
>
> Thereupon, Terach seized his son and delivered him to Nimrod. "Let us worship the fire!" bellowed Nimrod. "Let us rather worship the water which extinguishes fire," replied Avram. "Then let us worship water!" roared the tyrant. "Let us rather worship the clouds which bear the water," replied Avram. "Then let us worship the clouds!" cried Nimrod. "Let us rather worship the winds which disperse the clouds," replied Avram. "Then let us worship the winds!" exclaimed the king. "Let us rather worship human beings who withstand the wind," replied Avram. "You are just bandying words," said Nimrod, "I worship only the fire, and will cast you into it. Let the God in whom you believe save you from its effects!… Avram was cast into the fiery furnace and emerged unscathed.
>
> Haran was present [at the debate] and said to himself: "If Avram prevails then I am on his side and if Nimrod prevails then I am on his side." When Avram emerged, they said to him: "Whose side are you on?" He replied: "Avram's." They then cast

him into the fiery furnace but his innards were scorched; he died in the presence of his father Terach. Thus the text relates that "Haran died during his father Terach's lifetime, in the land of his birth in Ur Kasdim." (Breisheet Rabbah 38:13)

Scene One: Avram vs. His Father

This Midrashic account can be conveniently divided into two sections. The first describes Avram's souring relationship with his father and with his community, and the second tells of his hostile confrontation with proverbial Nimrod, tyrannical ruler of Ur, and with the bystanders at that debate. We might title the whole tale "Avram's Confrontations with Authority" but let us deal with each section in turn. In the first part, we are told that Terach was a purveyor of idols. This is a way of indicating that he was not simply another anonymous inhabitant of Ur, a peddler of vegetables or of earthenware pots, a government bureaucrat or a craftsman, a wagon driver or a porter. Rather, he was a salesman of molten images, a provider of gods to the masses. In other words, opines the Midrash, Terach was no outsider to the polytheistic culture of Ur; he was happily attracted to its blandishments and intimately connected to its ceremony. He was, in fact, personally and financially invested in its success, his idol shop even serving the community as a sort of local shrine.

Avram, therefore, is first introduced to us as an idolater who had been raised in a household, a community and a culture that was wholly devoted to idolatry. His father Terach and Terach's father before him had conscientiously adopted the values and traditions of their birthplace. They had imbibed a world view much concerned with the tangible, the temporal and the sensual, but hopelessly ignorant of the spiritual, the eternal and the absolute. And they had transmitted that way of life to their children and to their children's children after them. To employ the language of aged Yehoshua, successor of Moshe, who surveyed early Jewish history in a passage that was later incorporated into the Haggadah recited at the Seder: "Thus says God Lord of Israel: Your ancestors dwelt on the banks of the Euphrates from time immemorial, Terach the father of Avraham and the father of Nachor, and they worshipped other gods . . ." (*Yehoshua* 24:2)

Thus it was that in his father's absence, Avram was appointed by Terach to take his place as a proud and upstanding idol vendor. This appointment is indicative of the implicit trust that Terach put in his young son, of his hopes that one day Avram would faithfully (and profitably) continue the traditions of his ancestors. Terach perceived his young son Avram as idolatry's bright future, even as the city of Ur and its vaunted civilization were already in decline. We might paraphrase the Sages here: "Terach received the tradition from Ur and transmitted it to Avram . . ."

Avram, however, had different plans. Seizing upon the opportunity of being put in charge of the shop, Avram proceeded to put a serious dent in the idol sales by engaging potential customers in less-than-salesmanlike conversation. This section of the Midrash deals with doubts. It emerges that quite early in life, Avram had started to question the accepted norms of his society. While yet a child or a young lad, he had already embarked on the journey of enquiry that would eventually lead him to reject his father's faith and his people's way of life. But note how that investigation was essentially driven by rational considerations! In his interactions with the customers, Avram always returned to the same point: It is illogical for a grown person to worship a day-old object. In other words, young Avram charged polytheism with falsehood because it could not provide a reasonable explanation for existence.

Avram's new ideas engender conflict. No longer able to abide by his father's beliefs, Avram translates into action his conceptual break with his family and with the society around him by smashing the idols in his father's shop. He is the first iconoclast (breaker of idols) in human history! In so doing, Avram unleashes a process that will change forever the way that enlightened human beings apprehend the world and their place in it. This first scene of the Midrash ends with Avram irrevocably parting with his father Terach and with Terach's ancient way of life. Terach, unmoved by these new ideas and instead threatened by them, now appeals to a higher authority to intervene so that the natural order of things might be restored.

Scene Two: Avram vs. Nimrod

The second scene of the Midrash, more charged than the first, describes the exchange that takes place between Avram and Nimrod, king of Ur. Although the Torah itself does not link the name of Nimrod to the city of Ur, the Midrash consciously chooses to do so. The Nimrod of biblical fame, mentioned en passant in the earlier genealogy of Cham, is, according to *Breisheet* 10:8–12, a Mesopotamian tyrant, an empire builder and a gifted hunter. The Midrash intentionally inserts Nimrod at precisely this juncture, implying that Avram's revolution of faith represents a danger to all entrenched tyrannies that employ their absolute power to exercise unjust rule.

The scene opens with the two debating the respective merits of worshipping fire, water, clouds and the wind. We are struck by Nimrod's willingness to so readily surrender the worship of the first for the next in line, a sure indication of his mercurial and impulsive temperament and a sorry commentary on the capricious and irrational nature of polytheistic worship. We also note that each time Avram undermines Nimrod's demands, he does so by employing logic and reason, much as he did when he engaged his father's customers in debate. How are we to swear our allegiance to fire, Avram queries, when it can so easily be extinguished by water? Shall we then regard it as a god? And what of water being borne off by the winds? Are these not clear indications that these things can neither save their supplicants nor respond to their entreaties? For Nimrod, however, rational considerations are immaterial: When he demands that fire be worshipped by his subjects, then they must submit. If he suddenly substitutes water as the new bedrock of belief, then obey they blindly must.

There is an additional dimension to their exchange, for we know that fire, water, clouds and wind are natural forces that behave with erratic and destructive power. Any student of ancient history knows that all primitive polytheistic societies worshipped the forces of nature in the hopes of securing their favor and deflecting their displeasure. Avram's intent is therefore to cast doubt on the established faith of generations! Why worship a multiplicity of natural forces when each one of them is limited, irregular and undependable? Why attempt to engage deities who, much like their earthly counterparts, are endlessly locked in confrontation in a selfish attempt to secure supremacy?

But now, after the matter of the clouds, Avram unexpectedly redirects the discussion by interjecting the matter of man: "Let us then worship the human being who withstands the clouds . . ." At first glance, the insertion seems to be a non sequitur, for while water extinguishes fire, clouds bear water, and wind moves clouds, man does not exclusively or even prominently withstand the wind. But by invoking the place of human beings at precisely this point in the discussion, Avram bluntly intimates to Nimrod the real objective of the hunter king's theology: to justify the absolute rule of one human being over his brethren. Only a system that refuses to recognize any higher absolute authority whose law is binding on king and serf alike, can grant Nimrod the temporal powers that he so craves so that he might continue to hold the people of Ur in thralldom. In a world bereft of God, the mighty exercise their ruthless rule unchecked. It is no wonder that Nimrod, clearly perceiving that ethical monotheism spells the ultimate end of oppressive totalitarianism, wisely decides to dispense with Avram before his revolution can take hold among the subjects of Ur. But although he is cast into the fiery furnace (hence the place name אור that means "fire"), Avram miraculously survives. In Ur is thus kindled a great ideological conflagration ignited by Avram's views; his providential deliverance from the flames, constituting the only miraculous element in the story, points to his unexpected escape from the fiery wrath of the despot.

But that is not the end of the story. Haran, Avram's younger brother, is now asked to choose sides, but he is not saved from the flames. This is because while he mouths allegiance to Avram's God, his heart remains unmoved. Haran's new-found "faith" is opportunistic, conditioned by the desire to be on the winning team. His affirmation is not the patient product of sincere enquiry – a sort of spiritual storehouse amassed over the years – and it signals no deep-rooted willingness to be transformed. It is a faith that is superficial, spurious and pretend. It therefore cannot sustain in the face of life's vicissitudes, and cannot inspire when the believer is forced to contend with indifference or hostile opposition. The trust that will be needed in order to undertake the journey forth from irresolute Ur must be made of sterner stuff. So it is that Haran perishes, on the eve of the odyssey to Canaan, his innards scorched even while the outward façade of his faith remained intact. Like the other denizens of Ur who may have been moved by Avram's courage and even momentarily swayed by his persuasive words but who remained unable to extend a commitment to his God, Haran will remain behind.

Reevaluating the Text

Returning to the text of the Torah, we are now in a better position to appreciate its terse but allusive words. The introductory verses to Avram's journey focus on Terach and Terach alone, because Terach and his beliefs form the static backdrop for all of Avram's subsequent spiritual progress. To highlight the place name of Ur, when no other genealogy refers to geography, is to alert us to the allure of its corrosive civilization. In the Midrash and in the text, Terach and the culture of Ur are inseparable entities, for the man and his city are devoted to an idolatrous system of values that by definition cannot reject an unjust social order presided over by an unjust king.

In Charan, Terach dies (though not for some time after Avram leaves for Canaan. See *Breisheet* 11:32 and Rashi ad loc.), never to complete the journey. Avram's continuation of the trek to Canaan, alone but for loyal Sarai at his side and young Lot in tow, therefore represents his complete and irreparable rift with the past – with his society and culture, with his family and friends, and even with his own father left behind to die. Bearing in mind that momentous break and cognizant of the awesome emotional and spiritual fortitude necessary to carry it out, we are better able to understand God's "unexpected" choice of Avram as His own.

FOR FURTHER STUDY:

(1) See Maimonides' masterful and inspiring adaptation of the Midrash in his *Mishneh Torah*, Laws of Idolatry 1, and compare it to Ramban's commentary on *Breisheet* 12:3.

(2) Ramban and Ibn Ezra disagree forcefully about the birth place of Avraham our father with each one of them mustering an impressive array of proof texts to support their views. While the Ramban regards Charan as the true geographical origin of the family, I have, for the purposes of this discussion, adopted the view of Ibn Ezra who places Avraham's birthplace in Ur Kasdim and therefore regards *Breisheet* 12:1 as the proleptic beginning of the journey.

VAYERA

Avimelech's Pledge

Genesis 18:1-22:24

THE PARASHA begins with God's unexpected visitation to Avraham, after his prompt fulfillment of the command of circumcision. Three dusty wayfarers suddenly appear on the horizon at the heat of the day, and the aged patriarch quickly rises from his tent-flap perch to greet them. Graciously, he invites them to break bread but then proceeds, with the involvement of his wife and servants, to prepare a sumptuous feast in their honor. But it soon becomes apparent that the guests are no mere mortals, for they bear joyous tidings from God Himself: Sarah, despite her advanced years, will shortly conceive and give birth to a son.

Abruptly, the angelic visitors terminate the banquet, and two of them rise and advance in the direction of Sodom and its suburbs, as Avraham is informed of its imminent overthrow. Boldly, he steps forward to engage the deity in heated negotiation, attempting to win a reprieve for the sinful cities. God acquiesces to his demands for justice, but in the end, there are not to be found even ten righteous people – the critical mass needed to avert disaster. Sodom is destroyed, but Lot is miraculously spirited out to the hills with his two surviving daughters. There, in a dark and dismal cave, he writes his infamous epitaph, by fathering children from his own two girls.

Avraham and his household now relocate, pitching their tents in the region of the arid Negev. There, Avimelech the king of Gerar seizes beautiful Sarah, but divine intervention in the form of a threatening dream stays his hand. After Avraham's intercession on their behalf, Avimelech and his household are spared. In the end, not only does he release Sarah, but provides her with generous gifts as well. And as for Avraham, Avimelech proclaims to him: "Behold my land is before you, dwell wheresoever you see fit" (*Breisheet* 20:15).

The Theme of the Parasha and the Episode of the Akeda

Finally, the Parasha reports the timely realization of the angels' pledge, as Sarah gives birth to a son called Yitzchak, meaning "he will laugh." Dutifully, Avraham circumcises his son on the eighth day of his life, in accordance with God's covenant. Yitzchak grows and is weaned, and his proud parents prepare a feast to celebrate the event. It is then that Sarah decides to drive out Hagar and Yishmael, after the lad scorns all of the attention showered upon his young half-brother. With the banishment of Yishmael and his mother, Yitzchak's position as undisputed heir is secured.

On the whole, though the Parasha contains many discrete episodes, its overall theme is plain for all to see: it is the story of the fulfillment of God's oft-repeated promise. As Lot and Yishmael, the two anticipated guarantors of the future, fall by the wayside, it now becomes apparent that it is only through Yitzchak that the legacy of Avraham and Sarah will be preserved and transmitted. How patiently had the aged couple waited for a child, how many painful disappointments had they endured in the twenty-five interminable years since their arrival in the land of Canaan! But now God had at long last kept His word. Their bent frames buoyed by His beneficence, how tightly they now embraced their precious and only son!

The final episode of the Parasha, the *Akeda* or binding of Yitzchak, is now cast in sharper relief, for even as a disconnected event it surely would have represented the sorest test of Avraham's spiritual mettle. But following as it does on the heels of everything else in the Parasha – most of it a joyous paean to the birth of beloved Yitzchak – the *Akeda* becomes a faith trial of astonishing proportions.

The Visit of Avimelech

Most curious, though, is the passage that immediately precedes the *Akeda* and directly follows the banishment of Hagar and Yishmael. This short and obscure section describes an interchange between Avimelech and Avraham, their pedantic discussion concerning water rights, and the concluding of a covenant between them sealed by the presentation of seven sheep. The timing of the section seems to compound its obscurity, for it creates an inexplicable thematic wedge between the respective tales of Avraham's two sons. Both of these sons experience near-death moments that are averted by sudden divine intervention and both are vouchsafed a divine promise of offspring and achievement. But while Yishmael is lost in the wilderness and rejected as successor to Avraham, Yitzchak is proclaimed in the *Akeda*'s aftermath as the father of the budding nation. Why should the coherence of this glaring study in contrasts be interrupted by the visit of Avimelech?

The section reads as follows:

> It was at that time that Avimelech and Phichol his chief of staff said to Avraham: "The Lord is with you in all that you do. Now therefore swear to me by the Lord here that you will not deal treacherously with me, or with my son, or with my grandson. Rather, you shall act towards me and towards the people of the land in which you have dwelled with the very same compassion that I have shown to you." Avraham replied: "I will swear an oath."
>
> Avraham then rebuked Avimelech concerning the well of water that the servants of Avimelech had stolen [from him]. But Avimelech said: "I do not know who did this thing, nor did you tell me about it earlier, nor did I hear about it at all before now." Avraham took sheep and cattle and gave it to Avimelech, and they both concluded a covenant. Avraham set up the seven sheep by themselves, and Avimelech said to him: "What are these seven sheep that you have set up by themselves?" He responded: "You shall accept these seven sheep from me as a testimony that I have dug this well." Therefore that place was called Be'er Sheva, for there both of them swore an oath (נשבעו).
>
> They concluded a covenant in Be'er Sheva, and Avimelech and Phichol his chief of staff arose and returned to the land of the Philistines. He [Avraham] planted a tamarisk in Be'er Sheva, and there he called on the name of God the eternal Lord. Avraham dwelt in the land of the Philistines for many years. (21:22–34)

The Elements of the Encounter

The basic components of the passage are straightforward enough. Avimelech, who had allowed Avraham and Sarah to dwell in his land and is now struck by their astonishing success, demands that the powerful patriarch provide a pledge that he will not harm Avimelech's descendents after his demise. Avraham is more than prepared to swear to Avimelech's terms, but he is not prepared to overlook a breach of the contract by Avimelech's servants. If Avimelech demands that Avraham act towards him with "compassion," then he must be prepared to reciprocate. Thus, Avraham demands action "concerning the well of water that the servants of Avimelech had stolen from him" (21:25), and Avimelech concurs. Avraham, however, now taking a cue from his ally, insists that his rights to the disputed well at Be'er Sheva that he had dug be recognized in the treaty, and this he graphically reinforces by the presentation of the seven sheep. These seven sheep introduce an important word play, for their number, שבע in the original Hebrew, directly relates to the oath or שבועה that is undertaken at the location.

The episode concludes not with the departure of Avimelech and his retinue, as we might have expected, but rather with Avraham's interaction with his beloved God. Avraham plants a tree at Be'er Sheva and there he calls out in the name of the "eternal God." Just as the passage began with a God reference – Avimelech's amazement (or is it consternation?) at Avraham's achievements and his attribution of that triumph to divine intervention – so too does it conclude, with Avraham expressing profound gratitude to the eternal God who had granted him such goodness. Concerning this matter, then, Avimelech and Avraham have no disagreement: It is God who is responsible for the latter's success.

The core of the passage is an exploration of the limits of trust between parties that are bound up in some sort of a political but potentially rivalrous relationship. Avimelech feels the need to secure Avraham's pledge for the future, while Avraham insists on having his existing rights enshrined in the treaty as well. Neither of the protagonists feels that they can afford to leave the fate of their offspring to vague declarations of goodwill and friendship. The two men therefore conclude a formal covenant, a binding treaty that precisely spells out their respective responsibilities.

The Interpretation of the Rashbam

The medieval commentaries on our passage provide much technical information about the sealing of the treaty, but confine their comments to the local context. That is to say that they make no attempt to connect our passage to what precedes or else what follows it. A glaring exception in this regard is the Rashbam who provides us with one of his most controversial readings:

> When the Torah introduces the episode of the *Akeda* by saying that "it came to pass after these things" (*Breisheet* 22:1), it means after Avraham had concluded a treaty with Avimelech between their respective children and grandchildren and had given him the seven sheep. This angered God because the territory of the Philistines is regarded as the land of Israel and concerning them God commanded: "Do not allow any soul to live" (*Devarim* 20:16) . . . therefore, "the Lord now tested Avraham" which means that He caused him pain and grief . . . God said: "Have you become

> overbearing on account of the son that I gave you, so that you now conclude a treaty between yourselves and their offspring? Now go and offer your son as a burnt offering and then we will see what benefits were bestowed by your sealing of a treaty!" (commentary to *Breisheet* 22:1)

For the Rashbam, Avraham should not have concluded a treaty with Avimelech king of the Philistines. Doing so betrayed a lack of trust in God's pledge to one day cause Avraham's descendents to possess the land. Remarkably, Rashbam now links the *Akeda* to this treaty and then redefines what surely constitutes one of the Torah's most sublime moments as a petty punishment for Avraham's disbelief! While the attempt to connect the Avimelech episode with the *Akeda* is certainly noble, the results in this case are troubling and unsatisfying.

The Theme of Covenant

Cognizant of the Rashbam's attempt, let us consider a different approach. Let us begin by noting the obvious: Underlying the entire matter of treaties or covenants is the foundation of trust. That is to say that people who swear an oath to each other must obligate themselves to fulfill the provisions of the pledge. How else can a relationship be built and fostered between different parties with diverse but overlapping interests, if not by each one of those parties being prepared to abide by the agreed-upon terms? If Avimelech cannot depend upon Avraham and vise versa, then any treaty concluded between them, no matter how lofty its language or how noble the signatories' good wishes, is utterly ineffectual and worthless!

In a short textual moment (though perhaps after the chronological lapse of many years), God is about to call upon Avraham to take his beloved son to the land of Moriah. This is the same God who had pledged to Avraham that (1) He would provide him with offspring, and (2) He would grant him the land of Canaan, so that the nation of Israel could be forged from that offspring. God's binary pledge of children and land had been repeated with great frequency throughout the *parashiyot* of Lech Lecha and VaYera, and though we had all (Avraham, Sarah and the reader) been anxious about its fulfillment, God did not disappoint. In the end Sarah had a son that they joyously called "Yitzchak" for great was their mirth when God's promise finally came true.

In their minds, that son represented the future, the very same future that Avimelech clearly foresaw when he approached Avraham and demanded the conclusion of a treaty. "Do not betray me," he insisted, "and do not deal treacherously with my son or grandson either." But then Avraham introduced the matter of the wells, emphasizing that for there to be trust there must be mutual respect, for Avimelech could scarcely be a signatory to a treaty if he or his servants were already in breach of its provisions. Can one rely upon his fellow if that fellow is undependable? The rhetorical implication of the query is pronounced: What makes my God so reliable, Avraham seems to suggest, is that I know that He will not fail to uphold His side of *our* covenant, of the pledge that He extended to me when I left the land of Charan. God's word is unassailable and His commitment to His pledge is forever, for He is "God, the eternal Lord."

God's Pledge to Avraham

Although the passage describes the interaction of Avimelech with Avraham, anchoring their pact in oaths and pledges, responsibilities and obligations, constancy and dependability, it really serves as a foil for the ongoing story of the interaction of God with Avraham. Had not that interaction been consistently framed in the same terms? Hadn't God extended oaths and pledges, communicated responsibilities and obligations, demonstrated constancy and dependability, all of it revolving around the axis of Yitzchak's birth and then his growth and maturation into the progenitor of the nation? Avimelech looks towards the future, thinking of the fate of his son and his grandson after him, and for *the very first time* in his long and eventful life, Avraham is able to do the same! And while Avimelech fears treachery and betrayal and therefore insists upon a formal treaty, Avraham fears neither, for his God, the eternal Lord, the transcendent God who champions and demands moral conduct from His adherents, neither deceives nor acts with duplicity.

In the end, the seven sheep are accepted and the treaty is sealed. There will be no disputes about the ownership of the well and Avimelech's descendents will be safe. The Philistine king, his mind at ease, departs with his enforcer, and Avraham turns towards his God in gratitude. In His honor, Avraham plants a tree that because of its great longevity is a potent symbol of the future, and he then turns to Him in prayer. We can imagine his silent words to God as his aged heart overflows with gratitude and appreciation: "Thank You God for granting me a son, thank You for fulfilling Your pledge, and thank You for being dependable and worthy of my undying trust. While Avimelech may have wronged me, You never have. And while the treaty that we just now concluded with such fanfare may in the future after my demise be breached, You will never abrogate Your treaty with me, for You are eternal, Your essence is compassion, and Your seal is truth!"

Reevaluating the Episode of the Akeda

Enter the episode of the *Akeda*, for if we thought before our above analysis that the trial represented an astonishing test in light of the Parasha's general preoccupation with the birth of beloved Yitzchak, we must now adjust our conclusions not by a few degrees but rather by orders of magnitude.

> "God said to him: "Avraham!" and he said "here I am." He said: "Take now your son, your only son, the one whom you love, take Yitzchak, and go forth to the land of Moriah. Offer him there as a wholly burnt sacrifice upon one of the summits that I will show you!" (*Breisheet* 22:1–2)

What was to now become of divine dependability, of the fulfillment of His pledge, of the future of His promise? How to now reconcile the immutability, trustworthiness and constancy of God's word with His demands for Yitzchak's untimely and cruel return? Avimelech's fears of treachery and betrayal, forcefully countered by Avraham's own reassurances that one who champions an absolute and ethical deity can be depended upon, suddenly flooded into the patriarch's reeling mind. Is not a pledge holy and an oath of offspring sacrosanct? Ought not God's oft-repeated vow be at least as dependable as a treaty signed by the mercurial monarch of the Philistines?!

Avraham's willingness to go forward in the fulfillment of God's demand must therefore be understood not only against the backdrop of the Parasha as a whole, but especially in light of what immediately precedes it in the text. The treaty talk with Avimelech serves as a jarring juxtaposition, for Avraham's crisis of faith was now surely compounded by the terms of that pact. Avimelech had approached him and had spoken of compassion and trust, and Avraham – thinking of the example set by his own God – had set Avimelech's mind at ease. The king of Gerar sought a pledge concerning the future, and Avraham – casting a loving glance towards his precious Yitzchak – was prepared. The Philistine stressed that treaties and agreements are binding, and Avraham – recalling God's own fulfillment of His oath – agreed. But now God Himself was poised to break His promise, abrogating the very agreement whose terms Avraham had upheld with such devotion!

And yet, the aged patriarch betrayed no lack of trust as he dutifully arose the next morning and saddled his donkey, taking his son and the provisions for sacrifice, setting his sights for Moriah and for the unbearable encounter with God that awaited him there. Thus it is that Avraham's faith at that hour invites us to reconsider our own appreciation of his loyalty to God, challenging our unspoken thoughts that perhaps this man is not as exceptional as tradition has made him out to be! Avraham was now exposed for what he truly was: A possessor of a conviction and steadfastness so profound that we can scarcely stand the blinding illumination that it throws upon our own sordid doubts! If Avraham could continue to trust, in spite of all that he and Sarah had experienced, could we dare to surrender trust? If Avraham could maintain his faith, even as he imagined Avimelech now scoffing at his unshakable faith – for eternal God now seemed to renege on His word! – then what of us? And in spite of all of the indications to the contrary, as father and son embarked on their fateful journey to oblivion, God in the end maintained His trust, just as Avraham knew that He surely would: Yitzchak was spared, the patriarch was blessed, and the covenant with the nation of Israel was upheld.

We thus return to the comments of the Rashbam. Rather than the treaty with Avimelech highlighting the patriarch's reservations about God's pledge, rather than the *Akeda* serving as some sort of reprimand for Avraham's lack of faith, quite the opposite is true. The Avimelech episode is meant to cast Avraham's steadfastness in even sharper relief, his unwillingness to surrender his confidence in God even as the Philistine's words devastatingly echoed in his ears: "The Lord is with you in all that you do. Now therefore swear to me by the Lord here that you will not deal treacherously with me, or with my son, or with my grandson . . ."

It is instructive to note that the treaty with Avimelech was soon abrogated by the king or by his successor of the same name. After the death of Avraham, when Yitzchak and Rivka were forced by famine to return to the land of the Philistines, Avraham's earlier claims to the well were denied. In spite of the treaty of friendship that was supposed to have extended well into the lives of sons and grandsons, the jealousy of the Philistines won the day:

> . . . all of the wells that his father's servants had dug were sealed by the Philistines and filled with earth. Avimelech said to him: "Go away from us, for you have become more powerful than we are!" (26:15–16)

Thus the lesson was driven home most forcefully. In the final analysis, pledges of people, even when extended in friendship and sealed by official treaty, are never ironclad. New circumstances frequently demand re-evaluations and often the result is an abrogation of earlier promises. And though we often wonder, especially when buffeted by suffering and hardship, about the dependability of God in our own personal lives, His pledge to our ancestors is above reproach and His commitment to our future as a people is unwavering.

> A voice said: "Cry out!", and I said "What shall I cry?" "All flesh is like grass, and all of their compassion is like the flower of the field!" The grass becomes dry and the flower fades, for the wind of God has blown it and truly the people are like grass. The grass becomes dry and the flower will fade, but the word of our God shall endure forever. (*Yeshayahu* 40:68)

FOR FURTHER STUDY:

(1) While we have explored the juxtaposition of Avimelech's treaty with what follows, namely the *Akeda*, it should also be compared with what precedes. Considering the passages in succession – Yishmael's banishment, Avimelech's treaty and then the *Akeda* – yields an even sharper progression. The loss of Yishmael, at God's behest, must have surely highlighted to Avraham the preciousness of Yitzchak who remained. This sentiment was reinforced, as we have seen, by the treaty. God's demand to Avraham that Yitzchak now suffer immolation in His name thus becomes even more impossible to bear!

CHAYEI SARAH

The Tent of Rivka

Genesis 23:1-25:18

AFTER A LONG and productive life full of challenges enthusiastically engaged and setbacks overcome, mother Sarah dies and passes from the pages of biblical history. Avraham, while grief-stricken over the enormity of his loss, immediately sets out to secure a burial plot for her. Tentatively approaching the Chittite noblemen who hold deed to the lands in the Chevron region, Avraham turns to Efron their compatriot and requests to purchase from him the cave of Machpela and its surrounding fields. Though he conducts the negotiations with seeming magnanimity, Efron in the end reveals his mean-spirited miserliness, for he will not agree to sell the rock-strewn territory until Avraham has agreed to his inflated demands: four hundred shekels of fine silver currency.

Surprisingly, the patriarch readily surrenders the amount, for Avraham surely realizes that his purchase of Machpela will have far-reaching implications. He understands, as Sarah did before her own demise, that he will not live to see the birth of the nation concerning which God had so often and passionately pledged. He knows, after more than six decades of nomadic shepherding in Canaan and still bereft of landed property, that he will be long gone before his descendents are numerous and mature enough to claim Canaan as their own. But as their progenitor, Avraham also realizes that he must initiate the process of settling the land, though only symbolically and in death, by securing legal title to a portion of it. By establishing a family sepulcher for burial, by purchasing a plot for eternal repose, Avraham establishes a tangible and eternal connection with Canaan's fertile soil. Thus he ensures that his own descendents, though they may stray far from Canaan's borders and even farther from his legacy, will never be entirely cut off from their destiny. To Machpela they will return, if nothing more than as a pilgrimage to their ancient history, but in so doing they will remember.

Avraham and Sarah's Respective Deaths

In the narratives of Sefer Breisheet, few individuals loom as large as Avraham and Sarah. How lovingly the Torah traced their geographical and spiritual peregrination from Ur, how proudly it described their acts of compassion and righteousness in the new land, how it marveled at their steadfast trust in God even when He tested their faith severely. Though both of them pass from the scene in Parashat Chayei Sarah – the matriarch dying, as it were, in real time, the patriarch's death described only proleptically – they do not disappear before their worthy successors have been appointed. Yitzchak their son, in every respect a loyal bearer of their legacy, begins his life's journey with a new mate. The benevolent Rivka, her character tried and superbly vindicated by Eliezer's thirsty prayer at the well, willingly returns with Avraham's loyal servant from the far-off eastern lands of Mesopotamia to become Yitzchak's wife. Their marriage is presented by the Torah as the final narrative before the report of the death of Avraham, a sure indication that he dies a blissful man, for he knows with certainty that they will perpetuate God's mission. As the Torah poignantly puts it:

> Yitzchak brought her into the tent of Sarah his mother. He took Rivka as his, and she became his wife and he loved her. Then was Yitzchak comforted for the death of his mother. (*Breisheet* 24:67)

As surely as Yitzchak became the embodiment of everything that Avraham held dear, the transmitter of his values and the champion of his cause, so too Rivka enters the "tent of Sarah" to effectively perpetuate her role. Yitzchak finally ceases to mourn for his mother Sarah, not because he no longer feels the grief of her departure, but because he recognizes in Rivka the possibility of continuity. Sarah will live on posthumously through the deeds of her daughter-in-law, who in many respects will surpass her in achieving steadfast trust. After all, while Sarah too was called upon to sacrifice her son, in the end God relented. But wasn't Rivka later asked to surrender *both* of her own sons, driving an irrevocable wedge between herself and her firstborn Esav, even as she tearfully sent Ya'acov away to seize his future, never to see him again?

The Progression from Sarah to Rivka

The Midrash Breisheet Rabbah, quoted by Rashi with variations, describes the transition from Sarah to Rivka in telling terms:

> "Yitzchak brought her into the tent of Sarah his mother" – as long as Sarah was alive, a cloud was affixed to the entrance of her tent. When she died, that cloud ceased. But when Rivka arrived, the cloud returned. As long as Sarah was alive, the doors were opened wide. When she died, that generosity ceased. But when Rivka arrived, the generosity returned. As long as Sarah was alive, a blessing was associated with the dough. When she died, that blessing ceased. But when Rivka arrived, the blessing returned. As long as Sarah was alive, a lamp burned from one Shabbat night until the next. When she died, that lamp ceased. But when Rivka arrived, the fire returned. Yitzchak saw that she followed the example of his mother, preparing her dough and separating the *challah* in ritual fitness. When Yitzchak noted that she followed the example of his mother, separating the *challah* in purity and preparing the dough in purity, immediately: "Yitzchak brought her into the tent of Sarah his mother. He took Rivka as his, and she became his wife and he loved her. Then was Yitzchak comforted for the death of his mother." (Breisheet Rabbah 60:16)

Here, the Midrash employs some colorful comparisons to highlight the matter of Rivka's resemblance to Sarah. Sarah's dough was blessed, her tent was illuminated by perpetual candlelight, and a cloud hovered protectively above her door. What might be the meaning of these provocative images?

The Parallel of the Mishkan

The elements enumerated in the above Midrash that together describe the uniqueness of Sarah's household – a cloud, open doors, blessed dough and light – are all known to us from at least one other biblical context, and no doubt the ancient Rabbis were inspired by that other passage to reinterpret our text. I refer to the Tabernacle or Mishkan, that portable shrine of God that accompanied the people of Israel during the whole course of their wilderness wanderings. According to the account preserved in Sefer Shemot (chapters 25–27), the Mishkan was a rectangular building of prefabricated, gilded acacia boards that was provided with a finely embroidered covering of woven material and protective hides above. These were draped over the tops of the boards – for the building had no structural roof – and then fell down over their sides to be fastened by cords and pegs at the base, giving the entire edifice the appearance of a tent. For that reason, the Mishkan was often referred to in the text as "*Ohel Mo'ed*" or the Tent of Meeting (see *Shemot* 28:43, et al.).

The Mishkan, the locus in material space for the encounter with God's ethereal presence, was provided with a number of precious vessels, arranged hierarchically within its area. These vessels had ritual and ceremonial as well as symbolic and spiritual value. The ark of the covenant that alone occupied the most sanctified space of the Holy of Holies, was the repository for the engraved tablets of the Decalogue that Moshe had received at Sinai. This gilded object, surmounted by the winged cherubs, symbolically represented God's throne on earth. The Holy of Holies was divided from the other areas of the building by a beautiful embroidered curtain so that access to it was strictly controlled.

Beyond the curtain, in the more outer space of the "holy," was a small golden altar placed on center that was primarily used for the daily offering of incense, whose fragrant smoke ascending heavenwards symbolized the prayers of the people. Flanking it on either side were the golden menorah and the table of showbread. The former, a seven branched candelabrum heavily ornamented with motifs drawn from the world of trees and flowers, was lit daily with pure olive oil and served as a potent symbol of God's vital role in illuminating the human mind and soul with His wisdom. The latter, a gilded affair completely and perpetually covered with twelve specially shaped loaves of bread, signified God's constant involvement in the life of the nation of Israel (i.e., the twelve tribes) as provider of physical nourishment and sustainer of the body. Finally, in the outer courtyard, was an altar of bronze upon which the animal sacrifices were offered. The entire edifice was surmounted by a cloud, a tangible symbol of God's presence as well as of His mystery, as recorded at the close of the Mishkan narratives that conclude Sefer Shemot:

> The cloud covered the Tent of Meeting, and God's glory filled the Mishkan. Moshe was therefore unable to enter the Tent of Meeting, for the cloud rested upon it, and God's glory filled the Mishkan. When the cloud ascended from upon the Mishkan, then the people of Israel would embark upon all of their journeys. But if the cloud would not ascend, then they would not journey until such a time as it lifted. Thus, the cloud of God was upon the Mishkan by day and fire by night, in the view of all of the house of Israel during all of their journeys. (40:34–38)

The Ideal Jewish Home

It is not at all difficult to now recognize the link between the Tent of Meeting and the tent of Sarah and Rivka. Both edifices were essentially homes, the former serving as the august abode for the God-man encounter, the latter heroically attempting to duplicate it in mundane reality. Both highlighted the essential role of God in the human success of securing sustenance, for the former had the table of the showbread and in the latter "the dough was blessed." Both emphasized the involvement of God in providing inspiration, for the former had the perpetually lit menorah, and the latter had the "lamp that illumined from one Shabbat night until the next." And both, of course, were surmounted by the mysterious cloud, a concrete but elusive sign for God's incorporeal but real presence in the physical world. In essence, our Midrash suggests that Sarah and Rivka, by virtue of their exemplary conduct and virtuous deeds, their recognition of God's involvement in their lives and their steadfast trust in His salvation, had fashioned "Jewish homes" in the truest sense of the term, mirror images of God's own abode.

As matriarchal figures, their efforts and achievements that centered on the tent are understood by the Midrash to highlight their values, ideals that ought to characterize the homes of their descendents as well. And so we must ask ourselves in light of their example: Will our own homes be centers of strife and striving, sources of endless ambition and ruthless aspirations for the securing of evermore material possessions, in our futile belief that wealth confers immortality? Or will they instead be productive focal points for declaring labor's dignity, for fostering the profound recognition that materiality is but a noble means to a more noble end? To return to the Midrashic imagery, will we succeed in securing the blessed dough that fills the belly without leaving in the mouth the acrid taste of corporeal craving unrealized?

Will our homes be centers of learning and spiritual growth, places of illumination powered by the sincere desire to deepen our understanding of God and His Torah, and bright beacons that radiate the God idea into the surrounding moral darkness that threatens to engulf the world? Or will they instead be centers for banal and mindless living, hollow shells of concrete lit up by otherworldly blue flickers and bombarded with numbing noise telecast from static screens of glass? In short, will the inspiration of the "Shabbat lamp" light up our homes from one week to the next or will we seek our nirvana elsewhere?

The stark choices that are implied by our reading of the Midrash are amplified by an even more severe source, this time from the Mishna in Tractate *Shabbat*:

> Women die in childbirth because of three transgressions: for not exercising care concerning the laws of menstruation, the laws of *challah* and the kindling of the [Shabbat] lamp. (2:6)

We note immediately that two of our earlier elements associated with Rivka's tent, the blessed dough and the Shabbat lamp, are paralleled in the Mishna by the "laws of *challah* and the kindling of the lamp." The third element, the hovering cloud, must therefore be related to the laws of menstruation. But how can this be?

Social anthropologists make much commotion about the primitive blood taboos, prevalent in many ancient cultures, that they believe lie at the foundation of the Torah's laws of *Niddah*. While it is impossible to dismiss these claims entirely (see for instance the commentary of the Ramban to *Breisheet* 31:35 and *VaYikra* 18:19), they represent a very minor dimension of the matter. Much more significantly, the laws of *Niddah* impose powerful constraints on intimacy between husband and wife, as if to say that even life's most private moments must be inspired by the presence of God. In this sense, we may argue that the symbol of the cloud hovering above the matriarchal tent, the tangible expression of God's presence, is paralleled in the Mishna by the laws of *Niddah*, for both emphasize the overarching experience of God's involvement in the husband-wife relationship. In other words, the home that attends to these laws, inspiring intimacy with the recognition of God, transforms what is essentially a powerful but blind biological drive into a vehicle for fostering true and profound communion.

It may be instructive to note that while the Mishna in Shabbat clearly assigns the responsibility of these three laws to women, they also plainly devolve upon men. Anyone who bakes bread, male or female, is obligated to separate the *challah*. A man who dwells alone or else one whose wife is unable, must kindle the Shabbat lamps. The laws of *Niddah*, while addressing the monthly reproductive cycle of the woman, are clearly not performed in isolation. The impact of these laws is primarily felt, especially today in the post-Temple era, in the realm of relationship between the husband and wife.

Death in Childbirth

But what of the ominous "death in childbirth" that the Mishna assigns to a woman inattentive to these laws? The relevant Talmudic passage attempts to clarify the relationship between childbirth and these three things, but provides us with only an extrinsic linkage. "Sharpen the knife while the ox is fallen" goes the ancient adage (TB *Shabbat* 32a), morbidly highlighting the great danger that, until modern times, heralded childbirth. In other words, a situation of danger invites heavenly scrutiny of one's deeds, for the divine decision to save or else to let perish hinges on one's past conduct. Where merits are lacking, the argument goes, divine intervention will not be forthcoming. A woman's inattentiveness to these three laws is therefore brought to the consideration of the heavenly court at the time of childbirth, because that is precisely the moment of greatest vulnerability.

In light of our earlier analysis, though, there may very well be an additional aspect. Did the Mishna mean to suggest only a literal, causal and empirical connection between death in childbirth and the neglect of these three principles? As all of us know, such an assertion, if taken at face value, is tenuous at best. In the past, many God-fearing women have perished in childbirth while scoffers have survived! Or perhaps, was the Mishna indicating to us a more profound truth, namely that inattentiveness to these three laws, as the *defining components of a healthy and functioning Jewish home,* is destructive to any hope of Jewish continuity? In other words, if the proverbial *challah* is not taken – unbridled physicality for its own vulgar sake taking the place of the hallowed loaves, if the Shabbat lamp is not kindled – the unqualified endorsement of shallow popular culture and its skewed values taking the place of the golden glow of the menorah, and if the husband-wife relationship is but a hollow excuse for egocentric economic gain and selfish sexual gratification, then no proverbial Jewish children can grow up spiritually "well-adjusted" and wholesome in such an environment. It is as if these children, truly the future of the people of Israel, have been condemned to develop as spiritual orphans (i.e., death of the mother in childbirth), for their formative home life has been shorn of everything that is precious and meaningful.

This then is the meaning of first Sarah's and later Rivka's tent, powerful symbols of the necessity to transmit explicit values that must shape and inspire our homes, homes that must not be left undefined as materially comfortable but spiritually vacuous "machines for living." In these uncertain times, with Israel besieged from without by bloodthirsty foes, and from within threatened by indifference and apathy, we would do well to remember our matriarchs' example, for the future of the Jewish people depends upon it.

FOR FURTHER STUDY:

(1) The tent of Sarah had a fourth feature – "doors opened wide." This expression is a reference to her hospitality, as suggested as well by the events of *Breisheet* 18:1–8. The Mishkan parallel must be the courtyard, where the Israelites would congregate. The Rabbis actually regard the courtyard of the Mishkan as a quintessential רשות הרבים or public domain (see TB *Shabbat* 96b), emphasizing the people's unimpeded access to it.

TOLDOT

Of Blindness and Blessings

Genesis 25:19-28:9

WITH THE lives of Sarah and Avraham behind us, the Torah now begins to relate the story of Yitzchak and Rivka. Although they are important personalities in their own right, the principal significance of Yitzchak and Rivka lies in their being the link between trailblazing forebears and faithful progeny, that is between the past and the future. Therefore, this Parasha, while certainly describing important events in the lives of these two, places its primary emphasis on the story of their children, Ya'acov and Esav.

In broad outline, the events of the Parasha can be divided into three main sections. The first division, from *Breisheet* 25:19 to 25:34, describes the births of and subsequent rivalry between Esav and Ya'acov. The second, from 26:1 to 26:33, relates incidents in the lives of Yitzchak and Rivka during their sojourn in Gerar among the Philistines. The last part, from 26:34 to 28:9, narrates the struggle that ensues between the two brothers concerning the birthright and the blessing.

The Divisions of the Parasha

Let us table the structure of the Parasha in greater detail, according to the above tripartite division:

(I) 25:19–34

- the marriage of Yitzchak at the age of forty to Rivka.
- Rivka's barrenness, the heartfelt prayers for relief, her conception, the ensuing painful pregnancy, and her enquiry of God concerning its significance.
- the prophecy about the two nations that will emerge from her womb, the birth of the twins and their coming of age as each pursues markedly different interests, and Esav's sale of the birthright to Ya'acov for a bowl of pottage.

(II) 26:1–33

- the famine, the family's descent to lodge with Avimelech king of Gerar, the inhabitants' interest in Rivka, and the protection afforded to her by royal decree.
- Yitzchak's success at agriculture and husbandry, the jealousy which this arouses among the local peoples, and their resultant attempts to discourage his continued presence by filling in the wells which Avraham had dug.
- Yitzchak's redigging and renaming of the wells after the example of Avraham his father, the struggle between Yitzchak's shepherds and the local shepherds over new sources of water, and Yitzchak's successful claim to a newly dug well.

- the translocation of the family to Be'er Sheva, a divine vision that dispels Yitzchak's fears, the building by Yitzchak of an altar, his invoking of God's name, and the digging of a new well.
- the arrival of Avimelech and his entourage to negotiate a covenant with Yitzchak, the exchange of oaths between the two and the ratification of the treaty, the digging of a new well by Yitzchak's servants and the ascribing of the name "Shiva" to it.

(III) 26:34–28:9

- the marriage of Esav at the age of forty to Chittite women and their disfavor in the estimation of Yitzchak and Rivka.
- the aging of Yitzchak and the dimming of his eyes, his desire to bestow the blessing of the firstborn on Esav, and Esav's exit to secure the game which his father requests as a precursor to the blessings.
- Ya'acov's impersonation of his brother and the subterfuge undertaken at his mother's behest, and his securing of the blessings.
- Esav's discovery of the deception, his hatred of his brother and raging desire to kill him, and Ya'acov's flight to Charan in ostensible pursuit of a wife with his father's covenantal blessing in hand.
- the marriage of Esav to Machlat, daughter of Yishmael.

It will immediately be noticed that an overt bracketing effect organizes the material, in which the struggles of Ya'acov and Esav enclose the core events of the sojourn in Gerar. It should also be noted that many of these core events echo incidents from the lives of Avraham and Sarah. Thus, we find that Avraham and Sarah also descended to Gerar and that Sarah was in danger there of being seized by Avimelech. In the end, she emerged from the experience unscathed and in possession of a royal decree of protection (*Breisheet* 20). Further on, Avimelech and his chief of staff entreated Avraham to conclude a pact with them, and there was discussion concerning water rights, namely the well that had been unjustly seized by Avimelech's shepherds. The two concluded a treaty at Be'er Sheva and Avraham invoked the name of God (21:22–34).

Significantly, the final section of the Parasha that describes the stratagem employed by Ya'acov to secure the blessing also exhibits its own bracketing feature. Here, it is Esav's marriages that enclose the struggle over the blessings. His marriage to Chittite women introduces the section and his marriage to Machlat daughter of Yishmael concludes it, and with it, the Parasha. We will endeavor to keep these things in mind as we begin to consider some of the Parasha's salient themes.

The Theme of Infertility

The Parasha opens with a description of the marriage of Yitzchak to Rivka. Yitzchak was forty years old at the time of his marriage, and Rivka, like Sarah before her and Rachel after her (and perhaps Leah as well – see Midrash Breisheet Rabbah 71:1), was initially barren. This inability to conceive was not overcome until the protagonists called out to God to intervene. God acceded to their prayers, and in the cases of Sarah and Rivka, provided some cryptic pronouncement concerning the nature of the anticipated offspring.

The theme of childlessness is not confined to the narratives of Sefer Breisheet; it is found in other biblical instances as well. The mother of Shimshon, for instance, is initially unable to conceive (*Shoftim* 13:2), as is Channa the mother of Shemuel (*Shemuel* 1:1:2). The Jewish people in exile, after the fall of Jerusalem and the destruction of the Temple, are described by the prophet Isaiah as being barren and bereft of children, until God in His gentle mercy redeems and restores them to their land (*Yeshayahu* 54:1).

Of course, great anticipation and expectation on the part of anxious parents precedes the birth of every child. Pregnancy frequently heralds hopeful musings about the child to be, and dreams about his or her future. When a prolonged period of infertility comes before that pregnancy, those feelings and thoughts are magnified many times over. If recourse to prayer is an integral part of addressing the barrenness, and the prayers are subsequently answered, then an additional sense of destiny and mission invests the circumstance of the birth.

For this reason, the matriarchs were without exception barren. Their tearful entreaties addressed to the creator and the divine intervention secured by those prayers, made it very clear that the resultant child was not the straightforward outcome of a typical chain of events. Rather, that child, born out of intense longing and eventual triumph, embodied a unique and special task in life. In similar fashion, the twin birth of Esav and Ya'acov after Rivka's prolonged infertility, her and Yitzchak's poignant prayers and the divine oracle concerning their respective futures, indicated that each one of the children had an exceptional destiny to fulfill.

Esav and Ya'acov as Contrasting Archetypes

The peculiar nature of these disparate destinies is accentuated by the very unusual prophecy that portends their birth:

> Two nations are in your womb, and two peoples will separate from your belly. One nation will be more powerful than the other, and the greater shall serve the lesser. (*Breisheet* 25:23)

The truth of the pronouncement is soon borne out by the very different features of the newborn babies: The first is ruddy and full of hair, the second (who emerges while grasping the ankle of his brother) does not share these attributes. As the children grow, their characters diverge even further. Esav, the elder, takes to the hunt. An outdoorsman by nature, full of guile and craftiness, he enjoys the field and the killing of prey. Ya'acov, his younger brother, is of a more refined constitution. Adopting the pastoral pursuit of shepherding flocks, he gravitates towards a serene, contemplative lifestyle. Portentously, the text indicates that Yitzchak has a special love for Esav because of his provision of game, while Rivka prefers Ya'acov.

Let us briefly analyze the account of Esav's selling of the birthright, recounted in *Breisheet* 25:29–34. Returning home from the hunt in a particularly exhausted state, Esav finds his brother busy preparing a stew. "Allow me to devour this very red stuff" he exclaims, employing the unusual causative verb הַלְעִיטֵנִי (devour). This verb is otherwise unknown in biblical Hebrew, but in Mishnaic Hebrew it carries the sense of gorging down food after the manner of an animal (see for example Mishna *Shabbat* 24:3). Apparently, the exact ingredients of the stew in question are unimportant to Esav, so great is his hunger and so impetuous his desire. Ya'acov, sensing an opportunity, offers to exchange the stew for Esav's birthright, and the latter readily accepts: "Behold, I am going to die (of hunger?). Of what use to me is the birthright?"

Ya'acov extends the stew of lentils to Esav along with some bread, and the Torah then provides a list of five verbs to describe Esav's actions: "he ate, he drank, he arose, he walked off, and Esav despised the birthright." There is a great sense of impulsiveness expressed by these five verbs in quick succession, a feeling of dynamic abandon as Esav hungrily gorges on the stew, taking nary a breath, and rushes back to the hunt. Whatever the birthright's true significance, it is insufficient to give Esav pause for even a moment. He consciously exchanges it for a bowl of lentils, without a second thought, because he scorns its value.

Understanding the Birthright

What is the significance of the birthright and the blessing, the two things that constitute such a pivotal part of our Parasha? Or, to phrase the question differently, why is Ya'acov so interested in securing them? An ancient tradition suggests that the birthright was initially associated with the special role of serving and ministering to God:

> Why did Ya'acov our father risk his life for the birthright? It was because of what we have learned elsewhere, that before the construction of the Tabernacle, sacrifice at high places was permitted and the firstborn served as priests. After the building of the Tabernacle, the high places were forbidden and the service was limited to only the Kohanim. (Breisheet Rabbah 63:33)

According to this Midrash (quoting from Mishna *Zevachim* 14:4), being the firstborn in ancient Israel meant aspiring to a special life of connectedness to God and fulfilling a specific cultic function – the offering of sacrifices. This latter ritual role is referenced in *Shemot* 24:5, which describes the "lads of the people of Israel" at Mount Sinai who "offered burnt offerings and sacrificed peace offerings of cows to God." In the pre-Israel context of our story, living by the terms of the birthright meant being prepared to continue the spiritual legacy of Avraham and Sarah. That being the case, it seems hardly an appropriate vocation for a savage hunter whose greatest pleasures were temporal, corporeal, and sanguinary.

Perhaps we should understand Ya'acov's conduct here, often portrayed as being treacherously deceptive, as his means of overtly testing Esav's resolve. If the birthright means anything to him at all, he will certainly not exchange it for a bowl of lentils! After all, Ya'acov is completely up front about the terms of the sale: the birthright for a bowl of soup. The careful reader will notice that there is no attempt on Ya'acov's part to belittle the value of the birthright or else to portray it as a liability that Esav ought to dispense with. His remarks are strikingly neutral, allowing Esav to decide for himself whether the offer is worthwhile: "Sell me this day your birthright" is all that he exclaims.

By way of illustration, imagine for a moment a ravenous libertine roaming the darkened streets of Paris with a prized impressionist painting tucked under his arm, a bequest of his doting and over-indulgent father. Our famished sybarite searches the *arrondissement* for a café that is open but in vain. Suddenly, he encounters an industrious fellow who senses his distress and exclaims: "I will be only too happy to offer you this *pain ordinaire* in exchange for that Monet!" Let us now ask ourselves: Has an act of fraud been perpetrated? Or has the man who willingly parts with the painting instead demonstrated that he places no value whatsoever on the work of the French master? Lest it be argued that Esav was, through no fault of his own, clueless about the true value of the birthright, the earlier narratives of the book indicate that, from time immemorial, the birthright had been venerated. Was not Kayin, the firstborn, prepared to kill in order to secure the divine favor associated with it (see *Breisheet* 4:1–5)? Was not Yefet, the firstborn of Noach, given the special gift of "expansiveness" on account of his status (9:27)? Was not Avram, the firstborn of Terach, selected by God to transform the world (11:26)? If Ya'acov can be charged with anything in this exchange, it is with exposing Esav for what he truly is: a self-interested, coarse lout who has no respect for the spiritual or for the timeless.

To no one's surprise, then, not Ya'acov's and not Esav's, the birthright is peddled away for a pittance. Significantly, in the immediate aftermath of the sale, Esav expresses no regret, contrition, or remorse. Instead, his attitude towards the birthright is one of unmitigated disdain.

The Sojourn at Gerar

At this point, the Torah digresses from the subject at hand to describe the famine that strikes the land, "like the famine which occurred in the days of Avraham" (*Breisheet* 26:1). Yitzchak, Rivka and their children descend to Gerar and take up residence there. A series of incidents ensue, as detailed above in the second section of the summary. To briefly recap, the inhabitants' of Gerar express interest in Rivka, thinking that she is Yitzchak's sister. Avimelech discovers that she is in fact Yitzchak's wife and affords her protection. This of course parallels the almost identical experience of Avraham and Sarah in Gerar (*Breisheet* 20).

Yitzchak's material success arouses jealousy among the local peoples, and they attempt to discourage his continued presence by filling in his wells. Curiously, the Torah adds that these were the very wells dug by Avraham his father. Yitzchak, undeterred, re-digs the wells and assigns them the very names that his father Avraham had given them.

The family eventually relocates to Be'er Sheva, and Yitzchak is afforded a divine vision that dispels his fears. Just as Avraham his father had done in similar circumstances (12:7), Yitzchak proceeds to build an altar and to invoke God's name. Soon thereafter, Avimelech and his entourage arrive to negotiate a covenant with him. The two parties exchange oaths and ratify a treaty, just as Avraham had done years before at the very same location (21:22–34). The section is concluded with an unmistakable flashback to those events, as a new well is dug by Yitzchak's servants and named "Shiva." "And therefore the name of that city was Be'er Sheva until this very day." It will be recalled that the name "Be'er Sheva" was initially bestowed by Avraham at a much earlier time to commemorate his sealing of his oath (שבועה) with Avimelech (21:31).

What is the meaning of all of these parallels? Is it sheer coincidence that Yitzchak and Rivka undergo such similar life events as Avraham and Sarah? It is almost as if the later two have no independent, original experiences of which to speak. Clearly, the Torah must be indicating something consequential to us by narrating only those events that are analogous to moments in the life of Avraham and Sarah. It seems plausible that the point of the parallels is to emphasize to us that Yitzchak and Rivka are very much following in the footsteps of Avraham and Sarah, their parents. The trail that they had earlier blazed, the revolution in human thought that they unleashed by introducing ethical monotheism to the world, remains very much alive due to the concerted efforts of Yitzchak and Rivka. It is as if these two have actually *become* Avraham and Sarah, so closely do the events of their lives seem to overlap. At the very heart of this congruence lies a pertinent truth:

Avraham and Sarah are progenitors of a nation not because of their own personal accomplishments in acquiring faith and trust, but rather because they have succeeded in passing on their precious legacy to their son and to his wife, both of whom have enthusiastically embraced the same destiny. Yitzchak and Rivka together embody the principles that were faithfully transmitted by Avraham and Sarah, and their lives therefore bear so much resemblance to those of their parents.

Esav's Marriages

The account of the sojourn in Gerar thus also serves as a glaring foil to the brief two-verse account of Esav's marriages, which introduces the final section of the Parasha:

> When Esav was forty years old, he took as his wives Yehudit the daughter of Be'eri the Chittite and Basmat the daughter of Elon the Chittite. These wives caused vexation of spirit to Yitzchak and to Rivka. (*Breisheet* 26:33–34)

The report of these marriages constitutes a frightful juxtaposition and stands in blinding contrast to the sojourn at Gerar! Esav, the firstborn, the hope of the next generation, the promising scion to his parents' holy and demanding mission, here aspires to follow in the footsteps of his father Yitzchak, who also took a wife at the age of forty (23:20). But how disappointing, dismal and discouraging is his choice, for he decides to take Chittite (i.e., Canaanite) women as his wives! It will be recalled that Avraham his grandfather went to his grave only after having adjured his faithful servant not to take for Yitzchak "a wife from the daughters of Canaan" (24:1–4). As for Yitzchak himself, it was "unnecessary for Avraham to command his son concerning it, for he knew that Yitzchak would not abrogate the wishes of his father and the oath placed upon the servant, for Yitzchak was very much aware of the matter" (Ramban, commentary to 24:3).

Avraham correctly surmised that for his son to marry the daughters of Canaan would spell certain ruin for the ideology of ethical monotheism. The attractions of Canaanite polytheistic culture, the intense familial and communal connections that a Canaanite wife would introduce to the marriage, would create insurmountable obstacles to raising children committed to a different way of life, a life of responsibility and obligation. Had Yitzchak married a Canaanite woman, the death knell would have been sounded for the lifelong work of Avraham and Sarah, and all hopes of a future nation would have been dashed. Therefore, Avraham made his wishes crystal clear to his son Yitzchak and the servant, and the prohibition was faithfully upheld.

And yet cognizant of this, nay, in spite of it, Esav consciously turned his back on that mission and brazenly took Chittite wives, in contravention of his grandfather's injunction, and in contempt of his patrimony! No wonder that these wives caused vexation of spirit and "bitterness of soul" to Yitzchak and to Rivka. How dejected they must have felt and how disappointed in their firstborn son. In effect, while the sojourn at Gerar highlighted the determination of Yitzchak and Rivka to preserve their values at all costs, Esav's nuptials demonstrated his utter contempt for their efforts! And if his earlier peddling of the birthright could be defended by the accused as a rash act of youthful indiscretion, his marriages to Chittite women at the reflective age of forty are indefensible!

The Bestowal of the Blessing

Yitzchak ages and his eyes grow dim. With the specter of mortality ominously looming, Yitzchak decides that it is time to bestow the covenantal blessings on his firstborn son. "Behold, I am now old," he tells Esav, his eldest, "I know not the day of my death. Therefore, take your weapons, go to the field and bring me back game. Prepare for me the tasty food that I love and bring it before me, so that I might bless you before I die" (27:1–4).

In light of our earlier analysis, Yitzchak's conduct seems incomprehensible. How could he have intended to bless Esav after all that we know? Did the infirmities of old age cause Yitzchak to forget how Esav had so contemptuously flung the mantle of the firstborn from upon himself, so that he might instead devour his bowl of soup? Were not his son's subsequent intermarriages damning evidence of utter disdain for the precious legacy that Yitzchak and Rivka had so jealously guarded? The Ramban accentuates the paradox further:

> It was Yitzchak's intent to bless Esav so that he would merit the benediction bestowed upon Avraham to inherit the land. Further, Esav would be designated to fulfill the covenant with God, for indeed he was the firstborn. (27:4)

How then are we to understand Yitzchak's patent lack of judgment and his failure to exercise even a minimal amount of parental discretion? And how indeed to understand Rivka's recourse to deceit and subterfuge, in order to secure the blessings for Ya'acov?

The commentaries offer different approaches. Rashi suggests that Esav, true to his vocation of the hunt, was a master deceiver, a sly and skillful manipulator who was able to hoodwink his trusting father into believing that he was truly a pious and spiritual son (see his comments on 25:27). Only Rivka, it seems, was able to see through this carefully crafted facade. Of course, this explanation is difficult to sustain in light of our knowledge of Esav's blatant conduct in choosing wives.

Much more plausible is the approach of Rabbi Ovadiah Seforno (15th century, Italy), who senses in Yitzchak's premature blindness a metaphor for spiritual sightlessness as well:

> Yitzchak failed to recognize Esav's evil character, and should have protested his son's intermarriages. The attempt to bestow the blessing on Esav was a terrible error of judgment . . . The blindness with which he was stricken happened also to Eli (see Samuel 1:2:11–26), who failed to reprove his sons concerning their unacceptable conduct . . . (commentary to *Breisheet* 26:35, 27:1)

For the Seforno, Yitzchak is not at all deceived by Esav's behavior as Rashi would have us believe. On the contrary, he is well aware of it but willfully chooses to overlook it! Seforno's approach would of course explain Rivka's conduct as well. According to Rashi's approach, should we not be puzzled by her lack of communication with her husband? Why did she never speak to him about Esav's concealed character flaws and his unsuitability for the blessing? Why was there no conversation whatsoever between the two, as if a dysfunctional family dynamic exists in the household?

If, on the other hand, we adopt Seforno's interpretation, the picture is clarified. Rivka does not speak to Yitzchak about the matter because she has done so a thousand times in the past! And her words have fallen on deaf ears because Yitzchak has consistently decided to close them out! Blinded by his own shortsightedness, he is determined to select Esav as the spiritual heir, and no amount of reasoned arguments will sway him from his decision. Thus, there is no recourse for her except to prevail upon a reluctant Ya'acov to seize the blessings by deceit, to force Yitzchak's hand to do what destiny demands.

Seforno invites us to compare Yitzchak with Eli the High Priest, who presided at Shilo during its final days of decline. Eli's corrupt sons, Chofni and Pinchas, used their privileged positions to abuse the people who came to supplicate at the Mishkan and their old father remained impassive and silent. In much the same way, suggests the Seforno, Yitzchak averted his gaze from his firstborn's indiscretions, even as Esav flouted the conventions of his precious status.

Esav the Hunter

But having resolved the question concerning Rivka's conduct on the eve of the bestowal of the blessings, we are left with a larger question to ponder. What is it about Esav that Yitzchak finds so compelling, to the point of being prepared to ignore his most unsavory attributes? Does Esav possess any qualities whatsoever that make him a suitable choice for the office of firstborn? Cryptically, all that the Torah relates on the matter is that Yitzchak "loved Esav because he brought him from the hunt" (*Breisheet* 25:28). How might this fleeting reference to fatherly affection help us understand Yitzchak's motives?

We saw earlier that the designation of firstborn involved God-centered spiritual pursuits and was expressed in Sefer Breisheet as the readiness to perpetuate the legacy of Avraham and Sarah so that it might ultimately transform the world. This implies, of course, that the mission of the firstborn could not remain the preserve of individuals indefinitely. It had to eventually be translated into nationhood, just as the oft-repeated divine promises to Avraham and Yitzchak implied. The one who merited the patriarchal blessing had to carry upon his shoulders the onerous burden of founding a nation. Nation-building involves extraordinary ability, for not all men or women possess the crucial mix of ambition, determination, skill, foresight, and imperiousness that the calling demands.

The portrayal of Esav earlier in the story recalls another prominent hunter in the Hebrew scriptures: Nimrod the mighty. A descendent of Cham, his postdiluvial exploits were singled out for special mention in the Parasha of Noach:

> Kush begat Nimrod, who began to be a mighty man in the land. He was a mighty hunter before God who inspired a proverb: "He is like Nimrod, a mighty hunter before God!" The beginning of his kingdom was in Babylon, Erech, Akkad and Kalneh, in the land of Shin'ar. From that land he extended his rule to Assyria and built Nineveh, Rechovot-Ir and Kalach. Also Resen, between Nineveh and Kalach, it is the great city. (10:8–12)

The place names mentioned in this passage dot all of southern and northern Mesopotamia. "Nimrod the hunter" was a builder of cities and the founder of an empire. The Torah implies that there exists a definite connection between his prowess as a hunter and his aptitude as an emperor. The successful hunter possesses physical power, skill, determination, alacrity, and foresight. He also must be crafty, stealthy, and sly. He is not dissuaded by the sight of bloodshed and is able to maintain calm and resolve in the face of fear. In short, a conqueror of animals can easily adapt his abilities to become a conqueror of men.

In the words of the Ramban:

> Nimrod was the first man to rule by force over other people. He was the first king, for until his days there were no wars and no empires. First he overpowered the Babylonians and ruled over them by might, and then extended his dominion over Assyria, building fortified cities and tightening his grip . . . (commentary to *Breisheet* 10:9)

It is no wonder that the ancient near eastern king, whether he hails from Egypt, Assyria, or Babylon, is often represented, in literature as well as in art, as a hunter! The symbolism is trenchant: No other image captures so completely the king's essential characteristics and no other image is as successful in striking fear and foreboding into his subjects' hearts. The hunter iconography communicates the king's regal power as well as his ruthlessness. It visually broadcasts his nation-building charge: "I will sustain and protect my loyal subjects but brook no compromise with rebels!"

Astonishingly, it is the Midrash that first ties these disparate elements together. The Midrash relates that when Rivka dressed her son Ya'acov in the "desirous mantle of Esav her elder" as he prepared to seize the blessing (*Breisheet* 27:15), he donned "the garments that Esav had coveted from Nimrod!" (Breisheet Rabbah 65:16). In other words, avers the Midrash, Esav shared not only Nimrod's cruel aptitude for the hunt but his ruthless ability to be a ruler of men as well.

The Fateful Moment

Yitzchak grows old and begins to ponder the task that lies ahead. A nation must be founded whose ideas will conquer the world. Which of his two sons is better suited for the task? Will it be the placid and serene Ya'acov, who prefers introspection and solitude and the bleating of the sheep? Or will it be charismatic and dynamic Esav, who demonstrates unbridled enthusiasm, enterprise, and yes, an appetite for dominion? Confronted by the awesome choice, blinded by its terrible gravity, Yitzchak decides in favor of his true firstborn and selects Esav to receive the blessings of the covenant. It is a decision fraught with misgivings, for he knows well Esav's failings. But do it he must, for how else shall the nascent nation survive in a hostile world, if not by the power of the sword?

Rivka, insightful, perceptive and kind, knows otherwise. The future people of Israel will not secure their survival through arms or weapons. They will not win adherents to their cause by way of guile, coercion and bloodshed. They will not, by the exercise of military might alone, ride out the whirlwinds that will engulf them and threaten to overwhelm their ideas. Israel's survival and success will be a function of a quiet and persistent faith, an abiding trust that will fortify them so that they might endure the most horrific of attempts to destroy their grand vision. They will conquer the world not by the edge of the sword, but by gentle and impassioned words. In short, the nation of Israel shall look to Ya'acov as their founding father, and it is he who truly deserves the blessings of the covenant. And so Rivka takes matters into her own hands, setting right that which must be righted, defying Yitzchak even as she absolves him. The patriarch, when he discovers the subterfuge, will endorse her devious decision and confirm Ya'acov's blessing, even as he confronts Esav's anguish and his own terrible misjudgment.

Yitzchak Regains His Sight

Esav, enraged at his brother's deception, resolves to kill him and Ya'acov is forced to flee eastward to Charan, employing the pretext of looking for a wife. Yitzchak, now finally aware of his folly and convinced of Ya'acov's suitability, sends him off with the precious blessings of Avraham and the revived injunction not to take a wife from the daughters of Canaan, the very core principles of the covenant with God that Esav had so blatantly rejected! Ya'acov tearfully takes his leave, his family left splintered and stunned: There will be no reconciliation between Esav and his mother for the rest of her days and none between Ya'acov and his brother. At this juncture, however, Esav does something quite astounding:

> Esav saw that the daughters of Canaan were bad in the eyes of his father Yitzchak. Esav therefore went to Yishmael and took Machlat the daughter of Yishmael . . . in addition to his other wives. (*Breisheet* 28:8–9)

The Torah indicates Machlat's lineage to underscore that she is a descendent of Avraham and therefore a suitable mate. Even more striking than the genealogy is Esav's newfound compunctions and Yitzchak's regaining of his spiritual sight, for Esav has finally realized that his two Canaanite wives are bad "*in the eyes* of Yitzchak his father"! Esav will not go so far as to surrender his first Canaanite wives and attempt to reclaim his birthright and its responsibilities, but for Yitzchak, at least, the bout of blindness is finally over. In the aftermath of it all, Ya'acov will go forth to secure his rightful place.

FOR FURTHER STUDY:

(1) It is instructive that the only other hunter figure in the Pentateuch is Yishmael himself. According to *Breisheet* 21:20, Yishmael "dwelt in the wilderness and became an archer." The bow and arrow were standard equipment of the hunter, as indicated by Yitzchak's words to his firstborn son: "Now, take your gear, your quiver and your bow, and go out to the field to hunt me some game" (27:3). On two occasions, God extended to Yishmael a promise of nationhood and even empire (16:10–12 and 21:18).

VAYETZE

The Gods of Theft

Genesis 28:10-32:3

PARASHAT VAYETZE is a dramatic narrative of setbacks and progress, perseverance and success. Ya'acov, banished from home and hearth and the promised land of his birth by the murderous rage of his brother Esav, flees Be'er Sheva and wearily treads northeastwards towards Charan. As the flaming red orb sinks lower and lower, casting ominous black shadows across his path, Ya'acov recalls the abrupt and anguished parting from his beloved mother and father – how unexpectedly have things turned out! His father's parting blessings of land and legacy and the love of God now seem like a fleeting dream turned to dust.

Darkness falls. The solitary figure sets down his meager belongings, gathers some stones and arranges them about his head to keep the night demons at bay. Ya'acov sleeps fitfully, his brow fevered, his breathing fast, until God appears to him in a comforting vision of a towering ladder that connects heaven and earth, as silent angels rhythmically ascend and descend upon its rungs. God reassures the slumberer that He will be with him, that His protection will be upon him, that He will never leave him and that one day Ya'acov will return. Rising on the morrow with the heaviness lifted from his heart, Ya'acov journeys onwards, finally arriving at a well surrounded by shepherds and their flocks. There he meets and tearfully embraces his beautiful cousin Rachel, and in that cathartic moment he commits his future to hers.

Employed by Lavan

Entering the avaricious employ of his uncle Lavan, Ya'acov spends the next twenty years laboring mightily to secure wives and sheep, children and herds, his hard-won achievements all the while held in check by the wily Aramean. In the end, the two have an inevitable falling out, and Ya'acov, fearing the worst, contemplates escape. Fortified by a divine vision calling upon him to return home, he furtively gathers together his family and his flocks. Taking advantage of Lavan's temporary absence, Ya'acov takes flight westwards towards Canaan. But when Lavan receives word of his son-in-law's defection, he immediately gives chase. Pursuing Ya'acov with all of the self-serving single-mindedness that is his most notorious trait, Lavan traps the hapless patriarch at Mount Gil'ad and promptly unleashes a most disingenuous diatribe:

> Lavan said to Ya'acov: "What have you done by deceiving me (literally "stealing my heart")? You have led away my daughters like captives of the sword! Why did you hide your intentions to flee and deceive me (literally "steal from me")? Why

didn't you tell me? I would surely have sent you off with joy and song, with the drum and the lyre! You did not even let me kiss my sons and my daughters – now surely you have acted foolishly! It is within my power to harm all of you, but the Lord of your fathers said to me last night: 'Be careful that you do not speak to Ya'acov either good or bad.' Now, you have certainly gone your way, for you have yearned to return to your father's house, but why have you stolen my gods?!" (*Breisheet* 31:26–30)

No less than three times, Lavan accuses Ya'acov of theft: "You have stolen my heart, you have stolen from me, and you have stolen my gods." Interspersed among these three serious allegations of larceny are further claims of patent wrongdoing: "You have taken my daughters captive, you have denied me my children and grandchildren, and (most ludicrous of all!) you have deprived me of the opportunity to send you off with gladness and mirth." The effect of the whole is to publicly and perniciously cast Ya'acov in the most unfavorable of lights: "You are a liar and a cheat, a swindler and a charlatan! If it were up to me, I would punish your misconduct, but for the fact that your shiftless God seems to sanction if not downright encourage the misbehavior!"

Now anyone who has followed the tribulations of our gentle forefather during the course of Parashat VaYetze knows how utterly baseless and unfounded are the charges contained in Lavan's invective. How faithfully and loyally Ya'acov has served his uncle (31:6), even as the latter constantly changed the terms of his employment (31:7), all the time attempting to secure more at Ya'acov's expense. Beginning with the unjust substitution of Leah for Rachel under the wedding canopy (29:23–27) and continuing uninterrupted for a period of twenty years, Lavan has done everything in his power to deprive Ya'acov of what was rightfully his. Never has the Aramean lost an opportunity to cheat his nephew and son-in-law out of his wages (30:28–36), to unjustly hold him responsible for accident or loss (31:39), or to impose conditions of employment that were cruel and unreasonable (31:40). In short, never has Lavan been anything to his loyal son-in-law or even to his own daughters and grandchildren, except a selfish, insensitive and uncharitable miser (31:14), a rude and dishonest deceiver (31:15) and an incorrigible cheat (31:16). But true to his name that means "white," Lavan has always performed his evil work under the carefully cultivated guise of civility and propriety (29:13–14), uprightness and honesty (29:15) and genuine social concern (29:26). What a master of manipulation, an expert of exploitation and a genius of deceit!

The Theft of the "Terafim"

There is, however, one small but glaring inconsistency in this otherwise perfect contrast of genuine integrity (Ya'acov) versus surface veneer (Lavan), understated and uncelebrated honesty (Ya'acov) versus public persona and whitewashed wrongdoing (Lavan). It concerns one of Lavan's accusations, the only well-founded one of the bunch, a matter of most troubling material facts: the theft of his so-called *terafim* or household gods. Recall that Lavan had concluded his tirade against Ya'acov with the most damning accusation of them all: "Why have you stolen my gods?!" (31:30). Ya'acov disputed the claim vehemently, even inviting Lavan, in an act of unthinkable decency, to search through all of his possessions! But there could be no denying the truth, for the Torah itself indicated that on the eve of their hurried departure from Lavan's homestead, "Rachel stole the *terafim* that were her father's" (31:19). This petty act of pilferage was magnified by her brash concealment of the matter later on, for even as Lavan searched the tents, she surreptitiously spirited the gods into the saddle bag of the camel and then promptly placed herself immovable upon them. In her concluding act of fraudulence, she begged her father's indulgence for her failure to rise in his presence even as she feigned the symptoms of menstrual discomfort!

The questions raised by the episode are myriad: What are the mysterious *terafim* and why does Rachel steal them? Why does she then hide them from Lavan, all the while keeping Ya'acov blissfully unaware of her deed? What might be the deeper meaning of her polite excuse for not rising in her father's presence? Significantly, the classical commentaries were almost unanimous in their explanation of Rachel's motives. Representative is the view of the Rashbam:

> [She took them so that] they would not inform Lavan that Ya'acov desired to escape, as the verse states "there shall be neither *ephod* nor *terafim*" (*Hoshea* 3:4), "for the *terafim* speak vanity" (*Zechariah* 10:2). The ancients were wont to divine by them . . . (commentary to *Breisheet* 31:19)

Here the Rashbam relies on other biblical references in order to explain an otherwise obscure phenomenon. Elsewhere in the Tanakh, *terafim* appear as some sort of idolatrous images (prepared in human form) that were used for prognostication (see in particular *Shoftim* 17:5 and 18:1–4; *Yechezkel* 21:26). Now Lavan had already presented himself earlier in the narrative as a diviner (*Breisheet* 30:27), for when Ya'acov asked for payment for his labors, Lavan remarked that he had ascertained through divination that Ya'acov's hard work has been the source of his household's blessing (compare to Yosef as viceroy claiming to have uncovered the thief of his silver goblet through the art of divination, in *Breisheet* 44:5). In other words, says the Rashbam, Rachel feared that as the plans for their escape took shape and gathered momentum, Lavan would rely upon his occult skills and the instrument of the *terafim* in order to uncover the plot and then prevent them from leaving.

While the explanation of the Rashbam is intriguing, adopting it introduces more serious problems. Are to we assume that Rachel, a budding monotheist and mother of Israel, believed in the efficacy of discredited idols and feared her father's "powers" of prognostication? And if indeed this was so, then her attempt was in any case utterly ineffective, for very soon after their escape Lavan uncovered the plan through more conventional and reliable means – "it was told to Lavan on the third day that Ya'acov had fled . . ." (31:22). Lavan pursued them, quickly overtook them, and threatened them with destruction precisely because they had stolen those very gods – so much for thwarting her father's villainy!

While doubt remains to this day concerning the true nature of *terafim* and their cultic use, one thing is clear: Lavan regarded those objects as his precious household gods. He himself describes them as divinities (31:30), and one can only assume that when he later solemnly swears an oath in the name of the gods of Nachor (31:53), it is the image of the *terafim* that he sees before him. Bearing all of this in mind, we must offer a different interpretation. As we noted earlier, Lavan, though always careful to present himself as a paragon of virtue and civility, was actually a seasoned villain in disguise. The real Lavan, once shorn of his carefully crafted and cultivated facade, was revealed to be a malicious and menacing character. For twenty years he had been engaged in underhanded schemes to cheat Ya'acov at every turn. Never had his sullied hands been idle from attempting some new and outrageous act of theft at the expense of his honest and sincere son-in-law. One may go so far as to say that the gods that Lavan worshipped (for what man does not seek the blessings of the gods for his criminal and immoral acts?), insofar as such a man may be said to engage in worship, were the gods of cupidity and avarice. To them he paid homage and before them he prostrated himself in supplication. For Lavan, theft was a way of life!

Justice for the Gods of Theft

Now the time comes for Ya'acov and his household to flee. Ya'acov justifiably feels that he will not be able to secure Lavan's permission to leave and to return to Canaan his birthplace, and certainly (contrary to Lavan's vehement protests later on) he will not be sent off with the drum and the lyre, and joyous songs of farewell! Summoning his wives to the seclusion of the fields, he explains their need to escape. Lavan's own daughters, knowing their father only too well, offer not protests but rather cries of encouragement. Journeying forth from Lavan's homestead and looking back one final time to the location where all of them had spent twenty turbulent and pain-filled years, Rachel decides to steal the *terafim* "that were her father's" (31:19). Considering the matter from the broadest possible perspective yields but one interpretation for Rachel's otherwise inexplicable act: With her duplicitous deed she intends to mete out just desserts to the gods of theft, for they have been stolen in kind!

Soon Lavan catches them and unleashes his fury. Accusing Ya'acov of every indiscretion, he aims to expose his son-in-law as a common criminal while presenting himself, in contrast, as an upright champion of virtue. And the onlookers side with him! Hasn't Ya'acov fled under cover of darkness, does he not stand accused of seizing Lavan's gods? What else has he taken from Lavan's household while the latter has been away shearing the sheep? But now, Ya'acov takes up the challenge, allowing his father-in-law the unheard-of opportunity to search all of his things! Of course he does not know that Rachel has taken the *terafim*, nor may he, for his protest here must be absolutely sincere and truthful.

In the meantime, Rachel has relocated the *terafim* to the saddle of the camel, and in a final and fitting feat of ignominy, she gingerly places her bottom upon them. What an act of indiscretion towards the gods, but these are no gods of goodness and compassion, but rather of stinginess and greed. Thus it is that the *terafim* are not only stolen but denigrated and humiliated as well. Now, having roughly rummaged the tents of Ya'acov and of his wives in a fruitless search for his gods, Lavan unexpectedly encounters his daughter Rachel as she perplexingly sits upon the camel, a sardonic smile on her lips. Standing before her, the saddle bag slightly bulging beneath her seat, Lavan suddenly realizes where the *terafim* must be hiding. In the final act of the drama, Rachel offers a polite explanation for her inability to rise, a proper and civil response that must have caused her father to gnash his teeth in indignation, for he himself has rehearsed a similar script innumerable times! How often has Lavan himself secretly stolen from patient Ya'acov, all the while explaining his motives to the masses with the most sugared of words and phrases? But can he now ask Rachel to dismount, as the curious onlookers from both sides gather around them, in light of her gracious and eminently civil explanations?

Thus, by stealing the *terafim* from her father, Rachel has returned measure for measure to those symbols of vicious theft. By placing them in the saddle bag of the camel and sitting upon them, she has emphasized their utter contemptibility. By facing down her father and offering polite explanations in courteous tones, even as he knows (and she knows that he knows!) the true whereabouts of the *terafim*, Rachel administers the coup de grace: Lavan has finally been defeated at his own game! In the end, Lavan finds *nothing* of his goods among Ya'acov's possessions, neither gold nor silver, neither documents nor deeds, not even a simple needle and thread for the patriarch to sew up his tattered cloak. Thus it is that Lavan is trounced, his gods of theft themselves stolen, and his wild accusations exposed for all to see as being utterly groundless. And it is none other than Rachel his own daughter who has turned the tables against him, matching his lethal spars blow for vicious blow. We may unwittingly have stumbled upon Rashi's interpretation, albeit in truncated form, that Rachel's theft of the *terafim* was her noble attempt to "separate her father from idolatry!" (commentary to *Breisheet* 31:19).

An Unmistakable Wordplay

Now it is Ya'acov's turn to speak:

> Ya'acov became angry and strove with Lavan, saying: "What is my transgression and iniquity that you have pursued me so? You have handled all of my things but what have you found that is from your house? Place it down before your relatives and mine, so that they might judge between us! During the twenty years that I was with you, your sheep and goats never lost their young, nor did I consume a single ram from the flock. I never presented you with an attacked animal but rather made up the deficiency myself, for you so demanded. Whether stolen by day or by night, you held me responsible. By day I was consumed by scorching heat and by frost at night, and my sleep was snatched from my eyes. For twenty years I have been in your household – for fourteen years I served you for your two daughters, and six years for your sheep, and you changed my wages ten times! If the God of my ancestors, the God of Avraham and the dread of Yitzchak, had not been with me, you would have sent me away empty-handed. But God saw my plight and the effort of my hands, and last night He rendered judgment!" (31:36–42)

Lavan, finally exposed by Ya'acov for what he truly is, is momentarily silent. Though he will yet try one last time to emerge with the upper hand (31:43), he knows, along with all of the onlookers, that he has lost. He has been bested by the simple sincerity of his decent son-in-law and by the adroit daughter that stood by her husband, and the *terafim* have been bested as well. Nothing remains but to conclude a détente with Ya'acov (31:44), for Lavan can no longer defeat him.

While it is Rachel who has won the day, God has not been absent from the story. He has preserved Ya'acov from harm and vindicated him, just as He had pledged some twenty years earlier. In the course of his impassioned response, Ya'acov reintroduces divine providence to the scene as he inadvertently alludes to the kernel of the entire matter. Ya'acov states that "I never presented you with a torn animal but rather made up the deficiency myself, for so you demanded. Whether stolen by day or by night, you held me responsible." Here, Ya'acov lays out the evidence of Lavan's unfairness, for no shepherd should be made to pay for animals that have been unexpectedly attacked by wolves or wild dogs. No shepherd should be held accountable for animals stolen at night, when darkness falls and predators lurk (compare to *Shemot* 22:12). But Lavan did hold Ya'acov liable and the loyal patriarch did acquiesce!

Unbeknownst to himself, Ya'acov now employs a wordplay that goes unnoticed by all except for Lavan and Rachel, the father and daughter who had earlier locked tense glares over the disappearance of the *terafim*. In biblical Hebrew, a "torn animal" is called a *terefa* or טריפה. Though spelled slightly differently than *terafim* (תרפים), the similar sound is unmistakable to sensitive or else culpable ears. "I never presented you with a *terefa*," states Ya'acov, "but rather made up the deficiency . . . *stolen* by day or by night, you held me responsible!" As Lavan hears these impassioned words, he can also hear God's own, spoken through the agency of the patriarch: "Here you are, old man, bothered with the theft of *terafim*, with stolen gods that you worship so faithfully. Don't you realize that you yourself are the thief and the liar, that it is not futile *terafim* that are at stake but rather the unforgivable seizure of a poor man's honest wages? For the ostensible theft of your precious *terafim* you are willing to commit violence, but what about the real theft that has gone on in your household for the past twenty years?!"

Our Parasha thus presents us with a brilliant study in contrasts concerning sincerity and deception, appearances and reality, true virtue and feigned facades. Often, we are led astray by what we see or hear to make hasty and unwarranted judgments about people and their motives, but the God of justice knows better. Ultimately, falsehood is revealed for what it really is. The men and the gods that champion dishonesty as an instrument for self-advancement discredit themselves and, in the end, often suffer the fate of exposure that they deserve. Lavan the Aramean is not fondly remembered for his selfless acts of altruism or for his grandfatherly generosity. Instead, he is unfavorably recalled as a dangerous impostor, a fraud extraordinaire, and an impious con artist.

Our Sages understood the matter only too well when they proclaimed in the Haggadah that "One must go and learn what Lavan the Aramean attempted to do to Ya'acov our father, for Pharaoh only decreed the death of the males, but Lavan attempted to destroy everything!" Sadly, there is today no shortage of Lavan's protégés, filling to overflowing the world's halls of power, brazenly proclaiming their innocence even as they go about their dark business and heap scorn upon the blameless. But we need not look so far afield, for there are also more local varieties of Lavan, those that taint our communities with their hypocrisy and deceit. Perhaps (though we shrink from the thought) there is even a small Lavan or two that dwells within our own hearts, encouraging us to surreptitiously seek our fortune at someone else's expense. The Torah asks us to reject Lavan's overtures and instead to turn for inspiration to our father Ya'acov, who maintained his integrity in spite of the corrosive influence of his father-in-law. As Maimonides codifies in his *Mishneh Torah*, Laws of Hire 13:7:

> Just as the employer is enjoined not to rob the wages of the poor or else to withhold them, so too the employee is commanded not to steal from the employer by wasting time here and there such that the entire day is expended in deceitful sloth. Rather the employee must be strict about the use of his time . . . and must use all of his energies. Righteous Ya'acov proclaimed that he served Lavan with "all of his strength." Therefore he was rewarded for his efforts in this world as well, as the verse states "the man increased exceedingly much." (*Breisheet* 30:43)

FOR FURTHER STUDY:

(1) There are many similarities between the story of Ya'acov in the house of Lavan and the experience of the people of Israel in Egypt. In broad terms, both accounts speak of welcoming but wily hosts, opportunity and privilege insidiously transformed into oppression, threats of decimation defused by a hasty exodus, and murderous pursuit reined in by overt divine intervention that saved from harm. If our above analysis is correct, then we may add one more parallel to the list: the degradation of Lavan's *terafim*. These symbols of immoral and unjust polytheism suffer the same fate as the "gods of Egypt" that are laid low by God's mighty plagues on the eve of Israel's departure: "And I shall pass through the land of Egypt on this night, and I shall smite all of the firstborn in the land of Egypt, both man and beast, and *I shall execute vengeance upon all of the gods of Egypt, for I am God*" (*Shemot* 12:12).

(2) The dynamics of our Parasha – a tense relational triad consisting of a jealous and scheming father-in-law, a blameless and devoted son-in-law and a loving daughter committed to the welfare of her maltreated husband – is exactly analogous to the story of vengeful king Shaul, his talented son-in-law David, and Michal the wife of the latter who shields her husband from harm. Chapter 19 of *Shemuel I* preserves an account not unlike our own, in which otherwise mysterious *terafim* make an unexpected appearance as instruments of subterfuge, even as they remain concealed from plain view. While beyond the scope of this essay to analyze, the careful reader should note that there, just as here, the *terafim* are brilliantly manipulated by the industrious wife to expose the villainy of her father while highlighting the innocence of her husband for all to see.

VAYISHLACH

Ya'acov's Restoration

Genesis 32:4-36:43

TWENTY YEARS have elapsed since Ya'acov left home, fearfully fleeing the fury of his brother. Arriving alone and penniless at the house of Lavan his uncle, he now leaves that house with wives, children and great flocks. God has indeed preserved him and fulfilled His pledge to "keep watch over him wherever he will go" and now Ya'acov is poised to return to the land of Canaan and to the tearful embrace of his aged parents. Although two decades have passed, Ya'acov is justifiably apprehensive that his brother Esav has never forgiven his seizing of the birthright and the blessing, and may yet harbor malignant will towards him.

In the meantime, while Ya'acov tended the sheep of his wily uncle in Charan, Esav left the ancestral land of Canaan to establish himself in the rocky fastness of Se'ir. Indigenous peoples known as the Chorites had earlier inhabited this rugged region, southeast of the Dead Sea. But by employing a crafty combination of intermarriage and warfare, neutralizing the natives from within while overwhelming them from without, Esav's clan succeeded in quickly displacing them, thereby securing the land for themselves (*Breisheet* 36:2, 20–25; *Devarim* 2:12)

Ya'acov, however, is keenly aware that his return to Canaan is also his confrontation with the demons of the past. It will not be possible to enter the land stealthily; sooner or later a meeting and perhaps a clash with his twin brother is inevitable. Does his brother still feel lethal resentment towards him for having wrested the birthright and the patriarchal blessing from their old and blind father Yitzchak? Sending messengers ahead to ascertain Esav's intentions, he is alarmed by their report that Esav is approaching with a group of four hundred fighting men. Ya'acov responds to the news by adopting a multifaceted approach: He divides his own camp and prepares for war, he sends gifts to impulsive Esav in order to appease his ancient anger, and then he implores the God of his ancestors to save: "Rescue me now from the clutches of my brother, from the clutches of Esav, for I fear that he will smite me along with the mothers and the children . . ." (*Breisheet* 32:12).

Ya'acov's Prayer and Its Components

Ya'acov's anxious prayer, tense yet hopeful, sanguine while solemn, offers us an important study in the art of standing before God and imploring His mercy. Let us quote his impassioned words in their entirety:

> Ya'acov said: The Lord of my father Avraham and my father Yitzchak, God who said to me "return to your land and to your birthplace for I will deal goodly with

> you!" I do not deserve all of the kindness and all of the truth that You have done with your servant, for with my staff I traversed this Yarden and now I have become two encampments. Rescue me now from the clutches of my brother, from the clutches of Esav, for I fear that he will smite me along with the mothers and the children. But You had said, "I will surely bring goodness upon you, and I will multiply your descendents as numerous as the sand of the sea that cannot be counted." (32:10–13)

Structurally, the prayer employs a bracketing effect, for the divine pledges of protection, restoration and innumerable descendents neatly frame the core element of a plea for salvation ("Rescue me now from the clutches of my brother, from the clutches of Esav, for I fear that he will smite me along with the mothers and the children"). But that plea for salvation is appended to a statement of gratitude, for Ya'acov first recalls all of the kindnesses that God has bestowed upon him already. Empty-handed he had left Be'er Sheva to journey to Charan, bearing only his staff in his hand, while now he returns with a great household of wives, children, servants, flocks, livestock and camels.

When we carefully consider the content and form of Ya'acov's prayer, we realize that his poignant petition serves as the muse for the creation of formal prayer, the liturgy that only began to develop some 1,200 years later when the people of Israel returned from Babylonian exile! At that time, according to tradition, the gifted Ezra the scribe gathered around himself a cohort of sincere scholars and leaders, the so-called Men of the Great Assembly (אנשי כנסת הגדולה), who enacted a number of important laws to sustain the nascent community of Jews that gathered around the ruins of Jerusalem under the aegis of the Persian kings. One of the most important of these enactments was the composition of the daily prayer known as the *Shemoneh Esrei* or "Eighteen Benedictions," a paradigm that achieved final form in the aftermath of the destruction of the Second Temple and became the standard for Jewish worship until this very day (see TB *Megilla* 17b–18a). The *Shemoneh Esrei* is structurally predicated upon three basic elements: an opening series of three blessings of "praise" in which God's power is recounted, a middle section of twelve (later thirteen) blessings of "petition" in which God's assistance is requested, and three concluding blessings of "gratitude" in which God's kindnesses are recalled.

Ya'acov's prayer preserves this tripartite division, albeit with the critical elements arranged in a slightly different order: praise – "the Lord of my father Avraham and my father Yitzchak, God who said to me: 'Return to your land and to your birthplace for I will deal goodly with you!','" gratitude – "I do not deserve all of the kindness and all of the truth that You have done with your servant, for with my staff I traversed this Yarden and now I have become two encampments," and petition – "Rescue me now from the clutches of my brother, from the clutches of Esav, for I fear that he will smite me along with the mothers and the children." Additionally, we note that Ya'acov's prayer opens with a reference to the God of his father Avraham and his father Yitzchak, the one who pledged to "deal kindly with him." This sequence clearly inspires the opening blessing of the *Shemoneh Esrei* as well: "Blessed are you God, our Lord and the Lord of our ancestors, the Lord of Avraham, the Lord of Yitzchak and the Lord of Ya'acov . . . He who bestows merciful kindnesses." As Seforno perceptively remarks on our passage:

> The verse states: "Ya'acov said: the Lord of my father Avraham and my father Yitzchak" – Ya'acov first made mention of God's praise and His acts of kindness.

> He then recalled the merit of his own ancestors in the order adopted by the Men of the Great Assembly at the beginning of the *Shemoneh Esrei*. (commentary to *Breisheet* 32:10)

Of course, we must bear in mind that Ya'acov's prayer was the intensely personal and spontaneous outpouring of a man in distress, and not the ordered and routine service that constitutes the *Shemoneh Esrei* now. Nevertheless, it is striking indeed to discover that the leaders of early Second Temple Jewry, far removed in time, place and circumstance from Ya'acov their ancestor, looked to his prayer for their inspiration.

Resolving Maimonides

If our analysis is correct, that Ya'acov's prayer can be distilled into a structural division consisting of discrete elements of praise, petition and gratitude, then we have surely found the source for a puzzling remark of Maimonides. In his discussion of the origins of prayer, preserved in his monumental *Mishneh Torah*, Maimonides correctly asserts that before the innovations of Ezra and his court, prayer was an exclusively individual matter. People prayed when sudden adversity urged them or else when the desire for communion struck them, but at a time and with words that were both entirely of their own choosing:

> It is a positive command to pray daily, as the verse states…"serve Him with your whole heart" (*Devarim* 11:13) . . . the number of prayers is not dictated by the Torah nor is its liturgy, nor does prayer have a set time according to Torah law . . . *rather, the obligation of this command is thus: A person must plea and pray daily, expressing praise of the Holy One blessed be He, and afterwards asking for his needs with request and plea, and afterwards offering praise and gratitude to God for the goodness that He has bestowed,* each one in accordance with his abilities. If one were eloquent, then he would pour out his petition and request; if one were reticent, then he would express himself in accordance with his abilities, at any time of his choosing. Similarly, the number of daily prayers was also entirely personal. Some would pray once a day while others would offer multiple prayers . . . this was always the practice from the days of Moshe until Ezra . . . (*Mishneh Torah*, Laws of Tefillah 1:1–3)

What is unsolved in Maimonides' formulation is his assertion that the prayer required by Torah law (in contrast to the formulaic liturgy promulgated by Ezra) must incorporate praise, expression of needs and gratitude, the fundamental three elements that much later form the backbone of the *Shemoneh Esrei*. As the medieval commentary *Lechem Mishneh* (Rabbi Avraham di Boton, 16th century, Salonika) remarks on the above passage from Maimonides:

> One must ponder how our master (Maimonides) knows that this is a Torah requirement! The author of the Kiryat Sefer also wrote: I know not the source of this statement, and it is baffling to me! (commentary to 1:2)

The source, of course, is the patriarchal prayer of Ya'acov, his spontaneous, personal and plaintive plea to be spared from the wrath of his brother Esav. For Maimonides, Ya'acov's prayer constituted the model for Torah-mandated devotion to God. Therefore, while daily prayer was only enjoined after the giving of the Torah, and liturgy, timing and frequency were entirely Rabbinic innovations from a later age, the core ideas of praise, petition and gratitude were understood by Maimonides to have been prayer's defining essentials from time immemorial.

The Restoration of Ya'acov and the Return from Babylon

There may, of course, be more than an extrinsic link between Ya'acov's prayer and Ezra's *Shemoneh Esrei*, as implied by Seforno's interpretation. To put the matter differently, why should Ezra and his court have looked to Ya'acov's prayer as their inspiration, more than, say, to one of David's many petitions preserved in Sefer Tehillim, or to the entreaty and subsequent thanksgiving of Channa preserved in Sefer Shemuel (1:1:11; 2:1–10), or to Shelomo's dedicatory prayer preserved in Sefer Melachim (1:8:12–61) or to the innumerable other possibilities scattered throughout the Hebrew Bible? To be sure, many of the above references were incorporated into the formal prayer service one way or another, either as standards for sincere devotion or else as models for proper comportment, but it is Ya'acov's prayer that appears to have defined the formal liturgical parameters more than the rest.

Perhaps the answer lies in recalling the broader context of his outcry. Some twenty years beforehand, Ya'acov had fled eastwards towards Mesopotamia, effectively exiled by his brother's wrath and fearful of never returning. How uncertain the future seemed, how full of phantoms lurking just over the darkened horizon! In the house of Lavan, though his wily uncle had warmly welcomed him with open arms, it soon became apparent that Ya'acov's "refugee status" would be exploited to his acute disadvantage. As a rootless stranger from far off, Ya'acov could only clench his teeth and accept the terms of his vulnerability, all the while dreaming of one day being restored to Canaan, just as God had promised. Though he managed to establish his family and even to amass great wealth, Ya'acov always recognized that his sojourn was temporary and that eventually he would return. Finally forced by fate to flee once again, this time from Lavan's wrath, Ya'acov set his sights westwards towards his ancestral home. Though Lavan threatened him en route with overwhelming force, God again intervened and the former agreed to an uneasy pact.

But returning to Canaan carried its own perils, for waiting in ambush was his vengeful brother Esav, still fuming over his exclusion from the patriarchal blessings and from the unique status afforded to Ya'acov as the de facto firstborn. And so as he approached the land, Ya'acov offered his prayer, a tearful fusion of heartfelt pleas for divine protection as well as steadfast trust in the complete fulfillment of the pledge. Though "undeserving," Ya'acov asked for compassion, for God to answer him for the sake of His promise. And God responded. Finally the moment of confrontation arrived – Ya'acov's heart pounded fearfully, but Esav would not (could not!) harm him. The two parted amicably and Ya'acov finally continued home to claim his destiny.

Startling Parallels

Who could not fail to see, in the lengthy saga of Ya'acov's expulsion and return, the essence of the story of the Babylonian exile? Had not the Jews of Judah, in the aftermath of the First Temple's destruction, also been forced to wander eastwards to their ancient geographic source "between the rivers?" Hadn't they also suffered the ignominy and vulnerability of refugee status, laboring mightily to rebuild their lives while all the while subjected to the whims of their capricious hosts? Hadn't at least some of them preserved a dream, in spite of their lengthy sojourn on foreign soil, of one day returning home? Was not that dream ultimately realized only with the permission of the self-serving Persian kings? And didn't a hostile welcome await them around Jerusalem's ruins, in the guise of supposed "brothers" of Chorite, Ammonite and Arab stock who had claimed the land in their absence and now regarded themselves as Canaan's rightful heirs and as God's chosen (see *Ezra* 4 and *Nechemiah* 2)?

As the hapless Jews traveled westwards, elated over their "redemption" but apprehensive about their future, they no doubt turned (as Jews always have) to the Book of Books for guidance. Anxiously, they searched its ancient verses, seeking to find solace and inspiration, encouragement and hope. And they were not disappointed, for preserved within its narratives was a saga that was utterly familiar to them: the story of Ya'acov and his restoration. Cautiously, they marched forward, a pathetic train of horses, camels, donkeys and desperate men, a mere remnant of Judah's former glory and a small percentage of Babylon's burgeoning diaspora, but supremely confident nonetheless. God would protect them, God would restore them, surely God would fulfill His ancient pledge to their patriarch: "I will surely bring goodness upon you, and I will multiply your descendents as numerous as the sand of the sea that cannot be counted." And He did.

After much struggle, external adversity and internal apathy were overcome, rubble was cleared, ruins were restored and the Temple was rebuilt. Later, Ezra arrived and, ably assisted by many others, he inaugurated an era of religious and political stability, laying the foundations for the Second Commonwealth. Having decided that prayer could no longer be the preserve of the individual according to his personal whim but had to also strengthen the link between the individual and the community of Israel and its faith, he and his court began the process of formalizing the service. Finally ready to compose a liturgy that would simultaneously address the individual's needs while yet bringing together the people of Israel as a faith community, Ezra and his court drafted the *Shemoneh Esrei*. *Before their very eyes was the only patriarchal prayer whose broader context was a perfect reflection of their own struggle and redemption!* And so it was that the structure of the *Shemoneh Esrei*, its opening formula and its heartfelt plea for divine assistance, was modeled after the words of Ya'acov, who had sung God's praises, implored His mercy and thanked Him for His kindnesses some 1,200 years earlier.

FOR FURTHER STUDY:

(1) Consider the following Talmudic passage that draws together the main elements of our discussion, in a fashion that is surely more than serendipitous (TB *Berachot* 4a):

> Rabbi Ya'acov bar Idi contrasted the following verses: [God promised Ya'acov that he would protect him, as it states] "Behold I am with you and I will protect you wherever you go" (*Breisheet* 28:15). [Yet, Ya'acov was later afraid as] the verse states: "Ya'acov was sorely afraid" (*Breisheet* 32:8). Rather, he feared that perhaps his iniquities in the interim had caused him to forfeit that protection. This is just as we learned elsewhere: "Until your people traverse, God, until this people whom You have acquired pass over" (*Shemot* 15:16). From here the Sages derive that Israel should have been worthy of divine miracles [when they returned from exile] with Ezra, just as they experienced during the days of Yehoshua bin Nun [when they entered the land of Canaan for the first time]. But their iniquities caused them to

forfeit those miracles (and they could only return with the permission of Cyrus – Rashi ad loc.).

In essence, Rav Ya'acov posits that his eponymous ancestor was afraid of Esav, in spite of God's earlier pledges of protection, lest in the meantime his merits had been exhausted by iniquities. Though Ya'acov trusted God's promise implicitly, he recognized that twenty years had elapsed since He had made the pledge to protect him, on that dark night of his escape from Canaan and from Esav's anger! Perhaps, humble Ya'acov now surmised, he had in the interim forfeited God's guard. The Gemara then goes on to provide an example of just such a phenomenon – when the Jews returned from Babylon with Ezra they should have merited redemptive miracles just as their ancestors experienced at the time of the Exodus from Egypt, but the people of Israel's merits were insufficient and no miracles were forthcoming. As Israel traversed the Sea of Reeds on dry land, God had intimated future overt intervention at another redemptive moment, but the returnees from Babylon had to make due instead with securing the lukewarm backing of the kings of Persia even as danger lurked around Jerusalem's ruins. This, of course, is precisely the linkage that we have suggested above: the predicament of Ezra and his cohort as they embarked on their journey to the land brought to mind their ancestor Ya'acov's trek back to Canaan centuries before! How natural, then, for Ezra and his court to later construct the *Shemoneh Esrei* around the core of the patriarch's impassioned pleas!

VAYESHEV

Yosef the Dreamer

Genesis 37:1-40:23

WITH THE reading of Parashat VaYeshev, the focus of the Torah now shifts from patriarch Ya'acov and his travails to the thespian account of his beloved son Yosef. The story of Yosef and his brothers will occupy the remainder of Sefer Breisheet, making this narrative the longest in the book by far. Yosef's meteoric rise from slavery to become the administrator of Potiphar's estate, his wrongful imprisonment through the intrigues of a spurned woman and his unexpected release to become viceroy of Egypt and sustainer of his family are the stuff from which fantastic yarns are spun, but there is much more here than great literature. Rather, the story of Yosef is the intricate account of how a young man may transcend his immature egocentrism to stand in the presence of God. It offers us a profound statement about the subtle interplay between God's providence and human deed, between divine destiny and man's moral will. Human beings make their own choices but it is the veiled hand of God that determines the final outcome.

> Ya'acov dwelt in the land of his father's sojourning, in the land of Canaan. These are the generations of Ya'acov: Yosef was seventeen years old and shepherded the flocks with his brothers; he was a lad with the sons of Bilha and the sons of Zilpa, his father's wives. Yosef brought an evil report of them to his father. Yisrael loved Yosef more than all of his brothers, for he was the child of his old age, and he made for him a coat of colored stripes. His brothers saw that their father loved him more than all of his other sons and they hated him and could not speak peaceably with him . . . (*Breisheet* 37:1–4)

These verses constitute the Torah's first substantial statement about Yosef. The text indicates his age and pursuits, his relationship with his brothers and father, as well as his favored status. The trait that emerges most forcefully from the details, however, is not flattering: Yosef was terribly puerile. Although almost an adult, he spent much of his time prattling about his brothers' misdeeds. Oblivious to the sensitivities of his siblings, he delighted in reminding them of his special rank. Arrogant, proud and flushed with youthful impetuosity, he felt invincible. In a Midrashic portrayal, young Yosef was occupied with childish, self-centered activities; he was unable to see beyond his own shallow concerns and he certainly failed to foresee the consequences of his impulsiveness. In the colorful language of the Midrash, "How can the Torah refer to a young man of seventeen years as a mere 'lad?' Rather, Yosef behaved like a lad. He would pretty his eyes, walk haughtily, and primp his hair!" (Breisheet Rabbah 84:7).

> Yosef had a dream and told his brothers about it, and they hated him even more. He said to them: "Listen to the dream that I had! Behold, we were gathering sheaves in the field and my sheaf stood up tall. All of your sheaves turned towards it and bowed down to my sheaf!" His brothers said to him: "Will you then be king over us and rule us?!" They hated him even more because of his dreams and his words. Yosef had a different dream and recounted it to his brothers, saying: "Behold, I have had another dream! The sun, moon and stars were bowing down to me!" He told his father and his brothers about it, but his father rebuked him saying: "What is this dream that you have had? Shall I, your mother, and your brothers bow down to you to the ground?!" His brothers were jealous of him, but his father guarded the matter expectantly (*Breisheet* 37:5–11)

In his dream of sheaves, Yosef betrayed his ambitions – he believed himself to be superior to his brothers and deserving of their adulation. How he reveled in offering them his self-serving interpretation! Yosef's second dream was even more extravagant: Not only did he see himself as the center of his family, but as the center of the universe! The sun, moon and the stars paid homage to his greatness! Even Yosef's father, who had remained silent up until now, deemed it necessary to set him straight by publicly ridiculing his narcissistic visions.

Yosef's Great Potential

At first glance, Ya'acov's special attachment to Yosef is readily comprehensible. After all, Yosef was the son of beloved Rachel, Ya'acov's first and only true love. In the aftermath of her tragic and untimely death, Yosef and Binyamin were all that remained. But the Torah introduces another aspect by suggesting that Ya'acov's love of Yosef was because he was the "child of his old age." This is curious in light of the fact that Yissachar and Zevulun, Yosef's older half-brothers, could not have been much older than Yosef himself, and would therefore also have been children of Ya'acov's old age. At the same time, the expression cannot mean the "youngest child," since that was Binyamin.

These anomalies prompted the Ramban to explain that:

> It is the custom of elderly parents to select one of their younger children to be with them and to assist them. This child remains in close proximity to the parent and is referred to as a "בן זקונים" (child of old age) because of this role. It was Yosef whom Ya'acov chose for this task, and that is why we find later on that Yosef did not go with his brothers when they grazed their flocks in distant pastures. (commentary to *Breisheet* 37:3)

According to the Ramban, Yosef remained close to his father because his father depended upon him to provide reliable and responsible help. In spite of his character flaws, Yosef was a capable and industrious son who could be of critical assistance to his father. The narrative continues by informing us that in light of their special relationship, Ya'acov made for Yosef a coat of colored stripes. While the exact nature of this article of clothing cannot be ascertained, we know of one other biblical citation on the subject: the distressing tale of Amnon and Tamar recorded in *Shemuel II*, chapter 13. For our purposes, what is significant to note is that Tamar, one of the royal princesses, was clothed in a "coat of colored stripes, for this was the customary garb of the king's virgin daughters." It seems therefore that this particular type of garment was not only a fine, beautiful article of attire, but was also associated with authority. Those who wore it possessed special status and were marked for an elite leadership role.

It thus emerges that Ya'acov did not favor Yosef for superficial or sentimental reasons only. Ya'acov correctly perceived that Yosef was the most gifted and talented of his children. He remained in Ya'acov's constant company not only to help his ailing and aged father but also to receive his instruction. With outstretched hands Ya'acov extended to his son the coat of colored stripes, for Yosef was being carefully groomed to one day succeed his father as head of the household and leader of the budding tribes. "This coat," suggests the Seforno in his comments to *Breisheet* 37:3, "indicated that Yosef was to be the leader in the house and field, just as we find Elyakim being figuratively enrobed with the mantle of Shevna, as an expression of his assumption of authority" (see *Yeshayahu* 22:21).

We must therefore temper our earlier unflattering appraisal: Yosef may have been an immature and arrogant youth despised by his jealous brothers, but his father was perceptive enough to recognize in him prodigious natural talent. Put differently, of all of the brothers only Yosef had the audacity to dream of greatness and achievement. Alone among his siblings, he dared to imagine accomplishments more grand than the pastoral pursuit of minding sheep. Understood this way, the rage of Yosef's brothers comes into sharper focus. Yosef's brothers despised him not only because he conducted himself with superciliousness, but also because they knew, in the depths of their hearts, that his dreams would propel him forward to success even while they remained behind to tend the bleating flocks.

The account of Yosef's dreams aptly concludes: "His brothers were jealous of Yosef, but his father guarded the matter." The Midrash, always sensitive to subtle turns of phrase, portentously comments: "Rabbi Levi said: 'Ya'acov took a stylus and recorded the day, hour and place [of Yosef's dreams, for he knew that they would be fulfilled]'" (Breisheet Rabbah 84:12).

The Fateful Encounter

Yosef's brothers now depart the scene, taking the flocks to the greener pastures of Shechem:

> Yisrael said to Yosef: "Behold, your brothers are grazing the flocks in Shechem. Let me send you to them" and Yosef responded: "Here I am." Ya'acov said to him: "Go and see how your brothers and the sheep are doing and return to me with the report." Ya'acov sent him from the vale of Chevron, and he journeyed towards Shechem. A man found him wandering in the field and asked him: "What are you looking for?" Yosef answered: "I am searching for my brothers. Do you know where they are grazing the sheep?" The man said: "They have traveled from here. I heard them say: 'Let us go to Dotan.'" Yosef followed his brothers and found them in Dotan. The brothers saw him approaching from afar. Before he had come close to them they prepared a plan to kill him. (*Breisheet* 37:12–18)

These verses constitute the critical link between Yosef's dreams of grandeur and his sale by the brothers to the passing Yishmaelite caravan that would bring him down to Egypt. In other words, they are the decisive trigger that reduces the multiple, amorphous possibilities of Yosef's visions into a particular concrete reality. What might be the significance of the introductory exchange between Ya'acov and Yosef, to which Yosef responds: "I am ready"? Why was it necessary for us to know the location from which Yosef was sent? Most peculiar, why did the Torah record the chance encounter that took place between Yosef and the man who directed him to his brothers' whereabouts? Asking for directions while on a journey hardly seems a detail worthy of retelling, yet here Yosef's disorientation is given exceptional prominence.

We already know that Yosef and his brothers had a tense and hostile relationship. They resented his haughty demeanor and were infuriated by his self-serving words. They were jealous of all of the attention that their doting father showered upon him. How they despised that coat and all that it represented! For his part, Yosef did nothing to extinguish the smoldering animosity and instead reveled in stoking the coals. Now his father asked him to leave his protective embrace and to travel far away, towards an encounter with his brothers on alien turf. Was there perhaps a faint note of hesitation in Ya'acov's words, a subconscious fear of ineluctable fate about to unfold? Is Yosef's "here I am" just a brash attempt to brush off his father's misgivings and to dispel his own ambivalence towards the assignment? Or can we detect in his הנני, often a charged response to the undertaking of a fateful mission, an intimation of destiny?

Yosef embarked on the journey but became lost. Wandering aimlessly, he encountered a man who helped him find his way. This anonymous stranger provided Yosef with an essential piece of information concerning his brothers' whereabouts that allowed him to find them. But how significant that the man was merely a neutral bystander who unexpectedly became privy to their plans and communicated them to Yosef in a noncommittal fashion – "I heard them say: 'Let us go to Dotan'"! And how striking that the Torah carefully indicates not that Yosef encountered the man, but rather that the man "found him"!

The Ramban explains:

> Yosef had strayed from the path and knew not which way to go. He entered the fields because he knew that his brothers were to be found in grazing land. The Torah describes these things at length to indicate that many setbacks transpired that should have given Yosef pause and swayed him to return home. Yosef, however, out of love and deference for his father, pressed onwards. Also, the text indicates to us that the divine decree is true and that attempts to foil it are pointless, for God provided Yosef with a guide who unwittingly delivered him into the clutches of his brothers. This is what our Sages meant when they explained that this stranger was an angel, for this entire incident was meant to teach us that God's counsel will be established. (commentary to *Breisheet* 37:15)

By all indications, Yosef should have never met up with his brothers. He became lost and could not find them for they had moved on. Unenthusiastic from the start about his father's request, he now had ample reason to abandon the task and to go back home. Suddenly, a man found him and fatefully pointed him in the right direction. In so doing, a convoluted chain of events was unleashed that culminated in the descent of the tribes of Israel to Egypt. There, their initial privileged status gave way to harsh subjugation, until their emergence centuries later as a nation.

The Midrash remarks:

> Did Ya'acov then send Yosef from "the vale of Chevron"? Isn't Chevron in the hill country? Rather, said Rabbi Acha, it means that Yosef embarked on a journey that

represented the fulfillment of the deep and cryptic counsel that God established between himself and beloved Avraham who was buried in Chevron. Namely, "and they shall enslave and oppress them . . ." (Breisheet Rabbah 84:13)

According to the Midrash, Yosef's journey at his father's behest was not only a geographic trek from Chevron towards his brothers. There was another aspect to the matter, of mysterious and fateful proportions. To travel from the "vale of Chevron" meant to inadvertently unleash the cryptic divine decree (concealed as if in a deep valley) pronounced to Avraham:

> You shall surely know that your descendents shall be sojourners in a land not theirs, and shall be enslaved and oppressed, for a period of four hundred years. The nation that they will serve I shall judge, and then they shall depart with great substance. (*Breisheet* 15:13–14)

The Midrashic traditions later adapted by the Ramban thus acquaint us with the fundamental principle that underscores the entire saga of Yosef and his brothers: There is a divine design at work in human history, a cosmic orchestration of events calculated to bring about a deliberate and purposeful end. Human beings are the instruments that achieve that goal through the exercise of their completely autonomous freedom of choice. Most of the time, we remain oblivious to the transcendent consequences of our actions, but no encounter in life is accidental. God's counsel cannot be thwarted but the exact trajectory that leads to its fulfillment will be a function of the choices that we make within the circumscribed limits of our own control.

Yosef dreams while his brothers play out their petty animosities, Ya'acov unintentionally exacerbates matters through the provision of a trivial cloak, a harmless mission of patriarchal concern is engaged and the friendly stranger provides directions to where he thinks the brothers may have gone. Each one of these characters acts independently, completely unfettered by any divine fiat, and unburdened by any thoughts of a cosmic design. But in the end, the twisted threads of their choices converge, painstakingly woven together to reveal an unmistakable pattern.

The Self-Made Man

And so, Yosef was brought down to Egypt. Purchased by Potiphar, one of Pharaoh's chief ministers, he promptly proved himself to be an ambitious servant:

> God was with Yosef and he was successful, and he remained in the house of his Egyptian master. His master saw that God was with him, for everything that Yosef did, God crowned with success. Yosef found favor in the eyes of his master and served him, and his master appointed him over the house and over all of his things. From the time that Yosef was put in charge of the house and all else, God caused the household of the Egyptian to be blessed on Yosef's account. God's blessing extended to everything in the house and field. Potiphar entrusted everything to Yosef's care and supervised nothing except for the bread that he ate. Yosef was beautiful in form and appearance. (39:1–6)

The recurring words in this passage are "success" and "blessing." Beginning to live up to his potential, Yosef quickly rose through the ranks. Showing initiative, enthusiasm and conscientiousness, the Hebrew servant did his job and did it well. Potiphar his master was so impressed with him that he continually added to his responsibilities until Yosef was in complete charge of the estate, for everything that Yosef touched turned to gold. With rags-to-riches effect, the Semitic slave boy from Canaan soon became a self-made man, a sensation in a foreign land. We can only assume that Yosef realized his dreams by employing the tried and true methods of thinking ambitiously and working diligently towards the goal. Scarcely seventeen when he was sold into slavery – alone, completely indigent and thoroughly ignorant of Egyptian norms – he was probably by now in his mid-twenties and well on the way to financial security and even political power. In a few short years, he had achieved so much in spite of difficult odds while in the meantime his brothers had been tending the sheep!

Yosef's transformation was so sudden and startling that even Potiphar could only ascribe it to heavenly intervention. The hand of providence, so crucial in guiding the events of Yosef's life up until this point, was once again at work. The Torah itself emphasized God's involvement at every step of Yosef's success: "God was with Yosef," "God was with him," "God crowned everything with success," "God caused the household to be blessed," "God's blessing extended." During the earlier stages of Yosef's odyssey, God's involvement had been more oblique, concealed under layers of dreary human choices and seemingly random, trivial encounters. At this point, however, His providence was far too conspicuous to be mistaken for coincidence.

In this story of Yosef's lightning rise to prominence, there is only one individual who remained completely oblivious to the divine element in the whole enterprise, and that is Yosef himself! Blinded by his attainments, deluded by the illusion of self-achievement, Yosef failed to recognize any higher cause behind his meteoric ascent. Like the immature youth of seventeen who dreamt a dream but was too self-absorbed to hear the faint voice of God who inspired it, Yosef continued to believe that a man's accomplishments are his alone. Did he not labor long and hard under Potiphar's watchful gaze? Was he not a conscientious servant with a penchant for business and an eye to self-advancement? Who else was the cause of his promotion if not himself? Astonishingly, what Potiphar and his household could so plainly see, Yosef could not!

The brief account of Yosef's astounding success is concluded with a jolt: "Yosef was beautiful in form and appearance" (39:6). Besides all of his other talents, Yosef was also blessed with handsome features. Who could not be desirous of the young, talented, beautiful bachelor who enjoyed the confidence and trust of his master and the respect of his subordinates? While mainly serving as a segue for what must surely follow, the Midrash also detects the echo of an earlier moment:

> Yosef at this juncture may be likened to a hero who stood in the marketplace fixing his eyes, primping his hair, walking with haughtiness and saying: "I am handsome and I possess beauty. Am I not a hero?!" (Breisheet Rabbah 87:3)

This is almost the exact image that the Midrash employed earlier, to describe Yosef's immaturity on the eve of his first dream! Then, he was a selfish young man who behaved like a child and made choices that reflected egocentric and frivolous concerns. Now, suggests the Midrash, Yosef had come full circle, but although he had achieved the triumph predicted by his dreams, he had failed to achieve spiritual awareness. In essence, the Midrash suggests that Yosef's tragic flaw was his inability or unwillingness to see the guiding hand of God in the story of his success. But what is so terribly important about acknowledging God's role in our lives? What difference does it make if a person thinks that he has succeeded due exclusively to his own efforts or else because of God's ongoing intervention? The distinction, suggests the Torah, is actually immense, for the consequence of ignoring God's involvement is often the development of a character that is self-serving, self-centered and unconcerned with ultimate issues. Caught up in the realization of our dreams, we fail to heed the divine call that summons each one of us towards our higher purpose. What will it take for Yosef to finally cast off his spiritual fetters and to embrace his destiny?

Potiphar's Wife

> It came to pass immediately after these things that the wife of his master desired Yosef, and said "sleep with me!" (*Breisheet* 39:7)

Suddenly, Yosef was cast into a charged situation. Potiphar's wife took a liking to the youthful, attractive and ambitious administrator who had no other romantic attachments or family responsibilities to hold him back. Would he or would he not succumb to her wiles?

> He refused, saying to the wife of his master: "Behold, my master supervises nothing in this household, having given it entirely over to my responsibility. You alone, being my master's wife, have been withheld from me. How shall I perpetrate this great evil and sin against the Lord?!" Daily, she attempted to sway his heart, but he would not listen to her to lie with her and be with her. (39:8–10)

How admirable was Yosef's conduct, how effortlessly did he seem to brush off her advances! "He refused" the Torah observes, but the careful reader will detect a distinct note of wavering in that refusal. It was not an absolute, uncompromising negation, for Potiphar's wife was clearly not deterred. There was equivocation here, a heart that raced behind Yosef's noble words.

In the text of the Torah scroll there are no indications of vowels or punctuation. Nevertheless, oral tradition supplied these things to facilitate correct reading and eventually they were incorporated into the text. Tradition also devised a complex series of musical notes to allow for the text of scripture to be parsed into smaller phrases and to be liturgically sung. What is less well-known, but obvious once the fact has been pointed out, is that the musical notes themselves constitute an important source of interpretive material. This is because the notes that are attached to a given series of words in a verse impacts on the way that those words are broken up into meaningful phrases. To be specific, Yosef's refusal is marked by the note known as the שלשלת or "chain," because the symbol for this note resembles a vertical triple coil. The musical value of the note is a long, quavering tone consisting of three distinct inflections. It is a note that conveys a sense of prolonged hesitation, vacillation and indecision. There are only three other places in all of *Chumash* where the note occurs:

Breisheet 19:14–15 – "As dawn broke, the angels hurried Lot saying 'take your wife and two remaining daughters and escape, lest you be swept away in the cities' destruction.' *Lot hesitated* and the angels gripped his hand, his wife's hand and the hand of his two daughters, for God had mercy upon him, and they took them out and placed them outside of the city . . ."

Breisheet 24:11–12 – "The servant settled the camels outside of the city at the water well towards evening, at the time when the water drawers would come out. *He said*: 'God, the Lord of my master Avraham, happen before me this day, and act with kindness towards my master Avraham . . .'"

Va Yikra 8:22–23 – "He brought the second ram, for the inauguration, and Aharon and his sons placed their hands upon its head. *He (Moshe) slaughtered it* and, taking from its blood, placed it upon Aharon's right ear, right hand and right big toe . . ."

In the first instance, Lot was told to quickly leave Sodom or else to suffer immolation, but for him to do so meant not only physically departing, but also leaving behind everything that he had spent a lifetime constructing. His heart was still in Sodom, not to mention his possessions as well as his two married daughters who had refused to believe the story of impending doom. Warned to escape, he remained rooted to the spot, torn between the instinct of survival on the one hand, and on the other, the dreadful vision of everything that he held dear being incinerated.

In the second instance, Eliezer the servant of Avraham had embarked on a journey to fulfill the oath placed upon him by his beloved master. Avraham had invoked God's intervention to help the servant find a wife for Yitzchak, but Eliezer felt lost and in need of divine assurance. How would he find a woman to be Yitzchak's wife? Would she be from his family? Would she agree to return with him to the land of Canaan? As evening fell and the tired servant rested the camels, his pensive doubts converged on the mission still ahead. Looking heavenward, he haltingly offered a prayer, hesitant as well as hopeful, for God's intervention. In both of these situations the need for the שלשלת is apparent, for both contain great uncertainty and hesitation.

The third שלשלת, from the ceremony of the Mishkan's dedication, is less obvious. After many months of arduous effort, the project of the Tabernacle had been completed and was ready to function as the focal point for the experience of God's presence. Aharon and his sons had been designated to serve as the priests and through a series of unusual sacrifices were to be invested with their new roles. Moshe was no doubt proud of the people and of his brother. It would be his special role on this day to offer the dedicatory oblations, but from this point onwards, Aharon and his descendents would perform the divine service exclusively. As Moshe prepared the final ram, a fleeting regret crossed his mind, for he knew that he would never again have the opportunity to ritually serve in God's house. Could this be the significance of the שלשלת that accompanies his act of preparing the ram?

Let us now attempt to reconstruct Yosef's thoughts as Potiphar's wife enchants him. Yosef had always dreamt of greatness and instinctively knew that he would achieve it. He had suffered the "slings and arrows of outrageous fortune" but had persevered, painstakingly rebuilding his life while deftly advancing the self-fulfilling prophecy of his triumph. He was the toast of Potiphar's estate, held in high esteem by all of his subordinates. His master placed great trust in him, and Yosef *never* disappointed his expectations. Potiphar was no petty bureaucrat but one of Pharaoh's chief ministers, and Yosef's possibilities for advancement were endless. And now, fate handed him the trophy on a silver platter! Potiphar's siren graciously offered him the one thing that was denied by his master, and being at home in the world of palace intrigue, her oath to secrecy could certainly be relied upon. Should he not seize the moment to satisfy the lust that a young, good-looking success story such as himself had sublimated for so long? And by acquiescing to her honeyed words now, could he not enlist her support for later, to engineer the unsuspecting Potiphar's ouster and to wrest control of the household from his master's flagging grip?!

At the same time, a tattered memory of an earlier life with contrasting values suddenly flooded Yosef's mind. A long time ago in his childhood, Yosef was the apple of his aged father's eye. What love his father had for him, what expectations of success! Yosef, his father hoped, would continue the legacy of his illustrious ancestors. They had borne the burden of God's teachings with love and with absolute certainty of their calling. Ya'acov had dreamt of angels linking heaven and earth, of humanity and God joined in tender embrace, of devotion to a divine law that was the only possibility of perfecting a world steeped in destructive self-worship. And Yosef had been part of that dream! Although immature and full of reckless abandon, his father had trusted in him: with trembling hands, he had extended to him the coat of many stripes, for his father knew that Yosef would one day treasure the bequest.

In that instant between Yosef's apprehension of the seductress' words and the proffering of his refusal, a terrible eternity unfolded. Our Rabbis captured the dissonance only too well, for they claim that at his moment of weakness, seemingly about to succumb,

> The image of his father appeared to Yosef and said: "Yosef, in the future your brothers' names will be inscribed on the onyx stones that are set in the epaulettes of the High Priest, and your name shall be among them. Do you want your name to be erased from that inscription?!" (TB *Sotah* 36b)

The wife of Potiphar unwittingly placed Yosef in a fateful situation: For the first time in his life Yosef was forced to freely make a moral decision with far-reaching implications. To choose Potiphar's wife was to irrevocably repudiate any providence, any involvement of God, and any idea of a higher destiny that in one insightful flash could explain the convoluted series of coincidences that had brought Yosef this far. Conversely , to reject her advances was to at last submit to the spiritual stirrings that had gnawed at the back of Yosef's mind since his fateful encounter with the stranger so many years earlier. Was it not manifest for all to see that God had guided his steps all along, that he had not been abandoned to the whims of fortune but rather had been chosen to fulfill a redemptive role in the world?

Yosef Acknowledges God

> He refused, saying to the wife of his master "behold, my master supervises nothing in this household, having given it entirely over to my responsibility. You alone, being my master's wife, have been withheld from me. How shall I perpetrate this great evil and sin *against the Lord*?!" (*Breisheet* 39:8–9)

For the first time since we have met him, Yosef invoked the name of God. In all of his conversations with his brothers, his father, and the stranger, Yosef never mentioned God's name, for he had been willfully ignorant of His involvement. By citing it now at this critical juncture, torn between two worlds and two visions that could never be reconciled, Yosef exercised his God-given freedom of choice to redirect his life. From this point onwards, God's watchful providence would never be far from his mind and His name never absent from his lips. Later addressing the cupbearer, the baker, Pharaoh, and ultimately his brothers at their tearful reunion, Yosef referred to God as the source of his success with greater and greater confidence. To the butler and the baker he said: "*To the Lord belong interpretations*, tell me your dreams" (40:8), and when speaking to Pharaoh he sought no recognition at all: "*Naught is from me, the Lord will answer Pharaoh's welfare*" (41:16). With the brothers he shared the profound insight that he had acquired: "Do not be distressed or angry at yourselves, for *the Lord has sent me here to secure your survival*" (45:5).

We must note that it was not dread of his master that held Yosef back, neither fear of detection nor of punishment, but only the awesome disquietude of betraying his master's implicit trust and "sinning against the Lord." Having cast the die and chosen what is right, Yosef now suffered the consequences. Like many other noble men and women, Yosef discovered that sometimes the reward for moral action is not material success or acclaim, but rather anguish and humiliation. Falsely accused by Potiphar's wife of the very crime he had heroically eschewed, Yosef was cast into prison and condemned to an ignominious end. How swift was his downfall in the eyes of all of his incredulous admirers and jealous detractors! How unbearably tragic his undoing!

Bowed but not beaten, Yosef was not long discouraged:

> God was with Yosef and was gracious to him, and he found favor in the eyes of the warden. Yosef was put in charge of all of the inmates and oversaw all that they did. The warden could find no fault with Yosef's conduct, for God was with him and all that he did God crowned with success. (39:21–23)

In a deliberate throwback to his initiation into Potiphar's service, the Torah emphasizes once again that Yosef showed his talents and abilities. He could do no wrong as he slowly established himself as a capable administrator and won the confidence of the warden. Even in prison Yosef rose to the top! At the same time, the Torah makes it abundantly clear that God was the true author of his success: "God was with Yosef," "God was with him," "all that he did God crowned with success." These expressions are like harmonics to the chords that the Torah earlier sounded to explain Yosef's dazzling rise in the house of Potiphar.

> After these events, the cupbearer and baker transgressed against their master the king of Egypt. They were imprisoned in the ward of the chief executioner, in the dungeon where Yosef was incarcerated. The chief executioner appointed Yosef to be with them and to serve them and they were under guard for a full year. Both of them had a dream . . . (40:1–5)

The cupbearer and baker were disturbed by their dreams: "We have had a dream and there is no one who can interpret it," they exclaimed alarmed. "Yosef said to them: behold, interpretations belong to the Lord, tell me please what you saw." Once again, we note the centrality of dreams to the story. Our introduction to Yosef, which described the confrontational relationship between him and his brothers, revolved around his two dreams of sheaves and stars. Accused by the wife of Potiphar and thrown into prison, it is through the medium of dreams that Yosef now sees an opportunity to secure his release. By correctly interpreting the dream of the baker and especially that of the cupbearer, Yosef will be called to mind when the memory of the cupbearer is finally jogged. By later explaining the dreams of Pharaoh, Yosef will win the appointment to the office of viceroy and thus be positioned to preserve his family from famine. While the pivotal episodes in Yosef's life are conditioned by these visions, we note at this juncture a startling metamorphosis: In the episode of the butler and the baker, Yosef is no longer cast as a *dreamer* but has in fact become the *interpreter of dreams*! There are two fundamental questions which must now be asked: (1) why are dreams so important in the unfolding of Yosef's story? (2) How does Yosef become transformed from a dreamer into an interpreter of dreams?

In the Tanakh, a dream is never a figment devoid of meaning; rather, a dream is a form of divine communication. In the Hebrew Bible, personalities rarely experience direct dialogue with God. Instead, God communicates with them through prophecy, inspiration, visions and dreams. In Sefer Breisheet, for example, God speaks to Avraham (15:1, 12–13), Avimelech (20:3), Ya'acov (28:12; 31:10) and Lavan (31:24) through dreams. Avimelech and Lavan experience a single divine communication in which they are warned to follow a particular course of action. Avraham and Ya'acov, in contrast, often speak with God, and the dream is only one of a series of media by which He makes His will known to them.

Yosef's boyhood dreams, therefore, must be intimations of a divinely ordained destiny. He will be a leader and his brothers will bow down to him, but that is only the **superficial** reading of the vision. It also happens to be the only reading that Yosef is capable of in his immature state. On a more profound level, the sheaves of wheat of the first dream indicate that Yosef will be the instrument for securing sustenance for his family during the seven difficult years of famine soon to unfold, "for it was on account of grain that Yosef was elevated to the position of viceroy" (Radak, commentary to *Breisheet* 37:7). The more prophetic reading, however, remains beyond Yosef's ken until he himself is able to acknowledge the divine element in his own life, the guiding hand that orchestrates events to position Yosef for greatness.

Suddenly, Yosef was thrust by Potiphar's wife into making a staggering choice: Which model of human history shall he adopt? Will it be the mechanistic approach that denies a higher purpose and sees all of life's events as either self-authored triumphs and defeats or else accidents of nature? Or will it be the providential model that recognizes an all-powerful deity who created the cosmos with a purpose, who guides and instructs and also demands, who conceals His constant intervention under the guise of confluences and convergences? By forcefully choosing the latter, by acknowledging the deeper import of his own dreams, by surrendering to a higher purpose and casting off the superficialities that had earlier steered him, Yosef transforms himself into an *interpreter* of dreams. With the dawning awareness of providence comes a heightened sensitivity to the essence of events and so it is that the divine plan that eludes the cupbearer, the baker and the Pharaoh, is now obvious to Yosef.

The Cup-Bearer's Interminable Forgetfulness and God's Haste

The role of providence is reinforced by one final episode:

> Yosef said to the cupbearer: "This is the meaning of your dream. In three days time, Pharaoh will release you from prison and return you to your original office. You shall again serve him his cup as you were wont to do. Remember me upon your release, and deal kindly with me. Tell Pharaoh of my plight so that I may be released from this prison. For I have been kidnapped from the land of the Hebrews, and I have done nothing here to warrant being incarcerated." (*Breisheet* 40:12–15)

The critical phrase in Yosef's impassioned plea is "deal kindly with me" or "do an act of חסד with me" in the original Hebrew. Does this expression not call to mind God's earlier involvement both in the house of Potiphar as well as in the dungeon? "God was with Yosef and dealt kindly (ויט אליו חסד) with him, giving him favor (חנו) in the eyes of the warden" (39:21), "Yosef found favor (חן) in the eyes of Potiphar and he served him (39:4)." For Rashi, the implication is clear: By exclusively pinning his salvation on the intervention of the cupbearer Yosef suffered a spiritual retreat and therefore brought about the opposite effect, for "the cup-bearer remembered not Yosef, but rather forgot him" (40:23). Try as he might, the cupbearer could not remember his commitment to Yosef for God had expunged it from his conscience (commentary to 40:23). In the imaginative formulation of the Midrash that is intrigued by the double emphasis of "remembered not" and "rather forgot,"

> All day the cup-bearer made mental notes, but an angel came and erased them. All day the cupbearer tied knots to remind himself, but an angel came and loosed them. Said God: "You may forget him, but I will not!" (Breisheet Rabbah 88:7)

But there is another aspect to the matter besides Rashi's remedial reading: While Yosef will remain imprisoned for two more years until Pharaoh will have his dreams, the delay will ultimately work in Yosef's favor, for by interpreting the dreams of Pharaoh he will finally achieve his destined position of power. To have been remembered by the cupbearer immediately would have resulted in a premature release. Yosef would have gone his way and may never have had the opportunity to interpret Pharaoh's dreams later on. In other words, providential plans unfold slowly, convergences take time and the interpreter of dreams must therefore be a patient soul. Yosef had requested a show of kindness; God had bestowed it in a most unexpected fashion. Yosef pined away but God did not forget him, and when the confluence occurred, it overawed with its alacrity:

> Pharaoh was sorely disturbed by his dreams. He summoned all of the wizards and wise men of Egypt, but none of them could explain their import. The cup-bearer related: I hereby acknowledge my negligence . . . (*Breisheet* 41:8–9)

Finally, Yosef's fortunes are transformed, thus completing the threefold cycle of his rise and fall – in his father's house he had been chosen but by his brothers' animosity he had been deposed, in Potiphar's employ he had achieved success but by the revenge of his master's wife he had been ousted unjustly. Even in prison he had won admiration but by the butler's inexplicably deficient memory he had been condemned to an inexplicably prolonged incarceration. Now, in a climactic conclusion to the narrative, Pharaoh himself releases him and elevates him to preeminence, his star now shining with a brilliant luster that will wane no more.

More than any other account in the book of Breisheet, the story of Yosef is a study in divine involvement, a charting of the painful spiritual process by which human beings come to first recognize, then to accept, and finally, after many false starts and setbacks, to embrace God's destiny. Yosef's immature dreams of grandeur are dashed by the brothers, his stellar rise in Potiphar's house is suddenly arrested. Even his torturous attempts to climb out of the dungeon into which he had been unceremoniously cast are abruptly terminated by the butler's forgetfulness. But as the recognition slowly and inexorably dawns upon him that God has chosen him for a task, that his innate talents are not simply tickets to selfish attainment but rather instruments to effect the salvation of others and personal spiritual growth, it is at those moments of self-revelation that his misfortunes are suddenly transformed into successes, and it is precisely then that he is clothed in the garments of his mission.

The cycle repeats itself a number of times as Yosef gropes for this higher truth, but each repetition represents an incremental advance along the path of his enlightenment. Finally standing before Pharaoh, all of his pretensions now stripped away by successive trials, Yosef is at that moment utterly aware that "it is not through my powers, for *only the Lord* shall answer for Pharaoh's welfare" (41:16). It is precisely then that Yosef is prepared to assume the role of viceroy, to save his family from the scourge of famine by securing for them grain, while simultaneously preserving their progeny from spiritual demise by offering them the lofty example of his own life's choices. It is not enough to fulfill our dreams and live out our lives on the lowest material level. We must be cognizant of another, more exalted dimension of existence in which we strive to become not only starry-eyed dreamers, but interpreters of dreams as well.

FOR FURTHER STUDY:

(1) If we were to search for a motif that informs the entire story of Yosef, it is no doubt the theme of haste: Every pivotal moment in his life, whether good or bad, unfolds with astonishing speed as success inexplicably turns to failure and then back to success once again. And every one of these turning points is literarily linked with a donning or removal of a mantle, and in particular with the mantle of an overseer of one sort or another. When Yosef is chosen by his father to govern the brothers, he is invested in that august office (for which he is scarcely ready) with the donning of the coat of many colors. This beautiful cloak, of good quality but provincial weave, is immediately stripped off of him when he is attacked by his brothers, thus signifying his first and most painful fall. In Potiphar's employ, he is again clothed with the insignia of overseer as he rises to power, but the master's wife seizes the garment when her attempts at seduction fail, thus unleashing the inevitable process of Yosef's speedy decline. How tellingly does the Torah indicate that "she kept the garment next to her until [Yosef's] master returned" (39:16), thus recalling the initial presentation – also as evidence of downfall – of the coat of many colors to Ya'acov so many years earlier.

In prison, Yosef is again clothed, but this time in the rags of an inmate. After the memory of the butler is unexpectedly jogged, Yosef is summarily stripped of these tatters, to be first clothed in fresh garments when he initially appears in Pharaoh's presence (41:14), and later to be immediately covered with "garments of the finest linen and a necklace of gold" (41:42) when he assumes the position of viceroy. The question is therefore twofold: What is the significance of the recurring theme of urgency in the story of Yosef, and why is that transformative haste invariably linked with the donning or removal of external garb?

Let us begin with the second query first. In the Torah, as it is to this day, the clothing of an individual describes his or her station. A person's wealth, their occupation or role is symbolized by the clothing that they wear. It is not that one's clothing indicates anything at all about a person's real character or innate qualities. Rather, outward garb serves as the most obvious representation of either our aspirations or else our achievements; our clothing indicates status and a change in clothing indicates a change in status. When Yosef rises, he is invariably enwrapped; when he falls, he is without fail divested. It is the garment, then, that is the literary clue for charting the trajectory of Yosef's story.

But what about the theme of haste, the corollary to Yosef's wild swings of fortune and changes of attire? Here, the Seforno (commentary to *Breisheet* 41:14) provides a most intriguing interpretation:

> ...[it is] after the manner of all expressions of God's salvation which occur suddenly . . . Was this not the way of the Exodus when our ancestors were thrust out of bondage before their dough had time to rise? Indeed, this shall be the model for the future redemption as well, as the verse states "for suddenly the Master whom you are seeking shall return to His sanctuary"! (*Malachi* 3:1)

For the Seforno, an abrupt change of fortune is the hallmark of divine involvement in our lives. While God is constantly involved, we tend to overlook that fact until a situation is suddenly and unexpectedly reversed. Only then are we reminded of life's capriciousness, the vagaries of time and God's role in determining our fate.

MIKETZ

The Viceroy and His Brothers

Genesis 41:1-44:17

IN PARASHAT VaYeshev, we met Yosef. The precious offspring of beloved Rachel, the apple of Ya'acov's eye, the object of his brothers' venomous hate, few biblical characters can match Yosef for sheer dramatic effect. Clothed in a fine cloak of many colors, he used his privileged status in order to unfavorably report on the doings of his half brothers, the children of Bilha and Zilpa. Yosef delighted in stoking his brothers' wrath, recounting his dreams that foresaw success for himself and servitude for them. In the end, Yosef was even more accomplished than he ever imagined, but his place in posterity was not secured by his donning the robes of viceroy but rather by his steady evolution from self-made man into man of God. The narcissistic youth who dreamt of dominion eventually became a visionary who utilized his God-given talents to secure sustenance and life for his brothers, his family, and the people of Egypt.

What of Yosef's brothers? On the one hand, their significance in the story is a function of narrative necessity: they are required to drive the plot forward, catapulting Yosef to situations that will be transformative for him. On the other hand, their role is so central to the unfolding of the tale that we must wonder whether they too undergo a similar process of development. Can we chart their spiritual trajectory to conclude that they too are different people by the time the story exhausts itself with Yosef's cathartic revelation?

The chronology of the events is clear enough. Yosef takes center stage at the age of seventeen (*Breisheet* 37:2), is promptly trounced by his jealous brothers and sold into Egyptian servitude, and experiences a series of exhilarating triumphs as well as crushing disappointments until he stands before Pharaoh, interpreting the god-king's unsettling dreams at the tender age of thirty years (41:46). A further seven years of plenty (41:53) and two years of famine (45:6) elapse before he unexpectedly meets up again with his unsuspecting kin. There are therefore a total of twenty-two years that separate the first narrative from the last.

Reuven and Yehuda

Let us begin by briefly outlining the prominent events of the saga, insofar as they relate to the conduct of the brothers. Yosef shepherds the flocks with his half-brothers, the children of Bilha and Zilpa, but he thrusts them away by informing their father of their misdeeds. They are therefore not his allies when the ire of the other half-siblings, Leah's children, is aroused by the dreams. Later, Ya'acov sends Yosef to check on the wellbeing of the brothers and their flocks, who have traveled northwards from the homestead in search of greener pastures. When he arrives, they are ready:

> They saw him from afar and before he had approached, they devised plans of killing him. They said, each to his brother, "Behold, this master of dreams is coming. Now, let us kill him, throw his body into a pit and claim that a wild animal consumed him. Then we shall see what shall become of his dreams!" (*Breisheet* 37:18–20)

Enter Reuven, Ya'acov's firstborn, into the fray. Dissuading his brothers from committing premeditated murder, he instead suggests that Yosef be cast into a pit to passively perish of hunger and thirst. The Torah indicates however, that his true intention was "to save him from their hands in order to return him to his father" (37:22). Immediately, the other brothers heed Reuven's advice, strip Yosef of his coveted coat, and throw him into a dry well. They then break bread, callously deaf to Yosef's frightened pleas to be released. Suddenly, a caravan of Ishmaelite spice merchants appears on the horizon, their dusty camels swaying languidly in the heat. Yehuda suggests that they sell Yosef to the Ishmaelites, thus ridding themselves of his overbearing and meddlesome presence without resorting to bloodshed. Yosef is drawn out of the pit and sold for "twenty pieces of silver" (37:28), and so begins his incredible journey. Reuven, inexplicably absent from the sale, returns to the pit to release Yosef but discovers to his horror that he is too late. He dejectedly returns to his brothers, foreseeing all too well Ya'acov's aggrieved reaction.

The role of two brothers, Reuven and Yehuda, is thus spelled out explicitly, while allusion is made to the roles of some of the others. Reuven saves Yosef from immediate death but he does not prevent his exile, while Yehuda succeeds in preserving Yosef from fatal exposure but also is the direct cause of his sale into Egyptian bondage. The account of the brothers' dastardly deed concludes with their ritual dipping of Yosef's torn coat into goat's blood. The grisly trophy is then deviously presented to their aging father as proof of Yosef's tragic and untimely demise at the hands of "evil beasts"! Ya'acov enters a prolonged period of mourning over Yosef, and his dutiful sons arise to comfort him, all the while aware that Yosef is not really dead and that Ya'acov's intense grief is unwarranted.

With Yosef's auction to Potiphar, the involvement of the brothers in his life abruptly ends, and the Torah shifts its focus to describe his triumphs and travails in the house of his new master and eventually in the service of Pharaoh himself. Except for one puzzling episode concerning Yehuda and Tamar (chapter 38), the brothers completely disappear from the narrative until more than twenty years later when famine strikes Canaan and the brothers are forced at their aged father's behest to journey to Egypt in search of grain. But Ya'acov refuses to allow Binyamin, Yosef's younger brother, to accompany the others on their trek.

In Parashat Miketz, the brothers reenter the story, kneeling before the viceroy of Egypt who is none other than long-lost Yosef. He, dressed as an Egyptian lord and shielded from prying questions by an official interpreter, immediately recognizes them but they fail to discern his true identity. Yosef accuses his brothers of espionage, imprisoning them for three days and then demanding that they bring Binyamin before him in order to corroborate their counter-claims of no wrongdoing. As concerned students of the Torah, we grapple with Yosef's cruel conduct: is he driven by vengeance, is he obsessed with the fulfillment of his prophetic dreams, or might there be another way to explain his maliciousness?

The Reflexive Verb

Before we consider Yosef's behavior, let us frame the circumstances surrounding the brothers' descent: as hunger takes hold in the surrounding lands and Canaan too starts to suffer the effects, Ya'acov turns to his sons and asks them to go down to Egypt to secure provisions. "Ya'acov saw that in Egypt there was grain, and Ya'acov said to his sons 'what are you waiting for? Behold, there is grain in Egypt, descend and purchase some so that we might live and not die!'" (42:1). In the original Hebrew, Ya'acov addresses his sons by saying: "Why תתראו? Behold, there is grain in Egypt . . ." The verb תתראו is variously rendered by the commentaries as "why display yourselves (as full when in fact you are hungry)?", "why quarrel among yourselves?," or "why are you still here (rather than in Egypt securing sustenance)?." The word in question contains the common root ראה which means "see." What is unusual here is that the verb is in its reflexive form, a usage which occurs only one more time in the entire Tanakh (see *Melachim* 2:14:8). Adopting a more literal translation that takes account of the reflexive form might therefore yield "*why are you looking at yourselves?*," for a reflexive verb indicates that the action is done to oneself rather than to others.

We therefore posit another interpretation of the verb. As the famine intensifies, Ya'acov is surprised at his sons' lack of initiative. All of the surrounding clans have started to flock to Egypt in search of grain, but Ya'acov's sons remain static. "Why are you looking at yourselves?" he exclaims impatiently, "behold, there is grain in Egypt!" The brothers' lack of motivation and enthusiasm actually betrays their true emotional state. Having sold Yosef down to Egypt years before, they had been unwilling to live up to their crime ever since. At all costs they had avoided a journey to Egypt because descending there would dredge up misdeeds too painful to confront and too impossible to resolve. Had they not kept the truth from their own father these many years, first out of fear and then out of shame, suppressing feelings too tortuous to even acknowledge? Now their father was inadvertently asking them to come to terms with their past, with the cruel crime of transacting their own brother into a life of servitude and certain death. And so the brothers *looked at themselves* hesitatingly, ripe for introspection, for they realized that with their father's request the unavoidable day of facing Egypt and their past was fast approaching. But even while the brothers dreaded the descent to Egypt, Yosef patiently awaited their arrival for he knew that it would come.

The Brothers' First Journey to Egypt

Let us catalogue the several steps of Yosef's maltreatment of his brothers while noting their responses:

(1) **Yosef** – "Yosef saw his brothers and recognized them. He behaved cruelly towards them and spoke harshly . . . he said to them: 'you are spies, and you have come to ascertain the weakness of the country!'" (*Breisheet* 42:7–9)

Brothers – "They said to him: 'no sir, we are the sons of one father. We are truthful, we are not spies . . . we twelve are sons of one man in the land of Canaan. The youngest brother is with our father and one is no more.'" (42:10–13)

(2) **Yosef** – "Yosef said . . .'you are spies. Corroborate your claims by bringing your young brother here' . . . he placed them in prison under guard for three days. On

the third day he said: '. . . if you are truthful, let one of you be imprisoned, while the rest of you bring back provisions for your households. Bring your younger brother to me to corroborate your words so that you do not die.' They did so." (42:14–20)

Brothers – "The brothers said to each other: 'we are guilty concerning our brother, for we saw his distress as he cried out to us but we did not respond. Therefore this tribulation has befallen us!' Reuven said to them: 'I told you not to harm the child but you would not listen, and now his death is being requited!'" (42:21–22)

(3) **Yosef** – "Yosef turned from them and wept . . . he took Shimon and bound him before their eyes. He commanded that their vessels be filled with grain and that each brother's money be returned to his sack . . ." (42:24–25)

Brothers – "They took their provisions and placed them upon their donkeys and traveled from there. At the inn, one of them opened his sack in order to feed his donkey and saw his money in plain view . . . their hearts were afraid and they exclaimed: 'what is this that God has done to us?'" (42:26–28)

In this initial encounter between Yosef and his brothers, three discrete stages are discernable. First, Yosef speaks harshly to them and accuses them of espionage, then he incarcerates them for three days, and finally he imprisons Shimon alone and sets the stage for the next encounter by returning their money to them. The distress that Yosef engenders pivots around *accusations of spying* and is exacerbated by *unjust imprisonment*.

As for the brothers, they vehemently deny any wrongdoing and proclaim their complete innocence before the viceroy: "The youngest brother is with our father [in Canaan], and one is *no more*." Among themselves, however, they express guilt concerning their maltreatment of Yosef so many years earlier, regrets that are reinforced by Reuven's pained recollection of his attempts to dissuade them. In the meantime, Shimon is separated out for harsh treatment, and then on the way home one of the other brothers triggers another spasm of introspection with his discovery of the returned money at the inn. What is most remarkable is that throughout the ordeal, the brothers connect their predicament with unrelated events of more than twenty years earlier, evil deeds long since forgotten!

The Return to Canaan – Interlude of Grief

The brothers return to Canaan with heavy hearts. They describe to their aged father in halting words all that befell them and then must witness his grief: "Ya'acov their father said to them: 'you have made me bereft of my children. Yosef is no more, Shimon is no more. If you will take Binyamin, I cannot bear it!'" (42:36). Reuven tries to reassure his father and to convince him to release Binyamin to his care: ". . . kill my own two children if I fail to return Binyamin to you!", but Ya'acov is adamant that he will not risk another loss by allowing Binyamin to descend to Egypt. Thus, Shimon remains incarcerated for some time.

Time passes, the famine continues to rage and the family of Ya'acov begins to starve. Ya'acov again asks his sons to descend to Egypt in order to secure sustenance but now it is Yehuda's turn to respond: ". . . if you do not send our youngest brother we cannot go, for the man said to us not to appear before him without our youngest brother . . . send him with me. I will guarantee his safety . . . if I do not return him to you, then I will stand iniquitous before you until the end of time!" (43:3–9). This time, Ya'acov relents, dispatching Binyamin with a gift-offering for the viceroy as well as with the returned funds. With a tremulous voice, he offers blessings for their success and then the brothers depart and set their course for Egypt.

This intermission between the two encounters with Yosef is focused on Ya'acov and his grief. The brothers must see their father in mourning, stricken with fear over the fate of Shimon and terrified of losing Binyamin, his other favorite. We note that while Reuven's earlier attempt to win his father's confidence was rebuffed, Yehuda's pleas are now haltingly accepted.

The Brothers' Second Journey to Egypt

The brothers return to Egypt to stand once again in Yosef's presence:

(1) **Yosef** – "When Yosef saw Binyamin with them, he said to his servant: 'bring these men to my home and prepare a festive meal, for they will eat with me at noon.'" (43:16)

Brothers – "The brothers became afraid when they were brought to Yosef's house. They said: 'It is because of the money that was returned to our sacks . . . we will be falsely accused . . . and taken as slaves!' They approached the valet and explained . . . but he said: 'do not be afraid, for your Lord and the Lord of your fathers has given you treasure in your sacks. Your payment was received by me!' He released Shimon to them . . ." (43:18–23)

(2) **Yosef** – "Yosef returned home and they presented him with their gifts . . . He saw Binyamin among them . . . he quickly left their presence and wept . . . they served the meal, and he seated the brothers according to their age . . ." (43:26–33)

Brothers – "The brothers were amazed . . . Binyamin received a portion five times as great as theirs, and they drank and feasted with him (Yosef)." (43:33–34)

(3) **Yosef** – "Yosef commanded his servant to fill the brothers' sacks with grain and to return their money to them. He further said: 'Place my silver goblet in the sack of the youngest . . . as morning broke, they were sent on their way . . . They had scarcely left when Yosef's servant pursued them and apprehended them, saying: 'why did you repay kindness with wickedness? This goblet is my master's, he divines by it, and you have done a grievous deed!'" (44:1–5)

Brothers – "They said to him: 'why does our master say such things? . . . How could we dare steal anything from your master's home? If it is true, then the one with whom it is found shall die, and we shall all be your slaves!' He said: 'so be it. The one with whom it is found shall be my slave, but the rest of you shall go free.' The brothers quickly removed their sacks and opened them. He checked in all of their sacks, beginning with the oldest and ending with the youngest, and the goblet was found in Binyamin's sack! They tore their garments, loaded their donkeys and returned to the city . . ." (44:7–13)

In this second encounter between Yosef and his brothers, three stages are again evident. Firstly, Yosef invites the brothers to eat with him, a singular honor indeed to sup with the viceroy. Then, seeing Binyamin, he momentarily loses his composure, but then seats them according to age and they are served. That night, they sleep soundly for the first time in many months. Finally, at dawn they are sent on their way but then suddenly pursued, accused of stealing the silver goblet and forced to return. Now, it is accusations of *stolen money, plundered silver and ill-gotten gains*, all of it revealed to the all-knowing viceroy, that are the cause of the brothers' downfall.

Yosef's Revelation to His Brothers

In the final act of the drama at the opening of Parashat VaYigash, it is Yehuda who takes center stage. Responding to Yosef's claim of having ascertained their guilt through divination, Yehuda readily admits the brothers' culpability: "What shall we say to our master? How can we be righteous? The Lord has discovered your servants' iniquity! Behold, we are your slaves, both us as well as the one with whom the goblet has been found!" (44:16). Yosef refuses and instead demands only Binyamin's seizure and Yehuda responds with a pained description of their younger brother's death, Ya'acov's never-assuaged grief, and the certainty that Binyamin's arrest will result in their broken father's demise. Yehuda then offers to take Binyamin's place and finally Yosef relents: in this third and most emotional outburst, he breaks down and cries, at last revealing his true identity to his brothers!

How are we to understand Yosef's conduct throughout this ordeal? What does he achieve by subjecting his brothers to such intense emotional torment? It is difficult to see vengeance as his primary goal, as if Yosef desired to repay his brothers for all of the grief that they had brought upon him. After all, did he not twice cry as he advanced his scheme (42:24; 43:30), indicating his own distress at the pain that he imposed? For some direction, let us return to our structural analysis above. Recall that the two descents to Egypt and the two encounters with Yosef revolved around unjust incarceration and unjust gains respectively. In between the two descents, the brothers were forced to experience Ya'acov's intense grief. Note also that it was Reuven and Yehuda who took the most prominent roles as advocates in the saga, while Shimon and the "other brother" who discovered the money in his sack were forced to experience confusion and fear. From yet a broader perspective, we note that Yosef's entire orchestration wrested Binyamin from Ya'acov's protective embrace and placed upon the brothers the onus of his rescue, even at the cost of their own freedom.

In essence, what Yosef does through his carefully crafted artifice is *to force the brothers to relive the trauma of his own sale more than two decades earlier*! When the brothers first came down to Egypt, Yosef immediately recognized them. He exchanged some pleasantries and made some innocent enquiries but soon discovered to his dismay that the brothers were the same brothers and that they had never confronted their central role in his presumed demise. They spoke of Yosef as if he had somehow disappeared, "one of them is not" (42:13), as if they knew nothing of the circumstances surrounding his disappearance, as if they were blameless and completely innocent of any wrongdoing.

Yosef spoke harshly to them, recalling their own harsh and hateful words to him on the eve of their evil scheme – "they could not speak peaceably to him" (37:4). He accused them of espionage, no doubt recalling their own charges that he would tell damaging tales to their father – "Yosef brought evil reports of their conduct to his father" (37:2). Yosef then incarcerated them in a guarded prison referred to in the original Hebrew as the משמר and elsewhere in the story as the בור (40:3; 40:15) or pit! Is it not likely that the experience of three days of unjust incarceration in a dark dungeon was calculated to ignite in the minds of the brothers memories of their own nefarious injustice against him? Hadn't they thrown him into the deep pit in order to silence his exaggerated boasts and alleged acts of spying?

As for Shimon, Yosef singled him out for special treatment. Could it be that Shimon's imprisonment was an oblique reference to his own prominent role in Yosef's seizure? It will be recalled that the Torah never mentioned exactly which brothers were instrumental in formulating the plan to kill him. This was done out of deference, to conceal the shame of a dastardly act. All that was stated was that "one brother said to his fellow: behold, here comes this 'master of dreams.' Now, let us kill him and throw his body into a pit and say that a wild beast has devoured him. Then we shall see what will become of his dreams!" Nevertheless, the Rabbinic tradition preserved the identity of the perpetrators: "Yosef imprisoned Shimon for he was the one who cast him into the pit. He was the one who said to Levi: 'behold, here comes this master of dreams'" (quoted by Rashi, 42:24).

All of this inexplicable misfortune began to hit the mark, as the brothers painfully recalled the episode of Yosef's imprisonment and sale. Reuven, who had tried to rescue Yosef, returned once again in a role of advocacy, thereby revisiting his earlier intervention. His telling remark served as the catalyst for the brother's belated introspection. The brothers went back to their aged father in Canaan, and on the way "one of them" discovered his money at the inn when he opened his sack to give provender to his donkey. Could it be that this was Levi, the same Levi that according to Rashi was Shimon's accomplice in clamoring for Yosef's death? The discovery of the money, deliberately planted by Yosef, filled the brothers with dread, for they knew that now they would be accused of theft. It is Levi, then, who brought even more misfortune upon them!

Coming home, the brothers now faced their father's grief. He exclaimed that he had already lost Yosef years before, and now stood to lose Shimon and Binyamin as well. His pained protests at the prospect of releasing Binyamin, the remaining favorite, to their charge call to mind of course his reaction upon receiving the brothers' feigned report of twenty years earlier concerning Yosef's death. How terribly they had miscalculated the depth of their father's grief back then, to what great lengths had they subsequently gone in order to conceal their role in the affair! This time, however, any suppression or cover-up was impossible. It is as if the brothers now had to exclaim: "We are responsible for bringing this new disaster upon you and we must now suffer the results!"

Although Reuven attempted to win his father's confidence, Ya'acov rebuffed him: "My son will not go down with you!" (42:38). Eventually, the famine took its toll, and Ya'acov grudgingly agreed to send Binyamin under Yehuda's aegis. It is clear that providence orchestrated events just this way: Reuven may have been directly blameless in the events surrounding Yosef's sale, but he did fail miserably in not exercising his authority as firstborn in order to put a halt to the brothers' wicked scheme. That failure, a function of his refusal to act in order to save his father's most beloved son who was his direct rival, is thus relived here as Ya'acov now refuses him. The effect is to cast a burning question mark over Reuven's continued fitness to claim the coveted title of firstborn. Yehuda, on the other hand, was the first to raise the sinister suggestion of selling Yosef to the Ishmaelites. Although his intervention preserved Yosef's life, it also caused his descent to Egypt. Therefore, Yehuda must now relive his role by taking Binyamin, the "Yosef figure," down to Egypt, but this time under oath that he will protect him at all costs.

The second exchange between Yosef and the brothers revolves around the money that reappeared in their sacks, and the silver goblet (was no golden goblet available?) that mysteriously found its way into Binyamin's luggage. Try as they might, it seems that the brothers could not shake themselves of the כסף (money, silver) that so malevolently clung to them and to their possessions, bringing upon them such untold grief! Who could not fail to see the connection between these ill-gotten gains and the "twenty pieces of silver (כסף)" that constituted the price for Yosef's cruel auction to the Arabian traders plying their wares down to Egypt (37:28)? Yosef the viceroy remembered it only too well: the silver coins were patiently counted out, clanging loudly as shocked Yosef was tied up and handed over to the merchants. Lifted roughly onto a lumbering camel, he was carried off as his brothers' disdainful expressions receded and then disappeared. His brothers now relived that painful moment, but this time with the dawning awareness that every deed has consequences, that there can be no evasion from past crimes, that no amount of mental gymnastics can self-conceal an act of evil.

And what of Binyamin? In effect, Yosef's careful orchestration placed Binyamin in the exact situation that he himself had experienced so long ago. Like Yosef, Binyamin was his father's favorite and the only tangible memory of Rachel that remained. Yehuda finally secured Ya'acov's permission to take Binyamin in his care and when they arrived in Egypt, the viceroy showered him with inexplicable attention. Yosef then instructed his servant to conceal his silver goblet in Binyamin's sack and to then accuse him of theft. Demanding that Binyamin be turned over, the servant met with the brothers' refusal. Returning to Yosef they tearfully pleaded for his release and Yehuda stepped forward to entreat Yosef in consideration of Ya'acov's fragile state. "When our father sees that his son is no more he shall die, and we shall be guilty of having brought down our father to the grave in sadness!" (42:31). Finally, the brothers were transformed. This time, they defended their youngest sibling, not in spite of but rather because he was their father's favorite. This time, they could not bear the thought of seeing their father in mourning, even though for the last twenty-two years they had borne it well. This time, Yehuda was able to vocalize the words that admitted their culpability: "We have an elderly father, and a child of his old age whose brother has *died* . . ." (44:20). This time, the brothers were willing to suffer imprisonment so that Binyamin could go free.

Finally, now certain of his brothers' contrition, Yosef revealed his true identity. Had he done so at the moment of their initial meeting, his brothers could never have achieved the state of sincere *teshuva* (repentance) that characterized their reconciliation now. The story of Yosef's brothers teaches us that true repentance, although often precipitated by external events, must nevertheless come from within. Yosef could have secured his brothers' impassioned pleas for forgiveness much earlier in the narrative, had he revealed himself at their first encounter. But that "repentance" would have been nothing more than a shocked startle response devoid of any depth or authenticity. Our Sages say that "the Merciful One desires our hearts" (TB *Sanhedrin* 106b), for it is sincerity and truthfulness with ourselves that constitute the first steps in making real restitution. While the ultimate goal is to mend the hurt feelings and tragic misunderstandings that destroy relationships, that process must begin with an honest examination of our own soul.

FOR FURTHER STUDY:

(1) Don Yitzchak Abarbanel (15th century, Spain), in his loquacious comments to the Parasha, draws many of the same connections between the earlier conduct of the brothers leading up to Yosef's tragic sale and the viceroy's cruel behavior towards them now. Abarbanel offers two general approaches to the matter: (a) Yosef's orchestration was about settling accounts: Those that plan to commit a crime, even if providence foils their plans, must suffer punishment in the form of emotional torment; (b) Yosef wanted to be sure, before relocating his family to Egypt, that the brothers had overcome their jealousy and would show him the deference due to a viceroy. The first explanation thus sees Yosef's conduct as punitive while the second sees it as self-interested. I have instead suggested that Yosef's conduct was, ironically, magnanimous and even altruistic – it was an attempt to bring the brothers to self-transformation *for their sake*.

VAYIGASH

Yosef's Tears

Genesis 44:18-47:27

WITH THE impassioned pleas of Yehuda that open Parashat VaYigash, the dramatic story of Yosef draws to a close. Forcefully proclaiming his determination to not allow Binyamin to be seized by the viceroy, lest their aged father Ya'acov succumb to grief and die, Yehuda stands firm. "Now, then, let your servant remain in place of the lad as a servant to my master, while the lad goes with his brothers. For how shall I return to my father without the lad with me, lest I see the evil that will overtake my father?!" (*Breisheet* 44:33–34).

Finally convinced of his brothers' remorse, certain of their spiritual transformation, sure that they are sincere when they proclaim that they will not surrender Binyamin even at the cost of their freedom, Yosef reveals his true identity. In a cathartic moment of rare intensity, Yosef raises his voice and weeps, his anguished cries so vocal that they loudly echo through the august chambers of his palace. For twenty-two years, since the day that his cruel brothers had ignored his anxious entreaties and had instead sold him to a passing camel train of Ishmaelite traders, Yosef had wanted to cry, to cry for an old and doting father who had never ceased to mourn his disappearance, to cry for a family torn asunder by animosity and rage, to cry for a world in which the innocent often suffer immensely. But with superhuman strength he had held back his tears, even as the coat of many colors had been wrenched from his youthful frame, even as he had been unjustly cast into the dungeon by a master he had esteemed and served well, even as he had languished there for two additional years when the butler forgot his solemn pledge. Now, seeing his brothers form a protective phalanx around his own beloved Binyamin, hearing Yehuda's pathetic and poignant pleas for compassion, remembering in his mind's eye a far-off land and a promise and a precious legacy, Yosef could restrain himself no longer.

Yosef's Other Tears

Actually, though, this is not the first time that we have seen Yosef shed tears. When his brothers first descended to Egypt in search of grain, Yosef immediately recognized them and ascertained that they had neither confronted nor resolved their crime of his sale and presumed death. While Yosef had been tempered by his experiences to recognize God's guiding hand, and had shed his youthful self-centeredness to don the more substantial mantle of responsibility for others, his brothers had never undergone a similar transformation. In their ancient animosities they had remained locked, their father's anguish they had never assuaged, their own diabolism they had never faced. And so Yosef patiently brought them to self-realization by a carefully contrived series of steps. Most remarkably, though, as their defenses crumbled and the harsh truth stung their callous hearts first with misgivings, then with regret and finally with restorative *teshuva*, Yosef cried with them:

> "If you are honest" [said the viceroy], "let one of your brothers be imprisoned under guard while you go to bring grain for your famished household. But your youngest brother you must then bring to me so that your claims [of innocence] be substantiated, lest you die," and they resolved to do so. Then they began to say to each other: "Surely we are guilty concerning our brother, for we watched his pained plight as he called out to us for compassion but we would not hearken, and therefore this trouble has now come upon us!" Reuven said to them: "Did I not say to you not to sin against the boy? But you would not listen and behold, his blood has now been required!" But the brothers did not realize that Yosef understood them because the interpreter stood between. *He turned away from them and cried*, but then he returned and spoke, seizing Shimon and arresting him before their eyes. (42:19–24)

The brothers returned to Canaan, fearful and anxious, their minds reeling from the memories of their misdemeanor, but the homecoming afforded them no relief. Facing their father, they attempted to explain the strange accusations leveled against them by the viceroy and then tried to convince the old, broken man to allow precious Binyamin to leave his protective embrace! But Ya'acov was terribly reluctant, remembering only too well that with similar inexplicable suddenness he had lost beloved Yosef. In the end, though, famine won the day and to Egypt they returned. There, Yosef awaited them, first lowering their guard with a grand show of magnanimity, but then crushing their final resistance with the ploy of the stolen goblet of silver, now planted in Binyamin's sack! But in the interim, as they supped on delicacies with him and he plied them with pleasantries as well as probing questions, he recognized Binyamin:

> He lifted his gaze and saw Binyamin his brother, the son of his mother, and he said: "Is this your youngest brother that you spoke of?" He then said "May God show His grace to you, my son!" *Quickly, Yosef [excused himself], for his compassions for his brother were aroused, and he felt the need to cry. He entered the chamber and cried there.* He then washed his face and emerged . . . (43:29–30)

The opening cry of our Parasha, then, is Yosef's third and most pronounced bout of tears, and it is immediately followed by further crying as he embraces Binyamin (who cries in turn) and then kisses all of his brothers as he cries once more. In the end, Yosef cries again as he embraces his dying father Ya'acov at the end of the latter's life (*Breisheet* 50:1), and then a further final time as his brothers implore his mercy after Ya'acov's death (50:17). There is, in fact, no biblical character that cries as many times as Yosef! While the Torah mentions the shedding of tears concerning Hagar (21:16), Avraham (23:2), Esav (27:38, 33:4), Ya'acov (29:11, 33:4, 37:35 – also in the context of Yosef's disappearance), the infant Moshe (*Shemot* 2:6), Moshe and the congregation (*BeMidbar* 25:6), the people of Israel (11:10, 14:1, 20:29; *Devarim* 34:8), and even Egypt (*Breisheet* 50:3 – again in the context of Yosef, this time concerning Ya'acov's death), none of these other protagonists can match Yosef's tears for either frequency or intensity.

A Final Episode of Crying

There is, however, one final episode of crying concerning Yosef that is perhaps the most poignant of all, but here the commentaries part ways in a most startling fashion. After Yosef reveals himself and calms his brother's alarm, he makes concrete plans for the family's descent to Egypt. Providing his brothers with ample provisions as well as with wagons issued by Pharaonic decree, Yosef quickly dispatches them with instructions to bring Ya'acov and the entire household down to Goshen. Ya'acov is at first taken aback by the breathless news of Yosef's survival, but he eventually is convinced by the sight of the royal wagons, and his broken spirit is revived. The preparations are made, the household is packed, and the wheels of the laden ass-drawn carts begin to creak and turn. Taking leave of the sacred earth of Canaan for the final time (for he will return to it only after his death), Ya'acov is filled with misgivings, but he cannot deny the destiny that God has placed before him. For many days the caravan travels, turning westwards after Be'er Sheva to follow the coastal route down to Egypt. All the while, Ya'acov's thoughts focus upon Yosef, his beloved Yosef, who was but a youth of seventeen when Ya'acov had sent him on that fateful journey towards Shechem from which he had never returned. Although twenty-two years had elapsed, the memory of the events, the guilt and the anguish, were still fresh in Ya'acov's mind. And now he would be finally reunited!

> He sent Yehuda before him to Yosef, to pave their way to Goshen, and they arrived in the land of Goshen. Yosef hitched his chariot and went up to greet his father Yisrael at Goshen. He appeared before him, he fell upon his neck, and he cried upon his neck uncontrollably. Yisrael said to Yosef: "Now I am ready to die, after I have seen your face, for you are still alive!" (*Breisheet* 46:28–30)

While the text employs a maddening series of pronouns to describe the moment of their embrace, all indications point to Yosef as the subject of the cries: "He (Yosef) appeared before him (Ya'acov), he (Yosef) fell upon his (Ya'acov's) neck, and he (Yosef) cried upon his neck (Ya'acov's) uncontrollably." Surely the pattern of crying that had so far characterized sensitive Yosef is not to be broken now! He had cried for his estranged brothers, he had cried for Binyamin, and now he completes the circle of tears by crying for his aged father. Rashi tells us as much when he exclaims: "Yosef appeared before his father . . . and cried greatly upon him" (commentary to 46:29). According to Rashi, Yosef, who is clearly the subject at the beginning of verse 29 ("Yosef hitched his chariot and went up to greet his father Yisrael at Goshen"), is also the subject of the end of the verse ("*He* appeared before him, *he* fell upon his neck, and *he* cried upon his neck uncontrollably").

Following Rashi, we can imagine the scene: Yosef – tall and still youthful, upright and regal – gracefully dismounts from the shimmering royal chariot and then runs towards his hunched father who haltingly steps down from the laden wagon, his bowed head covered with white thatch. The old man's eyes are dim, his leathery face deeply creased, his voice muted. Yosef embraces him tightly, his tears now flowing freely, his body contorted by deep sobs. It has been twenty-two years since their last embrace, when Ya'acov had sent his beloved son to enquire about the brothers and the sheep, and Yosef, in spite of his misgivings, had acquiesced. How many times had Yosef played that scene over in his mind during the intervening two decades of separation from his beloved father? But now he was finally reunited, though Ya'acov was no longer the patriarchal protector figure of his youth and the lost years could never be recovered. How could Yosef not cry uncontrollably?

In contrast to Rashi who assumes that it is Yosef who weeps at the sight of his stooped father, the Ramban avers that it is Ya'acov who cries. Connecting the critical pronouns of 46:29 to the verse that precedes yields the following:

> Yosef hitched his chariot and went up to greet his father *Yisrael* at Goshen. He appeared before *him*, *he* fell upon his neck, and *he* cried upon his neck uncontrollably. Yisrael said to Yosef: "Now I am ready to die, after I have seen your face, for you are still alive!"

Since we were told at the beginning of 46:29 that Yosef went up to see his father Yisrael (i.e., Ya'acov) at Goshen, the pronouns at the end of the verse must be referring to Ya'acov. Yosef "appears" before his father, but then it is Ya'acov who "falls upon his neck" and "cries uncontrollably," even as Yosef supports his wizened frame. The Ramban concludes his remarks with a trenchant observation:

> It is indeed well-known whose tears come more easily, whether the old father who finds his beloved son alive after years of despair and mourning, or else the young son who has in the interim become a king! (commentary to 46:29–30)

Support for the Ramban's reading, that Yosef had long ago overcome his grief, may be adduced from the names of Yosef's children. Recall that after Yosef had been elevated to the position of viceroy by Pharaoh, the monarch gave him Assenat, the daughter of Poti-Fera the esteemed priest of On, as a wife. She bore him two sons in quick succession, both hopeful symbols of his rehabilitation:

> Yosef called the firstborn Menashe, "for the Lord has made me forget all of my burdens and all of my father's household." As for the second, he called him Efraim, "for the Lord has given me increase in the land of my affliction." (*Breisheet* 41:51–52)

As the names of the children indicate, Yosef's rise to the position of viceroy allowed him to finally overcome the painful trials of his past, so that even the memories of his father and estranged family began to fade, to be replaced by feelings of intense gratitude at having achieved so much success. We could very well imagine that, in accordance with the Ramban's reading, Yosef no longer had a *need* to cry.

While it is impossible to dispute the general cogency of the Ramban's psychological insight, here the matter must be different. Yosef was not like other kings who donned the crown and then promptly became disconnected despots, for as demonstrated above he continued to show unusual sensitivity. The story of his reconciliation with his brothers and his family is characterized by flowing tears from beginning to end, for Yosef cries no less than seven times, not including our disputed passage! Surely in the cathartic meeting between Yosef and Ya'acov – precious son and doting father, separated from each other for twenty-two arduous years, though in the meantime he had become the viceroy and second only to Pharaoh himself – Yosef could not remain silent and impassive! We must therefore conclude that Rashi's reading is more plausible.

A Striking Denouement

While Rashi's reading is more in consonance with the larger narrative, he goes on to introduce, in the name of the early Rabbis, a conclusion to the episode that is most startling: ". . . as for Ya'acov, he neither fell upon Yosef's neck in embrace nor even kissed him. Our Sages maintain that he was instead reciting the *Shema*!" (commentary to 46:29).

How are we to understand this unsettling tradition that refuses to ascribe to Ya'acov any eminently reasonable tears and instead describes the charged moment of the embrace as an occasion for him to busy himself with the ritual recitation of the *Shema*? We can readily appreciate the pathos of Yosef's tears at that encounter; ascribing stoic reticence to Ya'acov as his son falls upon him and sobs uncontrollably seems incongruous and bizarre! The bafflement is amplified by the fact that the mitzvah of the recitation of the Shema, a specific text spelled out in *Devarim* 6:4–9, is a biblical command that was not formally communicated to the people of Israel until centuries after Ya'acov's death. Clearly, then, the Sages did not intend for their words to be taken literally. Instead, they were attempting to communicate a more profound message through their provocative imagery, as the Midrash is often wont to do.

The "recitation of the *Shema*," is a concise statement about the intertwined truths of God's unity, His transcendence and His sovereignty. Elsewhere, the Sages speak of the recitation of the Shema as "the acceptance of the yoke of heaven" (Mishna *Berachot* 2:2), the complete emotional and spiritual acknowledgement of divine authority that must precede any meaningful acceptance of God's laws: "You shall love God your Lord with all of your heart, with all of your soul and with all of your might!" But because the Shema expresses utter subservience to God's will, it also implies acceptance of His judgment. We acquiesce to His will even when we fail to comprehend it; we accept His command even when we do not understand. Not surprisingly, the Sages derived the related concept of a person's obligation to "bless God concerning the evil just as he blesses Him concerning the good" from the text of the Shema itself:

> The verse states "You shall love God with all of your heart, all of your soul and all of your might" (*Devarim* 6:5) . . . all of your might implies that no matter what measure He metes out to you, acknowledge it and be exceedingly grateful for it . . . (Mishna *Berachot* 9:5)

Tzidduk Hadin – The Acceptance of God's Judgment

For twenty-two years, Ya'acov pined for his missing son and was never comforted. For twenty-two years he cried silently, his shoulders hunched by the tragedy of Yosef's presumed death, and by the crippling guilt that he, Ya'acov, had precipitated it. While the commentaries have often questioned the brothers' conduct in withholding the truth from Ya'acov, the truth that could have relieved some of the pain and perhaps even led to an earlier reunion, there was another Accomplice to their deed who also remained silent all of those years. Rashi himself was clearly bothered by the divine reticence, for he finds it necessary to elsewhere exonerate the Accomplice by suggesting that He too was sworn to secrecy by the brothers (see his commentary to 37:33)! But one cannot so easily dismiss the matter. When God wished to communicate with Ya'acov, He did so, and not less than five exchanges are recorded between God and the patriarch (*Breisheet* 28:13, 31:11,

32:29, 35:1, 35:9). But here, for reasons inexplicable to our limited human minds (but might it have been the unavoidable consequence of Ya'acov's own act of deception that he was forced to perpetrate against an aged and blind father?!), God remained silent and never alleviated Ya'acov's plight. Now it is true that Rashi mentions on two occasions that Ya'acov was at least afforded an inkling that Yosef was still alive (see his commentary to 37:33 and 42:1), a faint spark of divine inspiration that was just sufficient to sustain, but more than that was never bestowed upon his crushed spirit.

Now, standing before Yosef the viceroy, those futile years spent and gone forever, Ya'acov is not bitter. For a sanguine soul such as himself who has suffered so much but has never succumbed, resentment is not an option. For Ya'acov there can be no recovery of the past but only a hopeful look towards the future, to whatever is left that can yet be appreciated. The God whom he had championed, the God whom he had followed, the God whom he had never doubted but with whom he had often striven, is therefore now forgiven as well. Ya'acov "recites the Shema" and wholeheartedly accepts God's impenetrable judgment even as Yosef his beloved son sobs uncontrollably. And so the dramatic account is dramatically concluded. The acquisition of trust that is Yosef's triumph, the spiritual progress that is his fame, the restoration to inscrutable God and to his authentic self that are Ya'acov's crowning glories, all of these now come together in the tear-filled *Shema* that at long last fittingly completes the saga.

FOR FURTHER STUDY:

(1) Perhaps Jeremiah had our passage in mind when he prophesied about other tears of reconciliation, this time shed by mother Rachel, her grandson Efraim (i.e., the kingdom of Israel), and God himself at the time of Israel's redemption. These tears, like our those of our passage, combine joy over the present, sadness over the past, and wistful hopes for the future:

> This says God: A cry is heard in Ramah, lament and bitter weeping, it is Rachel weeping for her children; she refuses to be comforted because her children are no more. Thus says God: Withhold your voice from crying and your eyes from shedding tears because there is reward for your labor, says God, and they will return from the land of the enemy. There is hope for your future, says God, and the children will return to their borders. I have surely heard Efraim lamenting: "You have chastised me and I have been chastised, like a calf unbroken, return me and I will return, for You are God my Lord! Now that I have returned I feel regret and after my awareness I have struck my thigh. I am disgraced and humiliated, for I have borne the shame of my youth!" Efraim is a precious child to Me, a child dandled, and when I speak of him I remember him still. Therefore, My heart yearns for him, I will surely show compassion to him, says God. (*Yirmiyahu* 31:14–19)

VAYECHI

Ya'acov's Last Request

Genesis 47:28-50:26

FOR THE final seventeen years of his long but hard life, Ya'acov dwells in Egypt surrounded by his doting children and grandchildren, while comfortably maintained by Pharaoh's munificence. The unexpected reconciliation among his sons has restored his broken spirit, while beloved Yosef, whose authority is second only to the god-king himself, is able to attend to all of his physical needs. And although it was with serious misgivings that he had left Canaan's sacred earth behind, Ya'acov was sustained on the eve of his departure by a divine pledge that his descendents would one day return to their ancestral land. In the meantime, the stability and serenity that had so eluded him for most of his turbulent and tempestuous years – years consumed in abject fear of Esav, in oppressive servitude to Lavan and in painful mourning over Yosef – are now finally his. In tranquility he will breathe his last and then surrender himself to God's embrace.

As death approaches, Ya'acov summons his son Yosef and extracts from him a solemn oath:

> . . . do not bury me in Egypt. When I die and join my ancestors then you shall carry me out of Egypt and bury me with them. Yosef responded: "I shall fulfill your words." He (Ya'acov) said: "Swear to me!", and he swore to him, and then Yisrael prostrated himself at the head of the bed . . . (*Breisheet* 47:30–31)

Ya'acov can now die peacefully, for he knows that Yosef will fulfill his final wish and inter his earthly remains in the cave of Machpela at Chevron, notwithstanding the political and logistical complexities that Yosef will need to overcome in order to accomplish the mission. Thus it is that Ya'acov, at least in death, will be reunited with his ancestors and with the land that God had promised to him and to his descendents forever. And in the process, Ya'acov's children and grandchildren who have by now established themselves so successfully on the verdant shores of the Nile delta, will be pointedly reminded that Goshen, notwithstanding all of its fabled comforts, is neither their home nor their destiny.

Including Yosef's Children among the Tribes

Sometime later, Ya'acov becomes ill, and Yosef is summoned to his bedside. Sensing the mortality that now hovers ominously, Yosef brings his two children with him – Menashe and Efraim – to say goodbye. Upon Yosef's arrival, the aged patriarch strains himself to sit upon his sickbed and informs Yosef that the two lads will be counted among the tribes of Israel. Ya'acov said to Yosef:

> "Almighty God appeared to me at Luz in the land of Canaan, and He blessed me. He said to me: 'Behold, I will cause you to increase and to multiply, so that I shall make of you a multitude of peoples, and I shall give this land to your descendents after you in perpetuity.' Now therefore, your two sons that were born to you in the land of Egypt before my arrival in Egypt shall be counted as my own, for Efraim and Menashe shall be considered by me as Reuven and Shimon. But those that were born to you after them shall be considered as yours, for they shall be called by their brothers' names in their inheritance of land. As for me, when I arrived from Padan, my Rachel died in the land of Canaan en route, while there was yet some distance to Efrat, and I buried her there on the way to Efrat, also known as Beit Lechem." When Ya'acov saw the sons of Yosef, he said: "Who are these?" Yosef said to his father: "They are my sons that the Lord has given me here," and he responded: "Bring them near to me so that I might bless them!" (47:3–9)

As a whole, this section is about the election of Menashe and Efraim to the status of full-fledged tribes, in deference to Yosef's esteemed position as the firstborn of Ya'acov's beloved Rachel and acknowledged ruler of the other brothers. In his mind's eye, now inspired with the clarity of prophetic vision, the blind patriarch can already see his children's return to the land of Canaan. He thus informs Yosef that his two oldest children – Menashe and Efraim – will be counted among Ya'acov's own children as tribes in their own right. When the land is apportioned among the tribes of Israel, the respective families of Efraim and Menashe, marching under two separate tribal standards, will secure two shares of territory, as well as provide two independent representatives to the tribal council that will form the nascent nation's proto-government. But any other children born to Yosef after Ya'acov's arrival in Egypt will be included among the clans of their older brothers and therefore absorbed into the tribes and territories of Menashe and Efraim. Thus it is that the combined tribe of "Yosef" will potentially yield more power in Israel and exercise greater influence over national affairs than any of the other tribes. In effect, avers the Rashbam in his comments to *Breisheet* 48:5, Ya'acov anticipates that which the Torah will later enshrine in law – after the death of the parent, the firstborn shall possess "a double measure of all that was his" (*Devarim* 21:17).

The patriarch's fateful decision is immediately concretized by what follows. Seeing the two sturdy lads that flank Yosef but unable to make out their features due to his failing eyesight, Ya'acov enquires concerning their identities. Are they indeed the two eldest children of Yosef and therefore entitled to their special status, or are they perhaps some of the younger siblings that will not be counted as independent entities among the tribes? When Yosef informs his father that they are in fact Efraim and Menashe – "sons that the Lord has given me here" before Ya'acov's descent to Egypt – aged Ya'acov then responds that they must step forward to receive their blessings.

A Misplaced Verse

Most curiously, though, in the midst of a passage that is otherwise devoted exclusively to the issue of Yosef's enhanced tribal status and the securing of a blessing by his sons, Ya'acov unexpectedly recalls the death of beloved Rachel. A restatement of the section with the questionable verse highlighted underlines its seeming disconnection from the larger context:

> ". . . Now therefore, your two sons that were born to you in the land of Egypt before my arrival in Egypt shall be counted as my own, for Efraim and Menashe shall be considered by me as Reuven and Shimon. But those that were born to you after them shall be considered as yours, for they shall be called by their brothers' names upon their inheritance of land. *As for me, when I arrived from Padan, my Rachel died in the land of Canaan en route, while there was yet some distance to Efrat, and I buried her there on the way to Efrat, also known as Beit Lechem.*" When Ya'acov saw the sons of Yosef, he said: "Who are these"? Yosef said to his father: "They are my sons that the Lord has given me here," and he responded: "Bring them near to me so that I might bless them!" (*Breisheet* 47:3–9)

Why does Ya'acov abruptly digress to recall Rachel's tragic death en route? Why does he remember now the details surrounding her hurried burial? How is any of this connected to the matter at hand, namely the designation of Menashe and Efraim as separate tribes? The Radak attempts to provide a rational solution:

> This statement of Ya'acov was a form of apology to Yosef concerning Ya'acov's failure to bury his mother [Rachel] at Machpela as he had later done for Leah. Yosef should therefore not criticize his father's own request to be borne after his death to that very cave! Ya'acov said to him that he had not been negligent in this matter, for Rachel had died en route and he had to proceed slowly on account of their flocks and children. He could not leave all of them unattended even to bear her body to nearby Beit Lechem and surely not to the cave at Machpela that was more distant . . . Conversely, had he traveled to there at that slow pace, her body would have decomposed in the heat (for perhaps it was the summer months), and he had no provisions for preserving her; there were of course no embalmers in attendance when she died on the way. Therefore he buried her en route with dignity and set up a memorial upon her grave, a memorial that is still there until this very day. (commentary to 48:7)

The Difficulties Introduced by Radak's Explanation

For the Radak, Ya'acov's reference to Rachel's burial was an attempt to diffuse any lingering resentment on Yosef's part. After all, here was Ya'acov now asking his son to make special efforts to inter him at the cave of Machpela – efforts that involved the traversing of large distances – when he himself had not extended the same privilege towards Rachel! She had been chaotically buried on the way where she had tragically perished and her body was not brought either to Machpela or even to Beit Lechem! Therefore, avers the Radak, with his own wishes for burial at the cave of Machpela now obligating his son Yosef to undertake a long and treacherous journey, Ya'acov feels a special need to recall to his son the trying circumstances that prevented him from transferring Rachel's body to Chevron. There was certainly no lack of will on his part but rather a series of obstacles that were at the time insurmountable. It should be noted that Radak's comments are echoed by Ibn Ezra and Rashbam, as well as by Rashi (albeit with a Midrashic flourish).

While Radak provides an admirable explanation for Ya'acov's seeming digression, now infusing the patriarch's urgent words with a tone of noble contrition, the commentator's approach introduces some serious difficulties. First of all, the issue of Ya'acov's wish for an internment at Machpela had already been discussed with Yosef much earlier, in the Parasha's opening section, and had there been decisively resolved with a solemn oath (47:28–31). It was at that time that Ya'acov had broached the subject of being carried back to Canaan for burial and it was then that he had secured his son's agreement and pledge. If Ya'acov had felt the need to explain to Yosef the painful matter of Rachel's haphazard burial, then the verse in question should have been pointedly mentioned in that earlier context, rather than now! Our passage, unfolding at a later point in time when Ya'acov was already deathly ill, is not about his plans for burial at all but rather about Yosef's special status and about the designation of Menashe and Efraim as independent tribes, as we have seen.

Furthermore, we note that Yosef had been present at the time of his mother Rachel's death and burial (see 35:9–29). Surely he was aware of the difficult circumstances that faced the family at the time and of his father's great pain over his inability to convey Rachel's earthly remains to Machpela. Would Yosef really have felt antipathy towards his father, who had loved his mother Rachel more than anything and who had so bitterly mourned her untimely death? Is it not more reasonable to assume that Yosef, instead of harboring ancient resentment, would have wanted nothing more than to now extend to his father what had been so utterly impossible at the time of beloved Rachel's death?

The Literary Framework

Let us suggest a different approach that takes some of these concerns into consideration. We noted earlier that the topic of our passage was the designation of Efraim and Menashe as tribes, and by extension, the special status now accorded by Ya'acov to Yosef vis-à-vis the other brothers to be effectively considered as the firstborn son. This unique development was further emphasized by the qualification indicated by Ya'acov subsequently: only the children of Yosef born to him before the descent of Ya'acov to Egypt would be considered as "his sons," while any offspring born afterwards would not. But from the perspective of Yosef, the designation of his sons Efraim and Menashe surely had the effect of highlighting his own struggle and triumph! For twenty-two years he had been separated from his father, growing up in a strange land under the patronage of foreigners. In Egypt, Yosef married the woman assigned to him by Pharaoh and had children of his own, while his own father remained pathetically unaware.

In the meantime, the other brothers went about their lives, raising children of their own and building the extended family into a tight-knit clan. But Yosef had never been forgotten by his aged father, and broken Ya'acov had never ceased to mourn his tragic demise. Thus, when it became clear that Yosef was still miraculously alive and had not only survived but even prospered fabulously, Ya'acov was rejuvenated because his heartfelt hopes that he had never dared voice had finally been realized. And while there was no possibility now of reliving or else restoring those lost decades, at least Ya'acov could attempt to make some amends. And thus it was that as his strength ebbed and he felt death's approach, Ya'acov informed his beloved Yosef that he would now bestow upon him the precious privileges of the firstborn son, designating Efraim and Menashe as tribes.

It is as if Ya'acov now said to his son: "You were so painfully wrenched from my embrace and I was so unwillingly separated from you. Of your trials I knew nothing and of your accomplishments I was uninformed. I did not merit seeing you take a wife and marry, nor was I near you while your young sons grew up and became youths, and nothing can replace that which has been lost! But in my heart the memory of you always burned bright, and with it the memory of your beloved mother. Now I will bestow upon you the special status that you have earned by your merits. While your brothers may resent my decision they shall not dare dispute it, for they know that my deed is justified. Your children will be considered like my own, for it is as if they have grown up in my presence and under my tutelage along with my other sons."

Understanding Ya'acov's Digression

Ya'acov's seeming digression concerning the death and burial of Rachel can now be understood as an integral piece of his impassioned declaration to Yosef about the pain of their earlier parting and about his profound desire to rectify now that which can yet be rectified. When Ya'acov mentions Rachel's unexpected demise and hasty internment, it is not because he fears that his beloved son is angry with him for now requesting that which he could not earlier provide for Yosef's own mother. Rather, Ya'acov mentions Rachel's tragic death and burial because he intends to right an ancient wrong! How cruel fate had been to all of them! Rachel had been suddenly torn from him and later Yosef had been consumed by the wild beasts, and though Ya'acov was surrounded by his other wives and their children, the raw wound had never healed.

But now Yosef stood proudly before him with his own two sons, Ya'acov's grandchildren and the offspring that he had never dreamed that he would see. If only Rachel herself were alive to see it! She, however, had died on their return from Padan and Ya'acov had been forced to hurriedly bury her in a barren tract of land far from habitation. Cathartically, the measured words spill out of the old man as he relives the scene in his mind's eye. There was Rachel, her breathing stilled and her wracked body now motionless; there was Yosef, bent over in grief and sobbing uncontrollably; and there he was, powerless to prevent his love from being taken away from him and now brusquely faced with the prospect of continuing on alone even as a new child had been born. As the shovel struck the hard earth and dislodged the rocky clods to prepare the makeshift grave, Ya'acov wept.

The powerful memory of Rachel's death and the feeling of helplessness and desperation engendered by it are forcefully suggested by a single word:

> As for me, when I arrived from Padan, *my* Rachel died in the land of Canaan en route, while there was yet some distance to Efrat. So I buried there on the way to Efrat, also known as Beit Lechem . . .

In the original Hebrew, the text reads "מתה עלי רחל". This is literally rendered as "Rachel died upon me" and may be a reference to the suddenness of her demise (as in *BeMidbar* 6:9) or else to Ya'acov's intimations of responsibility for her tragic death (see *Breisheet* 20:3 and 26:9, as well as Rashi's comments to 31:32). Perhaps, in keeping with our reading, we may understand it as a forceful way of conveying Ya'acov's feelings of utter helplessness at that time. In modern English we might translate it as "my world came crashing down upon me when Rachel died," an apt description of the pathos of the situation and an emphatic indicator that the issue at hand was not Ya'acov's desire to be buried at Machpela but rather his sorrow at Rachel's death now coupled with his determination to see Yosef's stunning success through to its glorious end. In His mercy,

God had granted Ya'acov restoration, for Yosef had prospered mightily and had even sired sons of his own. As Ya'acov now blesses beloved Yosef and his offspring, it is only natural that he simultaneously recalls Rachel, his beloved wife and Yosef's mother. For while the past could no longer be repaired nor the dead by human hands revived, at least the future could yet be secured by conscious choices made by those still alive.

FOR FURTHER STUDY:

(1) Ya'acov's blessings to his children that follow our episode (*Breisheet* 49:1–28) reinforce the unique status of Yosef. The blessing extended to Yosef is the lengthiest and most luxuriant of them all. Although it does not mention Efraim and Menashe explicitly, the Ramban detects an allusion to them in verse 22:

> Yosef is a son like a fruitful vine, a fruitful vine planted upon a spring; its branches extend upon the ramparts . . .

For the Ramban, the "branches" are none other than Efraim and Menashe. Also see Moshe's blessing to the tribes in *Devarim* 33, where the two sons of Yosef are mentioned, to the exclusion of Shimon.

SHEMOT

The Valor of the Midwives

Exodus 1:1-6:1

WITH THE death of Yosef and of his brothers, the fortunes of the people of Israel take an abrupt turn for the worse. A new Pharaoh ascends to the throne of Egypt, solidifying his rule by appealing to his people's ancient proclivity for xenophobia:

> He said to his people: "Behold, the nation of Israel is more numerous and powerful than we! Let us deal with them wisely, lest they increase; in the event of warfare, they will join with our enemies, wage war against us and leave the land!" (*Shemot* 1:9–10)

The honored status enjoyed by the Israelites under the aegis of Yosef, the serene life that they carefully cultivated on the verdant Delta, the influence that they adroitly wielded in the august halls of the Great House, all of it is harshly swept away by a deluge. Relentlessly, the people of Israel are stripped of their historic and hard-won privileges by the neophyte god-king eager to prove his power. At first they are pressed into providing for the corvée, to strengthen and to build Pharaonic store cities, but this is soon followed by more ominous decrees. Hard fieldwork and the making of bricks, both thankless tasks of backbreaking drudgery, are imposed upon them with rigor. The Israelites attempt to maintain their crumbling resolve, deluding themselves with each new blow that the Pharaoh's inexplicable rage against them has been spent, but there will be no reprieve:

> The king of Egypt said to the Hebrew midwives – the name of the first was Shifra while the name of the second was Pu'ah. He said: "When you assist the Hebrew women at birth, then you shall look upon the birth stool. If it be a male child then you shall kill him, but if it be a female child then she shall live." (1:15–16)

The First Section of Sefer Shemot

But the midwives oppose the god-king's command, and instead allow the male children to live. Realizing that his directive will not be executed by these undependable sentimentalists, Pharaoh now pronounces the harshest decree of all:

> Pharaoh commanded all of his people saying: "All male newborn children you shall cast into the Nile, but all females you shall spare!" (1:22)

Thus concludes the first section of Sefer Shemot, on an unbearably bleak note. The people of Israel, innocent of wrongdoing, have been restrained and then enslaved by a brutal tyrant who will sanction even murder for the glory and grandeur of imperial Egypt. The only opposition to Pharaoh's wicked policies, from two minor and ineffectual women, is effortlessly overcome by his sweeping pronouncement of doom. And as for the Egyptians, nary a word of protest do they utter, even as they are called upon to perform infanticide.

In the meantime, the reader, animated by his innate sense of morality to side with the oppressed in refusing to countenance wanton cruelty, is left to ponder the imponderable: where was God? Where was the God of Avraham, Yitzchak and Ya'acov, who had so solemnly pledged to the patriarchs that He would redeem their children from foreign domination? Why was He silent as the people of Israel were beaten into submission and then condemned to bondage? How could He not allow Himself to respond even as the innocent male newborns were thrown into the raging river, their sharp and mournful wails muffled by its rushing waters? The text itself highlights His absence, for while the promise of God's name pervades the closing verses of Sefer Breisheet, in this first chapter of Sefer Shemot, He is barely mentioned even once! Yosef, it will be recalled, in his final words to his brethren that concluded the book, reminded them of His pledge:

> Yosef said to his brothers: "I will soon die, but the Lord will surely remember you and bring you forth from this land, to the land that He swore to give to Avraham, to Yitzchak and to Ya'acov." Yosef exacted an oath from the children of Israel saying: "The Lord will surely remember you, and you will bring forth my bones from here!" (*Breisheet* 50:24–25)

Finding God in the Narrative

When the opening verses of Sefer Shemot indicate that "a new king arose over Egypt, who did not know Yosef" (*Shemot* 1:8), they are telling us about much more than the changed political climate. These verses are emphasizing that God Himself, the faithful patron and protector who had sustained Yosef and his brothers and had been lovingly invoked by the viceroy on his deathbed, had been eclipsed by the sinister splendor of the ruthless god-king. Gone and forgotten were Yosef and his brothers; silenced was the God in whom they had so fervently trusted.

The hopeful reader, however, if he was careful in his reading, found His name in the most unexpected of places. As the midwives went forth from the presence of the king to do his nasty bidding, they were filled with terrible foreboding. Who would dare to oppose his might, to provoke his imperious disfavor? How could they, lowly midwives, resist a tyrant who clenched the golden crook and flail that held all of Egypt in sway? But what human being could kill an innocent child, even as he entered the world and filled his mother's relieved ears with his first throaty cries? Painfully aware of their terrible predicament, the midwives marshaled their inner strength and decided to do what was *right*. Only one thought could have stirred such fortitude, and only one Source could have inspired it: "The midwives *feared the Lord* and did not do as the king of Egypt had commanded them, for they caused the children to live!" (1:17). It was thoughts of God and their reverence for Him that braced the midwives, affording them the power to oppose the all-powerful. It was the memory of a God of goodness that sustained them, of a God of compassion and justice, of a God of reckoning and retribution. And thus it was that even as Pharaoh's massive monuments rose over Goshen, even as his proud obelisks towered over the brickworks to proclaim his eternal might, these two obscure women outshone him in radiance.

Asking ourselves once again concerning His involvement, as the heavenly beings themselves are wont to enquire about the "place of His glory" though it fills the universe to overflowing, we are now startled by the response: *God is to be found in the deeds of those who maintain their righteousness even as the world around them goes viciously mad*! In a heartless society bereft of His presence, in a situation so filled with brutality that to observe it even from the safety of scholastic detachment is to recoil in disgust, God is not absent as long as there are good people who do what is right in spite of it all. It is therefore through the agency of the midwives that God is introduced to the otherwise miserable landscape of the opening chapter of Sefer Shemot, for in their simple act of compassion they preserve His memory and His name from oblivion.

So while the spellbound social historian and the affected architect, the awestruck archeologist and the enthralled academic, look upon our Pharaoh's works and pronounce him an unqualified success, the Torah dares to voice an opinion less favorable. The true measure of a man, it proclaims, is not to be gauged by the number of bricks that his hapless slaves heap up to memorialize his name nor by the prestige that he secures for his adoring subjects. Rather, a person is appraised by his deeds of kindness and compassion towards the weak and the vulnerable, by his acts of justice and righteousness towards the oppressed and the downtrodden. And according to that evaluation, Pharaoh king of Egypt, "enduring-of-dominion-like-Ra-in-heaven," was a dismal and unmitigated failure!

But these two midwives who would not have merited even a brief footnote in any breathless account – ancient or modern – of Pharaoh's accomplishments, so lowly was their station and so minor their role, are here celebrated as the unlikely heroines of the narrative. And lest one make the mistake of assuming that a reckless act of justice or compassion under difficult circumstances is to be considered worthwhile only in accordance with its efficacy, the Torah goes to pains to tell us that the attempts of the midwives were ultimately unsuccessful. In the end, Pharaoh circumvented their goodness by pronouncing the ineffable: "All male newborn children you shall cast into the Nile, but all females you shall spare!" But the sad outcome of their efforts, says the Torah, does not lessen by even one iota the nobility of their deed. Their obscure names are thus preserved for posterity forever, while Pharaoh's own name, with the passage of the millennia, ultimately fades from even the most enduring of maniacal monuments to his self-aggrandizement. Before the transcendent one, all pretensions of temporal power melt away, revealing the invincible mettle of those that serve Him.

Textual Intimations

These truths are alluded to in a curious passage that describes God's intervention on the midwives' behalf:

> The midwives feared the Lord and they did not do as the king of Egypt commanded them, for they preserved the children. The king of Egypt therefore summoned the midwives, and he said to them: "Why have you done this thing and preserved the children?" The midwives answered Pharaoh: "It is because the Hebrew women are unlike the Egyptian women, for they are vigorous, so that before the midwife

> arrives, they proceed to give birth!" The Lord dealt kindly with the midwives, and the people multiplied and grew exceedingly. It came to pass that since the midwives feared the Lord *that He made houses* (בתים) *for them*. Pharaoh commanded all of his people saying: "All male newborn children you shall cast into the Nile, but all females you shall spare!" (1:17–22)

What exactly are the mysterious "houses" that God provides to the midwives in consequence of their devotion and loyalty? Most of the medieval commentaries understood the term metaphorically as an intimation of future descendents or offspring. Rabbi Avraham Ibn Ezra's formulation is typical:

> The term "houses" is to be understood as it is used elsewhere, where it states that "God will make a house for you" (*Shemuel* 2:7:11). The meaning is that He caused their descendents to increase, in reward for their preservation of the children of Israel. The Gaon, however, explained it to mean that He made for them houses in which He concealed them so that they could not be found! (commentary to *Shemot* 1:21)

Rejecting the Gaon's (Sa'adiah, 10th century, Babylon) literalism in spite of the imagery of divine protection that it brings to the passage, Ibn Ezra instead recalls the verse in Sefer Shemuel in which God responds to David's desire to build a Temple to His name. While God rejects David's overture as premature, He does promise him in turn a dynasty of descendents that will follow him. This dynasty is called in the text a "house," and parallels David's own aspiration to build a real house to God's glory. The "house of David" later becomes the biblical idiom for his dynasty. In a similar vein, the midwives are divinely provided with "houses" that Ibn Ezra understands to mean "descendents," directly paralleling their own good works in preserving the children of Israel. Ibn Ezra demands of us that we part with the literal meaning of the word "בתים" or "houses" in these contexts, and this is not unreasonable under the circumstances. After all, why should the midwives be rewarded with literal houses in consequence of their good deeds, and how would we anywise understand these houses to have been assigned to them in the course of the unfolding narrative? Are we to infer that they lacked domiciles until this point or else that they became real estate magnates sometime later on? If, instead, "houses" here means descendents (as it surely does in the proof text from Sefer Shemuel), then we have both a reasonable explanation for the term as well as a just dessert for their deed of compassion in preserving the children of Israel.

Pharaoh's Frantic Building

What is perhaps most striking about the idea that the midwives' offspring could be referred to as "houses" is that it is introduced in the midst of a narrative that portrays the Pharaoh's frenzied and feverish efforts to build his own "houses"! Thus, the people of Israel are set to work "building store cities for Pharaoh, namely Pitom and Ra'amses" (*Shemot* 1:11). They are oppressed with backbreaking toil, "with mortar and with bricks and with all manner of work in the fields" (1:14) so that the Pharaoh might be supplied with the endless numbers of blocks necessary for his own buildings. Even the birth stool referred to in the text, the low bench that the midwives are to attend to as they slay the newborn males, is called the "אבנים" (1:16), and while the commentaries debate the exact derivation, the root of the word is from the Hebrew for "stone" ("אבן")! In fact, the only other biblical usage of the term occurs in a verse that describes the potter doing his work at the wheel, fashioning vessels of clay upon the "אבנים" (see *Yirmiyahu* 18:3), and perhaps recalling once again the vast outlays of clay and mortar expended in our passage in homage to the god-king. And all that this arrogant man does, all of the buildings that he raises, all of the bricks that he impatiently demands, are for the sake of preserving his name, his dynasty and his descendents, for eternity! The houses of the midwives, then, stand in opposition to the houses of Pharaoh – the former built upon a foundation of goodness and decency, the latter erected on the broken backs of serfs.

Bearing all of this in mind, let us consider the significance of the word "Pharaoh," the only title by which the king of Egypt is ever called in the Torah. The word, in fact, is an Egyptian combination that means "Great House" and provides us with yet another reference to grand buildings and impressive structures. The Hebrew equivalent of "פרעה", however, is nothing more than a transliteration of the Egyptian term. Since it is a transliterated word, there are a number of possible renditions that would have been acceptable in biblical Hebrew. Conceivably, it could have been spelled "פרו" or else "פראו". Instead, the Torah spells it without exception as "פרעה".

This is not insignificant, for the biblical root פרע occurs in other contexts where it means "loose" (*BeMidbar* 5:18 – "he shall *untie* her hair . . ." – ופרע), "unchecked" (*Shemot* 32:25 – "Moshe saw that the people were behaving *without constraint* . . ." – "פרע"), or "unbounded" (*Mishlei* 15:32 – "He that *casts off* instruction despises his own soul, but he that heeds reproof acquires understanding" – "פורע"). Pharaoh's title, then, connotes not only an individual but also an archetype, the human being that refuses to abide by any limitations imposed by a higher sovereign. Pharaoh is not only a god in the eyes of his subjects but possesses divinity in his own eyes as well. Thus, he is free to behave without moral compunctions in his self-interested drive to achieve enduring and eternal fame. Or to recall the words that his successor later employs to rebuff Moshe's first attempts to secure the release of the Israelites, "who is God that I should hearken to his voice to send Israel forth? I do not know God, nor will I release Israel!" (*Shemot* 5:2). We therefore conclude that when the Torah transliterates this Egyptian term, it does so in a deliberately interpretive fashion (compare to another example of this technique in *Breisheet* 14:1–2 and see Rashi ad loc.).

The implications of all of this are quite remarkable. While Pharaoh frantically labors to erect his own buildings, cities of brick and monuments of stone, all in order to safeguard his name and to assure that his line will prevail forever, the midwives go about their own unsung labors, quietly preserving the children of Israel. And while Pharaoh's noisy efforts will, in the end, amount to naught, so that his grand memorials may endure for centuries but the eternity that he so craves will not be his, the descendents of the midwives, the counter-houses to Pharaoh's own, will never perish! Thus the Torah pointedly drives home one of its most important messages: while we may, like the Pharaoh, expend much effort in pursuit of material gains, often at the expense of others, God actually gauges our success as a function of our moral and spiritual accomplishments. A kind exploit, a compassionate act, a deed of justice and of righteousness, these are things out of which our eternity is made. The example of the midwives Shifra and Pu'ah lives on forever in our Torah, continuing to challenge and to inspire others to follow in their selfless ways. Try as he might, the potent Pharaoh, though buttressed by all of the resources that only a god-king can muster, will never achieve the staying power of two simple women who boldly chose to do what was right.

FOR FURTHER STUDY:

(1) The English poet Percy Bysshe Shelley (1792–1822) famously captured these sentiments in his poem "Ozymandias," the title of which is actually a Greek corruption of "Rameses" and refers to the indefatigable builder of whom our Parasha speaks:

> I met a traveler from an antique land
> Who said: "Two vast and trunkless legs of stone
> Stand in the desert. Near them, on the sand,
> Half sunk, a shattered visage lies, whose frown,
> And wrinkled lip, and sneer of cold command,
> Tell that its sculptor well those passions read
> Which yet survive, stamped on these lifeless things,
> The hand that mocked them, and the heart that fed;
> And on the pedestal these words appear:
> 'My name is Ozymandias, king of kings,
> Look on my works, ye Mighty, and despair!'
> Nothing beside remains. Round the decay
> Of that colossal wreck, boundless and bare,
> The lone and level sands stretch far away."

VAERA

Pharaoh's Hardness of Heart

Exodus 6:2-9:35

PARASHAT SHEMOT concluded with the first mission of Moshe and Aharon to Pharaoh, in which they demanded, in the name of the God of the Hebrews, the release of the Israelite slaves. That meeting ended in abject failure, for Pharaoh not only refused but also increased their burdens. Henceforth, they would be responsible for gathering their own straw with which to strengthen the clay bricks:

> That day, Pharaoh commanded the taskmasters and officers saying: "Do not provide the people with straw for bricks as before. Let them go and gather their own straw. However, you must place upon them the same quota of bricks as before, do not reduce it! They are indolent and therefore cry out: 'Let us go to sacrifice to our God.' Let the work become heavier for the people so that they will be occupied with it, and will not be misled by false ideas." (*Shemot* 5:6–9)

Thus began in earnest the struggle between Pharaoh and God, during which Pharaoh's stubbornness was countered by progressively harsher and more wondrous plagues. These culminated in the slaying of the Egyptian firstborn, a blow so grievous that the god-king finally capitulated. The unfolding saga of the plagues, accounting for the majority of the *parashiyot* of VaEra and Bo, is characterized by a formulaic pattern: divine warning is followed by Pharaonic refusal, pestilential visitation, Pharaonic acquiescence, relief from the affliction, and renewed noncompliance. The character most cited in these sections in none other than Pharaoh himself.

Why is it that Pharaoh repeatedly repudiates the dire urgings of Moshe and Aharon? Why does he allow his empire to be buffeted and then broken by stinging scourges that were entirely avoidable, if only he would have yielded? His early recalcitrance is comprehensible, for the god-king could hardly have regarded the wizened visages of the Hebrew leaders as even remotely menacing. The invisible God that they confidently invoked seemed too ethereal to constitute a threat to his robust rule. However, quite early on in the process, and certainly by the third or fourth plague, it became obvious to Pharaoh that his proud defiance was no match for the omnipotence of the absolute one, whose will could not be denied. The very magicians who handily duplicated the first two plagues of blood and frogs were quite ineffective by the third plague of lice. They themselves were stricken by the sixth plague of boils and by the eighth plague they were in the untenable position of pleading with Pharaoh to release the Hebrews! But all to no avail, for Pharaoh would not bow, not until darkness had obliterated his beloved sun god and death had taken his own firstborn child.

We will consider a number of explanations for Pharaoh's behavior. It is essential to bear in mind that a vexing theological enigma looms large in the background – Pharaoh's intransigence appears to have been imposed by divine fiat. Already on the eve of his appointment to be God's spokesman, Moshe was informed that He would harden Pharaoh's heart and that he would not submit before the deadly onslaught of the final plague (4:21–23). In our Parasha, the matter was reinforced (7:1–5). If it is God who intercedes to sway Pharaoh's autonomous decision, how can He then hold him responsible for the repudiation of Moshe's demands and then punish him with the full intensity of the plagues? As Rabbi Avraham Ibn Ezra succinctly puts it: "If God hardened Pharaoh's heart, then what is his transgression or his sin?" (commentary to 7:3).

Maimonides – The Choice Is Ours

Maimonides, echoing with some variation the words of Rashi who preceded him by almost a century, proffers an eloquent explanation in his *Mishneh Torah*, Laws of Teshuva, chapters 5 and 6. He begins his discussion by stating a fundamental tenet of the Torah:

> Every person is given complete autonomy to pursue the course of righteousness to become morally upright, or to follow the way of wickedness to become evil. This is what the Torah intimates concerning this unique capacity of the human being, when it states: "Behold the human being is like one of us, to know the difference between good and evil" (*Breisheet* 3:22). That is to say that the human being is completely exceptional in this respect, for only he is capable of distinguishing between good and evil, and of exercising an autonomous moral will without hindrance or constraint . . .
>
> This is a crucial principle that constitutes the foundation of the Torah and its commandments . . . God does not coerce human beings or decree upon them to do good or bad, but rather they have complete choice.
>
> If the deity were to decree upon the person to be righteous or evil, or were to shape his essential nature to of necessity follow a particular path, opinion, or deed (as the foolish astrologers maintain), how could He command us by the word of the prophets to "do this" or "don't do that," "improve your ways and desist from performing evil"? If it had already been determined at the moment of conception, that one's nature would inevitably be drawn towards a particular course of action that could not be averted, then where is the possibility of the Torah's fulfillment? By what law could God then punish the evildoer or reward the righteous? Shall the Judge of all the earth not do justice? (Book of Knowledge, Laws of Teshuva 5:1–4)

For Maimonides, the ability to distinguish between good and evil and to exercise a completely autonomous moral choice is at the core of the human personality. It is one of the essential qualities that separate man from all other creatures which act in accordance with instinctual drives that cannot be denied. In the absence of free will, self-obligation to the dictates of a higher law and the lofty dream of a higher purpose are absurdities. If moral autonomy does not exist then the extraordinary ideal of *teshuva* – a person's ability to experience sincere remorse for the past and to earnestly resolve to ennoble the future – is a baseless flight of fancy.

However, Maimonides continues:

> It is possible that a person can commit a sin so grievous or transgressions so numerous, such that the true judge determines that the transgressor, who committed those acts freely, henceforth will forfeit the opportunity of *teshuva*. Such a person loses the privilege of repentance from their evil, in order that they should die and perish on account of their act . . . Therefore the Torah states: "I will harden Pharaoh's heart", for he had initially transgressed of his own free will and dealt harshly with Israel who were sojourners in his land . . . thus, *teshuva* was withheld from him, and he was punished . . .
>
> Why then did God send Moshe telling him to let the people go and to repent if He had already informed him that he would not let them go? This was in order to indicate to all that when God withholds the option of *teshuva* from the transgressor, he will not be able to return, and will of necessity perish as a result of the wickedness that he had committed initially of his own free volition . . . Therefore, God did not decree that Pharaoh should oppress the Israelites . . . but rather, he himself decided to do so, and lost the opportunity of *teshuva* as a result. (Book of Knowledge, Laws of Teshuva 6:3)

Maimonides acknowledges that God did in fact deny Pharaoh the freedom to choose, but he regards the unusual intervention as a particularly harsh form of punishment reserved for only the most incorrigible of transgressors. From our first introduction to tyrannical Pharaoh and to his successors, the god-king had consistently chosen, freely and of his own volition, to oppress, brutalize, dehumanize and finally extirpate the hapless Hebrew slaves. He consciously embarked upon a vicious course that could, however, have been altered for the good, if only the monarch had so desired. But Pharaoh was immutable, for he persisted in his evil and resisted the call of his moral conscience even after Moshe and Aharon had addressed him with their softly-worded requests for relief. And so, posits Maimonides, after many opportunities had been offered and rejected, after five plagues had already unfolded and Pharaoh's heart remained adamant as stone, God intervened and eliminated his ability to henceforth freely choose, his earlier misdeeds thus condemning him to inevitable self-destruction.

Although we might be tempted to assign a psychological interpretation to this principle, such that conditioning created by repeated choices can sometimes result in terminal addiction, Maimonides intends a different reading. Moral autonomy is man's most precious possession. Besides God Himself, we are the only other beings on this planet who are endowed with this capacity. The moral will is therefore the primary expression of the bond that unites humanity with the creator, "for in the image of the Lord He made man" (*Breisheet* 9:6). By misusing the gift of free choice in order to do evil, man runs the risk of relinquishing it. *Teshuva*, which is nothing more than an emphatic expression of our freedom to change our course of action for the good, is therefore not an inalienable right, but rather a precious privilege that can be revoked.

Maimonides' reading introduces an ironic note to the drama by underscoring the extent of Pharaoh's retreat. In ancient Egypt, Pharaoh was regarded as the supreme authority; across the vast expanse of his desert kingdom, his pronouncement was law. His unwillingness to submit to the God of the Hebrews was a direct function of the unlimited temporal powers vested in him. In a land of absolutes of dazzling sun, burning sand, restorative river and obdurate rock, Pharaoh held utter sway.

Enter the God of Israel who dared to demand that the king of Egypt relinquish control over his serfs in order to grant them a brief respite from their back-breaking labor: "The God of the Hebrews has summoned us. Let us go a distance of three days into the wilderness in order to offer sacrifice to God our Lord . . ." (*Shemot* 5:3). For the first time in the history of the world, a God spoke out against the injustice of state-sponsored slavery and demanded the liberation of its defenseless victims from the tyrant's pernicious grip. Pharaoh responded with incredulity and disdain, as if an incorporeal, invisible and nameless God could dictate terms to the ancient world's most potent ruler! His ongoing refusal to grant the slaves their freedom and his freely exercised choice to instead increase their burdens were incrementally countered by the loss of his autonomy to change his ways. The vaunted monarch who styled himself a direct descendent of the sun and conducted himself with the bearing of a god, was in the end powerless even over the exercise of his own mind. The freedom to choose – the basic possession of every human being no matter how ignoble his station – was placed beyond humbled Pharaoh's reach! As our Sages colorfully put it: "The wicked are incapable of repentance, even as they stand at the gates of hell!" (TB *Eiruvin* 19a).

The Interpretation of the Seforno

How different is the approach of Rabbi Ovadiah Seforno who categorically rejects any divine complicity in taking away a human being's moral will:

> Surely God desires that the wicked return to Him rather than perishing, as the verse states: "As I live, says God, I do not desire the death of the wicked but only that he should turn away from his evil and live" (*Yechezkel* 33:11). Here, God tells Moshe that He will multiply His signs and wonders in order to cause the Egyptians to repent, for He will proclaim to them His greatness and compassion by these signs and wonders . . . Additionally, the purpose was also for Israel to observe and to revere . . . There is no doubt that had his heart not been fortified, then Pharaoh would have let Israel go. But this would not have been because of repentance or submission to the Almighty, nor because of regret for rebellious behavior, having finally recognized God's greatness and goodness, but rather because of his inability to suffer the plagues any longer . . . and this would not have constituted *teshuva* at all. *Had Pharaoh desired to submit to the Almighty and to return to Him in sincere repentance, nothing at all would have prevented him from doing so!* Therefore God says that "I will harden Pharaoh's heart" meaning that He will grant him the fortitude to bear the plagues so that he will not have to send forth Israel because of his fear of them . . . (commentary to *Shemot* 7:3)

Here, the Seforno posits a completely novel interpretation (though in outline it was already stated two centuries earlier by Ramban and by Ibn Ezra, the latter rejecting it!). The hardness of heart of which our passage speaks does not mean, as Maimonides understood it, a taking away of Pharaoh's freedom of choice. Maimonides had understood the metaphor of a "hard heart" to mean a heart incapable of being swayed, a heart insensitive and unfeeling, a heart that would not entertain thoughts of self-transformation or *teshuva*. Hardness of heart for Maimonides was synonymous with stubbornness, obduracy and inflexibility. A hard heart would not choose goodness, and God sealed Pharaoh's fate by perpetuating the very hardness of heart that the god-king had himself consciously nurtured by his ruinous choices all along. Such a heart, once the die of choice had been freely cast, would have to stay the course until the bitter end.

But for Seforno, the portal of sincere *teshuva* is never slammed shut, even in the face of a tyrant as vile as the Pharaoh. When God indicates to Moshe that He will harden Pharaoh's heart, He means to say that He will give the Pharaoh the fortitude and strength of spirit to bear the plagues. God will "strengthen" his heart and fill it with courage. This will, in turn, allow the monarch the opportunity to choose real and sincere repentance, rather than being coerced to let Israel go by the unbearable onslaught of the plagues. In other words, while Maimonides understood the hardening of Pharaoh's heart to mean the *taking away* of his ability to freely choose his moral course, for the Seforno the hardening of the heart constitutes the *restoration* of that very freedom! God hardens Pharaoh's resolve, thus granting him the endurance to withstand the plagues so that he might choose the good of his own accord! After all, for Pharaoh to exercise "compassion" and to let Israel go while a proverbial gun is pointed to his head is hardly *teshuva* at all. But with his heart fortified by God's saving power, Pharaoh will remain unbowed. He will therefore have the opportunity to make a free and conscious decision at any point during the process to reject cruelty, to condemn injustice, and to embrace the God of Israel in sincere *teshuva* by freeing Israel from bondage.

This brilliant approach at once relieves us of the knotty theological dilemma while also going a long way to explain the otherwise inexplicable disappointments introduced by the conclusion of last week's Parasha. How frustrated we felt when the dramatic build up towards redemption was dashed by Pharaoh's disdainful dismissal of Moshe and Aharon! How pained we were to see hapless Israel's increased sufferings as they were bidden to make bricks without straw! The enslavement dragged on, momentarily becoming even more unbearable. But for Seforno, if *teshuva* of the wicked is the goal, then patience is required. Had Pharaoh been vanquished in an instant, had Israel gone forth in a single stroke from dark slavery to blinding freedom, then surely God's might would have been confirmed, but His gentle call to *teshuva* would have been utterly lost in the tumult. Pharaoh's hold would have been broken, but the opportunity for his transformation would have been lost. The process of the plagues undoubtedly prolonged the suffering; forbearance for the wicked unfortunately means more victims. But, for Seforno, such are the ways of God. As the prophet Yechezkel described it some nine centuries later: "Do I then desire the death of the wicked?" says God Lord, "I want only that he repent from his ways so that he might live!" (*Yechezkel* 18:23).

FOR FURTHER STUDY:

(1) It would be convenient for us to confine our discussion to Pharaoh and his minions, tyrannical dictators all, who have filled the pages of human history with so much misery. There is, however, another Pharaoh with whom we are more familiar, a god-king who is not a vestige of antiquity or a current ruler of a far-off land. In the works of the ethicists who stressed self-mastery and heightened moral awareness, Pharaoh is a metaphor for a disagreeable aspect of the human personality that is alive and well to this day. Rabbi Moshe Chaim Luzzatto (18th century, Italy), in the context of a discussion concerning the importance of living an examined life that is not desensitized by habit and rote, writes:

> One of the evil inclination's most effective weapons is to overburden the human heart with cares and labors, leaving a person no time at all to consider the direction of his life. If a person would but contemplate his ways, he would surely begin to reconsider his priorities, and the ensuing remorse would no doubt bring about a complete abandonment of the transgression. This is similar to the counsel of the wicked Pharaoh who said: "Let the work become heavier for the people so that they will be occupied with it, and will not be misled by false ideas" (*Shemot* 5:9). His intent was not solely to frustrate any thoughts of resistance on their part, but also to prevent them any opportunity for even reflecting on their situation, by imposing upon them unceasing labor. This is exactly the same approach taken by the evil inclination . . ." (*Mesillat Yesharim* 2 – The Attribute of Caution).

It thus emerges that there is another dimension to our saga, one with which we can more readily identify. In every human heart there is a small voice that counsels us to pursue a life of material excess, of moral and spiritual apathy and of indifference to all that is holy. Held in its sway, we busily fill our days with labors, activities, and pastimes, rarely pausing to question the ultimate purpose of our endeavors. Caught up with life's burdens and worries, many of them self-imposed, we find little or no time to contemplate our enslavement. And when confronted like Pharaoh of old, there is a part of us that cries out with overbearing self-assurance: "Who is God that I should hearken to His voice?" (*Shemot* 5:2).

Cast in this light, the battle against the injustice of mighty Pharaoh takes on added meaning, for it is not only the universal story of wretched slaves achieving deliverance or even the particularistic narrative of Israel becoming a nation. The events leading up to the Exodus also tell the story of the self, of the ongoing struggle in each human heart to liberate the spirit from the bonds of lethargy that would otherwise overpower it. And at the core of the narrative, whether for Maimonides or for Seforno, is the principle of autonomy, the God-given ability of the individual to freely exercise his moral will and to determine the system of values that he will adopt. Pharaoh's abuse of that freedom and his wretched downfall, in spite of God's benevolence, is therefore a cautionary tale for us all.

BO

The Blood Service of the Paschal Lamb

Exodus 10:1–13:16

AS THE PLAGUES agonizingly draw to a close and the winds of freedom begin to blow, Pharaoh remains entrenched. Hostage to an adamance of his own making, he is unwilling to consider the sage counsel of his chastened advisors to release the Hebrews, even as disaster stares him squarely in the face. "God said to Moshe: I shall bring one more plague upon Pharaoh and upon Egypt and then he shall send the people forth, he shall surely drive you out completely" (*Shemot* 11:1).

As their last tense standoff is about to conclude, Moshe announces to Pharaoh and to his assembled court the most frightening plague of all:

> Thus says God: "At the stroke of midnight, I will go out in the midst of Egypt. All of the firstborn in the land of Egypt shall die, from the firstborn of Pharaoh who sits on his throne, to the firstborn of the slave girl who grinds at the millstone, as well as all of the firstborn animals. There shall be a great outcry in the land of Egypt, the likes of which there has never been, nor shall there ever be again. As for all of Israel, a dog shall not whet its tongue neither against man nor against animal, so that you may know the distinction that I shall draw between Egypt and Israel. All of your advisors assembled here shall come to me and bow down saying: 'Leave with all of your people!' and then we shall go." And Moshe left Pharaoh's presence in fury. (*Shemot* 12:4–8)

The Passivity of the Hebrews

Over the course of many months, nine plagues have been visited upon Pharaoh and the Egyptians. The invisible God of the Hebrews has patently demonstrated His superiority over the false gods of Egypt, His mastery of the forces of nature and His providence over the affairs of human beings. The Egyptians have borne the brunt of the plagues in a pathetic mixture of terror and wonder, as Pharaoh has impassively resisted their unavoidable message. As for Israel, they have for the most part witnessed the plagues as detached observers, internalizing the pertinent message without being subject to their painful effects.

It is notable indeed that for a people about to experience the refreshing air of national freedom, Israel remains completely passive. In fact, throughout the period of the plagues we have heard nothing of their preparations and plans for the Exodus. For an oppressed people chafing under cruel bondage and anticipating the aurora of liberation, they have been unusually inert. Have there been no clandestine meetings of the revolutionary council to discuss the dawning emancipation and to map out the setup of a provisional government? Why have we not heard of an aspiring cadre of firebrands gathering around the prophet and stirring up the people to acts of protest and to sabotage of the brick works? Where were the communiqués and leaflets issued periodically to buoy the people's spirits and to fan the flames of the insurrection? Instead, it appears that the Exodus is the only example in recorded history of a revolt of slaves in which their leader demanded and achieved deliverance, while the slaves themselves who longed to be free did nothing!

The significance of this "oversight" is abundantly clear: the Torah does not make mention of the people's active participation in winning emancipation because it did not take place. There was no popular movement to call for freedom and no band of inspired activists to oppose Pharaoh's decrees. When Moshe appeared to announce God's redemption, "the people believed" (4:31) but did nothing to realize the dream, and nothing more was asked of them. Standing back in awe and trepidation, they stoically beheld as God's mighty acts shook and toppled the oppressive regime of the Pharaoh. The participation of Israel was conspicuously absent from the process of the redemption because the Torah is emphasizing in no uncertain terms that divine involvement alone was responsible for the Exodus. To borrow from the language of the Haggadah, "if God had not taken out our ancestors from Egypt, surely we and our children and our grandchildren would still be slaves to Pharaoh in Egypt!" The Exodus therefore represents a meta-historical event that declares for all time that the world has an omnipotent God, transcendent and yet always present, absolutely surpassing the feeble limitations of pagan personification but never too distant from the aching heart of the serf.

The Taking of the Lamb

As the plague of the firstborn draws near, God issues a commandment whose fulfillment by the people constitutes their first tentative step away from enslavement and towards redemption:

> God spoke to Moshe and Aharon in the land of Egypt, saying: This month shall be for you the beginning of months, the first month of the year. Speak to Israel and tell them that on the tenth of this month each household is to take a lamb. If the household is too small to consume a lamb then let it join with a neighbor to together take a lamb . . . Guard the lamb until the fourteenth day of this month at which time the entire congregation of Israel shall slaughter it at evening. They shall take of its blood and mark the doorposts and lintel of the homes in which they consume it. They shall eat its flesh on that night, roasted and with *matzot,* and with bitter herbs shall they eat it . . . This is how you shall eat it: with girded loins, with your shoes on your feet and with your staff in your hands. Eat it in haste, it is a Pesach offering to God. I shall pass through the land of Egypt on this night, and I shall smite every firstborn in the land of Egypt, human as well as animal, and I shall execute stern judgments against the gods of Egypt. The blood shall serve as a sign upon the houses in which you dwell, and I shall see the blood and pass over you, and the destructive plague shall not be upon you as I smite the land of Egypt . . . (12:1–13)

The Paschal sacrifice, consisting of a lamb roasted whole and eaten in a state of preparation and haste, is the central element in the meal of redemption. As the surrounding night is punctuated by screams of dread and cries of anguish, the people of Israel will calmly consume their repast. The lamb is to be eaten with the unleavened cakes of *matzah* and the bitter herbs, and the doorways are to be marked with the blood of the lamb. Within the safety of their sealed homes they will wait for the night of terror to pass. Significantly, the badge of this blood is here described as the mechanism for warding off the dreaded visitation of the destroyer.

Transitory and Timeless Features

Gathered as close-knit and cohesive units, the former individuals of Israel, now finally coalescing into a nation, are to partake of the lamb's flesh in a state of impatient anticipation of the dawn of liberation. They are to be dressed and ready to leave Egypt at a moment's notice, demonstrating steadfast trust in God's promise even while the destroying angel performs his gruesome work. Similarly, the lamb is to be roasted whole, eaten with quickly baked unleavened bread and seasoned with nothing more elaborate than bitter herbs, to emphasize the hurriedness of the meal. There is to be no effort expended in the preparation of anything more time-consuming, for God's redemption will unfold in the blink of an eye and Israel must be ready to set forth (commentary of the Rashbam to 12:8–9). Of course, the ceremonial features of the meal are multi-dimensional: The *matzot* also recall the poor man's bread consumed in bondage, and the bitter herbs evoke the harsh servitude and the sting of the taskmaster's whip.

The "blood service" that accompanies the Passover rites is less comprehensible. While it is the placement of the blood upon the doorposts and lintel that conditions God's merciful passing over, the text does not at all spell out the meaning of this sign. Why should the portal be so stained at all? Why with the blood of the sacrifice and not with some other marker? To obfuscate matters more, why is it that only the very first Pesach in Egypt incorporated this ceremony? Or, to quote the Ramban who anchors his comments in early Talmudic traditions (TB *Pesachim* 96a):

> The prohibition of consuming the lamb while it is raw is for all subsequent generations, because all of the commands that pertain to the *actual body* of the sacrifice are eternal. Conversely, the extrinsic injunctions relating to those that consume it, such as the necessity for loins girded and shod feet, or the placement of the blood upon the portal, applied only to that first Pesach of Egypt. This distinction is clearly indicated by the rite of the so-called Second Passover that is to be observed by those who in future generations are unable, due to ritual unfitness, to celebrate the sacrifice at its proper time (see *BeMidbar* 9:1–14). There, the text indicates that the substitute sacrifice, offered exactly one month after the Pesach, is also to be consumed "with matzot and bitter herbs. None of its flesh is to be left over until morning, nor are any of its bones to be broken, for after the eternal manner of the Pesach sacrifice is it to be prepared." The verse thus specifies that the timeless features of the Pesach sacrifice are those that pertain to the consumption of its actual flesh. (commentary to *Shemot* 12:9)

An investigation of the traditional sources yields a number of basic approaches, each of which contributes an additional aspect to our understanding of this first commandment given to all of the people of Israel.

The Polemic against Idolatry

> "Draw and take lambs" – this is what is meant by the verse: "Those that serve idols shall be ashamed." When God told Moshe to command the people to sacrifice the Paschal lamb, Moshe was alarmed. "Master of the Universe! How shall I do this thing? Do You not know that the lamb is one of the gods of Egypt? Said God to him: "By your life, I swear that Israel shall not leave this land until they first slaughter the god of Egypt before their eyes, to indicate to them that their gods are powerless." And so it was, for that very night God smote the firstborn of Egypt and the people of Israel slaughtered and consumed the lamb. The Egyptians saw their firstborn dead and their god slaughtered and could do nothing, as the verse states: "Israel left Egypt on the morrow . . . and Egypt was burying their firstborn which God had smote, and against their gods He executed judgments." (*BeMidbar* 33:3–4; Midrash Shemot Rabbah 16:3)

According to this Midrash, the commandment to take and slaughter the Paschal lamb is understood as the final demonstration of God's omnipotence. Bowed and broken by the plagues, unable to withstand any more the irresistible message of God's dominance, Egypt must bear one final indignity: the wholesale slaughter and consumption of one of their popular deities by their formerly subservient nemeses. Its blood casually and conspicuously draping their doorways, the people of Israel eat the lamb in calm conviction, for no cruel taskmasters shall disturb their peace this night. What Moshe had earlier regarded as a dangerous act of provocation (see *Shemot* 8:22) is here commanded by God as a last, decisive indication that He alone is master of the fate of men, and that there are no other gods to oppose His will.

According to this reading, one can only assume that the blood was smeared on the *outside* doorframe, plain for all to see. Such is the view expressed by Rabbi Yitzchak in the Mechilta, Parashat Bo 6: "Rabbi Yitzchak said: The blood was smeared only on the outside, so that the Egyptians might see and their stomachs churn." This is an act of defiance, as the people of Israel thumb their noses at their former masters by fearlessly ridiculing their gods. Though the placing of the blood effectively singles out their homes for easy identification, Israel is unafraid of retribution, for God Himself has extended His protective canopy over them. "I shall see the blood and pass over you" is therefore not meant to imply a limitation on God's ability to otherwise identify the homes of the Hebrews. That would be a theological impossibility and completely at odds with the omniscience that God demonstrated during the course of the other plagues. Rather it is a statement in no uncertain terms that Israel's redemption hinges upon a brave act of conviction that publicly proclaims Egypt's utter defeat.

The Merit of Acts

A very different perspective is provided by a Midrash preserved in the Mechilta, Parashat Bo 5:

> "You shall guard the lamb until the fourteenth day of this month" – Why did the Torah ordain the taking of the lamb four days before its slaughter? Rabbi Matya ben Heresh explained: . . . the time had arrived for God to fulfill His oath

> to Avraham to redeem his children, but they had no *mitzvot* to perform in order to merit redemption. Therefore God gave them the twin *mitzvot* of the blood of the Paschal lamb and the blood of circumcision in order that they might merit redemption, as the verse states "I passed upon you and saw you wallowing in your blood, and I called to you: by your blood you shall live, by your blood you shall live!" (Yechezkel 16:6) . . . Thus, they were commanded to separate the lamb four days beforehand to indicate that one can receive reward only for acts.

In this formulation, the gods of Egypt are not at all of interest. The issue is merits, and merits are a function of acts. Belief in redemption is insufficient without acts of trust, and for Rabbi Matya acts of trust are the *mitzvot*. The people's passivity during the course of the plagues now had to be overcome by deeds, and the two deeds decreed by God were circumcision and the Paschal lamb. But these acts were not undertaken by Israel in order to highlight Egyptian impotence, as the earlier formulation suggested. Rather, they were about something else entirely.

Circumcision for adults is a painful experience, and the Hebrew males needed to be ready to suffer that pain in order to testify to their association with each other as well as with a common destiny. On the most fundamental level, circumcision is an indelible identifying mark that links together individuals to form a community or a nation. When individual people are marked with the same ineradicable sign then it is understood that they are part of a larger entity. In a similar way, the Paschal lamb is also about self-identification, for its blood marks the homes of God's followers. Eaten in units of the family and the clan, this sacrifice more than any other speaks of larger, national affiliations. For Rabbi Matya, it is precisely these two *mitzvot* that usher in the Exodus, for they both speak of assuming a national identity that is predicated upon recognition of the supreme God and adherence to His teachings. They are most appropriately the merits by which Israel secures their redemption. It is important to point out in this connection that the text makes the celebration of the Paschal sacrifice contingent upon being circumcised, for both are expressions of the same religious national themes (see *Shemot* 12:43–44). In all probability, the taking of the lamb four days before its slaughter was also the signal for the Israelites to perform the rite of circumcision, so that by the fourteenth day of the month they would have recovered (see Rashi on *Breisheet* 18:1).

Significantly, these are also the only two positive commandments in the Torah that carry the penalty of *Karet*, or spiritual excision from the community of Israel, for non-fulfillment. One who willfully abrogates either of these rites has rejected any connection to the destiny of the people of Israel, and is therefore spiritually expelled from their midst.

Overcoming Idolatry

We now turn our attention to the most striking of the sources, also a Midrash from the Mechilta (Parashat Bo 5):

> Moshe said to the people: "Draw yourselves away from idolatry and take instead the lamb commanded by God." Said Rabbi Yehuda ben Betayra: The verse states that the people did not hearken to Moshe [when he announced the impending redemption – see 6:9] because they were "short of breath and burdened with hard labor"! Is it possible that a person could be informed of glad tidings and not rejoice? If a person were told of the birth of his child would he not rejoice? If a slave was

> informed that his master was going to free him, would he not rejoice? Why then did the people ignore Moshe's encouraging words? Rather, it was difficult for them to part with idolatry!

According to this Midrash, the Paschal sacrifice constitutes a protest against idolatry. But it is not the idolatry of the Egyptians being derided, nor is it their gods being defiantly dispatched. Rather, it is the idolatry of the Israelites that must be extirpated! Sojourning in Egypt for generations, the people of Israel had adopted the erroneous beliefs and corrosive values of their oppressive hosts. Conditioned by the comfortable worship of the Egyptian pantheon, the personable and tangible gods of the river, earth and sky, Israel was unsettled by the prospect of a single, absolute, morally demanding God. With growing alarm they witnessed the demolishing not only of their cruel overlords, but also of their system of belief! As each plague drove home with greater force the futility of idolatry and their unsolicited selection as God's own, Israel stood passively by, hopeful for an end to their servitude but disconcerted by the prospect of freedom. Finally, with dawn about to break after the darkest night, God for the first time imposed a challenge on the people: slaughter the lamb god of Egypt whom *you* worship, loosen your embrace of idolatry, and demonstrate to *yourselves* that you are ready for redemption.

The placing of the blood on the doorway is therefore not to be understood as an act of confrontation but rather as a potent symbol of faith. As such, it is incongruous to associate the markings with the outside doorframe which tends to suggest a statement for Egyptian consumption. It is more probably the *inside* frame that was smeared, implying a message to be internalized by the people of Israel. Significantly, Rabbi Yishmael and Rabbi Natan, disagreeing with the opinion of Rabbi Yitzchak quoted above, both understood that the blood was in fact daubed on the inside frame as an exclusive sign for the people of Israel. In consonance with this reading, the theological difficulty of "I shall see the blood and pass over you" is also obviated – with the blood smeared on the inside of the doorframe, *only* an omniscient God could see it.

The Larger Context of the Pesach Sacrifice

A careful reading of the biblical context introduces another dimension to the matter and sheds light on the entire discussion. Recall some of the other features of that signal meal: Firstly, the Paschal lamb was consumed by household units that consisted of nuclear families, close relations, and invited guests. To adopt the Talmudic formulation of the perpetuated principle, the sacrifice could only be consumed by those who had been appointed ahead of time to partake (Mishna *Zevachim* 5:8). Secondly, these cohesive groups gathered in their huts and effectively shut themselves in, for none were to leave the secure embrace of kin and the protective heat of hearth until daybreak. With doorposts and lintel smeared with the Paschal blood, the people of Israel were to remain safely indoors, beyond the reach of the destroying angel, "for none of you shall trespass beyond the opening of your homes until morning" (*Shemot* 12:22). Thirdly, as the Israelites serenely partook of their meal of redemption, the silent night was repeatedly punctuated by the screams of the Egyptians, and even the sound sleep of Pharaoh was interrupted at the stroke of midnight: "Pharaoh arose at night, he and his ministers and all of Egypt, for there was a great outcry all over the land. There was not a household among them that did not experience a death" (12:30).

On that night, then, Israel was safe and secure within, while without, chaos and confusion reigned. As dawn broke, the screams subsided, the bolted doors were flung open, and the people of Israel stepped into the blinding light of freedom. The symbolism of the experience is now crystal clear: on that night of terror, a nation was born, and on the morrow they were brought forth. The threshold, consisting of doorposts and lintel stained with blood, thus defined the decisive moment in time and space that separated the protection and stillness of the "womb" from the harsh chaos of daylight. Crossing that verge, passing through that painful portal, was to experience that most excruciating and exhilarating of all experiences: *birth*!

The boldness of the metaphor also explains its singularity. The Exodus may be an eternal commemoration of emancipation from tyranny, the Pesach sacrifice a perpetual observance of God's saving intervention, but the particular features that address the theme of parturition remain unparalleled. A nation is born but once, and once crossed, the threshold of delivery cannot be retraced or crossed again. Remarkably, this very theme of birth finds expression in an astonishing vision communicated by God to the prophet Yechezkel, who addressed the exiled Judeans by the rivers of Babylon some eight hundred years after the events of the Exodus. Recalling the abject state in which God found their oppressed ancestors in Egypt, the prophet describes in coarse terms the disarray and inelegance of birth, and then God's compassionate involvement:

> The word of God came to me, saying: son of man, inform Jerusalem of its abominable conduct . . . As for your birth, on the day that you were born, your umbilicus was not cut, nor were you washed clean with water, conditioned with salt or swaddled in diapers. No one had compassion upon you to perform even one of these things to show kindness, for you were instead cast out into the field in your repulsive state on the day that you were born. I passed upon you and saw you wallowing in your blood, and I called to you: "by your blood you shall live, by your blood you shall live!" (*Yechezkel* 16:1–6)

Textual Parallels in Sefer Yechezkel and Allusions in Rabbinic Thought

In context, the harsh words of the prophet Yechezkel are a stinging rebuke to his compatriots, the people of Israel who forgot their humble origins and the God that sustained them from the beginning. Like an abandoned newborn, they had been forsaken under Egyptian bondage, covered with the mire of clay and mortar and utterly bereft of any human kindness, until God "passed over" them and raised their spirits with His fortifying words: notwithstanding their cruel predicament, they would endure, for the dreadful crimson coating of their birth would be transformed into the sanguine smudge of survival.

Yechezkel, then, clearly alludes to the experience of the Exodus as the process of the nation of Israel being born. While he sees with hindsight their terrible subsequent treachery, we see in foresight their moment of great promise. They are indeed like a newborn child, and thus it is perfectly plausible that the symbol for that torturous but transcendent moment be the blood placed upon the threshold of their shelters.

An extrinsic support for the above analysis is provided by the fact that the quoted passage from Yechezkel was early on incorporated into the traditional readings that accompany the Seder. When the Haggadah wishes to describe the abject but nevertheless hopeful state of the people as the servitude progressed, it cites *Yechezkel* 16:7, with some versions even concluding the reference with our earlier text, "I passed upon you and saw you wallowing in your blood, and I called to you: by your blood you shall live, by your blood you shall live!"

In light of the above, let us reconsider the Midrash Mechilta, Parashat Bo 5 that we saw before:

> "You shall guard the lamb until the fourteenth day of this month" – Why did the Torah ordain the taking of the lamb four days before its slaughter? Rabbi Matya ben Heresh explained: . . . the time had arrived for God to fulfill His oath to Avraham to redeem his children, but they had no *mitzvot* to perform in order to merit redemption . . . Therefore God gave them the twin *mitzvot* of the blood of the Paschal lamb and the blood of circumcision in order that they might merit redemption, as the verse states "I passed upon you and saw you wallowing in your blood, and I called to you: 'by your blood you shall live, by your blood you shall live!' . . . Thus, they were commanded to separate the lamb four days beforehand to indicate that one can receive reward only for acts."

Earlier, we noted that this Midrashic source emphasized that the redemption of the people was a function of the merits that they secured by hearkening to God's commands and performing acts of self-identification. Now, however, we also recognize that it highlights the clear link in Rabbinic thought between Yechezkel's blood of birth that covers the newborn and the blood of the Pesach sacrifice smeared upon the doorposts and lintels of the Hebrews. They are, it seems, one and the same. God's vengeful "passing through the land of Egypt" (ועבר ה' לנגף את מצרים – *Shemot* 12:23) is paralleled in Sefer Yechezkel by His compassionate "passing upon" the abandoned newborn (ואעבר עליך ואראך– *Yechezkel* 16:8), in order to save her from the certain death that would have otherwise been her fate.

We have thus seen a variety of sources that seek to explain the meaning of the Paschal sacrifice and the central ritual of the smearing of its blood. As the Exodus dawned, the people of Israel prepared to embark on their odyssey in the world as a liberated people. The freedom so hoped for and anticipated was extended to them only after they had taken the first critical spiritual steps, and it is this axiom that now emerges as the cornerstone of God's relationship to His people. Spiritual accomplishments are only possible if one is willing to take spiritual risks, by discarding the shackles of a comfortable culture in order to embrace a more profound approach to living, a sincere life of *mitzvot*. To do so requires courage, trust and not a small amount of determination.

FOR FURTHER STUDY:

(1) To recognize the motif of birth in the rituals that lead up to the Exodus adds a more profound layer of meaning to the discussion. Parenthetically, it also explains the Torah's insistence that Pesach be celebrated in the season of the spring (*Shemot* 23:15). But there are also larger implications: If leaving servitude and embarking on the path of freedom is akin to being born, then experiencing God's ongoing guidance in the wilderness, standing at Sinai to hear His words, and journeying to Canaan to settle it are the elements in the more lengthy and involved process of *national development*.

There are multiple experiences that separate the newborn infant from the responsible adult, many milestones that mark the route from self-absorbed and godless materiality to selflessness and spiritual enlightenment. This is true for individuals as well as for nations. The dynamic progress of the Jewish people towards an apprehension of God and a recognition of their singular mission may have commenced with their first halting steps over that bloodstained threshold, but that was only the *beginning* of their national story. That story is still being played out even now, more than three thousand years later.

BESHALACH

The Miracle at Yam Suf

Exodus 13:17-17:16

> And it came to pass that when Pharaoh sent the people forth, the Lord did not lead them by way of the land of the Philistines, although it was near. This was because the Lord said: "Lest the people have a change of heart when they see warfare, and return to Egypt." So the Lord caused the people to turn towards the way of the wilderness, to the Sea of Reeds, and the people of Israel went up from the land of Egypt armed . . ." (*Shemot* 13:17–18)

AS THE DRAMA of the Exodus unfolded, Israel embarked on its triumphant march from the house of bondage. Led by Moshe, who tenderly carried the bones of Yosef, the people went forward and set their bearings for freedom. The broad avenues of fabled Rameses – a colossal monument to hubris and greed, raised up by muck-encrusted hands to immortalize the god-king, constructed hurriedly under the cruel gaze of the impatient taskmasters – were now empty and eerily silent. Just a short while ago, the still desert air of this delta city, the seat of Pharaoh's imperial rule, was filled with the hum of activity and commotion. Weary work gangs scurried to and fro with their heavy burdens of brick and mortar, the cruel crack of a whip occasionally punctuating the undifferentiated din. But now there was otherworldly calm, an unnatural tranquility interrupted by intermittent cries as shovels struck dirt and another Egyptian body was mournfully lowered into the warm, black earth.

In the distance, the sounds of rejoicing and song could still be faintly heard, as the ragtag procession of liberated Israelites receded towards the shimmering horizon and then disappeared. The Egyptians were left to their own solitude to ponder the Hebrew God's mighty acts, the one who had proclaimed for the first time in the history of the world that slavery was unjust and imposed servitude a crime.

At Succot the people of Israel briefly rested, before continuing on to Etam to confront the vast and awesome wilderness that stretched beyond. Dutifully following Moshe and the mysterious pillars of cloud and fire that now led them along an unfamiliar route, they anxiously entered its maw. But then unexpectedly, God commanded the people to retrace their steps and to encamp before "Freedom Pass" (פי החירות), between "Migdol and the sea, opposite Baal Tzefon on the shore of the waters" (14:1). Portentously, God then told Moshe that He would harden Pharaoh's heart one last time so that He would be "glorified."

Meanwhile, Pharaoh and his henchman had a change of heart. Marshalling his best troops and six hundred of his most lethal chariots, the king of Egypt gave chase and quickly overtook the unsuspecting Hebrews as they calmly camped at the Sea of Reeds. Predictably, the people were thrown into a frenzied panic. The *matzot* that had tasted so sweet at that final meal in Egypt now turned bitter in the mouths of many. Had they not dutifully followed God's directives to offer the Paschal sacrifice just a few short nights earlier? Had they not hastily eaten the ritual repast in their full attire, prepared for the command to march? Had they not fearfully but obediently smeared the sacrificial blood on the doorposts and lintels of their former hovels, demonstrating their trust in a God who said that He would save?!

> Pharaoh drew close. Israel lifted up their eyes to see Egypt pursuing them, and they were very afraid. Israel cried out to God. They said to Moshe: "Were there not any graves in Egypt that you took us out to perish in the wilderness, what have you done to us to take us out of Egypt? This is the very thing that we said to you in Egypt repeatedly: Let us be, so that we may serve the Egyptians, for serving the Egyptians is preferable to dying in the wilderness!"

The Ramban is certainly correct in asserting that during those traumatic moments of turmoil that seemed to last an eternity, the people of Israel could not decide on a united course of action (commentary to 14:10–12). Many considered surrender, to swear renewed allegiance to the Pharaoh and to submissively offer to run back to the brick pits. Others, few in number, demurred. The Egyptian host, like a tempest fast approaching, would not be in a sympathetic mood. Surely they would not accept surrender. Would it not be better to oppose them, to die like free men instead of vanquished slaves? Some cried out to God, tearfully imploring His mercy and resolutely holding on to His promise. Not a few stood dumbstruck, shocked by the terror of imminent doom into an unfeeling stupor. In front of them all, the deep blue waters of the Sea of Reeds gleamed. The gentle waves lazily lapped at the soft sandy banks, but in the azure reflection the people saw the specter of death.

The Mentality of Slaves

Why did God bring the people of Israel to the shores of Yam Suf? Hadn't His other plagues upon Egypt been sufficiently impressive? Why was it necessary for Israel to experience in quick succession abject terror, absolute dread, utter hopelessness and then astounding salvation? Rabbi Avraham Ibn Ezra provides us with a critical glimpse into the situation by raising a question that begs for resolution (commentary to 14:13):

> One might ask why a great multitude of six-hundred-thousand people should fear their pursuers! Should they not prepare to fight for their lives and the lives of their children?

Ibn Ezra posits that Israel, with retreat impossible and faced with the prospect of being cut to pieces by the Egyptian charioteers, should have cried out about defending their lives! Confronted by an enemy force that could have numbered no more than a few thousand, the six-hundred-thousand men of Israel should have been planning a counter-attack. Yet, even as they railed against Moshe, words of insurgency were completely lacking. Expressing dejection and disillusionment, they failed to speak of resistance. Ibn Ezra continues:

> The answer is, however, that the Egyptians were the masters of the Israelites, and the generation that left Egypt had learned from its youth to bear the Egyptian yoke; its spirit was downtrodden. How could they now oppose their masters?!

Therefore, argues Ibn Ezra, the decision to fight for their lives was not even entertained by the newly-emancipated Hebrews. Burdened with a mentality that was conditioned to follow orders and to never object to their masters' commands, the people of Israel could not for a moment imagine defying Egyptian authority, even at the cost of their own lives. The brimming confidence shown by the people on that dawn of their redemption scarcely a few days earlier must have been flimsy indeed. Ibn Ezra's explanation corroborates the many ancient traditions asserting that the vast majority of Israelites had no interest in leaving Egypt to begin with (Midrash Shemot Rabbah 14:3) – had they not been "thrust out of Egypt" by their overwhelmed Egyptian overlords, they would have happily remained enslaved forever! To our Western ears, this disdain of freedom sounds incomprehensible, but we must attempt to comprehend the matter from a completely different perspective.

The life of a slave is a difficult one filled with toil, travail, exhaustion and the constant fear of sudden and violent death. The slave has few if any rights and many burdensome responsibilities. While dreams of relief are never far from his mind, he cannot fathom what existence might look like *after* liberation. This is because for all of its horror, the life of a slave holds one comfort: there is no necessity to take any initiative or to make any autonomous decision. For the slave who has been raised in servitude forever, choices are made by someone else, a master who wields authority with frightening intensity. As long as the quota of bricks is met, the drudgery of serfdom can therefore unfold with deadening predictability, dulling the senses and clouding the mind.

How alarming is the experience of sudden liberation! Suddenly all of life's givens evaporate and the small series of variables that were within the slave's purview abruptly increase by several orders of magnitude. In servitude, a familiar routine of oppression can be counted upon; in freedom, so much is unknown. Confronted by the reality of their liberation and not only a dream, the Israelites are paralyzed. A united course of action is impossible.

The Midrashic Account

Finding themselves closed in by the impassable waters on one side and by Pharaoh's whirling chariots on the other, the people of Israel cry out in desperation. Moshe attempts to comfort them with promises of divine salvation, but from all indications in the text, he himself does not know what God's plan might be! Unsure of how to proceed, Moshe calls out to God in prayer, but then his entreaties are cut short:

> God said to Moshe: "Why are you crying out to Me? Tell the people of Israel to move forward! Raise up your staff and stretch out your hand upon the sea to divide it, and let the people of Israel enter into the midst of the waters on dry land!" (*Shemot* 14:15–16)

The Midrash in Shemot Rabbah 21:10 vividly describes the scene:

> If they were to enter "the midst of the waters" how can the Torah call it dry land? And if they were to tread on dry land how could they be in "the midst of the

waters"? Rather, this indicates that the waters did not part until they had entered up to their noses, and only then was it made dry land!

The textual inconsistency that triggers the Midrashic reading could have been easily resolved without recourse to such an explanation, but the real purpose of the fanciful exegesis is to capture the essence of the charged moment. Through the eyes of the Midrash, we can see Israel as they desperately enter the waters at God's command. Wading in up to their ankles, they anticipate some sort of miraculous intervention, but none is forthcoming. As the waters reach their knees they are sure that God will not abandon them, but nothing happens. The waters now lap at their waists but still the heavens are silent. With water now up to their shoulders, their hearts begin to sink and thoughts of doom flood into their minds. But forward they go. The sea now at their noses, the hour of truth has arrived, for in a short moment they will drown! Suddenly the waters thunderously part and the people proceed through "the midst of the waters on dry land."

We tend to think of the parting of the Sea of Reeds as a miracle of "biblical" proportions and indeed it was. In a demonstration more impressive than any of the plagues that ushered in the Exodus, God showed His absolute mastery over the forces of nature as well as over the affairs of men. The Midrash, however, suggests another more significant dimension to the event. In essence, claims the Midrash, the true wonder at Yam Suf was not the parting of the waters at all, but rather the people of Israel's willingness to follow God's word. The trust that the people showed as they entered the waters, a spirited act that signaled their agonizing break with the slave mentality, was the real miracle at the Sea of Reeds. In the face of such fortitude, the waters had no choice but to part before them.

Incorporating the Midrashic account into the narrative yields a more nuanced reading. It is true that for the Midrash the people had faith and went ahead, but what other choice was there? God carefully orchestrated the events of the Exodus so that the people would arrive at the shores of Yam Suf with Pharaoh and his army in hot pursuit. There, they would have *no other option* but to enter the waters at His command, to grudgingly perform an act of initiative that would forever destroy the possibility of a return to Egypt, to a life of numbing bondage and to the paralysis of a slave. The Torah's repeated emphasis on "walls of water to their right and to their left" (*Shemot* 14:22, 29) must be intimating the compulsion of the moment, for in that tunnel-like state there existed only one path: to advance ahead. Their "free-will" act of trust was therefore divinely imposed, and there was no other viable alternative but to comply. The drawn-out plagues constituted for Israel an incremental process of instruction as their all-powerful taskmasters were cut down to size. The Paschal sacrifice on the eve of their departure, its blood defiantly smeared on their doorposts and lintels, was the first tentative expression of their independent will. At Yam Suf, Israel's descent into the deep at God's behest was therefore the natural continuation of the demanding march towards true independence. In effect, then, the Midrash augments the Torah's account – Israel's desperate desire to remain enslaved to no course of action, to maintain the passivity of serfdom at all costs, was shattered at Yam Suf by God's command. Outmaneuvered, not by Pharaoh but by God Himself, the people had no choice but to trust in Him and to go forward.

An Eternal Commemoration

Significantly, Rabbinic tradition discovered in the events of Yam Suf an eternal commemoration. Recall that as the people trembled and cried out to Moshe, he forcefully soothed them:

> Moshe said to the people: "Be not afraid! Stand fast and see the salvation of God that He will do for you on this day, for as surely as you see Egypt this day you will never see them again!" (14:13)

While Moshe's impassioned words appear to be *reassurance*, the Talmud (Yerushalmi *Succah* 5:1; Mechilta BeShalach 2 with minor variations) detected in them an *imperative*:

> Rabbi Shimon bar Yochai taught: There are three places in scripture where the people of Israel are enjoined not to return to the land of Egypt. Here, the verse states: "As surely as you see Egypt today, you will never see them again." Another verse states concerning the king: ". . . God has said to you that you shall not return by this way again" (*Devarim* 17:16). The third verse says in the admonition that "God will return you to Egypt in boats by the route concerning which I said that you shall not see it again . . ." (28:68)

Rabbi Shimon bar Yochai explains that Moshe's response to his panicked people was not simply words of encouragement as they stood opposite the Egyptian host with their backs to the sea – it was a divine command as well. God indicated at this critical juncture, through His prophet's measured words, that it is forbidden for the people of Israel to ever return to Egypt! Maimonides has the following to say on the matter:

> It is permitted to dwell anywhere in the world except for the land of Egypt, from the Mediterranean Sea and westwards for an area of 400 parasangs [a Persian distance equal to approximately 4.5 kilometers] square, opposite the land of Kush [Nubia] and opposite the [Sahara] desert. The entire region is forbidden for settlement. In three places the Torah warned us not to dwell there, as the verses state: "You shall not return by this way again" (*Devarim* 17:16), "you shall not see it again" (28:68), "as surely as you see Egypt today, you will never see them again." (*Shemot* 14:13)
>
> It is permitted to return to Egypt to secure merchandise or for business reasons or to conquer other territory. The prohibition only concerns dwelling there permanently. One does not, however, incur the punishment of lashes for the act, for at the time of entry it is permitted. If one subsequently decides to dwell there permanently, it is by then a passive act . . . (Book of Judges, Laws of Kings 5:7–8)

Here, Maimonides offers some important qualifications to the legislation, for not any return to Egypt is forbidden. Only one who descends to Egypt with intent to permanently dwell there is in direct violation of Torah law. One who temporarily visits for the sake of securing business or merchandise is permitted to do so.

The Reading of Rabbi Shimon

Why does Rabbi Shimon insist that Moshe's words at Yam Suf constitute the pronouncement of a negative *mitzvah* when the context seems to suggest otherwise? How are we to understand the transformation of Moshe's impassioned words into a formal commandment, introduced to the people at a most unsuitable time? Many commentaries adopt Maimonides' explanation for the prohibition of dwelling in Egypt: "That country's ways are more corrupt than any other land." In other words, the moral laxness of Egypt's inhabitants constitutes a danger to all those who dwell in its midst. It is, of course, difficult to support this thesis in light of what we know of many other ancient lands and cultures, and more difficult still to assign it eternal validity. Perhaps our story can yield another possibility.

Recall that the people of Israel had scarcely left the land of Egypt when God guided them to the shores of Yam Suf. While it is the case that they had marched forward from the house of bondage with the noble bearing of liberated men – "the people of Israel went out with hands held high [triumphantly]" (*Shemot* 14:8) – their newfound courage was mere euphoric posturing. Though they had witnessed the crumbling of Pharaoh's resolve before the God of Israel, they had yet to internalize the profundity of their new destiny. That is why just a short time later, confronted by the thundering Egyptian war machine and hemmed in by the sea, the people of Israel crumbled. Their proud manner vanished, their new identity dissolved, their desire to be bound no more in cruel bondage evaporated with the wet spray. They cried out against the God who had saved them, they derided loyal Moshe who had taken them out, and they resolved then and there to return to Egypt! In light of the above, perhaps we can now better comprehend the veiled meaning behind Moshe's words at that moment:

> Moshe said to the people: "Do not be afraid! Be steadfast and you will see the salvation of God that He will do for you this day, for as surely as you see Egypt this day, you will never see them again. God will wage war for you, while you be silent!" (14:13–14)

Rabbi Shimon maintains, in a profound reading of the underlying themes, that Moshe's response was not simply to offer the people words of strength in order to shore up their broken resolve, but to impress upon them an eternal truth: *there can be no return to Egyptian bondage, not now, not later and not ever*. There can be no return to the bearing of the slave who submits to his master and absorbs his blows, who casts off initiative and embraces hopelessness, who prefers the predictable terror of the brick pits to the challenge of exercising the moral will. Egypt may have been a geographical location, but in the conscience of the people of Israel it was also a *state of being*. The Torah prohibits the Jew from taking up permanent residence in Egypt not because it is necessarily more corrupt than other lands, but rather because such an act symbolizes the conscious desire to return to the demeanor of the slave and to his cursed lot. This prohibition of dwelling in Egypt is thus understood as the prohibition of taking on the slave identity anew, and it is first revealed to the people of Israel not in the book of Devarim concerning the king or else in the passage of admonition but rather at the shores of the Sea of Reeds. It is there that Israel wavers between abhorrence for their former taskmasters and a desire to be pressed into their service once again, between a nascent appreciation of autonomy's precious challenges and the enfeebling memory of slavery's refuge, between the cobalt waters of Yam Suf and the deafening whir of Pharaoh's chariot wheels. And it is there that God informs them, by way of Moshe's stirring words, that there is really only one possible choice – "Speak to the people of Israel and tell them to go forward!" (14:15).

FOR FURTHER STUDY:

(1) Recall that Rabbi Shimon bar Yochai cited three separate sources for the prohibition to dwell in Egypt – one from our Parasha, a second from the context of the king and a third from the "admonition." The above analysis addresses the reference drawn from our Parasha but the other two are just as telling.

In *Devarim* 17:14–20, the people of Israel are commanded to appoint a king. One of the provisions placed upon him involves horses: "However, he may not multiply horses for himself, lest he return the people to Egypt in order to multiply horses . . ." For the king of Israel to return to Egypt in order to secure horses is a dangerous act of dependence, mirroring our earlier discussion. Later biblical history preserves many moments of Egyptian meddling, their failure to fulfill expectations and even overt military intervention, all exacerbated by Israel's over-reliance on its neighbor to the south.

As for the admonition that spells out doom upon Israel for non-fulfillment of the Torah, what greater curse could there be than to return to Egypt as slaves? When the verse proclaims that "God will return you to Egypt in boats by the route concerning which I said that you shall not see it again . . ." (*Devarim* 28:68), it represents a complete unraveling of the Exodus dynamic! Leaving Egypt, we left slavery behind; returning to Egypt as slaves is utter national dissolution.

YITRO

Yitro and the Giving of the Torah

Exodus 18:1-20:22

AT THE CLOSE of Parashat BeShalach, the nomadic tribe of Amalek attacks the people of Israel while they are journeying in the wilderness of Refidim. According to the account in Sefer Devarim (25:17–19), they cravenly concentrate their assault on the weak and weary stragglers who trail behind the rest of the camp. Yehoshua, at Moshe's behest, raises a force and repels the marauders, and in the aftermath of the confrontation Moshe sets up a memorial altar and invokes God's eternal oath of retribution against them.

Parashat Yitro optimistically opens with the journey of Yitro from his desert redoubt of Midian, to meet Moshe and the people of Yisrael as they encamp in the wilderness of Sinai. Accompanied by Tzipora, Moshe's wife, as well as by Moshe's two sons, Yitro is met by the lawgiver, who recounts to his father-in-law all that God had done to Pharaoh and to Egypt on behalf of Israel. He also describes to Yitro their most recent adventures along the route, from all of which God had saved them. Yitro, gladdened by the news, blesses God and proclaims His greatness and uniqueness above all other gods. He then proceeds to prepare an offering, and Aharon and the elders of Yisrael join him for a sacrificial meal before God.

On the morrow, Moshe performs his role of adjudicating the peoples' civil suits, and is engaged in doing so from the morning until the evening. Yitro is surprised that there are no other official judges assisting Moshe in his work, and suggests that a hierarchical judiciary be established utilizing suitable candidates drawn from the people. This, he proposes, would allow the more straightforward cases to be heard by other officials. Moshe, whose expertise would be called upon only for the more difficult cases, would be able to devote the majority of his energies to the more pressing need of instructing the people in God's laws. Moshe graciously accepts his father-in-law's advice and begins to initiate it. The first section of the Parasha concludes with Moshe sending his father-in-law on his way, "and he returned to his land."

The subsequent section of the Parasha, beginning with chapter 19, is the most momentous in Sefer Shemot and describes the events surrounding the Revelation at Sinai. As the people camp at the foot of Mount Sinai, God reminds them of how He had taken them out of Egypt and had borne them on "eagles' wings" to bring them to this place. He then offers them the covenant of His Torah, so that they might thereby become His special treasure among the nations. The people in unison accept, and after intense preparations, they stand together to witness the awesome spectacle of the Decalogue.

Are these sections – Amalek, Yitro, the giving of the Torah – arranged chronologically, or is there some other ordering principle at work? When exactly does Yitro make his appearance at Sinai and when exactly does he leave? What inspires him to join the people of Israel and why is the account of his visit juxtaposed with the battle against Amalek on one hand, and the Ten Utterances on the other?

The Chronology of Events

> "Yitro the priest of Midian and father-in-law of Moshe heard of all that God had done on behalf of Moshe and His people Israel . . . and he journeyed towards them" – what did Yitro hear? Rabbi Yehoshua says: He heard about the battle against Amalek, which is recorded just prior to his visit. Rabbi Elazar HaModai says: He heard about the giving of the Torah and came to join them . . . Rabbi Eliezer says: He heard about the splitting of the Sea of Reeds. (Mechilta de Rabbi Yishmael, Parashat Yitro, beginning)

According to Rabbi Yehoshua, the sections of the Torah in the main follow a strict chronological order. If the section that precedes Yitro's visit describes the war against Amalek then that must have been the catalyst for his journey. Presumably, news of the surprising triumph of the freshly-freed slaves against the seasoned marauders spread throughout the region and Yitro discerned in that victory the hand of God.

Rabbi Elazar HaModai, in contrast, suggests that Yitro's arrival and visit is recorded out of order, for in fact he did not journey to meet the people at Sinai until **after** the giving of the Torah. Surely a minor desert skirmish with a trivial tribe of raiders was insufficient cause for Yitro to have undertaken such an arduous passage; it must have been tidings of much grander events that inspired him.

Rabbi Eliezer, perhaps taking his cue from the opening verse of the Parasha, understands that Yitro had received news of the most astonishing episode associated with the events of the Exodus: the crossing of the Sea of Reeds. When the text says that "Yitro . . . heard of all that God had done on behalf of Moshe and His people Israel, that God had taken Israel out of Egypt" it is for Rabbi Eliezer a reference to this most singular occurrence. According to his interpretation, Yitro's visit may have followed temporally on the heels of the contest against Amalek, but unlike Rabbi Yehoshua's view, it was not that battle that precipitated it.

Ibn Ezra's Explanation

A rather similar but expanded version of this disagreement is to be found at length in the classic commentaries of Rashi, Rabbi Avraham Ibn Ezra, and the Ramban. We will analyze the approach of the Ibn Ezra, who adopts the position of Rabbi Elazar HaModai. Ibn Ezra offers a number of converging lines of evidence for his view that indeed Yitro joined the people after the Revelation at Sinai had already taken place. In fact, Ibn Ezra argues, more than a year elapsed between the events of the Exodus recorded in the *Parashiyot* of Bo and BeShalach, and Yitro's appearance now. In the interim, the Torah had been given, the Tabernacle had been built, and the people were finally preparing to journey from Mount Sinai towards the Promised Land. Basing his interpretation on the subtle details recorded here, as well as in the *Parashiyot* of BeHa'alotcha and Devarim, Ibn Ezra assumes that the Torah occasionally records events in non-chronological order for the sake of overriding pedagogic purposes.

Thus, he argues, we find that Yitro offers a sacrifice to God in response to the news of the peoples' redemption (*Shemot* 18:12). This would imply that the Tabernacle with its sacrificial altar was already built, for prior to the giving of the Torah, we find no mention of another altar of sacrifice in regular use. Moreover, when Yitro questions the efficiency of Moshe's one-man judiciary, Moshe responds that he is busy from dawn until dusk because the people come to him for judgment: "When they have a disagreement, they come to me and I judge between them, and inform them of God's decrees and teachings" (18:16). What "decrees and teachings of God" could Moshe be conveying to the litigants if the Revelation had not yet taken place? Presumably, there was no significant corpus of civil law extant before the Torah was given to the people!

Most convincingly, when Moshe recalls in his twilight years the events of this time period, he appears to chronologically link Yitro's judicious advice with the journey from Mount Sinai towards the Promised Land:

> The Lord our God spoke to us at Chorev saying: "You have encamped at this mountain long enough. Now travel towards the land of . . . the Canaanite . . . and possess the land which God swore to your ancestors." At that time, I told you that I am not capable of bearing your burden alone. God has made you as numerous as the stars . . . select members of your tribes who are intelligent, wise and of renown, and I will appoint them over you . . . I appointed officers of thousands, hundreds, fifties and tens . . . and commanded them to judge justly . . . we journeyed from Chorev and traversed the great and awesome wilderness . . . until we came to Kadesh Barnea . . . (*Devarim* 1:6–21)

The appointment of these officers and judges which Moshe described as having occurred on the eve of their departure from Mount Sinai, is synonymous with the sage counsel of Yitro recorded in our Parasha: "Yitro said: 'Ascertain from among the people men of valor who are God-fearing, truthful and haters of bribery and appoint them over the people as officers of thousands, hundreds, fifties and tens. They will judge the people at all times . . .'" It therefore follows that Yitro must have arrived towards the very end of the peoples' sojourn at Sinai, long after they had received the Torah and soon after they had completed the building of the Mishkan.

Completing the puzzle, Ibn Ezra explains that the return of Yitro back to his home, which our Parasha records as the conclusion of the judicial reformation (*Shemot* 18:27), corresponds exactly with the narrative preserved in Sefer BeMidbar. There it states that on "the twentieth day of the second month in the second year of the Exodus, the cloud of glory lifted off of the Tabernacle, and the people began to journey from the wilderness of Sinai" (*BeMidbar* 10:11–12). And as the tribal units began to move forward towards the land after encamping at Sinai for almost a year, Moshe addressed "Chovav son of Reuel the Midianite, his father-in law, and said: 'We are going to the place which God said He would give to us. Accompany us and we shall be good to you, for God has spoken kindly concerning Israel.' He responded: 'I will not go, rather I shall return to my land and to my birthplace . . .'" (10:29–34). Thus, the Yitro who returned to his own land in our Parasha is the very same Chovav who decided to return home as the people left Mount Sinai and journeyed towards the land, because the two accounts are describing the exact same episode! While much of Ibn Ezra's evidence is not foolproof, his interpretation has the distinct advantage of being straightforward, elegant, and able to convincingly address all of the relevant contexts.

Yitro vs. Amalek; Yitro and Revelation

Having demonstrated that Yitro's visit in point of fact took place *after* the giving of the Torah, Ibn Ezra goes on to explain why the episode is recorded here out of chronological sequence:

> Since the text described earlier the dastardly act committed by Amalek, it notes in contrast the kindness of Yitro. Yitro had been gladdened by the news of God's redemption of the people, and he provides them with good and proper counsel regarding the establishment of a judicial system . . . just as we are enjoined to commemorate the cruelty of Amalek and to extirpate their memory, so must we not forget the kindness of Yitro and must preserve his descendents . . . (commentary to *Shemot* 18:1)

In other words, the justification for locating Yitro's visit at an earlier juncture in time than it actually occurred is didactic. It is to set up a glaring study in contrasts with the behavior of Amalek. In both cases, we have a non-Hebrew element responding to the news of Israel's miraculous delivery from slavery and bondage. Amalek counters the Exodus and the overt expression of divine providence that it represents by brutally attacking the Israelites. By rejecting the divine element in human history, Amalek scorns any higher moral law or spiritual dimension that it implies. If liberation from brutal slavery carries with it an obligation to acknowledge a God who will not brook oppression of body or dulling of soul, then let that exodus never occur!

Yitro, in contrast, also hearing news of Israel's salvation, is filled with joy. He resolves to join them and to link his destiny to theirs. He bears no animus towards their mission and in fact wishes to assist them in any way that he can. And his help is substantial, for he provides counsel that ultimately will set the foundation for righteousness and justice to prevail against oppression and violence. The judiciary that is established according to his recommendation is therefore the antithesis of the lawless "state of nature" – in which the powerful prevail and the weak are defeated – that is championed by Amalek.

There is, however, another implication to Ibn Ezra's comments. Recall that Yitro's visit is bracketed by *two* events: the battle against Amalek and the giving of the Decalogue. Ibn Ezra admirably explains the juxtaposition of Amalek with Yitro; at the same time, his exegesis should retain its cogency with respect to the linkage of Yitro with what follows it, namely the Revelation at Sinai. This is because if Yitro's visit is chronologically out of place at one end of the narrative, then it is also out of place at the other! What message is provided by the fact that Yitro's arrival is described not only in contrast to Amalek's villainy, but also as an introduction to the Revelation at Sinai?

Yitro is the first convert in Jewish history. The people had scarcely left Egypt when he traveled to meet them. Inspired by the Exodus, overawed by the expression of God's saving power, and genuinely appreciative of the profound goodness bestowed upon Israel, he embarks on an odyssey that will in the end take him away not only from Midian but from polytheism as well. In recognition of that profound shift, some traditions assert (and this is in consonance with Ibn Ezra's earlier comments) that Yitro's name is changed to "Chovav" or "Beloved" as reported in *BeMidbar* 10:29, for beloved is his character for resolving to join the people of Israel (see Ramban's commentary to *Shemot* 2:16). Thus, Yitro represents not the convert of convenience or of infatuation, but rather the wholly sincere individual who undertakes the awesome task of completely changing the direction of his life.

As the people stand at the foot of Mount Sinai and prepare to receive the Torah, they too will be asked to undergo a process not unlike that of conversion. In fact, Maimonides quotes a Talmudic tradition that the Revelation at Sinai provides the Halakhic paradigm for *all* future conversions:

> The people of Israel entered a covenant with God after three preparatory acts: circumcision, immersion, and sacrifice. Circumcision took place in Egypt prior to the consumption of the Paschal lamb, for [although it was a tradition from Avraham] the people had abrogated this practice over the course of time. Only the tribe of Levi had maintained the legacy of circumcision. Immersion took place in the wilderness as the people were encamped at Sinai, for the verse states: "Sanctify yourselves today and tomorrow and cleanse your clothing" (19:10). With respect to sacrifice, the verse says: "He sent forth the exalted lads of Israel and they offered sacrifice" (24:5) on behalf of all of the people. In similar fashion for all time, when a convert desires to enter the covenant, to find shelter under the wings of the divine presence, and to accept the yoke of the Torah, he requires circumcision, immersion and the bringing of a sacrifice. A woman requires only the latter two . . . nowadays, sacrifice is not offered but when the Temple is rebuilt, those sacrifices will be brought. (Laws of Forbidden Relations 13:1–5)

If indeed the receiving of the Torah at Sinai involved a process of conversion and demanded from the people not only the performance of ritual acts but also a paradigm shift in their outlook and worldview, then the most striking exemplar of one who met that challenge is none other than Yitro. A respected idolatrous priest among his own tribe, an important dignitary in his clan, Yitro leaves his esteemed past behind him and enters the wilderness in search of a more profound truth. His attachment to the God of Israel is not triggered by dreams of material gain, nor is it driven by a desire for honor, for he lacks neither in his native land. His odyssey is the earnest search of the restless soul who seeks communion with the creator and yearns for a relationship with the redeemer from servitude. Freely and of his own volition, Yitro embraces Israel and consigns his fate to their God.

Yitro's own acceptance of the Torah is thus purely motivated from the outset, as well as powerfully driven towards greater spiritual accomplishments. He therefore represents the sort of heartfelt commitment to Jewish faith and Jewish living that most of us fail to appreciate or to achieve! The Torah's narration of his story prior to the Revelation at Sinai, though he arrived after the event, thus serves as a forceful message to those of us born into the tradition who may take our covenantal status for granted. Meaningful acceptance and fulfillment of the *mitzvot*, as signified by the Revelation, must be transformative, for how can one remain static and unmoved when addressed by the "voice of the living God"? Yitro, the former priest and pagan, teaches us how to stand at Sinai suitably, how to receive the Torah authentically and how to live by its laws faithfully.

FOR FURTHER STUDY:

(1) See the Ramban's lengthy comments (*Shemot* 18:1) in which he follows his exegetical method of adopting a more conservative approach to chronology. For the Ramban, we are to assume that unless specifically and explicitly indicated otherwise, the events of the Torah are in chronological sequence. Therefore, Yitro arrives in the aftermath of the battle with Amalek and prior to the giving of the Torah at Sinai, according to the order that the events are recorded in the text. His attempts to address Ibn Ezra's evidence to the contrary are in this case less convincing.

Rashi adopts an intermediate view that breaks up Yitro's visit into two distinct components (18:1, 13). The first, in which he arrives with Tzipora and her children, is greeted by his illustrious son-in-law, and hears the full account of the Exodus, takes place *prior* to the Revelation as the order suggests. The second, however, in which he suggests an overhaul of the judicial system, occurs *after* the giving of the Torah. Rashi's approach, while solving some difficulties, introduces others.

MISHPATIM

An Eye for an Eye

Exodus 21:1-24:18

THE RAMBAN introduces his commentary to the Parasha of Mishpatim with the following synopsis:

> "And these are the laws which you shall place before them" (*Shemot* 21:1) – the divine intent was to present the people with these laws immediately after the Revelation at Sinai. Recall that the first of the Ten Utterances concerned recognition of God and the second prohibited idolatry. After that theophany had taken place, God reiterated these ideas: "You yourselves saw that I spoke to you from heaven" (20:19) parallels the first utterance of "I am the Lord." "You shall not fashion gods of silver or gold" (20:20) recalls the second utterance that prohibited idolatry. These laws about to now be presented continue the theme of "Thou shall not covet." For if a person is ignorant concerning the laws of the house, the field, or other forms of property, he might imagine to himself that they are his, and then covet them and seize them. Therefore, God commanded Moshe to place these laws before the people, so that they will behave with uprightness and not desire that which does not belong to them. Similarly in the Midrash Rabbah it is stated: "The entire Torah is predicated on justice, and therefore God presented these laws after the Revelation of the Ten Utterances." Thus, these laws that follow speak of the prohibition of idolatry, of the obligation to honor one's parents, and of the prohibition of murder and adultery, all of which are mentioned in the Ten Utterances.

Laws form the foundation of every functioning society. The rule of law ensures that individuals respect each other's person and property and behave responsibly when in a social context. When damage does occur, whether by premeditation, negligence or unforeseeable mishap, laws regulate restitution and impose punishment as appropriate. The Ten Utterances are universally regarded as fundamental principles and yet, the Ramban informs us, they are insufficient in and of themselves to create a moral and law-abiding society. "Thou shall not covet" is an upright and virtuous injunction, a majestic vision expressed with a remarkable economy of words, but in the absence of practical and detailed guidelines that spell out its parameters, it remains an exalted slogan with little hope of realization. Bearing this in mind, the Torah now presents the law code of Parashat Mishpatim, a comprehensive series of statutes that forms the natural continuation to the Ten Utterances presented in Parashat Yitro.

Civil Law and Ritual Obedience

Considering the Ten Utterances or the Parasha of Mishpatim, we at once notice a feature common to both that is striking as well as unique. Civil laws on the one hand, and ritual laws or exhortations to religious excellence on the other, are presented not as disparate and discrete disciplines but as organically related parts of a complete system. Thus, in the case of the Ten Utterances, laws of idolatry or Shabbat observance are juxtaposed with laws of murder or theft. In the much lengthier Parasha of Mishpatim, laws of slavery, torts or loans are presented in proximity to laws of forbidden foods, sacrifices, or holidays. This type of commingling is unparalleled in any other code of law that has come down to us from antiquity. All of the ancient near eastern compilations of law, for example, treat civil law and ritual law as two completely distinct frameworks that are invariably recorded as independent literary works.

The implication of this fact is staggering, for it suggests that the ultimate motive for the observance of rational and reasonable civil laws is exactly synonymous with the driving force that enjoins observance of the ritual and religious injunctions: the authority of a transcendent God. There is therefore no intrinsic difference between both realms, for they are complementary halves of a complete whole. The modern attempt to bifurcate social law from ritual, to swear allegiance to an enlightened "Prophetic Judaism" while denigrating or downgrading "archaic" ritual observance, is thus founded upon a selective reading of the sources.

We tend to accept civil law as more valuable and meaningful because it makes sense. Ritual, on the other hand, often defies easy and straightforward rational enquiry and is therefore discarded with greater ease. The structure of our Parasha, however, demonstrates that the authority of both is predicated upon the very same premise. The religious core values that motivate sincere ritual observance also are the soul of an impassioned crusade for social justice. Conversely, if social laws are meaningful only because their value is rational and obvious and not because they are the commands of an absolute deity, then such laws can never be the vehicles for the spiritual transformation of the human being. Put differently, the same Hebrew prophets who were filled with burning indignation for the plight of the widow, the orphan and the stranger, also inveighed against idolatry and the desecration of the Shabbat (see, for example, *Yeshayahu* 58:1–14). The ideal student of the Torah is therefore meticulous concerning the relationship with other people and their property, as well as being scrupulous with respect to the ritual laws.

Let us keep this critical binary relationship between civil law and ritual observance in mind as we examine one of the most misunderstood and maligned laws of this Parasha. A literal and superficial reading of its contents has served as a pretext to accuse the Torah of primitive vengefulness, and the God of the Hebrews of vindictiveness. The matter is presented in a section that relates the case of an injury inflicted upon an innocent bystander to a violent dispute:

> If two men strive together, and strike a pregnant woman who consequently miscarries, but no other tragedy ensues, then they shall be fined according to the claim filed by the husband in court. But if her tragic death follows, then you shall give a soul for a soul. An eye for an eye, a tooth for a tooth, a hand for a hand and a foot for a foot. A burn for a burn, a wound for a wound, and a bruise for a bruise. (*Shemot* 21:22–25)

This passage presents many difficulties of exegesis, but the most glaring one concerns the apparent legal sanction if not outright support for the so-called "*lex talionis*" or law of retaliation. Taken literally, the verses seem to indicate that if one inflicts an injury upon another, the Torah mandates that a similar injury be inflicted upon the perpetrator. This form of "justice" rightfully strikes us as barbaric and primitive, an appeal to the baser passions of the victim and society, rather than an attempt to inculcate a higher degree of civilized behavior.

The Traditional Reading – an Argument from Reason

It is essential to bear in mind that the unanimous consensus of the early Rabbinic sources such as the Mishna, Midrashei Halakha, and the Talmud, as well as that of the later commentaries, is that the passage in question is not to be understood literally. There is not a single source or opinion to be found in the vast corpus of traditional Jewish writings, early or late, Halakhic or homiletic, that argues seriously for a literal application of the principle. For the sake of brevity, we shall quote the words of Rabbi Avraham Ibn Ezra, but much of his evidence is in fact based upon earlier sources. In general, it may be said that the rejection of a literal interpretation is predicated upon rational and ethical considerations, but can also be convincingly supported by recourse to textual analysis and the investigation of parallel sources.

Ibn Ezra writes:

> "An eye for an eye" – Rabbi Sa'adiah explained that we cannot take this verse literally, for if a man struck the eye of his fellow and caused, let us say, a loss of vision equal to 30%, how would it be possible to inflict precisely the same injury on the perpetrator, with neither excess nor deficiency? The wound and the bruise present an even more difficult situation, for if the initial injury was sustained close to a vital organ, perhaps the retaliatory strike will result in the death of the perpetrator . . . and what of the blind man who harms the vision of his fellow? How shall retaliation be done to him? Reason cannot tolerate a literal interpretation of this verse! (expanded commentary to *Shemot* 21:24)

Here, Ibn Ezra maintains that logic argues against a literal understanding because it is not possible to apply the principle of retaliation with precision. This point is particularly cogent if we bear in mind that the underlying justification for retaliation in kind is the concept of *equivalence*. In other words, if the victim of an attack sustained an injury, it is only right that the aggressor should suffer the same injury. This represents a decidedly rough but particularly satisfying form of frontier justice in which the assailant gets his just desserts. But, says Ibn Ezra, the very desire to impose equality contests the literal interpretation, for the exact same injury cannot, in all probability, be inflicted upon the perpetrator.

The troublesome phrase in question is "then you shall give a soul for a soul. An eye for an eye . . ." In the original Hebrew, this is: "ונתת נפש תחת נפש. עין תחת עין . . ." What is the meaning of תחת? Often, this word carries a spatial connotation and means "under," but here and in many other contexts it implies "in place of." Thus, we are told that after the *Akeda*, Avraham offered a ram תחת his son Yitzchak (*Breisheet* 22:13) which is to say "in place of"; Ya'acov rebuked his wife Rachel by exclaiming "am I then תחת God who has withheld offspring from you?" (30:2). But rendering the phrase more colloquially as "a soul in place of a soul, and an eye in place of an eye" does not appear to obviate the difficulty.

An investigation of the parallel passage in Sefer VaYikra in Parashat Emor, however, begins to shed light on the textual aspect of the issue:

> A man who strikes and kills his fellow shall surely be put to death. One who strikes and kills an animal shall make payment (ישלמנה), a soul for a soul. A man who inflicts a disfigurement on his fellow, as he did so shall it be done to him. A break for a break, an eye for an eye, a tooth for a tooth, as a man inflicts a disfigurement on his fellow so shall it be given upon him. One who strikes and kills an animal shall pay for it and one who strikes and kills a man shall die . . ." (*VaYikra* 24:17–23)

The verses here emphatically contrast the case of killing a man with the case of killing an animal. For the former, capital punishment is enjoined, while for the latter, payment can be made. In language which echoes that of our Parasha, the Torah again appears to mandate retaliation for the bodily injury of another person. We are once more left to ponder the significance of "an eye for an eye, and a tooth for a tooth." This time, however, the text of the Torah *interprets itself*: "One who strikes and kills an animal shall make payment, a soul for a soul." The indication clearly is that one who kills his fellow's animal must pay for it and make restitution, for the verb ישלמנה comes from the root שלמ meaning "complete" or "whole." This is clearly a reference to the restitution or payment that can replace the loss and thereby restore the victim to a complete state. Yet the Torah unambiguously describes this arrangement as "a soul for a soul"! The implication is clear: the means of compensating the injured party for loss of his killed animal is not by killing the animal of the aggressor, but rather by necessitating that aggressor to make payment in kind.

At first glance, adopting such a reading also with respect to the injury of another human being appears to be contraindicated by the expression that follows the above verse: "A man who inflicts a disfigurement on his fellow, as he did (כאשר עשה) so shall it be done to him (כן יעשה לו)." There is, however, evidence from another biblical source that the turn of phrase is idiomatic rather than literal. In Sefer Shoftim, we are told that after the Philistines had burned his Timnite wife and father-in-law, Shimshon struck back and killed many of them. The tribesmen of Yehuda among whom he subsequently sought refuge were reluctant to shelter him, for they feared the inevitable retaliation of the ruling Philistines. "You are fully aware that the Philistines rule over us," they exclaimed to him, "what have you done to us?" Shimshon responded: "As they have done to me (כאשר עשו לי), so have I done to them (כן עשיתי להם)!" (*Shoftim* 15:11). Now surely, Shimshon did not mean to imply that he had inflicted the very same bodily injuries on the Philistines as they had done to him, for while they had burned his wife and father-in-law his response had been warfare. Rather, what he meant to say was that he had "repaid" them in kind for their act of cruelty by besting them in battle. Shimshon's use of the same idiom utilized in Parashat Emor to describe his response to the Philistine aggression demonstrates that it need not imply exact, equivalent reciprocity of injury. It therefore follows that the expression ". . . so shall it be done to him" employed in the passage from Parashat Emor can also be taken to mean "repayment or compensation" and not "equivalent retaliatory injury."

Reconciling the Literal Reading with the Traditional Interpretation

We are now able to provide a plausible exegesis for this difficult expression. The Torah could very well be interpreted to mean that when a person strikes and injures the eye or tooth of his fellow, the appropriate and just judicial response is the imposition of a monetary forfeiture on the aggressor in accordance with the value of the injured organ or limb. This, as we have seen, is the position that is maintained by the traditional post-biblical sources. Ibn Ezra, though, cognizant of the fact that a more literal reading of the text was not impossible, refused to rely exclusively on the rational and textual arguments. In the end he concludes:

> The general operative principle is that we are not able to offer a complete explanation for the commandments of the Torah without recourse to the oral tradition transmitted by our Sages. Just as we received the written Torah from our ancestors, so have we received the oral tradition, and both are equally authoritative.

Thus, although a literal reading of "an eye for an eye" may not be absolutely refutable on rational or textual grounds, it is ultimately negated by the existence of an authentic oral tradition to the contrary. We are thus left in the somewhat uncomfortable position of possessing a text which seems to indicate one thing – retaliation, and a tradition that insists on another – monetary compensation. Or, to phrase the conundrum differently, if the Torah really meant to teach us monetary compensation, then why did the biblical text employ an expression which could easily be misconstrued to mean bodily retaliation? Here, the Ibn Ezra provides an answer that captures the essence of the Torah's more profound message, although his characteristically concise and cryptic words require further elaboration:

> The expression "an eye for an eye" means that it would be *fitting* for the aggressor to forfeit his own eye, if he refuses to provide a ransom in the form of monetary compensation.

What might be the meaning of his words? Sometimes we fall into the trap of believing that money can solve all of life's ills. If an object breaks, money can replace it. If a body ails, money can heal it. If a soul languishes, money can comfort it. Human productivity is measured by economic output, human creativity by potential market value, human success by monetary worth. These deep-seated but skewed values are not an invention of the modern age but have been part of the social landscape since the concept of capital first seized hold of the human psyche. The danger that such attitudes engender is that they often lead to the commercialization of the human being, and his transformation from a divinely fashioned and unique personality into a mass-produced and standard good or service.

To express the problem in the terms of Parashat Mishpatim, we may mistakenly come to believe that when an injury is inflicted upon another person's property or body, money can heal the wound, assuage the pain, erase the anguish, and completely compensate for the damage. The adoption of such an attitude would indeed lead us to read "an eye for an eye" as implying exclusively monetary compensation and nothing else. Now it may indeed be the case that financial restitution is to be preferred to retaliation, and that surely needs no rational explanation. At the same time, however, the Torah wants to indicate to us that while monetary compensation is perhaps the best solution, it too is far from ideal. In the end, no replacement can ever be made for the injury inflicted, particularly if the loss of a limb or an organ is involved.

Thus, while the explanation provided by the oral tradition makes it clear that payment for bodily damages may absolve one of culpability in the realm of the secular and the social, the written Torah insists on couching the concept of monetary compensation in terms of "an eye for an eye." This striking phrase is meant to indicate that in the much more exalted dimension of the ethical and the authentic, money means nothing. Insofar as the real nature of the injury is concerned, the perpetrator must feel for the injured party *as if* he had to forfeit his own eye, *as if* financial restitution was only an imperfect and incomplete form of ransom for the crime, *as if no amount of money could ever replace that which was taken away*, for that is indeed the case. Ibn Ezra's reading that pays homage to the tradition while refusing to sacrifice the text alerts us to a more noble vision of compensation, in which the perpetrator extends not only financial restitution to the injured party but his heartfelt feelings of identification as well.

FOR FURTHER STUDY:

(1) See the Ibn Ezra's introduction to the Torah ("הדרך השנית") where he develops at length the concept of the necessity of relying upon an oral tradition to explicate the written text of the Torah. Something as fundamental as the astronomical and mathematical principles that govern the Hebrew calendar are not spelled out in the written Torah in any way that makes a practical formulation possible. How then are the people of Israel to regulate their national life and to observe the holidays enjoined by scriptural law? This example, and many others like it, indicates for the Ibn Ezra that the existence of an authentic and accurate oral tradition is not only an article of faith, but a *rational imperative* as well.

(2) See also Maimonides in his introduction to the Mishna, where he indicates that there has never been a divergent tradition that has read "an eye for an eye" literally. This makes the traditional oral interpretation as unassailable as the "use of the *etrog* on the festival of Succot, for since the days of Yehoshua bin Nun until now, we have not seen a single Jewish community interpret 'the fruit of a beautiful tree' (*Va Yikra* 23:40) as indicating any other species!"

TERUMA

The Missing Golden Altar

Exodus 25:1-27:19

> God spoke to Moshe saying: "Speak to the people of Israel and let them collect a contribution for Me, from every person whose heart moves him you shall accept a contribution. This is the contribution that you shall take: gold, silver and bronze; sky blue, purple, crimson, linen and goatskins; hides of rams dyed red, seal hides and acacia wood; oil for the lights, spices for the anointing oil and for the incense of spices; onyx stones and precious stones to set into the ephod and the breastplate. They shall fashion for Me a holy sanctuary, and I shall dwell among them. You shall fashion the Mishkan and its vessels just as I show you . . ." (*Shemot* 25:1–9)

THUS BEGINS the account of the wilderness Tabernacle, a lengthy and detailed narrative that takes up the remainder of Sefer Shemot. The short paragraph above that catalogues the required contributions provides us with an excellent summary of the elements involved: precious metals and woods for the vessels and building walls, valuable dyes and textiles for its tent-like covers as well as for the priestly garments, precious stones for the special vestments of the High Priest, and specially formulated oils and spices for anointing and kindling. The materials for the project are to be collected from the people of Israel as free-will offerings, emphasizing the fact that for service of God to be meaningful it must be both autonomous as well as sincere.

The Organizing Principle and a Glaring Omission

Our Parasha goes on to describe the Mishkan's most important vessels: the ark of the testimony, the table of the show bread, and the menorah. Attention is then turned to the curtains and boards of the building, as well as to the separations within that space, before interest is again focused on another vessel: the bronze altar. The account of our Parasha then concludes with a discussion of the courtyard enclosure. Structurally, the ordering principle that guides the textual organization of the various sections is the concept of *hierarchy*. The most important vessels are stated first, followed by a discussion of their enclosure: the ark is to be placed within the Holy of Holies, a sacred space that is separated from the rest of the building by a dividing curtain. The table and menorah are located within the building proper, but beyond the dividing curtain and in the area known as the Holy. The bronze altar, in contrast, is located outside of the building in the outer courtyard, an exterior enclosure that is again demarcated by curtains.

The ordering of the sections described above is utterly reasonable, except for one striking lacuna: the golden altar. This vessel forms an important part of the daily ritual, for an offering of pure spices is presented upon it morning and evening. Spatially, it too is located within the area of the Holy space, and centered between the table to the north and the menorah to the south. The opening passage of our Parasha quoted above alludes to it, for the "incense of spices" is the special preparation that is burned upon the golden altar. But curiously, these lengthy Mishkan narratives that so painstakingly describe the vessels, building elements and priestly garments in a most sensible and organized fashion, fail to explicitly mention the golden altar until the very *end* of the matter. It is only after spelling out the dedication ceremony to be celebrated at the completion of the edifice, as described at the conclusion of Parashat Tetzave, that the golden altar is formally introduced for the first time:

> You shall fashion an altar for the offering of incense, and you shall make it out of acacia wood. It shall be one cubit in length and one in width, perfectly square, and two in height, and shall have horns upon it. You shall gild it with pure gold, its top and its sides around, as well as its horns, and you shall fashion for it an ornamental crown around its top . . . You shall place it before the dividing curtain that is before the ark of the testimony, before the ark cover that is upon the testimony, the place where I shall meet with you. Aharon shall offer spiced incense upon it early in the morning, when he prepares the lights of the menorah he shall offer it. When Aharon kindles the lights at evening he shall offer incense again, it is perpetual incense to be offered before God for all generations . . . (30:1–10)

Comparisons and Contrasts

The textual formula that the Torah employs to describe the golden altar mirrors that of the ark, table and menorah. It consists of an imperative statement ("You shall fashion an altar for the offering of incense ...") that describes materials ("acacia wood"), dimensions ("one cubit in length . . ."), gilding ("you shall gild it with pure gold"), ornament ("you shall fashion for it an ornamental crown . . ."), and purpose ("Aharon shall offer spiced incense upon it early in the morning . . ."). For comparison, the passage concerning the table also begins with an imperative ("You shall fashion a table . . ."), and goes on to delineate materials ("acacia wood"), dimensions ("two cubits in length and one in width, and one and a half in height"), gilding ("you shall gild it with pure gold"), ornament ("you shall make for it a frame of one handbreadth height all around . . ."), and purpose ("you shall place upon the table bread for display before Me always") (25:23–30).

There are, however, two important differences. First of all, the detailed instructions of our Parasha do *not* indicate the exact spatial location of either the table or the menorah, as they do later for the golden altar. These pertinent facts are first mentioned in the discussion of the dividing curtain that follows the description of the curtains and boards:

> You shall place the dividing curtain below the hooks and within you shall place the ark of the testimony . . . You shall place the table outside of the dividing curtain, and the menorah opposite the table on the southern side of the Mishkan, while the table you shall place on the northern side. (26:33–37)

In contrast, the position of the golden altar is mentioned in the context of its construction as outlined above: "You shall place it before the dividing curtain that is before the ark of the testimony, before the ark cover that is upon the testimony, the place where I shall meet with you" (30:6).

Secondly, while the Torah describes the ritual functions of the table and the menorah, that they are for the display loaves and for kindling the lights respectively, it does not indicate any other specialized ceremonies associated with them. But the golden altar has an extraordinary function that is in addition to the diurnal ritual of incense offered morning and evening without fail:

> Aharon shall make atonement [by placing the blood] upon its horns once a year, from the sin-offering of the Day of Atonement. Once a year he shall atone for it forever, it is Holy of Holies to God.

The Commentary of the Seforno

In order to address these anomalies, we must first formulate a general theory of the Mishkan and it vessels. The Seforno relates:

> After mention of the ark, which is fashioned after the manner of a throne for God's presence (as 25:22 states: "I shall meet with you there . . ."), God commanded concerning the table and the menorah. Such is the custom to have these vessels before nobility, just as the Shunamite woman said that "we shall place for him there a bed, a table, a chair and a lamp" (*Melachim* 2:4:10). The crown around the top of the table relates to monarchy . . . for this vessel symbolizes the livelihood of the state . . . as well as its defense . . . The menorah is of a single piece, its lights unified . . . for both conceptual as well as practical knowledge must face the transcendent light and serve Him as one, for then all of them shall be enlightened . . . (commentary to *Shemot* 25:23–25, 31)

The Seforno concisely explains that the ark of the covenant, while functionally a receptacle for the two tablets of the Decalogue, was symbolically a representation of God's throne. The experience of God's presence in the world was associated with this vessel, a gilded box surmounted by two winged, angelic figures, and so it was placed in the most sanctified recess of the Mishkan. The table and the menorah corresponded to their mundane counterparts that could be found in the houses of the patricians and the people of rank. The Seforno brings support for his thesis from the story of the itinerant and miracle-working prophet Elisha. When he would traverse the northern region of Shunem, he would visit with an aristocratic woman and her husband. They would prevail upon him to stay with them, and they furnished a private room just for that purpose:

> It so happened on that day that Elisha passed through Shunem. There was to be found a powerful woman who would prevail upon him to break bread, and so when he would pass through the region he would turn aside there to break bread. She said to her husband: "I know that this man of God is holy, and he passes near us all the time. Let us make him a small upper chamber and we shall place for him there *a bed, a table, a chair and a lamp*, so that when he passes by us he can stay there . . ." (*Melachim* 2:4:8–11)

Seforno's association with the account of Elisha is most astonishing. He has the audacity to suggest that the table and the menorah are furnishings associated with living in a home, because the Mishkan is *God's abode*. Just as a noble has a table and lamp stand in his house, so too God has these appurtenances in His dwelling. The Mishkan is His house, its vessels are His furnishings, and when we enter its sacred precincts we are symbolically entering His domain. But God, of course, has no use for furniture! The coarse and concrete pagan deities physically dwelt in their temples in the form of idols. In their adherents' imaginations they actually consumed and were sustained by the food offerings placed before them. Not so the incorporeal and absolute God of Israel.

Therefore, Seforno explains, the table and menorah must also possess symbolic value, as already formulated by the Talmud in TB *Bava Batra* 25b: the golden table of the Tabernacle, laden with its showbread, was an expression of physical sustenance and of material success. Its twelve loaves (see *VaYikra* 24:5–9) indicated God's constant provision of nourishment to the people of Israel – the "Twelve Tribes" – much as an earthly monarch attends to the welfare of his people and defends their interests from harm. The menorah was a potent symbol of intellectual illumination, as if the ethereal fire perpetually set upon its golden boughs was about the diverse branches of human knowledge that all derived from the absolute source of all wisdom.

The table and the menorah framed the ark of the testimony that occupied the Holy of Holies just beyond the dividing curtain. As Seforno explained, the ark was the expression of God's throne, its cherubic figures hovering protectively over the precious contents: two tablets of the Decalogue that spelled out in remarkable economy the terms and conditions of the God-man relationship. In other words, God's presence among the people of Israel was predicated upon their fidelity to the Torah, their willingness and desire to actively seek Him out. Taken together, these three precious objects provided a concise and concrete summary of God's special bond with the people of Israel: His Torah guided them, His providence sustained them and His wisdom and spirit enlightened them.

Although the Seforno did not explicitly draw a link between the other furnishings of Elisha's chamber and the vessels of the Mishkan, such is the implication. Perhaps we go too far in associating the ark with the "bed" of Elisha's chamber, but the traditional sources do in fact draw just such a connection. The ark occupied the most private space of all, the Holy of Holies. Placed upon its lid were two golden figures called the *Keruvim*, which hovered protectively above it. In a most provocative statement, some of the Talmudic rabbis claimed that these *Keruvim*, described in our text as "facing each other" (25:20), but elsewhere as "facing the house" (*Divrei HaYamim* 2:3:13), would actually adjust their gaze in accordance with the state of the God-Israel relationship. When Israel fulfilled the will of God, the *Keruvim* would face each other, but when they strayed, the *Keruvim* would turn away (TB *Bava Batra* 99a). Rashi, in his commentary to the passage, boldly completes the metaphor:

> When Israel did the will of God, the *Keruvim* would turn their faces towards each other after the manner of *a man and a woman who were in love*, symbolic of the love that God had for the people of Israel. Thus were the *Keruvim* initially fashioned, face to face, in order that God's presence should manifest itself among the people of Israel and in order that they should fulfill His will. And when they did not fulfill His will, then the *Keruvim* would miraculously avert their gaze and face the wall.

There are inherent limitations to anthropomorphic readings, but we may yet profit from considering Rashi's startling remarks. The ark is symbolic not only of God's throne and sovereign presence in the material world, but of His desire to bestow His goodness, His Torah, on the people of Israel. When Israel "fulfills His will" and keeps His commands, then intense communion with God, a relationship of intimates and a genuine love are possible. When they stray from Him, then they experience the pain of separation and the travail of distance. God "turns away" in reaction to their infidelity. Connecting the strands, Seforno must therefore be intimating that the analog to the couch or bed of the noble's private chamber is the ark of the testimony in the Mishkan, for both objects bespeak the potential for consummating the most privileged, private and heartfelt of human longings. In this most intrepid of allegories, the intense love for another serves as the truest paradigm for the burning love of God.

The Analog to the Golden Altar

But what of the golden altar that is inexplicably absent from the account of the most precious vessels? Is it also parallel to an object in the chamber of Elisha, a correspondence that Seforno similarly left unstated? Let us begin by analyzing the significance of this altar in the daily Temple ritual. In contrast to the large altar of bronze located in the outer courtyard upon which the animal and bird sacrifices were burnt, the small and precious golden altar only received the incense. This consisted of a fragrant combination of spices (described at the beginning of Parashat Tetzave) that was twice daily offered upon burning hot coals that had been specially prepared for the purpose. The holy precinct would then fill with the ascending smoke, and the supplicant priest would bow and exit.

Although the Torah itself makes no attempt to explain the significance of the ritual, an early source already provides an interpretation. In a fleeting reference from the book of Psalms, David poetically exclaims:

> God, I call out to you, hurry to save me! Listen to my voice when I cry out to You! *May my prayer find favor before You as incense*, the lifting up of my hands as the evening offering . . . (*Tehillim* 141:1–2).

The service of the incense was therefore meant to represent Israel's offering of prayers to God. Unlike the tactile service of the animal sacrifice that had at its core the idea of substitution and submission, the incense offering consisted solely of fragrant smoke that ascended from the fire, ephemeral and elusive. What more fitting symbolism could there be for the poignant prayer of the human heart, uttered silently but sincerely, daily borne aloft to God on Israel's measured breaths, as delicate as a rising wisp of smoke?

The centrality of the golden altar in the ritual of atonement that pivots around a special incense offering, as spelled out in *VaYikra* 16:12–13, is now clear. The true repentance associated with Yom Kippur, the transforming *teshuva* that alone restores us to God's presence, is fundamentally a service of the heart. If we remain insensitive to God then the rituals of the day are of little worth. But if our *teshuva* is genuine, if our private prayers are real, then God is attentive to our cries and close to our broken hearts. The incense, the ascending fragrant smoke of Yom Kippur, is therefore symbolic not only of God's inscrutability – the impenetrable cloud that obscures His essence – but of our own intense desire to reach Him through prayer.

The Location of the Golden Altar

The important position assigned to the golden altar within the space of the Holy now makes sense. As the symbol of prayer ascending, it is placed exactly opposite the ark of the testimony and only separated from it by the thin partition of the dividing curtain. On either side, the table and the menorah guard the golden altar, for though these two objects speak worlds about God's involvement in our lives, it is the golden altar that speaks for **us**. We stand before God and pour out our prayers before Him, cognizant of His providence and enlightenment while transfixed by the awesome experience of His presence – the throne or couch that suggestively beckons beyond the curtain, an invitation to the spiritual intimacy for which we long.

But why then is the golden altar omitted from the account of the Mishkan, appended to its conclusion like some sort of afterthought? In fact, the lacuna is deliberate, a direct function of the golden altar's most unique status. The other vessels in the Holy space – the table and the menorah – describe God's ongoing intervention in our lives. He provides for our daily needs and defends us from physical harm, He inspires us with wisdom and ignites the flame of spirituality that gives meaning to our lives, and He of course guides us with His commands. The Mishkan is His house because its various vessels and their associated ceremonies highlight His eternal presence in Israel.

But the engine that drives the hallowed space and charges the Mishkan with meaning is the ritual that is performed by the sincere supplicant. If we cannot cry out to God, then no ceremony, no matter how august and noble, can save us from despair and oblivion. The golden altar – the service of the incense that embodies our most profound unutterable words – is therefore left until the very end, to emphasize in a most extraordinary way that the Mishkan remains painfully unfinished until its solemn space is animated by the *human prayer* that truly constitutes its intended purpose.

As for Elisha's seat (and here we can but speculate), might it be the analog to the golden altar? The ark is associated with the bed or couch, the table and menorah with their respective furnishings, leaving only the chair of the noble's chamber unaccounted for. But if our analysis is correct, that the golden altar is less about God's involvement and more about our own initiative, then perhaps the chair analogy is not absurd. Imagine, for a moment, Elisha in his chamber as he graciously receives the Shunamite woman and her husband in audience. Would the prophet himself not be seated upon his couch while they alight upon the chair, to pour out their hearts before him and to seek his inspired guidance? Could the chair, then, serve not only the noble himself but also those that appear before him asking his advice? Might the bed and the chair, placed exactly opposite each other to facilitate dialogue, perhaps be parallel to the ark and golden altar of the Mishkan?

The Priestly Blessing

Having established the respective purposes of the most important of the Tabernacle vessels, let us consider for a moment the dedication ceremony of the Mishkan described in Parashat Shemini (*VaYikra* 9). The Torah states that having concluded the requisite sacrifices without mishap:

> Aharon lifted up his hands to the people and blessed them. He then descended from having offered the sin-offering, the burnt-offering and the peace-offering. Moshe

> and Aharon came to the Tent of Meeting, they emerged and blessed the people, and God's glory appeared to the entire people . . . (*Va Yikra* 9:22–23)

According to an early tradition (Sifra, Miluim Shemini 30), the blessing that Aharon pronounced upon the people at that most auspicious event was the Priestly Blessing, spelled out later in the book of BeMidbar 6:22–27. Henceforth this special benediction was incorporated into the daily service of the Temple and is still recited in the synagogue to this day. By considering its formula we can ascertain why the Priestly Blessing is first introduced in connection with the dedication of the Mishkan:

> God spoke to Moshe saying: speak to Aharon and to his sons and tell them "thus shall you bless the people of Israel, say to them: may God bless you and protect you; may He cause His face to shine upon you and give you grace; may He lift up His face towards you and grant you peace." Let them pronounce My name upon the people of Israel and I will bless them . . . (*BeMidbar* 6:22–27)

These blessings, generous and comprehensive, address the basic elements of human existence and invoke God's beneficence upon them. But they are hardly generic. A careful reading of these verses reveals a most striking connection with our Parasha. "May God *bless* you and *protect* you" clearly addresses the *physical sustenance* and protection that Seforno related to the table. "May He cause His face to *shine* upon you and give you grace" is an unmistakable reference to God's central role in providing us with spiritual *enlightenment*, as embodied by the menorah. The third, most comprehensive and decisive blessing, "may He *lift up* His face towards you and grant you peace," cannot but refer to the golden altar, for from upon its polished crest the fragrant smoke of the incense *ascends* with our prayers.

Undoubtedly, the three vessels of the Holy space, though separated in the account of their construction in Parashat Teruma, are here brought together in precisely the correct progression. The priestly benediction can now be understood as the verbalization of their true meaning and the articulation of their purpose. The prayer that ascends heavenwards with the daily offering of incense fastens together earth and heaven, God and Israel, in perfect communion, fostering the peace and completeness for which we strive. No wonder that the Midrash Sifra quoted above, when citing the concluding verse of the dedication ceremony, confidently asserts in the absence of any textual proof that:

> Why did Moshe and Aharon enter the Mishkan together at that time? So that Moshe could instruct Aharon in the *service of the incense*!

FOR FURTHER STUDY:

(1) In Parashat Korach, a rebellion breaks out against the leadership of Moshe and Aharon, led by Moshe's charismatic cousin and hundreds of his supporters. Korach proclaims a democratic platform that is against despotism, nepotism and cronyism: "All of the congregation is holy and God is among them," he thunders, "so why do you lord it over the congregation of God?!" (*BeMidbar* 16:3). Gentle Moshe, taken aback by the unfair charges, invites the malcontents to a contest: "Let each one take his firepan, place fire upon it and offer incense to God tomorrow. The man whom God will choose is the holy one . . ." (*BeMidbar* 16:7).

Rashi wonders why Moshe chooses the incense offering as the test of choice. The answer may be a function of our analysis. The burning question concerning Korach relates to his authenticity: Are his motives pure? Does he truly have the interests of the people in mind? Are his accusations against Moshe and Aharon really about the welfare of Israel or more about his own aspirations? Moshe selects the incense because it represents sincerity of heart – it is the pure prayer of the supplicant reaching heavenwards to God! Therefore, let Korach and his cohorts offer the incense in order to ascertain whether or not their public platform matches their private intentions.

TETZAVE

The Robe of the High Priest

Exodus 27:20-30:10

PARASHAT TETZAVE is the natural continuation of Parashat Teruma. In Parashat Teruma, the Torah spelled out in exhaustive detail both the precious vessels of the Mishkan as well as the building elements – boards and curtains, covers and courtyard – that together constitute the housing for those precious vessels. Parashat Tetzave takes us from a description of the building and its vessels to a description of the garments worn by the officiating priests who were designated to perform the service:

> As for you, draw near your brother Aharon and his sons with him from the midst of the people of Israel so that he might serve Me – Aharon, Nadav and Avihu, Elazar and Itamar the sons of Aharon. Make holy garments for Aharon your brother, for honor and for glory. As for you, speak to all of the wise of heart that I have filled with a spirit of wisdom so that they will fashion the vestments of Aharon to sanctify him so that he may serve Me . . . (*Shemot* 28:1–3)

In great detail, the Torah now spells out these precious garments, clearly distinguishing between the attire of the regular Kohen and the more elaborate vestments donned by the Kohen Gadol or High Priest. The typical priest is to wear four garments during the course of performing his service: breeches, a tunic, a belt and a turban or miter. The Kohen Gadol, wears these four basic garments (with some variation in form) as well as four others layered upon them: a robe, an *ephod* or apron, a breastplate, and a headband. Concerning "the honor and the glory" of these priestly vestments, the Ramban says the following:

> Aharon ought to be honored and glorified by wearing garments of honor and glory . . . for these garments resemble garments of royalty in form. At the time of the Torah, the monarchy would have worn such clothing. The tunic signifies leadership just as Yosef was presented by his father with a "tunic of many stripes" (*Breisheet* 37:3) . . . Thus, Aharon was to be clothed as a king of ancient times . . . the miter is still worn by royalty and nobility to this day . . . the breastplate and *ephod* are regal attire . . . and the headband is a type of crown. The materials used to make these garments, namely gold, sky-blue, purple and crimson, are precious and rare . . .

For the Ramban, the Kohen Gadol represents a kind of sovereign, for his garments of office are fashioned out of unique and expensive materials and resemble the ornamented vestments of a king. But while outwardly the Kohen Gadol may resemble a regal figure bejeweled with the trappings of majesty, his true might is neither temporal nor political. Rather, he is a human being that ministers to God, living his life in His constant presence. For the Kohen Gadol, every moment is experienced in encounter with the divine.

With this in mind, let us consider one of the garments in particular, namely the robe or "מעיל." This outer garment was worn by the High Priest as the basic covering of the torso and legs, for it extended from the neck almost down to the feet. In form, it resembled a full-length robe or mantle, donned high about the neck and shoulders like a protective coat of armor (*Shemot* 28:32), while in color, it was as blue as a clear and cloudless sky (28:31). Attached to its hem were woven ornaments shaped like pomegranates that alternated with tiny golden bells. According to another view, these golden bells were housed within the woven pomegranates (28:33–34). When the Kohen Gadol walked in the Holy precincts and ministered before God, the bells would sound a melodious chime so that his movements "could be heard . . . so that he not die" (28:35).

What was the significance of the robe's entirely blue color, obtained from the precious marine dye known as "תכלת"? What might be the reason for the bells on the garment's hem and why the necessity for every stride of the Kohen Gadol to be announced by an audible signal? Most disconcertingly, what are we to make of the threat of death that awaits the High Priest for failing to make his steps heard? Before we can consider these specific questions, an analysis of the larger context is in order.

Considering the Broader Context: Before the Robe and After It

The descriptions of the *ephod* and the breastplate are introduced in the Torah before the robe. The *ephod* was an apron-like garment woven of precious fibers, secured by two shoulder straps set with onyx stones. Upon these stones were engraved the names of the twelve tribes, so that "Aharon might bear their names before God upon his two shoulders as a remembrance" (28:12). The breastplate was a small square ornament containing twelve different precious stones, each one of which was engraved with the name of one of the tribes of Israel. The breastplate was secured to the *ephod* top and bottom with four golden chains, two of them attaching to the front tabs of the shoulder straps and two to their backside. Secured inside the folds of the breastplate were the mysterious "*urim vetumim*," the "lights most perfect" understood by many commentaries to have been slips of parchment inscribed with the names of God (commentaries of Rashi and Ramban to 28:30).

While the *ephod* and the breastplate are presented as two discrete garments, it should be clear that they constitute an integrated unit. They are physically interconnected insofar as how they are worn by the Kohen Gadol and they share a common aesthetic language: each of them is woven from a yarn containing gold, blue, purple, red, and linen. Both of them also place an emphasis upon identical texts: The names of the tribes are to be engraved upon the precious stones that form the core of each scheme. For the *ephod*, the names of the tribes are engraved on the onyx stones that rest upon the shoulders; for the breastplate, they are inscribed on gems that are positioned upon the heart. In short, the *ephod*-breastplate unit highlights the great responsibility of the Kohen Gadol to represent the tribes of Israel before God at all times. It is for their welfare that he carries out his priestly duties and it is their needs that are uppermost in his heart. As the spiritual leader of Israel, he bears the burden of his office always; when he stands in God's presence with innermost thoughts revealed, the people of Israel stand with him. It is against this backdrop of the *ephod* and breastplate that our robe is presented. The verse actually describes it as the "robe of the *ephod*" (28:31), for the *ephod* and its attached breastplate are both worn on top of this sky-blue robe.

Succeeding the description of the robe is the account of the *tzitz* or headband. This golden strip, worn upon the forehead of the Kohen Gadol and secured by threads of blue to his ornamental turban, was inscribed with two single words: "קדש לה'" or "holy to God" (28:36). While the robe and breastplate emphasize the responsibilities of the Kohen Gadol towards the people of Israel and therefore incorporate the names of the twelve tribes, the headband addresses his status before God. The service that he performs and the instruction that he provides constitute a holy mission, and he recognizes that all of his works are performed under God's watchful gaze. The Kohen Gadol leads a life dedicated to God's service and to the propagation of the God-idea in the world. His crown of gold therefore proclaims not kingly power, but rather the unique human capacity, possessed by no other creature inhabiting the terrestrial plane, to be "holy to God." And unlike the crown of a king that loudly proclaims his exalted external status while saying nothing about his inner life, the commentaries rightly understand that the *tzitz* of the High Priest was as much about thoughts as about appearances. The dedicatory "holy to God" engraved upon its surface not only was a reference to the glorious office of the High Priest but also to the very personal deliberations that were processed behind that headband of gold, in the mind of the wearer who did God's service. Ibn Ezra elaborates by saying that:

> You must realize that the two temples near the forehead mark the location in the brain where the five senses come together, and there is to be found the seat of the imagination. From there higher thoughts proceed. Therefore the Torah indicates that it is through the agency of the *tzitz* that "expiation for the sacred offerings" is achieved, for perhaps the thoughts of those that sanctify the offerings may have been improper . . . (commentary to *Shemot* 28:37)

It should not surprise us, then, that in the world of the sacrificial service, some thoughts can actually render the offering unfit! The Mishna in Tractate Zevachim, chapters 1 and 2 details a number of scenarios in which the sacrifice is disqualified by the *thoughts* of the Kohen who performs the service, even while the external aspects of the ritual are in nowise altered. Without going into details, it is sufficient to note that thoughts do matter, and the more exalted the context, the more those thoughts matter. Just as a scribe who fails to explicitly have in mind the sanctification of God's name when he writes that name in the Torah scroll has rendered the scroll unfit (see Maimonides, Laws of Tefillin 1:15), so too must the High Priest dedicate his exclusive attention – spiritual and intellectual – to God's service.

Bracketing the Robe – the Explanation of the Rashbam

It thus emerges that the text brackets the robe with the description of the *ephod* and breastplate on the one end and the headband on the other. The *ephod* and breastplate are placed upon the sky-blue robe and worn in combination with it, while the headband, although disconnected from the robe physically, is nevertheless associated aesthetically by its own critical cord of pure blue. All of the other textiles that make up the garb of the Kohen Gadol are prepared from the hybrid fiber of gold, blue, purple, red and white linen. In sum, we have a dynamic arrangement of garments that together proclaim the special mission of the Kohen Gadol, a mission that is focused exclusively upon God and the people of Israel.

The Rashbam unravels the significance of the robe in his comments concerning its unique sky-blue color:

> The robe was entirely blue in color. It seems to me that since it was worn below the *ephod* and the breastplate that both serve as reminders, it is just like the sky-blue thread of the *tzitzit* that resembled the hue of the heavens and served as a reminder as well. Our Rabbis have explained concerning the blue thread of the *tzitzit* (TB *Menachot* 43b) that its color was reminiscent of the sea, and the sea recalled the sky that in turn evoked the divine throne of glory. So too, the robe was entirely sky-blue in color and incorporated no purple or scarlet. (commentary to *Shemot* 28:31)

The Rashbam draws our attention to the fact that the text refers to both the *ephod* and the breastplate as "reminders." The two onyx stones placed upon the epaulettes of the *ephod* are "stones of remembrance" (28:12), reminding Aharon of his august responsibilities towards the people. The twelve stones of the breastplate borne upon Aharon's heart serve as "a remembrance before God always" (28:29). As for the sky-blue robe, it was prepared with the same dye used to color the thread of blue for the *tzitzit* , as mandated in Parashat Shelach so that Israel might "remember" (*BeMidbar* 15:37–41):

> God spoke to Moshe saying: Speak to the people of Israel and bid them to make *tzitzit* (fringes) upon the corners of their garments for all generations, and they shall place a cord of blue upon the *tzitzit*. They shall have the *tzitzit* and you shall see it and *remember* all of the commandments of God and perform them . . .

According to the Rashbam, the overall theme of these three priestly garments is therefore "remembrance", not in the sense of recalling forgotten facts but rather as an ongoing and vital recognition, a constant appreciation of God's overarching presence and a conscious desire to live by His laws. The chromatic representation of this remembering was sky-blue because, as the Rabbis put it in the context of the *tzitzit*, this color resembled the sea, the sky and the throne of glory itself that is described in *Shemot* 24:10 as "sapphire as pure as the heavens." By relating the blue of the robe to the cord of the *tzitzit*, the Rashbam also links the ministering of the Kohen Gadol to the service of the people. Just as the Kohen Gadol pays heed, so too the people of Israel are later called upon to listen. Just as the Kohen Gadol was wrapped in the majestic robe, so too the people of Israel affixed the cord of blue – potent symbol of majesty – to the corners of their own garments. While unable to themselves share in his special service at the Mishkan, the people of Israel could yet partake of the Kohen Gadol's exalted mission.

For the Rashbam, the robe serves as the perfect backdrop for the *ephod* and breastplate, for all of them together proclaim "remember!" While the Rashbam does not include the *tzitz* in his triad, its fastening cord of blue ties it to the theme of remembrance and to the robe in turn, even as we note that *tzitz* is etymologically related to *tzitzit*! Aesthetically, the golden diadem perfectly mirrors the pomegranates and golden bells that gently tinkle upon the hem of the robe. The headband is worn high upon the head, the bells of the robe near the feet. The headband is worn against the linen turban, the golden bells opposite the woven pomegranates. And might not the sound of the golden bells down low, announcing the entry of the Kohen Gadol into the Holy precincts, be the auditory analog to the axiom engraved upon the golden crown high up – "holy to God"? In effect, then, the headband, *ephod* and breastplate are all joined in perfect conceptual and aesthetic union by the sky-blue robe. Together these garments, unique to the High Priest, affirm the potential of a human being to be enveloped in the experience of God, to be constantly sensitive to His sustaining presence, to be always inspired by His life-giving laws. The Ramban adds a provocative, mystical comment to the discussion:

> [The bells upon the hem of the robe] allude to what our Sages explained, that when the Torah states that "no *man* shall be present in the Tent of Meeting when the Kohen Gadol enters to atone for the Holy precinct, until he exits" (*VaYikra* 16:17) . . . this includes even the ministering angels! Therefore, God commanded that he announce his approach, as if to say "remove all *men* from before me!" (*Breisheet* 54:1) so that he might enter and serve the king in perfect seclusion . . . (paraphrase of commentary to *Shemot* 28:35)

As the Ramban understands it, when the Kohen Gadol approaches to serve God, announced by the gentle chiming of the bells upon the hem of the sky-blue robe, even the holy angels must clear the way from before him, thus sparing him from certain death should he enter their overwhelming presence! What a startling comment about the ability of a human being to transcend the petty and the mundane, to become sanctified to God's service and to briefly outshine even the holy *seraphim* in splendor!

Of course, we no longer have a Temple or priestly garments, but the Torah has preserved their memory for us with something more potent than mere material objects: the eternal text. For some, these texts describe old-fashioned curiosities; they are faint echoes of archaic artifacts now irrelevant and strange. But for the devoted student of the Torah who lives his life inspired by God's words, the descriptions of the priestly garments are forever relevant, because they are about engaging the fundamental challenge of being receptive to God's presence and always conscious of our mission. From head to toe, the Kohen Gadol is clothed with potent symbols of his charge and concrete reminders of its gravity. Every fiber of his being is dedicated to his task! The message for the people of Israel could not be more clear.

We shall let the Abarbanel have the last word:

> . . . what we can understand about the Mishkan and its vessels today is as meaningful now as when it was fully practiced. In this sense, the sacrificial service has not been suspended (although in practice it no longer exists), for study of those matters need not cease. Through comprehending their eternal message, a person can yet achieve subservience and closeness to God . . .
>
> Do not think for a moment that the descriptions of the Mishkan, its vessels and its construction, the sacrifices, the offerings of the princes at its dedication, the priestly garments as well as the rest of the ordinances that were practiced in antiquity, have no relevance for us today in our present state of exile. Indeed, one may be tempted to ask concerning the above, as well as regarding the agricultural laws that pertain to the land of Israel, or with respect to the laws of *tuma* and *tahara*, all of which are no longer practiced: what purpose do we achieve by studying and knowing them today?!

The answer is that one must realize that concerning all things mentioned in the Torah, no matter what they are, the main objective of their study is to draw us closer to God by perfecting our souls through their comprehension. The verse therefore states: "You shall observe the matters of this covenant and perform them, in order that you might be successful in all of your endeavors" (*Devarim* 29:8). Our Sages remark: "Observance" refers to study, and "Performance" refers to practice. Those singular individuals who strive to achieve perfect wisdom act in accordance with prior study and learning, and for them there is no appreciable difference between a matter that is applicable and one that is not. Therefore, what we know presently concerning the *meaning* of the Mishkan and its vessels is as beneficial to us today as on the very day of the events themselves. In this sense, the sacrificial service and the associated laws of ritual fitness and unfitness have never really ceased. Although the concrete acts themselves are no longer practiced, the study of the matters has not, and a man may yet acquire through their constant comprehension the precious commodity of submission before God, as the verse states: "A contrite and broken spirit is true sacrifice to God." (*Tehillim* 51:19)

FOR FURTHER STUDY:

(1) The commentaries wonder about the derivation of the unusual word "*tzitz*" and adopt three main approaches. According to the Ibn Ezra, the word is related to "*tzitzit*" or "tassel," whether of strings or of hair (see *BeMidbar* 15:37–41 and *Yechezkel* 8:3). In our context, the word connotes an ornament that is worn on the head next to the hair. The Rashbam, in contrast, relates the word to the verb form that means to "peak out or to be visible" (*Shir HaShirim* 2:9) and understands that the headband is so called because of its prominent placement upon the forehead. Finally, the Chizkuni opines that the word "*tzitz*" describes "a kind of adornment that sparkles and shines" and he derives the word from verb usages that suggest that meaning (*Yechezkel* 1:7 and *Tehillim* 132:18).

It is quite possible that all of these possibilities are themselves derivatives of a more fundamental definition, for the noun "*tzitz*" often means "a blossom or first flowering" (*BeMidbar* 17:23). If so, the basic definition of "*tzitz*" would be "that which bursts forth like a first flower" and this could then be related to a tassel or shock of hair (Ibn Ezra), a prominent protrusion (Rashbam) or a glint that catches the eye's attention (Chizkuni). The thrust of the matter is to suggest that the *tzitz* worn by the High Priest is not understated and hidden from view but rather is a public and prominent display piece, like a crown.

KI TISA

Image, Text and the Golden Calf

Exodus 30:11-34:35

AFTER THE blueprints for the precious vessels, the Holy spaces and the priestly garments had been commanded to Moshe in the lengthy readings of *Teruma* and *Tetzave*, our Parasha opens with the mitzvah of the half-shekel poll tax. All adult males are to contribute a half-shekel of silver towards the construction of the Mishkan, with the collected funds simultaneously serving as the vehicle for conducting a census of the people. The half-shekel contribution is introduced as a special measure for the particular task at hand, and is ultimately used for the casting of the silver sockets that support the wall planks of acacia wood (see *Shemot* 38:25–28). But the Torah's intent is also to state eternal statutes: (1) whenever a census of the people is undertaken, a contributed object is to be used in place of actually counting them; (2) the half-shekel Temple tax is to be collected every year from all adult males among the people, and is to be utilized for the purchase of communal sacrifices as well as for the maintenance and repair of the physical plant.

The Parasha goes on to describe the bronze laver, the anointing oil and the incense, before introducing us to the chief artisan charged with carrying out the sacred work – Bezalel son of Uri son of Chur of the tribe of Yehuda. This able craftsman is to be assisted by a compatriot with less illustrious lineage – Oholiav son of Achisamach of the tribe of Dan – thus implying that the Mishkan is not the exclusive preserve of certain powerful and well-connected tribes, but rather the patrimony of all Israel. After an emphatic reference to the need to observe the Shabbat, even as the work of building the Mishkan unfolds, the Parasha reaches its central and most lengthy narrative: the episode of the golden calf.

The literary effect is of course dramatic in the extreme, for after the Mishkan narratives have been unleashed, creating a rare momentum of anticipation and hope, the whole textual edifice proverbially comes crashing down. Recall how the Torah broached the subject by abstractly describing vessels and spaces and then went on to delineate the priestly garments while speaking more concretely of investiture. Finally, our Parasha spelled out practical plans for the gathering of contributions and confidently introduced the chief artisans. Suddenly and without warning, the entire endeavor was thrown into terrible disarray by Moshe's delay in descending from the mount and the people's disastrous reaction in fashioning a molten image.

Understanding the Transgression: Rashi vs. Ramban

The commentaries have discussed the transgression of the golden calf at length, and in their approach to the episode their explanations may be broadly broken down into two diverging schools of thought. There are those like Rashi who make no apologies about the sins of the people: Israel succumbed to idolatry and their intention in fashioning the golden fetish was to replace the transcendent and invisible God with a tangible and concrete image. When they excitedly exclaimed that "These are your gods, Oh Israel, who brought you forth from the land of Egypt!" (32:4) they committed the crime of polytheism. As Rashi puts it, "they desired many gods" (commentary to 32:1). And while Rashi maintains that the initial impetus for the fashioning of the idol came from the non-Israelite elements among the people – namely the "mixed multitude" (see *Shemot* 12:38) that had utilized the opportunity afforded by the post-plague collapse of the Egyptian state to also journey forth to freedom – he nevertheless maintains that Israel was quickly swept up by their villainous seductions to eagerly embrace the worship of the idol. In short, as far as Rashi is concerned, the fashioning and worship of the golden calf were grave deeds of idolatry as Israel "exchanged its glory for the figure of a grass-eating ox!" (*Tehillim* 106:20).

The Ramban on the other hand, following the lead of Rabbi Yehuda HaLevi (12th century, Spain) and the Ibn Ezra, maintains that the people of Israel were not initially interested in idolatry at all. Quite the contrary. Had they not just experienced the Revelation of God's presence and the thundering proclamation of His Decalogue at Sinai? Is it conceivable that they could have so easily cast off the effects of that transformative event to now embrace coarse and vulgar icons? Rather, avers the Ramban, what the people sought during those anxious hours prior to Moshe's return (for God had called him to the summit of the mount some forty days earlier to receive His teachings and His tablets – see *Shemot* 24:12–18), was a replacement for the lawgiver himself! Fearing the worst when Moshe failed to descend at what they believed to be the appointed time, the people felt leaderless and afraid. How would they traverse the inhospitable wilderness to the Promised Land without Moshe to guide them? Though they of course realized that in fact it was God's guidance that alone could guarantee their survival, they desired some sort of concrete symbol to serve as the focal point for God's providence, much as they believed that Moshe received ongoing divine inspiration and then was capable of leading them. As the Ramban himself so trenchantly remarks: "What they desired was another Moshe!" (commentary to 32:1). In the end, their misguided efforts spawned more ominous developments, for the less refined among them quickly adopted the golden object as a god in its own right. It was they who were later charged with worshipping idolatry and then punished accordingly. Nevertheless, for the Ramban, the initial intentions of the ringleaders were not malevolent.

Both of these approaches have their limitations. While Rashi's explanation accords with the straightforward reading of the text, it forces us to impose a most difficult premise. Could the people have remained so unmoved by the Exodus and by the Revelation, so utterly unconvinced concerning God's absoluteness and transcendence, even in the face of encounters with the divine that must surely rank as the most profound ever recorded in human history? And while the Ramban mitigates these difficulties by positing that the people did not initially succumb to idolatry at all but were only seeking a replacement for their dear but absent leader Moshe, his interpretation raises serious problems of its own. How could the people have thought that a lifeless, bovine image of gold could be their "leader"? In what sense did they believe that it would "guide" them through the wilderness to their destination? And why didn't the anxious throng simply ask Aharon to take the place of his brother, just as the elder prophet had been instrumental at the launch of the plagues (7:1–7), during the Exodus (12:1–3) and at Mount Sinai (19:24)? Hadn't Moshe himself appointed Aharon as a temporary leader in his place when he initially ascended the mountain (24:14)?

Considering the Textual Linkage

When we consider the episode from a textual standpoint, there appears to be an intentional and inverse parallel not between the calf and God (as Rashi suggests), or else the calf and Moshe (as Ramban suggests), but rather between the calf and the tablets of the Decalogue themselves! The entire episode, for example, does not begin with the account of the people's panic, as one would have expected (and as the chapter break misleadingly indicates), but rather with a tenuous verse, easily left out from a literary standpoint, that detachedly discusses these tablets of stone:

> When He finished speaking to him at Mount Sinai, He gave to Moshe the two tablets of testimony, tablets of stone written by the finger of God. The people saw that Moshe tarried in coming down from the mount, so the people gathered against Aharon and they said to him: "Arise and fashion us a god that will go before us, for this man Moshe we know not what has become of him!" Aharon said to them; "remove the rings of gold that are in the ears of your wives, sons and daughters, and bring them to me." All of the people removed the golden earrings from their ears and brought them to Aharon . . . (31:18–32:3)

This linkage is forcefully revisited when Moshe prepares to descend from the mountain, having been informed by God concerning the people's infidelity, and having already offered prayers on their behalf to avert His burning wrath:

> Moshe turned and descended from the mountain, bearing in his hands the two tablets of testimony. They were tablets written on both sides, from this side and that side they were inscribed. The tablets were the work of the Lord, and the text was the Lord's writing, engraved upon the tablets. Yehoshua heard the people's outcry, and he said to Moshe "there is a sound of fighting in the camp!" . . . (32:15–17)

As above, the account of the people's transgression is preceded by a superfluous reference to the tablets, and as above, the reference places special emphasis upon the *writing* engraved upon the stone. The narrative goes on to describe Moshe's approach, for when he saw the calf and the merrymaking, "he became angry, and he cast the tablets down from his hands, and he smashed them at the feet of the mountain" (32:19). Here, once again, the calf and the tablets are textually and temporally locked in tight embrace, for it is the *sight* of the calf that prompts their destruction. Finally, after Moshe destroys the fetish, chastises Aharon and punishes the perpetrators, he ascends to secure God's forgiveness. After much pleading and prayer, Moshe succeeds in restoring God's favor, a process that culminates in His charge to the lawgiver to "hew two other tablets of stone, and I shall write upon the tablets the very words that were on the first tablets that you shattered . . ." (34:1). In other words, the episode ends much as it began by associating the golden calf with the text of the tablets, for the ultimate lifting of the transgression's calamitous effects is signaled by none other than the preparation of new tablets with new writing engraved upon them.

Thus far, we have established an ongoing textual and episodic link between the golden calf and the tablets. The fashioning of the calf had been introduced by a superfluous mention of the tablets and its worship had then directly precipitated their destruction, while the subsequent obliteration of the molten image prompted their eventual restoration. Additionally, when the Torah described the tablets in these contexts, it never missed an opportunity to emphasize the unique writing engraved upon their surface, for not only had the letters been incised by God himself, but the words were curiously legible from both sides of the stone.

The seeming redundancy of all of this tablet talk should be noted, for we had already been informed long before the episode of the golden calf that the tablets were the special work of God and contained His words to the people. Recall that after the Revelation at Sinai that culminated in God's proclamation of the Decalogue, the deity bid Moshe to ascend to the mount in order to receive "the tablets of stone, the instruction and the commands, that I have written to guide them" (24:12). This reference is from the beginning of Moshe's forty-day repair to the summit of Sinai, and underscores the fact that all of the subsequent references to the tablets must be emphatic rather than informationally necessary. In this way, the Torah seeks to highlight something about the distinctiveness of the writing upon the tablets, something that stands in glaring contrast to their nemesis – the golden calf.

Iconography vs. Text

What is the difference between a molten image of gold and austere tablets of stone? Both are composed of a heavy and ponderous material, lifeless in its own right, that is then impressed with some other significance. But while the former communicates its meaning through the medium of concrete and tangible imagery, by material representation of a person, animal or thing, the latter speaks through the abstraction called "text." The message of a golden calf is immediate and obvious, for its eager worshippers need not exert any additional effort in comprehending its corporeal form or coarse symbolism, but tablets of text demand additional mental processing. That is to say that writing of any sort invites higher cognitive involvement, and when the subject matter of the text is complex or abstruse, conceptual rather than concrete, even greater effort must be expended in order to achieve comprehension.

Standing at the mountain and receiving the Torah, the people were stunned by God's *words*, by His thundering *commands* uttered out of the thick cloud cover and the impenetrable smoke that ominously swirled at Sinai's summit. Though their senses were inundated by an experience of the divine that could only be described as overwhelming, the Torah is careful to point out, in Moshe's reminisce of the event some forty years later, that they saw no image whatsoever of the deity:

> You drew near and stood at the base of the mountain, and the mountain burned with fire until the very heart of heaven, darkness, cloud and thick vapor. God spoke to you from the midst of the fire, but while you heard the sound of words, you saw no image, only a voice. He spoke to you His covenant that He commanded you to perform, the ten things, and He wrote them on two tablets of stone . . . you shall therefore be very careful for the sake of your souls, for you saw no image on the day that God spoke to you at Chorev out of the midst of the fire! (*Devarim* 4:11–15)

God's Inscrutable Uniqueness

What a strange God indeed, unlike any other worshipped in ancient times or most worshipped today, that had no image and no physical form whatsoever! At the moment of His much-anticipated Revelation to humanity, He broke with every convention known to man, for He did not appear as a body or a thing but only was heard as a voice, communicating not through tangible images but rather through intangible words! And while the people of Israel listened intently, they could scarcely comprehend the significance of the matter! For while they surely did not doubt God's existence or else His immediacy, they struggled mightily with His incorporeality. The gods with which they were familiar all had bodies and concrete form, molten images of every beast imaginable, all of them readily comprehensible and easily approached. But this God was different, for He demanded of His adherents not superficial and shallow devotion, after the manner of idolatrous adoration, but rather involved thought and study of His laws! He addressed His people with *words*, He gave them a *text*, and He required not the blind allegiance of their hearts but the intellectual commitment of their minds.

His service was not about empty ritual and drunken debauchery, man's finite body and its instinctual drives, but rather about our higher potential, the soul and the mind that could be nourished only by attentiveness to His words, by the laws that could repair human society even as they transformed the recalcitrant human heart. His banner was not inscribed with icons and images, tactile forms of recumbent and contemplative figures or else saviors nailed to a cross, all of them mere sensual representations readily comprehensible to the masses but correspondingly lacking any call to deeper study or devotion. Could the transcendent, the absolute and the ultimate be described by lifeless metal or insensible wood, even as the former's glitter could capture the eye with all of its splendor, while the latter's depiction of grotesque torment could hold the heart of the faithful in sway? No, God's banner was inscribed instead with *language*, with a text whose very abstraction stressed the chasm between finite man and infinite God, driving home the fundamental message that while in some contexts a picture may indeed be worth a thousand words, in the context of the divine it is worth none.

To commemorate the Revelation of His presence, God prepared to present His people with tablets of stone, unadorned and unimpressive, in and of themselves of little aesthetic or material value, but incised with words that if diligently studied and applied could change the world. But as Moshe tarried, the people anxiously pondered their new and strange destiny, for when they stood at Sinai's base they had (unwittingly?) agreed to champion in the world a God-idea that was not only revolutionary but peculiar in the extreme. Were they not themselves intimidated by a conception of the deity that, while freeing the body from its primitive preoccupations with magic, superstition, and the fear of capricious forces, would also obligate their minds to more constructive and complex pursuits? Anticipating Moshe's return bearing the tablets of text and emboldened by his seeming delay, the people approached Aharon and demanded in their place the fashioning of a molten image of gold! This was an emphatic statement on their part that they preferred a god that didn't demand so much mental and spiritual exertion, a god that could be appeased by trite formalities even as its empty ceremonial could numb their minds to the awesome and unsettling conception of a creator and liberator that was pure spirit, yet held utter sway over the material world. Aharon complied, and in complete contrast to the lengthy course of Moshe's forty-day immersion in the intricacies of God's wise statutes, the golden calf was fashioned almost instantaneously – a sure indication that the comprehension of its will would be correspondingly simple and straightforward.

It is for this reason that the Torah repeatedly contrasts the tablets and their unique divinely-inscribed text to the fashioning and worship of the golden calf, for like matter and anti-matter, the two cannot abide together for long. The God of Israel is a text-God – inscrutable but yet proximal, asking us to utilize our minds and demanding us to nurture our moral will, but refusing to be limited by our material constraints. He cannot be delineated by a form or an image and His interactions with the world can only be outlined in non-representational words. The gods of gold, in contrast, are nothing but form, for besides their coarse and vulgar materiality, there is no higher purpose, no moral demands and no allusions to more profound possibilities. With the gods of gold, what you see is what you get, and what you get is not very profound at all. How then could the God of text tolerate the worship of the gods of gold?

Literary Clues

The narrative provides us with a number of literary devices to highlight this binary but inverse relationship between the golden calf and the stone tablets. Recall that when the people approached Aharon to fashion for them a god, he attempted to delay by requesting their golden earrings. But the eager masses unexpectedly called his bluff and complied immediately, and Aharon was forced to do the dreadful deed:

> He took it [the gold] from them and he fashioned it with a stylus [חרט] and made it into a molten calf . . . (31:4)

The unusual "חרט" or "stylus" is a metal instrument that is used for carving or inscribing, and its only other biblical usage is in the context of writing. When God speaks to the 8th-century BCE prophet Yeshayahu and tells him to inform the people of impending disaster, He says to him: "Take a large scroll and write upon it with a common stylus (חרט) 'plunder approaches speedily, pillage with haste'" (*Yeshayahu* 8:1). Indicating that Aharon utilized a stylus to fashion the golden calf not only provides us with an intriguing but otherwise irrelevant detail but also highlights the perverse inversion inherent in the process – the very instrument that man would have used to inscribe the tablets with God's laws is here transmogrified into a tool of corruption. Who could fail to hear the echo of this *cheret* in the very description of the tablets' text, for "the tablets were the work of the Lord, and the text was the Lord's writing, engraved (חרות) upon the tablets" (*Shemot* 32:16). Although the grammatical roots are different, "*cheret*" ending with a "tet" and "*charoot*" with a "tav", and the pronunciation of that final consonant is (for some communities of Jews) quite different, the alliteration is nevertheless unmistakable.

Conversely, when God bids Moshe to fashion the second set of tablets from stone, He invites the lawgiver to "hew for yourself two tablets of stone," where the verb for "hewing", the 2nd person imperative פסל (*pesol*) is the same root that underlies every sculpted image or פסל (*pesel*) in the Tanakh! Thus, the shallowness of the molten image is rejected by God, to be forcefully replaced once again with a second set of tablets. The conclusion is thus inescapable that the people's desire to have a golden calf is neither their attempt to deny God's existence nor even to replace Moshe, but rather their projection in material form of the desire to rewrite the rules of their engagement with the divine. "Do not burden our minds with abstract text," they proclaim, "do not demand of us reflection and study! Do not enjoin upon us to develop a profound faith, or to labor mightily in the deliberation of life's complexities and in the resolution of its attendant moral ambiguities! Give us instead a god of gold, a simple and readily comprehensible explanation for everything, an easy engagement with the world and a naïve and superficial relationship with You, without all of the spiritual baggage that profundity introduces! Rather, let 'these be your gods, oh Israel, who brought you forth from the land of Egypt!'"

God, of course, will have none of it, neither then nor now. While much of modern existence – a popular culture that thrives against the backdrop of our media-based consumer society – champions the creed of the golden calf, stressing form over substance and fostering superficiality while denigrating spiritual and intellectual depth, the noble story of the tablets persists. The words of God engraved upon them have been written eternally upon our hearts and inscribed upon our minds, even if the divine letters sometimes seem very small and almost invisible. To follow the Torah is to connect with a tradition of intellectual study that is as relevant now as on the very day that the people of Israel stood at Sinai. It is to cleave to a heritage whose stress on learning and reflection is still unusual today, even among those other faith traditions that also search for "enlightenment."

The world gropes for transcendent meaning and for an encounter with the divine, but refuses to accept that spiritual and intellectual depth – profound effort of the heart and of the mind – are necessary for their real acquisition. And although the challenges that face the adherents of the tablets of stone may have changed in terms of the externals, at their core they are not much different at all. There are still only two basic choices before us, two fundamentally different worldviews of God and of our relationship with Him and with His laws, and they can in no wise be reconciled. Recalling God's summons to Moshe, we must cast off intellectual sloth, and choose the more demanding but ultimately more rewarding way: "Ascend the mountain towards Me and remain there. I shall give you the tablets of stone, the instruction and the commands, that I have written to guide them" (24:12).

FOR FURTHER STUDY:

(1) In *Avot deRabbi Natan* 2:3 there is a fascinating Midrash that is quoted with variations in many other places. In conflated form, the Midrash relates that when Moshe ascended on high to receive the tablets from God, there was consternation among the ministering angels that He would give His Torah to a mere mortal. Moshe prevailed, seized the tablets and began his descent. He was still carrying them when Israel fashioned the golden calf. At that moment, the letters flew off of the tablets and they fell from Moshe's grasp.

There is much to explore in this provocative Midrash. For our purposes, we note that once again, there is a direct connection drawn between the golden calf and the letters – they fly off when the idol is fashioned. The implication is clear: The essence of the Torah is a function of its text and without text there is only lifeless, heavy stone.

VAYAKHEL

Shabbat and the Mishkan

Exodus 35:1–38:20

THE LAST Parasha of Ki Tisa began with a command to the people to each contribute a half-shekel of silver towards the construction of the Mishkan. The laver or wash basin was then described as were additional details of Aharon's service. The ingredients of the anointing oil and incense, both of which figure prominently in the service, were then enumerated. Finally, Bezalel was named as the chief artisan of the undertaking, and a checklist of his skills, talents and responsibilities followed. The passage concluded with a succinct but strongly worded injunction concerning the observance of the Shabbat.

Parashat VaYakhel repeats the Mishkan/Shabbat juxtaposition: the section begins with God's decree to the people to observe the Shabbat, and then inaugurates the collection drive to gather materials for the Mishkan's construction. The Shabbat constitutes one of the greatest innovations of the Torah, and perhaps the most important ritual observance of the Jew. A cherished expression of Jewish identity, it would not be hyperbole to suggest that the survival of the Jewish people as a faith community has been due to the continued observance of the Shabbat. Throughout our long and checkered history but especially in the modern era, the relevance of Shabbat has been questioned, and its observance has been derided and ultimately discarded by many. Its prohibitions have been portrayed as antiquated, restrictive, and overly ritualistic. Even among the observant, many are hard-pressed to explain the underlying rationale behind the interdiction of putting on a light, driving a car or painting a picture, especially when these activities are, in our modern context, so effortless. We may conceal our ignorance with vague and ambiguous references to "tradition," but what is genuinely needed is a fundamental overview of the core ideas of Shabbat.

Through a close study of the Torah text as well as of the Talmudic and Midrashic explications, we will acquire a more profound understanding by examining the *purpose* of Shabbat – its core essence. We will find direction along the way by critically analyzing the fundamental vocabulary associated with its observance. Although at times it will seem as if we have strayed far from the fertile ground of our Parasha, we will in fact discover that the two most critical texts for our investigation are to be found in Parashat Ki Tisa and in our own Parashat VaYakhel.

Shabbat Breisheet

We must begin our research with the first mention of Shabbat in the Torah, for it is in that context that its primary features are spelled out. After the six days of creation are concluded, and their slow but steady progress from chaos to order and from inanimate to humanity is attained, the seventh day is introduced:

> The heavens and the earth and all of their host were completed. God completed on the seventh day all of His work that He had done, and He rested on the seventh day from all of His work that He had done. God blessed the seventh day and sanctified it, for on it He rested from all of His work that He had created and done. (*Breisheet* 2:1–3)

The repeating words in this text are "completed," "rested," and "done." "Shabbat," from the root שבת that is here translated as "rested," commemorates God's repose after His completion of creation. The difficulties raised by this translation are manifest, for how can we associate the idea of rest with a being who is omnipotent? How are we to understand the nature of His "work," a term that we employ to describe activity, toil, labor and especially effort? The notion of "resting from work" in our human frame of reference implies that physical exertion has taken place and that recuperation is needed. But understanding the terms in this fashion is impossible, for "surely you know and have heard that the Lord of the universe is God; He who has created the ends of the earth neither wearies nor tires, and His wisdom is unfathomable" (*Yeshayahu* 40:28).

For now, let us note that the word for "work" employed throughout the passage is without exception the Hebrew term מלאכה: "The heaven and earth and their entire host was completed. God completed on the seventh day all of His work (מלאכתו) that He had done, and He rested on the seventh day from all of His work (מלאכתו) that He had done. God blessed the seventh day and sanctified it, for on it He rested from all of His work (מלאכתו) that He had created and done." Let us also note that this first mention of the Shabbat is not an injunction or a command directed towards humanity, but rather an event in the life of God. In this passage, "Shabbat" is not actually used as a noun, but rather as a verb indicating that which God did.

Although the Torah introduces the notion of Shabbat as being coeval with the very dawn of human existence, there are no additional references to it in the book of Breisheet. The narratives of the patriarchs and matriarchs make not a single mention of its observance. Perhaps we should assume that as an abstraction Shabbat enters the world of human consciousness early on, but it is not crystallized into a set of formal practices until much later. It is not until the people of Israel have left the bondage of Egypt that Shabbat reappears, this time in an oblique reference to an observance taking shape:

> On the sixth day, the people gathered two measures of manna, two omer-measures per person, and all of the leaders of the congregation reported so to Moshe. He said to them: "Thus has God spoken that tomorrow is a holy Shabbat unto God. Bake what you intend to bake and cook what you intend to cook, and leave over the remainder until morning. The people left some over until morning as Moshe had commanded, and it did not become spoiled nor riddled with worms. Moshe said to them: "Eat it today for today is Shabbat unto God, today you shall not find manna in the fields. For six days you shall gather it, but on the seventh, the Shabbat, you shall not find it . . . God has given you the Shabbat and therefore gives you double measure on the sixth day. Remain in your places on the seventh day, and do not go out [to gather it] on the seventh day." The people rested on the seventh day. (*Shemot* 16:22–30)

The miraculous manna that began to fall after the people had crossed the Sea of Reeds and entered the foreboding wilderness would appear every morning with the rising of the dew. Intended to inculcate the profound lesson of ongoing trust in God's providence, the manna could not be stored up. Try as one might, only a single omer-measure could be gathered per person, any that remained on the ground ungathered vaporized in the heat of the late morning sun, and any uneaten and left for the morrow became rotten and inedible. A double amount, however, would fall on the sixth day, thus providing the people with provisions for the Shabbat. That twofold blessing carried with it a new responsibility: The people were bidden not to go out to gather manna on the Shabbat. For the first time, Shabbat is here presented as a formal observance possessing a prohibitive component, although it is the specific activity of "gathering" rather than a range of actions that is here curtailed. The text provides no elaboration concerning the mysterious concept of *melakha*, although it implies that baking and cooking are included in its definition since these activities must be completed before the onset of Shabbat. At the same time, the passage seems to indicate that the people had a previous familiarity with the notion of Shabbat, for otherwise a more direct and comprehensive introduction would have been in order.

Asseret HaDibrot – Melakha in the Imperative

At last, in Parashat Yitro, the Shabbat is presented as a broad and inclusive rite, in the fourth of the Ten Utterances. Its inclusion among these ten guiding principles secures its position as a central tenet of Jewish faith and observance, for Shabbat shares company with some of the most enduring ideals that humanity has ever known:

> Remember the Shabbat day to keep it holy. For six days shall you labor and do all of your work, but the seventh day shall be a Shabbat to God your Lord. You shall not do any work, neither you nor your son nor your daughter, nor your servant nor your maidservant, nor your animal, nor the convert that resides within your gates. This is because for six days God made heaven and earth, the sea and all that is in them, and He rested on the seventh day, therefore God blessed the seventh day and sanctified it. (20:8–11)

Here, the Torah establishes a direct link between our cessation of work on Shabbat and God's completion of His work after six days of creation. We are to work for six days and rest on the seventh just like God. By implication, the activities with which we are occupied during the six days of the week and from which we are bidden to desist, are the very ones corresponding to God's own acts during the first six days. It is of extreme consequence that the Torah consistently utilizes the term "*melakha*" to describe the work from which we are to refrain on the Shabbat: "For six days shall you labor and do all of your work (מלאכתך), but the seventh day shall be a Shabbat to God your Lord. You shall not do any work (מלאכה) . . ." It should be recalled that this expression was also used to describe God's activities during the first six days of creation; during those six days, God did *melakha*. In spite of the fact that in the Ten Utterances the text more clearly delineates the command to observe the Shabbat, it sheds no new lexicological light on the meaning of *melakha*.

At this juncture, it is important to point out that the Hebrew language does possess a number of synonyms (each with a different shade of meaning) for the word "work."

These include most commonly *avoda* (עבודה), but also *maaseh* (מעשה), *amal* (עמל), *peulah* (פעולה), and *alilah* (עלילה). Notwithstanding this lengthy list of worthy analogs, only one of them (עשה) ever occurs in both contexts of creation and the Ten Utterances and only then as a verb in conjunction with *melakha*. We can therefore draw two important conclusions. Firstly, we now know that *melakha* is associated almost exclusively with the act of creation and that cessation from it constitutes the central pillar of Shabbat observance. Secondly, we realize that whatever *melakha* is, it must differ fundamentally from *avoda* and its synonyms, for the Torah consciously avoids use of any other term when Shabbat is the topic of discussion.

The next mention of Shabbat in the Torah occurs in a fleeting reference from Parashat Mishpatim: "For six days shall you do your work (מעשיך) but on the seventh you shall cease (תשבות). This is in order that your ox and donkey may rest, and that the son of your maidservant and the convert may have respite" (*Shemot* 23:12). This verse addresses the animals, the servants and the converts – disenfranchised all. The ox and the donkey were the beasts of burden in antiquity; the son of the maidservant and the convert were marginalized members of society frequently associated with menial labor. While this reference provides no new insight into the prohibited activities of Shabbat, it does speak worlds about the social revolution that the Shabbat unleashed. It was novel enough that according to the Torah a day each week had to be set aside in order for people to liberate themselves from their weekday pursuits. But that work animals and poor members of society could also partake of that rare gift, not as a function of patrician charity but rather by basic right, was unprecedented. Slavery reduces men to beasts of burden. The Shabbat that releases both from toil restores dignity to creation.

Shabbat, Bezalel and the Mishkan

We now turn to Parashat Ki Tisa. Here, as in the Ten Utterances, the observance of Shabbat is spelled out at some length. As in previous contexts, its most salient feature is cessation from *melakha*:

> God spoke to Moshe saying: As for you, speak to the people of Israel and say "But observe My Sabbaths, for it is a sign between Me and you for all generations, so that you might know that I your God sanctify you . . . For six days shall work (מלאכה) be done, but the seventh day shall be a Shabbat consecrated to God, whosoever does work (מלאכה) on the Shabbat day shall be put to death. The people of Israel shall observe the Shabbat, to keep the Shabbat for their generations as an eternal covenant. Between Me and the people of Israel it is a sign forever, for six days God made the heavens and the earth and on the seventh day He ceased and was refreshed. (31:12–17)

For the first time, Shabbat is presented as a sign of the covenant between God and the people of Israel, highlighting the particularistic nature of the observance. The Shabbat of Breisheet was universal; this Shabbat is unique to the people of Israel. Additionally, consequences for non-observance of the Shabbat rites are here introduced, and they are severe: "Whosoever does work on the Shabbat day shall be put to death." The reference to Shabbat in the Ten Utterances spelled out no penalty for its abrogation. Now, rejection of Shabbat by performance of *melakha* is considered a capital crime.

But it is actually an *earlier* passage in Parashat Ki Tisa, juxtaposed to the above Shabbat reference, that for the Rabbinic tradition was the most critical. It concerns Bezalel the chief artisan of the Mishkan:

> God spoke to Moshe saying: "Behold, I single out by name Bezalel son of Uri son of Chur from the tribe of Yehuda. I have filled him with the spirit of God, with wisdom, understanding, knowledge, and the ability to execute all manner of work. To weave designs, to work with gold, silver and bronze. To cut stones and to fit them, to carve wood and to do all manner of work. Behold I have provided as his assistant Oholiav son of Achisamach of the tribe of Dan and in the heart of all of the wise I have placed wisdom, so that they will do all that I have commanded you: the tent of meeting and the ark for the testimony, as well as the lid that is upon it and all of the other vessels of the tent . . ." (31:1–7)

One of the most gifted characters mentioned in all of Tanakh, Bezalel is a capable artisan in every media. Full of wisdom and insight, he is comfortable working with textiles, metals, stone or wood. The rare combination drew the attention of the Ramban, who wondered about the significance:

> While the people of Israel were in Egypt they were broken by the heavy work of brick and clay; they never learned the fine arts of working with gold, silver and precious stones, and never saw them at all. How remarkable then, that there should be found among them a gifted and wise artisan capable of working with silver, gold, stone, wood, textiles, embroidery and weaving. Even among those who have studied these arts before the wise, it is not possible to find one who is expert in all of them. Even those who are familiar with these crafts, if they are burdened with the coarse toil of brick and mortar, soon lose their dexterity and their ability to execute fine, detailed, and beautiful work. In addition to practical skill, Bezalel was also filled with wisdom, insight and knowledge so that he understood the profound mystical meaning of the Mishkan and all of its vessels, why they were commanded and to what they allude. Therefore, God said to Moshe: "Behold this great wonder!" so that Moshe and the people of Israel would realize that He filled Bezalel with all of this ability so that he could construct the Mishkan, for so it was His will that the people construct this edifice in the wilderness for His glory. God announces the generations from the beginning as it says concerning Yirmiyahu: "Before I formed you in the womb I knew you, and before you were born I already designated you as a prophet to the peoples." (commentary to 31:2)

Textually, Ramban's comments are triggered by the unusual introductory remark of God to Moshe: "Behold, I designate by name Bezalel son of Uri son of Chur from the tribe of Yehuda . . ." Ramban explains that to be "designated by name" involves a selection which is unusual and unexpected. On the one hand, avers the Ramban, it is unreasonable to assume that the people of Israel had any exposure to the fine arts during their years of bondage. According to all indications in the Torah, the people of Israel were involved with back-breaking labor in the brick pits and fields, and were certainly not enrolled at the great art academies of the Delta. Assuredly, then, Bezalel did not receive a formal education in the arts. On the other hand, even if Bezalel was a "natural" who possessed innate abilities, his talented hands would have become blunted and dulled by the rough and crude work of bricks and mortar.

Even more extraordinary, notes the Ramban, Bezalel was proficient in *every type* of craftsmanship. Gifted goldsmiths are not usually talented weavers as well, and sculptors of stone cannot generally execute filigree in silver. But here was an artisan who was adept in every medium – metalwork, woodwork, stonework, weaving, and design! Ramban adds that Bezalel possessed keen spiritual insight and wisdom so that he truly comprehended the meaning of the great undertaking with all of its allusive details. The Ibn Ezra alerts us to another unusual talent: not only was Bezalel a gifted artisan, but also a master teacher, as indicated by *Shemot* 35:34. Rare is the artist who can articulate the process by which he came to his inspiration and can then guide others so that they might create beauty as well.

For the Ramban, there is only one way to explain all of Bezalel's exceptional expertise: divine inspiration. This is the significance of the unusual introduction: "Behold I have designated by name . . . I have filled him with the spirit of God." To be "designated by name" means more than simply to be selected by God. It means to be given the spiritual, intellectual and practical wherewithal, at precisely the right moment, to fulfill a mission – to be the architect of the house of God.

Bezalel as a Paradigm

Who is Bezalel as an archetype? What does he represent in the story of human history? What is the true significance of his exceptional aptitude? Considering all of his talents, pondering the range of his skills, deliberating upon the gravity of his mission, a single, startling conclusion emerges. Bezalel, like God Himself, is a *creator*. Charged with a sense of purpose, guided by insight and understanding, and sensitive to a task that will transform raw materials into things of utility, meaning and beauty, Bezalel initiates a grand process of design that is a faint reflection of God's own work at the dawn of creation. The act of creation that brought the cosmos into being, the supreme exercise of absolute wisdom that shaped nonexistence into matter and rendered chaos into order, cannot be duplicated by finite man. Nevertheless, a simulacrum of that moment, a semblance of its infinite grandeur, is repeated every time a spark flies from the anvil and an amorphous natural element is shaped by human ingenuity. Bezalel creates just as God creates. Inspired with wisdom, electrified with fervor, he directs his God-given spark of creativity to transform the world.

> Said Rav Yehuda in the name of Rav: Bezalel knew how to join the letters by which heaven and earth were created. Concerning him it says that he was filled with "a spirit of God, with *wisdom*, *insight* and *knowledge*," and concerning God's act of creation it says: "God with *wisdom* founded the earth, and with *insight* established the heavens" (*Mishle* 3:19). Furthermore, it states: "with *knowledge* did He expose the deep." (3:20)

In this Midrashic statement of our Sages, from TB *Berachot* 55a, Bezalel is portrayed as a creator who employs the very same methods and tools that God utilized to forge the cosmos. From a rational perspective, the letters of the Hebrew alphabet constitute the basic building blocks of language. Metaphorically, they represent the elemental fragments from which all other matter was derived. Mystically, the Hebrew letters possess innate spiritual potential waiting to be actualized. The Midrash draws upon all of these aspects in crafting a parallel between God's act of creation and Bezalel's fashioning of the Mishkan. Just as God manipulated and arranged the atomic particles to fashion a world of complexity, order, beauty and meaning, so too Bezalel takes the basic raw materials of metal, stone, wood, and fiber to create an edifice of splendor and spiritual significance.

Consider for a moment the processes involved in Bezalel's work. Without exception, they tell the story of how the awesome power of human creativity bridges the chasm between the abstract idea and the concrete product. In metalworking, unimpressive and ineffectual ore is remarkably converted into a useful, lustrous object. When working with stone, a rough and ordinary-looking mineral is transformed into a precious gem. As a woodworker, one changes a formless and dull block of timber into a beautiful and purposeful vessel. In the act of spinning thread and weaving, fibers from an animal (wool) or vegetable (linen) source are remarkably transmuted into a fine piece of textile. In all of these four progressions, ingenuity is the necessary link between the purposeful conception and the intelligent result. Along the way, a raw material is reshaped by human intervention and given a new and wondrous form.

The Definition of Melakha

Let us consider again the passage from Parashat Ki Tisa describing Bezalel's election:

> God spoke to Moshe saying: "Behold, I single out by name Bezalel son of Uri son of Chur from the tribe of Yehuda. I have filled him with the spirit of God, with wisdom, understanding, knowledge, and the ability to execute *all manner of work*. To weave designs, to work with gold, silver and bronze. To cut stones and to fit them, to carve wood and to do *all manner of work*. Behold I have provided as his assistant Oholiav son of Achisamach of the tribe of Dan, and in the heart of all of the wise I have placed wisdom, so that they will do all that I have commanded you . . . (*Shemot* 31:1–6)

Notice that the phrase "all manner of work" occurs twice. It first occurs as the tangible expression of the divine spirit of wisdom, understanding and knowledge with which he is endowed. It occurs again as a generic summary of the processes of weaving, metallurgy, stonework and carpentry. In other words, "all manner of work" describes a category of specific activities that are purposeful, creative, and transformative, that employ intelligence and ingenuity to refine matter and to shape it. In the original Hebrew text, "all manner of work" is כל מלאכה! The operational definition of *melakha* for which we have been searching is thus indicated by the paradigm of Bezalel. As a gifted artisan and craftsman, as a creator whose work is a reflection of God's own work, Bezalel does not perform *avoda* but rather *melakha*.

To reformulate our analysis, Shabbat commemorates God's cessation from the act of creating the universe. The Torah enjoins the curtailment of *melakha* as the commemoration of that fact. The labors of Bezalel in constructing the Mishkan capture the essence of the concept of *melakha*. We now appreciate that *melakha* is not a general and all-inclusive definition of labor, work and toil. Rather, it is a specific class of activities that are characterized by purposefulness, the exercise of intelligence and creativity, and a process of transformation that reshapes a coarse and crude material into a useful product.

It is indeed significant that the word "*avoda*" never occurs as a freestanding noun in any passage describing creation, Shabbat or the Mishkan. Conversely, of the approximately sixty times that the term "*melakha*" occurs in the Torah, more than half refer to its curtailment on Shabbat and the holidays, while the vast majority of other half occur in the context of the construction of the Mishkan. The conclusion is therefore inescapable: when the Torah forbids the performance of *melakha* on Shabbat, it is ruling out those activities specifically associated with Bezalel's undertaking that recall God's own act of creation.

The Mishna in Tractate *Chagiga* 1:8 asserts:

> Release from vows hovers in the air and has no scriptural basis. The laws of the Shabbat, Festival offerings, and Temple trespass are like mountains suspended by a hair, because *their respective texts are meager and their laws are numerous*. Torts, rules of the Temple service, laws of *Tuma* and *Tahara* and laws of forbidden relations have much scriptural basis for support. All, however, are essentials of the Torah.

The observation of this Mishna is the same one that has puzzled many of us. The laws of Shabbat observance are numerous, detailed and complex. Very few of these forbidden activities are explicitly spelled out in the text of the Torah, and vague, ambiguous references to "you shall not do any work" do not seem adequate to explain the overwhelming edifice of Shabbat practice. Like proverbial mountains hanging by a hair, the laws of the Shabbat appear to some to be a fanciful and not terribly convincing invention of the Rabbis! But, suggests the Mishna, by what a hair those mountains hang! By stating that "you shall not do any *melakha*" while indicating from the context of creation on the one hand, and Bezalel and the Mishkan on the other, exactly what *melakha* entails, the carefully worded text of the Torah need not state any more. It becomes abundantly clear to anyone who critically and carefully studies the text, as our Sages most eminently did, that *melakha* has little or nothing to do with physical exertion, and everything to do with human creativity that shapes and reshapes physical matter.

The Thirty-nine Avot Melachot

The text of our Parasha states:

> Moshe assembled the entire people of Israel and said to them: "*These are the things* that God has commanded to be done. For six days you may do work (*melakha*) but the seventh day shall be a holy Shabbat to God, whoever does work (*melakha*) on it shall be put to death. Do not kindle a fire in your habitations on the Shabbat." Moshe said to the entire people of Israel: "This is the thing that God has commanded. Collect from among yourselves an offering to God, all those of generous heart shall bring the offering to God, of gold, silver and bronze . . . all those who are wise-hearted among you shall come forth to make all the things which God has commanded, namely the Mishkan . . . and the ark . . ." (*Shemot* 35:1–20)

Just as Parashat Ki Tisa connected the designation of gifted Bezalel with the observance of the Shabbat, Parashat VaYakhel also contains the very same critical juxtaposition in reverse order. Shabbat observance and the building of the Mishkan are twice joined in context because they are also joined in concept. According to ancient and well-founded tradition, there are thirty-nine main categories of activities that delineate the types of work forbidden on the Shabbat. The conceptual source for these thirty-nine is none other then the main activities associated with the building of the Mishkan. As Rabbi Yehuda HaNasi states in the Mechilta de R. Yishmael Parashat VaYakhel: "*These are the things* refers to the thirty-nine main categories of forbidden Shabbat activities that Moshe told the people orally." Rabbi Yehuda understands that embedded in the connection between Shabbat and the building of the Mishkan is the definition of *melakha* for which we have been searching. The somewhat different Talmudic formulation states:

> The thirty-nine categories of forbidden labor recorded in the Mishna relate to the work of the Mishkan . . . one is only liable for an activity that was similarly performed in the Mishkan. They planted . . . and harvested (the flora that furnished the vegetable dyes used in the coloring of some of the materials – Rashi ad loc), you shall not do so, etc . . . (TB *Shabbat* 49b)

Consider these thirty-nine activities as they are listed in the 7th chapter of Mishna *Shabbat*:

1. Plowing
2. Sowing
3. Harvesting
4. Sheaf making
5. Threshing
6. Winnowing
7. Selecting
8. Sifting
9. Grinding
10. Kneading
11. Baking
12. Sheep shearing
13. Bleaching
14. Combing raw materials
15. Dying
16. Spinning
17. Warping
18. Constructing two heddles
19. Weaving two threads
20. Separating into threads
21. Tying a knot
22. Untying a knot
23. Sewing
24. Tearing
25. Trapping/hunting
26. Slaughtering
27. Skinning
28. Tanning
29. Scraping pelts
30. Marking out
31. Cutting to shape
32. Writing
33. Erasing
34. Building
35. Demolishing
36. Kindling fire
37. Extinguishing fire
38. Finishing touches of a product
39. Carrying from public to private domain or within the public

While it is difficult to fully comprehend the parameters of some of these activities based upon this concise list, it is nonetheless possible to organize the thirty-nine things into a series of broader groupings. The first category consists of numbers 1–11, and clearly relates to the practice of *agriculture*, spelling out all of the activities necessary to wring forth "bread from the earth." Category two, numbers 12–24, describes the processes involved in fashioning *textiles*. The third group, consisting of numbers 25–31, describes the control and judicious use of *animals*. The fourth group, 32–33, concerns *writing*, and the fifth group of 34–35, concerns *building*. The sixth group of activities 36–37 relates to *fire*, and the final two groups of 38 and 39 are the unrelated actions of *completion* and *carrying*.

Evaluating these categories from an anthropological and social historical perspective reveals a remarkable common denominator. Each one of them represents a *revolution in human development*! Agriculture ushered in the age of independence from a nomadic way of life, and freed early man from the time-consuming and wearisome task of gathering food for survival. The making of textiles, the remarkable conversion of coarse fibers into materials, provided clothing for warmth as well as many other useful products. The use of animals to give us food for sustenance and hides for survival was another important break with more primitive living, and inaugurated a relationship with the other species from which we still benefit. Writing was one of humanity's greatest inventions, allowing knowledge and information to be transmitted around the world and across the generations. The dawn of recorded history is a function of writing. Human buildings are unlike any shelter constructed by other species, for they are complex manipulations of materials and forms. The construction of a free-standing shelter was a development that allowed humanity to leave the darkness of the cave. Fire was perhaps mankind's greatest invention, for so many other human activities depend upon the ability to harness this force. Through the use of fire, we have transformed our lives and the world around us. The category of completion includes the various processes that human beings employ in their production of diverse objects. The specialization of labor that is a hallmark of civilization is based upon this category. Finally, the act of carrying from the private to the public domain and visa versa constitutes the foundation of commerce. Commerce is about the transfer of goods and materials, and is a direct function of their transportation between the private and public domain. Complex societies are founded upon elaborate networks of commercial traffic that are fundamentally expressions of "carrying."

Humanity and the Rest of Creation

It is now apparent that the creative enterprise contained in the Torah's description of Bezalel's work is echoed and amplified in the traditional list of thirty-nine אבות מלאכות or "major categories of forbidden labors." Precisely those acts that are necessary to build the Mishkan are expressions of the human creativity that alters nature and reshapes it to fit an anthropomorphic mold. Let us proceed one step further. The thirty-nine categories not only trace the story of human progress and the ongoing ability of humanity to modify their surroundings, but also encapsulate the essential distinction between humanity and the rest of creation. No other species on this planet engages in the vast majority of these thirty-nine pursuits. Those that do activities resembling planting, cutting or building do so at a level of complexity that is limited, and perform within circumscribed limits that are a direct function of their particular instinctive capabilities. The leaf-cutter ant may do "farming," but is incapable of growing anything other than mushrooms. The common spider may spin an orb of astounding strength and ethereal beauty, but is not capable of building anything else. Only the human being has the ability to develop complex solutions that address such an astoundingly wide array of situations.

The forbidden *melakhot* therefore speak of what makes us uniquely human, the aspects of our constitution that separate us from the other species. The *melakhot* address the creative spark in man, which is part and parcel of what we variously refer to as "intelligence," "consciousness," "freedom of choice," "awareness of God" or "the soul." All of these intangible spiritual qualities describe facets of the human personality that at its core is a reflection of "the divine image" in which we were created. But when we employ the power of this divine image to materially transform the world, then we have done *melakha*. In other words, *melakha* does not describe those activities that all creatures engage in. Every animal on this planet performs at sundry times activities that are required for its physical survival. By and large, these activities involve physical exertion, toil and drudgery. But in so doing they are not performing *melakha*. *Melakha* is a special type of activity that only human beings can perform. To phrase the matter in Halachic terms, if one wishes one may lift heavy furniture all day long to the point of physical exhaustion and not be in direct violation of Shabbat, but to effortlessly strike a match or nonchalantly pick a flower is to brazenly abrogate "you shall not do any *melakha*."

Surely it is not an accident that Bezalel's name means literally "in the shadow of the divine" or אֵ־ל – בְּצַל. In the same way that an object casts a shadow that resembles it and describes it but does not quite equal it, Bezalel employs his divine image to create and to transform, just like his creator. Only almighty God is capable of ultimate *melakha*, fashioning matter *ex nihilo*; Bezalel emulates God by using his intelligence to shape and to transform the material world around him. Bezalel, filled with "the spirit of the Lord" (*Shemot* 31:3) and about to embark on the project of building the Mishkan, is like God at the dawn of creation when the "spirit of the Lord hovered upon the face of the waters" (*Breisheet* 1:2). *Melakha*, then, is a higher activity, an expression of our unique essence and capacity. *Melakha* and *malakh* (מלאך – angel) derive from the same root.

The Essence of Shabbat

What then is the purpose of Shabbat? Why does God demand of His people that one day in seven they cease from purposeful, deliberate, creative pursuits that effect a physical change in the world? For a generation living at the cusp of apocalypse the answer has never been more clear. God has endowed us with abilities and talents that allow us to occupy the most exalted place in the scheme of things. As creators, we alone can bend the world to suit our purposes. As creators, we alone can transform nature to meet our goals. But precisely because we are blessed with unrivalled potential, we are in great danger of succumbing to the erroneous and destructive belief that we are gods in our own right. When our creativity knows no limits, when it is allowed to freely act without constraint, when we refuse to acknowledge the God who demands responsible conduct, the result is not constructive creation but rather the atomic bomb. As perhaps no previous generation has ever understood so well, we are realizing with frightening urgency that human creativity can very easily destroy the world and turn our existence into a living hell. The institution of the Shabbat, when correctly understood and sincerely appreciated, represents the dream that a better world can yet be fashioned by human hands. The key to that elusive possibility remains the acknowledgement that, notwithstanding our unrivalled accomplishments in extending our reach to the edges of the solar system and beyond, we are still the work of a creator who not only fashioned the cosmos but also gave us the precious gift of self-mastery.

FOR FURTHER STUDY:

(1) It is very significant that during the entire experience of slavery and bondage in Egypt, the people of Israel are *never* described as performing *melakha* but rather as being oppressed with *avoda*: "The Egyptians enslaved (ויעבידו) the people of Israel with backbreaking labor. They embittered their lives with hard work (עבודה), with clay and brick and all manner of work (עבודה) in the field. All of their work (עבודתם) was imposed with harsh rigor" (*Shemot* 1:13–14). *Avoda* is the work of the slave, but *melakha* is the creative spark of the free human personality. *Avoda* is performed by the *eved* (slave), but *melakha* is etymologically related to *malakh* (angel or messenger). The great injustice of slavery is that it dehumanizes people and reduces them to beasts of burden, for the animal does *avoda* but never independently does *melakha*.

(2) In Hebrew, there is no verb conjugation for the root מלאך as there is for עבד. Rather we say לעשות מלאכה which means "to do" or "to make" or "to fashion" *melakha*, and this is an indication that *melakha* is a more refined pursuit.

(3) When electricity first became widely available at the turn of the 20th century, there was a lively discussion and debate among the Halakhic decisors as to whether use of this new dynamic force was a violation of Shabbat law or not. Differences of opinion existed concerning the *melakha*, if any, that was performed by utilizing electricity. Was it a form of completion (the closing of the electric circuit), a variation of fire (the electric spark or the incandescent filament), or the idea of bringing something new into existence? In the end, the weight of opinion ruled that its use on Shabbat was forbidden. From a conceptual standpoint, this decision was undoubtedly the right one, for no other force in the modern world transforms our lives as much. Electricity is the engine that drives every industry, powers every transformative process, and continues to shape and reshape nature like no other. The harnessing of the electric spark was as significant for the modern age as was the discovery of fire for the ancients. How senseless to imagine that simply because turning on a light switch is effortless it therefore cannot be characterized as "work"! In fact, as our earlier discussion indicates, activating a light is the essence of what *melakha* is about.

PEKUDEI

The Bronze Altar

Exodus 38:21-40:38

THE LATTER half of Sefer Shemot concerns a single topic: the construction of the Mishkan or Tabernacle. Stretching over five lengthy *parashiyot*, the story of the Mishkan's fabrication is divided into two main sections. The first, comprising the *parashiyot* of Teruma (25:1–27:19) and Tetzave (27:20–30:10), is phrased in the imperative and relates God's commands to Moshe. The second, composed of *parashiyot* VaYakhel (35:1–38:20) and Pekudei (38:21–40:38), describes the fulfillment of those detailed provisions by the artisans and the people of Israel. Unusually, there is almost perfect symmetry between the two sections, so that all of the descriptions concerning the vessels, building elements and priestly garments related at the outset as part of the divine directives are repeated almost verbatim in the narratives of implementation.

In the center is the Parasha of Ki Tisa (30:11–34:35) that jarringly bifurcates the otherwise perfectly balanced account, and although that Parasha begins with topics that are germane to the Mishkan undertaking (30:11–31:17), its focus quickly shifts to the debacle of the golden calf and the smashing of the tablets of the Decalogue. The placement of the golden calf passage precisely at the pivot point between the sections is intended to sound a note of caution: the noble desire to provide transcendent God with a physical abode, a tangible location where we might encounter and worship Him, is one that is fraught with real danger. How easily can concrete symbols for profound truths become garish and crude objects of shallow veneration! How quickly can the worship of God be supplanted by the worship of the self, in the form of a golden calf!

The Bronze Altar and Its Placement

In an attempt to encapsulate some of the most salient ideas associated with the Mishkan, we will consider the bronze altar or מזבח הנחושת that is mentioned towards the end of Parashat Pekudei and then figures so prominently in the narratives of Sefer VaYikra that immediately follow. This large, square bronze platform, dominating the outer courtyard that surrounded the Mishkan, was the location where the animal sacrifices took place. Its lengthy ramp extended southwards towards the linen curtains that marked the perimeter of the space. Upon its fiery top, the daily communal sacrifice burned morning and evening on behalf of all of the people of Israel, while during the interval the personal sacrifices of individuals – burnt offerings, guilt offerings, sin offerings, and thanksgiving offerings – were presented. On Shabbat, new moon, or holidays, additional communal sacrifices were offered. In fact, the Rabbis relate that for the altar to be idle at all was inauspicious; if there were no sacrifices that were slated to be brought, then special communal offerings would be presented so that the bronze altar would never be inactive (Mishna *Shekalim* 4:4; TB *Succah* 56a).

In contrast to the animal sacrifices, the services of the incense, showbread and kindling of the lights associated with the golden altar, table and menorah respectively, were performed in the building proper, in the space known as the קודש. This holy precinct was separated from the inner sanctum housing the ark of the covenant by a richly-embroidered dividing curtain, and the activities associated with this sheltered space were of a more sanctified ritual value than those executed in the exterior, uncovered courtyard. Although other vessels might be holier, no other vessel could match the bronze altar either in size or unceasing operation.

The bronze altar was first introduced by the Torah in Parashat Teruma:

> You shall fashion the altar out of acacia wood, it shall be five cubits in length and five cubits in width, so that the altar shall be square, and three cubits in height. You shall fashion its projections on its four corners so that they are part of it, and you shall cover it with bronze. You shall prepare its shovels to clear its ashes, its sweepers and its basins, its forks and its firepans, all of its vessels shall be fashioned out of bronze. You shall make for it a screen after the manner of a bronze network, and you shall make four rings upon that network at its extremities. You shall place it below the molding of the altar, so that the network extends to half of its height. You shall prepare staves for the altar, staves of acacia wood, and you shall cover them with bronze. The staves shall be brought into its rings, so that the staves shall be on both sides of the altar when it is borne. You shall fashion it hollow out of boards, as it was shown to you upon the mountain, so shall you do. (*Shemot* 27:1–8)

The altar is composed of a number of discrete elements. First there is the frame itself, made out of boards of acacia wood covered with bronze overlay. Then there are the four curious projections on each of the four corners, and the screen-like ornamental network that divides the altar's height into two. This division was important ritually: certain sacrifices had their blood placed above it while others had the blood thrown below. Finally, there are the appurtenances such as the shovels and sweepers to remove the ash, the basins to receive the blood, the forks to turn the sacrificial meats and the firepans to collect the glowing coals.

But most remarkable about the altar is the last provision, mentioned at the conclusion of the section: "You shall fashion it hollow out of boards, as it was shown to you upon the mountain, so shall you do" (27:8). While we may have surmised that the bronze boards of the altar framed it on all sides as well as on top, so that the fire was kindled upon the bronze covering and there the sacrifices were consumed by the flames, it actually emerges that the altar had no top at all, save for the projections on each of the four corners! Instead, the bronze boards enclosed the sides of the altar while the top was left wide open. How then were the sacrifices presented upon it? In this connection, Rashi quotes an early Rabbinic tradition insisting that: "They would fill its hollowness with earth when the people would encamp . . ." (commentary to 27:5).

Filled with Earth

Rashi's interpretation that the overlaid acacia boards were nothing more than a frame for the real altar that consisted of earth is echoed by the other classical commentaries. As the Rashbam states: "When they would encamp, then they would fill it with earth and sacrifice upon it . . ." (commentary to 27:8). The Seforno on the same verse offers a more detailed formulation: the altar was like "a box with neither a bottom nor a top . . . for they would fill its cavity with earth at the time of their encampment and upon that very earth 'the perpetual fire would be kindled'" (*VaYikra* 6:6). As the Seforno describes it, the "bronze altar" was really just a casing without top or bottom, a sort of mold placed directly upon the ground into which earth would then be poured. All of these interpretations obviate an otherwise serious difficulty: what prevented the overlaid wooden top from becoming scorched by the searing sacrificial flames? It emerges from this discussion that the flames were never in contact with anything except the sacrifice and the earth itself.

In reconstructing the altar's accurate form, the commentaries direct us to another context entirely – the aftermath of the Revelation at Sinai:

> God said to Moshe: Thus shall you say to the people of Israel – you saw that I addressed you from the heavens. You shall not fashion besides Me gods of silver or gods of gold, do not make them for yourselves. *You shall fashion for Me an altar of earth* and you shall sacrifice upon it your burnt offerings and your peace offerings, your sheep and your cattle, for at whatever place that I shall cause My name to be mentioned, there shall I come to you and bless you. And if you fashion for Me an altar of stones, then you shall not build it out of hewn stones, for by lifting up your sword upon it you have defiled it. You shall not ascend to My altar by stairs, so that your nakedness not be uncovered upon it. (*Shemot* 20:18–22)

Here, the Torah enjoins the construction of an earthen or stone altar. Reconciling this description with the "hollow overlaid boards" of Parashat Teruma yields the bronze altar of the commentaries. But why is it that of all of the vessels of the Mishkan, only the bronze altar was organically attached to the earth? What could be the significance of a sacrificial service that was performed upon a summit of dust, so that no contrivance intervened between the consuming fire above and the hallowed ground of the courtyard below?

Hierarchy and Intrinsic Worth

The strict hierarchy that informs the entire structure and organization of the Mishkan, expressed in terms of spaces, materials and utility, argues for a secondary status for the sacrificial service performed upon the bronze altar. The most sanctified spaces of the Mishkan complex were those associated with the building proper – the Holy of Holies and the Holy – and not the space of the exterior courtyard. The most precious materials – the gold and silver, the sky blue, purple and crimson – were utilized in the fashioning of the vessels and curtains for the interior spaces of the building, while the more mundane bronze and simple white linen were reserved for the external altar and for the curtains that surrounded the courtyard. The most exalted and ethereal services – the offering of the incense, the kindling of the lights and the presentation of the loaves – were performed in the Tabernacle itself, while the exterior courtyard was reserved for the service of the animal sacrifices.

All of these distinctions provide circumstantial evidence for Maimonides' controversial claim that animal sacrifice at the Mishkan was a divine concession rather than an ideal, a compromise with the primitive forms of worship that were then current among all peoples of the world. As Maimonides explains in his Guide to the Perplexed (3:32), service of the gods through sacrifice was familiar to the ancient Israelites through their contact with other nations, and not easily surrendered by them in favor of more "advanced" forms of worship such as prayer or meditation. Maimonides explains that according to the Torah, sacrifices were to be performed only at the Mishkan and only under the watchful gaze of the stern priests, in order to introduce strict constraints on this mode of worship. Israel was thus to be weaned from idolatry incrementally.

While Maimonides does not develop the theory further, his approach would shed light on the distinctions that we noted earlier: The real service that spoke of worshipping God with the heart and with the mind would be performed in the sheltered space of the Mishkan proper where the ignorant masses dared not tread. Here the sweet-smelling incense ascended from the miniature golden altar like a wispy and delicate prayer, the kindling of the flames upon the menorah's seven branches proclaimed God as the source of all wisdom, and the twelve heavy loaves placed upon the golden table asserted that "not by bread alone does man live but by all of the words of God . . ." (*Devarim* 8:3). Beyond the richly embroidered entrance curtain that shielded these devotions from ignorant eyes, the Israelite throngs would observe the animal sacrifices, filling the outer courtyard with their excited chatter.

But we need not take our cue from Maimonides in his Guide, especially since the same Maimonides in his code argues that the sacrificial service has an intrinsic albeit suprarational value (see his *Mishneh Torah*, Laws of Trespass 8:8). Therefore, instead of regarding the service of the bronze altar as inferior to the service performed within the building proper, so that we view the former as an allowance for the immature masses while the latter speaks to the more refined and select devotees, we may instead regard both services as necessary and intertwined elements of the same spiritual progression. The matter of serving God is a process rather than an event; it is composed of a series of successive steps of approach calculated to culminate in an authentic encounter with the divine. And while the ultimate objective of the supplicant is intimate and unfiltered communion (symbolized by the entry of the High Priest into the Holy of Holies on the Day of Atonement), the architectural ordering of the Mishkan implies that there is much work to be done along the way. There are no shortcuts that could allow a person to sidestep the preliminary preparations. It is as if the Mishkan was organized like a series of concentric circles, each one of which represented a higher level of spiritual sensitivity. The service of the bronze altar was therefore not a Maimonidean diversion, but rather the critical first step in the process of approach and the prerequisite for everything that followed. But what, exactly, is the content of this first step? In what way does the service of the bronze altar launch us upon an encounter with the divine?

Understanding the Sacrificial Service

Consider the remarkable commentary of the Ibn Ezra, as amplified and expanded upon by the Ramban. In his rejection of Maimonides' rationale for the sacrifices, the Ramban states:

> . . . It is preferable to accept that the reason for the sacrifices relates to the fact that all human deeds are accomplished through the exercise of thought, speech and action. Thus, God commands that when a person transgresses and offers a sacrifice

> to atone, that he must place his hands upon it as an expression of the action, confess with words as an expression of the speech and burn in the fire the innards and the kidneys that are the vehicles of one's thoughts and desires. The limbs of the animal are expressions of the person's arms and legs that do all of his bidding, and the blood sprinkled upon the altar is an expression of the supplicant's own lifeblood. Thus, a person should ponder, having performed this service, that he transgressed the will of his God with his body and with his soul and ought to accordingly suffer a similar fate, if not for the compassion of the creator that accepted a substitute in his place – a soul for a soul and sacrificial limbs of the animal in place of his own! The portions for the priests are so that these teachers of the Torah are preserved through his efforts so that they might pray on his behalf . . . (commentary to *Va-Yikra* 1:9, middle section)

Here, the Ramban introduces the provocative idea of *substitution* to explain the matter of the sacrificial service. Acknowledging the obvious argument that an absolute and incorporeal God has no need for physical sustenance, the Ramban avers that the purpose of sacrifice relates more to the needs of the devotee rather than to those of the divine. Slaughtering the animal, dismembering its limbs, sprinkling its blood upon the altar and offering the flesh upon the fire, the supplicant is supposed to feel the gravity of his misdeeds, as if he were deserving of a similar, sorry end were it not for divine compassion. While the Ramban's explanation might strike us as somewhat grotesque, his main point is well taken: the sacrificial cult is calculated to unleash a spiritual transformation of the supplicant and not simply to assuage his guilty conscience.

We can temper the Ramban's theory by suggesting that rather than sacrifices starkly speaking of direct and unqualified substitution, they more symbolically speak of *selective personification*. In other words, it is not the hapless devotee that is being metaphorically consumed by the flames for his gross misdeeds but rather *his animal nature*. The sacrifice of the animal upon the altar is really a way of indicating that connection with God can be accomplished only if a person is willing to forego his animalistic passions and submit his coarser character traits to the refining flames. The baser instincts – the selfishness, the greed, the lust and the hubris – that we gleefully exercise to our spiritual detriment, must be overcome if we are to meaningfully acknowledge and revere God. A man enslaved to his base passions so that he is inconsiderate of his fellow's body or things, cannot be ushered into His awesome presence. And so these strivings must be harnessed and directed, the baser matter incinerated so that the supplicant might yet advance.

Connecting the Strands: Earth and Animals

Thus we return to the altar of earth, for the earth is symbolic of our material selves, the bodies of flesh that we inhabit and must make holy. Here the earth is raised up high in its square shining frame, held in check as it were by the structure of divine laws, as a powerful expression of our desire to consecrate the mundane and soar heavenwards to God. While we are undoubtedly creatures of the earth, fashioned by the creator out of its dust (*Breisheet* 2:7), still we seek to transcend, to rise above the stifling physicality that holds us back. Therefore the bronze altar is left uncovered so that the animal sacrifices that speak of overcoming coarse desire take place upon the heaped up earth. While this earth betrays our terrestrial origins it also directs us heavenwards towards higher accomplishment.

While we are, like all other creatures, of this world, we are also, unlike any of them, capable of surpassing its limitations to encounter God. The animal self is offered to Him, the base passions are overcome, and the lowly earth from which we were fashioned is exalted.

FOR FURTHER STUDY:

(1) According to Maimonides' immortal formulation, the Sages have a tradition that:

> The location of the altar must be very precise, and can never be moved. As the verse states: "This shall be the altar of burnt offering for Israel" (*Divrei HaYamim* 1:22:1). At the very location of the Temple, the binding of Yitzchak had taken place (centuries before), for God had commanded Avraham to "go to the land of Moriah, to offer Yitzchak upon one of the mountains that I will show you" (*Breisheet* 22:2). And in the Book of Divrei HaYamim (2:3:1) it states that "Shelomo commenced the building of God's House at Jerusalem on Mount Moriah where God had appeared to David his father, at the place that David had prepared . . ."
>
> It is a well-established tradition that the place where David and Shelomo erected the altar at the threshing floor of Ornah the Yevusi was the very place where Avraham had prepared his altar upon which to sacrifice Yitzchak. It is the same place where Noach had built an altar when he disembarked from the ark, and the same location where Kayin and Hevel had sacrificed to God. *The first man, Adam, offered sacrifice there after he had been created, and in fact was created from earth drawn from that very place. As the Sages put it: "Man was fashioned from the place of his atonement."* (Book of Service, Laws of the Temple 2:1–2)

In this rendering, Maimonides connects the location of the altar at the Temple in Jerusalem to a series of events in biblical history. If we rely exclusively upon textual evidence, however, only the tradition linking the binding of Yitzchak with the building of the Temple is unassailable (see *Divrei HaYamim* 2:3:1 and *Breisheet* 22:14), for the Torah does not explicitly record Adam's presumed sacrifice, nor does it state the location of Kayin and Hevel's altar. In fact, the Torah itself seems to argue against Noach offering sacrifice at the site of future Jerusalem, for the text makes it clear that the ark landed at Mount Ararat in eastern Turkey!

But Maimonides, of course, is teaching something more profound than historical or geographical facts. For him, the altar at the Temple in Jerusalem expresses the universal human aspiration for communion with God. By heaping up the mundane earth to fashion an altar reaching for the sky and by offering upon its summit the creatures that speak of our baser nature, these sensitive souls articulated their intense longing for something higher, for the source of all being who transcends the terrestrial plane and its profane pursuits.

Concluding his remarks, Maimonides says in the name of the Sages that this very altar of dust of which we speak was the raw material from which humanity was first formed: *"Man was fashioned from the place of his atonement."* With this, he reminds us that there exists a perfect affinity between the fundamental nature of the human being and the innate yearning to sanctify that nature through an intense encounter with God. Maimonides' tradition thus corresponds perfectly to the deep symbolism that informs the altar of heaped-up dust and the animals that are raised up heavenwards upon it.

VAYIKRA

Studying the Laws of the Sacrifices

Leviticus 1:1–5:26

SEFER VAYIKRA is without doubt the least appreciated book of the Chumash. Many of us are stirred by the inspiring narratives of the patriarchs and matriarchs, marveling at their strength of spirit in overcoming all manner of adversity while intrigued by their personal and familial struggles that seem to us so painfully familiar. We therefore readily identify with Sefer Breisheet.

Most of us also feel connected to the story of the oppression in Egypt and the Exodus, finding inspiration in the fact that the birth of the Israelite nation was precipitated by the first human rights struggle in recorded history. The oppressive Pharaoh, vile, self-serving and vain, is a fitting archetype for all of the modern-day despots and dictators who enthusiastically follow in his footsteps. More than three millennia after the god-king's downfall at the hands of the God of Israel, we can still hear His thundering demands that we take an active role in constructing a better and more just world.

As for Sefer BeMidbar, its concerns with structure and order, censuses of tribes and their judicious arrangement, remind us that in pursuit of Godliness organization matters. As a counterpoint, its awesome narratives about journey and passage, tracing the perilous route from the arid wastelands of the Sinai to the Promised Land of milk and honey, provide us with much material for reflection. There is more than geography in that journey; there is the precious process of self-transformation. What thoughtful soul could not but be moved?

Sefer Devarim, the repetition of the Torah's instruction and Moshe's recounting of Israel's trials and triumphs, secures its place in our hearts on its literary merits alone. In soaring language approaching the sublime, the words weave an intricate tapestry – now exhorting, now cautioning and now inspiring, but never tedious or irrelevant. Episodes are re-examined through the lens of hindsight, judgment is intensely passed on earlier indiscretions, and Moshe firmly urges the people of Israel to remain true to their calling.

Relating to Sefer VaYikra

But Sefer VaYikra is something else entirely. Its single-minded fixations with cult and custom, sacrifices and ceremonial, ritual defilement and the notion of the holy, all strike us as old-fashioned and atavistic, vestiges of an archaic past thankfully left behind in the wake of the Temple's destruction almost two thousand years ago. We can scarcely begin to relate to its painstaking and formalized descriptions of sacrificial modes of worship or else its scrupulous attention to disqualifying conditions that make entry into the Mishkan forbidden. If these contrivances are the media for expressing devotion to God, then much of Sefer VaYikra appears to teeter precariously on the brink of primitiveness and irrelevancy!

But for the Rabbis, surprisingly enough, Sefer VaYikra was a venerated text and a thing of adoration. According to an ancient practice still observed in some communities, a small child's first tender educational experiences were grounded in this *Chumash*: "Says the Holy One blessed be He: Let the pure ones [the children] come and occupy themselves with purity [the contents of Sefer VaYikra]!" (quoted in commentary of Siftei Kohen to Shulchan Aruch 245:8). A Jew's first practical instruction in Torah and *mitzvot*, the initial development of his textual and analytical skills in study and his earliest and most vivid memories of stories and events were all derived from his primary study of Sefer VaYikra. How shocking, some of us may think, that one would intentionally expose (and before all else!) innocent and impressionable minds to such disturbing subject matter.

According to a statement in the Midrash that complements the above custom, Sefer VaYikra was regarded as a particularly powerful source of enlightenment:

> Said Rabbi Shimon: There are five mentions of "light" [in the passage of *Breisheet* 1:1–5] corresponding to the five books of the *Chumash*. "God said: Let there be light" parallels Sefer Breisheet, for with that book God occupied Himself and then created the world. "And there was light" matches Sefer Shemot, for in its narratives the people of Israel went forth from great darkness [slavery in Egypt] to light. *"God saw the light that it was good" is analogous to Sefer VaYikra, for it is full of so many mitzvot.* "God separated between the light and the darkness" refers to Sefer BeMidbar, for in that book a division was drawn between those that left the land of Egypt and those that entered the new land. "Gods called the light – day" relates to Sefer Devarim, for it too is full of so many *mitzvot* . . . (Breisheet Rabbah 3:5)

For Rabbi Shimon, the unique fixation of Sefer VaYikra with ritual or ceremonial injunctions was itself the source of its metaphorical light. The other books of the Torah certainly had their messages of illumination, whether these related to meaning, redemption, or destiny. But for the Rabbis, what made Sefer VaYikra exceptional, its inherent goodness, was its single-minded focus upon ceremonial and cultic laws and its numerous ordinances concerning holiness. By simple computation, there are about 247 *mitzvot* that are mentioned in Sefer VaYikra, making it the most commandment-intensive *Chumash* by far, for it contains almost half of the Torah's total number of 613 commandments. By comparison, Sefer Devarim – the other source of "intense light" in the Midrash of Rabbi Shimon above – contains 200 *mitzvot*, while Sefer Shemot, running a distant third, has but 111. Completing the picture, Sefer BeMidbar contains 52 commands, and Sefer Breisheet has only 3!

In this connection, it should be noted that there are correspondingly few narrative sections in Sefer VaYikra at all. Unlike Breisheet that is entirely narrative, and Shemot that is primarily narrative with some laws that are introduced only against its narrative background, VaYikra is almost exclusively about injunctions. Its few narratives (if we may even employ the term here) only serve as introductions to more laws! Thus, for example, the tragic but exceedingly concise tale of the untimely death of two of Aharon's sons, those that offered "strange fire" at the dedication of the Mishkan (*VaYikra* 10:1–5), is immediately succeeded by a much lengthier passage spelling out the appropriate laws that are to be exercised by Aharon and the surviving brothers in the aftermath of the disaster (10:6–20). We would be hard pressed to provide another narrative section in all of Sefer VaYikra!

Sefer BeMidbar reverts back to the narrative model, for that book describes the physical peregrinations and associated spiritual challenges of the people of Israel as they journeyed from Egypt towards the land of Canaan. And while it is true that Sefer Devarim also contains much legislative material and a dearth of narrative, such is to be expected, for at its very outset Moshe introduces the book as the repetition of the Torah. Nevertheless, insofar as Moshe's reminisces are concerned (and there are many in the book), there is decidedly more narrative in Sefer Devarim than there is in Sefer VaYikra. The correspondence is thus clear: more narrative indicates less *mitzvot*, more *mitzvot* mean less narrative, for the Torah's guiding message is effectively conveyed in two distinct but analogous ways – by the recounting of a story as well as by the proclamation of laws and ordinances.

After the Destruction

It stands to reason that as long as the Mishkan or Temple stood and the service was intact, the study of Sefer VaYikra focused upon practicalities. The "how to" of the sacrifices trumped the "why" because it addressed the more pressing needs of the devotee and his priestly agents. But with the cessation of the sacrificial service and the subsequent end of the related practices concerning *tuma* and *tahara* (ritual unfitness and fitness, respectively) so long ago, the Rabbis early on were forced to formulate alternative approaches to the matter. In consequence of the Roman conquest and the dissolution of the Jewish state, it was no longer possible to ascend with one's offering to the Temple at Jerusalem and to follow the ministrations of the Kohanim as they received it and presented it upon the altar. The holy house lay in ruins, its magnificent precincts turned to dust and ashes, its beloved altar stones overthrown and shattered. Nothing remained of God's house but a persistent memory of its grand dimensions and the echo of the Kohanim's footsteps, much of it eventually committed to writing and incorporated into various tractates of the Mishna.

Thus it was that the text took the place of the Holy precincts, the inscribed words became the mode of worship, and recitation of rites was replaced by patient and thoughtful study. Remarkably, not only were the ancient traditions preserved in this fashion but they were given new meaning and immediacy as a result. Paradoxically, the sacrificial service could now be evaluated with greater clarity, for as long as the acts were ascendant, the thoughtful interpretation of those very acts was correspondingly less urgent. Who needed to understand the intellectual or spiritual profundity of a sin-offering as long as the selected animal could be impressively brought to the altar and transformed into wisps of smoke upon its fiery summit? What need was there to ponder the deeper meaning of corpse defilement when its provisions were lived and experienced as daily realities?

But when all of these things were suddenly taken away, wrenched from our bosom by cruel and arrogant overlords, there was nothing left for us to grasp but the Torah's eternal text and the recollection of the rites. No enemy could seize the holy words or else the thoughts that now took on supreme significance, for these intangible things required almost no material vehicles for their preservation or transmission. If need be, they could be preserved in the sanctuary of the human mind, committed to memory and recited by heart. With the painful lack of the physical Temple and the cessation of the sacrificial service, inspiration would have to be sought and found elsewhere. As the Rabbis poignantly put it:

> . . . Rabbi Yochanan says: For the Sages who are occupied with the laws of the Temple service, it is *as if* the Temple was rebuilt in their days. Resh Lakish remarked: "What is meant by the verse: 'This is the law (haTorah) for the burnt offering, the meal offering, the sin offering and the guilt offering, the dedication offering and the peace offering' (*Va Yikra* 7:37)? It indicates that whoever studies Torah, it is *as if* they have sacrificed the burnt offering, the meal offering, the sin offering and the guilt offering." Rava demurred. "If so," he said, "then the text should have said 'This is the law – the burnt offering, the meal offering, etc'" [omitting the preposition to imply equivalence]. "Rather," said Rava, "whosoever occupies himself with the study of the Torah has **no need** for the burnt offering, the meal offering or the guilt offering . . ." Said Rabbi Yitzchak: "What is meant by the verse: 'This is the law (haTorah) of the sin offering (6:18) . . . this is the law (haTorah) of the guilt offering (7:1) . . . etc?' Rather, whoever is occupied with the study of the sin offering, it is *as if* he has offered a sin offering; and whoever is occupied with the study of the guilt offering, it is *as if* he has offered a guilt offering"! (TB *Menachot* 110a)

The above selection from the Rabbis indicates a lack of consensus. The 3rd century CE Eretz Yisrael sage Rabbi Yochanan opens the discussion by addressing the new reality. He suggests that even in the absence of a Temple and a sacrificial service, it is still possible to experience something of their import by studying their associated laws. Rabbi Yitzchak, at the end of the selection, concurs, and applies the principle specifically to the role of the sacrifices in securing atonement. How could one make amends for the commission of indiscretions that would, in Temple times, have necessitated the presentation of a particular offering? The answer is that by undertaking the **study** of those very matters, one may yet approximate the act of offering the sacrifice itself.

The intermediate view, that of Resh Lakish, is more novel, for he entirely eschews any need for direct substitution of the specific text for the defunct deed. Simply studying Torah, any Torah, can take the place of the departed cult and presumably accomplish the same objectives as offering the sacrifices at the Temple altar. And 4th century Babylonian sage Rava, of course, goes even further, for he claims that study of Torah does not take the place of the sacrifices but actually renders them completely unnecessary. One who studies Torah need not concern himself with matters of burnt offerings and guilt offerings, for real and meaningful atonement can be achieved by more cerebral and spiritual pursuits. The study of the Torah effects expiation.

We should not misconstrue the views of Resh Lakish and Rava to imply that one should dispense with any direct study of the Temple ritual itself and be content to be occupied with other more relevant areas of the Torah in their stead. Certainly the Rabbis of the Mishna and the Talmud, including Resh Lakish and Rava themselves, were anything but uninvolved in the profound study of the sacrificial cult and its myriad details. One full order of the Mishna is devoted to these laws, and numerous volumes of the Talmud painstakingly discuss them! Every aspect of the service is scrutinized, every feature examined. Sages far removed in time and space from Jerusalem's fabled hilltops and the Temple's broken ramparts discussed the laws of sacrifice with a zeal and an immediacy that easily puts us to shame. It therefore must be that Resh Lakish and Rava do not intend to downplay the study of the sacrifices or else to suggest that other texts are more important. Rather, they offer us a precious alternative, a consolation prize as it were, in light of the Temple's destruction and the tragic demise of its ceremonial: Study Torah and you will achieve what previously could be accomplished only by the cultic rites.

The veneration for the ancient ceremonies and the associated laws never waned in our tradition. Thus it was that the Shulchan Aruch, the 16th century code of law authored by Rav Yosef Karo, preserved the ardor for a shrine and for a service both long extinct. Commenting in the very first chapter of that monumental work, a chapter in which he sets down the daily devotions from the moment a person awakes in the morning, he relates:

> (3) It is appropriate for all those who are imbued with fear of heaven to be upset and anxious concerning the destruction of the Holy Temple. (4) It is better to recite less supplications but with sincerity and concentration than to recite more but bereft of these things. (5) It is a good practice to recite the chapters concerning the *Akeda*, the manna and the Ten Utterances, as well as the sections concerning the burnt offering, the meal offering, the peace offering, the sin offering and the guilt offering . . . (7) After reciting the section of the burnt offering, he should say: "May it be Your will that this recitation be accepted as if I had sacrificed a burnt offering . . ."

The Mishna's Textual Observation

But at the same time, the concrete absence of these things ironically affords us a rare opportunity. We may study these matters from an abstract and conceptual perspective (for nothing else of them remains) and extract meaningful insight from the effort. We may plumb the texts for implications that perhaps even eluded the ancient practitioners of these matters. We may thoughtfully reflect on the significance of details that survive only as cherished words and phrases. Only a profound meditation on the *texts* themselves could have produced the following Mishnaic observation:

> Concerning the animal offering, the verse refers to it as a "sweet-smelling savor" (*VaYikra* 1:9, 13). And so too concerning the bird offering, the verse refers to it as a "sweet-smelling savor" (1:17). And so too concerning the meal offering, the verse refers to it as a "sweet-smelling savor" (2:2, 9). This comes to teach you that whether one does much or else does little, the main thing is to focus one's heart towards heaven in sincerity. (TB *Menachot* 110a)

The narrow concern of the above Mishna may be in fact only the sacrificial service. It notes how the Torah refers to each type of voluntary sacrificial category – whether presented from animals, birds or grain – as a "sweet-smelling savor." Now presumably, the monetary value of one's sacrifice that is voluntarily presented is a direct function of one's financial means. The wealthy can afford to bring large or small cattle, the less endowed can only afford to present birds, and those suffering from poverty can ill afford anything but a simple offering of grain. But, remarkably, the Torah describes all of these sacrifices with the same potent phrase signifying divine favor and acceptance – they are all regarded as a sweet-smelling savor to God and are all received in love.

The Mishna therefore introduces a new idea behind which lurks not a concrete observation but rather a *textual* reflection: would we as devotees of God standing in the hushed precincts of His paved courtyards necessarily conclude that meager gifts are just as accepted as grand ones? Watching the busy ministrations of the priests at the altar, would we not reason that a more expensive presentation to God should in fact find greater favor in His eyes than one that is of a lesser grade? But when we can focus on the text rather than on the act, posits the Mishna, then the true value of a sacrifice can be gauged. And what emerges from the *study of the text* is that divine acceptance of the offering is not a function of financial assets but rather of sincerity. A small sacrifice brought with love and proper intent, when circumstances preclude the presentation of anything larger, is just as meaningful and just as beloved before God. And it surely follows that even a luxurious offering presented with self-serving insincerity cannot match the modest sacrifice of the earnest worshipper.

Afterwards, students of the text took the matter even further, for the Shulchan Aruch quoted above adapts the principle to prayer as well: "It is better to recite less supplications but with sincerity and concentration, than to recite more but bereft of these things." And the later authorities, coming full circle, then adapted it to the study of Torah itself! If one is burdened with cares and can therefore devote only a small amount of time to the study of Torah, but one carries out that study with diligence and concentration and with a spirit of sincerity, then that study is as precious in God's eyes as the accomplishments of the more gifted scholars who have time on their side (see Shulchan Aruch 1:4 and Mishna Berura note 12).

One could, of course, apply the principle even more broadly, for any endeavor undertaken with proper concentration and intent is more valuable than one undertaken without those motivations. And that is exactly the point of the discussion. The sacrificial service may strike some of us as outdated and bizarre, its overly detailed provisions anachronistic and strange, but to reject the study of these matters is misguided in the extreme. Our tradition remembers the Temple service fondly, and the experience of the divine associated with its hallowed spaces inspires us even today to seek God's presence in the temple of our hearts. To dismiss the sacrificial service is therefore to forfeit a treasured memory of closeness and communion; it is to give up a precious desire for atonement both personal as well as national; it is to fail to utter a silent prayer for the strength to overcome self-alienation and estrangement. But it is also to forego the opportunity for more profound enlightenment, for there is so much insight to be gleaned from even a small and seemingly superfluous textual anomaly. May all of our own efforts in the study of these matters be regarded also as a "sweet-smelling savor" to God, and may they be undertaken with sincerity and with love.

FOR FURTHER STUDY:

(1) Although often passed over in many prayer services, the daily morning liturgy preserves a lengthy preliminary section composed almost entirely of readings drawn from the *parashiyot* of sacrifice in Sefer VaYikra and from the associated Rabbinic texts. The purpose of the inclusion is threefold: (a) to recall the Temple and its ritual and to pray for its restoration; (b) to reinforce the tradition mentioned above that study of the sacrificial service is akin to offering sacrifices; and (c) to suggest that sacrifice and prayer are two sides of the same coin.

We often mistakenly think that prayer *took the place* of sacrifice but that is simply not true. Prayer and sacrifice are two independent and complementary modes for encountering God, and until the Temple's destruction, they were practiced concurrently. After the destruction of the Temple when sacrifices were suspended, prayer took on additional importance.

Significantly, the preliminary section ends with the following formula: "May it be your will, God our Lord and Lord of our ancestors, that the Temple be speedily rebuilt in our days, and grant us our share in Your Torah, and may we serve You with reverence as in days of old and former years."

TZAV

The Perpetual Fire

Leviticus 6:1-8:36

PARASHAT TZAV continues with a description of the sacrificial service that was introduced in Parashat VaYikra. In great detail, the Torah spells out the rituals of the burnt offering, meal offering, investiture offering, sin offering, guilt offering, and peace offering. Then, the Parasha spells out the unique service celebrated by Aharon and his sons at the Mishkan's dedication, the so-called מילואים or week-long inauguration that is completed in the next Parasha of Shemini.

> God spoke to Moshe saying: "Speak to Aharon and to his sons and say: This is the law of the burnt offering – it is the burnt offering that shall remain upon the hearth of the altar all night long until the morning, and the fire of the altar shall burn it. The Kohen shall don his linen garments and shall wear linen pants upon his flesh, and he shall remove the ashes of the burnt offering consumed by the fire of the altar, and he shall place them next to the altar. He shall then take off his garments and don other clothes, and shall remove the ashes to beyond the camp to a ritually fit place. The fire upon the altar shall burn upon it and shall not be extinguished, and the Kohen shall kindle wood upon it every morning. He shall then arrange the burnt offering upon it and burn the fat of the peace offerings upon it. A perpetual fire shall be kept burning upon the altar and must not be extinguished."

In Parashat VaYikra (1:1–17), the Torah first related how the burnt offering was to be slaughtered and skinned, how its blood was to be presented, and how its flesh and fat were to be placed upon the altar fire. Our passage now completes the account by describing how the offering is to be consumed by the altar fire, how the resulting ash is to be removed to a location next to the altar and from there to a site "outside of the camp." But when we consider the passage more carefully, we discover that it revolves in particular around the matter of the "fire." This fire is mentioned no less than four times in the passage and is the main subject. The verses do not describe the consumption of the burnt offering and the disposal of the ash in their own right, but rather as direct functions of the altar fire that figures so prominently in those processes. Highlighting the fire element in the above passage yields the following:

> ... this is the law of the burnt offering – it ... shall remain upon the hearth of the altar all night long until the morning, and the *fire of the altar* shall burn it. The Kohen ... shall remove the ashes of the burnt offering consumed by the *fire of the altar*, and he shall place them next to the altar ... The *fire upon the altar* shall burn

upon it and shall not be extinguished . . . *A perpetual fire* shall be kept burning upon the altar and must not be extinguished.

The Respective Formulations of Maimonides and the Ramban

The early Sages (TB *Yoma* 43b) disagreed concerning the fire of the altar and they anchored their respective opinions in the above texts. Some maintained that there were no less than four separate fires that burned simultaneously upon the sacrificial altar, as the above four fire references imply, while others only counted two. The prevailing (and compromise) view spoke of three discrete altar fires: one for the burning of the sacrifices, another for the provision of the coals needed to offer the incense and a third simply to provide a perpetual flame. Maimonides codifies the matter in his Book of the Temple Service, Laws of the Daily and Additional Sacrifices 2:4–5:

> Three hearths of fire were arranged upon the altar daily. The first was the great hearth upon which were offered the daily sacrifice as well as the other sacrifices. The second was next to it and was smaller, and burning coals were retrieved from it with a firepan in order to offer the daily incense. The third one had no other purpose except to provide a perpetual fire, as the verse states, "A perpetual fire shall be kept burning upon the altar and must not be extinguished." According to tradition, when the verse states "it shall remain upon the hearth of the altar all night long until the morning" it refers to the large hearth; when it says that "the fire of the altar shall burn it" it refers to the second hearth of the incense, and when it relates "the fire upon the altar shall burn and shall not be extinguished" it refers to the perpetual flame . . .

Significantly, the Talmudic tradition that spoke of three hearths and not one also maintained that there is a prohibition or a negative command concerning the flame of the altar: under no circumstances is it to be extinguished. This is learned from the fourth and final reference to the altar fire that occurs in our passage: "A perpetual fire shall be kept burning upon the altar and must not be extinguished." Maimonides states that "one who extinguishes the fire of the altar is liable to receive lashes. Even one who puts out only a single coal, and even one who removes the coal from the altar and then extinguishes it, is liable to receive lashes" (2:6). Rashi goes further, asserting that one who extinguishes the flame upon the altar has violated two negative commandments (commentary to *Va Yikra* 6:6)! The Ramban elaborates on the procedural aspects of the mitzvah in his comments to *Va Yikra* 6:2, emphasizing the need to maintain the flame:

> "The fire of the altar shall burn it" – this means that the fire should continue all of the night because it is a positive command for the Kohanim to place much wood on the altar during the day so that the fuel is not entirely consumed, lest the flames go out. In my opinion, when it states that "a perpetual fire shall be kept burning upon the altar and must not be extinguished" it means that the Kohanim are commanded to *preserve* the fire . . . they must be careful concerning this and arrange much wood so that the fire burns all day and all night. This command is then amplified by the prohibition that warns them that the flame must not be extinguished ever. For this reason, our Sages maintain that there was a second hearth just for providing a perpetual fire [and not for sacrifice].

It therefore emerges there is more to the altar fire than meets the eye. It must be kindled, generously fueled and preserved, and under no circumstances may it be extinguished. Day or night, rain or shine, it must burn brightly upon the altar's summit, even when no sacrifices are being consumed. The daily sacrifice is called in the text the קרבן תמיד (*Shemot* 29:38–46, et al.) or "perpetual sacrifice" because it was offered twice daily according to a rigid and repetitive ritual. The incense offering is referred to as קטורת תמיד (30:7–8) for the very same reason. But the fire of the altar that must burn continually surpasses both. What exactly might be the significance of the perpetual flame that was kept burning always?

Understanding the Perpetual Flame

The commentaries provide a number of possible explanations in place of the Torah's reticence on the matter. The Chizkuni champions a rational approach. He suggests that the perpetual flame is an expression of our great esteem for the service of God. We show our respect for that service by ensuring that the flame that feeds it is always burning. Quoting the early Rabbinic tradition that maintains that even during the journeys through the wilderness the flame of the altar was never entirely extinguished but rather placed in a vessel and shielded with a perforated cover of bronze, the Chizkuni says: "It is God's honor that His hearth should never be idle" (commentary to *VaYikra* 6:6). Like an eternal flame devotedly cared for to remind us of a loved one, or a lighthouse beacon faithfully lit to guide ships safely to shore, the fire of the altar is never extinguished. It is to be kindled daily upon the multiple hearths and at least a glowing remnant of it is to be kept alive at all times.

Many other commentaries, however, interpret the matter of the altar fire more symbolically. Typically, this means linking the theme of fire with the soul of man, with his intellect and with the life force that animates his every thought and deed. The formulation of the Sefer HaChinuch (Rabbi Aharon HaLevi, 14th century, Spain) is most compelling:

> By way of introduction: it is known to us and to every wise man that great miracles performed for human beings by the Lord in his goodness are always accomplished in a hidden manner. The things appear to unfold according to the laws of nature or close to them. Even concerning the splitting of the Sea of Reeds which was an incontrovertible miracle, it is written that "God caused a strong eastern wind to blow upon the sea all night, rendering the sea into dry land, so that the waters split" (*Shemot* 14:21) . . . For this reason, He commanded us to kindle a fire upon the altar in spite of the fact that the fire descends from heaven. All of this is to conceal the miracle . . .
>
> According to the straightforward interpretation, we might say that this matter is similar to what we explained concerning the showbread, namely that a person merits divine blessing in accordance with the acts that he does in conformity to his creator's will. Thus, blessing may be found in our mundane daily bread – our livelihood and sustenance – because of our attention to God's command concerning the showbread in the Holy precinct. By way of a parable, one could say that the blessing extends to its related things. Similarly, by attending daily to the command of the fire we may merit blessing in the matter of *the fire that is within us*. And what is this fire within if not the life force of the person . . . for by it a person is animate

> and active, and it therefore requires an additional measure of blessing . . . for in direct accordance with a person's deeds they receive their reckoning or else God's blessing rests upon them. (Mitzvah #132: "The Command to Kindle Fire upon the Altar Daily")

The Life Force and the Theme of Perpetuity

The Sefer HaChinuch begins by referencing an ancient tradition concerning the altar fire. After the completion of the inauguration sacrifices on the eighth day, the Torah relates that:

> A fire went forth from before God and consumed the burnt offering and the fats that were on the altar, and all of the people saw and cried out and fell upon their faces. (*Va Yikra* 9:24)

According to the Rabbis, this verse implied that really there was no need to kindle a flame upon the altar at all because the initial flame descended from the heavens! In spite of this, the Sefer HaChinuch maintains, the sons of Aharon were bidden to kindle it because we prefer to downplay God's miraculous involvement by increasing human initiative. In comments that constitute a powerful maxim for living, the Sefer HaChinuch argues that while God is fully capable of intervening in human affairs with supernatural effect, He rarely if ever does so. Rather, His involvement is veiled, concealed within the predictable and appearing to the detached observer to be nothing more than the routine unfolding of the laws of nature. Even our astonishment concerning an overt miracle such as the splitting of the Sea of Reeds is tempered when we take note of the fact that the Torah describes a mighty eastern wind blowing across its surface all through the previous night, as if that might have been sufficient cause for the sea to open wide in order to allow the people of Israel to traverse its bed on dry land. The supernatural nature of the miracle, though still intact, is correspondingly decreased by the introduction of a less than miraculous variable.

As for the fire of the altar, human beings are called upon to follow God's example by obscuring His supernatural involvement – we *appear* to "kindle" and maintain a flame that is actually miraculous in origin because it really descends from on high! This startling inversion, in which God bestows overt miracles only to invite human beings to obscure His involvement by highlighting their own contribution, is consistent with Sefer HaChinuch's comments elsewhere concerning the centrality of both natural laws as well as human reason in setting the parameters of our encounter with the divine. Whereas devotees of other gods emphasize the extraordinary and stake their faith on the paranormal and miraculous, the Torah asks of us to undermine that very approach. The implications of all of this are profound: our role as human beings in the service of God is to do all that we can in order to secure our own fate. God, it seems, is not particularly interested in overawing us with a display of His power. He is much happier to appear to surrender His omnipotence by inviting our involvement and resourcefulness.

For the Sefer HaChinuch, there is a connection to be drawn between the service of God that we perform in the Mishkan and many of our mundane activities that resemble the divine service in outline. For instance, by performing the commandment of preparing the showbread – the twelve loaves that were specially baked for display on the golden table – a person merits God's blessing for their own "bread" or livelihood. The blessing of God extends to those things that are the mundane analogs to our ritual devotions. In this reading, the fire of the altar that we so fervently tend is analogous to the fire that burns within the human being, the life force that animates and sustains, the source within of warmth and light. By maintaining the altar fire and the service of God that it symbolizes, we merit in turn God's attention to our own altar within, to the "fire" that we depend upon in order to survive. This is not only mere symbolism. For living things, warmth and body temperature mean life and motion while coldness is stasis and the chill of death. It is the divine spark within us that transforms our existence from the lifeless state of the inanimate and the dead to the flourishing state of consciousness, sentience and awareness of God.

The progression of the Sefer HaChinuch goes a long away towards mitigating the paradox that underlies the God-man relationship. On the one hand, we acknowledge and serve an absolute deity whose existence is in no way dependent upon our efforts or those of any other being, whose knowledge is perfect and whose involvement in our lives is all-embracing – "There is nothing besides Him!" (*Devarim* 4:35). On the other hand, as independent moral agents and authors of our fate, we act to secure our lives with utter autonomy and freedom, as if we alone could determine the outcome. The Sefer HaChinuch's altar fire is both the symbolic locus of the God-man encounter as well as the point of resolution of the paradox: absolute God sends miraculous fire from heaven but then makes room for human beings to take part by providing fire of their own. In fact, He bids them to do so even as their actions seem to undermine His own transcendence! And when they act in consonance with His will for self-concealment by taking initiative, they invite His interest and care for their own little fires – their very lives – that brightly burn within them. God obscures His overwhelming presence, lovingly invites the human initiative and then rewards that enterprise with His involvement and concern. It may therefore be said that while we act independently, we only do so as a function of God limiting Himself in order for our choices to be actualized. But God deeply cares about the choices that we make and hopes that we will choose in consonance with His will so that we might live. God therefore grants us the opportunity to choose Him!

The altar fire is characterized by constancy, the daily sacrifice and incense offering by stability and permanence, and the human soul by its wish for eternity. The life force that animates the body is but an expression of the glimmer of godliness within that is our everlasting essence. Ultimately, all expressions of life, permanence and indestructibility are bound up with the absolute one who forever sustains. Our innate desire to connect to God is matched by God's desire to be so engaged by us. This is the true significance of the fire upon the altar that must never be extinguished.

FOR FURTHER STUDY:

(1) A perpetual fire is also associated with the menorah, especially its "western branch." Significantly, if this branch is found to be extinguished when the Kohen enters to prepare the lamps, it is rekindled from the fire of the bronze altar (TB *Tamid* 33a). Perhaps this constitutes another expression of the "partnership" model that Sefer HaChinuch advocates: it is the human being that is ultimately responsible for introducing the light of God into the world and the pivotal role played by humanity is God's desire.

SHEMINI

The Fervor of Nadav and Avihu

Leviticus 9:1-11:47

FINALLY, AFTER much anticipation, the dedicatory ceremony of the Mishkan reaches its climax. After Aharon and his sons had been bathed and then clothed in the regal garments of their office, after they, the vessels and the building proper had been anointed with the holy oil, after all of the requisite sacrifices had been presented and offered, after Moshe and Aharon had movingly blessed the assembled congregation of Israel, the glory of God manifests itself to the people:

> A fire went forth from before God, it consumed the sacrifices upon the altar – the burnt offering and the fats – and when the people saw it they cried out, and prostrated themselves upon their faces . . . (*Va Yikra* 9:24)

What a fitting finale to the narrative of the Mishkan's construction! Recall how Moshe had excitedly first communicated the command concerning the Mishkan to the multitude (*Shemot* 35:4–19) and how they had immediately began the process of gathering materials. The text had taken pains to point out that everyone had generously contributed to the undertaking, presenting their gold, silver, copper, precious stones, wood, dyed wool, linen and skins (35:20–29). In fact, God's command had been so well received that the contributions soon exceeded even the substantial needs of the artisans, and Moshe had to call upon the people to cease presenting their donations (36:4–7). The work then commenced in earnest as each building element, precious vessel and priestly garment was lovingly fashioned in strict accordance with God's directives. About six months after the project began, it was completed without mishap (39:32), and when the unassembled work was presented to Moshe, he emotionally blessed the people for their efforts (39:43).

Then, the setting up of all of the various elements was undertaken. The enclosure of the courtyard was erected, the building of the sanctuary and the Holy of Holies was completed, and the dividing curtains were hung in place. The holy vessels were arranged in their respective locations and everything was completed according to the illuminating refrain that is repeated in the passage from Sefer Shemot no less than seventeen times: "just as God had commanded Moshe."

Unexpected Tragedy by Fire

But the joy of the people on a job well done and their euphoria at the awesome sight of the divine glory filling the silent spaces was short-lived. Scarcely had the fire descended from on high to consume the last of the inaugural sacrifices when tragedy struck:

> The two sons of Aharon, Nadav and Avihu, each took their firepans, placed within them fire and upon that incense, and they offered before God an unfamiliar fire that He had not commanded them [to present]. A fire went forth from before God and consumed them, and they died before God. (*VaYikra* 10:1–2)

It is, once again, the theme of fire that informs this section, for it was the awesome fire of divine approval that immediately preceded it, the presentation of the unfamiliar and unwarranted fire of Nadav and Avihu that lies at its core, and the destructive fire of divine punishment that concludes it. Put slightly differently, we may say that the indiscretion of Nadav and Avihu, whatever its import, is effectively bracketed by two similar manifestations of God's consuming fire. Initially, it is that divine fire that approvingly consumes the presented offerings of Aharon and his sons, but then that very same fire menacingly consumes the hapless brothers themselves. Not surprisingly, the chapter break – not the product of Jewish tradition – that separates the former fire from the rest is contradicted by the original Hebrew text that actually preserves the entire account as a single undivided passage. In the Hebrew, then, the section reads as follows:

> . . . A *fire* went forth from before God and it consumed the sacrifices that were upon the altar (ותצא אש מלפני ה' ותאכל על המזבח) – the burnt offering and the fats – and when the people saw it they cried out, and prostrated themselves upon their faces. The two sons of Aharon, Nadav and Avihu, each took their firepans, placed within them *fire* and upon that incense, and they offered before God an unfamiliar *fire* that He had not commanded them (to present). A *fire* went forth from before God and it consumed them (ותצא אש מלפני ה' ותאכל אותם), and they died before God . . . (10:1–2)

We may go one step further by now noting a glaring contrast. While that first fire of endorsement precipitated a popular outcry of joy and a display of reverential worship on the part of the assembled congregation of Israel, the second fire of devastation occasions a stony silence of pained resignation on the part of Aharon the father of the victims:

> Moshe said to Aharon: this is in accordance with what God spoke, for He said that "I will be sanctified by those that are close to Me, and I will be glorified in the sight of all of the people." But Aharon remained silent. (10:3)

What prompted Nadav and Avihu, Aharon's trusted firstborn and his brother next in line, to present an unauthorized offering on the most solemn occasion that the people of Israel had ever celebrated? What exactly was the nature of the "unfamiliar fire" that suddenly brought about their untimely demise? What did Moshe mean by his cryptic words of comfort, and why did Aharon remain so frustratingly quiet in response?

The Rabbinic Interpretations

We should properly begin our investigation by noting that the Sages themselves were unable to come to any consensus concerning the crime of the two. In the Talmud (TB *Eiruvin* 63a), Rabbi Eliezer charges them with the irreverent offense of pronouncing a Halakhic decision in the presence of their mentor Moshe:

> Said Rabbi Eliezer: The sons of Aharon died only because they pronounced a decision in the presence of Moshe their teacher. What did they [mistakenly] deduce from the text? They reasoned the following: Since the Torah states [concerning

> the burnt offering] that "the sons of Aharon the priest shall place fire upon the altar" (*VaYikra* 1:7), therefore here as well, although the fire descends from the heavens, it is nevertheless a mitzvah for it to be brought from a human source.

In the Midrash, in contrast, the sons of Aharon are accused of ministering in the holy precincts while in a state of drunkenness (!):

> Said Rabbi Yishmael: The two sons of Aharon died only because they entered the Tent of Meeting while drunk. In the text following their death, God commands Aharon and says: "You must not drink wine nor strong drink, neither you nor your sons, when you enter the Tent of Meeting lest you die, it is an eternal statute forever . . ." (10:8–9). We may therefore infer that they died only on account of wine. (Midrash VaYikra Rabbah 12:1, 5)

Both of these traditions are inspired by the textual cues provided by the passage itself. Rabbi Eliezer considers the larger context: if the opening premise of Sefer VaYikra is that an integral part of the ongoing sacrificial service is the placement of the fire upon the altar by the ministering priests, then that must be true at the time of its inauguration as well. Even though the inaugural sacrifices were consumed by a heavenly fire of approval, Nadav and Avihu mistakenly reasoned that it was nevertheless necessary for the officiating priests to provide their own fire. Had they but shown deference to Moshe their teacher, he would have pointed out to them the error of their syllogism before they recklessly applied it with such tragic results.

Rabbi Yishmael, on the other hand, considers the narrower context of the episode. After the death of the two, the report of the unceremonious removal of their corpses from the holy precincts and the special provisions placed upon the surviving family members not to observe formal mourning practices (*VaYikra* 10:2–7), there is then the passage that interdicts the consumption of intoxicating beverages by the ministering priests (10:8–9). This is immediately followed by the conclusion of the narrative in which Moshe instructs Aharon and his remaining sons to consume the sacrificial offerings in spite of the tragedy (10:12–20). The prohibition concerning intoxication is separated from the rest of the text by a paragraph break both before and after, and Rabbi Yishmael therefore considers the short section to be the core of the narrative. Hence, it must be the case that Nadav and Avihu were guilty of ministering to God while under the influence of alcohol.

The History and Character of the Two

Both traditions fail to address the fundamental questions: What could possibly have motivated the two sons to act so carelessly, whether in the unguided practical application of erroneously deduced concepts or else in the throwing of caution to the wind with the imbibing of intoxicating drink? And why again is the matter of fire so seemingly central to the story?

In order to assist us in formulating a theory, it is helpful to briefly trace the history of the two brothers. In the genealogy preserved at the opening of Sefer Shemot, when Moshe and Aharon stood poised to embark upon their mission to Pharaoh, Nadav and Avihu as well as their two younger brothers Elazar and Itamar were all listed as the children of Aharon and Elisheva daughter of Aminadav (*Shemot* 6:23). Now this Elisheva, Aharon's wife, was the sister of none other than Nachshon son of Aminadav, who later achieved singular prominence as the tribal chief of Yehuda (see *BeMidbar* 1:7, 2:3). It therefore seems plausible that Nadav the firstborn (was he named for his grandfather?) as well as Avihu were destined for achievement early on, for they were descended from prominent forebears on both their father's as well as their mother's sides of the family.

This grooming for greatness soon bore fruit, for when the people left Egypt, arrived at Sinai and received the Torah, Nadav and Avihu figured prominently in the episode. Recall that after God had pronounced the Decalogue from Sinai's fiery peak, He summoned Moshe to approach the mountain accompanied by a delegation of elders. Counted among that illustrious group were none other than Nadav and Avihu, who alone (but for their father) were singled out by name:

> God said to Moshe: ascend to God, you, Aharon, Nadav and Avihu as well as seventy of the elders of Israel, and you shall prostrate yourselves at a distance. (*Shemot* 24:1)

And while only Moshe was then invited to Sinai's summit, the rest of the delegation was afforded a rare and precious glimpse of God's grandeur:

> Moshe and Aharon ascended, Nadav and Avihu, and seventy of the elders of Israel. They perceived the Lord of Israel, and beneath His feet was like the manner of sapphire stone, as pure in color as the very heavens. He did not stretch forth His hand against the nobles of Israel, and they experienced a vision of the Lord, and they ate and they drank. (24:9–11)

Piecing together the terse references, we may now construct a promising profile. As Aharon's first sons, the two were from the outset expected to fill priestly positions of prominence, as all firstborns in the Torah were initially expected to do (though few actually succeeded in the mission!). As direct descendents of Nachshon son of Aminadav, they also bore the additional burdens of political and spiritual leadership of the people. And as esteemed members of the "inner circle" that alone was granted a unique divine encounter, the two were no doubt imbued with a heightened sensitivity to God's overarching presence.

Having experienced the awesome spectacle of the inauguration, having personally participated in the preparatory sacrifices, having witnessed the descent of the divine fire that signaled acceptance of the prescribed rites, the two brothers were filled with genuine religious fervor. The glory of God had been revealed to them, just as it had been when they stood transfixed at Sinai and God's fire flashed forth from the thick cloud. For a precious moment, time stood still and eternity beckoned, just beyond the dividing curtain that shielded God's radiance from undeserving eyes. Filled with uncontainable enthusiasm, the two took up their firepans. Electrified with spiritual ecstasy, they placed upon them fire and fragrant incense. Solemnly, they approached the divine presence in a spontaneous outburst of religious zeal. The smoke slowly began to ascend heavenward before it was met by a blinding flash from above. In an instant, the two were overtaken, their souls incinerated by tongues of fire that tellingly left their vestments and bodies intact (*VaYikra* 9:5).

In a word, the transgression of Nadav and Avihu was not precipitated by a lack of sensitivity but rather by an *abundance* of it. In the great pageant of ritual and worship that was the inauguration of the Mishkan, every sacrificial and ceremonial detail to be performed was spelled out ahead of time by divine fiat, so that no man might exercise best-intentioned impulsiveness. Singular moments of spiritual transcendence and connectedness to God are simultaneously moments of great danger, for one who is swept up in rapture can presume too much and overstep his bounds. Though we often tend to celebrate God's mercy and forbearance, we must not lose sight of His overwhelming might. Love of God (intense though it may be) that is not tempered by reverence and fear, is in the end self-defeating, for it cannot stop a man from breathlessly rewriting His laws in order to "better serve Him."

The fire of God that initially consumed the sacrificial offerings was met by the fire of Nadav and Avihu that burned so brightly and uncontrollably in their souls. But then that divine fire, provider of warmth and illumination, turned destructively against them, fittingly consuming their spiritual enthusiasm while leaving their corporal frames unscorched. Moshe meant what he said when he pronounced the dead brothers to be those that are "close" to Him, sanctifiers of His name in life as well as in death, for Nadav and Avihu truly were servants of God. But the deity does not brook unwarranted familiarity in the awesome act of worship even from His most loyal subjects.

Notice that Rabbi Eliezer did not simply charge the two with pronouncing **any** Halakhic ruling in Moshe's presence (a breach of protocol that alone would have merited censure), but singled out their penchant for religious over-enthusiasm in particular: "They reasoned the following: Since the Torah states [concerning the burnt offering] that 'the sons of Aharon the priest shall place fire upon the altar' (1:7), therefore here as well, although the fire descends from the heavens, it is nevertheless a mitzvah for it to be brought from a human source." And notice how Rabbi Yishmael connected their indiscretion with intoxication, for although strong drink is often cited as a source of emotional or spiritual inspiration, it can also cloud one's cognitive judgment, removing inhibitions that would otherwise keep a person at a safe distance from flames that provide heat and light but also can consume the careless.

As for Aharon's silence, it is the most fitting of all. Who realized more than the aged priest the great dangers inherent in unbridled religious enthusiasm? Who understood better than he did, having once stood powerless to stem the crowd excitedly clamoring for a golden calf, that the best intentioned acts of worship can so easily degrade into coarse and corrosive idolatry? Had he not himself raised up the altar before that bovine thing and proclaimed a "festival to God tomorrow" (*Shemot* 32:5), dangerously stoking the people's passions for unrestrained adulation? His beloved children, whom he hoped would one day succeed him in the service of God, now lay dead at his feet, but how could he blame the deity for their demise? Nadav and Avihu were consumed by an inner fire that could not but be matched by an outer fire from above. Did the poet-king perhaps have them in mind when he bid his beloved to

> Place me as a signet upon your heart and as a seal upon your hand, for love is as powerful as death and yearning as cruel as the grave, its flames are the flames of God's consuming fire! (*Shir HaShirim* 8:6)

And did God Himself perhaps have them in mind as well when He twice warned Moshe at the Revelation to distance the people and the priests from the mount, lest "they break forth to ascend towards God, and He then break forth upon them" (*Shemot* 19:24)? Did God perchance anticipate their burning enthusiasm when He warned that only Moshe was to draw close to Sinai's summit while they and the elders "were not to approach" (24:2)?

All religions speak of divine mercy and love, inviting us to lovingly embrace God in turn. And who is there that does not want to experience that intimate concern of God in his own life? Who is there that does not yearn to serve God sincerely, with enthusiasm and passion? One of the most unique contributions of the Torah to religious discourse, however, is the development of the contrary notion: worship of God, if it is to be genuine, must also be predicated upon reverence and fear, for reverence provides the restraints that love refuses to recognize. Nadav and Avihu tragically perished at the very moment that God's presence was most intensely felt. But through their death, the two brothers communicated a fundamental lesson that was to inform the service of the Mishkan and the Temple (and for that matter the synagogue) for all time: "Moshe said to Aharon: this is in accordance with what God spoke, for He said that 'I will be sanctified by those that are close to Me, and I will be glorified in the sight of all of the people.'"

FOR FURTHER STUDY:

(1) While the Torah itself keeps silent concerning the exact indiscretion of the sons, and the early Rabbis and medieval commentaries adopt many explanations in order to fill in the gap, it is instructive to consider the earliest interpretation of the event. The calamitous episode of the death of Uza, recounted in Sefer Shemuel 2, chapter 6, constitutes the *haftarah* of our Parasha. The context describes how David, after his ascent to the throne of Israel, his conquest of Jerusalem and its designation as the capital of all of the tribes, attempted to relocate the ark of the covenant from its temporary abode at Kiryat Ye'arim in the Judean foothills to his new city. But scarcely had the festive public procession began when Uza lay dead, felled by a "divine wrath" kindled when he stretched forth his hand to secure the ark of the covenant as the oxen conveying its wagon stumbled and slipped.

There are many general similarities between the circumstances surrounding the death of Nadav and Avihu and those that informed Uza's untimely demise. In both narratives, the broader context concerns the challenge of forging disparate tribes into a unified nation. In both stories, the centrality of the ark of the covenant and its relocation is highlighted, and in both accounts a national celebration of dedication is unexpectedly clouded by a catastrophe. Drawing more specific parallels, we note that both tragedies revolve around brothers (Nadav and Avihu vs. Uza and Achyo) who were integral to the process of the inauguration and who perished while the eyes of all of Israel were upon them. Their respective fathers, namely Aharon in Parashat Shemini and Avinadav in Sefer Shemuel, remained outside of the relevant narrative, peripheral to the account of their children's untimely death and detached or mute in their response.

The most striking parallel, however, and the one that long ago inspired the designation of this section of the prophets as the *haftarah* for Parashat Shemini, surely concerns the inexplicability of the respective crimes. Like Nadav and Avihu before him, why is it exactly that innocent Uza was struck down? Did he not intend to preserve the ark from harm by holding it steady even as its cart unexpectedly tottered? Were his intentions not noble, his rash action an instinctive response that had only God's glory as its objective? Should he have rather allowed the ark to ignominiously fall to the ground?

See the commentary of the Radak (*Shemuel* 2:6:6) who attributes the blame for Uza's death to David himself, for breaking with the accepted tradition of bearing the ark on the shoulders of the Levites to instead convey it by a new wagon. Here again, we have a sincerely motivated but innovative act of religious enthusiasm on David's part that precipitates a tragedy. And what of David's innovation? Why would he have wanted to introduce a practice that was not sanctioned by precedent? No doubt he surmised as follows: The Torah did not explicitly prohibit the conveyance of the ark by wagon and only discouraged it by implication. Perhaps that was legislation limited to the wilderness wanderings when the ark would have to be conveyed from place to place at regular intervals. But to now bring it up to Jerusalem in order to install it in its new and more permanent location called for another method, something more grand and stately. Let the ark be carried aloft upon a new wagon, entirely set apart in the festive procession from the throng of Israelite pedestrians! And (do we assume too much?) let that conveyance be an echo of the Philistines' own act (when they were forced to return the lethal trophy in *Shemuel* 1:6:7–14), not in order to ape the pagan practices of the surrounding peoples, but rather in order to forcefully suggest that the wanderings of the ark were over! Let the circle of infamy be closed, as it were, by restoring the ark to its glory using the very same method that decades earlier had recalled the ark's exile among the Philistines! For an emotional expression of David's enthusiasm on the matter, see *Tehillim* 132.

If our earlier analysis is correct, then the narrative of Uza's death also constitutes an important cautionary tale. We break from explicit tradition, even when motivated by sincere and genuine intentions, at our own peril. Our profound desire to glorify God and to elevate His service cannot come at the expense of His clearly defined laws. And ultimately, it is the people of Israel who bear the brunt of those well-intentioned attempts to rewrite ritual. Coupled with the account of Aharon's sons, a complete picture thus begins to emerge. Their infraction was also one of spontaneous but earnest innovation, as they attempted to serve God with unsanctioned fire. After all, could the dedication of God's house fail to include a more human component, now that all of His detailed provisions had been faithfully fulfilled? But whereas their act did not have wider repercussions, David's decision did. The individual who autonomously chooses his own way will impact only upon himself, but the leader who decides will naturally affect others as well. Thus, we may infer that these two narratives – Nadav and Avihu on the one hand, and the death of Uza on the other – are complementary, inviting us through their overlapping literary structures to interpret one against the other.

TAZRIA

Making a Case for *Tzara'at*

Leviticus 12:1-13:59

PARASHAT TAZRIA introduces us to what is undeniably the most difficult of topics that are addressed in Sefer VaYikra, namely the laws of debilitating skin disorders. At great length, the Torah describes various strange ailments that may afflict an individual's body, or even his garments or his house. While the Parasha opens with the laws of confinement associated with childbirth, it abruptly goes on to spell out in exhaustive detail the condition of צרעת, or the one so afflicted who is referred to as the צרוע or the מצורע. According to the Torah's description, the malady may strike the skin, the scalp, or the beard. It may occur in the aftermath of a previous lesion or a burn. It may afflict garments of wool or linen. It may even strike the stones, mortar, or plaster of a house! In all cases, it is the Kohen or priest who must examine the infection and diagnose it.

While *tzara'at* is often identified by modern scholars with leprosy due to the Torah's association of some strains of the illness with a whitening of the afflicted skin, no other features of a typical leprous condition are indicated in the text. The loss of sensation, paralysis, wasting of muscle and deformity that occur as chronic leprosy progresses, are completely absent from the Torah's description of the illness, thus rendering such an identification clearly unwarranted. Certainly, a clinical case of leprosy cannot infect articles of wool or linen, nor can it contaminate the walls of a house! Thus, we are forced to conclude that the conventional linkage of *tzara'at* with leprosy, a linkage that renders this unusual sickness into nothing more than an unfortunate but natural bacterial infection, is untenable.

Significantly, the Torah is silent concerning the causes of *tzara'at*. It strikes suddenly and without warning. Sometimes, the Kohen may be able to immediately identify the symptoms and declare the afflicted individual as *tamei* or ritually unfit, but more often than not a seven-day incubation period is required in order to make a definitive diagnosis. And sometimes, a further seven-day period is needed if the first quarantine fails to provide conclusive results. In all cases, the waiting period is characterized by isolation from others, as the potential *metzora*, his garment or his house, awaits the judgment of the Kohen. In the end, either if the condition turns out to be harmless or else after it has run its course, the Kohen pronounces the ailing person *tahor* or ritually fit, and only then may he be re-admitted to the encampment.

Finding an Explanation Elsewhere

While academics have searched in vain for a medical explanation for *tzara'at*, the classical Jewish sources recognized early on that a meaningful explanation for the condition must be sought elsewhere. Writing in the 13th century, the Ramban remarked that "[the *tzara'at* associated with garments] is not at all a natural occurrence and does not typically occur in the world, and so with respect to the plague of the house . . ." (commentary to *VaYikra* 13:47). In other words, there is no rational explanation for these conditions and no straightforward biological chain of cause and effect that could account for them.

The juxtaposition of the condition of *tzara'at* with the matter of childbirth that textually introduces it (12:1–8) is thus rendered all the more jarring, for while the latter also necessitates some form of temporary isolation that includes unfitness to enter the precincts of the Mishkan, the condition itself is medically unremarkable in the extreme. Childbirth is a profound and transformative experience that may at times be also dangerous, but it is certainly not "unnatural." Nothing could be more mundane from a detached medical point of view. The course of the condition is predictable, the symptoms conventional, and the prognosis inevitable. The course of *tzara'at*, on the other hand, must be regarded as progressing completely beyond the realm of what may be regarded as medically anticipated.

As indicated in the text, the features of the malady are quite multifaceted and may include the appearance of white blotches on the skin, white hairs that have sprouted on raw skin, lesions or burns that have become infected, or yellow hairs that have sprouted on the affected skin of the scalp or beard. It is therefore difficult to isolate a set of common denominators that characterize the condition, especially in light of its aforementioned ability to infect garments and houses as well. There is, however, a single textual feature that unites all of the various forms of the disorder, and it is this feature that may help us to propel our investigation forward.

The Torah indicates that whosoever is stricken with *tzara'at,* be it person, garment or house, must be subjected to a period of *isolation and confinement*. During that duration, the afflicted person is unable to participate in any social intercourse, is barred from entering the hallowed precincts of the Tabernacle or partaking of hallowed sacrificial foods and is instead effectively shut in. To quote the colorful language of the Torah:

> The *tzarua* who suffers from the ailment shall have torn clothes and unkempt hair and shall cover his face with his cloak. He shall call out: "*Tamei, tamei*!" For as long as he is afflicted with the ailment he shall be considered as *tamei* and shall dwell alone outside of the boundaries of the camp. (13:45–46)

If it is a garment that is definitively infected, as characterized by a progressive spread of the noxious discoloration, then that garment is to be burned. If the discoloration does not spread but also does not disappear, then the garment is to be laundered and confined for a further seven days. If no change is noted, then that garment must also be burned. If, however, the infection has shown signs of subsiding, then the infected fibers alone must be stripped from the garment and discarded.

With respect to houses, a definitive infection results in the afflicted stones being removed and discarded outside of the camp, while a doubtful case requires a seven-day waiting period followed by a reexamination of the affected premises. If the discoloration has in the meantime spread, then the affected stones are to be removed and discarded and a second period of seven days is to be kept. If after the second round the malady has returned, then the entire house is to be demolished and its rubble is to be relocated outside of the camp. Thus, taken together, it is the notion of isolation or confinement, whether of person, garment or house, that dominates the discussion of the *metzora*.

Tuma and Tahara

While it may be tempting to see in the recurring theme of isolation a medical necessity to quarantine a harmful pathogen, the ongoing involvement of the Kohen – his contact with the infected person and periodic entry into the contaminated premises of the afflicted house – negate the possibility that harmful bacteria are the culprits. Most telling of all, however, is the recurring terms that the Torah employs to describe the consequences of the condition, for without exception, the Torah describes the condition in terms of *tuma* and *tahara*. One who is afflicted is *tamei*; one who has recovered and presented the requisite sacrifices is *tahor*.

These loaded terms, often mistranslated as "impure" and "pure," "unclean" and "clean," actually address another dimension entirely. Suffice it to say that they almost always describe a state of ritual disqualification insofar as the Mishkan or its environs are concerned. Thus, one who is *tamei* may not enter the sacred precincts or partake of sacrificial foods. It can be conclusively demonstrated from the text that *tuma* and *tahara* have nothing to do with physical hygiene or medical health, and everything to do with subtle spiritual states. These two terms, really mirror images of each other bound up in a tight binary relationship, describe the parameters of a person's suitability to stand in God's presence, as signified by either admittance or else exclusion from the boundaries of His house. The fact that the Torah chooses to use these terms here is another indication that *tzara'at* must be understood as something other than a medical condition.

It is therefore not surprising that when the ancients came to ponder these laws, they arrived at the inescapable conclusion that the condition of *tzara'at* is a function not of viral or bacterial pathogens or else exposure to dangerous chemical substances, but rather is intrinsically connected to the spiritual state of the ailing victim's soul. More specifically, the Rabbis (see TB *Arachin* 15b–16b) associated the ailment of *tzara'at* with the particular transgression of *lashon hara* or disparaging speech, as implied by the episode of Miriam described in Sefer BeMidbar 12:

> Miriam and Aharon spoke disparagingly of Moshe concerning the dark-skinned wife that he had taken . . . God heard . . . The man Moshe was exceedingly humble, more so than any person on the face of the earth. Suddenly, God addressed Moshe, Aharon and Miriam saying: "All three of you go out to the Tent of Meeting" . . . God descended in a pillar of cloud and hovered at the opening of the tent. He called Aharon and Miriam and both of them approached. He said: "Hear My words. If there is a prophet among you, I appear to him in a vision or else in a dream. Not so with respect to My servant Moshe, for he is most loyal in all of My house . . . why were you not afraid to speak against My servant Moshe?" God was angry with them and He departed. The cloud lifted off of the tent, and behold, Miriam was as *metzora'at* as snow. Aharon turned towards Miriam, and behold, she was *metzora'at* . . . Moshe cried out to God saying: "Almighty, please heal her now!" God said to Moshe: "If her father had spit in her face would she not be ashamed for seven days? Let her be isolated outside of the camp for seven days and only then readmitted." So Miriam was shut out of the camp for seven days, but the people did not travel onwards until she was readmitted . . . (*BeMidbar* 12:1–16)

In the case of Miriam, we note many of the classical features of the *tzara'at* condition as detailed in our Parasha: a harmful and horrifying whitening of the skin that precipitates a stern exclusion from the presence of God and from the camp of Israel. The quarantine lasts until such time as "healing" takes place, designated here, just as in our Parasha, as a period of seven days. The episode of Miriam, however, provides us with one additional and critical detail concerning the malady: her sudden affliction was brought upon her through the misuse of speech, for she had deliberately spoken ill of her brother. The exact nature and content of Miriam's verbal broadside need not concern us here. What is important for our purposes is to recognize that she was guilty of employing hurtful words and that Moshe her brother was offended by them.

For the Rabbis the linkage was not only well-nigh undeniable, it also admirably provided a rationale for the striking requirement of exclusion from the camp. The *tuma* designation was now rendered comprehensible as well: a clear indication that the Torah was concerned with spiritual and ethical categories of behavior, since the term almost invariably describes a flawed spiritual state of being. And it was the Kohen who was designated to diagnose the disorder – not because he is the ancient equivalent of the physician but rather because he is elsewhere called upon to provide religious instruction, spiritual guidance and the possibility of repairing one's relationship with others and with God. It is Maimonides who weaves together the various strands of our investigation into a cohesive idea, which he presents as a fitting conclusion to his lengthy and detailed codification of the laws of *tzara'at* (Laws of *Tumat Tzara'at* 16:10):

> "*Tzara'at*" is a general term that includes many distinct conditions that differ one from the other. A whitening of human skin is called *tzara'at*, a loss of some scalp or beard hair may be *tzara'at*, a discoloration of garments or the house is *tzara'at*. This condition that afflicts garments or houses to which the Torah refers by this term is not a natural occurrence but rather a miraculous sign that would transpire in ancient Israel in order *to dissuade them from engaging in evil talk*. Thus, if one engaged in disparaging speech, then the walls of his house would become discolored. If he repented, then the walls would recover, but if he persisted, then . . . the garments upon him would be afflicted . . . if he persisted, then his very skin would be stricken and he would be *publicly separated and isolated* so that he would be unable to engage in the chatter of the wicked, namely foolish words and evil speech. Concerning this very thing, the Torah warned when it said: "Observe diligently the laws of *tzara'at* . . . remember what God your Lord did to Miriam on the way as you left the land of Egypt . . ." (*BeMidbar* 24:8–9)

To speak ill of someone else is not only to cause grave emotional and spiritual discomfort to the victim but also to tear asunder the social fabric, for individual people can be brought together as family or as community only in direct proportion to the amount of trust that underlies their relationships. It is only fitting, therefore, that the *tzaru'a* is relocated to the outside of the camp where he must dwell in complete isolation until such time as he relents, recognizing the danger to family and to community that his evil speech engenders.

Consequences of the Rabbinic Interpretation

By explaining an ostensibly medical ailment as a spiritual failing of the character, the Rabbis surely rescued our Parasha from oblivion. What had seemed to the reader to be a baffling and irrelevant condition, of interest only to overachieving medical sleuths who peruse ancient texts aspiring to unlock obscure mysteries of diagnoses, suddenly became relevant and real. And what had appeared to be an infrequent and unusual ailment, strange in the extreme and of little import, was now revealed to be widespread and endemic. Who could not readily comprehend the scourge of *lashon hara*? Who had not experienced, at some point or another, its deleterious effects? And who could not personally identify with the insane delight associated with its propagation? With the linkage of the Rabbis, the vast amount of verses that the Torah devotes to the arcane subject of *tzara'at* suddenly becomes entirely appropriate (if not insufficient!), for the overabundance of text is nothing but a reflection of the pervasiveness of this sad phenomenon that poisons so many of our social interactions.

We may of course justifiably wonder: if the identification of the Rabbis is correct, why is it that this ailment of *tzara'at* is no longer extant? Surely the *lashon hara* that is its root cause is very much still with us; why then has the condition so completely disappeared? Could we not still benefit from the corrective and rehabilitative course of treatment prescribed for it? Might not the astonishing effects of *tzara'at* quickly eradicate the blight of *lashon hara* from our midst, as no amount of instruction and exhortation have yet succeeded in doing?

We return again to the words of the Ramban that we quoted in passing earlier:

> The text speaks of a garment that is infected with *tzara'at* (*VaYikra* 13:47). This condition is not at all a natural occurrence and does not typically occur in the world, and so with respect to the plague of the house. Rather, when the people of Israel are whole in their relationship with God, then God's spirit is upon them constantly to preserve their bodies, garments and houses in good repair. When sin or transgression happens with one of them, then a blemish occurs on their flesh, their clothing or their domicile to indicate that God has withdrawn from them. Therefore, the text states that "I shall place the plague of *tzara'at* upon a house in the land of your inheritance" (14:34), for it truly is God's plague upon that house.
>
> Behold, this matter only occurs in the land that is God's inheritance, for so the verse states: "When you enter the land of Canaan that I give to you as an inheritance (14:34). This is not because the matter is an obligation of location, but rather because it may only happen in the chosen land where God's glorious presence resides . . . and so I believe it is the case with respect to plagues of the garments as well . . . (commentary to 13:47)

The Ramban introduces two related ideas to explain the phenomenon of *tzara'at*. First of all, he posits that the ailment is supernatural and is a direct function of one thing only: the withdrawal of the divine presence. No doubt he was inspired by the report concerning Miriam that "God was angry with them and He departed. The cloud lifted off of the tent, and behold, Miriam was as *metzora'at* as snow" (*BeMidbar* 12:9–10). In that passage, the onset of Miriam's ailment was clearly marked by the departure of His cloud – the manifestation of His presence – and for the Ramban this was not merely a confluence of events but rather a sure case of cause and effect. God's presence sustains us, His involvement preserves us, and when we banish Him by our deeds then His protective support dissipates. *Tzara'at* then, is a direct consequence of divine distancing.

But the Ramban qualifies this thesis by remarking that these effects can only be experienced by the individual "when the people of Israel are whole in their relationship with God." In other words, the feeling of God's absence is only pronounced when there is a profound experience of His presence to begin with. When the people of Israel are "whole" with God and close to Him, when they bask in the radiance of His words and perform the commands of His Torah, when they choose as a nation the path of observance and fulfillment, then the individual who strays unleashes a dynamic that breeds a physical symptom for his spiritual estrangement. But if the people of Israel are anywise insensitive to His presence and alienated from His Torah, then how shall His absence be even recognized and let alone felt in a tangible way? The absence of a loved one sows sorrow and fosters longing; the absence of a stranger leaves us unmoved.

But for the Ramban there is a second aspect to the matter. When we speak of the profound experience of God's presence then we must confine our discussion to primarily one locale: the land of Israel. It is there that the *Shechina* resides and it is there that the most intense expression of His immediacy is to be sought. God's glory indeed fills the cosmos but the substantial experience of that glory is more circumscribed. While we may seek out and celebrate God's closeness in good deeds and in noble thoughts, it is also to be found in physical space. And while we tend to identify this physical space with sacred houses of worship where we engage in prayer and thanksgiving, God is also to be found in a special land, in a particular city, and in a Mikdash from whence His glory radiates outwards. But like the first premise of the Ramban's theory, this postulate also depends upon human sensitivity, for if the human heart is stubborn as stone and the human mind is numb, then even one who stands at the very portals of the Holy Temple at Jerusalem will remain impassive. How shall the man indifferent to his soul and apathetic to the divine spark be distraught by the departure of God from his life?

For the Ramban, there are therefore two conditions that must be met in order for *tzara'at* to be possible: first of all, the nation of Israel must be living its collective life in connection to God. This condition pertains to all forms of the ailment. Second of all, they must be living that life in the land of Israel, the locus of connection. This condition pertains to *tzara'at* of houses and garments. Only under such intense conditions of attachment to the divine is the physical manifestation associated with the spiritual ailment of *tzara'at* even possible. Is it any wonder then that *tzara'at* is no longer extant?

When we read the sections that detail the illness of *tzara'at*, our natural tendency is to recoil in horror. What strange and terrible affliction is this that marks one's body and necessitates its quarantine? But the Rabbis alerted us to a different reading that suddenly casts the horror in a different light – is not speaking disparagingly of another human being and undermining with hurtful words his or her reputation and legitimacy also a plague upon our societies? And now the Ramban has opened our eyes to an additional dimension: how far we truly are from the presence of God, how insensitive and estranged, when we can scarcely even notice that such behavior is destructive! When the hopeful among us dream of a resumption of certain Torah laws that others regard as hopelessly antiquated, perhaps we are really dreaming of something else: of the day when Israel and God will finally be reconciled, when His gentle demands for sensitivity to others will be heeded, and when His overarching presence will be felt in every fiber of our lives. *Tzara'at* as a medical condition may no longer be evident or identifiable in our day, but as with other seemingly archaic and atavistic laws of the book of VaYikra, the object lessons of *tzara'at*, as understood by our tradition, are as pertinent as ever.

FOR FURTHER STUDY:

(1) It should be noted that the Ramban's interpretation was actually advanced earlier by Rabbi Yehuda HaLevi, the great poet philosopher who lived in Spain in the 12th century and shared the Ramban's sensitivity for matters of Jewish nationhood and the Jewish land. Disenchanted with the indifference of his compatriots, HaLevi eventually left what was, until that point, the most comfortable and affluent diaspora in Jewish history and journeyed towards the land of Israel, then under the control of the crusaders. Opinions are divided concerning whether or not he reached his goal. Rabbi HaLevi's formulation of the idea may be found in his monumental *Kuzari*, 2:62.

METZORA

Purification Rites of the *Metzora*

Leviticus 14:1-15:33

God spoke to Moshe saying: "This shall be the matter of the *metzora* on the day of his purification: he shall be brought before the Kohen. The Kohen shall go out of the camp and see that indeed the afflicted one has been healed from the plague of *tzara'at*. The Kohen shall command that two clean living birds be brought for the individual undergoing purification, along with cedar wood, scarlet and hyssop. The Kohen shall command that one of the birds be slaughtered, upon water from a living spring that has been gathered within an earthenware vessel.

"He shall then take the living bird, along with cedar wood, scarlet and hyssop, and he shall immerse them along with the living bird into the blood of the slaughtered bird that is upon the water from a living spring. He shall then sprinkle seven times the one undergoing purification from *tzara'at*, and when he has purified him, he shall release the living bird into the wide open field . . ." (*Va Yikra* 14:1–7)

THUS BEGINS Parashat Metzora, with a detailed account of the purification rites for one who has emerged from the condition of *tzara'at* and now waits impatiently to rejoin his kin and his community. In many respects, these rites are particular to the *metzora* (or to the related situation of house *tzara'at* – see 14:33–57), but there are also a number of points of contact between these rites and those associated with relieving other forms of *tuma*.

Tracing the Outline of the Process

Let us begin by outlining the process of purification, supplementing the biblical text with relevant material gleaned from the Mishna *Nega'im* 14:

First of all, the Kohen must ascertain that the *metzora* has indeed been healed from his condition, much as the Kohen was initially responsible for declaring him *tamei* and causing his banishment from the community. Then, while the *metzora* is still residing outside of the encampment of Israel, two birds are taken, of a species that is both undomesticated as well as *tahor* (fit for consumption). Additionally, the Kohen must take a new earthenware vessel, and fill it with a small amount of water drawn from a flowing spring. In volume, the water should measure one *revi'it* or approximately 90–150 ml. One of the birds is then slaughtered above the vessel, and its blood is drained into the waters. The Kohen then takes the cedar wood, hyssop and a ribbon of wool that has been dyed scarlet and bundles them together, securing the grouping with part of the scarlet ribbon. The living bird is brought together with the bundle, so that its wingtips, head and tail are all in contact with it, and then all of the items are ceremoniously immersed into the earthenware vessel. The Kohen then sprinkles the liquid seven times upon the hands of the *metzora*, and then the living bird is released to its freedom.

Afterwards, of course, the *metzora* must follow the rest of the ritual as it is described later in our text: he must shave all of the visible concentrations of hair upon his body and immerse himself, before entering the confines of the camp. In this transitional stage, he may not have relations with his wife for a period of seven days. On the seventh day, he must again shave the hair of his body and immerse a second time, but he remains unfit to partake of sacrificial meats until the presentation of his offerings on the eighth day. These eighth day offerings consist of a sin offering, a burnt offering and a guilt offering, the attendant meal offering and a special presentation of oil. The specific species for the offerings are adjusted in accordance with the financial state of the supplicant, and the exact ceremonial of the presentation that includes the placement of some of the blood and oil upon parts of his body is described in 14:10–20.

Considering the Precedents

What might be the significance of these things? Why must the *metzora* present two birds at the outset and why is one of them then set free? What about the three species of cedar wood, scarlet and hyssop, as well as the need for the living waters of a free-flowing spring? Although it may not be possible to ascertain the meaning of all of the specific items that are needed for the complex choreography of the purification, we may at least succeed in tracing the general thrust of the matter.

We begin our investigation by noting that at least insofar as the basic scheme is concerned, we have already encountered a similar ceremonial. Recall that as the people of Israel were poised to leave the land of Egypt and the plague of the firstborn was about to strike, God commanded the people to prepare the Paschal lamb. This special sacrifice, a statement of Israel's trust in God as they took their first tentative step away from Egyptian polytheism, was slaughtered on the eve of the fourteenth day of Nissan. The blood of the lamb was gathered into a receptacle and then smeared upon the lintel and doorposts of the Hebrew huts in order to ward off the destroyer from their households. In that context, the Torah specified that the people were to take "a bundle of hyssop and to dip it into the blood that is in the receptacle . . ." (*Shemot* 12:22), thus providing us with a tantalizing precedent for the purification rites of the *metzora* that also include a dipping of hyssop into a mixture of blood and spring water.

Besides the Pesach sacrifice, we also find a similar series of steps associated with the purification rites of one who has come into contact with a human corpse. As spelled out in Parashat Chukat (*BeMidbar* 19), corpse *tuma* can only be relieved by the puzzling ceremony of the *para aduma* or red heifer. In this scenario, a perfectly red-haired cow that has never been utilized to draw the plow is slaughtered beyond the confines of the camp. Its body is then completely incinerated in a specially prepared bonfire, and the ashes are carefully gathered. These ashes are subsequently mixed as needed into a vessel containing spring water, and the Kohen then takes a bundle of hyssop, dips it into the mixture and sprinkles it upon the *tamei* individual on the third and seventh day. After the sprinkling of the seventh day, the person immerses himself in a *mikvah* and after nightfall is *tahor*. He is then free to enter the confines of the Mishkan as necessary or to partake of sacrificial meats.

In all three of the situations, a liquid that is either blood, water or else a mixture of both is first gathered into some sort of receptacle, typically an earthenware vessel. Next, a bundle of organic material that is either exclusively hyssop or else includes the plant as a major ingredient is dipped into the liquid and some sort of sprinkling or smearing is then done with it. Afterwards, the status of the afflicted individual is transformed. It is Rabbi Avraham Ibn Ezra who not only links the three ceremonials together but maintains that the paradigm for them all is the Pesach sacrifice of *Shemot* 12:

> Behold, the purification rites of the *metzora*, the house stricken with *tzara'at*, and the individual who has come into contact with a human corpse are all similar. All of them are modeled after the Pesach sacrifice in Egypt. (commentary to *VaYikra* 14:4)

Taking our cue from the Ibn Ezra, we notice that when considering the Pesach in Egypt more closely, other similarities suddenly materialize. First of all, the Pesach sacrifice marks Israel's emergence as a nation. On that night of horrors, even as the destroyer sowed death among the Egyptians, the firstborn of Israel were spared. On the morrow, they left Egypt as a free people. Finally, they were liberated from the bondage of the brick pits and ready to take their place in the world as God's own. The Pesach sacrifice acted as the catalyst that catapulted them forwards in their national spiritual development; the threshold of their homes, ceremoniously marked with its blood, marked the verge of the process. Once they crossed that doorway and journeyed forth there would be no turning back. In a similar vein, both the *metzora* as well as the one who suffers corpse defilement undergo a series of rites as they move from their oppressive present situations to something more sublime. In essence, the *metzora* and the *tamei* feel a measure of that which is at the heart of the Exodus experience: *transformation*.

Exile and Redemption

But if it is transformation that we discern when reflecting upon the triad, then we must consider it more closely: what precisely is the nature of the transformation? When we speak of the Israelites in Egypt, we may describe their transformation in specific geographic and existential terms: *exile and redemption*. Banished from Canaan because of famine, the people descended to Egypt. There, though they initially enjoyed material plenty, they suffered from spiritual want. When their hosts' welcome was exhausted, they were enslaved. Their estrangement from God was now mirrored by their physical exile far from their land and from the familiar landscape of Canaan. When Israel left Egypt, they embarked on an odyssey that would eventually bring them first to Sinai and then finally, decades later, back to the Promised Land. Much as Israel had surrendered their spiritual patrimony when they left Canaan's verdant hills behind, they first had to reclaim it at Sinai before completing the redemptive process of their return to the land.

As for the *metzora*, stricken with a condition that our Sages maintain is a consequence of spiritual deficiency, he is banished from his home and from the larger encampment of Israel. In effect, he too suffers the estrangement of "exile" and dislocation so that he might ponder his sorry state and begin the process of spiritual repair. How he pines for restoration to his family and community, eagerly anticipating the day when the Kohen will pronounce him fit! But how the days seem to drag on interminably! When the day of his redemption finally dawns, he too takes the ritual objects associated with the Exodus from Egypt – the blood and the hyssop – and marks the moment of his transition. Then he begins the arduous process of securing complete restoration to the camp and to his former life.

The *tamei* also experiences physical exile and spiritual estrangement, for he is barred from entering the holy precincts of the Temple as long as he remains in his state of *tuma*. Insofar as exile means distance from one's place of origin and familiar landscape, the *tamei* is in exile. The center of his national life and concern, the symbol of his connection to his God and to his people, the holy Mishkan or Mikdash, is painfully out of bounds as long as he is *tamei*. Can there be a more anguished banishment than this?

Purification from Death and Emergence to Life

We have thus far noted two dimensions to the discussion. First of all, Israel in Egypt, the *metzora* sent far from the encampment, or the *tamei* who may not enter the Temple, all experience a transformation when they return to their former more ideal states. That transformation is marked by the ritual of the blood/water and the hyssop, with each one of the three ceremonies possessing a unique character of its own. Second of all, the transformation of which we speak is immediately comprehensible when we recast it in more familiar terms: exile and redemption. The Exodus is akin to the *metzora*'s return to the camp or the *tamei*'s re-entry into the courtyard of the Temple, as each one reclaims their true destiny, seizes a forward trajectory and sets their sites for the "promised land." The journey may be long and arduous, plagued by setbacks or failures, but there can be no doubt about the destination.

The theme of exile and redemption is one that naturally emerges as a common denominator when we consider the three from the starting point of the Exodus, as Ibn Ezra suggests. But what will another starting point yield? What if we were to begin our discussion with the matter of the purification rites from death? Any man who has come into contact with a human corpse is ritually unfit to stand before God. The Temple is where we experience God's presence – the source of all life – and when we are tainted with death we must therefore pause at its portals and not enter the sacred enclosure; *tuma*, the antithesis of life and all that is vital, bars our entry. We do not blame the human being for being mortal; we only protest against the state of death that our poor moral choices have introduced into the world.

While in a state of *tuma*, we suffer spiritual estrangement and experience a different form of exile, exile from life and from vitality. When we are ready to emerge from that state to once again stand in the presence of God, we prepare by undergoing the rites associated with the red heifer. It is in this dimension that the elements of the rites acquire greater clarity. Now, a mixture consisting of living waters and ashes, potent symbols of life and death respectively, is sprinkled upon the individual with the aid of the organic hyssop, a tenacious plant that thrives in even the most arid and ashen environments. In this way, the moment of transformation is marked by the taking of items that mark the passage, as the *tamei* person transcends morbidity to secure life.

As for the Exodus from Egypt, surely the emergence from death to life must be counted as one of its most salient themes. This is of course true on a literal level – the male children flung into the Nile, the Israelite bondservants beaten and killed, the murderous regime that state-sponsored slavery inevitably imposes upon its victims – all of it overthrown by the events of the Exodus. But there is the more subtle form of resurgence as well. In Egypt, though the budding tribes of Israel preserved a common language and shared a common fate while laboring for their taskmasters, they were not able to exercise any form of self-determination that is the hallmark of a national existence. All of this was transformed by the Exodus, as they became a people and began to make the kinds of choices that up until that point had been the exclusive preserve of their overlords. Seizing the hyssop and smearing the blood upon the threshold, they came back to life as the *people of Israel*, their atrophied lungs now taking in the invigorating and restorative air of national freedom.

And what of the *metzora*? Does he too move from a state of death to one of life, as he presents his offering and is then readmitted to the camp of Israel? His estrangement from his family and community and his banishment outside of the camp certainly imply some loss of vital energy, some cutting off from the vigor that a social context confers. If we are prepared to adopt the Rabbinic explanation for his sorry state then the link becomes even more cohesive. For the Rabbis, a man is punished with *tzara'at* for speaking evil of others, for making disparaging remarks, for misusing the precious gift of speech with which only the human being is endowed. As Rashi explains in the name of the ancient Rabbis:

> . . . the plague (of *tzara'at*) happens on account of evil speech that involves prattle. Thus, birds are required for the purification rites because they chirp and chatter constantly and noisily . . . (commentary to *VaYikra* 14:4)

Significantly, when the Aramaic Targum of Onkelos (2nd century, Israel) translated the matter of the "breath of life" that God blew into the nostrils of inert Adam in order to bestow upon him vigor and animation, he translated the term as "the breath of speech" (see *Breisheet* 2:7)! Perhaps we do not go too far in asserting that the *metzora* who has misused speech has introduced death into his community and sown destruction by his hurtful words.

The purification of the *metzora*, then, must perforce imply a transition not only from exile to redemption but from death to life as well. The living waters, drawn from a flowing spring, are symbols of life, for where there is water there is vitality. The two undomesticated and vibrant birds, that ideally must be equivalent in appearance, size and value (Mishna *Nega'im* 14:5), signify the two antithetical states and the emergence from the one to the other. One of the birds experiences death while the other, held tight with the hyssop while dipped into the waters, is set free into an open space, "the field," signifying the *metzora's* re-emergence into a state of pristine potential. The whole world beckons, just beyond the completion of his purification! As the Chizkuni explains in a slightly different formulation but with the same intent:

> The sending forth of the bird symbolizes the dissipation of the *tzara'at* state. Previously he was like a lonely bird trapped upon a roof, distant from all other people. But now he is permitted to rejoin his kin, just like this bird that had been captured but now was free to rejoin its fellows. (commentary to *VaYikra* 14:7)

The three situations – the slave in bondage in Egypt, the *metzora* banished from the camp, and the person who has touched the corpse – all inhabit the same static dimension. All have experienced, in one form or another, the sting of exile and the stupor of death, whether physical and real, or spiritual and no less real. Though we do not presently have a Temple, *tzara'at* is a thing of the past and the Exodus happened long, long ago, the lesson of these things is still germane. Our goal must be to overcome apathy and to seize life – physical and spiritual, individual and national – as our destiny.

FOR FURTHER STUDY:

(1) The link between exile and death is drawn most forcefully by the prophet Yechezkel in his famous vision of the "dry bones." This prophet was active in Babylon at the end of the First Temple period, among the Jews who had been exiled before the final destruction of Jerusalem. It was a time of great upheaval, calamity and despair. In chapter 37, Yechezkel has a vision of a valley filled with very dry bones that are miraculously restored to life by the breath of God:

> God said to me: son of man, these bones are the entire house of Israel, behold they say "our bones are dry, our hope is lost and we have been cut off!" Therefore, prophesy and say to them: Thus says Almighty God "Behold, I will open your graves and I will raise you out of your graves, My people, and I will bring you to the land of Israel. You will know that I am God when I open your graves and when I take you out of your graves, My people. I will put My spirit into you and you shall live and I will place you upon your land, and you will know that I am God, for I spoke and I fulfilled says God!" (*Yechezkel* 37:11–14)

ACHAREI MOT

The Laws of *Tuma* and *Tahara*

Leviticus 16:1-18:30

THE BIBLICAL laws of *tuma* and *tahara*, inadequately translated as "unclean" and "clean," constitute one of the most significant, if least understood, foundations of the book of VaYikra. These provisions are to be found scattered throughout many of the *parashiyot* of the Torah, but the core of the matter is in the *parashiyot* of Shemini, Tazria, Metzora and Acharei Mot (*VaYikra*, chapters 11–16). In order to emphasize that the terms "uncleanness" and "cleanness" are deficient and misleading, we shall intentionally use *tuma* and *tahara* without translation.

We shall examine some of these laws with the intent of coming to a more profound appreciation of the matter, at least insofar as broader themes are concerned. Along the way we may achieve a more cautious respect for an important aspect of Torah legislation that most people unfortunately regard as obscure, enigmatic and absolutely obsolete. For the purposes of brevity, we shall begin our discussion by listing data gleaned from a large number of textual sources. We shall endeavor to create a concise but comprehensive guide that makes, however, no attempt at exhaustiveness. We would do well to begin our investigation by recalling the sage advice of Maimonides, who concluded his discussion of the Laws of Immersion by remarking:

> It should be clear and obvious that the laws of *tuma* and *tahara* are decrees of the Torah that would not necessarily have been formulated by the exercise of human reason and logic. These laws are rather included among the חוקים, that is, divine injunctions without an obvious rational basis . . .

Generally speaking, we may divide up the laws of *tuma* and *tahara* into three distinct realms. The first addresses *sources* of *tuma*, namely those items that serve as generators of this condition. What sorts of things are *tamei*, and by what mechanism is *tuma* transferred from one thing to another? The second speaks of *processes* of *tahara*, namely the ritual procedures that are necessary in order to dissipate a state of *tuma* and reinstate a condition of *tahara* in its place. How does a person or an object overcome a state of *tuma* and achieve *tahara* in its stead? The third concerns the *impact* of *tuma*, for what limits does this curious condition impose upon the person or object so affected? It should be stated at the outset that for the most part, the laws of *tuma* and *tahara* are no longer practiced today in any form, with the exception of particular circumstances that I shall enumerate.

Sources of Tuma

According to biblical law, there are a number of distinct objects or situations that act as sources of *tuma*. The first category of things relates to physical death. Thus, the human corpse is regarded as one of the most virulent sources of *tuma* (*BeMidbar* 19:11), as is the dead reptile or "creeping thing" (*VaYikra* 11:29–31) as well as the carcasses of various "clean" animals (11:39), "unclean" animals (11:26–28) and "clean" birds (17:15). Parenthetically, "clean" and "unclean" in this context refer to what we call today "kosher" and "non-kosher," namely those creatures ritually fit for consumption and those disqualified from consumption. In all of the above cases, contact (which may include indirect carrying or, in the case of the corpse, even overshadowing) with the dead object renders the person, vessel or foodstuff *tamei*. In some cases, that *tuma* can be communicated to another object in turn, but usually to a lesser degree.

The second category of *tuma* arises as a function of various afflictions associated with the living human being. The זב (15:2) is a male who suffers from some sort of flux or discharge (erroneously translated as gonorrhea), the זבה (15:25) is a female similarly afflicted, the נדה (15:19) is the menstruating woman, the יולדת (12:2) is the woman who has given birth, the צרוע (13:2 et al.) has one of a number of possible skin conditions (erroneously translated as leprosy, as we have seen). All of these individuals, as well as the male who has experienced a seminal emission (15:16), are considered to be in a state of *tuma*, and their bodily secretions are similarly *tamei*. Curiously, the woman who has given birth to a male child is *temeia* for a period of seven days, but if a female child has been born, the period of *tuma* is twice as long – fourteen days.

Finally, we have forms of *tuma* that are associated with specific sacrificial rites that render *tamei* those involved with their preparation. The burning of the red heifer as well as contact with the resulting ash (*BeMidbar* 19:7 et al.) are sources of *tuma*, as are various bullock sacrifices (*VaYikra* 4:3) that are associated with certain transgressions of the High Priest (פר כהן משיח), particular sins of the congregation of Israel (פר העלם דבר של ציבור – 4:13), or else elements of the Yom Kippur service (16:3 – פר יום הכיפורים). In all of the above, those individuals involved with burning the sacrificial carcass outside of the camp are rendered *tamei* for their efforts! Additionally, some he-goat sacrifices, such as that of Yom Kippur (16:27 – שעיר של יום הכיפורים) as well as that of the congregation of Israel (*BeMidbar* 15:24), have a similar effect. Lastly, the scapegoat of the Yom Kippur service (*VaYikra* 16:26), banished to the desolate wilderness bearing the iniquities of the people of Israel, causes its sender to enter a state of *tuma*.

The detailed regulations and various contingencies associated with the above items are very involved and beyond the scope of this essay to explore. Bear in mind that the largest of the six orders of the Mishna is none other than "Taharot," which deals at great length with this subject matter! Our intent is to arrive at some general understanding of the conceptual framework, without attempting to entirely integrate every particular into this structure, an undertaking that would be onerous and of necessity contrived. For the present, therefore, let us content ourselves with noting that thus far *tuma* has some association with either physical death, the functioning or malfunctioning of the male and female reproductive organs, or else sacrifices associated with rather serious transgressions. If we exclude this last category of sacrifices, then the state of *tuma* does not appear to be generated by axiological considerations but rather by biological imperatives. That is to say that the onset of *tuma* is typically not a function of a person's ethical conduct but rather a result of the body's self-regulated processes of growth and decay.

Processes of Tahara

Just as the sources of *tuma* include a broad array of items or situations, so too the process of *tahara* associated with each involves a different ritual. Thus, in order to effect *tahara* for an individual who has come into contact with a human corpse, sprinkling with a solution composed of red heifer ashes dissolved in spring water must take place on the third and seventh day, followed by immersion in a *mikvah* or specially constructed ritual pool of water. For contact with one of the carcasses enumerated above, ritual immersion is sufficient, and the *tahara* is then completed with the onset of nightfall. For the זב, זבה or יולדת the presentation of special sacrifices is also ordained. The individual afflicted with צרעת undergoes a complex and involved ceremonial including the presentation of two birds, one of which is set free. It should be noted that in all cases, the *tahara* rite does not impact on the actual source of *tuma* itself, be it the corpse, the flux, the carcass etc., but rather on the *person* or *vessel* who came into contact with that source. In other words, there is no way to purify the corpse from its *tamei* state. Only the person or object that touched, carried or overshadowed the corpse, thus becoming *tamei* in the process, can be restored to a state of *tahara* according to the prescribed rituals.

The above outline illustrates that it is difficult to speak of a general process of *tahara* that is universally efficacious. What can be concluded, however, is that all rites of *tahara* involve the element of water, whether it is the spring water of the sprinkled ashes of the red heifer, the immersion in the waters of the *mikvah*, or the "living spring waters" associated with the *tahara* of the צרוע.

The Impact of Tuma

Of what consequence is it to be in a state of *tuma*? It should be obvious by now that being *tamei* does not express itself in the realm of the physical, but rather constitutes a state of being. With some celebrated exceptions, the state of *tuma* imposes absolutely no qualifying conditions upon the individual so affected, with the exception of one: He or she is denied entry into the precincts of the Mishkan or Mikdash (the Tabernacle in the wilderness and later the Temple at Jerusalem) and is not permitted to participate in the associated activity of consuming sacrificial meats or sanctified foods. The degree to which one's entry is curtailed is a function of the specific *tuma* with which one is affected, for the Temple compound contains varying areas of sanctity. This qualification is such a glaring feature of the state of *tuma* that Maimonides adopted it as the underlying rationale for this entire otherwise inexplicable series of laws. Writing in the Guide to the Perplexed (3:37), he remarks:

> We have already explained that the purpose of the Temple was to inspire the visitor with feelings of reverence and awe [of God]. It is well-known that any encounter, no matter how exalted or noble, loses its efficacy when it is experienced regularly, and its effect on the human soul and personality correspondingly decreases. Therefore our Sages have suggested that it is not preferable to visit the Temple too regularly . . . This being the case, the Torah legislated such a multitude of forms of *tuma* and barred those individuals in a state of *tuma* from entering the Temple, in order to limit the possibility of being in a state of *tahara* and therefore

the opportunity of entry. If a person is able to avoid contact with an animal carcass, he will be less able to avoid contact with a dead reptile or creeping thing, for they are quite commonly found in houses and in foodstuffs. If he succeeds in averting them, he will surely come into contact with a יולדת, זבה, זב, נדה, or touch the objects upon which they have alighted . . . All of these regulations are a means of limiting one's access to the Temple and discouraging habitual entry to its precincts . . . thus preserving the reverential character of the place and safeguarding the purpose of instilling humility before God.

Although we may disagree with Maimonides' underlying thesis that the incredibly complex and involved laws of *tuma* are simply legislated as impediments to Temple entry, we cannot deny the linkage. Being in a state of *tuma* effectively bars one from treading upon its hallowed ground. It is for this very reason that observant Jews to this day will not ascend certain areas of the Temple Mount, for some forms of *tuma* (such as that associated with corpse contact) cannot be removed in the absence of as-of-yet-unrestored rituals. It is not disconnection for the place but rather, paradoxically, intense reverence for it that currently self-excludes many Jews from the area of the Temple Mount.

So far, we have investigated some of the basic foundations of the laws of *tuma* and *tahara*. We have made no attempt to integrate what we have seen into any sort of a larger idea, although we have already began to notice certain repeating motifs that may in fact be intertwined. The death quality of *tuma*, the water element of *tahara* and the looming presence of the Temple are all factors in this complex equation. What can be stated conclusively at this point is that *tuma* and *tahara* appear to exist in some sort of a binary relationship. Either one is in a state of *tuma* or else one is in a state of *tahara*, but there exists no intermediate state between the two. Additionally, although the exact meaning of *tuma* remains at this point obscure, it should be clear that the matter has absolutely nothing to do with physical hygiene. This is borne out by the simple fact that those items that we clean-conscious moderns would consider to be particularly harmful and unhealthy are not generators of *tuma* at all! As Rabbi Yehuda HaLevi pungently remarks in his *Kuzari* (2:61) "urine, excrement, and the like, notwithstanding their noxiousness and pathogenic qualities . . . are not sources of *tuma*, whereas a seminal issue is!" If *tuma* and *tahara* are not expressions of unclean and clean, then what exactly are they?

Tuma of Vessels

Let us begin to unravel the mystery by investigating some tangential *halakhot* that will, in the end, provide the key to comprehending the matter. Bear in mind that the following discussion has little relevance for today's reality, and hearkens back to the time when the Temple stood at Jerusalem. As we have already seen, sources of *tuma* such as the human corpse or the animal carcass can convey *tuma* to people or to objects that come into contact with them. However, not all objects are equally susceptible to *tuma*. Certain objects remain immune to many of its injurious effects, even insofar as the most serious corpse *tuma* is concerned. The Talmud in TB *Shabbat* 58a states: "Vessels fashioned out of stone or earth [unfired] are not susceptible to *tuma*, neither according to Torah law nor according to Rabbinic enactment." The Mishna in Tractate *Keilim* ("Vessels") elaborates:

> Vessels made out of wood, hides or animal bone are unsusceptible to *tuma* when they are fashioned as flat surfaces, but can become *tamei* when they have a receptacle

(2:1) . . . earthenware vessels are susceptible to *tuma* insofar as their airspace is concerned, but not when contact with *tuma* takes place on their outer surface (2:2) . . . vessels made out of metal are susceptible to *tuma* whether they are flat surfaces or have a receptacle. (11:1)

According to the above sources, we may broadly speak of a number of categories of vessels. Some vessels, namely those made out of *stone* or *unfired earth*, never become *tamei*, even when they come into direct contact with a corpse or other primary source of *tuma*. Other vessels can become *tamei* but only when they are fashioned with a "receptacle," which is to say some sort of an inner volume that can be used to hold something. A *wooden* vessel, for instance, when fashioned as a flat surface such as a tabletop, cannot become *tamei* according to Torah law. A wooden bowl, on the other hand, will become *tamei* if a source of *tuma* comes into contact with it, and will have to be ritually immersed in the *mikvah* in order to restore it to a state of *tahara*. *Metal* vessels, in contrast, are susceptible to *tuma* even as flat surfaces such as a simple tray, and certainly when they are in the form of "receptacles" such as cups, bowls, boxes, etc. The *earthenware* vessel, perhaps the most unusual of the group, becomes *tamei* when *tuma* is suspended within its inner airspace (even if no direct contact with the sides of the vessel takes place), but not when *tuma* touches its outer surface, even when direct contact does take place! Additionally, alone among all of the other receptacles, the earthenware vessel, once it has contracted *tuma*, cannot be returned to a state of *tahara* even by immersion in a *mikvah*. Only by breaking it into useless shards is it purified! How are we to comprehend these confusing laws and to formulate some sort of an underlying principle based upon them?

Human Potential and the Lifeless Vessel

When the human artisan takes a rough piece of stone and reshapes it to suit human needs and aesthetics, a transformation of its shape and surface qualities has clearly taken place. Nevertheless, the inert stone material remains untransformed by the human intervention, for the elemental substance is just as it was. The outer surface qualities of the stone may loudly proclaim the work of man, but its essential substance and materiality are as fixed as before. With respect to wood, however, some additional processing must take place, for before the human being can begin to act upon the physical mass of the wood, he must first accomplish some sort of transformation of its essence. The wood in its crude and original state is unsuited for work. The tree must be felled, its bark stripped away, its substance dried and treated before it can be effectively reshaped. In other words, in contrast to stone, the wooden material itself begins to speak of the human potential invested in it, for the wood must first be removed from the state of nature and introduced to the world of man. In the case of metal, the effect is even more pronounced, for metals rarely occur in nature in usable forms. First, suitable ore must be mined, then it must be crushed and sifted, until finally it can be refined and transformed in the fiery crucible.

The consistent pattern that emerges is that as the degree of human potential invested in the material or object increases and the expression of that investment becomes more pronounced, so too does the susceptibility to tuma. In consonance with this principle governing material qualities, the utilitarian qualities of the object or its ability to "hold" things also increases its risk of becoming *tamei*. This is because possessing the form of a receptacle confers upon the vessel greater potential for human use. A bowl is potentially more useful to us than a flat tray, because a bowl, by virtue of its inner volume, can hold a greater variety of objects or liquids. Its external form enhances its usefulness for our purposes, and this is expressed in the world of *tuma* and *tahara* as a heightened sensitivity to contracting *tuma*.

Nowhere is the anthropogenic impact more pronounced than in the case of the earthenware vessel, for although its elemental clay material is as inert and lifeless as stone, something unusual takes place when man introduces fire to the equation. The chemical makeup of the clay is actually transformed by the heat so that the resulting material becomes impervious to water, proclaiming an alteration that forever separates the earthenware from its more humble origins. It is this starkest of contrasts – the most static matter transmuted by man's most profound spark of inventiveness – that is highlighted by the laws of the earthenware vessel. Its outer surface remains resistant and impenetrable to any type of *tuma*, but simply suspend *tuma* within its airspace, the potentially useful volume bound by its terra cotta perimeter, and the earthenware vessel becomes inalterably *tamei*; nothing short of completely shattering its visage can return it to a state of *tahara*.

The fundamental principle that emerges is that *tuma* and *tahara* are not arbitrary or irrational states of being, but rather are intrinsically related to the human condition, to the human potential that God has given us to shape the world to our ends. Wherever we find a greater degree of human potential that has left its mark on the world, there we will find a greater susceptibility to *tuma*. And *tuma* is nothing less or more than the counterweight of *tahara*: both express the concretization of human potential and the impact of that concretization on the world around us.

Reconsidering the Generators of Tuma

Returning to the generators of *tuma*, they now are suddenly more comprehensible, for the most virulent type of *tuma* is that conveyed by the human corpse. The human being, perhaps alone in the cosmos, has the unique potential to apprehend God, to spiritually develop and to grow, and to permanently alter the moral (not to mention the physical) state of the world. When the human being expires and his body dies, that potential is forever dissipated. Although Jewish tradition asserts that the spiritual soul of man lives on forever, the ability to accomplish, to improve, and to impact with sublimity on this physical world of mundane cares is spent with the demise of the house of clay within which the soul fleetingly and often contentiously dwelt. As our Sages wistfully describe it, "when a person dies, he is freed from mitzvah obligations" (TB *Shabbat* 30a). The potential inherent in the performance of a mitzvah or in the fulfillment of a divine command is, for the Torah, the most pronounced expression of the human being's capacity to transcend deadening equilibrium in order to *become*. Death, however, truncates that opportunity, for there can be no more momentum in the grave.

All members of the first category of *tuma* sources discussed above are related to this notion, for the specter of death hovers over them all. The dead animal, reptile, or bird is *tamei* because the world of man and the world of the lower creatures are intertwined, and in their passing we too experience the dismal ache associated with corporeal decay. Who can remain spiritually immune to the effects of life's ebb and the body's ruin, for wherever the life force futilely fades away, *tuma* encroaches.

The second category of *tuma* generators, almost all related to the function or malfunction of the human reproductive organs, pertains to the same theme, for not only does the cessation of physical life invite the state of *tuma*, but even the dissipation of *potential* life.

The זב and זבה both suffer from some sort of issue involving a disruption of their capacity to reproduce, as if the possibility of generating new human life has been temporarily curtailed. The נדה or menstruating woman has shed the ovum that might have been, that could have become, that had the potential to assume the form of a living human being. The loss of that potential, blameless and natural though it may have been, is the dynamo that drives the state of *tuma*, for human existence can never remain undefined. If *tahara* cannot be present, then by default *tuma* takes its exalted place, for the spiritual condition of man abhors a vacuum. In analogous fashion the male also becomes *tamei* when he has experienced a seminal issue, even when a single one of the hundreds of millions of gametes released by his willful act of intercourse has wondrously spawned new life. Once again, it is the loss of potential human life contained in all of the non-fertilizing sperm that allow for *tuma* to intrude.

The pregnant woman contains within her body the miracle of new life in formation. Upon releasing the fetus in the act of birth, she has introduced that new life into the world, but in the process has become shorn of the potential that was latent within her. What is regarded as a new beginning for her offspring, is for her, paradoxically, a moment of loss, for the miraculous translation of that potential life into real life has left her bereft of the promise that was heretofore developing within her body. She therefore enters a temporary state of *tuma* soon relieved by the counting of days, immersion in a *mikvah*, and the bringing of prescribed offerings. As for the curious twofold measure of *tuma* associated with the birth of a female, the fourteen days of confinement versus the seven days attendant upon the birth of a male (*VaYikra* 12:1–8), we may now appreciate it as something other than unfair bias. Rather, it is the acknowledgement of the female's unique capacity to nurture nascent life within her body. Since the female infant is herself capable of one day sustaining, nourishing, and giving birth to new life, the delivery of that child constitutes a "double loss" of potential insofar as the mother is concerned. This results in a state of *tuma* lasting twice as long as that associated with the birth of a male!

In light of all of the above, we may now confidently conclude that the state of *tuma* is cohesively bound up with *the state of death*. Physical death, whether of man or beast, as well as death of the potential for human life even in its incomplete forms, even the spiritual death that necessitates the presentation of those certain sin-offerings outlined above, are the breeding grounds that spawn the doleful condition of *tuma*. The condition persists until it is relieved by immersion in a *mikvah*. In some cases of *tuma*, other rites are enjoined as well, but immersion in a *mikvah* at some stage of the process is always required.

The Roots of the Mikvah: Of Jericho and Job

What exactly is the *mikvah*, spelled out explicitly in Parashat Shemini and alluded to in many other related contexts? In the discussion of the "crawling things" that convey *tuma* when dead, the Torah remarks: "However, the spring or pool, a gathering of waters shall be *tahor*, but he who comes into contact with the carcass of these things shall be *tamei*'" (11:36). This "gathering of waters" in Hebrew is מקוה מים, the scriptural basis for the familiar term "*mikvah*." Although the text fails to spell out its features in more exact detail, it is clear that water is its defining element.

The commentaries are in universal agreement that מקוה, from the biblical root קוה, means a gathering of waters, just as we find concerning creation, when God gathered the deep waters that covered the terrestrial surface and caused the dry land to emerge. "The Lord said: 'Let the waters be gathered (יקוו המים) from under the heavens to one place, so that the dry land will emerge,' and it was so" (*Breisheet* 1:6). Curiously, though, this very same root has at least two other distinct meanings. It is the foundation of the familiar תקוה or "hope," as well as the basis of the less-well-known קו or "twisted cord."

Occasionally, these latter two meanings are brought together for literary effect to produce an unusual play on words. Thus, when Rachav the harlot hides the spies that Yehoshua had sent to spy out the city of Jericho and later aids their escape through her well-situated window, she asks for her life and for the life of her family in return. The men advise her: "Behold, we will soon attack the city. Tie this cord of scarlet in the window by which you lowered us down, and gather your parents and family into your home . . . if any harm shall come to whosoever shall be inside your house, we shall be held accountable . . ." (*Yehoshua* 2:18). Here, the pivotal *cord* of scarlet, the means of her deliverance and thus a dazzling symbol of hope, is תקות חוט השני.

In a less optimistic context, as the anguished Job contemplates his misery and awaits his bitter and untimely end, he laments: "My days expire faster than the weaver's shuttle, to be ended without *hope*" (*Iyov* 7:6). Here, Job sees his life fleetingly passing before him, just as quickly as the weaver thrusts the shuttle of yarn through the extended threads of the warp. They will end "without hope," rendered in the original Hebrew as **באפס תקוה**, a poignant play on words, because תקוה can also refer to the *yarn* or *cord* of the shuttle, the cord that Job sees suddenly running out before the fabric can be completed! His own life, like the weaver's yarn, will be cut off before he has accomplished all that he had wished, and dejectedly he watches, as his hope for better days vanishes.

Rabbi David Kimchi explains in his *Sefer HaShorashim* or Book of Biblical Roots that the three meanings of the root קוה, namely (1) gathering, (2) hope and (3) cord, are in fact completely unrelated, notwithstanding the fact that they all share the same exact consonantal basis. The *mikvah* is therefore to be rendered the "gathering of waters" and is constructed as a pool within the earth or rock (and not upon it) into which rainwater is naturally collected. For the Radak, the *mikvah* has nothing to do with either hope or twisted cords!

It is the Ramban, in an unrelated context (commentary to *Breisheet* 1:1), who provides us with an insight that can propel our investigation forward. In an involved discussion concerning the nature of the primordial matter, the Ramban suggests that in the initial act of creation, God brought forth from absolute nothingness a primary substance so incorporeal that it lacked any physical qualities whatsoever. It is called in the account of the Torah "*tohu*" (תוהו), and perhaps corresponds to what modern physics refers to as "energy." Using that potential-laden medium, God fashioned the first tangible substance, tenuous and transitory (the earliest unstable elements?), from which all other matter was ultimately derived. It is referred to as "*bohu*" (בהו), literally "in it," for it contains in its latency the possibility of everything else in the material cosmos. Working with these remarkably prescient definitions, the Ramban goes on to explain an otherwise obscure verse from SeferYeshayahu. The context of the verse is a frightful vision of destruction that God will visit upon rebellious Edom, the archetypal plunderer of the Jewish state: ". . . their land will become as burning pitch . . . it shall be forever desolate . . . a habitat for the . . . owl and raven . . . for He shall stretch upon it the line (קו) of '*tohu*', and stones of '*bohu*'" (*Yeshayahu* 34:9–11). The Ramban explains:

> The קו or line belongs to the builder, it is his plumb line, and with it he marks out his plans for the building and what he hopes to accomplish. The usage is similar to that of the verse: "Hope (קוה) for God and be strong hearted" (*Tehillim* 27:14). The stones are the form that the building assumes . . .

In other words, says the Ramban, this "*tohu*" or pure potential is analogous to the קו or line of the builder, for both suggest the possibilities and plans waiting to be realized in the material world. The stones or building blocks, in contrast, speak of the following stage, namely the "bohu" or primary matter that must be arranged and rearranged in order to yield the building. In Isaiah's eschatological vision, God's plans for Edom will also come to fruition, for in the end His retribution will be visited upon it.

For our purposes, what is important is that the Ramban suggests an explicit linkage between two meanings of the root קוה. The line is called a קו because it is related to the hopes and aspirations, the תקוות, of the builder who wields it. The meanings that for the Radak were disparate, for the Ramban are the same. The yarn or thread (תקוה) of the weaver also quite naturally belongs to this definition, for it too speaks of the potential cloth that awaits realization. We may easily relate the third meaning of the root to this framework as well, for to *gather* something up is to augment its potential for purposeful use. By gathering the waters, God not only reveals the dry land, but also increases the potential of the seas, for they are now concentrated in a more localized volume. And so it is with every other material. To be scattered is to have less potentiality, while to be consolidated is to have more. In short, קוה speaks of promise, of opportunity and of potential.

Let us now apply this idea to the matter of the *mikvah*. Bear in mind that the Hebrew language organizes words not only by definition, but by grammatical form as well. The morphology of "*mikvah*" relates it to an entire category of nouns that all mean the "place of xyz," where "xyz" is the relevant root. Thus, to be precise, the word "*mikvah*" actually means the "place of קוה." Up until now we have understood the term to mean "the place of the gathering [of waters]," and this has provided us with an eminently plausible reading. Now recognizing, however, that the "gathering" of קוה is the same as the "hope" of תקוה as well as being related to the קו of the "thread or line," we may confidently translate the term "*mikvah*" differently. The *mikvah* is actually the *place of potential* because the gathered waters that it contains are a concrete expression of the hopes and aspirations of all who enter its fluid embrace.

The *mikvah*, therefore, becomes the repository of hope and the reservoir of aspiration, for water is the generative element that more than any other fosters life. We are alive because of water, and in its absence we wither and perish. If there are worlds in the cosmos besides our own Earth that contain life similar to what exists on our planet, then those worlds must also have water, for without this precious liquid, survival is impossible. To enter the organic waters of the *mikvah* is therefore to be reinvigorated with an expression of the life force, to shed the death and demise of *tuma* and to be created anew. It should come as no surprise that the mystical teachings relate the *mikvah* to the watery womb and the act of immersion to the time before birth. To submerge completely in its waters (as the Halakha mandates) is to return to the pristine moment during which we effortlessly drifted, untroubled and safe in the warm sea of our mother's buoyant embrace, borne aloft by indistinct and pleasant dreams of life's endless potential. How tragic indeed that modern scientific approaches have one-dimensionally understood the *mikvah* as a primitive form of hygiene that can be thankfully dispensed with, now that we have indoor plumbing! What an utter misreading of what *tuma* is about and of what the experience of immersion can be!

Tahara and the Temple

The rites associated with *tahara* invariably involve the waters of the *mikvah*, because *tahara* is the emergence from the state of *tuma*, the death grip that seeks to seize us whenever we are confronted by the specter of mortal passing. When in a state of *tuma*, entry to the Temple precincts is curtailed, for the Temple is the place in which we experience God's immediacy and closeness, and God is *life*. Bearing in mind the "negative theology" of Maimonides who explains that we cannot speak with certainty of what God is but only of what He is not, we might with assurance say that God is not dead! Quite the opposite, for God is the life force that animates the cosmos. Of all things, God alone is absolute and unconditional existence, undiminished and unlimited life that knows no cessation and no end. God's proper name itself, the ineffable Tetragrammaton or four letter appellation, is predicated upon a grammatical root that simply means "Timeless Being" or "Eternal Existence." When in a state of *tuma*, therefore, one cannot stand in God's immediate presence, for first the veil of death must be lifted by immersion and *tahara*. To return to the words of the *Kuzari*, authored by Rabbi Yehuda HaLevi: ". . . God's presence (שכינה or "indwelling," the experience of which was centered at the Temple) was associated with the people of Israel in the same way that the soul animates the body . . ." (2:62).

In a deliberate and provocative mixing of the metaphors, the Torah and books of the prophets often portray the Temple not only as the source of proximity to God and therefore eternal life, but as a source of "living waters" as well. This is imagery that has its roots in Eden, for the Torah's description of that ideal state of eternal life in perfect harmony with God and the rest of creation speaks of "a river that issued out of Eden to water the garden . . ." (*Breisheet* 2:1). The notion is alluded to in a number of other places (see for example *Yoel* 4:18, *Zechariah* 14:8), and most especially in Yechezkel's vision of the restored Temple (*Yechezkel* 47:1–13), where the Eden parallel is vividly revisited:

> . . . behold, on the banks of the stream [that issued forth from under the threshold of the Temple gate], on either side, were all manner of fruit trees. Their leaves did not wither, nor did they cease giving forth their fruits. Monthly, their fruits would grow anew, for the waters of the stream issued forth *from the holy Temple*. The fruits were for eating and the leaves had curative qualities.

What we saw elsewhere as an implied linkage is here spelled out explicitly: the Temple and the *mikvah* are both bound up in a tight matrix that stands in glaring opposition to the state of *tuma* and the death that hovers over it. We have therefore come full circle. The state of *tuma*, associated with death, excludes one from the place of life, the Temple, until one performs rites of *tahara* that restore the state of life. The concept of *tuma* reminds us that the world is not yet perfect, that there is still sickness, sadness and mortality. These realities often operate independently of the moral choices that we may personally make, and are better understood as forces that impact upon the world as long as humanity as a whole remains committed to destructive plans. At the same time, however, we are inspired by the assurance of the *mikvah* that life will one day triumph, death will be vanquished and the state of Eden will be restored:

> He will destroy death forever and Lord God will wipe the tears away from every face. He will remove the reproach of His people from upon the whole earth, for God has spoken (*Yeshayahu* 25:8).

FOR FURTHER STUDY:

(1) In addition to the *tuma* restrictions placed upon the נדה insofar as entry to the Temple compound is concerned, there is also the curtailment of marital intimacy associated with the onset of the menstrual period. Modern social scientists have attempted, with some degree of malice, to link the two, as if the woman's "unclean" state is the root cause of the Bible's enjoinder upon intimacy. These claims have been buttressed by scholarly comparisons with other primitive cultures that developed taboos against harmful bodily issues and especially against blood. Although echoes of such ideas can be found within the corpus of Jewish tradition (see for example the comments of the Ramban on *VaYikra* 12:4, and especially on *Breisheet* 31:35), there are also alternative views that are equally valid. The Ra'avad, Rabbi Avraham ben David of Posquieres, one of the foremost Talmudists of the 12th century, had the following to say in his introduction to the *Ba'alei HaNefesh*, an authoritative treatment of the laws of menstruation:

> In order that a man should know that there is a God above who is sovereign over him, man was given laws and ordinances to govern his relations with woman, just as we find in every other area of human endeavor. One who owns a field must adhere to the Torah's commands with respect to plowing, planting and harvest, for mixed kinds are forbidden and a portion of the harvest must be shared with the poor . . . when a person desires to partake of his bread, he must first invoke God's name and bless Him before and after . . . garments must not be composed of a mixture of wool and linen . . . the male body also is governed by Torah law, for circumcision must be performed upon it . . . a person's time is informed by the observance of the Shabbat and the holidays during which *melakha* (creative labor) is forbidden . . . so too, relations between a couple are guided by the Torah's laws, for they are commanded to separate at the times of her period and childbirth . . .

In other words, for the Ra'avad, the menstruant's state of *tuma* is quite distinct from the limits that the condition places upon marital intimacy, for the latter are part of the larger matrix of Torah commands that bear upon every facet of human life. No aspect of human existence is removed from the purview of the Torah's concern, for every mundane activity in which we engage has the potential and the obligation to bear the imprimatur of God's nearness. It may very well be that the "government has no business in the bedrooms of the nation," but the same is not true of God. If we are to live lives of exemplary conduct and heightened sensitivity to all that is good, spiritual and true, then excluding God's presence even from its most sequestered moments is inconceivable. In this particular case, then, the *tuma* state must be separated from the prohibition upon intimacy, with the former relating to the "death of potential" that we have been discussing and the latter relating to the acceptance of God's authority.

KEDOSHIM

Love Your Fellow as Yourself

Leviticus 19:1-20:27

THE FIRST half of Sefer VaYikra concentrates in the main upon laws associated exclusively with the Kohanim and with their sacrificial service. As the book progresses, a shift in focus takes place, towards laws that encompass the entire people of Israel. This change of emphasis begins near the end of Parashat Acharei Mot, when the Torah tabulates the list of forbidden relations that the people of Israel are to shun. It continues in a more pronounced fashion with our Parasha which begins with an unusual introductory phrase: "Speak to the *entire* congregation of Israel and say to them 'Be holy, for I God your Lord am holy'" (*VaYikra* 19:2). As Rashi perceptively notes: "The statutes of Parashat Kedoshim were stated to the multitudes of Israel, because the majority of the Torah's basic principles are contained herein."

The laws of Parashat Kedoshim are numerous and variegated. They address such diverse topics as reverence for one's parents, the prohibition of idolatry, laws of sacrifice, laws concerning the gifts to the poor from the produce of the field, the prohibition of consuming the fruit of a tree during its first three years of growth, Shabbat observance, the fair and equal treatment of converts, as well as a host of others. In short, it may be said that the foundations of Parashat Kedoshim are the twin principles of בין אדם למקום and בין אדם לחבירו, namely those laws that govern our relationship with God and those laws that govern our relationship with other people. What is particularly striking in the Torah's formulation, however, is the conscious commingling of these two seemingly distinct realms. Laws that we might otherwise consider to have a purely "ritual" basis are freely interspersed among laws that pertain to social responsibility and concern for the welfare of other people, and vice versa. This makes the Torah's formulation distinct from every other code of law that has come down to us from antiquity.

A Basic Law

One of the laws mentioned in Parashat Kedoshim is well-known to all students of the Torah. In fact, it proclaims an idea that has been adopted by all civilized human beings, in every part of the globe. Any person who possesses even the most rudimentary system of moral values lives by this principle or one of the innumerable variations of it, whether they are a Jew or a gentile, a believer or a skeptic, ritually observant or completely secular. We might test the matter by addressing the following query to any individual whose path we cross: "If there is a single postulate by which your relationship with other human beings is governed, what is it?" The response proffered will no doubt be a variation of the Torah's fundamental imperative "*love your fellow as yourself*" (19:18).

We shall examine this concept in greater depth, studying its context, considering its related themes, and exploring its scope as it finds expression in the primary sources and in the classical commentaries. We shall consider how the Torah's formulation of the principle is unique and in fact mirrors the larger structure of Parashat Kedoshim of which this law is but a small part.

The Local Context

> . . . Do not pervert justice, neither give special consideration to the poor nor show deference to the great, but judge your people fairly. Do not go around as a gossiper among your people, do not stand idly by over your neighbor's blood, I am God. Do not hate your brother in your heart, but rather surely admonish your fellow and do not bear iniquity because of him. Do not take revenge nor bear a grudge against the children of your people, but *love your fellow as yourself, I am God*. Observe My decrees: Do not crossbreed your livestock, do not plant your field with diverse species of seeds, and do not wear a garment that contains a mixture of wool and linen . . . (19:15–19)

The broader matrix into which "love your fellow" is integrated is an assorted series of laws that in the main attempt to foster equitable and amicable relationships with other people. We are not to show partiality in judgment, we are not to destroy confidences through slander nor are we to harbor ill will towards another even in the secluded recesses of our own minds. We are enjoined to abjure revenge and to transcend resentment, to love each fellow as much as we love ourselves. Surely this series of laws has the potential to transform human society, to refine and to ennoble it, and to create a community and a commonwealth predicated upon the precious principles of justice, trust, and love. How is it then that our civilization, while enthusiastically paying homage to these ideals or to others like them, seems so far from realizing a vision of the good as expressed in our Parasha?

One of the recurring phrases in Parashat Kedoshim, which may in fact be considered its characteristic refrain, is the expression "I am God," or "I am the Lord your God." This expression occurs nineteen times in the Parasha (!), primarily in its first half. What is the significance of these repeating words that serve as the postscript for so many laws? In the frame of reference of the Torah, these words constitute either a categorical admonition concerning consequences or else a passionate exhortation to carry out and to fulfill. The words of the Torah are binding because they are the words of the living God.

The difference between the truncated "Love your fellow as yourself," and the Torah's statement of "Love your fellow as yourself, *I am God*" is thus decisive. While the former is an invitation to propriety and social etiquette, it is forever subject to the whims and weaknesses of capricious human hearts and ultimately unenforceable. It can therefore never constitute anything more than an admirable slogan, a plea for goodness anchored in the shifting sands. While any number of upright individuals may be true exemplars of the ideal in their personal lives, having decided to adopt the principle as their own particular creed, they cannot thereby change the world. On a communal, national or global level, the destiny of the many is more often decided by the less scrupulous and the more brutal, who jettison the noble standard in favor of a more pragmatic principle:

Might makes right. Thus, while no rational individual would ever deny the principle's centrality, civilization as a whole develops in the shadow of its ongoing abrogation.

"Love your neighbor as yourself, I am God" represents, on the other hand, the only potential for the creation of a just and moral society. Although admittedly there may be no human means of ensuring concrete compliance with this principle, any person who sincerely recognizes the sovereignty of God over their lives will provide the most effective means of enforcement possible: the regulation and the control of the self. There are, of course, no guarantees that those who earnestly pledge to live by God's laws will succeed in vanquishing their greedy self-interest. Nevertheless, a precept formulated as an obligation, as an emphatic demand of an absolute being who brooks no moral compromises, carries an axiological weight far more substantial than a mere maxim for living.

That God is the critical component in this equation is attested to by what probably constitutes the most glaring juxtaposition in the entire Torah:

> Do not take revenge nor bear a grudge against the children of your people, but love your fellow as yourself, I am God. Observe My decrees: Do not crossbreed your livestock, do not plant your field with diverse species of seeds, and do not wear a garment that contains a forbidden mixture of fabrics . . . (19:18–19)

The principle of loving one's fellow as oneself, of extending to others the type of treatment that one would want to receive in turn, is an idea so eminently reasonable that no rational human being could ever deny its indispensability in serving as the basis of a functioning society. But here, this paradigm of common sense is followed by the prohibitions of forbidden mixtures! These so-called "decrees" or "חוקים" represent a body of laws that by definition defy rational explanation, whose sole justification for fulfillment is the fact that they are ordained and commanded by a transcendent God. The stern imperative to "Observe My decrees" in spite of their suprarational status thus serves as the dazzling contrast to the lyrical and logical "Love your fellow as yourself." The message of the Torah in linking the two is eminently clear. In the final analysis, the bedrock for both types of legislation – the laws that govern our treatment of other people as well as the laws that define our relationship with God – is entirely the same: the recognition of a supreme God and the acknowledgement of His moral absolutes. According to the Torah, it is this affirmation alone that can provide the potential for the creation of a better world.

Hillel and the Proselyte

A very famous Talmudic passage sheds an entirely different light on the dictum of "Love your fellow." The incident recorded in TB *Shabbat* 31a is part of a larger trilogy of stories that provide much grist for additional study, but for the purposes of brevity we shall address only the tale that is directly relevant to our discussion:

> Our Sages related: a heathen once came before Shammai [preeminent sage in 1st century BCE Israel] and said to him: "Accept me for conversion on condition that you will teach me the entire Torah as I stand on one foot." Shammai pushed him away with the builder's cubit that was in his hand. The heathen then came before Hillel [Shammai's colleague and president of the Sanhedrin] who accepted him for conversion. Hillel said to him: "What is hateful to you, do not do to your fellow. This is the entire Torah, and the rest is commentary. Go and learn."

At first glance it is difficult to reconcile Hillel's remarkable words with the principle enunciated by the Torah. Why didn't Hillel simply quote to the heathen the well-known verse from Parashat Kedoshim that appears to convey the same message? In what ways does his negative formulation (what is *hateful* . . . do *not* do . . .) differ from the positive one (*do love* your fellow...)? How can Hillel claim that this principle constitutes the entire Torah, when in fact we have seen that even when considered solely against the backdrop of its local context in Parashat Kedoshim, it is but a single law among many?

Rabbi Akiva's "Important Principle" and Its Relation to Hillel's Dictum

Before returning to Hillel's maxim, let us first consider another Rabbinic source that seems to return matters to their proper perspective:

> "Do not take revenge nor bear a grudge against the children of your people" – one may, however, be vengeful towards others. "Love your fellow as yourself" – Rabbi Akiva said: This is an important principle of the Torah. Said ben Azzai to him: "This is the book of the generations of humanity . . ." (*Breisheet* 5:1) is a more inclusive principle. (Sifra Kedoshim 7, 4:12)

Rabbi Akiva was the fabled 2nd century CE sage whose contributions to Jewish life during the tumultuous period of oppressive Roman domination are counted among the most significant in all of our tradition. On the one hand, his words appear to more accurately reflect the scope of the commandment to "love your fellow." Unlike Hillel who spoke of the *entire* Torah, Akiva's more modest assessment speaks of *an* important principle. On the other hand, the nature of his disagreement with ben Azzai and the proof text that the latter proffers are both enigmatic. Most troubling of all, however, is the initial part of the above source that seems to condone vengefulness towards the "others" who stand in contrast to the "children of your people."

Does Hillel fundamentally disagree with Rabbi Akiva's statement or is it possible to reconcile the two? Do ben Azzai and Rabbi Akiva differ or are they perhaps addressing two different aspects of the same issue? Could it be that all three of the views are complementary rather than at odds with each other? Let us begin by noting that there is a direct line of transmission that connects Akiva to his illustrious forebear. Hillel's most influential student was a certain Yochanan ben Zakkai who ultimately achieved great prominence on the eve of the Second Temple's destruction (see TB *Succah* 28a). Later generations credited him with saving normative Judaism from the flames by reconstituting the assembly of the Sages at Yavne where they instituted critical innovations that allowed the people of Israel to survive in the hostile post-Temple era. In deference to his immense contribution, they bestowed upon him the title of "Rabban" (our master), though this honorific was typically reserved for ruling descendents of Hillel himself who traced his ancestry to King David. Counted among Rabban Yochanan ben Zakkai's most important disciples were Rabbi Eliezer ben Hyrcanus and Rabbi Yehoshua ben Chananya – and Rabbi Akiva was one of their most important students in turn! Therefore, we must consider the possibility that Rabbi Akiva was both cognizant as well as loyal to Hillel's earlier formulation. How then to explain the discrepancies?

Addressing the Audience

Let us take note of the respective audiences in the two sources. While Hillel is responding to a challenge voiced by an incredulous potential convert, at the time of their fateful meeting the man is still a "heathen." The heathen or נוכרי of the Rabbinic world was an individual who worshipped idols, and could therefore not be depended upon to necessarily act according to any moral compunctions. Hillel therefore suggests to the man that there is a principle of the Torah that speaks to the lowest common denominator, a fundamental idea that is universal in scope and constitutes the touchstone of even the most rudimentary moral system: What is hateful to you do not do to your fellow. It is an idea that demands no concern for the other, that requires no interest in their welfare, and that imposes no preoccupation with their wellbeing. It is neither an intense feeling of love nor even a more modest desire to improve the lot of another human being that underlies Hillel's dictum. In fact, one might go so far as to say that Hillel's formulation is actually selfish in origin: I must avoid hurting another or harming their property solely in order to escape a similar fate befalling myself.

In spite of these limitations, Hillel is forcefully enunciating to the heathen the idea that true moral development begins with a dawning recognition: to desist from harming another is the beginning of the emergence from the proverbial mire. The nasty, brutish and short life that is the lot of humanity in the primitive state of nature can be immeasurably improved by the adoption of this most obvious of principles. If only the heathens (as well as the gentiles and the Jews!) could refrain from hating, harming or hurting their fellows, the world would be eminently more livable!

Akiva, in contrast, speaks of something else entirely. The Torah says: "*Love* your fellow as yourself." Whatever else this reciprocal phrase means, it surely implies a dimension of moral conduct that far surpasses what Hillel recommends. Love, the loftiest of human emotions, is predicated upon an intimate relationship with another and demands a genuine care and concern for that other's property and person. In its more comprehensive versions, love insists upon the selfless surrender of one's own interests for the advancement of another's. Thus, while Hillel speaks of what is hateful, Akiva speaks of love. While Hillel speaks of desisting, Akiva speaks of deed. While Hillel responds to the heathen, Akiva speaks to the Jew. In other words, Hillel, addressing humanity and not Israel, formulates the minimalist principle that the Torah expects all civilized people to adopt as the starting point for their moral development. But Rabbi Akiva reminds us that there is also an abundantly more elevated standard of morality that the Jew must observe with respect to his co-religionist.

The Contribution of Ben Azzai

What is the source for Hillel's idea? Where does the Torah speak of a basic, fundamental moral principle that encompasses all of humanity? The reference is provided by ben Azzai. It will be recalled that in retort to Rabbi Akiva's characterization of "love your fellow" as an "important" principle of the Torah, ben Azzai voiced what he deemed to be a more "inclusive" statement: "This is the book of the generations of humanity." This verse is from the early chapters of the book of Breisheet and introduces the Torah's first genealogical list. The descendents of Adam, the first man, are individually enumerated and their life spans are recorded. In its entirety, the verse states: "This is the book of the generations of humanity – on the day that the Lord created humanity, *He fashioned him in the image of the Lord.*"

The Torah was the first and only ancient code to promulgate the revolutionary idea that all human beings, irrespective of race, color or creed, were descended from a single man and woman who were fashioned in the "divine image." This implied that all members of humanity were related to each other by a common bond of blood, and that all were equal in the sight of their benevolent creator. Parenthetically, it must follow that in a polytheistic system recognizing a multiplicity of quarrelsome gods, there cannot possibly be an idea of a single, united humanity. The cruel enslavement of others, the oppression of nation by nation or of a man by his fellow that was celebrated in other cultures was thus renounced by the Torah at the outset, as an abrogation of the fundamental dignity invested in the human being by God Himself.

All people have the right to be treated with respect and honor by virtue of their "divine image." This basic, elemental dignity is bestowed not by man's fancy but by God's fiat. Jew or non-Jew, heathen or monotheist, all were created in "God's image." This is the idea advanced by ben Azzai's proof text, and Hillel's principle is its direct corollary. Rabbi Akiva does not disagree with either his colleague or his predecessor, but comes to impress upon us that there is an additional obligation placed upon the Jew with respect to his fellow, and it is burdensome indeed. It is the responsibility of love. In another departure from prevailing thought, the Torah advanced the notion that to be part of the Jewish people was to accept an obligation to be concerned with the welfare of other Jews to a degree heretofore extended only to one's closest relatives. To love your fellow as *yourself* constitutes an extreme commitment, for the average person recognizes no more intense love than that which he feels for his own being!

Thus, in the final analysis there need not be any disagreement among the sources. There are different levels of responsibility, arranged like concentric circles, that inform our relationship with others and with the world. To the world, to humanity at large, one must show deference, for all are created in God's image. But this deference to all cannot be entirely unconditional, for other human beings may not feel bound by the moral constraints of the Torah. When willfully harmed by the "heathen," a Rabbinic epithet for one who does not behave according to any accepted standard of civilized or moral behavior, one may have to *react* in kind. Not to do so is not only to invite further aggression, but to foolishly cultivate a threat to one's survival. Thus, in the language of the Sifra, one may exercise vengeance in *response* to an attack by the "other."

Towards the Jewish people, however, the Torah demands that the individual Jew show a heightened sensitivity, a love that implies concern and care and that to a large measure must be unconditional. To act with love towards one's fellow because that is the will of God is to nurture a moral outlook that ennobles not only the community or the nation but the entire world as well.

FOR FURTHER STUDY:

(1) See the disagreement of Maimonides (Laws of Opinions 6:3–4 and Laws of Mourning 14:1) and the Ramban (commentary to *VaYikra* 19:17) concerning the literalness of the Torah's command to love one's fellow "as one's self." Also see the Mishna and Gemara in TB *Sanhedrin* 45a concerning the extension of the principle even to the criminal convicted of a capital crime!

EMOR

The Holiday Cycle

Leviticus 21:1-24:23

PARASHAT EMOR opens with a series of injunctions pertaining to the Kohanim and to their service in the Mishkan. The Torah goes on to describe a number of sacrificial laws before directing our attention to the holiday cycle. The holidays and their respective rituals are delineated one at a time, but in keeping with the primary thrust of Sefer VaYikra, the particular sacrifices associated with each of them are spelled out as well. The Parasha then concludes with laws pertaining to the menorah and its oil, to the table of showbread and its loaves and then to the account of the blasphemer.

Concerning the holidays, the Torah commences the discussion with a brief reference to the Shabbat, and then proceeds to detail the laws of Pesach, the very first festival of our people. The text states:

> These are the set times of God, holy convocations that you shall declare in their proper times. On the fourteenth day of the first month at eventide shall be Pesach unto God. On the fifteenth day of this month a holiday of *matzot* shall be observed unto God, and for seven days you shall consume *matzot* . . . (*VaYikra* 23:4–6)

The ritual observances of the holiday reflect the memory of the events associated with the Exodus. The Pesach sacrifice of the unblemished lamb that inaugurated the eve of redemption and the unleavened bread that so eloquently marked the transformation from servitude into sudden and unexpected liberation, are here presented as the central commemorations. No mention is made here of the season of the Exodus, although it should be recalled that on the morrow of that tumultuous night, Moshe had reminded the people that "today you go forth, in the month of the spring" (*Shemot* 13:5).

Towards the end of the section, the Torah mandates the celebration of a corresponding seven-day festival in the "seventh month":

> . . . on the fifteenth day of the seventh month, the festival of Succot (literally "booths") is to be celebrated for seven days unto God . . . when you gather in the produce of the land . . . for seven days you shall dwell in booths . . . in order that your descendents will know that I caused the people of Israel to dwell in *succot* when I took them out of the land of Egypt. I am God your Lord. (*VaYikra* 23:33–44)

Here, the binary foundation of the holiday is more explicit, for it is associated with the agricultural ingathering from the fields as well as with the journey forth from the land of Egypt into the inhospitable wilderness.

Pesach and Succot are linked by more than their common commemorative content. They also share an underlying temporal structure since they are celebrated at exactly opposite poles of the year. Pesach ushers in the season of the spring when the barley begins to ripen and the wheat is young and green. Succot is celebrated exactly six months later and marks the commencement of fall, as the farmer gathers in the last of his crops from the field, leaves his temporary booth where he had slept while guarding his harvest and begins to look forward to the winter rains. While in our passage these critical agricultural aspects of Pesach and Succot are more muted, elsewhere in the Torah they are the focal point. Thus, with respect to Pesach, the text in Parashat Mishpatim states: "Observe the festival of *matzot*. For seven days you shall eat *matzot* as I have commanded you, *in the time of the month of spring*, for at that time you left Egypt . . ." (*Shemot* 22:15). Concerning Succot, the Torah there designates it as "the festival of the ingathering at the end of the year, *when you gather in your produce from the field*" (22:16).

In essence, then, the holidays of Pesach and Succot exhibit an unmistakable duality. On the one hand, they possess a decidedly historical character, for Pesach celebrates the redemption from Egypt, while Succot recalls the journey through the wilderness in the aftermath of that exodus. On the other hand, they clearly commemorate agricultural seasons, for Pesach inaugurates the ripening of the barley and the wheat while Succot marks the end of the farming year and the anticipation of the autumn rains. What might be the significance of this duality, which is highlighted in almost every mention of these holidays in the Torah? Why do they commemorate agricultural as well as historical events?

The Solar Year and the Phases of the Moon

From an astronomical angle, the dual aspect of these festivals is mirrored by the two systems that are used to mark them. On the one hand, these holidays are tethered to the spring and to the fall respectively, agricultural seasons that are a function of the earth's revolution around the sun. As the earth proceeds around the sun, with its axis of rotation at a slight tilt of 23.5° to the plane of its orbit, the length of the daylight increases to usher in the spring and decreases to announce the onset of fall. That is to say that the seasons of the year are completely dependent upon the sun.

At the same time, the actual calendar dates of the holidays of Pesach and Succot are spelled out in the Torah as "the fifteenth day of the first month" and the "fifteenth day of the seventh month" respectively. These designations are functions not of the sun but of the moon, for they depend upon the lunar calendar that the Torah introduced on the eve of the departure from Egypt: "This month (החודש) shall be for you the first of months . . ." (12:2). As Rabbi Avraham Ibn Ezra points out, the Torah's consistent use of the term "*chodesh*" to describe "month" indicates a lunar count. The word, he explains, comes from the root חדש signifying "new," and therefore signifies renewal, "for renewal pertains to the light of the moon, for although it has no light of its own, its appearance waxes and wanes due to the light of the sun . . ." (beginning of commentary to 12:2). In a similar vein, the English word "month" is itself derived from the Old English word for "moon"!

What is singularly striking, however, is that the Torah insists that both of these time systems be simultaneously employed as the foundation of the calendar. That is to say that while the holidays must fall during their appropriate agricultural seasons, their specific dates are reckoned according to the phases of the moon. This bifurcation has the potential to create difficulties, for the solar year (the period of a single complete revolution of the earth around the sun) is approximately 365.25 days long, while a period of twelve lunar months is only about 354 days long. This is because each lunar month, describing a complete revolution of the moon around the earth, constitutes about 29.5 days. The effects of this discrepancy quickly accumulate; holidays marked exclusively by the phases of the moon begin to "migrate" across the solar seasons by a rate of about 11 days per year (365 – 354 = 11).

It should be emphasized that from an astronomical point of view, both of these systems are completely independent. The phases of the moon and its revolution around the earth have absolutely nothing to do with the rotation of the earth around the sun. The fact that we tend to speak of "twelve months" in a year is an arbitrary convention, and is based upon an early recognition that over the course of a solar year approximately twelve lunar renewals would be observed. While it may be convenient to employ a calendar of twelve solar months since these are easily divided into four seasons of three months each, one could conceivably divide up the 365 days of the solar year any which way. The ancient Aztecs, for example, divided their solar year into eighteen periods consisting of twenty days each.

The method of synchronizing the seasons of the sun with the months of the moon is the basis of the Jewish calendar, and explains the periodic introduction of a "thirteenth month" to harmonize the discrepancy. Briefly, since a solar year is longer than twelve lunar months by about eleven days, this means that over the course of three years, the incongruity grows to about a full month (11 x 3=33). Therefore, approximately every three years (actually seven times during the course of nineteen years) an additional month is added to the Jewish year to achieve synchronization. We may contrast this system with the completely solar calendar employed in all countries historically associated with Christianity, or the exclusively lunar calendar used in all Muslim countries. For the Christian, the seasons always begin on the same calendar day of the year; for the Muslim, the festivals migrate over the years across all of the seasons.

To sum up thus far, we have noticed that the Torah unerringly refers to Pesach as an agricultural festival of the spring, and to Succot as an agricultural festival of the fall. These designations are seasonally dependent and relate only to the sun. At the same time, the Torah always references the historical basis of these festivals, and sets their formal dates as a function of lunar months that, strictly speaking, are completely independent of the agricultural seasons and the sun. Again, we ask: what might be the significance of this duality?

The Festivals of Nature

Early in human history, mankind recognized that survival was a function of the seasons. The luminous rays of the sun warmed the earth, the gracious rains revived it, and it, in turn, brought forth its bounty. When cultivated conscientiously, the black soil could miraculously transform seeds into sustenance. But there were other awesome and capricious forces at work, for an unexpected period of intense heat could burn up its beneficence, and an unforeseen storm could swiftly sweep it away. So it was that early man, seeking to relieve the anxiety of the unknown, thought it prudent to seek the favor of these natural forces which he identified with different divinities. The forces of nature were worshipped as gods, perceived at once as terrifying in their power but also munificent in their life-giving love. These gods, never completely independent of each other, were themselves subject to primordial forces beyond *their* control – the mysterious fates that could upset their plans and toss their decrees to the winds.

The Torah forcefully parted ways with this conception of the world, by categorically proclaiming that a single God had fashioned the cosmos and that He sustained it continually. The forces of nature were not erratic and mercurial gods at odds with each other, but rather the manifestations of an underlying structure that had been called into being by a willful creator. The different seasons, overt expressions of these assorted powers of nature, were themselves functions of the sun, the most mighty and majestic of them all. But even this sun was not a god in its own right, but only the creation of an absolute being and utterly obedient to His rule. Today we live in a world that has for the most part progressed to a theology of monotheism in one form or another, and we take the idea of a single supreme deity for granted. Three or four thousand years ago, however, the Torah's towering message that at once freed man from the clutches of magic and superstition while simultaneously burdening him with the responsibility to exercise his moral will, was regarded as astonishing.

Thus, the ancient milestones of spring and fall, celebrated by humanity from time immemorial as pivotal events in the lives of the gods, were henceforth to be observed as expressions of the creator's omnipotence. Pesach and Succot proclaimed God's complete mastery over nature, His indispensable involvement in the processes of cultivation and harvest, growth and decay, life and death. The Torah-enjoined festivals broadcast for the first time the revolutionary message that the contradictory forces of the cosmos, though they might seem awesome and overwhelming, were themselves entirely under the dominion of a single and non-corporeal God who transcended the inherent limitations of material existence that held the lesser divinities in sway.

The Festivals of History

But that was not enough, for a God of nature, mighty though He may be, was not necessarily an involved God, an immediate God, or a God who cared. The transcendence of an absolute deity could be easily mistaken for remoteness, His otherworldliness for abstraction. The forces of creation might be awesome and breathtaking, but, by the very same token, their vastness renders them impersonal and detached. The seasons of the sun progress unceasingly at their own pace, indifferent to any human cares and unheeding of our concerns.

"I am God your Lord who brought you out of the land of Egypt!" thundered the deity at Sinai, articulating for the first time in the history of the world the notion of a God that was aware, attentive, near at hand, and involved. This was a God who was aware of the Israelites' oppression, attentive to their cries in servitude, near to their pain, and intimately involved in their liberation. The Exodus was not in the main about a God who could overpower, but about a God who could redeem. Human destiny was no longer to be regarded as a function of impersonal fates, but was rather proclaimed to be the result of moral choice. The gods of Egypt, among whom the Pharaoh occupied a most honored position, could be bought off with incantations and bribed with offerings, but the God of Israel could only be supplicated with deeds of kindness and acts of compassion. The gods of Egypt, responsible for regulating the august cosmic order, could not deign to occupy themselves with a matter as trifling as the injustice of slavery.

With the same suddenness as the act of creation that brought forth matter from utter oblivion, this new notion of a God of concern burst forth upon the world, carried forward by a freed people of Israel too immature to fully internalize its significance. In order to impress it upon them, they were given new observances to commemorate the great historical events that heralded their deliverance, to recall God's intimate involvement that had brought them forth from Egypt and sustained them during the course of their wanderings. There was an aspect to these events that did not relate to the seasons of the year at all, to the events of nature or to the cycles of agriculture, but only to the unique and special bond between God and the people of Israel. It was an aspect that was best expressed by coupling it to the phases of the moon, for the lunar calendar (in contrast to its solar counterpart) is exclusively about man's history.

The Sun and the Moon – Two Ways to Mark Time

If the seasons of the sun are about God's mastery of nature, the phases of the moon are about man's imprint on time. The solar seasons have their own rhythms that unfold independent of our existence, but the lunar calendar is artificial and contrived. It is an expression of how *we* mark time as human beings and how *we* choose to gauge the progress of our lives, for according to astronomical reality there is no such thing as a "lunar year" of twelve or thirteen lunar months. A true lunar year is the length of time that it takes the moon to complete one full orbit around the earth. From the perspective of natural science, the only period that matters when we speak of the moon is therefore 29.5 days. When we speak of twelve lunar months and we refer to that construction as a *year* then we have created that artifice and we assign it its validity, for its parameters are products of our ingenuity. It therefore follows that by remembering the momentous events of our national birth according to a lunar reckoning, we celebrate man's role in the world, and especially his privileged status as the most precious subject of God's concern. The solar calendar is about God's overwhelming involvement with nature, but the lunar calendar is about God's interaction with man. By dating the holidays of the Exodus and the wilderness according to the lunar cycle, the Torah is insisting that we remain cognizant of God's other attribute: His immediacy and intimacy, His ongoing participation in the ebb and flow of our unfolding human lives. We recall the great historic moments of God's involvement in the life of the Jewish nation by marking them according to a calendar predicated upon human methods of measuring time's ceaseless passage. The Torah therefore demands that we embrace a paradox: There is a God of creation, but there is also a God of history. The creator who transcends is one and the same with the liberator who cares; the awesome God of reverence is synonymous with the approachable God of love. The revolution that the Torah unleashed was the idea that these two fundamental expressions of God's involvement with the universe are in truth a perfect oneness that is inseparable.

Thus, Pesach is the holiday of the spring, but is also the season of our redemption from Egypt. Succot celebrates harvest, but also recalls our traversing of the hostile wilderness. The seasons of the sun and the phases of the moon must be synchronized, for they speak of a unified conception of God that alone has the power to transform us. Most of us are probably comfortable with the notion of a creator, even perhaps an all-powerful one, but we would prefer to keep Him at arm's length. God may have created the cosmos, but we have confined Him to the margins – overwhelming, absolute and irrelevant. Conceptually, not much separates the notion of no God from the notion of an unaware, uncaring and removed God, for the impact on our lives is in either case negligible. Conversely, a God who is appreciated exclusively through the prism of the historical moment, a God of love and redemption who cares intensely and intervenes, a personal God who is not also the Transcendent and Unfathomable, *becomes* a person. In pagan mythologies, not much separates the gods from their devotees – both have coarse desires, material needs and tragic faults. To embrace only the God of history is therefore to commit the grievous error of incarnation. Only the conception of an omnipotent *and* concerned God, who is capable but who also demands, who is strong enough to intervene but who also takes account, who nurtures but at the same time obligates us to grow, can make a difference to our lives. This is the true significance of Pesach and Succot, the festivals not only of the fruits of the soil but of the fruits of the soul as well.

FOR FURTHER STUDY:

(1) See the commentary of the Ramban to *Shemot* 23:16 – "You shall celebrate three festivals to Me. Observe the holiday of matzot… [Also observe] *the* holiday of the harvest . . . and *the* holiday of the ingathering . . ." He comments: "I do not know why the Torah introduces the two latter holidays with the definite article, since this is the first time that they are mentioned in the Torah. Rather it should have stated: "*a* holiday of the harvest . . ."

While the Ramban goes on to provide a technical solution to the question, according to our analysis above the answer is straightforward. The Torah introduces the holidays of harvest and ingathering with the definite article, because they were *already known* to the ancient Israelites! Seasonal festivals – whether at spring or harvest – are not innovations of the Torah, for they are commemorated by all people and cultures, ancient as well as modern. What was innovative was the Torah's insistence that these times were to be celebrated not as pagan festivals of thanksgiving dedicated to the forces of nature, but rather as commemorations of God's mastery of the seasons and, by extension, His essential role in ensuring human survival.

(2) For the most forceful statement of the role of human beings in reckoning the lunar calendar, see the words of Rabbi Akiva in the final Mishna of chapter 2 of Mishna *Rosh HaShanah*, where he exclaims: "The text states that 'these are the set times of God which you shall declare in their proper time' (*VaYikra* 23:4). This verse indicates that even if the High Court is incorrect in their calculation of the New Moon, the holiday falls according to their reckoning!"

(3) The fundamental dichotomy concerning God's interaction with the universe – creator vs. redeemer, transcendent vs. intimate – is of course the product of our need for a taxonomy rather than a real division in God's nature. Sometimes, we refer to the two aspects of God's interaction as the attribute of justice and the attribute of mercy, sometimes as Elohim and the Tetragrammaton and sometimes, from our perspective, as fear and love. But to push the division too far may lead to dualism, a belief system that the Rabbis vehemently rejected. As Yeshayahu famously wrote: "That they might know from the rising of the sun until its setting that there is none besides Me, I am God and there is nothing else. I am the one who fashions light and creates darkness, who makes peace and creates evil, I am God who does all of these things!" (*Yeshayahu* 45:6–7).

BEHAR

The *Shemitta* or Sabbatical Year

Leviticus 25:1-26:2

> God spoke to Moshe at Mount Sinai saying: "Speak to the people of Israel and say to them 'when you enter the land that I am giving to you, the land shall have a rest period, a sabbath unto God. For six years you may plant your fields, prune your vineyards and harvest your crops. But the seventh year is a sabbath of sabbaths for the land. It is God's sabbath during which you may not plant your fields nor prune your vineyards . . .'" (*VaYikra* 25:1–4)

IN CONTRAST to many of the other parashiyot of Sefer VaYikra, Parashat BeHar is devoted to a single main topic, namely the *Shemitta* or sabbatical year. The Torah spells out its primary observance: It is a year during which we desist from agrarian pursuits and allow the land to experience rest. At first glance, the purpose of the precept seems eminently environmental, to allow the land to lie fallow so that intensive and ceaseless agricultural cultivation does not exhaust its life-giving fertility. Upon closer examination, however, it emerges that in fact there are entirely different considerations at work, and these find expression in some of the year's other unusual practices.

The Theme of Relinquishment

In addition to desisting from working the land, the Torah stipulates that ownership or control over the produce that grows of its own accord during the seventh year is to be relinquished, for the landowner is enjoined to allow all who desire to partake of the land's natural yield:

> What grows [of its own accord] while the land is resting may be eaten by you, by your male and female servants, and by the workers and residents who live with you. All the crops shall also be eaten by the domestic and wild animals that are in your land. (25:6–7)

As Maimonides explains in his monumental code:

> It is a positive command to forfeit ownership over all the produce that the earth brings forth in the seventh year, as the verse states: "You may plant your land for six years and gather in its crops. But during the seventh year you must leave it alone and withdraw from it. The needy among you will then be able to eat from your fields just as you do; the beast of the field will consume whatever is left over. This

> applies also to your vineyard and to your olive grove" (*Shemot* 23:10–11). Whosoever locks his vineyard or else fences in his field during the seventh year abrogates this commandment. Similarly, one who gathers in all of the produce into his own house [to prevent others from partaking of it] violates this precept of the Torah. Rather, he must declare it all ownerless so that anyone may lay equal claim to it; he himself may store up small amounts as would one who gathers from abandoned produce. (*Mishneh Torah*, Laws of Shemitta and Yovel 4:24)

The Yovel or Jubilee

Therefore, not only is the earth to experience a break from the farmer's plowshare and pruning hook during the seventh year, but even the fruits and other bounty that his land produces by itself are to be shared equally with all. He is not to prevent even the beasts from partaking of the earth's natural munificence. His farm and vineyard are to remain open and accessible so that anyone, man or beast, may enter and freely partake of the earth's natural bounty.

In this connection, we should note that the term שמיטה comes from a Hebrew root that literally means "to let go of." This highlights the fact that the primary characteristic of the seventh year is that it is a year during which we let go of our ownership over the land and its produce. According to this reading, then, curtailing agricultural activities has less to do with allowing for soil recharge and more to do with impressing upon the farmer that he does not exercise ultimate control over his land. The prohibition on agriculture and the necessity to guarantee access are thus seen to be complementary.

The Torah goes on to detail how the observances of the seventh year are amplified with the celebration of the *Yovel* or Jubilee that is marked every fiftieth year, at the culmination of seven sabbatical cycles:

> You shall count seven cycles of the sabbatical year, seven years seven times, so that the seven cycles of sabbath years equal forty-nine years. You shall sound the *shofar* blast in the seventh month on the tenth day of the month, on the Day of Atonement you shall sound the *shofar* throughout all of your land. You shall sanctify the fiftieth year and proclaim liberty throughout the land for all of its inhabitants, for each of you shall return to your ancestral inheritance and family. It is a *Yovel*, the fiftieth year for you; you are neither to plant, nor to harvest the field's produce and the vineyard's yield. For it is the *Yovel* and it shall be holy unto you, you shall consume the produce from the field. During this *Yovel* year, each of you shall return to his ancestral land. (*VaYikra* 25:8–13)

Sharing many of the features of the seventh year, the Jubilee that occurs every fiftieth year is also observed by ceasing from cultivating the land. The earth is to be given rest and to remain idle. In contrast to the sabbatical year, however, the Torah commands that the *Yovel* year is to be inaugurated with the blast of the *shofar*, with this solemn ceremony taking place on the Day of Atonement. While both the sounding of the *shofar* as well as the Day of Atonement are about *teshuva*, soul-searching and expiation, the convergence here is unusual. Typically, the *shofar* is sounded on Rosh HaShanah (23:23–25), the process of *teshuva* is engaged in earnest and it continues to gather momentum until the climactic conclusion of Yom Kippur ten days later (16:29–30). But here, Rosh HaShanah is overlooked entirely as the *Yovel* is instead announced by a *shofar* blast on Yom Kippur itself. On the one hand, sounding the *shofar* on Yom Kippur of *Yovel* would seem to be an emphasis of the *teshuva* theme. On the other hand, it is not immediately apparent what special process of *teshuva* might be associated with the onset of the *Yovel* year that was not already engaged ten days earlier on Rosh HaShanah.

In another departure from the *Shemitta* year observances, the Torah enjoins that during the *Yovel* year, all lands are to revert back to their ancestral owners and all slaves are to be freed. Though one may have sold his field or village home (i.e., home in an unwalled city) to someone else, the sale is not absolutely final, for when the *Yovel* falls, the land or house must leave the possession of the buyer and return to the original owner. Similarly, the Hebrew slave who opted to remain with his master after his six years of service have been completed, must leave at the *Yovel* and return to his home and former life. It should be noted that these other *returns* – of land to its ancestral owner and of the slave to his original state – also strike a "*teshuva*" cord, albeit a more concrete one.

The Interpretation of the Akedat Yitzchak

One of the most moving explanations for the practice of the sabbatical and *Yovel* years is provided by Rabbi Yitzchak Arama, the 15th century Spanish scholar, in his classic homiletic commentary called the "Akedat Yitzchak":

> [The purpose of the sabbatical year is] to open our ears and to arouse our hearts by erecting for us great and awesome markers [of time]. How easily are our eyes blinded by the blandishments of this world, its deceits and futilities, which cause us to sell our souls into eternal servitude of the earth after the manner of a team of senseless mules! Did we not accept upon ourselves to serve God out of love?
>
> In order to liberate us from this self-imposed prison of desire that tightly binds us in its powerful embrace to the vanities of the hour, God has illuminated for us a clear means of marking our time in this world – our days, our weeks, and our years – that we cannot overlook except through willful blindness. The work of six days and the cessation from labor on the seventh is true testimony that the world was purposefully brought into being by a creator . . . Acknowledgement of this fact is the necessary starting point for all spiritual development. (Akedat Yitzchak 69)

For the Akedat Yitzchak, not only are we enjoined to record the passage of time on a weekly basis through the observance of the Shabbat, but on a yearly basis as well through the observance of the sabbatical year. The purpose of both is fundamentally the same: to impress upon us that God created the world. Philosophically, the doctrine of creation is essential, for if the cosmos has existed eternally, independent of God's will, it inescapably follows that it has no ultimate purpose or direction. By extension, our lives would therefore have no meaning or higher purpose, for God's role in human destiny would be correspondingly trivial. Only if the universe is the product of an omnipotent and involved *creator* does human life have transcendent meaning and ultimate worth.

The approach of the Akedat Yitzchak offers us an invitation to translate a philosophical construct into concrete reality. We are material beings and the earth is our abode. How devoutly we cultivate its soil, and how devotedly we seek to dominate its riches. Our best years are spent in endless pursuit of extracting its resources, of amassing its wealth, of attempting to thwart the implacable mortality that patiently awaits us all. How painstakingly we gather landed property, precious *terra firma*, so that we might erect upon it stalwart houses of stone in which to guard our gold. But, alas, we are in fact but "dwellers in houses of clay . . . crushed before the moth!" (*Iyov* 4:19). The seventh year beckons us to look at life from a different perspective. Its primary observance is cessation from cultivating the soil, for how easily we can be blinded by that pursuit to imagine that we can maintain our grasp forever. Its hallmark is relinquishment of ownership, for in reality we cannot hold on to the earth or to its precious produce in perpetuity.

The Motif of Seven

The number seven underscores the sabbatical year, for in the Torah's frame of reference, seven represents the basic cycle of time. But this cycle is not only a convenient means of keeping count. The six days of creation are expressed in Hebrew in ordinal terms (first day, second day, etc.) for they derive their meaning from the Shabbat, the seventh day that serves as the reference point. The process of creation as it unfolded during those six days – inanimate to living, simple to complex and instinctive to sentient – expresses the dynamic of purposeful movement towards an encounter with God. It culminates in the Shabbat, the "Crown of Creation." A cycle of time predicated upon the number seven is therefore one that speaks not of amorphous minutes and hours, days and years indistinguishable in their monotony, but rather of precious and unique moments awaiting sanctification. What is true of days and years – the weekly Shabbat and the periodic *Shemitta* – is true of decades as well:

> You shall count seven cycles of the sabbatical year, seven years seven times, so that the seven cycles of sabbath years equal forty-nine years. You shall sound the *shofar* blast in the seventh month on the tenth day of the month, on the Day of Atonement you shall sound the *shofar* throughout all of your land. You shall sanctify the fiftieth year and proclaim liberty throughout the land for all of its inhabitants, for each of you shall return to your ancestral inheritance and family. (*VaYikra* 25:8–10)

By marking the temporal aspect of our existence according to the repeating seven-year cycle, we remain always cognizant of life's priorities, for the period of a *Yovel* is a *lifetime*. A person may merit to experience two Jubilees, at most three, but the average person will see but one. The typical human life span, though steadily increasing in the developed world, still allows for no more than about fifty productive years.

The Lifetime of the Jubilee

The interval of the *Yovel* therefore represents the period of time during which a person can make their mark in the world. But what should be a person's direction and what should be his goal? How shall we determine what is of consequence and what is only ephemeral, transitory and of little value? The answer to these questions is heralded by the blast of the *shofar* on the Day of Atonement that inaugurates the *Yovel*. The practicing Jew knows of a *teshuva* that colors each and every day, for thrice daily he mentions it as part of his devotions. He knows as well of a *teshuva* that ushers in every new year, for on Rosh Hashanah the Torah mandates the sounding of the *shofar* to remind him. But here the Torah speaks of the *teshuva* of a lifetime! The freedom that the *Yovel* announces is not only the physical freedom of the slave and the economic liberation of the land from its most recent owner, but the emancipation of the human spirit from the iron grip of acquisitiveness. To internalize the message of the *Yovel*, to understand the haunting summons of its *shofar* blast, is to relax our grasp on the illusion of physical permanence that land possession affords, "for you are but strangers and temporary residents with Me" (25:23). Our life spans, even when considered only in relation to the brief epoch that constitutes recorded human history, are short. For the human psyche land represents permanence, and our attempts to hold on to it at all costs are a futile and pathetic grasping for immortality. But the land and wealth that we amass will not afford us the eternity that we crave, for its source is to be found elsewhere. Thus, the season of the *Yovel* is poignantly ushered in by the cry of the shofar on the Day of Atonement to summon us to redirect our remaining productive years to worthwhile endeavors.

To again quote the Akedat Yitzchak:

> The purpose of the gift of the land of Israel is not in order that we might devote our labors to it for the sake of extracting its riches and wealth, thus becoming its servants in the process. This is the intention of all other nations in their respective lands . . . The purpose is rather that we should search for spiritual perfection in accordance with the will of the creator; the land provides the necessary sustenance for this endeavor to be pursued. In order to reinforce this essential truth, the Torah commands that the earth be worked for six years and relinquished during the seventh. This is to clearly indicate that not through the exercise of material acquisition is the purpose of life realized but rather through spiritual growth and perfection.

FOR FURTHER STUDY:

(1) See the passage in *Shemot* 21:1–6 that speaks of the Hebrew slave. If after his requisite six years of labor he desires to stay on, he is to be brought before the court where his ear is pierced against the door. Then he serves his master "forever" (לעולם). Traditional sources explain, however, that "forever" means until the *Yovel*, for afterwards he must go free in consonance with our Parasha. This exegesis has often been accused of being divorced from the text, for the verse clearly states "forever." According to the above analysis, though, the intent of this "forever" is to imply "for a lifetime," and indeed the interval of the *Yovel* from the perspective of the individual human being is in fact just that. See also the commentary of Rabbi Avraham Ibn Ezra there.

(2) Consider the perfect parallel between the seven weeks that separate Pesach from Shavuot, which falls on the "fiftieth day," and the seven sabbatical cycles that culminate in the *Yovel*. In both cases there is an intimation of progress, of direction, and of dynamic movement from physical liberation to spiritual redemption. Shavuot celebrates the giving of the Torah, the awareness that bereft of spiritual purpose we are never truly free at all. *Yovel* commemorates the potential of living our most productive years unfettered by the misplaced desire for material permanence that distracts us from our true spiritual purpose.

BECHUKOTAI
The Blessings of the State of Nature

Leviticus 26:3-27:34

If you will follow My decrees and observe My commandments to fulfill them, then I will provide your rains in their season; the earth will bring forth its produce and the trees of the field will yield their fruit. Your threshing season will last until grape harvest, and the grape harvest will continue until planting, and you shall eat your bread to satiation and shall dwell in security in your land.

I will grant peace in the land and you shall lie down to sleep without fear, and I will rid the land of dangerous animals and the sword shall not pass through your land. You shall pursue your enemies and they shall fall before you by the sword. Five of you shall pursue one hundred of them, and one hundred of you shall pursue ten thousand of them, and your enemies shall fall before you by the sword. I shall turn towards you and shall make you fertile and numerous, and shall establish My covenant with you.

You shall eat the previous year's crops for a long time and will have to eventually clear them out to make room for the new. I will put My sanctuary in your midst and My soul shall not cast you away. I will walk in your midst and I shall be your God, and you shall be My people. I am God your Lord who brought you forth out of the land of Egypt where you were their slaves; I broke the bars of your yoke and caused you to walk upright. (*VaYikra* 26:3–13)

PARASHAT BECHUKOTAI marks the completion of Sefer VaYikra, as the book is solemnly sealed by an eternal covenant between God and the people of Israel. As His special nation, Israel is expected to follow the statutes of the Torah, to faithfully observe its teachings and to fulfill its commands. In consequence, they are to enjoy God's copious blessings – rain in its due season, bountiful harvests, peace and security, abundant health, and the experience of God's overarching closeness in their midst. But if they fail to observe the Torah, then disaster will befall them – not only will their land be barren and their natural vigor exhausted, but warfare will overwhelm them and their enemies will cast them into exile, far from God's presence.

The Uniqueness of the Blessings

While the Torah speaks of "reward and punishment" on any number of occasions, our section of Parashat BeChukotai is nevertheless unique. First of all, the blessings and curses spelled out in our section are strikingly comprehensive, for they leave no aspect of human experience unaddressed. Physical health and sustenance, emotional well-being and stability, spiritual satisfaction and fulfillment and every other possible blessing that inspires our earthly existence with worth and meaning, are all presented as the natural outcome of serving God in sincerity. And sickness and poverty, anxiety and fear, alienation and depression and all of the other myriad demons that haunt humanity and crush it with their oppressiveness, are even more prominently highlighted – as the inevitable consequences of abandoning God and abrogating His commands.

Secondly, while the Torah more often than not speaks to the individual Jew and charges him or her with the holy burden and noble responsibility to uphold its teachings, our section speaks to the nation, to the people of Israel and to their political state. In exhaustive detail, the text describes the great promise and potential on the one hand, and the unparalleled capacity for self-destruction on the other, that nationhood, a homeland, and political independence confer.

As the Ramban so perceptively remarks:

> These blessings are all-inclusive and apply to the entire nation, and they will be fulfilled when all of our people are righteous. That is why the passage repeatedly refers to "the land" – "the land will give forth its produce" (26:4); "you shall dwell in security in your land" (26:5); "I will make peace in the land . . . I will cause evil beasts to cease from the land and the sword shall not pass through your land." (26:6)

Finally, other passages in the Torah tend to appraise the human condition in realistic terms. Many of the Torah's commands are predicated upon a recognition of our inherent limitations and some of them even offer a concession to our penchant for malevolence. Of course, these *mitzvot* concurrently attempt to refine our moral coarseness in order to lift us out of the morass so that we may yet behold God. But by and large the Torah accurately portrays a human landscape in which social ills such as poverty, injustice and distrust are alive and well, and in which societies – even decent societies – must constantly struggle to eradicate evil, inequity and suffering from their midst. In other words, the Torah describes the nature of man for what it is – inspired with a divine potential for the good, but often consumed with a nasty self-interest that spells his moral doom. But our passage of blessings, in contrast, paints a picture of man and of Israel that is so overwhelmingly good that the commentaries early on proclaimed that its primary applicability must be eschatological! Here, for the first time in the Torah since our expulsion from the Garden of Eden, material plentitude is coupled with a cohesive and intimate relationship with God. The vivid images of abundance, health, peace and tender attachment to God portrayed in this passage suggest an ideal state or utopian vision in which the tense bifurcation of the physical and the spiritual has been finally resolved.

Turning again to the Ramban in his commentary to verse 12,

> These blessings in their entirety will not unfold except when all of Israel fulfills the will of their Father, and the heavens and earth have been perfectly established upon their foundations. Nowhere else in the Torah are there blessings as comprehensive as these, for they are the elements of the covenant and its conditions that pertain between the Holy One blessed be He and ourselves. Understand that Israel *never* achieved these blessings in their entirety, neither as a collective nor as individuals, for their merits were insufficient . . . and therefore we find our Sages referring to

these verses as descriptions of the future age . . . for they were not fulfilled, but will yet be fulfilled at the time of perfection, i.e., the messianic age.

The Vision of Isaiah

This remarkable period, consistently described in the prophetic books as an age of universal harmony that will spell an end to the scourge of sickness, the wantonness of war, and the ignominy of injustice, is celebrated in a well-known passage from Sefer Yeshayahu 11.

> A shoot shall spring forth from the trunk of Yishai and a sprout from his roots will blossom. The spirit of God shall rest upon him, a spirit of wisdom and understanding, counsel and might, knowledge and fear of God . . . He shall judge the poor with righteousness . . . and smite the wicked with the words of his mouth. The wolf shall dwell with the lamb and the leopard with the kid, a calf, young lion and fatling shall be together, and a small child shall guide them. The cow and bear shall graze together, and together they shall cause their young to lay down, and the lion shall consume straw like an ox. An infant shall play over the lair of the python and shall stretch forth his hand upon the adder's den. There shall be neither evil nor destruction on all of My holy mountain, for the earth shall be filled with knowledge of God as the waters cover the sea . . . (*Yeshayahu* 11:1–9)

In this portrayal, the messianic figure who is a divinely inspired but unequivocally human descendent of the Davidic line, will arise from the national ruins to uphold the rule of law and to undermine corruption. A fantastic change will correspondingly take place in the natural order, as carnivores will mend their brutal ways and placidly dwell in harmony with their former prey. A small child will oversee the transformation as he casually plays with the python, for repair will finally be secured for the cursed serpent's primeval crime of alienating man from the earth that bore him.

Maimonides vs. the Ramban

Maimonides is quick to point out the metaphorical meaning of this passage from the book of Yeshayahu, in his celebrated description of the messianic age in his Laws of Kings 12:1.

> Do not think that during the messianic era any of the laws of nature will be suspended or that new changes will be introduced into the order of creation. Rather the world will continue to operate according to these natural laws. That which Yeshayahu describes as "the wolf shall dwell with the lamb and the leopard with the kid" is in fact a parable and an allegory. The meaning of the matter is that the people of Israel will dwell in security with those wicked nations who are compared to the wolf and to the leopard . . . as all of them will finally acknowledge the true doctrines and will cease from engaging in robbery and corruption. Rather, these nations will consume only permitted things, at peace with Israel, as it then states "the lion shall eat straw like the ox." All similar passages concerning the messiah are to be understood as allegories, and during that age it will become apparent to all what the meaning of the allegory was and to what matter it alluded.

A well-established Talmudic tradition in TB *Sanhedrin* 91b asserts that the only substantial distinction between the present time and the messianic era will be the cessation of the people of Israel's oppressed state as they once again secure political sovereignty.

Maimonides, basing himself upon this source and no doubt also relying upon the same rational considerations that underlie all of his thinking, is quite content to reinterpret seemingly fantastic prophetic descriptions of that time as parables and similes. The meat-eating lion will not really change its diet of hapless herbivores, for the basic laws of nature according to which the world operates will never be suspended. For Maimonides, the messianic era is not a time of marvelous miracles and extraordinary wonders. Rather, it is a period of a transformed human condition that is heralded by the vindication of Israel's faith and by her long-awaited liberation from the clutches of the brutal regimes that sought to destroy her.

The Ramban, in contrast, understands the matter quite differently, as he explains in his commentary to our Parasha. His starting point is a curious verse from our section, concerning which the Sages disagreed in the Midrash:

> "I will grant peace in the land and you shall lie down to sleep without fear, and I will rid the land of dangerous animals and the sword shall not pass through your land" (*VaYikra* 26:6). What does the Torah mean when it says that the land will be rid of dangerous animals? – Rabbi Yehuda explained that God will cause the dangerous beasts to be removed from the world. Rabbi Nehemiah explained that God will cause them to cease from harming others.

The Ramban elucidates the matter by explaining that Rabbi Yehuda understood the biblical verse according to its straightforward reading. Since the land will be full of plenty and the cities full of people, wild animals will not enter the settled areas and they will thus cease to present an immediate menace to people. According to Rabbi Nehemiah, however, the meaning of the verse is not that God will distance these evil beasts from our cities, but rather that He will cause the evil *of the beasts* to be removed from the land. In other words, according to Rabbi Nehemiah, a fundamental transformation of the natural order will take place, and indeed the words of Yeshayahu will be fulfilled according to their plain meaning – the wolf will lie down with the lamb in tranquil concord!

Ramban continues:

> The view of Rabbi Nehemiah is the correct one, for when the Jewish people fulfill the *mitzvot* of the Torah, the land of Israel will come to resemble the state of the world at its pristine beginning, before the transgression of the first humans. At that time, beasts and creeping things did not harm or kill people . . . as the verse states "an infant shall play over the lair of the python" etc., for the carnivorous nature of the dangerous beasts only came about as a result of the transgression of man who was condemned to become their prey . . . At the time of creation, the verses state that the diet of the wild animals was to be the grass of the field – "as for the beasts of the land and the birds of the heavens and all of the animals that creep upon the earth, I give them all manner of vegetation to consume" (*Breisheet* 1:29–30), for that was to be their eternal nature. They only became carnivorous because of transgression, as I have explained . . . Therefore, when a time of completeness is reached, the vicious temper of the animals in the land of Israel will come to an end, for they shall all revert back to their initial nature that was placed in them at the time of their creation. Thus, during the days of the redeemer who will be a descendent of Yishai, concerning which Yeshayahu spoke, peace will return to the world and cruelty will cease . . . (commentary to *VaYikra* 26:6)

The Land of Israel and the Garden of Eden

With his explanation, the Ramban draws a direct parallel between the paradisiacal garden described at the outset of *Breisheet* on the one hand, and the land of Israel in the messianic era on the other. In that initial ideal state, the natural order was in perfect balance. Humanity dwelt in harmony with other creatures, and they in turn lived peaceably among themselves. God's overarching presence was felt in that well-watered and verdant garden and man and woman lived their lives in constant experience of His closeness. Strife and struggle, brutality and bloodshed, anger and anguish were unknown. The destructive alienation of man from his God, from his world, and from himself had not happened, for human ears were attuned to the divine call and the human heart beat sensitively to its message.

But then the world was transmogrified into a place of ferocity and death. All creatures began to struggle mightily for their survival, and a "nature, red in tooth and claw" took the place of the ideal state. The first human beings were exiled from the Garden of Eden and sent into a world turned hostile and savage. Having embraced a life of spiritual rupture, their descendents soon introduced more ominous innovations: injustice and murder. Nevertheless, some of them – the more sensitive souls – preserved a wistful memory of that garden, so that humanity has ever since attempted to find its way back.

It was the arrogant transgression of Adam and Chava that upset the ideal equilibrium, for by abrogating God's command they introduced a new and dangerous element into the fabric of creation – human hubris that refused to accede to a transcendent authority. Most strikingly, the Ramban posits that the effects of that momentous decision were not consequential for only humanity but rather for the entire order of creation. The harmony and peace that had initially characterized the animal kingdom dissipated, to be replaced by the "unnatural" order of predator and prey. The great beasts that had been initially created as gentle grazers of vegetation now became fearsome killers. And, most tragic of all, the relationship between God and man now became distant and estranged.

Clearly, the Ramban, animated as he is by the soul of the mystic, perceives the matter in other than rational terms. According to his interpretation, what we heedlessly refer to as the "state of nature" – the bloodshed and death that is the inevitable product of the struggle for survival – is actually *unnatural* in the extreme! We might summarize the difference between Maimonides and the Ramban in the following way: While Maimonides sees the human condition and the state of the world for what it is, the Ramban perceives what it once was and what it ought to be.

Returning to Eden – Implications of the Ramban

What then is the way back to that ideal state? The Ramban explains that when the Jewish people return to the Torah, to a vision of the world predicated upon sensitivity for others and reverence for God, when we are ready to surrender the will to dominate for the desire to serve, then the messianic era will dawn. That time will be one of peace, plenty, tranquility and spiritual fulfillment. Nature will cease being the artificial construct full of barbarity and outrage that it now is, and the land of Israel will epitomize the ideal state of Eden. Though this transformation might strike us as miraculous and the skeptic would dismiss it as doubtful, the Ramban suggests that it is in fact nothing more than a return to the untarnished, pristine world that God initially fashioned. There is no miraculous transformation, then, but only decisive restoration.

Our perceptions of the world of nature tend to be shaped by our urban experience. Living in comfortable cities and spacious, safe homes, our primary contact with "wild beasts" is through the innocuous experience of the neighborhood zoo. Colored by a romantic vision of the wilderness, we tend to forget that in reality, the world of nature is not the pleasant chirping of morning starlings outside of our window, but rather the relentless struggle for survival that necessarily spells life for some creatures and a cruel, sudden, and painful death for others. If we candidly look at nature for what it truly is, we are shocked by its vulgarity.

But, explains the Ramban, what is most shocking about the natural world around us is that it is nothing but a *reflection* of ourselves! That is to say that the state of nature is a direct function of our moral and ethical choices. If we as humans champion acts of avarice, injustice, and viciousness, routinely condoning all manner of individual and collective oppression, then we should not be surprised that a lion can heartlessly tear an antelope to shreds. If the cruelty of the beasts is a perfect mirror image of our own ethical failures, how can it be otherwise? Conversely, if the day finally dawns when nations can live in peace with each other, if the sun finally rises on cities filled with fellowship and righteousness, if we as individuals can repair the tattered state of our relationship with others and with God, then, avers the Ramban, the literal fulfillment of "the wolf dwelling with the lamb and the leopard with the kid" is indeed not far off.

FOR FURTHER STUDY:

(1) See the Ramban's clever reinterpretation of the famous tale of the miracle-working Rabbi Chanina ben Dosa, recounted in TB *Berachot* 33a. The Talmud relates that a neighborhood was plagued by a lethal reptile that had injured a number of people. When shown its lair, the rabbi placed his heel upon the opening. The bite, however, resulted in the death of the reptile and not the rabbi! He then took the creature to the Beit Midrash and proclaimed: "Behold, my children! It is not the reptile that kills but rather sin that kills!" Typically, Rabbi Chanina's remarks are understood to mean that righteousness has a prophylactic effect. The Ramban, however, explains it in accordance with his theory above: "It is not the *nature* of the reptile to kill but rather human transgression that inspires it with that nature!"

BEMIDBAR

The Theme of Passage

Numbers 1:1-4:20

PARASHAT BEMIDBAR introduces the fourth of the Five Books of Moses, Sefer BeMidbar. This book as well as the Parasha are so-called because of one of the first words in the section: "God spoke to Moshe in the *midbar* of Sinai at the Tent of Meeting, on the first day of the second month in the second year of the Exodus and said . . ." (*BeMidbar* 1:1). The opening events of the book find the people of Israel still encamped in the environs of Mount Sinai, where they have been stationed for almost a year. During the time that has elapsed since the Exodus, the people have achieved a number of impressive accomplishments, but not without many setbacks great and small.

They crossed the Sea of Reeds, but on its shores they fell prey to fear, discontent, and the desire to return to Egypt. They stood at the foot of the mountain to receive God's Torah, but soon thereafter they succumbed to the spell of the golden calf. They built the Tent of Meeting to house the tablets and to serve as an abode for God's presence, but its dedication was marred by the untimely demise of Aharon's overzealous sons. Sustained by manna from the sky and by water brought forth from impervious rock, the people have yet to master the precious life skills of confidence, reliance and an abiding trust. God proclaimed His guiding laws, but the people continue to struggle with the consequences of their brash declarations of endorsement. As Sefer BeMidbar unfolds, we shall see how the many threads of its narratives are skillfully woven together to frame an eternal message: sincere realization of the Torah's *mitzvot* is not the result of mechanistic performance but rather of profound internalization.

Taking a Census

> God spoke to Moshe in the *midbar* of Sinai at the Tent of Meeting, on the first day of the second month in the second year of the Exodus and said: "Count the entire congregation of Israel according to their families and their clans, each male according to name. You and Aharon shall count them from the age of twenty and above, all those who go out to war in Israel."

Rashi considers this opening census in the context of the other times that the people have been counted since the Exodus, and comments:

> Because of God's love for the Jewish people, He counts them constantly. At the time of the Exodus, He counted them; after the incident of the golden calf, He

> counted them [to ascertain how many remained]. When the time came to manifest His presence among them He counted them again, for the Mishkan was set up on the first of Nissan, and on the first of Iyar He counted them.

For Rashi, counting is an expression of concern and care for the things being enumerated. In other places, the Tanakh employs the parable of the shepherd and the sheep to highlight the special relationship between God and His people (see for instance *Yeshayahu* 40:10–11 and *Tehillim* 23), and no doubt for Rashi the theme of lovingly counting Israel is related to this powerful image. This theme actually colors the entire book, for in the early Rabbinic sources it is often referred to as "*Chumash HaPekudim*," popularly adapted as the "Book of Numbers." Tellingly, the book both begins and ends with a census of the people, the one taken on the eve of the journey from Sinai, and the other almost forty years later at the Plains of Jericho.

The Explanation of the Ramban – Preparations for Battle

Ramban, in contrast to Rashi, adopts a more rational approach to the matter of the census, one that is grounded in the immediate context:

> The reason for ascertaining their number is like a ruling power that is about to embark on a war, for the people are now poised to enter the land and to fight the Amorite kings who guard its entrance from the east, as well all of the other kings on the other side of the Yarden . . . Moshe and the tribal princes had to know the number of fighting men . . . for the Torah does not rely on the miracle of "one chasing a thousand" (*Devarim* 32:30). Thus, the text states "all those who go out to war in Israel" because the count is for the sake of preparing the nation for battle. Also, they must know the number of people so that they can distribute the land that they conquer, for were it not for the incident of the spies, they would have entered the land immediately. (commentary to *BeMidbar* 1:45)

Ramban thus highlights what he takes to be the book's dominant theme: in contrast to Sefer Shemot that describes the events surrounding the Exodus, and in contradistinction to Sefer VaYikra that is concerned with the Mishkan and the laws relating to its ongoing operation, Sefer BeMidbar speaks of the *preparations* undertaken by the people for entering the land of Canaan. The census with which the book begins constitutes the first step in preparing the people for conquering the land.

"Preparations," of course, implies activities that are of a provisional nature, undertaken for the sake of a particular objective. Preparations are generally not ends unto themselves but only means to an end. They are therefore temporary rather than permanent measures. In his introduction to Sefer BeMidbar, the Ramban first emphasizes the transitory aspect of its narratives. As he explains, since the account is primarily concerned with the journey from Sinai to Canaan, the *mitzvot* that unevenly punctuate its passages tend to be momentary and of immediate relevance, rather than eternally binding commands:

> This entire book speaks only of those commandments that were meant for a particular time, namely during the period of the people's sojourn in the *midbar*. Also, it recounts the great miracles that were wrought on their behalf during their journey, in order to recall God's wondrous acts. The book later describes how God began the process of destroying their enemies before them, and also commands

> how the land is to be divided up among them. There are no commandments in this book that are binding for all times except for some sacrificial laws, which were first spelled out in Sefer VaYikra but remained incomplete until concluded here.

A broad outline of Sefer BeMidbar thus begins to emerge: it is in the main focused upon the journey towards the land, and as such essentially describes a temporary condition. The path stretching from Sinai to Israel, from the giving of the Torah to the possibility of its comprehensive fulfillment, is the subject of its narratives. The fundamental character of most of its *mitzvot* is therefore decidedly different than elsewhere in the Torah, for it is less concerned with the eternal acts to be practiced upon reaching the destination, and more concerned with the lessons to be internalized during the critical course of the passage. Looming large on the horizon, effectively filling the void between the point of departure and the destination, is the *midbar*. This geographical zone, often translated as "desert," conjures up images of sun-baked sand dunes stretching to eternity and laden camels languidly swaying across an endless expanse. As we shall see, however, this conception of the *midbar* is both imprecise as well as misleading.

The Memory of the Midbar

The significance of the *midbar* experience may be gauged by the fact that some forty years after the opening events of the book, the Torah returns to make a number of pointed references to it. These occur in the form of recollections addressed by Moshe to the new generation that finally stands on the banks of the Yarden, about four decades after the disastrous episode of the spies. After briefly recalling the sojourn at Sinai, Moshe tersely describes the journey away from the mountain, for which the preliminary preparations take place in our Parasha. "We traveled from Chorev, and traversed the great and awesome *midbar* that you saw, by way of the ridge of the Amorites as God commanded us, and we arrived at Kadesh Barnea" (*Devarim* 1:19). Here, the *midbar* is recalled as "great and awesome," a characterization implying an impressive but fearful territory.

In a lengthier passage forming part of his exhortation to the people to not grow complacent in their new land, Moshe again remembers the *midbar* as a place of sinister dangers as well as of divine concern:

> Be careful lest you forget God your Lord, not to observe His commandments, laws and decrees that I command you this day. Lest you eat and be satiated, and build fine houses in which to dwell. Lest your cattle and sheep increase, and you amass silver and gold, and all that you possess increases. Lest your heart becomes arrogant and you forget God your Lord who took you out of the land of Egypt, from the house of bondage. He who led you through the great and awesome *midbar*, the dwelling place of the snake, the fiery serpent and the scorpion, a place of great thirst for lack of water; He who extracted for you water from the impenetrable rock. He who fed you manna in the *midbar*, a form of sustenance that your ancestors knew not, in order to afflict you and to test you, so that it would be good for you at the end. Say not in your heart "my power and the strength of my hand have wrought for me this wealth!" Rather, remember God your Lord for He gives you the strength to gather wealth, in order to fulfill His covenant that He swore to your ancestors, this very day. (*Devarim* 8:11–18)

In his farewell song at the conclusion of Sefer Devarim, Moshe returns one last time to the memory of the *midbar*, again describing it as a place of both foreboding desolation as well as of providential care: "He (God) found them (Israel) in the land of the *midbar*, in a barren and howling wasteland; He enveloped them and protected them, keeping them safe as the pupil of His eye" (32:10). In all of these references, the *midbar* is invoked not as a fleeting memory of a featureless topographical location, of a stretch of land uneventfully traversed and promptly forgotten, but rather as some sort of formative experience that left its profound mark on the national psyche. What might be the thrust of the *midbar*'s message?

Understanding the Grammatical Basis

The Hebrew language, like other Semitic tongues, recognizes families of words that are grouped not according to meaning, but rather according to grammatical form. Thus, *midbar* is based upon the three-letter consonantal root דבר. This root is introduced by a מ prefix marked with a long vowel called *chirik*, and has a penultimate consonant containing the emphatic *dagesh* and marked by the vowel called *kamatz* (or, in the case of the construct form, *patach*). Other familiar words that fit this same pattern include the following: משפט or "court," מקדש or "temple," מקלט or "refuge," משגב or "fortress," מצפה or "lookout," מזרח or "east," and מזבח or "altar." It will be noticed that in all of the above cases, the *forms* of the words are almost identical, although the *meanings* are of course completely different. Examining the matter further, we in fact discover that the general grammatical form "miXYaZ" means "the place of XYZ" where "XYZ" is the three-letter consonantal root. Thus, to translate the above terms more accurately if less idiomatically, we render *mishpat* as "place of judgment" (hence a court), *mikdash* as "place of holiness" (hence a temple), *miklat* as "place of being let in" (hence a refuge), *misgav* as "place of strength" (hence a fortress), *mitzpah* as "place of seeing out into the distance" (hence a lookout), *mizrach* as "place of the rising" (hence the east where the sun rises), and *mizbeach* as "place of slaughter" (hence an altar).

The term "*midbar*" would therefore mean "place of דבר," where דבר is the elemental root. But what is the meaning of DaBaR and how does it relate to our investigation of *midbar*? Here, Rabbi David Kimchi offers us assistance with his grammatical work entitled *Sefer HaShorashim* or the Book of Grammatical Roots. Commenting on the "*midbar* of Sinai" (*Shemot* 19:1) and "the great *midbar*" (*Devarim* 1:19), Radak explains:

> This term refers to a desolate place, uncultivated and unsettled. Grazing land is also called *midbar*, whether it be far or close to the city. Another meaning of the root is "manner" or "way," as in "the sheep shall graze after their manner (כדברם)" (*Yeshayahu* 5:17). Here, the usage is similar to the Aramaic translation of the verse "and he *led* his flocks" (*Breisheet* 31:18), which is ודבר. It is correct to say that *midbar* therefore refers to a place of grazing because there the shepherd must lead the flocks to pasture. Similarly, we find "I shall place them as דברות on the sea" (*Melachim* 1:5:23), which refers to large timbers tied together and directed down the coast, namely rafts.

Radak explains that the fundamental meaning of דבר is "to guide" or "to lead." The *midbar* is frequently associated with grazing land because to there the sheep are led to pasture. The shepherd and his flock are enemies of the farmer who industriously cultivates his plot of land. Where agriculture thrives, the sheep and goats are not welcome. Therefore, they must be grazed in unsettled areas far from human habitation. Rather than signifying the sterile and stifling environment of the desert, the *midbar* is any place that is desolate, uncultivated and vacant. It may be temperate and even fertile, for its defining characteristic is not its climate or its annual precipitation but rather its population density. That is to say that the *midbar* is any area that is bereft of human habitation.

Referring to its usage in Aramaic, also a Semitic language, Radak explains that the verb form means "to guide" or "to lead," and offers the example of Ya'acov leading his flocks back to Canaan after his escape from his belligerent father-in-law Lavan. Radak detects a further variation of the root in the description of King Shelomo's plans to build the Temple. Solomon secures the services of Chiram, king of Tyre, who agrees to provide dressed timbers of cedar and spruce from his extensive forests in Lebanon. Chiram, sensitive to the vast outlays of labor that would be required to carry the huge timbers overland from the Lebanon mountains to Jerusalem, instead suggests floating them down the Mediterranean coast and landing them at the port of Yaffo. The biblical דברות are the rafts made of these timbers lashed together, so called because sailors must *guide* them down the coast, or else they float aimlessly away.

Late in biblical history, this usage of דבר became archaic. By the time the building of Shelomo's temple was recalled in a parallel passage from the book of Divrei HaYamim (2:2:15) that dates from the early 2nd Temple period, these דברות had become more comprehensible רפסדות, a usage later adopted by modern Hebrew. But the Aramaic language continued to make use of the archaic form (see, for instance, the Rabbis' comments about Yehoshua having to lead the people into the land with self-confidence and independence: "דבר אחד לדור ולא שני דברים לדור", quoted by Rashi on *Devarim* 31:7)

Now although Radak fails to explicitly make the connection, for he confines his discussion to flocks of sheep, it is clear that the term *midbar* impacts on the human dimension as well. Any large tract of land that is completely desolate and uninhabited can be traversed safely only by one who is intimately familiar with the terrain. The novice who enters the expanse of the wilderness without proper guidance, though he may have provisions aplenty, puts his life in danger, for he may easily become lost and disoriented and may never emerge. Referring to our earlier analysis, the term *midbar* is therefore most accurately translated as "*the place of being led*"!

Submitting to God's Guidance

The profound meaning of this book's title is therefore a penetrating comment on its entire contents. At Sinai, God proclaimed His Torah and the people listened. Receiving a new set of norms and rituals, they offered formal acceptance and perfunctorily pledged their performance but remained far from the ideal of being spiritually transformed. Encamped at the foot of the mountain for close to a year, they solidified their commitment and slowly adapted to a new way of life. Preparing to break up camp to commence their journey to the Promised Land, they were still bereft of the precious possessions of complete trust in God and the recognition of utter dependence on His providence. The acquisition of these critical faith values would be essential to inoculate them against developing a conceited belief in their own abilities and an arrogant worship of their accomplishments, flaws that would spell their doom in the new land. But the journey from Sinai to Kadesh Barnea and on to the plains of Jericho could have taken many routes.

"We traveled from Chorev, and journeyed across the great and awesome *midbar* that you saw, by way of the ridge of the Amorites as God commanded us . . ." (*Devarim* 1:19), Moshe reminded the people, explaining that there was divine intent and purpose in directing Israel to enter the wilderness and to traverse its desolate expanse. The *midbar*, the place of being led, represented not only a geographic zone but a spiritual challenge as well. To enter the *midbar* meant to submit to the realization that without God's ever-present and loving guidance, survival was impossible. The passage across its stark and lonely landscape drove home the essential lessons that were so necessary for the people to internalize, not only that they might endure its immediate trials, but also that they might overcome the more formidable spiritual perils that awaited them on the other side of the Yarden. At first forced to submit to God's guidance, who led them unwillingly into the *midbar*'s howling grasp, they would, by the end of the journey, longingly recall the overt expressions of His continuous, sustaining intervention. To develop steadfast trust in God's guidance and an unshakeable recognition of His role in securing our survival is to realize a spiritual achievement of the highest order. The experience of the *midbar* was divinely orchestrated in order to provide the people with the optimal conditions for them to succeed. They were to remember it always, so that they might carry their new-found trust with them even after they had left its desolate embrace and embarked upon a new life in which God's involvement may have been just as real but was not nearly as manifest.

Moshe's directive to the people to never forget the journey through the *midbar*, stated in *Devarim* 8:2, suddenly takes on additional meaning:

> Remember the whole journey on which God led you for forty years in the wilderness, in order to afflict you and to test you, to ascertain what was in your heart, to see if you would keep His commandments or not.

As the Ramban insightfully explains on the passage:

> The people did not know what counsel to adopt for themselves when they entered the great wilderness, a place of no food, and had no reserves of manna. For each day the manna came down from the heavens anew and "as the sun become hot, it melted", though the people hungered for it. All this they did to keep God's commands and to journey according to His guidance. Now God could have led them by way of the populated cities that were around them, but instead He brought them into the trial of the wilderness, for He knew that as a result of this experience, they would keep His commandments forever.

FOR FURTHER STUDY:

It is instructive to note how other constructs employing the root דבר are informed by the above analysis that explains the core meaning as "to guide" or "to lead":

(1) The infinitive לדבר means "to speak" and is often regarded as a synonym of לאמור, "to say." Nevertheless, Rabbinic exegesis tended to differentiate the two forms by insisting that לדבר constituted a harsher form of speech, a לשון קשה (see Rashi's commentary to *BeMidbar* 12:1 and *Devarim* 2:17). Perhaps this is because אמירה indicates a true dialogue of equals, whereas דיבור implies a form of speech in which the conversation is one-sided – the speaker *guides* the conversation and the listener submits to his words.

(2) The term עשרת הדברות or עשרת הדברים is frequently translated as the "Ten Commandments," a usage that has absolutely no basis in the traditional literature. Bearing in mind the fundamental importance of these ten things but cognizant that they are but the foundation of a much larger edifice, we might be more accurate by translating the term as the "Ten *Guiding* Principles."

(3) The Hebrew word for "bee" is the well-known דבורה. Now it is true that the ancients did not employ a scientific methodology, as we know it. Nevertheless, we do ourselves a disservice by underestimating their powers of observation, for they were very keen observers of the world around them to a degree that would probably put us to shame. Could it be that they noticed that a bee that had discovered pollen would do a "dance" in order to lead the other bees to the source? Or perhaps they recognized that the hive's survival depended upon a single queen who alone "led" her workers and drones?

(4) Radak's comments may have unwittingly brought us full circle. Recall how Rashi had explained the census at the book's opening as an expression of divine concern which we had understood to imply "as a shepherd counts his sheep." The shepherd, to employ Radak's derivation, guides his sheep to pasture in the *midbar*, "the place of being led." Rashi's imaginative imagery and Radak's rigorous analysis thus intersect!

NASO

The Nazir

Numbers 4:21-7:89

PARASHAT NASO completes the tally of the three primary Levitical families, a process that was initiated towards the end of last week's Parasha with the designation of the family of Kehat as the bearers of the Mishkan's most precious vessels. The Torah now enumerates the responsibilities of the other Levitical families of Gershon and Merari, and then provides an accounting of the tribe's number. As Ramban explained in his introductory remarks to Sefer BeMidbar, the theme of the book is that of journey and passage, and this Parasha's Levitical census closely relates to this idea. After all, the three Levitical families of Kehat, Gershon, and Merari are together responsible for the dismantling, transport, and assembly of the Mishkan and its vessels at each station along the way to the Promised Land. In order to properly organize the tribe for this work, the exact number of their able-bodied members must be ascertained.

After the census of the Levites, the Torah goes on to detail various laws: rules that govern the sanctity of the camp, expiation rites for the transgressions of theft and for swearing false oaths, and the remarkable ceremony prescribed for the *sotah*. We will focus on the passage that follows all of the above, namely that of the *nazir*.

> God spoke to Moshe saying: "Speak to the people of Israel and say to them that a man or a woman who explicitly takes an oath to be a *nazir* unto God, shall refrain from wine and strong drink, vinegar, beverages of grapes, and grapes whether fresh or dried. During the entire period of being a *nazir*, he shall consume nothing processed from grapes of the vine, neither from their seeds nor from their skins. All the days of the oath of being a *nazir*, he shall not cut the hair of his head with a razor; until the days of the oath unto God are completed, he shall be holy, and the hair of his head shall be left alone to grow long. All the days of his oath to God, he shall not come into contact with a human corpse. He shall not defile himself even on the occasion of the death of his mother, father, brother, or sister, for the *nezer* of his God is upon him. All of the days of his oath, he shall be holy unto God." (*BeMidbar* 6:1–8)

The Torah, while pointedly omitting to mention any preliminaries as to why a person might choose to become a *nazir*, here spells out the three distinct practices that the *nazir* is expected to faithfully observe: (1) a thorough rejection of any products of the grape; (2) a proscription on the cutting of the hair with a razor so that it may grow long unimpeded, and (3) a prohibition concerning any contact with the dead, even in the case of one's immediate family. What is the significance of these three constraints? And what, for that matter, is the exact meaning of the word "*nazir*"?

The Approach of the Ibn Ezra

The medieval commentaries adopted a remarkably positive view on the matter of the *nazir*. Rabbi Avraham Ibn Ezra explains that the practices proscribed for the *nazir* by the Torah are intended to fashion for him a framework of splendid isolation, so that he might further his daring decision to withdraw from all that society foolishly considers fashionable. "A man or a woman who explicitly takes an oath (יפליא) to be a nazir unto God . . ." (6:2) is understood by the Ibn Ezra to be a reference to a vow that is not only definitively enunciated in the formal sense, but also remarkable (פלא – "wondrous") for its sobriety, "for the majority of the world's people are led along by their desires" (commentary to 6:2). Wine, suggests the Ibn Ezra, clouds one's judgment, numbs one's sense of decency and can thus interfere with and degrade one's service of God. By taking on a temporary vow of abstinence from the intoxicant and its derivatives, the *nazir* expresses a concrete aspiration to overcome the temptations of this world.

In fact, explains Ibn Ezra, the *nazir* is so-called because he wears a figurative crown or נזר upon his head, for his mane of long hair singles him out as one who has broken the bonds that otherwise hold us fast to the fleeting and futile pleasures of this world. As he puts it:

> Realize that all people are enslaved to the enticements of this world. The true king, the one who wears a crown of kingship upon his head, is the one who has liberated himself from desires. (commentary to 6:7)

For Ibn Ezra, then, letting the hair grow long is a means of publicly identifying the individual who has become a *nazir* and marking him in an exemplary fashion. His loosened tresses are symbolic, like the crown that is placed upon the head of a royal personage, indicating to all that "here is a man or woman who is in sovereign control of the self!"

The interpretation of Ibn Ezra, that the *nazir* is a monarch who rules over his desires, assumes two things. Firstly, we are to understand that the Torah's proscription of wine and grape products in this context is a function of their potentially intoxicating nature and not due to some sort of inexplicable taboo. "Most transgressions are the result of wine," he avers (6:2), and while the Torah nowhere draws this connection explicitly, there are at least two episodes in Sefer Breisheet that reinforce his reading. Recall that Noach, in the aftermath of the flood, turned to viticulture and planted grapes. Soon thereafter, he became drunk and then "uncovered his nakedness in his tent." Cham, his son, witnessed the disgrace and told his brothers who promptly covered him (*Breisheet* 9:18–29). Later on, after the fiery overthrow of Sodom, the young daughters of Lot fled with their father to a secluded mountain cave. Convinced that the world had ended and that their prospects for marriage and for procreation were nonexistent, they plied their aged father with wine and slept with him, so that they might conceive and repopulate the world (19:30–38).

The second assumption of Ibn Ezra is that the three prohibitions associated with the *nazir* – wine, hair cutting and corpse defilement – are not discrete and unrelated matters but are instead interconnected. The defining prohibition for the *nazir* is the consumption of wine. Overcoming its blandishments represents the conquest of desire and the long hair is a public announcement of that victory. As for the distancing from death, he who seeks sanctification of the spirit must, like the Kohen, abjure death and avoid its injurious effects.

Significantly, although the direct context of our Parasha appears to limit the duration of the nazirite vow and to consequently downplay the desirability of living one's entire life according to its strictures, Ibn Ezra elsewhere makes it clear that a life of separation is not to be disparaged. Commenting on the Torah's lengthy list of forbidden sexual relationships presented in *VaYikra* 18, Ibn Ezra explains that the emphatic "I am God" repeated there in verse 6 as the refrain indicates divine approval for the ideal of restraint:

> . . . God loves the one who is separated to serve Him and to listen to His words, as is suggested by the paradigm of Mount Sinai, as well as by the "First." Is this not man's essence? (commentary to *VaYikra* 18:6)

The mention of Mount Sinai is a reference to the preparations enjoined upon the people as the day of Revelation drew near:

> God said to Moshe: "approach the people and sanctify them today and tomorrow and let them wash their clothing (and immerse). They shall be prepared for the third day, for on the third day God will descend on Mount Sinai in the sight of all the people." (*Shemot* 19:10–11)

When conveying God's words to the people, Moshe explained the significance of these days of preparation: "Be ready for three days and *do not come close to a woman*" (19:15). Thus, the ideal state of Revelation, a brief but unparalleled interval during which the experience of God's closeness and immediacy was unrivalled, is made possible by a recess from sexual contact.

As for the cryptic "First" mentioned in Ibn Ezra's comments above, is a reference to the first human beings. In his commentary to *Breisheet* 2:17 and 3:6, he suggests that their consumption of the desirous but forbidden fruit of the tree of knowledge awakened in humanity a sexual appetite that would henceforth constitute a constant source of frustration between man and woman, as well as a potential cause of alienation from God. Man's "essence" is to strive for spiritual progress, but when his physicality is given the opportunity for unbridled expression, this most important of objectives is subverted. The strictures of the *nazir*, while differing substantially from the preparations enjoined at Sinai or the commandment given to the first human beings, is nevertheless related to them both in purpose: to cultivate self-restraint.

Ramban's Emphatic Endorsement and Seforno's Qualification

Although Ibn Ezra may fail to make a categorical argument for the merits of a permanent state of naziritehood, the Ramban's comments are unequivocal. The background to his comments concerns the ascription of sinfulness to the *nazir* who had become defiled (*BeMidbar* 6:11). This was understood by some early Rabbinic opinions to represent a clear polemic against the self-denial of life's permitted pleasures such as wine:

> Rabbi Elazar HaKappar explained: Why does the text say that "he [the Kohen] shall atone for him for having sinned upon the soul"? Concerning which soul did this *nazir* sin? Rather, it is because he denied himself wine! Now if this *nazir* who

> refrained only from wine is called a sinner, one who refrains from everything else all the more so!

The Ramban emphatically disagrees with his assessment:

> the reason for the sin-offering brought by the *nazir* at the conclusion of his vows is not stated in the text. The rational explanation appears to be that this man is actually committing a transgression by *concluding* his vows, for up until now he has been separated in his holiness and in his service to God. It would have been more fitting for this man to remain a *nazir* forever, sanctified unto his God . . . he therefore requires atonement for deciding to return to the defilement associated with the desires of this world. (commentary to *BeMidbar* 6:11)

The Ramban explains that the *nazir* achieves an ideal state through his abstention, and ideal states ought to be perpetuated. In deciding to adopt the strictures only temporarily, the *nazir* commits an offense that requires atonement! Thus, while he clearly echoes the sentiments of Ibn Ezra, the Ramban goes even further in his praise of abstention.

In this connection, it is worthwhile to consider the words of the Seforno. Like his earlier counterparts, Seforno understands that the ideal of the *nazir* is

> to be separated (נזור) from habitual pleasures . . . in order to be dedicated completely to God, to be occupied in the Torah, to follow His ways and to cleave to Him.

Nevertheless, Seforno proffers that the Torah is very *selective* in its choice of abstentions for the *nazir*. He is to be separated only from wine, but this in no way constitutes a license to

> abuse himself through fasting, for such conduct would lessen one's strength and cause a proportional reduction in his ability to serve God. The purpose is not for the *nazir* to become an ascetic and to punish his body through self-flagellation after the manner of the monastic priests. Rather, let him abstain from wine only, for this will lessen levity and subdue his inclinations, without weakening the body's strength. (commentary to 6:3)

In a similar vein, the emphasis on allowing the hair of the head to grow long allows the *nazir* to "cast behind himself all concerns of beautification and attention to his hair" (commentary to 6:5). But here as well, "separation from material desires" is accomplished without recourse to general self-abasement and the extensive neglect of the body. For the Seforno, the prohibition of trimming the hair is not calculated to afford the *nazir* with a glorious mane to signify his mastery of desires, as Ibn Ezra had suggested. Rather, the Seforno perceives the matter to be directly analogous to the abstention from wine. Wine symbolizes life's empty pleasures, hair and our preoccupation with it symbolizes superficial fashion and our over-concern with appearances. In another departure from the interpretation of the Ibn Ezra, Seforno maintains that the word "*nazir*" is derived from a root that means "separate," for separation and abstention are at the core of the *nazir*'s concern.

The essential life-affirming nature of these two restrictions is amplified by the third – the prohibition of coming into contact with a corpse. Like his counterpart the Kohen Gadol (High Priest), who alone shares a similar ban on being in attendance at the death or burial of even immediate family members (*VaYikra* 21:10–12), the *nazir*'s mission is bound up with life. Being in God's presence is connecting with the source of all life. Therefore during the period of his vows, the *nazir* renounces death. But what the Kohen Gadol acquires through lineage and appointment, the nazir accomplishes through the exercise of his own free will. He therefore merits to be holy unto God, to "be illuminated by the light of life, and to be a teacher and guide to the generation" (Seforno's commentary to *BeMidbar* 6:6).

The Seforno's contribution to the discussion is enlightening, for he is suggesting that the Torah's purpose in presenting us with the paradigm of the *nazir* is not to disparage physicality or to malign materiality, as if there exists an unbridgeable chasm between the reality of the body and the ideal of the soul. Quite the contrary, for the ultimate success of the spirit in this world is predicated upon the healthy functioning of the body. Rather, the restrictions of the *nazir* serve as gentle reminders that one's goals in life must be to transcend the immediate and the shallow – the desire to drink to inebriation or to look beautiful as a narcissistic end unto itself. These two activities are paradigms for pursuits that, left unchecked, deflect us from our objective and may ultimately consume us. To become a *nazir* is to appreciate the higher value of things, to recognize not only life's preciousness but also its ultimate purpose, and to communicate these hard-won truths to others.

Often we trumpet the platitude that the Torah does not advocate mortification of the body but rather its sanctification. This is fundamentally true, but when we consider the matter more carefully through the prism of the *nazir*, we may in fact come to the conclusion that true sanctification is impossible without first having acquired the perspective afforded by abstinence. We must bear in mind that we are acculturated to social norms that venerate the body and idolize wealth, even as the needs of the spirit are glaringly overlooked. Often, we justify our over-attention to material pursuits by misinterpreting the Torah's ideal of sanctification of the physical as a license for its unmitigated embrace; we indulge our base material and physical drives in the name of הידור מצווה or "beautification and adornment of mitzvah performance," when really it is unbridled desire in disguise. We may be living Torah-observant lives in the narrow sense but still be very far from the ideal of living in God's presence.

Our Parasha reminds us of the challenges before us: How shall we navigate the desires of this world without becoming overwhelmed by them? How shall we justifiably care for and nurture our material bodies without becoming enslaved in the process? The *nazir* points the way to a higher dialectic, in which the body and its passions are not to be rejected or suppressed, but nevertheless must be tempered in the interests of nurturing our spiritual growth and development.

FOR FURTHER STUDY:

(1) The disagreement concerning the place of abstinence and asceticism in the service of God is an ancient one. The Rabbis of the Talmud, for instance, vehemently disagreed about the value of fasting, as related in TB *Ta'anit* 11a–b. That discussion was in turn directly related to the *nazir*, as mentioned above. See TB *Nazir* 2b and the Tosafot there for more on the matter.

(2) While the Torah itself does not explicitly link wine with immorality, the prophets do so on numerous occasions. See, for example, *Yeshayahu* 5:11–17 and 28:1–13; *Amos* 6:1–10.

BEHA'ALOTCHA

Chovav and the Ark

Numbers 8:1-12:16

OUR BOOK optimistically began with a census of the people of Israel, as they prepared to undertake the march from Mount Sinai to the Promised Land. The organization of their camp, predicated upon four tribal units grouped around the Mishkan, was spelled out at some length. The first Parasha of BeMidbar concluded with a census of the tribe of Levi and a detailed description of the responsibilities pertaining to the Levitical clan of Kehat. Parashat Naso continued by delineating the responsibilities of the other two Levitical clans of Gershon and Merari. The topics of the *sotah* and *nazir* were then discussed, with each of their respective rituals rigidly revolving around the Mishkan. That Parasha finished with a lengthy and repetitive formulary describing the offerings presented by the twelve tribal princes of Israel on the occasion of the Mishkan's dedication.

Parashat BeHa'alotcha now opens with a brief mention of the kindling of the menorah. It then describes the formal investiture of the Levites into the service of the Mishkan, in place of the firstborn who had been rejected due to their prominent role in the sin of the golden calf. Immediately following the account of the Levites' election (*BeMidbar* 8), the Torah anachronistically narrates the celebration of the Paschal sacrifice that actually preceded the census at the book's outset. This Pesach constitutes the only recorded observance of the rite during the entire wilderness experience. When some of the people are unable to perform the Pesach ceremonial due to ritual unfitness, the Torah mandates the unusual opportunity of a compensatory observance, to be performed exactly one month later. This so-called "Pesach Sheni" or Second Passover is the only example of a holiday ritual for which the Torah offers another chance.

What then follows (9:15–23) is a proleptic description of the journeys through the wilderness. First, the divine cloud would lift off of the Mishkan and then the camp would begin to move. The duration of Israel's encampment at the next location would be dictated by the cloud's continued presence. As long as the cloud remained stationed above the Mishkan, the people would encamp; as soon as it began to journey, the people would follow its lead. With the trek from Sinai now imminent, the Torah introduces one last item: the silver trumpets (10:1–10). Moshe is to fashion these precious instruments and to use them to rally the tribal princes or the people (in accordance with the specific notes that are sounded), or to signal to them all that the camp is to break up and their peregrinations are to begin.

When we consider this narrative progression in its totality, it emerges that the Mishkan is the thematic glue that binds all of the subject matter together. This movable building, a traveling sanctuary for God's presence, is the foundation of the camp's structure and the focal point of its cares. The census of the Levite clans and their respective ritual assignments all pertain to the service of the Mishkan. The journeys narrated in Sefer BeMidbar loyally follow its rhythms, for when this building is dismantled the people begin their trek and they mark their arrival at the next destination by fabricating it anew. The momentous events recorded in the other books of the Torah all take place at fixed geographic locations: Canaan (*Breisheet*), Egypt (*Shemot*), Sinai (*VaYikra*), and the Plains of Moav (*Devarim*). Only Sefer BeMidbar has no geographic anchor – it is the account of Israel's journey towards the Promised Land. The impermanent Mishkan, a perfect mirror for Israel's transitory state during this time, is therefore at the center of the story.

Embarking Upon the Journey

The day of journey from Mount Sinai finally arrives, just three short weeks after the census of the people had been taken:

> On the twentieth day of the second month of the second year, the cloud lifted from upon the Tent of the Testimony. The people of Israel journeyed from the wilderness of Sinai according to the order of their travels, and the cloud came to rest in the wilderness of Paran. (*BeMidbar* 10:11–12)

As the journey commences, Moshe addresses Chovav in a hope-filled exchange that serves as the culmination of this entire series of narratives:

> Moshe said to Chovav son of Re'uel the Midianite, Moshe's father-in-law: "We are traveling to the place concerning which God said 'I shall give it to you,' come with us and we shall deal kindly with you, for God has spoken good things concerning Israel." But he said: "I shall not go, rather to my own land and to my own birthplace I shall go." He (Moshe) said: "Please do not abandon us, for you know our encampments in the wilderness, and you shall serve as our eyes." They journeyed forth from the mountain of God for a distance of three days, and the ark of God's covenant traveled before them at a three-day distance in order to search out a place of rest for them. The cloud of God was upon them by day, when they traveled forth from the encampment. (10:29–34)

Moshe's tone is hopeful as he invites Chovav to join the people on the journey to the land. But Chovav, whose name means "beloved one," expresses misgivings. He desires instead to return to his own "land and birthplace." Moshe pleads with him to accompany them, but the text leaves it unclear as to whether in the end he is convinced to join the people of Israel on their fateful trek, an ambiguity later echoed in a difference of opinion among the commentaries. What is abundantly clear, however, is that his reluctance is motivated by a strong identification with his *own* land and birthplace – "I shall not go, rather to my own land and to my own birthplace I shall go." The passage thus serves as a fitting close to the entire section, for Chovav conveys an emphatic message to the people of Israel that they must internalize if they are to succeed: Ancestral land is a precious asset and connection to one's birthplace ought to be one of life's strongest attachments. Canaan – Israel's ancient patrimony – beckons. It will be up to the people to seize it and to make it their own.

The camp now breaks up and begins its ponderous march, with the tribe of Yehuda (and its two associated tribes of Yissachar and Zevulun) serving as the vanguard. The other tribes follow suit, but the journey does not unfold in accordance with the strict ordering principles outlined earlier in the book. In general, the ark would embark after the departure of the first two tribal standards and the Levitical families of Gershon and Merari that traveled between them (2:17). This was done so that by the time the ark arrived with the other holy vessels borne by the family of Kehat, the Mishkan building and enclosure would already be assembled and ready for their immediate placement (see 4:4–20 and 10:11–28). But as they now go forth from Sinai, the ark of the covenant breaks ranks – rather than traveling in the midst of the standards, it goes *before* the entire congregation. The discrepancy can be easily explained: The people of Israel were anxious as they left Sinai behind and entered the fearsome wilderness once again. Journeying ahead of them at a three-day distance in order to pave the way, this visible symbol of God's presence ameliorated the anxiety and inspired the people with confidence. As they slowly made their way through the barren landscape, a protective cloud shielded them from the harsh elements (10:33–34). The message was therefore clear: God leads and God protects!

Expectation, Enthusiasm and Hope

There is, however, another aspect to the anomaly of the ark leading the way, highlighted by Rashi in at least two places. Commenting on our section, Rashi remarks that it is striking that when Moshe announces to Chovav that the people are set to journey towards the land, he includes himself among them: "*We* are traveling to the place concerning which God said 'I shall give it to you,' go forth with us and we shall deal kindly with you, for God has spoken good things concerning Israel." This is in spite of the fact that every student of the text knows that Moshe was later denied entry to the land at the episode of the "waters of Meriva" (see 20:1–13). Rather, avers Rashi, when Moshe stated that "*we* are traveling to the place" he meant to indicate that

> "... we are going there immediately, for at the end of these three days we shall enter the land." This first journey was undertaken with the intention of entering the land of Israel. But the people soon fell prey to grumbling. It was for this reason that Moshe included himself with them, for the decree banning him from the land had not yet been promulgated and he thought that he was entering with them ... (commentary to 10:29)

In other words, when the ark traveled before the people at a distance of three days, it did not do so in order to search out an appropriate location for their next encampment, for there was to be *no* intermediate encampment at all until they actually entered Canaan! The ark leading the procession was therefore not so much about nurturing reassurance as much as it was about fostering enthusiasm, heightening anticipation and introducing haste. As Rashi explains in the parallel passage from Sefer Devarim, in which Moshe recalls this tumultuous and tragic journey,

> Moshe said to the people: "Look what you have done! The shortest path from Chorev (Mount Sinai) to Kadesh Barnea (the southern entrance to Canaan) is by the way of Mount Se'ir, and even so it is a distance of eleven days. But you traversed that distance in three days ... for the divine presence was so anxious on your behalf to expedite your entry into the land. But because you transgressed, He caused you to aimlessly wander the region of Mount Se'ir for a period of forty years!" (commentary to *Devarim* 1:2)

Placing the ark at the vanguard casts Moshe's conversation with Chovav in a completely different light. "God has spoken kindly concerning Israel" refers not only to the gift of the land but also to His intent to swiftly bring them to Canaan's gates. When Chovav expresses reservations, Moshe appeals to Chovav's ability to provide "guidance," which we understood as a reference to the Midianite nomad's intimate familiarity with the wilderness and a seeming indication that the journey to the land will be lengthy. But the passage in its original Hebrew could just as easily be interpreted as expressing the past tense: "Please do not abandon us, for you *did know* our encampments in the wilderness, and *you served* as our eyes." If so, the reference is not to Chovav's imminent role as a wilderness guide – unnecessary considering the ark's lead and the short duration of the journey – but rather to his *past* role as spiritual guide or witness. Rashi's comments in this connection are consistent:

> . . . you knew about our encampment in the wilderness and served as eyes for the miracles and wonders performed for us . . . (commentary to *BeMidbar* 10:31)

For Rashi, Chovav experienced the miracles that God had wrought for the people in the wilderness as they camped at Sinai after the Exodus. He felt the divine concern for their welfare and he was acutely aware of His desire to speedily bring them to the land. When he heard of Israel's miraculous triumph over Egypt, he journeyed from afar, out of the maw of the Midianite wastelands, in pursuit of the God of Israel (*Shemot* 18:1–12). What better paradigm could there be for the people of Israel than a man so inspired by his witnessing of divine intervention that he overcame his own fears and misgivings, to eagerly follow God wherever He might lead?

Of course, if this is the import of Moshe's invitation, then the Ramban's postscript must perforce be adopted:

> It is my opinion that Chovav acquiesced and indeed accompanied them . . . (commentary to *BeMidbar* 10:31, amplified by his remarks to *Shemot* 18:1, end)

The opening narratives of Sefer BeMidbar, permeated with optimism and full of hope, are thus fittingly concluded by this exchange between Moshe and Chovav. The Torah's point in including the passage is to drive home a central point: trust in God is never a free ride. When God asks of us to be steadfast and to be faithful, to be inspired and to be bold, then we must maintain our composure even when difficult trials stand in our path. What Israel needed most as they finally journeyed forth from Sinai towards the Promised Land, God paradoxically could *not* give them. They would have to acquire it on their own. While the ark could enthusiastically guide them and the protective cloud could shield them from harm, the people would have to decide whether to now embrace the destiny that God extended towards them. Moshe's intention in inviting Chovav to join them was to provide his people with living proof that steadfast trust was possible.

The Other Half of the Parasha

All of this positive momentum is unexpectedly derailed by the events that now quickly unfold. As the ark begins its propitious journey, the people are suddenly seized with a spirit of complaint (*BeMidbar* 11:1–3). Quickly, this degenerates into a desire for meat, fish and all of the other culinary pleasures of Egypt. The oppressive bondage that only a short time ago was left behind with relief, is now recalled with fondness. The miraculous manna is found by the people to be wanting, for they desire a return to Egyptian fare, and by extension, to Egyptian ways (11:4–35). The Parasha inauspiciously ends with Miriam's verbal broadside against Moshe (12:1–16). It is not unreasonable to trace a straight line from these episodes to the spies' failed mission and the people's rejection of the land in next Parasha, to the rebellion of Korach recorded next, and even to the downfall of Moshe and Aharon that unfolds in Parashat Chukat.

These opposing episodes, constituting the second half of Sefer BeMidbar, describe the other side of the wilderness coin: the people's unwillingness to take up the challenge of journeying to Canaan to there realize the Torah's mandate to be God's nation. As they begin to traverse the wilderness of Sinai towards that bright but uncertain future, their misgivings become palpable and eventually are expressed by a profound reluctance to go on. In the end, they will be condemned to perish in the wilderness that they refuse to leave behind. In many ways, however, that harsh sentence is not an exaggerated outburst of divine displeasure but rather an inevitable outcome of their own spiritual immaturity.

Parashat BeHa'alotcha is therefore the pivot between two opposing draws – the call of a land budding with potential but whose possession depends upon making autonomous choices and accepting responsibility, versus the seductive inner voice that rejects any higher purpose and seeks comfort in the spiritual torpor represented by Egypt. The great divide between the two is highlighted in the Torah by an unusual feature. The exact turning point of the account is a well-known couplet of verses that has entered the liturgy as part of the Torah service. In context, Moshe invokes God's protection as the journey towards Canaan commences, for he knows that Israel's entry into the land will not go unopposed:

> When the ark began to journey, Moshe proclaimed: "Arise, God, and let your enemies be scattered, may those that hate You flee from before You." When the ark came to rest, Moshe said: "Rest Your presence upon the myriads and thousands of Israel." (10:35–36)

As it turns out, these verses separate Moshe's conversation with Chovav from the people's first grievance and are bracketed in the original Hebrew text by a very curious backwards letter "נ". According to one view in the Talmud, the short section constitutes an independent book of the Torah (!), and the eighty-five letters that it contains are therefore the benchmark for determining the continued sanctity of a worn-out Torah scroll:

> A worn-out Torah scroll that does not have eighty-five valid letters, corresponding to the section of "when the ark began to journey . . ." may not be saved from a fire that breaks out on the Shabbat [if this involves its transfer from the private to the public domain] . . . (TB *Shabbat* 115b–116a)

Sefer BeMidbar is therefore composed of *three* separate volumes: the first that extends from the book's beginning until these verses, these two verses themselves, and the last section of the book from just after these verses until the end. As Rabbi Shemuel bar Nachman colorfully elaborates in the name of Rabbi Yonatan:

> When the verse states that "Wisdom has built her house and has hewn her seven pillars" (*Mishlei* 9:1), it refers to the *seven* books of the Torah!

The Torah marks the disparate sections of Parashat BeHa'alotcha by employing the reversed letter "נ" to bracket these verses. But in essence, as Rabbi Shemuel bar Nachman explains, the entire book of BeMidbar can be divided into two thematic halves: optimistically and enthusiastically preparing for the journey, and then losing the resolve just as it is commenced! Navigating a desolate wilderness – geographical as well as existential – is this book's most abiding challenge. The journey of the ark at the vanguard – the intimation of God's guidance and ongoing support – is its eternal promise. It is this profound truth that the Torah communicates with its judicious placement of these two short verses, for they encapsulate the essence of the matter. Moshe's invitation to Chovav and the journey of the ark are therefore complementary. Often we travel – we know not where, nor how we shall ever reach the destination. Sometimes we undertake the voyage reluctantly, bowed by indecision and plagued by misgivings. We fall prey to doubt, to disbelief and to the denial of God's concern and expectations. But by taking Chovav's lead and following the ark, by submitting to God's guidance and to His direction in our lives, by embracing His enthusiasm for granting us success, we can yet reach the Promised Land.

FOR FURTHER STUDY:

(1) The commentaries disagree about the identity of Chovav, with the matter depending upon the placement of a modifier. For Rashi, who identifies Chovav with Yitro, the verse reads as follows:

> Moshe said to Chovav – son of Re'uel the Midianite – Moshe's father-in-law . . . (*BeMidbar* 10:29)

Accordingly, Chovav is Moshe's father-in-law who is synonymous with Yitro, and Yitro's father is Re'uel the Midianite. When Moshe rescues Yitro's daughters from the shepherds at the well, they return home and report to "Re'uel their father" (*Shemot* 2:18). This must mean their *grandfather*, as Rashi here (*BeMidbar* 10:29) and Rashbam there explain. Our analysis follows their identification.

Alternatively, we could divide up the ambiguous verse this way:

> Moshe said to Chovav – son of Re'uel the Midianite Moshe's father-in-law . . . (*BeMidbar* 10:29)

This parsing yields a different reading. Chovav is the son of Re'uel and Re'uel is Moshe's father-in-law. This therefore makes Chovav Moshe's brother-in-law and the *son* of Yitro! Ibn Ezra mentions this possibility in his comments to *BeMidbar* 10:29 but ultimately leaves the matter unresolved. If Re'uel is Yitro, then *Shemot* 2:18 that refers to "Re'uel their father" can be read in the most straightforward way.

Ramban in his comments to *Shemot* 2:16 adopts Rashi's reading and posits that Yitro was given the new name "Chovav" after his conversion, "because all those that convert are given a different name in Israel," and this new name reflects his beloved status as a sincere convert.

SHELACH

Moshe's Missing Prayer

Numbers 13:1-15:41

PARASHAT SHELACH, always read at the onset of summer time as the grapes start to ripen and the green fields turn inexorably to burnt brown, constitutes the historic turning point for the generation that had left the land of Egypt. Only fifteen short months had elapsed since the Exodus and a scarce few weeks since Israel had journeyed forth from Mount Sinai in the direction of the Promised Land, when the twelve tribal leaders were sent forth with much fanfare to spy out fertile Canaan. It was from the southern oasis of Kadesh Barnea that the spies advanced, bearing with them not only the solemn burden of Moshe's charge, but also the buoyant expectations of the people of Israel. Searching out the land for a period of forty days, traversing its hills and valleys from south to north and then southwards again, the spies indeed discovered that it was a verdant land full of promise. There was plentitude in Canaan, trees and fruits in abundance, sources of fresh water and grasslands for grazing sheep. But the countryside was also dotted with villages and towns – small but fortified bastions of Canaanite settlement – as well as large and strongly defended cities.

Upon their return, the spies displayed the large and redolent fruits that they had gathered, informed the people of their findings, and then concluded their report with the almost unanimous assessment that conquering the land would be impossible. Two of them, Yehoshua and Calev, vehemently and courageously disagreed, but their impassioned and faith-filled words were soon drowned out by the other spies' sinister tales and then by the people's uncontrolled sobs. God's anger was kindled against Israel, and in a burning outburst of divine displeasure, He threatened to destroy the people entirely. Stepping into the breach, Moshe deflected His wrath (*BeMidbar* 14:11–20), but he was unable to avert the subsequent sentence that condemned them to perish in the wilderness:

> God said to Moshe: "For how long will this people provoke Me? For how long will they not trust in Me, in spite of all of the signs that I have done in their midst? I will strike them down by the plague and make of you a greater and more powerful nation"!
>
> Moshe responded to God: "The people of Egypt will hear that You have brought up this people from their midst by Your strength . . . If you kill this people as one then the nations that have heard of Your reputation will proclaim: it is beyond God's ability to bring this people into the Land that He swore to them, and so He slaughtered them in the wilderness. Now let Your power increase, Lord, just

as You have stated: 'God is long suffering and full of mercy, He forgives iniquity and rebellion . . .' Forgive the iniquity of this people in accordance with Your great mercy, as You have borne this people from Egypt until this moment."

God said: "I forgive in accordance with your words . . . however . . . all of the men that saw My glory and the wonders that I did in Egypt and in the wilderness, yet still tested Me these ten times and did not hearken to My voice, will surely not see the land that I swore to give to their ancestors. All those that incensed Me will not see it!" (14:11–23)

Moshe's Prayer at the Episode of the Golden Calf vs. His Deafening Silence Here

While Moshe's pleas were impassioned and sincere, invoking God's mercy while appealing to His name, he remarkably made no further attempts to soften the decree. This was in glaring contrast to his heroic conduct in the aftermath of the other great wilderness debacle, the sin of the golden calf that had occurred about one year earlier. At that time, not only did Moshe, as here, successfully cancel the initial threat of destruction (see *Shemot* 32:7–14), but he went on, unlike here, to tearfully plead the people's case for eighty consecutive days and nights (see 32:31)! In the end, he succeeded in restoring almost entirely God's confidence and His promise, and in the process Moshe secured the second tablets of stone. But here, Moshe fell uncharacteristically silent, his initial prayer less than efficacious, a subsequent prayer on his part entirely non-existent, thus leaving himself open to the charge that his own love for the people had perhaps dissipated in the interim.

The lacuna is forcefully highlighted by Moshe's own recounting of both pivotal events, as he recorded them in Sefer Devarim some forty years later. Note how in the following lengthy passage, Moshe clearly mentions both episodes, but assigns a disproportionately meager amount of text (a single fleeting verse!) to the sin of the spies, and in that connection neglects to mention undertaking any efforts whatsoever to annul the divine pronouncement. Significantly, the sin of the spies is bracketed on both ends by the memory of the golden calf:

> I fell down before God like at the outset, for forty days and for forty nights. I ate no bread nor drank no water, because of the sin that you had transgressed, to do evil in the sight of God and to anger Him. This was because I was terrified by the anger and rage that God showed towards you to destroy you, but God listened to me at that time also. God was also very angry at Aharon and sought to destroy him, and I prayed on Aharon's behalf at that time. As for your transgression that you had fashioned, that calf, I took it and burned it in the fire and beat it into fine dust, casting its dust into the stream that descended from the mountain. At Tavera, Masa and Kivrot HaTa'avah you also angered God.
>
> When God sent you from Kadesh Barnea saying: "Arise and possess the land that I have given you!" you rebelled against the word of God your Lord and did not trust in Him nor hearken to His voice. You have been rebellious with God from the day that I have known you.
>
> I fell before God for the forty days and the forty nights that I fell down, for God had spoken of destroying you. I prayed to God and I said: "Almighty God, do not destroy Your people and possession that You have liberated by Your greatness, that You took out of Egypt with a strong hand. Remember the merit of Your servants

> Avraham, Yitzchak and Ya'acov and do not turn to this people's stubbornness, or to their wickedness or to their transgression. Lest the inhabitants of the land from whence You brought them forth exclaim that it is beyond God's powers to bring them into the land that He spoke of to them, and in His hatred of them He brought them forth to exterminate them in the wilderness. But they are Your people and Your inheritance, that You have brought forth with Your great power and with Your outstretched arm!" (*Devarim* 9:18–29)

These final lines of Moshe's reminiscence are extremely telling, for in them he describes how he was able to placate God's wrath concerning the golden calf by appealing to the glory of His reputation. "What would the nations say," argued Moshe, "if You were to destroy the people in the wilderness? Would they not then erroneously conclude that You were too weak to bring them into Canaan, and therefore chose instead to annihilate them in the wilderness?!" How striking it is that while Moshe does initially employ a similar stratagem here in order to forestall the people's immediate and utter destruction (see *BeMidbar* 14:11–16), he fails to press on with that argument after God issues His decree to deny the generation of the wilderness entry into the land. Were Moshe's assertions about God's tarnished reputation rendered any less cogent by the fact that Israel's entry would now be delayed by some forty years rather than revoked entirely? Would the said nations not similarly question God's supposed omnipotence in the face of a four-decade-long postponement?

The Ramban perceptively notes in his commentary to 16:1 that the people's disappointment in Moshe's performance at this juncture may very well have provided the initial spark that later ignited the first serious bout of discontent with his leadership since the Exodus. That despair was soon after skillfully stoked by Moshe's megalomaniacal cousin Korach to become a burning insurrection. The Ramban relates:

> As long as Israel was in the wilderness of Sinai, nothing bad befell them. Even in the matter of the golden calf, admittedly a grievous and public sin, the number of those who perished was small while the rest were saved by Moshe's prayer, for he fell down on their behalf for forty days and forty nights . . . But then they entered the wilderness of Paran and some were burned by the fires of Tavera and many perished at Kivrot HaTa'avah. *When they sinned concerning the spies, Moshe did not pray on their behalf and the decree was not averted.* Rather, the tribal leaders fell by plague before God, while the rest of the people were condemned to perish in the wilderness and to there die out. Then the soul of the people became bitter and they said in their hearts that only failures befell them as a result of Moshe . . .

How are we to understand Moshe's reticence at the sin of the spies, his utter lack of enthusiasm in undertaking any serious effort to avert the disastrous decree of decimation? Why didn't the lawgiver throw himself down in supplication, even offering to forfeit his own future if only the people of Israel could be saved (as in fact he did at the sin of the golden calf, see *Shemot* 32:22–33)? In short, why is Moshe's conduct here so glaringly different than his own comportment at the sin of the golden calf? Where is Moshe's missing prayer?!

The Punishment of the Spies: Retribution or Rehabilitation

Before we can answer the question, we must first dispel a serious misconception that for many of us informs our understanding of the account of the spies. The fact is that we tend to view the episode of the spies as another typical biblical paradigm for the matter of crime and punishment. As the passage is so often superficially understood, the people of Israel sinned grievously by displaying too little faith in His power, and God responded in kind by punishing them harshly. In accordance with this reading, we search for a rough correspondence between the crime and the punishment, a smug and satisfying "measure for measure" that could explain the destructive dynamic, and thus we fall upon the following verse in which God expresses His disappointment: "According to the number of days that you spied out the land, namely forty days, you shall bear your iniquity for forty years, one day per year, one day per year, and you shall thus know My fury!" (*BeMidbar* 14:34).

In constructing the syllogism, we fail to realize that such a facile interpretation of the episode casts God as a terribly vengeful and vindictive being, for there is no other way to account for a symmetry that is so lopsided in the extreme. Do forty *days* of traversing the land justify forty *years* of wandering in the wilderness? Do the indiscretions of the spies, representatives of the people though they may have been, justify the wholesale punishment of the entire generation? Additionally, as we stated earlier, such an interpretation also raises serious and irresolvable questions concerning Moshe's conduct, for why wouldn't he pray to God to mitigate His decree? Why would he stand idly by as his people are condemned to perish by a slow and pernicious process that has no purpose but to punish?

But what if we are not dealing with a punishment at all, and not even with a "crime" in its most narrow sense? What if the episode of the spies was calculated instead to provide Israel with an indicator of their own spiritual condition, a divinely-orchestrated means of measuring their national state of readiness to confront the challenges of conquering and settling the land of Canaan? In other words, God commanded the sending of the spies not in order to test Israel – only to award them a dismally failing grade and then to expel them altogether – but rather in order to bring to light *for their own sake* the people's state of mind. Canaan beckoned, but entering it would require resilience, fortitude, and no small amount of courage, notwithstanding God's recurring promises of assistance. If Israel was truly up for the challenge, then they would have been heartened by the reports of the land's fertility and not discouraged by the reports of what should have been obvious in any case: The Canaanites would defend their land. But if in the spies' assessment conquest was utterly impossible, then better to spend additional time nurturing the necessary resolve so that Israel might one day confront their destiny and triumph. The impassioned entreaties of Yehoshua and Calev therefore had to be shrilly voiced only to be rejected, for in so doing the people of Israel were simultaneously rejecting the still, small voice within them that spoke courageously and confidently of entering the land and prevailing.

Viewed in this way, the forty years of wandering were not an abusive form of punishment but rather an opportunity (painful though it may have been) for development and growth. Israel would spend a generation of time in the wilderness, buffeted by deprivation while sustained exclusively by God's concern, maturing into a nation not of formerly oppressed slaves but of truly free men. The liberated slave may succeed in shedding his tatters to externally embrace comfort and tranquility and thus resemble those who are free, but he rarely overcomes the gnawing self-doubt and deep-seated existential fear that together preclude truly great achievement.

Thus, Israel was condemned, condemned to grow and to mature. As Rabbi Avraham Ibn Ezra so eloquently puts it in his insightful comments concerning the people's inability to confront the Egyptian host at the Sea of Reeds, a situation of palpable panic not unlike the moment of their reaction to the spies' report,

> . . . God who alone does wonders and who alone reckons the deeds of mortals, brought it about that all of the males who came out of Egypt perished, for they did not possess the strength of spirit necessary to fight and to prevail against the Canaanites. A new generation had to arise after that of the generation of the wilderness, who had not experienced exile and thus possessed a confident spirit . . . (commentary to *Shemot* 14:13)

As for Moshe's missing prayer, it is now blatantly obvious why it is not here. For what should Moshe have prayed, after the people demonstrated not only a lack of trust but an essential deficiency of spirit? Should he have prayed that God relent, only so that the people should quickly march to Canaan's borders, there to crumble and to take flight back into the wilderness at the first sign of setback? Since the decree of forty years was not punitive but rather pedagogical, any prayer to relieve the decree would have constituted a destructive distraction from the task at hand: the building of Israel's self-worth that is the prerequisite for any true spiritual development and meaningful accomplishment. We may thus reframe the burning question: How can I believe and trust in God unless I can believe and trust in myself? And how can I trust in myself while lacking self-worth and self-respect?

The sin of the golden calf, on the other hand, constituted a fundamentally different infraction. It was a transgression of doctrine, a brazen attempt to preserve an entrenched attachment to idolatry that was disguised in the more benign trappings of intermediation and incarnation. The people strayed in their thoughts from the pure monotheism that God demanded of them, they fashioned a concrete icon to take the place of incorporeal God, and they sinned grievously by worshipping it as their liberator. God was upset at their infidelity and He sought to punish them and then Moshe averted disaster and restored equilibrium by appealing to His compassion. Thus God's hand was stayed and their failure was soon rectified, for their infraction was an infraction of the *mind*. Erroneous doctrines can be easily corrected by appealing to the intellect and then reworking the equation. But at the episode of the spies, the people betrayed their deepest self-doubts. Concerning these failures of the *heart* and of the spirit there could be neither punishment nor immediate correction, but only the slow and arduous work of divinely-mandated restoration over the course of a lifetime.

In the end, of course, the people of Israel were primed and ready, and under Yehoshua's able leadership they traversed the Yarden and entered the land. Conquering and settling it took many, many decades and though there was no shortage of setbacks along the way, the people persevered and eventually fashioned their state. Centuries after their entry into Canaan, they built the Temple at Jerusalem and inaugurated a brief but glorious period of national self-actualization. Searching for the source of their eventual triumph, it is very easy to look elsewhere than to our Parasha. But that would be an error, for it was precisely within the formative crucible of the lengthy wilderness wanderings, ostensibly precipitated by the failure of the spies but actually demanded by more fundamental needs, that Israel's resolve was forged.

FOR FURTHER STUDY:

(1) See Maimonides' trenchant remarks in his Guide to the Perplexed 3:32, where he charts that generation's greatest challenges:

> ... it is not within the nature of the person who has been raised in servitude and slavery and conditioned to make mortar and bricks, to quickly wash his hands of that dirt and immediately engage the giants of Canaan in battle ... God led them through the wilderness so that their spirits might be strengthened, for adversity breeds courage while complacency breeds cowardice. In that place a generation was born that was not conditioned to be submissive or to be slaves. All of this was accomplished by divine commands through the agency of Moshe – "By God's word they encamped and by His word they journeyed; the charge of God they kept, by God's word and Moshe's works ..." (*BeMidbar* 9:23)

KORACH

Rebellion and Reform

Numbers 16:1-18:32

KORACH IS Moshe and Aharon's infamous cousin, who seeks to unseat the two brothers from their positions of leadership. Blessed with a true demagogue's sense of timing, Korach steps into the fray in the immediate aftermath of the catastrophe of the spies. The people of Israel, just recently denied entry into the Promised Land and condemned to perish in the inhospitable wilderness, are seething with disappointment, and Korach quickly seizes upon that discontent to advance his own political aspirations. Claiming to represent the people's best interests, he gathers around himself a disgruntled group of malcontents, some of them upset at the election of the tribe of Levi in place of the firstborn, others distressed by Aharon's seemingly selfish cornering of the priesthood, and still others dissatisfied with Moshe's ineffectiveness in averting God's wrath concerning the spies.

> Korach, the son of Yitzhar, the son of Kehat, the son of Levi, joined forces with Datan and Aviram the sons of Eliav, and On son of Pelet from the tribe of Reuven. They arose before Moshe, along with two hundred and fifty men of Israel, all of whom were princes of the congregation and men of renown. They gathered against Moshe and Aharon and said to them, "You have enough! Is not the whole congregation holy, is not God in their midst? Why then do you raise yourselves above the congregation of God?" (*BeMidbar* 16:1–3)

Quickly, things come to a head. Korach and his cohorts take up Moshe's challenge of the firepans and two hundred and fifty of them are summarily incinerated by divine fire. Datan and Aviram, two of Korach's most ardent supporters and Moshe's most bitter opponents, are miraculously consumed by a sudden earthquake that swallows them, their families, and all of their worldly possessions. The people of Israel, who had thrown their support behind Korach and his men and now bemoan their unnatural demise, are stricken with plague; many perish before Aharon arrests the death by supplicating God with an offering of incense.

The View of the Ibn Ezra

In contrast to the outline presented above that places Korach's rebellion after the episode of the spies and assumes that the Torah's narratives are arranged chronologically, some commentaries disagree. Obviously, how one views the timing of the rebellion impacts in turn upon how one understands Korach's motives, the grievances of his allies and the reaction of the people of Israel to the events. We will first consider the explanation of Rabbi Avraham Ibn Ezra who places Korach's rebellion at a much earlier time than its presentation in this week's Parasha:

> This episode took place in the wilderness of Sinai, when the firstborn males were substituted by the Levites who took on their role. The people of Israel thought that Moshe our master had acted of his own accord to elevate his brother Aharon to the priesthood, to appoint his clan of Kehat to the unique role of transporting the holy vessels of the Mishkan, and to designate his tribe of Levi to minister before God. Those same Levites, however, opposed Moshe because he had made them subservient to Aharon and his descendents, the Kohanim. Datan and Aviram, who hailed from the tribe of Reuven, were angered by the fact that their tribe's preeminence had been eclipsed by that of Yosef [composed of the two tribes of Efraim and Menashe]. Perhaps, they reasoned, Moshe had so acted because he favored his apprentice Yehoshua, who descended from the tribe of Efraim. Korach himself was a firstborn, as the text clearly indicates (see *Shemot* 6:21). His clan of Kehat was stationed on the southern boundary of the Mishkan and its members were therefore in close contact with the tribe of Reuven who were also arrayed on the south. As for the rebellious princes of the congregation, they too were firstborns who in the past had been used to offering the sacrifices, and they therefore took their firepans . . .

Ibn Ezra begins by adopting an approach that he employs at other junctures in the Torah: the section describing Korach's rebellion is recorded out of strict chronological sequence. It properly belongs to the opening of Sefer BeMidbar, to the narratives that describe the organization of the tribes around the Mishkan and the election of the tribe of Levi to minister before God. It was at that time that the Torah formalized the rejection of the firstborn Israelites from serving in the Mishkan, in favor of the tribe of Levi:

> God spoke to Moshe saying: "Bring forth the tribe of Levi and present them to Aharon the priest, so that they may serve him. They shall safeguard his trust and the trust of the entire congregation before the Tent of Meeting, to perform the service of the Mishkan. They shall safeguard all of the vessels of the Tent of Meeting and keep the trust of Israel, to perform the service of the Mishkan. You shall put the Levites at the disposal of Aharon and his sons – they are given over to him from Israel. Appoint Aharon and his sons, and they shall guard their priesthood; a non-priest who serves shall die."
>
> God spoke to Moshe saying: "Behold, I have separated the Levites from among the people of Israel in place of all of their firstborn; the Levites shall be mine. For the firstborn had been Mine; from the day that I smote all of the firstborn in the land of Egypt I sanctified every firstborn in Israel to Me; they shall be Mine, I am God." (*BeMidbar* 3:5–13)

For Ibn Ezra, Korach's rebellion was sparked by the rejection of the firstborn from serving in the Mishkan. Traditionally, the firstborn from among all of the Israelites had ministered before God but after the transgression of the golden calf, in which they played a villainous role, they were rebuffed. When Moshe descended from the mountain and saw the revelers worshipping the golden calf, the tribe of Levi rallied at his call to arms, and executed God's vengeance (see *Shemot* 32:25–29). It was in consequence of this act of loyalty, in contrast to the insufferable treachery of the firstborn, that the tribe of Levi secured for itself the special task of performing the service in the Mishkan.

Ibn Ezra reminds us, however, that this substitution did not go unchallenged, for "it was a very enraging act and an affront to the non-believers to remove the firstborn from their position of service and to install Moshe's tribe in their place . . ." (commentary to *BeMidbar* 16:28). After all, the earlier arrangement ensured that many households in ancient Israel had direct involvement in the ongoing service. The election of the Levites effectively recast the service as less "democratic," for now a particular group would have exclusive rights to ministering in the Mishkan. Thus, Ibn Ezra explains, the most prominent participants in the rebellion were, one way or another, attempting to revoke the disqualification of the firstborn. The people of Israel, themselves now distanced from unimpeded access to the precincts of the Mishkan, therefore supported the rebellion enthusiastically. Most curious of all, however, was the behavior of Korach himself: although he was a Levite and therefore a beneficiary of the latest privileges, he was apparently acting as a firstborn in his rejection of the new order.

In retrospect and with the hindsight of centuries, we may appreciate how the rejection of the firstborn had far-reaching positive consequences. Had the service of the firstborn been sanctioned by tradition, the veneer of democratic participation by the people would have been maintained. Many (but not all!) households in Israel would have had a representative serving in the Mishkan or Temple. However, the more primary role of these ministers to God would have been undermined, for it was as impartial judges and teachers of the Torah that they were to excel (see *Devarim* 17:8–9, 33:8–11, etc). That is to say that had the firstborn been appointed as teachers and judges, any possibility of their unbiased involvement in the lives of the people would have been compromised, for family and clan ties would surely win the day over justice and truth. The Levites, on the other hand, had no special attachment to any one segment of the people over another.

In addition, the Levites' exclusion from having a tribal territory (in accordance with *BeMidbar* 18:20–24) tended to discourage the rapacious land acquisitions and concentration of wealth that characterized the priesthood in other cultures. It ensured that the Levites were uniformly distributed throughout the country, thus increasing their potential to raise the level of literacy of the people as a whole. Such limitations would have been impossible to enforce with respect to the firstborn, who could not have been individually barred from owning land or compelled to wander far from home and hearth.

Unfortunately, Ibn Ezra does not explain why the rebellion of Korach is related out of chronological sequence. When Ibn Ezra elsewhere invokes his exegetical principle of "the Torah not possessing a strict chronological arrangement," he discovers a didactic objective to explain the Torah's narrating of events out of order. To recall an earlier example, although Yitro's arrival at the Israelite encampment at Sinai is narrated *before* the events of the Revelation (*Shemot* 18:1–27), Ibn Ezra maintains that Yitro in fact only joined the people of Israel *after* they had heard God proclaim the Decalogue (ibid., 20). Therefore, the report of Yitro's arrival must be recorded out of order! But, as Ibn Ezra there explains, the Torah diverges from the strict chronological sequence for the sake of a clear educational goal: to emphatically contrast Yitro's act of compassion and kindness with the dastardly deed of Amalek that is recorded immediately prior to his visit (17:8–16).

Perhaps here as well the Torah wanted us to evaluate Korach's act in light of the episode of the spies that immediately precedes it in the text. Those ten leaders had been given a mandate from the people and should have served them with sincerity. Instead, they brought ruin upon Israel by succumbing to their own personal sentiments of fear and inadequacy. Unlike the spies, a true leader of the people is not overcome by despair even when confronted by difficult challenges. Unlike Korach, a true leader of the people is not driven by selfish ambition or by the appetite for power, but only by the genuine desire to serve his constituents well.

Ramban and the Incident of the Spies

The Ramban adopts a contrasting approach to that of Ibn Ezra. Elsewhere in his commentary to the Torah, the Ramban is consistent in his rejection of the assumption of non-chronological sequencing. The narratives of the Torah are in order unless we are specifically told otherwise, such as by the employment of an introductory phrase indicating an event out of sequence (see for instance the passage in *BeMidbar* 9:1–5). Therefore, the episode of Korach's rebellion must have taken place in the aftermath of the narrative of the spies. The Ramban explains:

> This incident took place in the wilderness of Paran at Kadesh Barnea after the debacle of the spies . . . As long as Israel was in the wilderness of Sinai, nothing bad befell them. Even in the matter of the golden calf, admittedly a grievous and public sin, the number of those who perished was small while the rest were saved by Moshe's prayer, for he fell down on their behalf for forty days and forty nights. At that time, the people of Israel loved Moshe as they loved themselves and would not have tolerated any insurrection against his leadership. Therefore Korach silently endured the election of Aharon to the priesthood and the appointment of Elizaphan his younger cousin to the leadership of the clan of Kehat (3:30), while the firstborn tolerated the appointment of the tribe of Levi in their stead.
>
> But then they entered the wilderness of Paran and some were burned by the fires of Tavera and many perished at Kivrot HaTa'avah. When they sinned concerning the spies, Moshe did not pray on their behalf and the decree was not averted. Rather, the tribal leaders fell by plague before God, while the rest of the people were condemned to perish in the wilderness and to there die out. Then the soul of the people became bitter and they said in their hearts that only failures befell them as a result of Moshe. It was then that Korach chose to act, correctly surmising that his attempted coup would enjoy broad support among the masses. (commentary to 16:1)

The Ramban adduces support for his interpretation from the words of Datan and Aviram. These two allies of Korach sarcastically contrasted the "land (of Egypt) flowing with milk and honey" out of which Moshe had led them, to the barren wilderness in which the people now found themselves, so that they despaired of ever entering the land of Canaan to secure "a plot of field or vineyard." In other words, avers the Ramban, Datan and Aviram and their supporters were not so much angered by the election of the Levites as they were by the prospect of the dismal denouement that awaited them in the wilderness.

For the Ramban, Korach's rebellion may have hatched out of some of the same misgivings that Ibn Ezra detected, but those angry sentiments would have been held in check if not for the incident of the spies. The disappointment and despair that the people experienced after God sealed their decree for death were the fuses that caused Korach's smoldering defiance to explode. Ramban's linkage has thematic implications as well: Both incidents, that of the spies and that of Korach, have at their core the same dissatisfaction with Israel's leaders. The spies railed against Moshe's confident counterclaims that Israel could enter the land and triumph (*Devarim* 1:29–33), while Korach bitterly questioned his illustrious cousin's motives in appointing Aharon to the position of High Priest and the Levites to the role of serving God at His house.

Insincere Motives and Genuine Reform

In the end, Korach's challenge was roundly defeated: Datan, Aviram and all that was theirs were suddenly swallowed by an earthquake announced by Moshe, while the two hundred and fifty men of renown were incinerated along with their provocative incense offerings. Korach's fate was no more fortunate, though the text refrains from explicitly spelling it out. But while the exaggerated assertions of the spies were undermined by two courageous men from their own midst, no one in our Parasha offers a rebuttal to Korach's claims. What of the impassioned manifesto advanced by him and his party? What of his provocative assertion that "the entire congregation is holy and God is in their midst. Why, then, do both of you exercise rule over the congregation of God?!" Democratic in tone and populist in content, Korach's passionate words justifiably strike a resonant chord in the ears of the people. Why then was his platform for reform expunged, just as utterly as he and his reckless retinue disappeared from sight?

Commenting in the Mishna (*Avot* 5:17), our Sages offered the following pertinent observation:

> All disagreements that are for the sake of heaven will in the end be established. However, disagreements that are not for the sake of heaven, will not be established. What is an example of a disagreement that is for the sake of heaven? That of Hillel and Shammai. What is an example of a disagreement that is not for the sake of heaven? That of Korach and all of his cohorts.

The Mishna here draws a sharp distinction between disagreements joined by antagonists who are animated by earnest motives versus arguments initiated by pugnacious people that trumpet populist slogans but really have sectarian interests in mind. As the 16th century commentator Ovadiah of Bertinoro (Italy) explains:

> If the objective and final purpose of the dissenters is to ascertain the truth, then such an argument will bear fruit, for out of disagreement and sincere discussion the truth will emerge. Thus, the divergences between Shammai and Hillel eventually led to the conclusion that the Halakha follows the house of Hillel. A disagreement that is engaged with insincere motives, however, such as with the goal of securing rule or for the love of supremacy, will yield nothing of permanence. Thus, Korach and his supporters sought honor and power for themselves, and in the end they perished.

The claims of Korach may have had merit, but since they were animated by impure motives they were disqualified. A more equitable distribution of honors and a more democratic process for the selection of leaders – the essential elements of Korach's platform – strike us as positive proposals, and rightly so. But when power-hungry demagogues reform the existing order, their calls for improvements often yield results that are more destructive than the wrongs they set out to right. History offers us innumerable examples of agitators who seized power under the banner of improving the lives of the masses, but then turned that power against the very people that they came to serve.

Shemuel, Descendent of Korach

In Rabbinic literature, Korach is portrayed as being excessively caught up with his own illustrious lineage and with his dreams for the future:

> Korach, who seemed so wise, what caused him to act so foolishly? He was led astray by his visions of the future. He saw that from him would descend a famous dynasty, for Shemuel the prophet was among his progeny. This is the same Shemuel whom the text equates with Moshe and Aharon, as it says: "Moshe and Aharon were His priests, and Shemuel called His name" (*Tehillim* 99:6) . . . Korach said: "Is it possible that all of this greatness will issue from me and I will remain silent?" He did not, however, discern matters properly, for his children did *teshuva* and therefore Shemuel descended from them. But Moshe was able to ascertain . . .

Significantly, the Rabbis drew a link between Korach the anti-hero of our Parasha and Shemuel the prophet who was his offspring. According to the pedigree preserved in *Divrei HaYamim* 1:6:7–13, Shemuel was in fact a direct but distant descendent of Korach:

> The descendents of Kehat [were]: Aminadav his son, *Korach* his son, Asir, Elkana and Aviasaf his sons, Asir's son Tachat, Uriel his son, Uziah his son, Shaul his son, Elkana his son, Amasai and Achimot his sons, Elkana his son, Tzofai his son, Nachat his son, Eliav his son, Yerocham his son, Elkana his son, and *Shemuel* his son . . .

For the Rabbis, it was visions of Shemuel's future greatness that led Korach to undertake his rebellion. What might the Rabbis have intended by their linkage? Shemuel the prophet presided over one of the most tumultuous periods in biblical history. While the people of Israel had entered the land centuries before his birth, had settled it and had adapted to an agrarian life, they had failed to achieve tranquility. The period of the judges that preceded Shemuel was characterized by instability, disunity and long stretches of moral and religious decline. The Canaanite gods and the anti-values that they championed exerted a powerful influence over the people of Israel. Although the Tabernacle stood at Shilo, it was controlled by a corrupt priestly oligarchy, which plodded on in woeful ignorance of the august responsibilities of their office. While Shemuel was still a youngster, the holy precinct was destroyed by the marauding Philistines, a cataclysmic event that had the refreshing side-effect of shattering the people's illusions that divine assistance could be secured through shallow devotions.

Into the vacuum created by the loss of the national shrine and made more acute by the absence of reliable leadership or impartial religious guidance, stepped the young Shemuel, full of divine inspiration, sincere motivation and honest concern. During the course of his tenure, he succeeded in arresting the spiritual decline, holding off the Philistine onslaught and providing the people with a credible model of administration. Most importantly, Shemuel presided over the transition from the period of the Judges to the age of the monarchy and it was under his tutelage that Shaul, the first king of Israel, was selected and invested into office.

The connections between Korach and his able offspring are thus not at all arbitrary, but actually reflect two antithetical models of how to effect social change. Though Korach mouthed catchphrases of concern, in reality he was an egocentric soapbox orator consumed with visions of grandeur. Though he agitated for change, for an overthrow of the "oppressive" priesthood and its replacement with a more egalitarian arrangement, his real agenda was self-advancement. His initiative failed because it was driven by conceit. His direct descendent Shemuel, a member of the same honored caste and in possession of the same coveted genes, also effected a social and political revolution. Motivated by selflessness, he succeeded – not by the violent overthrow of the unjust order that preceded him but rather by its incremental and steady repair. How significant that it was Shemuel who supervised the appointment of Israel's first king, a radical development that weakened the tight grasp of the priesthood upon the people by providing the exact sort of checks and balances that Korach had demanded so many generations earlier! In a way, then, Korach's reforms did not die. Though he himself perished due to narcissistic pride, the equitable plan of which he spoke was planted in the national consciousness. There it lay dormant for a very long time, to be reintroduced by a descendent who possessed the nobility of character and the care for the people that Korach so glaringly lacked. And that made all of the difference.

FOR FURTHER STUDY:

(1) The glaring contrast between Korach's appealing but insincere platform and Shemuel's genuine reforms is indicated by an intriguing textual cue in our story. When Moshe turns to God after Datan and Aviram ignore his noble summons to make peace, he exclaims in hurt and exasperation:

> ". . . do not accept their offering! I did not seize *even one of their donkeys* nor did I harm any one of them!" (*BeMidbar* 16:15)

What Moshe means to say is that in spite of Korach's claims to the contrary, he never abused his position of authority to take anything belonging to the people, not even an insignificant donkey to ride upon. His leadership was above reproach.

When Shemuel prepares to step down from leadership after the appointment of the new king, he calls an assembly of the people:

> Shemuel said to all of Israel: "Behold, I hearkened to you concerning everything and appointed a king upon you. Now, the king goes before you and I am very old and my sons are with you. I have served you from my youth until this day. Testify against me this day, before God and before His anointed one. Whose ox did I seize? *Whose donkey did I seize*? Whom did I oppress? Whom did I tyrannize? From whom did I accept bribes to look the other way?! I will make restoration!" But they said: "You have not oppressed us nor tyrannized us nor taken anything from anyone!" He said to them: "May God serve as witness against you, and may his anointed one serve as witness on this day that you have found nothing in my hands!" and they said "[He is] witness!" (*Shemuel* 1:12:1–5)

In this telling exchange, Shemuel highlights his honesty – though he led the people for decades, he never abused his position of authority to take anything from them, he never showed favoritism or accepted bribes and he judged them righteously. The phrase concerning the banal "donkey" is the trigger that invites us to compare and contrast the two accounts. In both, an aged leader who had fulfilled the duties of his office with utmost integrity suffers the rejection of his people. In both, the leader emphasizes that he is utterly above reproach and that the fault therefore lies elsewhere, namely with opponents or constituents who are not as authentic. In effect, Shemuel's integrity – an echo of Moshe his predecessor – highlights Korach's insincerity in demanding reforms. To put it differently, Korach's democratic platform could not be implemented except by his virtuous descendent because it is not enough for an aspiring leader to trumpet populist slogans; he must also be honest! Corrupt men who seize control never improve the lot of the proletariat.

CHUKAT

The Striking of the Rock

Numbers 19:1-22:1

PARASHAT CHUKAT opens with the ritual of the *para aduma*, or red heifer. According to the proscriptions of the Torah, one who has come in contact with a human corpse is deemed טמא, or ritually unfit to enter the precincts of the Mishkan or the Mikdash. In order to emerge from this state of *tuma*, the said individual must first be sprinkled with the מי חטאת or waters of purification. After its slaughter outside of the camp and the ritual sprinkling of its blood, the body of the red heifer is set alight. As the bonfire burns, cedar wood, hyssop and crimson are added to the flames. The resulting ashes are collected and are then combined with spring water; a bundle of hyssop is dipped into the mixture and, with it, the individual is sprinkled on the third and seventh days. After immersion in a *mikvah* at the conclusion of the rite, the person returns to a state of *tahara* or ritual fitness, and is again able to enter the Tabernacle or Temple area.

The very next passage of the Torah relates that "the entire congregation of Israel came to the wilderness of Zin in the first month, and encamped at Kadesh. There, Miriam died and was buried . . ." (*BeMidbar* 20:1). As Rashi points out, at this juncture the Torah abruptly begins to narrate events that took place at the *conclusion* of the period of wandering, which had commenced almost forty years earlier:

> The emphatic expression "the *entire* congregation of Israel came to the wilderness of Zin in the first month" implies that the congregation of which the Torah now speaks was whole and complete, for the generation of the wilderness had perished, while this new generation had been separated for life.

Ibn Ezra adds to Rashi's startling comments by observing that the Torah records not a single event or prophecy that occurred in the intervening thirty-eight years since the aborted mission of the spies! In effect, we move in a heartbeat from the episode of the spies and its aftermath to the account of the new generation preparing to enter the land, covering an interval of almost forty years in the space of a fleeting verse or two! How fitting it is, therefore, that the section concerning the red heifer serves as the transitional narrative, as we proceed from the account of the generation of the Exodus to the story of their descendents. Those who had left Egypt had been condemned to their sad fate and had passed on; their children now stood ready to cast off the pall of death and to solemnly embrace life in the new land. Therefore, the rite of the red heifer, necessary to effect the change of state from corpse defilement to the life-giving presence of God, functions here as the textual link between the generations.

This somber study in contrasts between parents and offspring, dissipated potential and actualization, death and life restored, sheds light on the events that follow, which are among the most inscrutable in the Torah.

> The congregation did not have water and they gathered against Moshe and Aharon. The people strove with Moshe, exclaiming "if only we had perished along with our brethren, before God! Why then did you bring God's congregation into this wilderness, to die along with our flocks? Why then did you take us out of Egypt to bring us to this evil place? It is not a place of sowing, or of figs, grapes or pomegranates, and there is no water to drink!" Moshe and Aharon left their presence to go to the entrance of the Tent of Meeting, and fell upon their faces in supplication. God's glory then appeared to them. (20:2–6)

Following a well-worn script rehearsed at every previous occasion of discomfort and deficiency, the people cried out in bitter complaint and bemoaned their sorry state. The vivid memory of Egyptian bondage, more alluring with each passing year, was recalled by the people to comfort them in their thirst.

Moshe's Failure

> God spoke to Moshe and said: "Take the staff and, together with Aharon your brother, gather the people. Speak to the rock in their presence and it will give forth its waters; you shall extract water for them from the rock and provide water for the congregation and its flocks." Moshe took the staff from before God's presence as he had been commanded.
>
> Moshe and Aharon gathered the congregation in front of the rock, and he said to them: "Listen you rebels! Shall we extract water for you from this rock?" Moshe lifted up his hand and struck the rock twice with his staff. The water poured forth from the rock and the congregation and its flocks drank.
>
> God spoke to Moshe and Aharon: "Because you did not trust in Me, to sanctify Me in the eyes of Israel, therefore you will not bring this congregation into the land that I have given them." These were the waters of struggle, at which Israel strove with God, and He was sanctified by them. (20:7–13)

Commanded to speak to the rock, Moshe instead strikes it, and in consequence is denied entry into the land that he so desired to see. What is the meaning of this inexplicable episode? How are we to understand God's unusual directive to speak to the rock and Moshe's failure to fulfill His words? To paraphrase the Ramban in his comments to 20:7, is God any less sanctified by a rock that miraculously gives forth water under blows than by one that is addressed with words? The commentaries have advanced a myriad of explanations for God's unusual command and Moshe's unfair downfall, with Ibn Ezra adducing no less than eight possibilities, and Rashi, Maimonides and Ramban advancing more. The plethora of interpretations is a sure sign that the text is too obscure to furnish us with a definitive answer.

The Precedent at Chorev

Let us attempt to furnish an approach, in consonance with the theme of the "generations" introduced above. Although most people are familiar only with our Parasha's account of

Moshe striking the rock, there is in fact an antecedent recorded in Sefer Shemot 17. After Israel had successfully traversed the Sea of Reeds and their Egyptian overlords were swept away by its waters, the people entered the hostile and foreboding wilderness of Shur. There they found no water and cried out and God sweetened the bitter waters of Marah for their consumption. The people continued on to the wilderness of Tzin, entering its vast, inhospitable expanse a short but arduous month after their exodus from Egypt. In Tzin, the people cried out again to God and He provided them with miraculous manna to assuage their hunger. Israel then commenced to travel in accordance with God's command and they encamped at Refidim:

> . . . and there was no water there for the people to drink. The people strove with Moshe saying: "give us water to drink!" Moshe said to them: "why do you strive with me and why do you test God?" The people thirsted for water and railed against Moshe, saying: "why did you bring us forth from Egypt, to kill us, our children and our flocks by thirst?" Moshe cried out to God saying: "what shall I do for this people, for soon they will stone me!"
>
> God said to Moshe: "Pass before the people and take the elders of Israel with you. Take in your hand the staff with which you struck the Nile and go. Behold, My presence is before you there at the rock in Chorev; strike the rock so that water will pour forth, and then the people can drink." Moshe did so in the presence of the elders of Israel. The place was therefore called Masa uMeriva, for Israel strove with God and tried Him, saying: "Is God in our midst or isn't He?" (*Shemot* 17:1–7)

Comparisons and Contrasts

The conspicuous parallels with our passage are striking. In both cases, the people entered a barren, arid wilderness, there called סין and here called צין. In both cases, it was a scorching thirst that provoked tempers and incited the people to cry out against God. In both cases, the people pined for the soothing mirage of the sojourn in Egypt and contrasted it with their wretched state. In both cases, Israel bemoaned their predicament and threatened to come to blows with Moshe. In both cases, water was miraculously brought forth from unyielding rock by Moshe and the people's thirst was quenched. The earlier place was therefore named מסה ומריבה and the latter מי מריבה, with the theme of "striving" as well as the alliteration common to both.

There are, of course, a number of glaring contrasts between these two events which are removed from each other in time by a period of almost forty years. In the first case, Moshe alone was commanded to secure God's gift of free-flowing water in the exclusive presence of the elders of Israel. In our Parasha, on the other hand, the miracle was done by both Moshe and Aharon in the presence of all of the people of Israel. At Refidim, Moshe was specifically commanded to "strike the rock" with the staff while at the wilderness of Zin, although Moshe was bidden to "take the staff," he and Aharon were told to "speak to the rock." How are we to understand these two episodes that the Torah clearly wants us to correlate? How are we to interpret the fact that the entire experience of the wilderness is effectively bracketed by these two incidents, the former transpiring just as the people begin their journey into its unforgiving expanse and the latter unfolding as they finally emerge alive from its lethal embrace? Can a careful reading of both passages *against each other* shed light on the obscure nature of Moshe's indiscretion in our Parasha?

The key to unraveling the mystery depends upon correctly interpreting the inverse symbolism of rock and water. These two primary elements, both at the core of the events, are connected by a process that sees one transformed into the other. As the Ramban parenthetically remarks in our Parasha, the expression that the rock "will give forth its waters" implies that the water is to issue from the essence of the rock itself. It will not emerge from the ground beneath, once Moshe has exposed its source, after the manner of a concealed spring (commentary to *BeMidbar* 20:8). Thus, the Torah does not speak of two unrelated substances that share only wildly contrasting properties, but rather of two materials that are inextricably bound up together in the matrix of transformation. That is to say that when addressed by God's command, the inanimate, unyielding rock, devoid of any inherent moisture, is to undergo a change and become free-flowing, life-giving waters. What might be the significance of the metamorphosis?

In scattered references throughout the Tanakh, the human heart is provocatively compared to impervious rock. Capable of inattention, gross indifference and utter insensitivity to the word of God, the human heart can sustain a life of self-centeredness and the inability to feel another's pain. Unyielding as rock, hard as adamant stone, the human heart can condone acts of injustice and commit deeds of cruelty that even the most vicious of carnivores could not conjure up. How fitting that Pharaoh's brutal intransigence – the same Pharaoh who could shamelessly enslave a nation and command that their offspring be mercilessly cast into the Nile – is consistently described in the early chapters of Sefer Shemot as "hardness of heart." Yet, that same human heart can become soft and feeling, animated and concerned, full of compassion for the plight of another and touched by the spirit of contrition to make amends. The hard and deadened heart can yet be a life-giving fountain, a source of vitality and vigor, a wellspring and reservoir of love and benevolence. According to the Torah, it is the word of God alone that has the ability to effect such a profound transformation of the human psyche.

When sincerely touched by God's healing message, the human being can marshal the strength necessary to overcome the lethargy and lifelessness of a detached and insensitive heart in order to initiate the process of moral and spiritual renewal. The prophet Yechezkel who witnessed the social and religious degradation that led to the destruction of the First Temple, looked forward to better days, when God would gather the scattered remnant of His people from the four corners of the globe and bring them to their land. At that time, says God:

> I shall sprinkle you with pure water and you shall become pure, pure from all of the defilement of your idolatry and transgressions. I shall give you a new heart and shall place a new spirit within you; *I shall remove the heart of stone from your bodies and give you in its place a heart of flesh*. I shall put My spirit within you and shall cause you to follow My statutes and to observe and fulfill My laws. You shall dwell in the land that I gave to your ancestors, and you shall be My people and I shall be your God . . . (*Yechezkel* 36:24–28)

In this passage, a conscious nexus is drawn between the cleansing waters and the senseless stone that is transformed – God will sprinkle them with life-giving and purifying waters and their deadened hearts of stone will be revived, to become receptive to His word.

The Two Models

To return to our context, it appears that the Torah provides us with two possible models for affecting transformation. In the first model, employed at the commencement of the journey into the wilderness, the rock was violently struck in order to change it into water and it was divinely-mandated force that caused the rock to transform. Moshe hit the rock and, in a sense, it was coerced to provide water. The rock was treated as a hard and unyielding object that had to be smashed in order to compel compliance.

The second model, in contrast, raises another possibility. The rock can be coaxed to give forth water, not by intimidation and overwhelming force, but rather by words of encouragement and inspiration. There is no divine directive to strike the rock as Moshe stands at Mei Meriva, addressing a generation nurtured by the life-altering experience of the wilderness, but only the command to *speak*: "Speak to the rock and it shall give forth its waters . . ."

As the people left the land of Egypt, their spirits broken by centuries of slavery and their hearts conditioned by its harsh and brutal oppression, they embarked on a journey that was meant to ultimately remake them into a "kingdom of priests and a holy nation" (*Shemot* 19:6). But on the eve of their exodus they had not dreamt of ethical refinement or of spiritual enlightenment, for the dehumanized slave is taught early on by cruel necessity to surrender any goals more exalted than self-preservation. At that early point in their moral development, God's basic directives to transcend callousness and to overcome insensitivity must have been unbearable impositions against which the scarcely-freed slaves chafed. For them, the path to transformation – to change their pharaonic hearts of rock into springs of living waters – had to be paved by the blows of scarcity and deficiency, by the punishing experience of a wilderness arid and inhospitable, by an endless journey across an expanse that held no promise of life-giving waters.

As they entered that wasteland, God commanded Moshe to strike the rock in the presence of the elders to indicate that it would be their role to initiate the difficult process of the people's change through harsh acts and threats of punishment. Sadly, the people, like the unyielding rock before them, were to be only objects in the process. Their gross moral immaturity could allow for no other approach. But while it is sometimes necessary to shock a hardened heart out of its coarse and unfeeling stupor, it is no way to raise a person to become sensitive, compassionate or gentle.

Thus, God led Israel into the wilderness, His patience tested by their provocations while His wrathful responses were tempered with compassion and love. Slowly, Israel matured, coming to the realization that life is more than survival, that the boon of freedom is to embrace a higher purpose, that while bricks and bread may sustain the body, only the word of God can transform the heart. And then finally, as the experience of the wilderness drew to a close, its lessons well-learned and internalized, the new generation stood prepared to take its place in the land. Moshe was again bidden to drive home the lesson that adamant hearts could become thinking and feeling hearts beating with compassion and holiness. But this time, no force was to be used on the people, no assault was to be made on their indifference through blows. That same rock, if it is sensitive and open to change, could be made to become water through words, through God's gentle message, for it is this approach that alone carries the hope of effecting real and long-lasting change.

Moshe's act of indiscretion, his misuse of the staff because words were to be extended in its stead, is characterized by the Torah as failing "to sanctify God" in the eyes of the congregation. It is so called because rather than indicating to the people that they could change through yielding to God's word, Moshe reinforced the message that force alone can ensure compliance with God's Torah. But, as we all know, this approach has limited success and never produces meaningful life-long results. Only by opening our minds to hear God's word, by being sensitive to the message of spiritual transformation that the Torah unfailingly affirms, is there the possibility of changing hearts of stone into life-giving springs of water. As Rashi so poignantly puts it, had Moshe but spoken to the rock instead of striking it, the people would have understood:

> If this lifeless rock that neither speaks nor hears nor requires sustenance can yet fulfill the word of God, how much more so are we capable of doing so! (commentary to *BeMidbar* 20:12)

FOR FURTHER STUDY:

(1) See the account preserved in Avot DeRabbi Natan 6:2 of Akiva ben Yosef the ignorant shepherd, who embarked, at the telling age of forty, on his own journey of spiritual transformation, eventually to become the illustrious Rabbi Akiva. It seems that the catalyst for Akiva was an unusual rock that was located next to the spring from which he watered his sheep. Over the course of many years, the gurgling waters had worn down the rock and etched a deep groove in its surface. Though Akiva had probably seen the rock many times before, on this particular occasion the sight of it was accompanied by a dawning recognition: "If soft waters can carve out adamant rock, then the words of Torah can yet penetrate my heart of flesh!" In essence, Akiva's epiphany at the age of forty parallels Israel's transformation after forty years of wilderness wandering, while his exclamation echoes Rashi's interpretation of our passage.

BALAK

"A Star Shall Shoot Forth out of Ya'acov"

Numbers 22:2-25:9

AS THE BOOK of BeMidbar begins to wind down, the people of Israel finally draw close to their destination. At the wilderness of Zin, the inhospitable badlands located in the Negev region, Miriam passes on and the people thirst for water. There, Moshe and Aharon strike the rock and they too are condemned to perish. Soon thereafter, the people reach the mount of Hor, Aharon is told to ascend to its summit and there he dies, leaving Moshe to continue as leader alone. Journeying from the place of Aharon's demise, the people are attacked by the king of Arad, but remarkably prevail against him. They then circle around the southern shores of the Dead Sea, approaching the land of Canaan from the east. Skirting the territory of the hostile Edomites and inhospitable Moavites, Israel soon encounters the antagonistic Sichon king of the Amorites, who engages them at Edre'i. Israel miraculously triumphs against this regional superpower, and then goes on to defeat the even more intimidating Og king of Bashan. Suddenly and unexpectedly, Israel finds itself in possession of a great swath of territory on the eastern side of the Jordan River, including lands considered by Balak the King of Moav to have constituted his people's unassailable patrimony:

> Balak son of Tzippor saw all that Israel had done to the Amorite. Moav greatly feared the people for they were numerous, and Moav recoiled from before the people of Israel. Moav said to the elders of Midian: "Now this congregation will consume all around us just as the ox consumes the vegetation of the field," and Balak son of Tzippor was the king of Moav at that time. (*BeMidbar* 22:2–4)

Concluding that besting the Israelites in battle was impossible, the king of Moav and his Midianite cohorts instead opted to attempt to overwhelm them through supernatural means. Quickly, Balak dispatched emissaries to Bil'am son of Be'or, a well-known occultist from the lands of the east, whom he charged with the mission of pronouncing a fateful (and fatal) curse against the people of Israel. Though Bil'am tried mightily to execrate Israel, time and time again he was forced instead under divine duress to exalt them. Balak's disappointment was palpable but Bil'am was powerless to alter his course. As the Parasha unfolds, he and those around him come to the unmistakable conclusion that neither incantations nor magic can affect the ineluctable destiny of the people of Israel, for their fate is in God's hands alone.

Taken together, the remarkable victory over Sichon and Og and the utter inability of Bil'am's sorcery to stem the Israelite tide, both point to a single truth. The God of

Israel is neither bound by the statistical probabilities of the scientists nor is He subject to the provisional pronouncements of the prognosticators. According to all of the empirical data, Israel should not have trounced the devastating forces of the Amorite kings who held all of the lands east of the Jordan under their heel. But defeat them they did, astounding not only themselves but all of the petty Transjordanian kingdoms and the Canaanite city-states as well. As for Bil'am, his spellbinding prowess was celebrated throughout the eastern lands, but try as he might, he could not confine the God of Israel with his diablerie. And with each successive failure, the deflating reality weighed more heavily upon him: All-powerful and absolute, incorporeal and of perfect oneness, it is God alone who determines the fate of nations and who guides the history of His people Israel.

Three times Bil'am the seer attempts to pronounce his malediction against Israel and three times he is precluded from doing so by divine intervention. In the subtle shifts of language that characterize his three pronouncements, the Ramban detects not only three independent prophecies but an important chronological progression as well. As he understands it, Bil'am's blessings unwittingly chart the entire sweep of Israel's history as a nation, describing first the Exodus from Egypt, then the entry and conquest of Canaan, and finally the founding of a monarchy, events that together trace an outline of approximately three-hundred-and-fifty-years.

The Fourth and Last Prophecy and Ibn Ezra's Interpretation

There is a fourth proclamation that Bil'am offers, this time without any of the sacrificial preparations and preliminary remarks to Balak that highlighted his first three attempts to secure divine favor. Undaunted by Balak's increasingly irate disapproval, Bil'am presents his fourth oracle unsolicited, as he admits defeat and sets his sights homeward. This time, he peers far into the future, inspired by a vision of Israel's absolute triumph over all of its foes:

> "And now," said Bil'am, "I am returning to my people. Let me counsel you as to what this nation shall do to your people at the end of days!" He proclaimed his oracle and said: "These are the words of Bil'am son of Be'or, the words of the man with the seeing eye. This is the pronouncement of the one who heard the words of the Almighty, who knows the knowledge of the most high, who perceived a vision of the all powerful, falling down but with open eyes. I see him but not now, I gaze upon him but not soon. A star will shoot forth out of Ya'acov, a scepter shall rise from Israel, who shall crush the princes of Moav and demolish all of Shet's descendents. Edom shall be their possession, Se'ir their enemies shall be their possession, and Israel shall be triumphant. A ruler shall issue forth from Ya'acov, and he shall destroy the remnant of the city . . ." (*BeMidbar* 24:14–19)

In his other three prophetic pronouncements, Bil'am utilizes obscure metaphors and indefinite references, but his fourth and final prophecy is particularly cryptic: When is the "end of days?" What or who is the "shooting star?" Who are "the descendents of Shet" (Seth)? Who is the "ruler from Ya'acov" and what city will he destroy? The commentaries disagree concerning the import of Bil'am's prophecy and its exact historical framework, and we will examine two possibilities and their ramifications. It should be borne in mind, however, that notwithstanding the numerous textual ambiguities, the thrust of Bil'am's message is crystal clear: In the end, Moav and his allies will be utterly vanquished while Israel will be triumphant.

> "It seems to me," says Rabbi Avraham Ibn Ezra, "that this prophecy concerns David. 'I see him, but not now' is an apt description, since David would only arise four hundred years hence . . . David did in fact 'crush the princes of Moav' (*Shemuel* 2:8:2) . . . and it is known that David exercised dominion over Edom and the mount of Se'ir . . ." (commentary to *BeMidbar* 24:17–19)

Ibn Ezra understands that Bil'am sees the future downfall of Moav at the hands of the Israelite monarch David, who succeeded King Shaul and united the people of Israel behind him. David, an enlightened ruler and gifted warrior, vanquished all of the hostile nations surrounding Israel, namely Moav, Amon and Edom, and laid the groundwork for an empire. The "end of days," therefore, does not mean the "end of time," but rather "far off in the future." The mention of "a scepter" is a clear reference to some form of royalty, just the sort that King David would effectively wield. The scepter reference is twinned by the text to the metaphor of a "shooting star" whose shining path is clearly visible in the heavens, for David's dominion would be manifest to all of the surrounding nations.

Though taking note of the sweeping historical progression that characterizes Bil'am's first three pronouncements, Ibn Ezra nevertheless maintains that the eastern seer's oracles are addressed primarily to Balak and to his people Moav. It was in fact David who first dealt them a crushing defeat, and Ibn Ezra is content to confine the extent of Bil'am's charged words to a relatively short period of history, namely about four hundred years. Ibn Ezra feels no necessity to assign Bil'am's pronouncements a significance more far-reaching than that. He maintains that Bil'am's forward-looking vision of a future Israelite monarchy is more than sufficient to highlight to Balak and his cohorts not only the inefficacy of their wretched attempts to curse Israel when God desires to bless, but also the profound difference between true prophecy and mere soothsaying.

The Interpretation of the Ramban – Eschatology

In contrast to Ibn Ezra, the Ramban identifies in Bil'am's prophecy the unfolding of a more momentous process. Commenting on the general outline of Bil'am's words, Ramban remarks:

> All of Bil'am's prophecies see progressively farther into the future. First he pointed out that Israel is God's portion and inheritance, and then he spoke of their conquest of the land and domination of its kings. Thirdly, he saw them securely dwelling in their land and becoming abundant upon it. He saw them appoint a king that would vanquish Agag (Amalek), and establish a kingdom that would achieve victory under David . . .

So far, Ramban's outline closely resembles that of Ibn Ezra. Concerning the fourth prophecy, however, he radically parts ways with his predecessor. As Ramban explains, "in this fourth vision, Bil'am goes on to see the messianic age, and he therefore describes his vision as 'not now' and 'not soon,' because it will unfold only far off in the future . . . It is God's counsel that He will fulfill at the end of days" (commentary to *BeMidbar* 24:14).

For the Ramban, the expression "end of days" implies the messianic age, and this usage is in fact documented in the books of the prophets many times (see *Devarim* 4:30, 31:29; *Yeshayahu* 2:2; *Yirmiyahu* 30:34; *Yechezkel* 38:16). As for the metaphor of the shooting star, ". . . since the messiah will gather in the dispersed people of Israel from the ends of the earth, he is referred to as a 'shooting star' that traverses the sky from the ends of the heavens . . ." (commentary to *BeMidbar* 24:17).

Continuing the theme, the Ramban explains:

> A ruling scepter shall arise out of Israel that will crush the corners of Moav and demolish all of the descendents of Shet the son of Adam, who is the progenitor of all humanity. Bil'am meant to inform Balak that his people of Moav would not be vanquished by Israel now, but at the end of days they will not escape the scepter that shall rule over them . . . As for Edom, its downfall will transpire at the hands of the messiah, because our present exile under the domination of Rome is associated with Edom . . . for they disputed our rule, and concerning them it was stated "one nation shall overpower the other" (*Bereisheet* 25:23) . . . Edom and Se'ir the enemies of Ya'acov shall be inherited by them . . . (commentary to *BeMidbar* 24:17–18)

The Ramban understands Bil'am's final words to be a prophecy of cosmic proportions. Bil'am sees not only the entry of the tribes into Canaan and their settlement of the land, events that began to unfold soon after his return eastward to his home, but he also perceives the final chapter of Israel's national history and the ultimate purpose of their election: the dawning of the messianic era. The remnants of Israel, destined to be dispersed to the four corners of the earth and to languish interminably under the cruel conditions of exile, will in the end be gathered and restored to their land under the capable rule of the messianic king. There they will finally overcome the enemies that had beset them from ancient times, the very ones that until the end of days continued to dispute their mission and their claim. The proverbial Edom, Ya'acov's twin and nemesis, the personification of the Roman empire and its heirs that destroyed the Second Temple and scattered the Jews worldwide, will in the end submit to Israel's rule and the irresistible message of redemption that their God shall proclaim. The arrival of the messiah will herald a new era of human history, of concord, harmony and peace, of reconciliation between God and man and between man and himself, and Israel's role in the realization of that most noble of visions will be decisive.

Larger Divergences vs. Similar Reactions

The disagreement between the Ibn Ezra and the Ramban may in fact point to a larger divergence. Ibn Ezra is a rationalist who sets the parameters of his interpretation in accordance with the immediate context of the passage. If the first three pronouncements of Bil'am are historically confined to the period of Israel's entry into their land and to the founding of their first state, then it is reasonable to assign Bil'am's fourth pronouncement to this era as well. Why search for intimations of far-off and final events when it is possible to adequately interpret the verses in question as referring to known and documented occurrences that are also momentous? The Ramban, on the other hand, animated by the soul of a mystic and the mystic's preoccupation with the "end of days," sees in Bil'am's words a future vision of ultimate significance.

At the same time, it should be noted that Ibn Ezra is quick to emphasize that his reading is not at all calculated to undermine belief in the messianic future:

> The foolish ones believe that by explaining "a star shall shoot forth out of Ya'acov" as a reference to David constitutes a denial of the messiah's coming. God forbid that it should be so! The messiah's arrival is explicitly spelled out in the prophecy of Daniel as I have explained, for there he mentions the rise of the Syrian Greek kings, the appearance of Hasmoneans, the building of the Second Temple and the years of its final siege, as well as the exile and the redemption that will follow it. Moreover, we need no additional prophetic pronouncements, for Moshe's words in *Devarim* 30:4–5 are the main thing: "Though your dispersion may be at the ends of the earth, God your Lord shall gather you from there . . . and God your Lord shall return your captivity and have mercy upon you, and He shall return and gather you in from among all of the nations to which God your Lord scattered you . . ." (commentary to *BeMidbar* 24:17)

In the final analysis, both Ibn Ezra as well as the Ramban may be reacting, each in his own way, to a famous Rabbinic tradition concerning the interpretation of this verse:

> Rabbi [Yehuda the Prince – redactor of the Mishna] used to explain: "a star (כוכב) shall shoot forth out of Ya'acov" – read not a star (כוכב) but rather a deceiver (כוזב)!" When Rabbi Akiva would see ben Kosva he would explain: "This man is King Messiah!" Said to him Rabbi Yochanan ben Torta: "Akiva, your cheeks will have sprouted with grass and King Messiah will still not have arrived!" (Midrash Eichah Rabbah 2:5)

The historical background to the disagreement between Rabbi Akiva and Rabbi Yochanan ben Torta is the aborted Bar Kochva rebellion of 132–135 CE. After the destruction of the Second Temple by the Romans in 70 CE, the defeated province of Judea continued to be ruled from Caesarea by a series of rapacious and oppressive governors. Heavy taxation and religious oppression took their toll on the large remnant of Jews who chafed under the Roman yoke. Finally, after six decades of abusive rule, a well-planned rebellion broke out during the reign of the emperor Hadrian, having been sparked, in part, by his decision to erect a pagan temple on the ruins of Jerusalem. The leader of the revolt was a very charismatic and gifted warrior by the name of Shim'on bar (son of) Kosva. Under his rule, the Roman garrison was driven from Jerusalem, commemorative coins were minted and for a brief moment the Jews enjoyed relief. The legions, however, soon returned with an overpowering vengeance and the rebellion was put down with great cruelty. Bar Kosva died defending his last redoubt of Beitar in the summer of 135 CE, and with his death were extinguished the last vestiges of Jewish sovereignty until the dawn of the modern state of Israel. The Romans laid waste to the Judean countryside and the remaining Jewish population, now a minority in their own land, was henceforth concentrated in the Galilee. In a final act of contempt, the Romans renamed Judea as "Provincia Syria Palaestina" in honor of the Jews' ancient nemeses, the Philistines! This was later shortened to Palaestina, from which derives the modern word "Palestine."

Significantly, it was none other than the illustrious 2nd century CE sage Rabbi Akiva who provided bar Kosva which much-needed support. Throwing his substantial influence behind the imposing warrior, who held in his hands the rekindled hopes of national restoration, Rabbi Akiva proclaimed bar Kosva to be the much-anticipated messianic king who would rescue Israel from their oppressors and rebuild the Temple on its ruined site. Rabbi

Akiva was already an old man when the rebellion broke out, but his pronouncements enhanced bar Kosva's stature immeasurably while many of his students filled the warrior's burgeoning ranks. Seeking a scriptural allusion for bar Kosva's aspirations, Rabbi Akiva found it in our parasha, reading Bil'am's prophecy concerning the "star that would shoot forth from Ya'acov" as a reference to bar Kosva himself! Cleverly, Rabbi Akiva preserved the messianic fervor of the verse and its charged imagery of the overarching shooting star while making use of the warrior's real name. Utilizing a skillful transfer of letters, Shimon bar Kosva (כוסבא) now became "Shimon bar Kochva (כוכבא), prince of Israel"!

Some (many?) of the Sages disagreed with Rabbi Akiva's judgment and declared that the venerable and aged scholar would be long dead before the messiah would arrive. And when Rabbi Yehuda the Prince considered the matter with almost a century of hindsight, he too linked bar Kosva to the verse in question, this time reading it as a reference to the false messiah that the failed warrior turned out to be! Once again reinterpreting the warrior's name, he pronounced him to be not "bar Kochva" who had inspired Rabbi Akiva or even "bar Kosva" whom he was, but rather "bar Kozva" – deceiver of Israel! In the end, the abortive revolt was decisive for the future of the Jewish presence in the land of Israel, for in its aftermath the much-dwindled population of Jews became a minority, their former capital was plowed over to become a pagan city, much of their former territory was utterly desolated, and even the name of their land was expunged from history in a strong-handed attempt to break their ancient connection with it.

Returning to Ibn Ezra and Ramban: Reconciling Their Views

Perhaps Ibn Ezra still heard the echo of Rabbi Yehuda's words in his ears when he decided to interpret the verse as a reference to more successful leaders, to David who overcame the Moavites and made them his vassals. To refer to King Messiah as that star that would shoot forth from Ya'acov was to employ a metaphor that was still tainted by Rabbi Yehuda's caustic and sarcastic comment, a thousand years after the revolt had so miserably failed. The Ramban, on the other hand, took up the theme inspired by Rabbi Akiva's enthusiastic endorsement, even though in the end the messianic hopes that the sage pinned upon bar Kochva had not been realized. Though in his failure bar Kochva thus joined the long line of Jewish national leaders who had not lived up to their potential, the eschatological echoes of the verse in question could still be heard, and so the Ramban returned to the reading that the early Sages seemed to favor – the "shooting star" was none other than the messianic king that would one day restore the Jews to their land and the Temple to its former glory.

Though the Ibn Ezra's interpretation seems on the surface completely at odds with that of the Ramban, there is in fact a profound connection between the two. The genius of Jewish tradition and the key to its remarkable survival has always been its ability to comprehend human history as a purposeful progression, to transcend present adversity by grasping tightly to a glimpse of eternity, and to see in seemingly unrelated events God's unmistakable involvement. David was Israel's first ideal king, possessing a rare combination of military prowess, political talent, genuine concern for justice and a profound spiritual sensitivity. Through the tumultuous events of his own life, he also came to understand and to champion true *teshuva* and rapprochement with God. It was through David's inspiration that the disparate tribes of Israel began to coalesce into a nation centered around Jerusalem, that they were able to battle and overcome their foes, and that the necessary material and spiritual foundations for the building of the Temple and the ideal state were first set down.

Though that state achieved optimal form for only a very short period before its decline, by coming into real existence it became the sustaining inspiration for all later visions of the good and the right, all subsequent dreams of the Jewish people achieving their national purpose and radiating the truth of God's teachings to all humanity, and all future hopes of a messianic era that the prophets of Israel so glowingly described. No wonder the messianic figure was regarded not only as a "descendent of David" in the narrow genealogical sense but as the embodiment of his example as well. There is therefore less than meets the eye separating the explanation of the Ibn Ezra from that of the Ramban. When Bil'am perceives in his prophecy the ascent of David and the scope of his exploits, he unwittingly also catches a fleeting glimpse of the end of days. Then, the messiah who is David's descendent will succeed in completing the awesome task of nation-building and Temple-building, of completely restoring Israel to their land and returning them to God, of proclaiming to all the world the truth of God's teachings. The messiah, in other words, will follow in the footsteps of his illustrious forebear David and complete his unfinished task.

FOR FURTHER STUDY:

(1) Rashi raises the possibility that Bil'am's final prophecy refers both to David as well as to the messianic king who is his direct descendent (commentary to 24:17, 19). In Rashi's opinion, Bil'am's final prophecy that brims with so much anticipation must be referring to Israel's greatest successes as a nation – the reign of their first king who brought them renown, and the rule of their final king who will restore their fortunes as in days of old. Rashi thus bridges the gap between Ibn Ezra and the Ramban.

(2) It is based upon Rabbi Akiva's example that Maimonides famously rules that the messianic king need not perform any miracles in order to win our allegiance:

> Do not imagine that the messianic king must perform signs and wonders and supernatural feats such as resurrecting the dead or similar things. It is not so! After all, Rabbi Akiva was one of the great Mishnaic Sages and he was the armor bearer (!) for ben Kozva the king. He said concerning him that he was the messiah; he and all of the Sages of his generation thought that he was the messiah until he was killed on account of transgressions. After he was killed, they realized that he was not [the messiah]. The Sages did not ask him to perform a sign or wonder. The essence of the matter is this: This Torah – its statutes and its laws – are eternal and we may neither add to them nor subtract from them. (*Mishneh Torah*, Laws of Kings 11:3)

PINCHAS

The Theme of Succession

Numbers 25:10-30:1

AT THE END of Parashat Balak, the people of Israel succumbed to the seductions of the daughters of Moav and joined them in the worship of their pagan god Baal Pe'or. Adopting its licentious rites, Israel strayed from God and faltered; God unleashed a plague and demanded that the ringleaders be punished. But in the meantime, a prince of the tribe of Shimon defiantly consorted with a Midianite princess in the eyes of all of Israel. Shocked by the debacle, Moshe and the leaders of Israel were paralyzed to act; it was Pinchas the son of Elazar, Aharon's son, who forcefully brought an end to the matter by summarily dispatching the two.

Pinchas' act of zealousness earned him divine approval, and it is God's "covenant of peace" with him that serves as the opening passage of our Parasha. While the Parasha goes on to introduce many matters, mostly pertaining to Israel's imminent entry into the land, it is noteworthy that they are presented against the backdrop of Pinchas' fervent deed. The juxtaposition is important: The entry into Canaan cannot but precipitate conflict – the existing social order that is founded upon a polytheistic worldview will stand in direct opposition to Israel's monotheistic, ethical values. The immoral rites of Baal Pe'or, though confined to the Jordan's eastern plains, were a small expression of much broader cultural norms that characterized the entire region. A vicious outcome was inevitable wherever coarse idolatry held sway: the obscene worship of many gods fostered the cruel oppression of many men, and the people of Canaan excelled at both. Pinchas' severe and selfless act should thus be viewed as paradigmatic for what would be required of the people of Israel once they crossed the Yarden River, for numerous versions of Baal Pe'or awaited them on its western shores. A just and stable Israelite state could only be secured by expunging Canaanite idolatry.

Counting the People of Israel

> God spoke to Moshe and to Elazar son of Aharon the Kohen saying: "Count the entire congregation of Israel, from the age of twenty and above according to their clans, all those who go forth to wage war." Moshe and Elazar the Kohen addressed them at the plains of Moav, on the shores of the Yarden across from Yericho, saying: "From the age of twenty and above, just as God commanded Moshe and the people of Israel when they left the land of Egypt.'" (*BeMidbar* 26:1–4)

This census of the people calls to mind the earlier one undertaken at the very opening of the book (1:1–47), as the people prepared to leave Mount Sinai and to commence their journey towards the land. The divine pledge to the generation of the Exodus that they would enter the land flowing with milk and honey (*Shemot* 3:8), which had been suspended after the sin of the spies, now stood to be realized through their children. Our census therefore has the effect of neatly closing the circle of the book by recalling its inaugural episode.

The tribes are counted according to their designated arrangement around the Tabernacle as described in *BeMidbar* 2:1–47. But there is one exception – though the tribes of Yosef were typically led by the ensign of Efraim, here it is Menashe that is enumerated first: Reuven, Shimon and Gad; Yehuda, Yisachar and Zevulun; Menashe, Efraim and Binyamin; Dan, Asher and Naftali. In the earlier census Efraim was counted before his brother (1:32–35). Presumably, the enhanced status of Menashe this time around is a result of the tribe's central role in the conquest of Sichon and Og, the Amorite kings. Later on, Menashe will achieve prominence by joining Reuven and Gad in settling the Transjordanian territories (32:39–42).

Moving on to the actual numerical data, the census total this time is somewhat less than the earlier one. Originally, the people numbered 603,550 (1:46). Here, they comprise 601,730. Thus, in almost forty years they have exhibited slightly negative population growth! This stands in glaring contrast to the almost supernatural increase of Israel that was reported at the beginning of Sefer Shemot, when the people first came down to Egypt (*Shemot* 1:7). The puzzling decrease in numbers is addressed by the 13th century commentator Chezekiah ben Manoach (the Chizkuni), who explains:

> This census figure is smaller than that of Midbar Sinai (the census of the generation of the Exodus, described at the beginning of Sefer BeMidbar) by an amount of 1,820. Had the people numbered more at this juncture, then they would have thought: "Since we are now numerous, we will be able to conquer the land. Had we been less, we would be unable to do so." Therefore, God did not want their current population to exceed that of Midbar Sinai in order to demonstrate that they were nevertheless able to conquer Canaan, for there are no limits on God's ability to effect salvation whether there are many or few. (commentary to *BeMidbar* 26:51)

The Chizkuni understands that the smaller number of fighting men on the eve of the entry into Canaan is to emphasize to the people of Israel that ultimately their military successes will not be a function of numerical superiority but rather of God's intervention. This is a central theme in the Tanakh, one that is invoked many times. Perhaps the early 2nd Temple period prophet Zechariah captures it best when he addresses the anxious leader Zerubavel son of Shaltiel with words of encouragement, after the latter had led the first small wave of émigrés back to the land after a lengthy exile in Babylon: "This is the word of God to Zerubavel saying: 'Not by might nor by power but rather by My spirit, says the God of hosts'" (*Zechariah* 4:6).

But the Chizkuni's argument is compromised by the fact that the difference between the two census figures is so small. If an emphatic statement of divine involvement was called for, then one would have expected a drastic decrease in the second census figure, rather than a difference of a mere few tenths of a percent. An example of just such a drastic decrease is to be found in the book of Shoftim, where reluctant Gideon is told by God to raise a militia to battle an overwhelming force composed of hordes of Midianites and their eager allies, who had descended upon the fertile Israelite hill country like a "swarm of locusts" (*Shoftim* 6:3–5). There, in a passage that probably serves as Chizkuni's inspiration, Gideon's initial force of 32,000 fighters is progressively whittled down by God until it numbers only 300! This God does deliberately, in order to make very clear that when the victory does come, it will not be ascribed to anything other than His assistance:

> God said to Gideon: "The people that are with you are too numerous for Me to give Midian into their hands, lest Israel glorifies itself against Me and says 'My own power has saved me.'" (7:2)

It should be noted that the Chizkuni once again raises the issue with the census of the tribe of Levi. In our counting, the Levites number 23,000 (*BeMidbar* 26:62), a slight gain over their census figure almost forty years earlier when they tallied 22,000 (3:39). The Chizkuni comments:

> This matter proves that the task of bearing the ark of the covenant must have taken its toll on them because they are counted from the age of one month and during the course of thirty-eight years their tribe only increased by 1,000! The number of the Israelites, who all perished from above the age of twenty years old, was similar to what it was at the time of the first census in Midbar Sinai.

In both cases, the Chizkuni is sensitive to the data and provides us with a local but unconvincing solution.

A Common Theme

A careful reading of the larger context that follows the census may shed some light on the matter:

> God spoke to Moshe saying: "To these shall the land be divided into sections according to number. The many shall receive more and the few shall receive less, for each shall receive a portion according to their number. The land shall be divided by lot . . ." (26:52–55)

This passage that looks forward to the distribution of the land of Canaan amongst the Israelite tribes is followed by the census figures for the tribe of Levi, whose clans were counted separately from the general population and numbered 23,000 in total. The verse relates that "they were not counted among the people since they did not receive an allotment of land among the people of Israel" (26:62). With the count of Levi completed, the section concludes:

> These were the countings undertaken by Moshe and Elazar the Kohen, who counted the people of Israel at the plains of Moav by the banks of the Yarden across from Yericho. Among them was not to be found a single man who had been counted by Moshe and Aharon the Kohen in the wilderness of Sinai. For God had decreed that they would surely perish in the wilderness, and there remained not a man of them, excepting Calev son of Yefuneh and Yehoshua son of Nun. (26:63–65)

Immediately thereafter, the five daughters of Zelofchad boldly approach Moshe and the tribal leaders, and ask to receive a plot of land on account of their late father, who had no sons. While the Torah stipulated that the males counted in the census were to receive a plot of land in Canaan, to be later passed on to their sons, no provision was made for daughters. Moshe refers the matter to God who proclaims that "the daughters of Zelofchad have spoken well. You shall surely give them an inheritance of land among their father's brothers, and you shall transfer their father's inheritance of land to them" (27:7).

There are therefore four discrete sections that comprise this first part of the Parasha: (1) the census of the people which, as we have seen, yielded a total roughly equivalent to that provided by the initial census almost forty years earlier (26:1–51); (2) a divine imperative to apportion the land by lot among those counted in the census (26:52–56); (3) a separate counting of the tribe of Levi who were excluded from receiving an estate of land (26:57–65); (4) the episode of Zelofchad's daughters, who successfully petition to receive an estate in the land of Canaan (27:1–11).

The larger theme animating the entire passage can now be ascertained: it is the idea of *succession*, especially as it pertains to the land of Canaan that Israel stands to possess imminently. While the second census records the count of the tribes much as the first census did, this time the tallies are comprised of the children who have taken the place of their condemned parents and will merit inheriting the land that their elders spurned. The count is undertaken by Moshe with able assistance from Elazar the Kohen, who was explicitly designated as the successor to his father Aharon (20:22–29). The land will be divided among the tribes of Israel; since the tribe of Levi will not receive any tribal territory (18:20–24) but only scattered cities (35:1–8), they are therefore counted separately. This discrete count of the Levites once again mirrors the opening of the book, when that tribe was enumerated separately from the others so that Mishkan-related tasks could be assigned to them to the exclusion of the Israelites. As for the daughters of Zelofchad, singled out in Rabbinic tradition as exemplars for the womenfolk who "cherished the land" (see commentary of Rashi to 26:64, 27:1), their claim emphasizes the theme of succession on the individual level. They regard themselves as the sole and legitimate successors to their departed father and request to receive his portion of land in order to perpetuate his memory west of the Yarden.

The almost identical census figure is now comprehensible but it has nothing to do with the Chizkuni's theory. While the Chizkuni invoked an authentic theme that is elsewhere essential, here we may draw upon the larger context to inform the specific exegetical question in a more reasonable manner. The very similar census figure and the zero population growth that it implies are potent suggestions that although the generation of Egypt died out, they have been effectively followed by their children, the generation who will enter the land. This is true of the Israelite tribes as well as of the tribe of Levi whose number also roughly corresponds to the earlier figure. The doubling effect emphasizes the point: the dreams of the generation of the wilderness have not turned to dust with their demise, because their progeny will continue their legacy in the new land. It is this land that serves as the focal point for the narratives of succession, for the people of Israel have an enduring bond to that place that can never be broken: "A generation passes and a generation comes, but the land abides forever" (*Kohelet* 1:4). It is therefore as if the generation of the wilderness has been completely succeeded by their children – so much so that the census numbers for both, though separated by almost four decades, are almost indistinguishable!

"Ascend to Mount Neve"

Nowhere is the theme of succession more strongly spelled out than in the section that follows, as God bids Moshe to ascend Mount Nevo in order to see the land that lies on the other side of the river: "You shall see it and then die, just as your brother Aharon perished. For you both abrogated My word at the wilderness of Zin, when the congregation strove [with you], and you failed to sanctify Me in their eyes . . ." (*BeMidbar* 27:13–14). As the Ramban insightfully notes:

> . . . this is not a commandment that God insists be fulfilled now, for if that were the case then Moshe would have to ascend to the mount immediately! Rather, God is informing Moshe of what will eventually transpire, namely that he will soon ascend the mount and see the land. Since God had said that "among these shall the land be divided into sections according to number," He informs Moshe here that the said apportioning will not be carried out by him. Moshe will instead ascend to the heights before Israel journeys from the plains of Moav, and then he will die. Moshe will receive no portion in the land but will only see it from afar . . . (commentary to 27:12)

Moshe's response to the divine disclosure is most remarkable. It is devoid of regret and contains no hint of bitterness. Instead, the aged lawgiver reminds us that the welfare of the people is a leader's most important concern, until the very end. Moshe informs God that He must appoint his *successor*:

> Moshe spoke to God saying: "May God the Lord of all spirits for all mortals appoint a man to lead the congregation, to go before them and to come before them, so that God's congregation be not as a flock of sheep that have no shepherd!" God said to Moshe: "Take Yehoshua the son of Nun, a man who has spirit, and place (וסמכת) your hand upon him. Stand him before Elazar the Kohen and before the entire congregation and charge him in their sight. Place your glory upon him so that the congregation of Israel follows him . . ." Moshe did as God commanded . . . (27:15–22)

Yehoshua, Moshe's loyal disciple since the time of the Exodus, is now formally appointed to succeed him. We first met Yehoshua at the battle against Amalek, when the people were attacked soon after they had left the land of Egypt (*Shemot* 17:8–16). He appeared again as Moshe's faithful protégé at the sin of the golden calf, when he waited expectantly for the return of his master from the encounter with God at Sinai (32:17). We next met him at the incident of Eldad and Medad, defending Moshe's honor (*BeMidbar* 11:28–29). Finally, we anxiously followed his appointment as one of the twelve spies, and marveled at his steadfast refusal, along with Calev son of Yefuneh, to adopt the self-defeating report of the other ten (13:8, 14:6–10).

The above list indicates that Yehoshua was present and involved in every single formative event that the people had experienced during the course of the last forty years. He never strayed from Moshe's side and always was a source of support for him. He never failed to exhibit steadfast trust in God. There was therefore no one more worthy than him to become Moshe's successor, and no one more capable of transmitting the teachings after the master's death.

This transfer of leadership to Yehoshua represents the strongest possible expression of the theme of succession and serves as the appropriate conclusion to the Parasha's first half. Here, Yehoshua is invested as Moshe's fitting replacement with a formal act called by the Torah the "placing of the hands," or סמיכה. The act of placing one's hands on one's successor symbolizes the transfer of power and authority, as well as suggesting confidence in the successor and conviction that he will excel. It is therefore not only the passing on of the reins of power that is implied here, but also the faithful and accurate transmission of a body of teaching. It naturally follows from this paradigm that future scholars must be attached by the chain of tradition to their predecessors, from whom they receive teaching and instruction. In the language of the Sages, "Moshe received the Torah from Sinai and transmitted it to Yehoshua, and Yehoshua to the elders, and the elders to the prophets . . ." (Mishna *Avot* 1:1). Moshe will soon die but his accumulated teachings and wisdom, the very Torah that he received from God, will continue to live on, because Yehoshua will perpetuate it and transmit it in turn.

Our Parasha therefore speaks of many successions: the generation of the Exodus is replaced by the generation of the entry, Aharon's role is filled by Elazar, the Levites are succeeded by their children, Zelofchad is followed by his trustworthy daughters, and Moshe is himself succeeded by his illustrious pupil. In all of the cases, however, and most especially in the case of Yehoshua, the physical replacement of the deceased is quite secondary to the spiritual continuity of their legacy.

Long ago, the Torah understood that Israel's survival would ultimately depend upon its ability to transmit its heritage to succeeding generations. The faithful preservation of a memory of an encounter with God and of the way of life obligated by His teachings would be Israel's keys to eternity. Against all odds, Israel has succeeded, albeit with heavy losses along the way. Although the formal chain of this "placing of the hands" or *semicha* may have been broken since the time of Roman hegemony (see TB *Sanhedrin* 14a), one day to be repaired as a precursor to the messianic age, the spirit of Moshe's transmission to Yehoshua lives on, as the broader context suggests. By actively attaching ourselves to the tradition and assenting to pass it down, we too become an indispensable link in the eternal chain that is Israel, preserving our people and safeguarding our unique contribution to human civilization.

FOR FURTHER STUDY:

(1) Note that at the moment that Moshe was informed by God that he must ascend Mount Nevo because he would not enter the land, he made no attempt to maneuver his own sons to become his successors. Instead, he implored God to select the person that was most fit to lead the people of Israel after him. God selected Yehoshua. This highlights an essential feature of Moshe's authentic leadership – as he saw it, the people deserved the best candidate for the job, not the most well-connected!

MATOT

The Lands East of the Yarden

Numbers 30:2-32:42

THE PEOPLE of Israel, encamped just east of the Yarden River at the plains of Moav, complete their final preparations for entering the land. Not long before, they had defeated Sichon and Og, the mighty Amorite kings who ruled over the Transjordan from the Wadi Arnon that empties into the Dead Sea midway along its eastern shore, all the way up to the foothills of snow-capped Mount Chermon in the Lebanon mountains. In later biblical tradition, that triumph continued to loom large as a remarkable expression of God's saving power:

> He struck down great kings — for His mercy endures forever.
> He slew mighty monarchs — for His mercy endures forever.
> Sichon king of the Amorite — for His mercy endures forever.
> And Og, king of the Bashan — for His mercy endures forever.
> He gave their land as an inheritance — for His mercy endures forever.
> An inheritance for His servant Israel — for His mercy endures forever.
> He remembered us in our degradation — for His mercy endures forever.
> He redeemed us from our adversaries — for His mercy endures forever.
> He gives food to all flesh — for His mercy endures forever.
> Praise the God of heaven — for His mercy endures forever.
> (*Tehillim* 136:17–26)

The Appeals of Reuven and Gad

As the Parasha winds down, a number of the tribes approach Moshe and sheepishly broach the subject of settling the recently conquered territory as their own:

> The people of Reuven and Gad had immense flocks. They saw that the land of Y'azer and Gil'ad was pastureland. The people of Gad and Reuven said to Moshe, Elazar the Kohen and the princes of the congregation: "Atarot, Divon, Y'azer, Nimra, Cheshbon El'aley, Sevam, Nevo and Be'on – the land that God struck down before the congregation of Israel – is grazing land, and your servants have flocks."
>
> They said: "If we have found favor in your eyes, then let this land be given to your servants as an inheritance, and do not cause us to pass over the Yarden River." (*BeMidbar* 32:1–5)

The two tribes of Reuven and Gad, blessed with large herds, began to wonder whether the vast tracts of fertile grazing land that they then occupied might not better meet their material needs than the rocky Canaanite highlands. Perceptively, the 15th century Spanish commentator Rabbi Yitzchak Abarbanel detected in their measured words a wavering note of hesitation. As he describes it:

> Initially, these tribes voiced their request in allusive terms for they were ashamed to state it explicitly . . . therefore, the text of the Torah introduced a paragraph division after their first statement. Moshe understood their intent but chose not to reprove them immediately. Rather he remained silent to allow them to openly divulge their request. When they saw that Moshe remained silent and did not respond to their intimation, they were forced to ask again with greater directness. Hence, the text states that "They said" a second time . . .

We can certainly imagine these tribes' reluctance to be more direct as they stood before Moshe and the tribal leaders. After all, hadn't thirty-eight years been dissipated in purposeless wandering in the wilderness because of an earlier generation's reluctance to enter the new land? Understandably, Moshe was incensed:

> . . . shall your brethren go to fight while you remain here? Why do you break the people's resolve to cross over into the land that God gave to them? Just so did your fathers behave when I sent them from Kadesh Barnea to spy out the land . . . Now you have arisen in their place as a brood of sinful folk, only to increase God's anger against Israel. By turning away from Him you will cause Him to leave them in the wilderness even longer, and you shall thereby destroy this people! (32:6–15)

What a striking encounter between Moshe and them, the disconnection mirroring the two divided territories of Canaan and the Transjordan. On the one side stood the aged lawgiver, flanked by Yehoshua and Elazar the Kohen, the new leaders of the people. Moshe remembered the debacle of the spies only too well. How that mission ended so tragically because the people had lacked the steadfastness to trust in God's assistance! Perhaps the troubling thought of his own more recent exclusion from entering the land also lurked in his mind, for he wished nothing more than to lead the people to their promised destination. Couldn't these tribes recognize the folly of their ways in rejecting the very future that he so desired?

On the other side, separated from Moshe by only a few paces, stood the tribes of Reuven and Gad. Certainly, they had fully shared in the people's fate up until this point and had borne the communal calamity imposed by God's decree. Had they not sufficiently "paid the price?" Besides, why did God grant them victory over those vast tracts if not to settle them? Wasn't the natural division imposed by the meandering Yarden River rather inconsequential, in light of their cohesive connection to the other tribes and to the shared destiny of the people of Israel?

> They approached him and said: "We shall build sheep pens for our flocks and towns for our children. We shall quickly proceed at the vanguard of Israel until we have brought them to their place, while our children remain in the fortified towns because of this land's inhabitants. We will not return to our own homes until the people of Israel have received their possession. But we will not possess with them on the other side of the Yarden because our possession is rather to be on its eastern side!" (32:16–19)

Animated by a curious mixture of kinship and independence, defiance and compromise, the two tribes spelled out their plan: they *would* fight with their brethren and help them to secure their Land, but in the end they *would not* settle it with them. After the territories in Canaan would be secured, they would return to their own homes east of the Yarden. With resignation, Moshe acquiesced and placed an oath upon them in the presence of Yehoshua, Elazar and the tribal leaders. Significantly, he bound them to their commitment with a "double conditional," an uncommon legal formula that highlights the binding nature of a pledge by spelling out not only the responsibilities that devolve upon the obligated party but also the consequences of non-fulfillment:

> Moshe said to them (Elazar the Kohen, Yehoshua bin Nun and the tribal elders of Israel): "*If* a strike force of the people of Gad and the people of Reuven traverse the Yarden with you, to wage war before God so that the land is conquered by you, *then* you shall give them all of the land of Gil'ad as a possession. But *if* a strike force does *not* traverse with you, *then* they shall inherit with you in the land of Canaan . . ." (32:29–30)

Returning from Canaan

In the end, Reuven, Gad and half Menashe fulfilled their oath and dutifully accompanied the people over the Yarden to fight on their behalf, as recorded in the early chapters of Sefer Yehoshua (4:12–13). Canaan was eventually conquered, and after a good many years the battle for the land subsided. With the end of the fighting, Yehoshua released them from their vow:

> At that time, Yehoshua summoned the tribes of Reuven, Gad and half Menashe. He said to them: "You have observed all that Moshe, God's servant, commanded you and have hearkened to me in accordance with all that I commanded you. You have not abandoned your brethren for many days until now, and you have carefully observed God your Lord's command. Now, God your Lord has granted rest to your brethren just as He spoke, therefore turn now and go to your tents in the land of your possessions that Moshe, God's servant, granted you on the Yarden's other side. But be very careful to fulfill the commands and the teaching that Moshe, God's servant, commanded you – to love God your Lord and to follow His ways, to keep his commands and to cleave to Him, to serve Him with all of your heart and with all of your soul." Thus, Yehoshua blessed them and sent them on their way, and they returned to their tents. (*Yehoshua* 22:1–6)

The two-and-one-half tribes finally returned home, but when they reached the shores of the Yarden they left their mark in the form of a large and highly visible cultic object:

> They reached the region of the Yarden in the land of Canaan, and there Reuven, Gad and half of Menashe built a massive altar next to the Yarden. When the people of Israel heard of their deed . . . they gathered against them with arms . . . (*Yehoshua* 22:9–12)

Interpreting their act as an invitation to idolatry, as an attempt to set up an alternate center of worship to rival the national shrine recently constructed at Shilo (*Yehoshua* 18:1), the people of Israel sent the fiery Pinchas son of Elazar the Kohen accompanied by ten tribal elders, to dissuade them. Again, just as they had done almost two decades earlier when they stood before Moshe in our Parasha, Reuven and Gad explained their true motives and calmed Israel's fears:

> . . . Mighty Lord God, Mighty Lord God, He knows and Israel will know that if [we did this] in rebellion or as a trespass against God, He will not save us this day. We did not build this altar to rebel against God, we did not erect it to offer sacrifice . . . we were rather concerned that in the future, your children would say to ours: "What do you have with God the Lord of Israel? Did God not place a boundary between us, Reuven and Gad, the Yarden River? You have no share with God!" . . . we therefore decided to build this altar . . . as a witness between us and you for generations to come . . . that we will serve God . . . so that your children will not say tomorrow to our children "you have no share with God!" . . . Pinchas the Kohen, the congregation's princes and the leaders that were with him heard the explanation offered by Reuven, Gad and Menashe, and they received it favorably . . . (*Yehoshua* 22:21–30)

The structure of the above passage from Sefer Yehoshua closely parallels that of our Parasha. Like our Parasha, the tribes of Reuven and Gad decided on a striking unilateral move (to build an altar), the ire of Israel was aroused when their motives were justifiably misinterpreted (as idolatry), Reuven and Gad mollified the people and explained that their intent was noble and above reproach (to maintain their connection to the tribes in Canaan), and only then was the matter finally resolved to everyone's satisfaction. Unlike our Parasha though, in which Reuven and Gad feared Moshe's reaction but never doubted their decision, here their misgivings were more palpable. By consciously choosing to remain on its eastern side, Reuven, Gad and Menashe now realized that they had driven a wedge between themselves and the rest of Israel. Though they had fought on their behalf when the people entered Canaan, though they wished to participate in the national service of God centered at Shilo, they knew that henceforth their role in shaping Israel's destiny would be smaller. The uncertainties that earlier had worried Moshe now worried them: Israel might come to resent their non-involvement in the daily trials and triumphs of national life in Canaan, and might eventually reject their claim to be part of the people.

Understanding Moshe's Motives

All of the above explains with greater clarity the role of Menashe in the settlement of the Transjordanian territories. The initial petition as presented to Moshe in our Parasha was offered by Reuven and Gad only. Only after the matter was resolved by their swearing an oath, did Moshe assign some of the territories to Menashe (*BeMidbar* 32:33):

> The sons of Machir, son of Menashe, captured the Gil'ad and drove out the Amorites who were there. Moshe gave the Gil'ad to Machir son of Menashe, and he dwelt there. Yair son of Menashe went and captured their farms, and called them Chavot Yair. Novach went and captured Kenat and its villages, and called it Novach after his own name. (*BeMidbar* 32:39–42)

Moshe's conduct is rather puzzling in light of his earlier reluctance to entertain the appeal of Reuven and Gad. Why would he in the end strengthen a claim that he had regarded as potentially ruinous, by assigning yet another tribe to the lands east of the Yarden? The Ramban explains:

> At the outset, the tribe of Menashe did not approach Moshe. But after Moshe apportioned the land to the two tribes, he realized that it was a territory too large for their needs. He therefore requested volunteers to settle it with them. Some of the members of Menashe agreed, perhaps because they also possessed flocks, and he therefore gave them their appropriate portion . . . (commentary to 32:33)

We may go one step further than the Ramban and posit that Moshe *intentionally* selected Menashe, with due deliberation and care. Recall that Moshe feared that Reuven and Gad had abandoned the national destiny by casting their lot with the territory of Sichon and Og. Recall also from Sefer Yehoshua that in hindsight Reuven and Gad themselves had serious misgivings about the consequences of their decision: perhaps the rest of the people of Israel would one day reject them and come to regard them as a selfish and irrelevant diaspora.

Moshe considered the matter and acted to limit the danger. By actively *assigning* part of Menashe to the lands east of the Yarden while the bulk of this important tribe would settle on its western side, Moshe introduced a mechanism to preserve a cohesive connection between all of the tribes on both sides of the river. The bulk of Menashe's descendents would remain within Israel proper but the common culture, history and dialect that they shared with the families to the east would ensure that a strong link was maintained. In this way, the other Transjordanian tribes would also not be completely cut off from the national enterprise and would have an interest in maintaining their connection to their compatriots. In other words, rather than seeking volunteers for the task as the Ramban explained, Moshe deliberately allocated part of the tribe of Menashe to the Transjordan in order to solidify the tribal union.

In the end, not only Reuven, Gad and part of Menashe settled east of the Yarden. As Rabbi Avraham Ibn Ezra conclusively demonstrates from the lineage lists preserved in *Divrei HaYamim* 1:2:21–22, Yair son of Menashe was actually a member of the tribe of Yehuda who was descended from Menashe on his mother's side only: "Chezron [of Yehuda] took the daughter of Machir father of Gil'ad as his wife . . . she bore him Seguv, whose son was Yair, who possessed twenty-three towns in the land of Gil'ad." This Yair was an illustrious warrior who hailed from Yehuda and helped conquer the frontier lands, as recounted by Moshe in Sefer Devarim:

> At that time, we possessed this land: from Aroer that is on the banks of wadi Arnon and half of Mount Gil'ad and its cities I gave to the tribes of Reuven and Gad. The rest of the Gil'ad and the Bashan that was the kingdom of Og I gave to half of the tribe of Menashe – this was the whole region of the Argov and the whole of the Bashan that is called the land of Refaim. Yair son of Menashe conquered the entire region of Argov until the border of the Geshurite and the Ma'achatite and he called them – that is the Bashan – by his name "Chavot Yair" until this very day (*Devarim* 3:12–14)

Thus, not only were the eastern tribes joined to their western brethren by the tribe of Menashe, they were also connected via an important family from the tribe of Yehuda. The point is this: No one – not Moshe, not Reuven or Gad, not Menashe and not

Yehuda wanted to see the ominous predictions of detachment and dissension come true!

But in the end, the worst fears were realized. In spite of Moshe's great efforts, in spite of everyone's best intentions and most fervent hopes, the bonds between Reuven and Gad and the other tribes could not be preserved. Though regarded as part of the Jewish people and often active in the issues of the day, Reuven and Gad eventually suffered an ignoble end that mirrored their own conscious choice generations earlier: exile by the Assyrians to distant lands, never to be heard of again.

> They trespassed against the God of their ancestors and strayed after the gods of the land that the Lord had destroyed from before them. The Lord of Israel inspired Pul king of Assyria and Tilgat Pileser, and they exiled the tribes of Reuven, Gad and half Menashe. He brought them to Chalach, Chavor, Hara, and the river of Gozan until this very day . . . (*Divrei HaYamim* 1:5:25–26)

The Midrash puts it most acerbically, in attempting to pinpoint the cause of their downfall:

> The tribes of Gad and Reuven were wealthy and had many flocks. Because of their love of their possessions, they decided to dwell outside of the land of Israel. Therefore, they were exiled before any of the other tribes . . . what brought this fate upon them? The fact that they separated themselves from their brethren because of their wealth, as the verse states: "The tribes of Reuven and Gad had immense flocks . . ." (BeMidbar Rabbah 22:7)

As they prepared to cross the Yarden, Reuven, Gad and half Menashe painfully realized that spatial separation does matter and distance from the land of Israel is decisive. The most sincere oaths of allegiance, the most moving of monuments and memorials, even taking an active part in fighting the people's wars, could not in the end sustain a shared destiny with those that dwelt in the land. Only by settling in that land with the tribes of Israel could the two-and-one-half tribes have shared in the national enterprise in the most comprehensive and meaningful way. In the end, the destiny of Israel was decided in Canaan without them, and the bleating flocks that they favored over their brethren proved to be their tragic undoing.

FOR FURTHER STUDY:

(1) See Devorah's harsh criticism of the tribe of Reuven for not participating in the battle against the oppressive Sisera king of Chatzor, recorded in Sefer Shoftim chapters 4–5. As she ironically put it: "Why did you dwell among the sheepfolds to listen to the bleating flocks?! There were great searchings of the heart among the clans of Reuven!" (*Shoftim* 5:16)

MASEI

The Commandment to Settle Canaan

Numbers 33:1-36:13

PARASHAT MASEI concludes the book of BeMidbar. It opens with a lengthy listing of the people's journeys through the wilderness and goes on to delineate the territory of the land of Israel. The Parasha then describes the institution of the Levitical cities, introduces the legislation concerning the cities of refuge, and concludes with an account of the daughters of Zelofchad marrying within their own tribe. Without exception, all of the material in the Parasha pivots around the point of the people's imminent entry into the land.

In many ways, it would not be an exaggeration to suggest that the entire narrative thrust of the Torah is directed towards the land of Canaan. Recall that the account of the patriarchs and matriarchs begins with God's sudden charge to Avraham to leave his Mesopotamian birthplace and to journey westwards to "the land that I will show you" (*Breisheet* 12:1). The backdrop against which the remaining narratives of Sefer Breisheet subsequently unfold is that land. The protagonists, the founders of the people of Israel, live out their lives on its rocky soil and, when forced to leave it, pensively dream of their eventual return.

The oppressiveness of exile and the promise of redemption that inform the book of Shemot are again bound up with the idea of the land. God's pledge to redeem His people from bondage and His wonders in the land of Egypt, the providential care with which He guides them through the wilderness as they take their first halting steps as a free nation and the Revelation of His instruction at Mount Sinai are all in order to soon bring them to their land, a "land flowing with milk and honey" (*Shemot* 3:8). The construction of the Mishkan, imbued with God's glory, introduces the people to the concept of holiness in space, an idea that will stand them in good stead when they arrive at their destination.

The people remain encamped at Sinai for some time. There they learn the precious lessons of faith in God, of trust in His ability to sustain and of attentiveness to a higher moral law and a more exalted calling. The laws of the wilderness Mishkan that form the core of Sefer VaYikra – the sacrifices, the holiday observances and the overwhelming idea of holiness – are bound up with perpetuating the experience of God's presence. But the ultimate intention of Israel's sojourn at the base of the mountain is to prepare them for their new life as a self-governing nation in their own land. The Torah was never intended to be an exercise in conceptual thinking but rather a way of life – to be experienced and practiced as a concrete and comprehensive reality.

Finally, as the book of BeMidbar begins, the tangible preparations for entering the land are commenced. The adult males of military age are counted, the tribes are tightly organized and the journey begins. Although terribly delayed by the episode of the spies that unfolds shortly after the people leave Sinai, the goal of entering the land remains fixed on the horizon, to be attempted again some thirty-eight years later by the children of the generation that had left the land of Egypt. As Sefer BeMidbar concludes, the people of Israel stand at the very gates of the land, encamped expectantly at the plains of Moav just east of the Yarden River and awaiting the directive to go forwards.

The book of Devarim, constituting Moshe's final words of instruction, exhortation and encouragement, contains a striking series of admonitions and warnings to the people. The Torah's ongoing polemic against idolatry is spelled out in this book with unusual forcefulness, as the allures of Canaanite polytheism are roundly and repeatedly condemned. In conjunction, the praise of the land, its beauty and its fertility, are described. Again and again, Moshe's expresses his poignant desire to himself cross the Yarden and enter the land, seamlessly interweaving the unattainable wish with his lofty vision of Israel's national destiny that is soon to unfold.

The Commandment to Settle the Land

Bearing this brief introduction in mind, let us consider the Torah's command to settle the land, particularly as it is understood by the Ramban. The command to settle Canaan is forcefully expressed in the following passage from our Parasha:

> God spoke to Moshe at the plains of Moav, at the Yarden across from Yericho saying: Speak to the people of Israel and say to them, "You are passing over the Yarden and entering the land of Canaan. You shall drive out the inhabitants of the land from before you and destroy all of their shrines. Demolish their idolatrous images and obliterate their high places of worship. Drive out the inhabitants of the land and settle it, for I have given the land to you to as a possession. Divide the land by lot according to your families, so that the numerous receive a larger portion and the few receive less. It shall be theirs according to the lot, by their tribes they shall possess it. If you fail to drive out the inhabitants of the land from before you, then those that you allow to remain shall be as thorns in your eyes and thistles in your sides, for they shall pain you in the land upon which you shall dwell. That which I contemplated to do to them, I shall do to you instead . . ." (*BeMidbar* 33:50–56)

Although the above passage sounds unduly harsh, its tone of wariness must be understood against the background of Canaanite culture. Israel was the *only* nation of antiquity to espouse a vision of a single, absolute God whose primary will concerning human beings was to guide them towards moral and ethical behavior. The conflict with the Canaanites was not a clash over territory, resources, or trade routes but rather over values. The corrupt and corrosive effects of idolatry had to be extirpated in order for the nation of Israel to have any hope of fulfilling its more exalted mission in the world.

The Five Books of Moses related the ongoing *internal* struggle of Israel to live by the word of God and to embrace His commands. Would the people have trust in Him, would they accept His *mitzvot*? While contact with other nations took place after the Exodus, it tended to be minimal and only under tightly controlled conditions. During the period of the wilderness wanderings, the war against idolatry was an abstract conflict, a theoretical construct that pitted Israel against its own ingrained and primitive ideas, but not against other peoples. The remainder of the Tanakh, however, the flurry of narrative and prophetic books composed after the entry into the land and constituting the lion's share of biblical history, were almost without exception about the *external* challenge of the people to resist the siren call of idolatry, to reject the allure of serving the deities of the surrounding nations, the many gods who made no moral or ethical demands and who could be effortlessly appeased by empty rituals and murderous rites. Every people with whom ancient Israel made contact – whether of a cultural, commercial or military nature – was committed to a diametrically opposed worldview and to antithetical values. We moderns, living in a world that has largely abandoned classical forms of polytheism and their moral equivocation, can scarcely imagine the cultural struggle waged by ancient Israel – often reluctantly and always alone (!) – against every other belief system.

The Torah's warning concerning the "remaining inhabitants" was meant to foreshadow what may transpire, for the eyes blinded by thorns

> cannot see nor understand, so that you will be easily taught to follow their abominations and to serve their gods . . . straying from Me . . . After they have become thorns in your eyes and have led you astray from serving Me, they will become thistles in your sides, causing you pain and suffering and plundering your possessions . . . and then they will fight against you and besiege you and I will completely drive you out of the land from before them! (commentary of the Ramban, 33:53)

God's forceful admonition – "that which I contemplated to do to them, I shall do to you instead . . ." – is a veiled reference to exile, for if the people of Israel fail to supplant Canaanite civilization with a more just and upright society, then their God-given rights to the land will be forfeit, and their fate will be no different than that of the inhabitants that they were commanded to drive out. This divine threat constitutes a startling indication that Israel's deed to Canaan is not a function of some sort of mystical, organic entitlement but is rather a conditional form of ownership that can only be guaranteed by ongoing adherence to God's word. For Israel to stray from God is therefore to forfeit the land and to be driven out just like the Canaanites before them.

The Commentary of the Ramban

We shall now turn to the Ramban's comments concerning the Torah's injunction to settle the land. It is instructive to note that the Ramban, in a move highly unusual for his time and place, settled in Israel towards the end of his life, taking up residence in Jerusalem. After successfully defending his faith and his people at the celebrated dispute with the Dominican friars held before King James of Aragon at Barcelona in 1263, Ramban was forced into exile from Spain and arrived in Israel in 1267. There he remained until his death in 1270. He relates:

> [The verse says:] "Drive out the inhabitants of the land and settle it, for I have given the land to you to as a possession." In my opinion, these words constitute a positive commandment, for they are enjoined to dwell in the land and to possess it, for He has given it to them, and they must not reject God's inheritance. If they would instead go to conquer the land of Shinar or the land of Assyria or other lands with intent to settle there, they would abrogate God's command. The hyperbolic statements of our Sages concerning the mitzvah to dwell in the land of Israel

> and not to leave it . . . are derived from here, for this verse constitutes a positive command that the Torah repeats in many other places (commentary to 33:53).

Here, the Ramban explains that the people of Israel are commanded to possess their land, to dwell in it and not to leave it, for doing so would constitute an act of rejection of God's gift. Apparently, the directive enjoined upon Israel to create a nation loyal to God's laws involves more than simply being sovereign over a particular territory. For the Ramban, the land of Israel itself is necessary in order to accomplish the goal, and other territories – pleasant and expansive though they may be – will not do. Ramban uses even more emphatic language in his critical remarks to Maimonides' "Book of the Commandments," where he attacks the latter's failure to include the mitzvah of settling the land of Israel in his tally of the 613 commands:

> The fourth [omission of Maimonides] is the command to possess the land that God gave to our ancestors Avraham, Yitzchak and Ya'acov, and not to allow it to be in the possession of another nation, nor to allow it to remain desolate . . . and it is a mitzvah for all generations. Our Sages speak in astonishing tones concerning this commandment, for they say that "whosoever leaves the land to dwell outside of it ought be regarded as one who worships idols" (TB *Ketubot* 110b) . . . Therefore, this is a positive commandment forever that obligates each individual, even during the time of exile . . . The Sifre adds: "When Rabbi Yehuda ben Betayra, Rabbi Matya ben Cheresh, Rabbi Chananya nephew of Rabbi Yehoshua and Rabbi Natan had to leave the land of Israel, they journeyed as far as Palatia. They remembered the land of Israel and began to cry, rending their garments. They recalled the verse 'you shall possess it and dwell in it and observe the laws.' They concluded: 'Dwelling in the land of Israel is equivalent to all of the other *mitzvot*!'" (*Hassagot HaRamban*, Mitzvat Asei 4).

According to the Ramban, dwelling in the land of Israel is a necessary condition for Israel to succeed at the task of nation building and to achieve its mission in the world. Sovereignty over another land is insufficient. Autonomy anywhere else is inadequate. This interpretation, at its core based upon the bedrock of Rabbinic tradition and the biblical text, casts the subject in an entirely different light. Without the Ramban we might have imagined that the land is merely a *vehicle* for Israel to become a people. After all, devoid of a land, it is not possible to exercise national independence or to implement national policies in accordance with Torah principles. Without the Ramban we might have imagined that the Torah highlights the land because comprehensive living encompasses not only the individual or the community, but the people as well. Does the Torah have nothing to say about social policy, national defense or the regulation of commercial activity? But if that were all that the land makes possible, then any land would do. There should be no objection to the people of Israel exercising national rule over a different land and there instituting the Torah's directives as a people. The Ramban is therefore suggesting much more than nationalism in the sense of political and cultural independence. What he intimates is that there is a unique *spiritual* quality to the land of Israel that is a function of the divine energy that is focused upon it always. In spite of the fact that topographically and climatologically its hills and valleys may seem indistinguishable from other lands in the Mediterranean basin, the land of Israel is fundamentally different because it is imbued with the experience of God's presence. "It is a land that God your Lord searches out; the eyes of God your Lord are upon it always, from the beginning of the year until the end" (*Devarim* 11:12).

The "Holiness Code" of the Book of VaYikra

Support for the Ramban's thesis can be found in the book of VaYikra, in the lengthy sections that call upon Israel to be holy and to refrain from immoral and immodest sexual practices. After an exhaustive list of forbidden relationships and abhorrent rituals that were practiced by both the Egyptians as well as by the Canaanites, the Torah concludes:

> Do not become defiled (תטמאו) by all these things, for the nations that I am driving out before you became defiled (נטמאו) by them. The land became defiled (ותטמא), and I was cognizant of its iniquity, and the land vomited out its inhabitants. Therefore, you shall keep My decrees and laws and not perform any of these abominations . . . for such did the people of the land before you and the land became defiled (ותטמא). Let not the land vomit you out should you defile it (בטמאכם), as it vomited out the people before you . . . (*VaYikra* 18:24–28)

The recurring use of the root טמא in this passage, often mistranslated as "impure" but always associated with some sort of spiritual failing or deficiency, coupled with the bold metaphor of the land "vomiting out" its inhabitants, highlights the unique spiritual characteristics of the land of Israel. Those who dwell in it, be they Canaanite or Israelite, must live up to more stringent moral demands or else invite exile from it. The driving out of the Canaanites that the Torah invariably connects with the command to settle the land is thus recast. Their expulsion is the natural and inevitable consequence of their incorrigible moral and spiritual corruption, rather than a conquest of native peoples in order to colonize their land and take their place. Concerning Canaan there is no such thing as indigenous rights to the land; ongoing possession depends upon ongoing merit. With unparalleled boldness, the Torah announces in our Parasha that the fate of the Israelites, God's own, will also be a function of their conduct and that the privilege of dwelling in the land can be just as easily withdrawn from them!

In a lengthy essay on the above verses, the Ramban explores the unique attributes of the land, suggesting that God exercises a more profound and intimate degree of providence over its borders. Concluding his remarks, he states that:

> The people of Canaan were not the only ones guilty of these crimes, for the passage explicitly charges the Egyptians with similar conduct! Nevertheless, the land of Egypt was not expected to vomit out its people, nor any other land to expel its inhabitants, for the matter is completely a function of the exalted state and sanctity of the land of Israel . . . (commentary to 18:25, end)

For the Ramban, dwelling in the land of Israel is a special privilege as well as a great responsibility. Securing its borders is a divine command, but it is a command that must be associated with a commitment to live an exemplary national and individual life. The promise of redemption that has sustained us for so long is predicated upon a vision of a better world, a more just society and a heightened sensitivity to God's presence. The land of Israel lies at the focal point of this vision, the necessary environment for it to unfold, but it is the *people* who dwell in the land that will determine the course. If Israel can live up to the spiritual potential of the land in which they dwell, then they can yet achieve their mission, long ago assigned to them by God Himself as they stood at Mount Sinai and prepared to receive the Torah: "Now if you will hearken to My voice and observe My covenant, then you shall be My treasure from among all of the peoples, for the earth is Mine. You shall be for Me a kingdom of priests and a holy nation . . ." (*Shemot* 19:6).

FOR FURTHER STUDY:

(1) More than many other medieval commentaries, the Ramban introduces to the student comprehensive and far-reaching ideas. Often, however, these must be assembled from the more local comments that he makes in various places. Concerning the spiritual aspects of the land of Israel and its centrality to Israelite destiny, compare Ramban's comments in our Parasha to what he relates in *Breisheet* 26:5 concerning the patriarchs' fulfillment of *mitzvot*, *VaYikra* 13:47 concerning plagues of garments, *VaYikra* 26:6–7 concerning the messianic era and *Devarim* 11:18 concerning *mitzvah* fulfillment outside of the land.

DEVARIM

Rebuke and Remedy

Deuteronomy 1:1-3:22

These are the words that Moshe spoke to all of Israel on the other side of the Yarden, in the wilderness, in the plain, opposite Suf, between Paran and between Tofel, and Lavan and Chatzerot and Di Zahav. Eleven days' journey from Chorev by way of Mount Se'ir, until Kadesh Barnea.

And so it was in the fortieth year, on the first day of the eleventh month, that Moshe spoke to the people of Israel in accordance with all that God commanded him to convey to them. This was after he had struck down Sichon the king of the Amorites who dwells at Cheshbon, as well as Og king of the Bashan who dwells at Ashtarot in Edrei.

On the other side of the Yarden in the land of Moav, Moshe began to explicate this Torah by saying: "God our Lord spoke to us at Chorev saying 'it is long enough that you have dwelt at this mountain. Turn and travel forward and come to the mount of the Amorite and to all of his neighbors – those that dwell in the plain, the hills, the lowlands, the dry lands and the coast of the sea – the land of the Canaanite and the Levanon, all the way until the great river, the Euphrates. Behold, I have given you the land, come and possess the land that God pledged to your ancestors, to Avraham to Yitzchak and to Ya'acov to give it to them, and to their descendents after them . . .'" (*Devarim* 1:1–8)

THUS BEGINS Sefer Devarim, the final book of the Torah. In soaring, exhortative language, Moshe foretells his people's future and vividly recalls their past. Forty years have elapsed since the time that he took them out of Egyptian bondage, a generation has lived out its allotted years and has perished, and now the people finally stand ready to possess the new land. Encamped with them on the Yarden's eastern side, the aged shepherd spends his final months reviewing the Torah's teachings with his flock, explicating what had been obscure and introducing the suddenly relevant, inspiring them to be devoted to God while impressing upon them the grave dangers of idolatry that lie in wait just beyond the rushing waters.

The discourses of this book are confident yet guarded, the expressions hopeful but cautious. Cognizant of his imminent demise, Moshe recounts to the people their triumphs and failures, their moments of trust in God's guidance as well as their many reversals. Since his objective in addressing the people at this juncture is to instruct and to guide, Moshe highlights certain features of the events while downplaying others; the effect of the whole is not a rewriting of Israel's wilderness history but rather a profound meditation on its implications. Hovering over his words, like some vivid vision of the painfully unattainable, is the land of Canaan, its windswept, rocky peaks and its verdant vales, its dry and foreboding wastelands and its fertile and terraced slopes, all of it proximal, tangible and immediate, yet just beyond the grasp of the dying leader.

A Tripartite Division

From the broadest perspective, we may divide the Sefer Devarim into three main sections, each one reflecting a distinct didactic motive. The first relatively small section of the book, constituting Moshe's introductory remarks, is comprised of the initial four chapters. In this section, Moshe recalls the journey from Sinai, the sending of the spies, the wilderness experience, and the recent conquest and settlement of the Amorite territories. He goes on to describe his personal disappointment at being denied entry to the land, but then warns the people that their own success at settling it will be contingent upon their remaining loyal to God's teaching. His words are primarily expressed in tones of *admonishment*, and apprehension is heard in his measured breaths. The section concludes with Moshe's partial fulfillment of the Torah's injunction to designate cities of refuge (see *BeMidbar* 35:9–34), as he selects three cities from the lands east of the Yarden, leaving to his successor the task of designating the corresponding three western cities.

The next section of the book, comprising its largest component, is Moshe's lengthy *explanation of the Torah*. It begins in *Devarim* 5 with a recollection of the Revelation at Sinai and a restatement of the Decalogue, and then goes on to describe the many *mitzvot* that the people have received. Various ritual, civil and holiness laws are explicated, seamlessly interwoven with forthright locutions of counsel and forewarning. In this section, Moshe is determined to impress upon the people that soon they will face very real challenges as they cross the Yarden and enter the land. Their success will depend upon fortitude, perseverance, and unswerving loyalty to God's instruction. This central portion of the Sefer concludes with 27:8: "Write upon the stones all the words of this Torah, clearly and completely."

The final segment of the book, from 27:9 until its conclusion, is perhaps the most exalted and inspiring. The subject matter is the formal *sealing of the covenant* with God, but the language is lyrical and poetic. The section contains many intimations of Moshe's end and many poignant expressions of parting, as if he and the people can bid each other farewell with only the greatest reluctance. Moshe first details the terms of the covenant, the so-called "blessings" and the "curses" (27:9–29:8), and then convenes the people to accept its provisions (29:9–28). The covenant is sealed and Moshe prepares to take his final leave. He offers his parting oration (30:1–20) and is called upon by God to finally hand over the leadership of the people to Yehoshua's able but trembling hands (31:1–30). Moshe concludes with a striking song that spells out Israel's past history and future destiny (32:1–52). He then blesses the people and reluctantly ascends Nevo's summit to die (33:1–34:12).

The preamble to Devarim's first section of urgent admonitions is the series of puzzling verses with which our Parasha begins. Some of the place names mentioned, such as Tofel and Di Zahav, are otherwise unknown. Concerning the rest, it is unclear whether they come together in order to designate a very specific location or rather are an extended list of different places. This much, however, is clear: it is with an unmistakable sense of place and time that Moshe offers his words to the people. These first few verses contain no less than thirteen geographical designations and four or five temporal ones!

Rashi's Explanation – Words of Censure

But why all of this specificity surrounding the matter of Moshe's final addresses, as if we do not know that the people are encamped at the eastern banks of the Yarden (*BeMidbar* 33:48–49) or that the forty years of wilderness wandering are about to come to an end (33:50)? Would it not have been sufficient to indicate that Moshe offered his homilies on the eve of his death as the people were positioned to enter the new land? We will begin by considering the explanation of Rashi:

> These are words of rebuke. The text recounts all of the places where Israel angered God and therefore the events are recalled only in general terms out of deference for the honor of Israel . . . (commentary to *Devarim* 1:1)

As Rashi understands it (and his explanation is drawn from much earlier Rabbinic sources), these opening lines of Sefer Devarim are intended to set the tone for the whole book. Moshe's final addresses to the people are intended to guide and to exhort, to caution and to warn, and he therefore begins by briefly and obliquely referencing all of the locations where Israel betrayed a lack of trust in God or else showed themselves ungrateful for His blessings. For example, in the *wilderness* after crossing the Sea of Reeds they cried out impatiently for food (*Shemot* 16:3), and at the *plain* they disastrously strayed after the daughters of Moav (*BeMidbar* 25:1), etc. Rashi quotes the words of Rabbi Shimon bar Yochai concerning a number of the more obscure geographical references:

> We have reviewed the entire text of the Torah and have found no places by the names of Tofel or Lavan. Rather, Moshe meant to rebuke them concerning their impetuous words (תפל) about the manna that was white (לבן), as they said: "Our souls are sick of the meager food!" (*BeMidbar* 21:5) . . . as for Di Zahav, he rebuked them for the calf that they fashioned from the masses of gold (זהב) that He had bestowed upon them . . .

Similarly for Rashi, the mention of the "eleven days' journey from Chorev by way of Mount Se'ir, until Kadesh Barnea" (*Devarim* 1:2), is an allusion to the people's greatest failure – the sin of the spies:

> Moshe said to them: "Look what you have done! There is no shorter route from Chorev to Kadesh Barnea than the route of Mount Se'ir, and it too takes eleven days. You, however, traversed it in three days' time . . . for God was so anxious to bring you into the land. But because you failed, He therefore caused you to circle round the environs of Mount Se'ir for a period of forty years! (commentary to 1:2)

In effect, Rashi relates to the place names and times as if they were allusions to events, thus dispensing with the need to identify obscure locations or to clarify durations of time that are not cited elsewhere. The straightforward reading of the text may be otherwise, but let us for now accept Rashi's approach. Let us consent to the external controls that Rashi imposes in order to focus upon the internal meaning. If in fact these are episodes rather than locations or times, it is nevertheless curious why there should be a need to recount Israel's setbacks by way of allusion only. Is it really the case that these failures have been intentionally shrouded in order to preserve Israel's dignity? After all, doesn't Moshe later dwell upon many of these very ignominies at length, each time squarely laying the blame upon his people Israel? Doesn't he say concerning their role in the affair of the spies that "you did not want to enter the land, and you rebelled against the word of God you Lord . . . and did not have trust" (1:26, 32)? Doesn't he exhort them (6:16) not to test God as they did at Masa, when they cried out for water (see *Shemot* 17:1–3)? Won't he later exclaim with exasperation, before going on to describe the sin of the golden calf in great detail, that "you are a stiff-necked people! Remember and do not forgot how you angered God your Lord in the wilderness, from the very day that you left the land of Egypt until you have arrived at this place, you have been rebellious with God!" (*Devarim* 9:7)? Why then the need to speak in circumlocutions, to mention places and times that refer only indirectly to Israel's infamy, if anywise these failures will later be elaborated upon at great length?

The answer, of course, relates to the character of the book of Devarim as a whole. While there is much information in the book concerning the commandments – emphasis, elaboration and even innovation – the purpose of the book is not simply to review the known or else to introduce the novel. Moshe's divinely-mandated mission, as the people prepare to become a nation in their own land, is to *warn* them concerning the perils and to *guide* them to success. Though Rashi speaks of "rebuke," what he intends is more akin to constructive criticism. Moshe's words of admonition are not proffered out of a spirit of vindictiveness by an old man embittered by his tragic fate; they are not meant to fulfill a disillusioned leader's need for self-justification as the end of his term draws near. Rather, Moshe speaks out of concern for his people and with the benefit of hindsight that his years confer, so that Israel might understand from their setbacks that they must strive for more. He teaches and instructs, unleashing in his listeners the self-realization that will inspire them to learn from their mistakes and to go forward. The essence of Sefer Devarim, then, is *didactic*.

It is for this reason that Moshe dare not begin his remarks with explicit references to downfall, with a lengthy litany of obvious failures, with Israel's tragic mistakes plainly spelled out for all to see. The true teacher will first engage his listeners, drawing them close with words of love even as he makes clear that his message may be painful. He does not overwhelm his followers with long lists of ruin so that he may impose upon them his own vision of what is right. Rather, the true teacher provides the cues that guide us towards self-understanding, so that we may discover for ourselves what must be rectified and be inspired to make amends. According to Rashi's reading, then, Sefer Devarim begins by revealing its teaching methodology.

The Introduction of the Ramban

In his introduction to Sefer Devarim, the Ramban spells out some of the book's most salient features, echoing Rashi's opening comments:

> The topic of this book is known to be the repetition of the Torah. In it, Moshe explains to the generation about to enter the land the majority of the *mitzvot* that are necessary for the people of Israel. None of the subjects addressed in the priestly code [of Sefer VaYikra] are mentioned here, not the sacrifices nor the matters of priestly ritual fitness and the service, for these things had already been explained to them and the Kohanim are careful, not needing additional warnings.
>
> As for Israel, however, the book admonishes them with respect to the familiar and customary *mitzvot* mainly in order to explicate them more fully, and sometimes only for the purpose of warning them forcefully. For instance, concerning matters pertaining to idolatry, the book sounds many, many cautions one after the other,

as well as stern admonishments and descriptions of frightening consequences, all of which are calculated to impress upon them the gravity of the transgression.

Here, the Ramban indicates both what Sefer Devarim glaringly omits as well as what it seems to persistently repeat. Absent from its verses is any significant treatment of the priestly laws or of the associated sacrificial service – these topics constituting the bulk of Sefer VaYikra. The Kohanim, it seems, are dependable students who internalize their lessons well and are not in need of a review or a reprimand. On the other hand, Sefer Devarim spends an inordinate amount of time explicating the perils of idolatry, the harsh consequences that await those that succumb to its immoral wiles. The reason for both the omission as well as for the repetition is the same: Sefer Devarim addresses the new generation of Israelites that will be shortly traversing the Yarden River and entering the Promised Land. The challenges that the people of Israel will face mainly concern the corrupt Canaanite culture that will everywhere confront them, "on the high mountains and upon the hills and under every leafy tree" (*Devarim* 12:2). Their success in settling the land and remaining loyal to God's teachings will depend upon their ability to avoid idolatry – the allure of the licentious rites and moral relativism that everywhere held the ancients in sway.

Thus, while we often refer to the book as "*Mishneh Torah*" or "repetition of the Torah" (a usage itself introduced by the text in 17:18), it is in fact a very selective repetition, for Moshe's eloquent remarks are not meant to simply review the *mitzvot* but rather to provide the people with the tools that they will need in order to triumph.

The Ramban goes on to address our larger section that makes no mention of *mitzvot* at all and instead focuses exclusively upon matters of reproof:

> Before Moshe began to explain the Torah, he first admonished the people and reminded them of their transgressions. How much had they rebelled against Him while they were in the wilderness! How compassionate had God been in the face of their constant provocations! Moshe here intended to recall His kindnesses with them as well as to caution them not to repeat their misdeeds, so that they might not be destroyed by their transgressions.

The binary message of Israel's rebelliousness and God's compassion underlines the entirety of Moshe's opening remarks but it is not meant to frighten or to shame the people into compliance. Rather, the Ramban avers, the mention of Israel's infamy and God's graciousness is a conscious strategy on Moshe's part to provide Sefer Devarim with the most fitting introduction possible:

> This was intended to fortify their hearts by indicating that He would always relate to them with the attribute of compassion. *Let no man say that "possession of the land is impossible, for no person can be without sin and God's unforgiving attribute of justice will destroy!" Therefore Moshe our teacher informs the people that the Holy One blessed be He is a compassionate one full of compassion*, for His forgiveness and forbearance constitute a great support for the people to serve Him, as the verse states: "Forgiveness is with You, in order that You might be revered (*Tehillim* 130:4)."

Complementing Rashi's reading, Ramban explains that Moshe recalls Israel's myriad indiscretions and God's constant corrections not in order to dishearten the people but rather in order to inspire them! God is patient and forgiving. When they enter the new land, Israel will undoubtedly err, transgress His words and abandon His Torah. Though God may react with harshness, His objective is rectification. He does not desire Israel's downfall but rather their recovery and success. For Rashi, therefore, the first few **verses** of Sefer Devarim recount Israel's failures, but only in a veiled fashion calculated to foster reflection and repair. For the Ramban, the first few *chapters* preserve the account of Israel's failures, but the purpose is actually to highlight God's patience and tenderness – in spite of their constant provocations, He is their compassionate God who loves them and desires their welfare. The message of both commentaries, in spite of the painful subject matter, is affirming and positive.

The meaning for us in all of this is profound: Sometimes, we convince ourselves that we are already so far from fulfilling God's expectations that there really is no point anymore in attempting to do so. Why bother trying to live a life that would make God proud if we have no realistic chance of ever succeeding? The task is too daunting and the standard too high! Sometimes, it is too overwhelming to even face the failure! But, says Moshe, while there can be no choices without consequences, there is also the constant opportunity to make amends and to restore God's confidence in us. No one, at least in God's eyes, is incorrigible. Israel in the wilderness may have tested Him sorely and constantly rebelled against His word, but God never gave up on His people. When they were ready to return to Him, He was always receptive. Though He reminded them of their transgressions, He was never vindictive. Divine compassion and the human ability to make amends are the bedrock upon which Sefer Devarim is founded. Could there be a more heartening thought for us as we read Parashat Devarim, with Tish'a Be'Av once again just around the corner?

FOR FURTHER STUDY:

(1) For the Ramban, the multiple names of verse 1 are not, as Rashi explains, allusions to misdeeds. Instead, they are geographical place names that are meant to pinpoint the *exact* location in which Moshe's final addresses to the people took place. As the Rashbam explains with greater clarity:

> According to the straightforward meaning, all of the names mentioned in this first verse are locations, for the text often provides multiple pieces of information in order to specify a particular place. For example, in Parashat Lech Lecha we are told that Avraham pitched his tent "east of Beit el, that is, Beit El to the west and the Ai to the east . . ." (*Breisheet* 12:8). In Parashat BeShalach the people were told to encamp "before Pi HaChirot, between Migdol and the sea, opposite Baal Tzephon." (*Shemot* 14:2). At the end of Sefer Shoftim, we are informed of a "festival to God celebrated yearly in Shilo, north of Beit El, east of the road that goes northwards from Beit El to Shechem, and south of Levona" (*Shoftim* 21:19). All the more so, is it important to tell us where Moshe recounted the *mitzvot* . . . (commentary to *Devarim* 1:1)

For the Rashbam and the Ramban, the Torah specifies the location of Moshe's last discourses with great precision in order to highlight their importance.

VAETCHANAN

"Observe" and "Remember" Were Pronounced Together

Deuteronomy 3:23-7:11

PARASHAT DEVARIM concluded with Moshe's recollection of the astounding victories over Sichon and Og, the powerful Amorite tyrants who ruled over the Transjordanian highlands. The remarkable events occurred at the end of the wilderness journeys, as the people of Israel finally drew close to their destination. The triumphs ushered in Israel's wars of conquest and ignited in Moshe the fervent hope that God's decree barring him from entering the land of Canaan had been relaxed, but to no avail:

> I entreated God at that time saying: "Almighty God, You have begun to show Your servant Your greatness and Your forceful hand, for there is no power in heaven or upon earth that can match Your deeds and Your strength. Let me please pass over so that I may see the good land that is on the other side of the Yarden, this fine range of mountains and the Levanon." But God was angry with me because of you and He would not listen to me. God said to me: "It is enough! Do not continue to speak to Me any more concerning this matter! Rather, ascend to the top of the heights and lift up your eyes to the west, to the north, to the south and to the east, and see it with your own eyes, for you will surely not pass over this Yarden. Charge Yehoshua and strengthen and encourage him, for he will traverse before this people, and he will cause them to possess the land that you will see." We encamped in the valley, opposite Bet Pe'or . . . (*Devarim* 3:23–29)

Resigned to his fate with finality, Moshe now turns his attention to the people of Israel. In soaring words, he encourages them to cleave to God's instruction even as he warns them about the perils of idolatry. He recalls for them the pivotal events of their wilderness sojourns, and he then begins to explicate for them God's statutes and laws. In the course of his remarks, Moshe remembers the decisive moment of the Revelation at Sinai – reinforcing for the people the theme of binding covenant, emphasizing to them the notion of divine immediacy, and loudly proclaiming God's Decalogue for the benefit of the new generation.

Since Sefer Devarim is introduced from the outset as Moshe's own impassioned words to Israel and his personal recalling of their history, it is only natural that there should exist discrepancies between his retelling of events and the events themselves, as they are recorded elsewhere in the Torah. Often these incongruities amount to nothing more than didactically-inspired shifts in nuance; they can be easily resolved by considering the nature of the different audience that now receives Moshe's teachings. For the generation about to enter the new land, the lessons to be gleaned from the experiences of the Exodus or the wilderness wanderings must necessarily be different, at least in some respects, than for those that actually lived through the events. It is therefore reasonable for Moshe's words in Sefer Devarim, when recalling an earlier event in Israel's history, to reflect an altered sensibility.

For example, Moshe's recounting of the sin of the spies is markedly different in Sefer Devarim (1:22–2:1) than the narrative that is recorded in Sefer BeMidbar (13:1–14:45). In startling contrast to the actual event, Moshe here places the burden of responsibility for the debacle *exclusively* upon the people of Israel, as if God had never commanded him to send the spies at all! In Moshe's version, it was Israel who initiated the mission (*Devarim* 1:22), it was Israel who ignored the spies' glowing report (1:25–26) and it was Israel who failed to trust in God in spite of Moshe's encouraging words (1:27–28). The discrepancies can be readily explained: Moshe's intent in Sefer Devarim is not to objectively recall the events of the past but rather to communicate guiding instruction for the future. He therefore recalls those features of the episode that underscore Israel's power to choose and the consequences of such choice. His message is clear: It is Israel's judicious exercise of their autonomy that will determine their fate in the new land.

Occasionally, however, the clash of texts is more difficult to resolve. What are we to make of Moshe's version when his *verbatim* repetition diverges from the original? This happens more rarely, but our Parasha presents us with the most celebrated example: the Decalogue – the ten guiding principles that God proclaimed at Sinai. Our discussion will be guided by the explanation of Rashi here as well as by the contrasting remarks of the Ibn Ezra in his commentary to Sefer Shemot (chapter 20). We may discover that their different solutions point to a larger disagreement between them.

The Overall Context of the Decalogue

Moshe's depiction of the Decalogue's general context, understandably more concise in our account, is accurate. His mention of the covenant (*Devarim* 5:2), his description of the overwhelming immediacy of the God-man encounter (5:4), his recounting of the awe-inspiring fire that enveloped the mountain (5:4), and his reference to the special role that he played in the communication of God's word (5:5) all correspond to the version in Sefer Shemot (*Shemot* 19:16–25). The Decalogue itself (*Devarim* 5:6–17) is mostly synonymous with the original (*Shemot* 20:2–13). Though there are occasional words that are rearranged and syntactical features that are not the same (especially concerning the use of the conjunction), the overall convergence of the two texts is unmistakable, with one glaring exception: the command concerning the Shabbat. Here, the differences of vocabulary and of emphasis are striking. In Sefer Shemot 20, the fourth utterance reads:

> *Remember* (זכור) the Shabbat day to sanctify it. Six days shall you labor and do all of your work, but the seventh day shall be a Shabbat to God your Lord. Neither you, nor your son, daughter, servant, maidservant, beasts nor convert that dwells within your gates shall do any manner of work. *This is because in six days God made heaven, earth, the sea and all that they contain, and He rested on the seventh day. Therefore, God blessed the Shabbat day and sanctified it.* (20:7–10)

In Moshe's recounting, however, the command concerning the Shabbat says as follows:

> *Observe* (שמור) the Shabbat day to sanctify it, *as God your Lord commanded you.* Six days shall you labor and do all of your work, but the seventh day shall be a Shabbat to God your Lord. Neither you, nor your son, daughter, servant, maidservant, *ox, donkey or any* beasts or the convert that dwells within your gates shall do any manner of work, *in order that your servant and maidservant shall rest as you do. You shall remember that you yourself were a slave in the land of Egypt and God your Lord took you out of there with a strong hand and with an outstretched arm. Therefore God your Lord commanded you to fulfill the Shabbat day.* (*Devarim* 5:11–14)

Here we note that while some of the deviations between the two texts are slight, others are glaring. The opening word is, for example, entirely different! In Shemot, we are bidden to remember and here we are bidden to observe. Moshe's elaboration on the generic "beasts" mentioned in Sefer Shemot is notable but not necessarily at odds with the earlier text. But concerning the impetus for the Shabbat observance, there appears to be no convergence at all. In Sefer Shemot, the reason advanced for the Shabbat relates to the act of creation: because God created the universe in six days and ceased from His activity on the seventh day, so too must we acknowledge His central role in the cosmic order by following His example. But in Sefer Devarim when Moshe spells out the reason for the Shabbat, God's creation is completely omitted. Instead, the Shabbat is to be marked because of its critical thematic link with the servitude in Egypt – its observance can foster a profound identification with those that are less fortunate. Because we were slaves who tirelessly toiled, we must ensure that our own servants are granted a day of rest. Because God rescued us from bondage and oppression, therefore we must be sensitive to those who labor for us. The emphasis, then, is not the creation of the world but rather the Exodus, not the abstract truth of God's almighty transcendence but rather His tangible concern for the vulnerable and the downtrodden.

How then to explain Moshe's reiteration? If Moshe purports to tell the people of Israel exactly what transpired at Mount Sinai, then how can he take so many liberties with God's own pronouncements? What, in fact, did God actually utter as the people of Israel stood expectantly at the mountain's base, and for what purpose would Moshe modify matters in his parting address to the people?

The Explanation of Rashi

Rashi offers a well-known interpretation from the ancient Rabbis:

> [Our verse states:] "Observe the Shabbat day" – [But] in the first Decalogue, it says "Remember the Shabbat day . . ." Both of them were stated in one utterance and as one word, and both were heard as one . . . (Mechilta of Rabbi Yishmael, Masechta Yitro 7)

This explanation, immortalized in Rabbi Shelomo Alkabetz's (16th century, Safed) "*Lecha Dodi*" hymn that is intoned on Shabbat eve, essentially maintains that there is *no* discrepancy between the two accounts at all. In fact, God simultaneously uttered both words – "Remember" and "Observe" – at Sinai, and both words were miraculously heard and understood by Israel in the same moment. Moshe's version in our Parasha simply fills in the missing word that was not spelled out in Sefer Shemot. For Rashi, adopting this interpretation clearly introduces a miraculous element to the moment that the Torah itself did not describe.

Concerning the other discrepancies, great and small, Rashi is not fazed. "Observe the Shabbat day to sanctify it, *as God your Lord commanded you*" is understood by Rashi to mean "as God commanded you *before the giving of the Torah*, for at Mara they were commanded concerning the Shabbat" (commentary of Rashi to *Devarim* 5:11). For Rashi, Moshe reminds the people of Israel that the command of the Shabbat actually preceded the Decalogue – for the people arrived at Mara in the immediate aftermath of their exodus from Egypt and the crossing of the Sea of Reeds (see *Shemot* 15:22–26). In Sefer Shemot, the reason advanced for the Shabbat is that its observance commemorates God's act of creation, while here in Sefer Devarim the Shabbat rest highlights the thankless lot of the slave and the need to identify with his plight. "Grant rest to the slave," the Torah seems to be saying, "because you know only too well the injustice of ceaseless toil." Rashi, however, offers us a different reading:

> "Remember that you were a slave in the land of Egypt" – for this very reason God redeemed you, so that you might be His servant and observe His commands.

For Rashi, what Moshe highlights for the new generation of Israel is a message that is relevant to them as they prepare to enter the land and to settle it as free men: freedom is a gift as well as a precious responsibility. God took Israel out of Egypt and rescued them from slavery to Pharaoh so that they might exercise their newfound autonomy to perform His will. The goal of freedom, then, is not to live life with abandon but rather to embrace obligation to a higher purpose and to strive for a greater good. For Rashi, Moshe invokes Israel's slavery in Egypt not as an alternative explanation for the Shabbat. As enunciated in Sefer Shemot's version of the Decalogue, Shabbat is predicated upon the recognition that God created the heavens and the earth. This recognition is at the very core of the Shabbat idea. Our Parasha's reference to slavery does not constitute a contradiction to the earlier Decalogue but rather complements its message: while the God of creation bestows freedom, He also demands accountability.

For Rashi then, there are two ways to resolve textual or thematic discrepancies in the Decalogue: either divergences are deliberate pedagogic strategies on Moshe's part and not genuine inconsistencies, or else, as in "remember" and "observe," they do not really exist at all.

The Interpretation of the Ibn Ezra

Rabbi Avraham Ibn Ezra authored two versions of his commentary on Sefer Shemot. One of them is similar in style to his commentaries on the other books of the Torah and, like them, is characterized by a cryptic conciseness that for the uninitiated appears to border on obfuscation. The other is a much lengthier and developed version that relates not only to the straightforward exploration of the immediate context but also offers more involved thematic discussions. These two are known respectively as the פירוש הקצר ("concise commentary") and the פירוש הארוך ("lengthy commentary"), and occasionally they are even at odds with each other! Sometimes an explanation that is offered by the Ibn Ezra in the פירוש הקצר is rejected by him in the פירוש הארוך and sometimes it is the other way around. For the purposes of this discussion, we quote his comments from the lengthy commentary:

> Thus says Avraham the author: It is the convention of Hebrew speakers to sometimes explain their words at great length and with clarity, while at other times they express the necessary ideas with an economy of language, so that the listener might understand the essence. *Realize that the words are like material bodies while the message is like the spirit,* for the body is to the soul only a vehicle. Thus it is the convention of all wise men, whatever language they may be speaking, to preserve the message while not being concerned with using the exact same words, since the message is anywise the same. (introductory commentary of the Ibn Ezra to the Decalogue, *Shemot* 20:1)

Here, Ibn Ezra shares with us the essence of his idea. Whenever there is a repetition of a biblical text, whenever an episode or a law is repeated in the Torah, the second version may employ different words. This is because the purpose of the repetition is to convey the essential *meaning* to the reader and not to reiterate matters verbatim. The words themselves, says Ibn Ezra, are only vehicles for the communication of the idea, much like the physical body is a vessel for the more essential soul to complete its tasks. Therefore, we need not be perturbed by these two linguistically distinct versions of the Decalogue because only the underlying message of both need be the same. In other words, for Ibn Ezra there are no contradictions between diverging texts – the choice of words may be different, but the essential meaning is the same.

Concerning the specific issue of "remember" and "observe," Ibn Ezra elaborates:

> Now I will speak concerning "remember" and "observe." Realize that the meaning is preserved and not the actual words. Recall that Yitzchak told Esav that he wanted to bless him "before I die" (*Breisheet* 27:4). When Rivka related the matter to Ya'acov, however, she reported that he said "so that I might bless you *before God* before I die" (27:7). Why did she add the words "before God" (if Yitzchak himself did not say them)? The answer is that she realized that Yitzchak was God's prophet and that the blessing that he would utter would be a form of prophecy. She therefore told Ya'acov "before God", because she was explaining to him the *reason for the blessing.*
>
> Moshe spoke in a similar manner. *The Decalogue in Sefer Shemot is the precise word of God, without addition or deficiency*, and these words alone were recorded on the tablets of the covenant . . . but the Decalogue preserved in Parashat VaEtchanan is the words of Moshe. The proof for this is the fact that it twice mentions "as God your Lord commanded you (*Devarim* 5:11, 15)."
>
> At the base of the brain is the faculty of memory and it is there that images are stored. Memory thus includes observance. The meaning of "remember" is to be always cognizant of the day of the week, so that the seventh day be observed and no labor be performed on it. The *reason* for remembering is therefore to observe. When God uttered "remember," all of the listeners *understood* it to mean "observe," *as if* both of them had been uttered simultaneously!

For Ibn Ezra, then, there is no need to introduce the miraculous as Rashi asks of us, to proclaim that both words had been uttered by God at the same time and astonishingly grasped by the people of Israel. In fact, there is no need to reconcile both versions of the Decalogue at all, because God only uttered the first and original one! The second Decalogue, introduced in our Parasha, is Moshe's record of what God had said, but not recalled by him (inaccurately as it were) as some sort of an exact, precise and literal rendering. Rather, Moshe's intention is only to communicate the deeper meaning of God's words and what He intended the people of Israel to understand. When God told us to remember the Shabbat, He did not mean that we should recall it from time to time like some neutral piece of data, but rather that we should be aware and mindful of it. This awareness is not an exercise in abstraction but rather a means to an end: we remember the Shabbat in order to cease from *melakha* on that day! The fundamental objective of *remembering Shabbat is therefore in order to observe it* and God's intent in His original pronouncement was the communication of that truth. Moshe's repetition of the Decalogue is not to quote what God said but rather to remind Israel what He meant.

Likewise, when Moshe informs us that the purpose of the Shabbat is to recall the servitude in Egypt and to relieve the slave of his labors, he is not communicating a different version of the divine utterance preserved in Sefer Shemot that focused the discussion on God's creation. Rather, Moshe here indicates the *reason* why the slave was granted rest to begin with. Earlier, God had related that all members of the community are to partake of the Shabbat rest, including "you, your son, daughter, servant, maidservant, beast and convert that dwells within your gates" (*Shemot* 20:9). But why ought the servant and the maidservant to enjoy the restfulness of Shabbat? The text in Sefer Shemot does not elaborate, but

> Moshe here tells us the reason (for God's command): When God indicated in the first Decalogue that the slave ought to rest, this was in order that you might recall that you too were a slave in Egypt like him, and God redeemed you from there . . .

Ibn Ezra's explanation for resolving the discrepancies between the Decalogues is both reasonable as well as comprehensive. He succeeds in working out every one of the divergences while making no demands upon the student to suspend his logical faculties. It is because of this that Ibn Ezra is characterized (and characterizes himself) as a rationalist – not because he disputes the Torah's divinity, the accuracy of its transmitted text or even the matter of miracles. Rather it is because he champions the intellect with which God has endowed the human being. God is surely capable of miracles but we do not invoke them in order to resolve textual anomalies in the Torah.

FOR FURTHER STUDY:

(1) Consider Ibn Ezra's lyrical introduction to the Torah in which he lauds man's rational faculty and regards its exercise as the most important means of understanding the word of God. The specific context of his words is his rejection of the allegorical approach popular in Christian circles that refused to take the *mitzvot* literally and instead attempted to explain them as metaphors:

> . . . every *mitzvah* small or great must be weighed in the balance of the heart, because the Eternal One has taken of His wisdom and implanted understanding in our hearts. If reason cannot bear the literal reading or else it conflicts with what our senses plainly indicate, then and only then do we search for an allegorical meaning. This is because the rational faculty is the foundation and the Torah was not given

to a being devoid of understanding. The angel that connects the human to his God is discernment! Therefore, anything that reason does not reject we shall explain according to its straightforward meaning and grammar, and we shall establish it upon its foundation and we shall believe that this is its truth. Why should we grope like blind men, twist the meaning according to our agenda and transform the obvious into the allegorical?!

EIKEV

The Security of the Promised Land

Deuteronomy 7:12–11:25

PARASHAT EIKEV is a continuation of Moshe's impassioned exhortations to Israel, the last of his introductory addresses before he begins the explication of the laws with the following reading of Parashat Re'eh. In Parashat Eikev, Moshe again charges the people of Israel to remain loyal to God's teachings, spelling out the consequences whether good or evil that will befall them as a direct result of their national choices. Once more, he offers them words of strength and encouragement assuring that if they merit God's assistance and help, then the daunting challenge of conquering and settling the land will be accomplished without mishap or setback. And as always, but this time with unusual urgency, he cautions them not to fall prey to Canaan's fetishes of gold and silver, the alluring molten images and their ceremonies that if adopted by the people of Israel will quickly spell their doom.

Moshe reminds the people of the Exodus, when God forcefully intervened to reduce the oppressive Pharaoh and his threatening minions to naught. He recalls the transformative experience of the wilderness wanderings, when steadfast trust in God's providence was acquired not in spite of but rather because of deprivation and want. How the people longed for sustenance and how they anxiously thirsted for water! Only years later, with the hindsight afforded by a lifetime, came Israel's realization that what they truly lacked during that formative period was not food and drink, clothing and physical comfort, but rather a recognition of human dependence upon God and an unshakable faith in both His power as well as His concern to sustain and to preserve them:

> He afflicted you and caused you to hunger, He fed you the manna that you did not know, neither you nor your ancestors, in order to inform you that not by bread alone does man live but rather by all of the words of God does man live! (*Devarim* 8:3).

Moshe, though painfully aware that he himself will not live to enter it, then embarks upon an extended praise of the land of Israel. Describing for his expectant listeners its fertility and its plenty in the most attractive terms, his hopeful words contrast forcefully with his earlier intimations of catastrophe:

> You shall know in your heart that as a parent chastises his child, so too does God your Lord chastise you. You shall observe the commands of God your Lord, to walk in His ways and to revere Him. For God your Lord brings you to a good land, a land of water streams, of springs and deep pools, issuing forth in the valleys and

> from the hills. It is land of wheat and of barley, of grapes, figs and pomegranates; it is a land of olive oil and (date) honey. It is a land in which you shall eat bread without deficiency, you shall lack nothing in it; it is a land whose stones shall yield iron and from whose mountains you shall extract copper. You shall eat and be satisfied, and you shall bless God your Lord concerning the good land that He has given you. Be on guard lest you forget God your Lord . . . (8:5–11)

As the commentaries insightfully point out, the noun "land" occurs in this brief series of seven verses a total of seven times, a sure indication that it is in fact the passage's key expression. Here, Canaan's bounty is tantalizingly spelled out – its abundant sources of water, its golden grains, redolent fruits and luxurious liquids, even the metallic resources embedded deep in its rocky hills. The land's blessing will provide a surfeit of good bread and sweet water, precisely the staples for which the people hungered so mightily during their extended period of aimless wandering through a parched and inhospitable wasteland. But Canaan's rewards will not be extended to the people gratis; in fact, quite the contrary. If the trying experience of the wilderness provided ample opportunity for the people to express discontent and rancor, unveiled resentment and exaggerated complaints, then the produce of the land's fertile hills and valleys will surely demand of them a different, countervailing response: "You shall eat and be satisfied, and you shall bless God your Lord concerning the good land that He has given you." The text thus presents us with a glaring study in contrasts: the scorched and arid wilderness versus the well-watered slopes of the land, the people's pained and impetuous outcries versus their measured and sincere praises of the provider.

Egypt and Canaan

The uniqueness of the new land, just beyond the Yarden but forever beyond Moshe's reach, is the theme that concludes this Parasha as well, where yet another contrast is spelled out:

> For the land that you now enter to possess is not like the land of Egypt from which you have gone forth, where you would plant your seeds and then irrigate them after the manner of the garden of vegetables. But the land which you go over to inherit is a land of hills and vales; from the rains of the heavens you shall drink water. It is a land that God your Lord seeks constantly, the eyes of God your Lord are upon it from the beginning of the year until its end. (11:10–12)

In this passage, the Torah contrasts the new land that the people of Israel will soon enter with the land of Egypt that they had long ago left behind, though they still remember it fondly. The latter had to be cultivated through irrigation, while the former depends upon the rains of the heavens. The reason for the startling difference between the two landscapes is suggested by the text: rainfall in Egypt is quite rare. The verdant valley, bounded on either side by the inhospitable sand and rock of the Sahara desert, is instead sustained by the life-giving waters of the Nile River.

This mighty river has its beginnings in the vast lakes of the African interior. Along its entire length, some 6,000 kilometers until it disgorges as a delta into the Mediterranean Sea, many civilizations grew up. The river valley of Egypt that constitutes the final 1,000 kilometer stretch of the Nile, is exceptionally fertile, for the winter and spring run-off of the river is full of nutrients supplied by organic detritus. The ancient Egyptians cultivated their narrow valley industriously, often coaxing two or three crops out of the black earth each growing season. But the work was intensive – the water of the river had to first be directed into large irrigation channels and then brought to the fields at some distance from the water's edge. Later in the season, water had to be stored up in reservoirs, for with the onset of the autumn, the level of the river would begin to decline until the next inundation some eight months later. And of course, it was necessary to carry out much ongoing maintenance of the complex water systems, ensuring that all of the channels, ditches and conduits were in good shape, neither clogged by debris nor rendered inefficient through neglect and disrepair.

In the Canaanite hill country, by contrast, there were no major rivers, only small springs, often seasonal, that were fed by the sometimes intense winter rains. And while the Nile valley was a flat and featureless plain, the hill country of Canaan was uneven and irregular. The hills had to be terraced so that agriculture could be sustained along narrow strips of arable land while the Canaanite farmer depended upon the rainfall exclusively in order to cultivate his crops. It should come as no surprise, by way of digression, that the sun god was worshipped with special zeal during every period of ancient Egyptian history, while in Canaan the storm god Baal, ostensible master of the winds, the rains and the thunderbolt, was venerated with particular affection and fear. In any case, in our passage the Torah seems to be favorably contrasting the land of Egypt with the land of Canaan, as Moshe impresses upon his expectant listeners that life in Canaan will be less arduous, with the physical effort necessary for sustaining agriculture appreciably less due to the direct irrigation provided by the rainfall.

This is in fact Rashi's reading and he quotes an ancient Rabbinic opinion on the matter:

> "[The new land] is not like the land of Egypt" (*Devarim* 11:10) – but rather *better* than it. This assurance was extended to the people of Israel when they left the land of Egypt, for they had said: "Perhaps we will not come to a land as good and as beautiful as this one!" . . . for the land of Egypt is more praiseworthy than all of the other lands, as the verse states "it is like the garden of the Lord" (*Breisheet* 13:10), and . . . the land of Ra'amses where the Israelites dwelt is the choicest land in Egypt, as the verse states "Yosef settled his father and his brothers. He gave them a landed possession in Egypt in the choicest area of Ra'amses, just as Pharaoh had commanded" (47:11). But even that land is not as good as the land of Israel! [For in Egypt] you irrigated the fields after the manner of a garden of vegetables – for which rainfall does not suffice and it must be watered by foot and shoulder, [holding the water and transporting it to the fields]. In the land of Egypt one had to bring water from the Nile with one's feet and then water the fields and one had to disturb one's sleep and expend effort, for the lowlands could be thereby irrigated but not the highlands, and one had to raise the water from the lowlands to the high. But this land [the land of Israel] drinks water "from the rains of the heavens" (*Devarim* 11:11) – you may continue to sleep in your bed while the Holy One Blessed be He does the work for you, irrigating the lowlands and the highlands, the exposed tracts and the unexposed tracts as one. (commentary to 11:10)

For Rashi then, Moshe provides the people with the assurance that, their fond memories of Egypt notwithstanding, life in the new land of Canaan will be appreciably less labor-intensive.

Ramban's Opposing View

In glaring contrast to Rashi, the Ramban provides an alternative and more sobering reading. After quoting Rashi at length, the Ramban retorts:

> The straightforward reading of the passage is that it is stated as a warning, for God means to say to them that "if you observe all of the commandments then you shall possess a land flowing with milk and honey," for God will grant the rains of your land in their due season and the land shall give forth its produce. But realize that this new land is not like the land of Egypt that can be irrigated from the water channels and reservoirs like a garden of vegetables, but it rather is a land of hills and valleys that gets its water from the rainfall and in no other way. It therefore always requires God's sustaining hand to provide it with rain, for it is a very arid land that needs rainfall all of the year. *If you abrogate the will of God so that He will not sustain it with desirable rains, then it becomes a poor land indeed, that can be neither planted nor cultivated, and no crops shall grow upon its slopes.*
>
> All of this is reemphasized in the following section that "if you shall surely hearken to My commandments . . . then I shall grant the rains of your land in their proper season – the early rain and the late rain" (*Devarim* 11:13–15) – that is, always; but if you fail to hearken to My commandments, then God shall "stop up the heavens so that there will not be any rain, and you will be quickly lost – by famine – from upon the good land" (11:17), for you will not be able to live in it when the rainfall fails.
>
> This section therefore provides a *warning* in accordance with the laws of nature and from it we may deduce that even though God is capable of all things and He could effortlessly destroy the inhabitants of Egypt and dry up their rivers and channels, nevertheless the land of Canaan would be more quickly lost should He withhold His powerful rains. The ill person requires more merit and prayer that God should heal him than the well person requires, in order to preserve his healthy state. So too is the divine measure concerning the poor and the wealthy, though God illuminates the eyes of both . . . (commentary to 11:10–12)

For the Ramban, our section contrasts the land of Egypt to the land of Canaan but not, as Rashi maintains, in order to highlight the ease of living that awaits the Israelites on the other side of the Yarden. Quite the opposite. Life in Egypt is actually easier, for the river provides its people with a dependable source of water. The Egyptian farmer labors mightily in order to irrigate his tract of land, but he need rarely fear that his source of water will suddenly dry up. The Nile rises and falls according to a fairly predictable seasonal pattern but it seldom fails entirely. The situation of the farmer in Canaan, however, is many times more precarious. Because he depends upon the rainfall for his sustenance, his is a life of uncertainty and existential insecurity. He raises his eyes heavenwards in anticipation of the winter rains and if those rains fail to materialize, then he and his family are in acute danger. The issue for the Ramban, then, is not the *physical* effort that must be expended in order to wring sustenance from the earth, but rather the *emotional* and *spiritual* outlay that must accompany the process. Put differently, the Egyptian farmer can afford to be complacent for he knows that his source of water (and hence the sustenance that grants him life) is stable, sound, secure and steady. But the Israelite farmer must always be vigilant, for his agricultural successes are tenuous, tied as they are to the vagaries of the seasonal rains.

Lot's Choice

It is instructive to note that Ramban's reading is supported by a citation that Rashi had mentioned above in praise of Egypt: recall that after the shepherds of Avram and Lot had a falling out over insufficient grazing land, Avram offered to solve the dispute by inviting Lot to choose his territory:

> . . . if you go north, then I will go south, and if you go south then I will go north. Lot lifted up his eyes and he saw that the Yarden valley was entirely irrigated. This was before God had destroyed Sodom and Ammorah so that it was *like the garden of God and the land of Egypt*, all the way to Tsoar. Lot therefore chose for himself all of the Yarden valley and he departed . . . (*Breisheet* 13:9–11)

For Lot, seeing the lush and irrigated plain of the Yarden watered by springs located along the river's length, not only was a palpable reminder of Egypt to where the family had temporarily relocated after famine struck Canaan (12:10). It was also – and this is most striking – a subconscious memory of Eden, the mythical garden of God where sumptuousness and serenity reigned!

For Rashi in the name of the Rabbis, life's comforts for the people of Israel in the new land will surpass even Lot's wildest dreams, for when the rains fall in their season then the terraced slopes of Canaan provide Nile-like bounty, but without all of the labor associated with irrigation. But for the Ramban, Lot's desire for the ease of the Yarden valley expresses the same kind of fatal attraction with Egypt that Moshe now warns against: The new land is not like Egypt, where water from the Nile is never lacking and life along its banks is inherently more stable. That is precisely the spiritual danger associated with it! Just as surely as Lot's fateful choice spelled his eventual doom, for he was quickly swept up by Sodom's allure and could not extricate himself from its mire even as the maelstrom approached, so too living along the verdant banks of the Nile carries its own dangers: complacency, a spiritual smugness spawned by abundance, and the estrangement from God that lacking nothing often breeds.

The interpretation of the Ramban goes a long away towards explaining the maddening stress that sometimes overwhelms those that dwell in the land of Israel, until this very day. Sometimes, the challenges seem so insurmountable and the state of stability and equilibrium an elusive and far-off dream. But this very quality of volatility, the shifting sands that seem to underlie so many of our accomplishments in the land, can yet be the source of our strength. For the Ramban, life in the land of Canaan is inherently tenuous for a profound but simple reason: How much harder it is to lose sight of almighty God's ongoing involvement when life itself hangs in the balance! How much easier it is to reach out to God in supplication once the illusions of self-sustainability have been stripped away! For while the farmer in Egypt can mistakenly believe that his efforts will surely secure his survival, the farmer in Israel knows otherwise. They will labor mightily, for such is the lot of man, but it is merciful God alone who will bestow success. Put differently, the dweller in Canaan need never feel abandoned, for dwelling in the land will ensure that he continually seeks out God as his source of strength and comfort. The dependency upon the seasonal rains, and the inherent instability associated with that way of life, are the invitation to reach out to God and to forge an ongoing relationship with Him. And God will not disappoint: "It is a land that God your Lord seeks constantly, the eyes of God your Lord are upon it from the beginning of the year until its end" (*Devarim* 11:12).

FOR FURTHER STUDY:

(1) The comments of the Ramban underscoring the spiritual dangers of Egypt are echoed in a famous remark concerning the curse placed upon the primeval serpent, attributed to the Rebbe of Gur, Yitzchak Meir Rotenberg Alter (19th century, Poland). Recall that in the aftermath of Adam and Chava's transgression, the serpent was cursed by God to "slither upon its belly and to eat the dust of the earth all of the days of its life" (*Breisheet* 3:14). The Rebbe rhetorically asks:

> What sort of a curse is it to eat the dust of the earth? After all, that means that wherever the serpent goes, it will find its food in abundance, as implied by the Rabbis in TB *Yoma* 75a: "If the serpent ascends to the roof it obtains its food and if it descends to the ground it obtains its food!" Rather, the curse is that since the serpent will always find its sustenance readily available, it never needs to turn its eyes heavenwards, to supplicate God and to foster a connection with Him!

The fear of deprivation creates an opportunity for us to build a relationship with God; dependable abundance often breeds estrangement.

RE'EH

The Central Shrine

Deuteronomy 11:26-16:17

PARASHAT RE'EH opens with additional rites to be fulfilled when the people of Israel enter the land, and effectively constitutes the beginning of Moshe's explication of the laws of Sefer Devarim. First, Moshe instructs the people that the "Blessings" and "Curses" are to be publicly proclaimed as they assemble according to tribe in the valley between Mount Gerizim and Mount Eval, after their arrival in the land, and there the war against idolatry and immorality is to be formally initiated (*Devarim* 11:26–32). Moshe goes on to warn the people not to succumb to the attractions of polytheism, cautioning them to wipe out any traces of its widespread worship so that the true God can be served faithfully.

In glaring contrast to the rampant service of idols that takes place "on the high mountains and hills and under every leafy tree" (12:2), the worship of the God of Israel is to be confined to one central temple whose location "God will choose." In consonance with the revolutionary idea of a single, absolute deity, there is to be a single, definite sanctuary where that God is to be served: ". . . there you shall bring your burnt offerings and sacrifices, your tithes and donations, your vows and free-will offerings, the firstborn of your cattle and sheep" (12:6). No local sacrificial shrines are to be erected to God's service, for although prayer is deemed efficacious at every location, sacrifice is an affront when practiced outside of the Temple's precincts.

Moshe reinforces the polemic against idolatry with a series of extreme pronouncements directed against the false prophet (13:2–6), the "inciter" (13:7–12), and the city "led astray" (13:13–19). In all three cases, the elements responsible for the idolatrous undoing are to be destroyed, as the message is forcefully driven home that idol worship cannot be tolerated.

The Parasha then turns to the subject of holiness and, concerning consumption, discusses the permitted and forbidden creatures. Two agricultural laws are afterwards explicated: the rituals of the second tithe and the principles of the Shemitta cycle. In both instances, it is the overarching moral implication of the observances that is highlighted: "The poor shall not cease from the land. Therefore, I command you saying: you shall surely open your hand to your poor relation or countryman" (15:11).

Finally, the seasonal holiday cycle of the three pilgrim festivals of Pesach, Shavuot and Succot is described, and the Parasha concludes much as it began – with a mention of the necessity for a single, central shrine: "Three times a year shall all of your males appear before God your Lord at the location that He shall choose . . ." (16:16).

The History of the National Shrine

What exactly is the necessity for one central sacrificial location for the worship of God? Why is the Torah so adamant that no offerings are to be presented outside of the confines of the Temple? Certainly, the requirement constitutes a fundamental break with prevailing polytheistic practice that endorsed a myriad of sacrificial worship sites dedicated to different deities and scattered the length and breadth of the land. This was especially true in Canaan, where highly heterogeneous landscapes tended to encourage regional and sectarian outlooks, whether in politics, commerce or religion.

Thematically, we tend to draw a straight line from the portable Mishkan in the wilderness to the permanent Temple at Jerusalem, as if the Torah's insistence that sacrificial worship be confined to a single location was forever part and parcel of Israel's biblical history. A careful reading of the sources, however, reveals a more complex picture, as the following lengthy citation from the Mishna *Zevachim*, chapter 14 illustrates:

> Before the Mishkan was erected, sacrifice upon the high places was permitted and the service was performed by the firstborn. After the establishment of the Mishkan, however, the high places were forbidden and the service was performed by the Kohanim. The most holy sacrifices could be eaten only within its perimeter curtains, while sacrifices of lesser sanctity could be consumed anywhere within the Israelite encampment.
>
> When the people came to Gilgal, the high places were again permitted. The most holy sacrifices could be eaten only within the perimeter curtains of the Mishkan, while sacrifices of lesser sanctity could be consumed anywhere.
>
> When the people came to Shilo, the high places were forbidden. [At Shilo] the Mishkan had no ceiling. It was provided with walls of stone below, while the covering above was made of curtains, and it constituted the "resting place" (מנוחה). The most holy sacrifices could be eaten only within its perimeter curtains, while sacrifices of lesser sanctity as well as the second tithe could be consumed anywhere within its field of vision.
>
> When the people came to Nov and to Giv'on, sacrifice upon the high places was again permitted. The most holy sacrifices could be eaten only within the perimeter curtains, while sacrifices of lesser sanctity could be consumed among any of the cities of Israel.
>
> When the people came to Jerusalem, the high places were forbidden and were never permitted again, for it constituted the "possession" (נחלה). The most holy sacrifices could be eaten only within the perimeter walls [of the Temple Mount], while sacrifices of lesser sanctity and second tithe could be consumed only within the city wall. (Mishna *Zevachim* 14:4–8)

The Progression in the Mishna

The above *mishnayot* describe a number of related issues that require further elaboration. In pre-Mishkan days, and dating back to the beginnings of Hebrew history, there was no central sanctuary for the people of Israel, and sacrifices could be offered to God at any location. These so-called "high places" were makeshift altars that were typically located upon the summits of hills or other elevations, while the sacrificial service associated with them would entail little in the way of formal ritual or mandated ceremonial. Any family could take an active part in the ceremony through the agency of their firstborn who would perform the requisite rites. The narratives of Sefer Breisheet correspond to such a reality, for everywhere the patriarchs are described as building makeshift altars and offering spontaneous sacrifices to God (see *Breisheet* 12:7; 12:8; 13:4; 13:18; 21:33; 22:13; 26:25; 28:22; 31:54; 33:20; 35:7; 46:1).

The situation changed dramatically with the completion of the Mishkan about a year after the Exodus, during the beginning of the wilderness wanderings (14th century BCE). This building and its appurtenances, described in exhaustive detail in the second half of Sefer Shemot, ushered in a new period in Israel's religious development. Henceforth, the sacrificial service became a centralized affair, carried out under the rigorous and exclusive jurisdiction of the Kohanim, the priests who descended from Aharon. The reformation had the welcome result of putting an end to informal sacrificial services that, even among Israelites, were more often than not devoted to idolatrous worship rather than homage to the one true God (see, for instance, *VaYikra* 17:1–7). Also, the institution of the Mishkan was an important vehicle for fostering unification of the fractious Israelite tribes, who now rallied around a single central sanctuary.

After the people left the wilderness and crossed into Canaan under the leadership of Yehoshua (13th century BCE), the high places were again permitted, at least as long as the Mishkan was sited at Gilgal and the wars of conquest were being waged. Gilgal, just west of the Yarden and opposite the city of Yericho, was the place where Israel first encamped after they crossed the swollen waters of the river on a radiant spring day some forty years after the Exodus. At Gilgal, the people of Israel renewed the rite of circumcision (*Yehoshua* 5), there they celebrated their first Pesach in the new land, and during the course of the wars of conquest they always returned to Gilgal to regroup. Although sacrifice upon the high places was permitted while the Mishkan stood at Gilgal, the centrality of the national shrine was nevertheless highlighted by the stipulation that certain grades of sacrifices, the most sanctified communal variety, could only be offered and consumed within its boundaries.

Eventually, towards the end of Yehoshua's lifetime, after the tribal territories of Yehuda and Yosef had been apportioned and with the rest of the land soon to be allotted by the aged leader, the people of Israel established the Mishkan at Shilo (13th century BCE):

> The entire congregation of Israel gathered at Shilo and there they set up the Tent of Meeting, for the land was conquered before them. There remained seven tribes from among the people of Israel who had not apportioned their territories . . . Yehoshua cast lots for them in Shilo before God, and there Yehoshua divided the land for the people of Israel according to their tribal divisions. (*Yehoshua* 18:1–10)

The town of Shilo, located some thirty kilometers northeast of Jerusalem, is nestled in the scenic highlands of Efraim, among the rugged hills that form the topographical backbone of the land of Canaan. After the Mishkan's relocation, the high places were again forbidden, and the Shilo sanctuary became the only acceptable venue for the sacrificial service. Also, as the people began to plant crops in the new land and harvested the produce, the practice of the second tithe that is stipulated in our Parasha, began. This portion of the crop – separated every 1st, 2nd, 4th, and 5th years of the agricultural cycle – was to be brought and consumed in the proximity of the Mishkan.

In the end, the sanctuary at Shilo was destroyed by the Philistines (11th century BCE), a traumatic event described in the opening chapters of Sefer Shemuel that ushered in a period of intense instability. Eventually, the sanctuary was re-established, first at Nov and later at Giv'on, and during this time, the high places were again permitted.

Finally, the Temple was built in Jerusalem by Shelomo (10th century BCE), and worship upon the high places was discontinued forever. The sweep of national history concisely described by these Mishnayot – from the aftermath of the Exodus until the building of the Temple – corresponds to a period of over 400 years and includes the most pivotal moments in biblical history: the Exodus, the entry into Canaan, the conquest and beginning of settlement, the period of the Judges, and the dawn of the monarchy. According to the traditional chronology, the Mishkan stood at Gilgal for 14 years, at Shilo for 369 years, and at Nov and Giv'on for 57 years (see Maimonides, Laws of Beit HaBechira 1:2). Taking into account the 40 years of wandering in the wilderness, a total of 480 years therefore elapsed from the Exodus until the building of the Temple at Jerusalem (40 + 14 + 369 + 57 = 480), just as recorded in Sefer Melachim 1:6:1.

The Architectural Account

Interestingly, the Mishna was not content to simply describe the ritual ramifications of the Mishkan's peregrinations, but described its architectural progressions as well: "[At Shilo] the Mishkan had no ceiling. It was provided with walls of stone below, while the covering above was made of curtains . . ." Before Shilo, of course, the Mishkan was a temporary tent-like structure exclusively, as the Exodus narratives describe. Its walls were made of gilded boards of acacia wood that were disassembled and reassembled at every encampment in the wilderness, and its roof consisted of a series of curtains and animal hides that gave it a most tent-like quality (see *Shemot* 26). Hence, the Torah often refers to it as the "Tent of Meeting," and the term "Mishkan" is often translated as "Tabernacle" (40:2, etc.). Once established at Shilo, however, the temporary and modular walls of acacia wood, fastened together using an ingenious system of golden bars and rings, were stored away forever, and the walls of the Mishkan were built out of stalwart stone. The cover of textiles and skins, however, was retained. At Jerusalem, the Temple was constructed with permanent walls of stone as well as with a sturdy roof of cedar beams, and every interior surface was extravagantly covered with pure gold (see *Melachim* 1:6:9, 22).

Considering this architectural account carefully, a startling observation emerges: the architectonic progression in the building envelope of the Mishkan perfectly parallels the story of the people of Israel as they themselves experience the process of securing permanent settlement in the land! In other words, as long as the people were confined to the wilderness, the Mishkan was an exclusively temporary affair that reflected that nomadic condition. As soon as they entered the land and embarked on the wars of conquest, a precarious transition began to unfold, underscored in the ritual life of the Mishkan by the interim suspension of the ban on sacrifice at the high places.

Eventually, after Yehoshua completed the wars of conquest, the Mishkan was established at Shilo, but this time as a fixed sanctuary taking on the trappings of permanence. While the tent-like and temporary cover was preserved, the walls were fashioned out of impervious rock to indicate that the people of Israel had achieved an important milestone in their national development – they had succeeded in entering the land and had started to strike down roots in its fertile red earth. Historically, the period of Shilo corresponded to the rule of the Judges, a tenuous era during which central authority was lacking, inspiration was in short supply, external threats were myriad, and tribal unity was still an unrealized dream. But the process of securing the land, though plagued by struggle and setbacks, was nevertheless underway.

In the end, the Mishkan at Shilo was destroyed by the Philistines, a technologically advanced but morally primitive coastal people who opposed the Israelite expansion at every step. For a time, instability reigned, until the prophet Shemuel arose to guide the people and to later lay the groundwork for the establishment of the monarchy. At this time, the Mishkan was again temporary, now at Nov, then at Giv'on, as first King Shaul and finally David ascended to the throne. In the meantime, the high places returned to vogue, highlighting the provisional character of the era as well as its dangerous instability.

It was David who decisively succeeded in unifying the tribes and in neutralizing Israel's enemies, eventually founding the national capital in Jerusalem and initiating the process of building the Temple. Shelomo his son built that edifice, upon sacred Mount Moriah, as the prolonged odyssey of the people of Israel finally came to an end. The national stability, unity of purpose, security from external threats and cultural ascendancy that Israel enjoyed during the brief period of his reign corresponded to the building of the Temple, a building that was structurally permanent in every sense of the term. Again, the fortunes of the people were perfectly mirrored by the fate of their holy place, for towering above Jerusalem, the Temple told the story of Israel finally achieving stability and rootedness in their land.

Actually, the connection between the Mishkan and the process of Israel's settlement of the land should not be that surprising. As the concrete expression of God's abode on earth among the people of Israel, the fortunes of the Mishkan ought to reflect the travails and triumphs of the Jewish nation. As much as God's presence is among them and His concern is not far removed, the Mishkan or Temple reflects that condition. No wonder that in the biblical frame of mind, the exile of the nation of Israel from its land as well as the promise of their eventual restoration were both inextricably bound up with the fortunes of the Temple: its tragic destruction on the one hand and the prophetic vision of its ultimate rebuilding on the other. And thus it is that the ancient yearning for the Temple's re-establishment upon its holy mountain, never entirely extirpated from the national Jewish heart even by exile's harsh travails, corresponds to our eternal longing for a complete reconciliation with the God of Israel.

Linking the Narrative Books of the Prophets to the Fate of the Mishkan

To complete the picture, we note that these epochs of Israel's biblical history closely follow the chronological outline of the prophetic books of the Tanakh. Sefer Yehoshua is almost entirely transitional, and the narratives told within its pages therefore correspond to the Mishkan leaving the wilderness, arriving at Gilgal and, towards the end of the book, finally arriving at Shilo as the settlement drive begins in earnest. The events of Sefer Shoftim, full as they are of the painful struggle to found a nation and to unite it around its mission, all take place while the Mishkan stands at Shilo, more established and secure but vulnerable nonetheless.

Sefer Shemuel opens with the Mishkan's destruction, as the uncertain and perilous passage from the rule of the Judges to the founding of the monarchy unfolds. Without exception, the events of the book transpire while the Mishkan is temporally located first at Nov and then at Giv'on, while all the while the rival high places enjoy a resurgence – a direct expression of the uncertainty of the times.

Finally, Sefer Melachim begins with the ascent of Shelomo to the throne. Full of talent and spiritual ambition, thoughtful enough to make good use of all of his father David's thorough preparatory work, Shelomo quickly consolidates his rule and then embarks upon the most memorable accomplishment of his illustrious reign: the building of the Temple at Jerusalem. The remainder of Sefer Melachim, of course, is bound up with the physical fortunes of this edifice, and when the people of Israel are exiled to the rivers of Babylon at the book's conclusion, the Temple is razed to the ground.

This Shilo-Jerusalem nexus, representing two distinct but linked stages of national consolidation – the beginning of settlement on the one hand and the securing of permanence on the other – is suggested by an illuminating verse from our Parasha that holds the key to comprehending the matter. As Moshe prepares to take his leave of the people forever, he again exhorts them to follow God's commands and encourages them to remain steadfast in the new land:

> Do not do as all of us now do here today, everyone as he sees fit in his own eyes. For you have not yet arrived at the state of rest (מנוחה) or possession (נחלה) that God your Lord gives to you. You shall traverse the Yarden River and dwell in the land that God your Lord causes you to possess, and He will grant you rest from all of your enemies around and you shall dwell in security! Then, at the place that God your Lord shall choose to cause His name to dwell there you shall present all that I command you, your burnt offerings and sacrifices, your tithes and dues, and all of your best vow offerings that you shall promise to God . . . (*Devarim* 12:8–11)

Moshe tells them that although the process of settling the land will be drawn out and difficult, mirrored by the relaxation of the Torah's prohibition concerning the high places, one day they shall enjoy national peace and tranquility, and at that time they will build a sanctuary to God and serve Him there exclusively. One day they will achieve the state of rest that will mark their securing of a viable and permanent state, to be reflected by the establishment of an enduring edifice to God's glory, a Temple. Significantly, the early sources identified this state of rest with Shilo and the state of possession with Jerusalem (Sifre Devarim 66), as spelled out in the Mishna quoted above:

> When the people came to Shilo, the high places were forbidden. [At Shilo] the Mishkan had no ceiling. It was provided with walls of stone below, while the covering above was made of curtains, and it constituted the "resting place" (מנוחה) . . . When the people came to Jerusalem, the high places were again forbidden and were never permitted again, for it constituted the "possession" (נחלה) . . .

Perhaps, then, we have found an answer to our earlier query. While it is obvious that the designation of a single national shrine has many advantages, the text of our Parasha alludes to more subtle truths. Not only does a central location foster political unity while discouraging dangerous heterodoxy, not only does it reflect the unique Israelite conception of a single, transcendent deity and its critical corollary of an absolute morality, but it also speaks worlds about the historic destiny of the people of Israel. Israel as a nation has a mission in the world, and our Parasha makes clear that our mission is bound up with a land. Geographically scattered among other nations, possessing political and economic power but shorn of national sovereignty, we shall never achieve it. Settled in Canaan but subject to ongoing external threats, or else rooted in the land but blinded by the materiality that the other nations so ardently worship, achieving our destiny will also continue to remain beyond our grasp.

It is only by recognizing Israel's existential need for a central sanctuary – the necessity for national unity, for recognition of the one God and for the embrace of absolute moral standards – that there is hope for the fulfillment of Israel's mission, a mission that is mirrored by the fortunes of that place. To truly understand Shilo and Jerusalem and the stages in between is to realize that history has a purpose and Israel a goal. The Exodus unleashed a process of God-involvement in human history that the people of Israel were chosen to champion and to advance. That process unfolded as Israel entered the land and settled it, and continued to unfold even when Israel was forced into exile. Now in repossession of our ancient patrimony, we stand at a historic crossroads. If we can overcome disunity and religious apathy to again champion the God-idea and the ethical conduct that it must imply, then the rebuilt Temple at Jerusalem can yet serve as the meeting point for all of mankind, so that God's healing instruction can issue forth from its holy precincts to repair our tattered world: ". . . for you have not yet arrived at the state of rest or possession that God your Lord gives to you. You shall traverse the Yarden River and dwell in the land that God your Lord causes you to possess, and He will grant you rest from all of your enemies around and you shall dwell in security! Then, at the place that God your Lord shall choose to cause His name to dwell there you shall present all that I command you . . ."

FOR FURTHER STUDY:

(1) The link between the Exodus and the building of the Temple is actually introduced very early in our national history. Recall that after the Israelites successfully traversed Yam Suf, they sang a paean to God praising Him for His overthrow of the cruel Egyptians. In the song, Israel expressed not only gratitude for the present salvation but also profound hopes for the future. Anticipating their journey towards the land, they prayed that their enemies would melt away so that they could enter and settle it unopposed:

> Bring them in and plant them upon the mount of Your possession,
> You have established a place for Your dwelling God,
> the Temple, Almighty, Your hands have established!
> God will reign forever and ever! (*Shemot* 15:17–18)

These impassioned words, eschatological in tone, anticipate the building of the Temple and present it as the culmination of the project known as the "Exodus from Egypt." While the people of Israel glimpsed transcendence and responded with impassioned song, they could scarcely have appreciated that the process would take almost five centuries!

SHOFTIM

Returning from the Front

Deuteronomy 16:18-21:9

As ISRAEL encamps on the Yarden's eastern bank, anxious to enter the new land but also filled with apprehension, Moshe continues his final address. He has already reviewed with them the pivotal episodes of their national history, recalling the Revelation, the golden calf and the incident of the spies. He has reminded them of their astounding victories, first over Pharaoh and later over the Amorite kings, emphasizing to them that they need not fear as long as they remain steadfast in their faith. And he has impressed upon them repeatedly that their achievements as a people will depend upon the choices that they make: keep God's charge and succeed, abrogate it and perish.

Now Moshe turns his attention to national concerns, to the instruments and to the institutions that will regulate Israel's life as a people in the new land. First, he describes the need for a functioning judiciary, for devoted judges who are accessible yet impartial, learned but involved. He calls for officers, who will fearlessly enforce the rulings of the judges and ensure that the laws are observed (*Devarim* 16:18–20). Next, he emphasizes the necessity of a priesthood, not only to perform the rituals but also to interpret the Torah, to instruct the people in God's ways and to inspire them to follow Him (17:8–13). Then, he raises the issue of a king, setting out the parameters of a monarchial system that is meant not to replace God with a temporal ruler but rather to complement His dominion with good and equitable governance (17:14–20). Finally, Moshe mentions the matter of a prophet, reassuring the people that God's direct communications to them will continue even after his demise (18:15–22). The discussion concerning these four critical offices – judiciary, priesthood, king and prophet – that together constitute a rudimentary but effective system of checks and balances, is interspersed with a number of references to the hazards of idolatry and to the attendant need to extirpate it utterly. Where idolatry thrives, Moshe indicates, Godliness withers and moral corruption holds sway.

There is one more topic that is featured prominently in our Parasha and in many other sections of Sefer Devarim, a matter that is especially pertinent to a people about to enter a new land, and that concerns the issue of warfare. In fact, most of the second half of Parashat Shoftim is devoted to this subject (chapter 20), and the discussion continues into the next Parasha as well. As Sefer Devarim progresses and the people draw closer and closer to their destiny, the discussion takes on a more practical as well as a more urgent quality. Our Parasha introduces the subject with an inspirational flourish, and this is quickly followed by the particulars concerning what might be termed "non-obligatory warfare."

This type of conflict, known in the Rabbinic sources as מלחמת רשות is a type of war in which it is resources and not lives that are at stake. Israel, after its biblically-mandated borders have been secured, may choose to engage in *milchemet reshut* in order to obtain additional assets or else to enhance its strategic depth by seizing the territory of belligerent but currently non-engaging foes. Since this type of conflict is regarded as being less urgent than a direct response to unprovoked enemy attack, the Torah provides a number of important exemptions from what would otherwise amount to universal conscription:

> When you go out to war against your foes, if you should see horses, chariots and armies that outnumber you, then do not be afraid of them, for God your Lord is with you who took you out of the land of Egypt. When you draw close to the battlefield, then the priest shall step forward and address the people. He shall say to them: "Hearken Israel, today you draw close to wage war against your enemies. Let not your heart be irresolute, neither fear nor be afraid nor be frightened from before them! For God your Lord goes before you, to fight your enemies on your behalf and to save you!"
>
> The officers will then address the people saying: "Is there a man who has built a new house but has not yet dedicated it? If so, then let him return to his house, lest he die in battle and another man dedicate it instead. And is there a man who has planted a vineyard but has not yet eaten of its fruit? If so, then let him return to his house, lest he die in battle and another man eat of it instead. And is there a man who has betrothed a woman but has not yet taken her in marriage? If so, then let him return to his house, lest he die in battle and another man take her instead." Then the officers shall continue to say: "Who is the man that is afraid and timorous? Let him go and return to his house, so that he will not melt the hearts of his fellows like his own!" When the officers have finished addressing the people, then they shall appoint the captains of the army to lead the people . . . (20:1–9)

Not Succumbing to Fear and Despondency

The overall theme of the section concerns the necessity of the armed forces to maintain their composure, to enter the fray with confidence and with fortitude. Even when the odds seem less than sanguine, many a more powerful foe has been defeated by a combination of strategy, motivation, and the conviction that one's cause is just. The message that the priest is to forcefully convey to the people as they advance to the battlefield is that God will not abandon His people to defeat, as long as they trust in Him.

Perhaps the exemptions from active service that follow the address of the Kohen are to be understood as directly related to this underlying theme. Let these four types of "warriors" leave the battlefield, for how can they be expected to fight with fortitude when their minds are so clearly preoccupied with other thoughts? Success on the battlefield depends foremost upon concentration and focus; all of life's myriad plans, hopes and dreams must be effectively held in abeyance until victory is achieved. The house builder, the planter of the vineyard and certainly the one engaged to marry cannot be devoted with single-mindedness to the task at hand because their other concerns refuse to be ignored and can thus become a lethal distraction. In effect, all of these three can be understood as constituting a thematic expansion of the final exemption in the list: the one who is afraid to fight. This man whose craven heart is consumed by dread is sent home because he may come to weaken the resolve of his compatriots. Panic can spread quickly through the ranks, and the fearful man is therefore wisely exempted before his feelings of timidity become contagious. But in essence, the coward is excused because he too cannot concentrate on the matter of the clash, so consumed is he with his own fears and uncertainties. In essence, the justification for all four of the exemptions may have been inspired by the same fundamental idea. Understanding the matter this way sheds light on the structure of the passage as a whole: isn't the section entirely about overcoming fear? Let us read the verses again with the key words highlighted:

> When you go out to war against your foes, if you should see horses, chariots and armies that outnumber you then do not be *afraid* of them, for God your Lord is with you who took you out of the land of Egypt. When you draw close to the battlefield, then the priest shall step forward and address the people. He shall say to them: "Hearken Israel, today you draw close to wage war against your enemies. Let not your heart be *irresolute*, neither *fear* nor be *afraid* nor be *frightened* from before them! For God your Lord goes before you, to fight your enemies on your behalf and to save you!"
>
> The officers will then address the people saying: "Is there a man who has built a new house but has not yet dedicated it? If so, then let him return to his house, lest he die in battle and another man dedicate it instead. And is there a man who has planted a vineyard but has not yet eaten of its fruit? If so, then let him return to his house, lest he die in battle and another man eat of it instead. And is there a man who has betrothed a woman but has not yet taken her in marriage? If so, then let him return to his house, lest he die in battle and another man take her instead." Then the officers shall continue to say: "Who is the man who is *afraid* and *timorous*? Let him go and return to his house, so that he will not *melt the hearts* of his fellows as his own"! When the officers shall finish addressing the people, then they shall appoint the captains of the army to lead the people . . . (20:1–9)

This eminently rational approach to the passage, no doubt inspired by a reading of the broader context, is independently advanced by three of the medieval commentaries, a sure sign that it is on the mark. The Rashbam, the Ibn Ezra, and the Ramban all agree that the house builder, vine planter and engaged suitor are released from battle because of their inability to focus upon the fray. In effect, their exemption is not fundamentally different on an emotional and psychological level than the man stricken with fear of battle who cannot keep his mind on the immediate task – defeating the enemy. As the Ramban concisely puts it, borrowing from the vocabulary that the Torah utilized to describe the one whose *heart* is stricken with fear:

> The Torah commanded concerning all three of these that they should return [from the front] because his *heart* is upon his home, his vineyard and his wife, and he will therefore flee . . . (commentary to 20:5)

Rashi's Reading

Remarkably, though, Rashi offers a completely different reading than his colleagues, arguing that the builder of a new home returns from battle "lest he die in battle and another man dedicate it, and this is something that torments the soul . . ." (commentary to 20:5). Although Rashi does not repeat the comment concerning the other exemptions, they presumably all relate to this overarching idea. How troubling and disconcerting it is when young men die in battle, their vivid plans for the future tragically and suddenly cut short by a cruel and capricious fate! And when a young man has already began the process of building his life in earnest, by erecting a home, planting a vineyard or engaging a woman, then the tragedy is magnified, for the loss now encompasses a wider circle of constructive potential destroyed. That someone else should complete the task began by that young man is paradoxically not a source of comfort but rather of greater vexation, for it highlights the gaping hole that his untimely demise has rent in the fabric of his family and larger community of which he had been part.

For Rashi then, what is at stake is not the morale of the fighters in battle but rather that of the civilians that remain behind and constitute the home front. In order that the people of Israel not lose their resolve, in order that particularly tragic losses are minimized (though every loss is indescribably tragic), these three are released from service lest they perish in battle. Significantly for Rashi, the exemption granted to the man afraid of fighting, the fainthearted individual sent home so as not to unsettle and unnerve his company, is completely independent of these three and unrelated to their discharge.

Support can be adduced for Rashi's unconventional reading from a seemingly unrelated passage from Sefer Yirmiyahu. There, the prophet addresses the people of Jerusalem who had been exiled to the rivers of Babylon towards the very end of the First Temple period. The destruction of the Jewish commonwealth happened incrementally over the course of many years, and there were a number of waves of exile to Babylon even before Jerusalem was besieged and conquered. In this poignant passage, Yirmiyahu conveys God's comforting words to the people. They are to build new lives for themselves in Babylon, for they will not be returning to Jerusalem any time soon:

> These are the words of the scroll that Yirmiyahu the prophet sent from Jerusalem to the rest of the elders of the diaspora and to the priests, prophets and all of the people that Nevuchadnezzar had exiled from Jerusalem to Babylon… [It said]: Thus says God of hosts Lord of Israel to all of the deportees that I have exiled from Jerusalem to Babylon: "Build houses and dwell in them, plant gardens and eat their fruit. Take wives and beget sons and daughters, and take wives for your sons and give your daughters in marriage to men and let them beget sons and daughters, and increase there and do not become less. Seek the peace of the city to which I have exiled you and pray on its behalf to God, for in its peace you too shall have peace . . . for thus says God: in accordance with seventy full years for Babylon shall I remember you and establish with you all of My good words, to return you to this place . . ." (*Yirmiyahu* 29:1–9)

Yirmiyahu, in his efforts to convince the émigrés that they would be remaining in exile for a lengthy period of time, describes three pursuits that are indicative of striking down roots in a new place and restoring lives that had been destroyed: building houses, planting gardens, and taking wives in marriage, the very three things (and in the same order!) that had been presented in our Parasha as the basis of the permission granted to return from the front. The exiles from Jerusalem, their earlier lives shattered and demolished, their home towns in ruins and their former fields abandoned and unsown, are reassured by Yirmiyahu that in Babylon they will yet prosper. God will show compassion towards them and ultimately restore them to their land, but until that time they are to rehabilitate themselves and rebuild their lives on foreign soil.

A Modern Application of Rashi's Reading

Rashi's explanation is thus vindicated, for it is precisely because the three pursuits enumerated in the Parasha and in Sefer Yirmiyahu are in the national interest, especially in times of war, that they must be continued even as the battle rages. For the house to remain incomplete, the vineyard untended and the woman bereft of her future husband, is for society at large to surrender to despondency, to be overwhelmed by the war and to give up hope of a brighter future. Now surely it is true that in the end the house can be completed by someone else, the vineyard tended by another, and the woman married to a new suitor. But Rashi wants to emphasize that the Torah's objective in this legislation is not simply that Israel should prevail in the short term through military means but rather that they should also triumph in the long term, by continuing to celebrate life: to build cities, to cultivate the earth and to raise children even during the course of the conflict. Let these men return and eschew warfare so that they might show their compatriots through their concrete acts of building a future that real victory over the enemy means never succumbing to despair. Let the creative pursuits of building cities, planting fields and raising children serve as a signal to all that life will triumph over death and Israel over its enemies!

Rashi's life-affirming reading resonates for us as well, even as we are removed from the original biblical context of his remarks by thousands of years. For more than a century, from the time that Jews began to return to the land of their ancestors en masse in order to reconstitute their state and up until the present day, the people of the modern state of Israel have been subjected to unrelenting attack by their foes. Sometimes this warfare has been overt and obvious for all to see; often, it has been "low intensity" and largely unreported in the world media, but it has never ceased for even one single moment. Jews in the land of Israel have had to defend themselves constantly from enemy armies and from terrorist attacks, from the unremitting incitement fomented by their supposed peace partners as well as from constant calls from near and far for the dismantling of their enterprise.

Miraculously, however, the Jews of Israel have managed not only to survive but to prosper as well. Their democratic state has become a local superpower – a cultural, political, financial and scientific marvel thriving in a lackluster regional landscape otherwise populated by oppressive, entrenched oligarchies characterized by economic and technological stagnation, state suppression of individual rights and widespread cultural decay. Largely, this remarkable success has been fueled by the very optimism that the Torah demands of us in our section. Even while engaging in warfare, the people of Israel have insisted on continuing to build. Even as so many precious sons have been lost, Israel's thirst for life has not been quenched and their dreams for a better future have not been shattered. As a people, we are called upon to not only endure but to flourish, not only to survive but to thrive and to increase. This is accomplished by insisting on continued building and growth, physical as well as spiritual, even as destruction sometimes stares us in the face. May God grant us the fortitude to prevail.

FOR FURTHER STUDY:

(1) TB *Sotah* 44a, in a life-affirming observation based upon the three exemptions enumerated in our Parasha, supports Rashi's exegesis:

> Our Rabbis taught: [The verses list] one who builds (a house), one who plants (a vineyard) and one who betroths. The Torah thus teaches us about proper conduct, namely that a man ought to first build a house, then plant a vineyard and only then get married. Shelomo also similarly said in his wisdom: "Establish your livelihood outside and get ready what you have in the field, and then build your home." (*Mishle* 24:27)

The Talmudic rabbis are suggesting that the thoughtful way of conducting one's affairs is to first secure a home and a livelihood and only then to become married, so that one will be able to house and support one's family. For our purposes, we note that the three pursuits of our Parasha are here understood to be the basis of a successful approach to living. See also Maimonides in his Laws of Character Traits 5:11. *Devarim* 28:30 links the tragic termination of these three things to the dissolution of society.

KI TETZE

Sending Away the Mother Bird

Deuteronomy 21:10-25:19

MOSHE'S LIFE and the book of Devarim that constitutes his parting words draw inexorably closer to their conclusion. His impassioned exhortations that opened the book had been followed by a systematic review of the Torah's *mitzvot*, in order to prepare the people for the new life awaiting them on the other side of the Yarden River. Parashat Ki Tetze is replete with a great variety of those *mitzvot*; in fact, there is no Parasha in the Torah that contains more. While many have been presented elsewhere in the Torah, some are introduced here for the very first time. One of the most intriguing of these *mitzvot* concerns the "bird's nest," and as we shall see, the commentaries' analyses of this passage yields some very valuable ideas.

> If you come across a bird's nest on any tree or on the ground, and it contains baby chicks or eggs, you must not take the mother along with her young. You shall surely send away the mother first and only then may you take the young, in order that you might enjoy goodness and length of days. (*Devarim* 22:6–7)

In general, the Torah text does not offer the reader a rationale for specific *mitzvot* and this case is no exception. The outline of the act, however, is clear: an individual who happens to pass a nest and desires to take the eggs or chicks for himself may not do so as long as the mother bird is present. Rather, the mother bird must first be sent away and only then may the young be taken. The Torah then indicates a reward for proper observance of the rite: goodness and length of days. Rabbi Avraham Ibn Ezra provides an interpretation that is compelling:

> The reason for this mitzvah is that expunging the mother with her young constitutes cruelty of heart, as the Prophet Hoshea describes "the mother dashed to pieces with her young" (*Hoshea* 10:14). This is also the rationale for the Torah's prohibition concerning slaughter of the cow and her offspring on the same day (*Va Yikra* 22:28).

In his characteristically terse comments concerning *Shemot* 23:19 forbidding one "to seethe a kid in its mother's milk," Ibn Ezra remarks:

> There is no need for us to search for the rationale behind this injunction, for even the wise cannot explain it. Perhaps the Torah prohibits this act because it is cruelty of heart to boil a kid in its mother's milk, just as we are forbidden to kill a cow and its offspring on the same day or *to take the mother bird along with its young*."

For Ibn Ezra, it is clear that all three of these *mitzvot* draw their inspiration from a single source: to kill a mother creature and its offspring at the same time betrays an inexcusable lack of sensitivity to life. Significantly for the Ibn Ezra, it is not the feelings of the mother animal that are at the core of the legislation, for he nowhere states that the aim of the injunctions is to minimize her pain on seeing her offspring taken from her or put to death. In fact, in the case of seething the kid in its mother's milk, or slaughtering the offspring on the same day, the mother is not even necessarily present. Rather, it is the *character of the person* that is of paramount concern – the indiscriminate destruction of life, symbolized by the mother perishing along with her young, is what is too abhorrent for the Torah to countenance.

This reading is supported by the Ibn Ezra's proof text from Sefer Hoshea, for in context the verses there describe the ghastly aftermath of a skirmish in which the enemy wantonly exterminated not only the lives of the vanquished but their own moral conscience as well: ". . . Therefore shall a tumult arise among your people, and all of your fortresses shall be plundered, just as Shalmon conquered Bet Arbel on the day of battle, when the mothers were dashed to pieces with their young" (*Hoshea* 10:14). The identity of Shalmon and the battle of Bet Arbel have been lost in the sands of time, but the prophet chillingly preserved the memory of flagrant disdain for the sanctity of life: mothers slaughtered along with their children.

Parenthetically, we may now better appreciate Ya'acov's anxious characterization of his brother Esav on the eve of their confrontation. Recall that when Ya'acov was fearfully preparing to meet his estranged brother after an absence of twenty-odd years, he implored God's mercy: "Please save me from the hands of my brother, from the grasp of Esav, for I fear that he will strike me and slay the mothers along with the children" (*Breisheet* 32:12). Esav's predilection for barbarity, his lack of any moral compunctions, is implied by Ya'acov's plea: Esav will spare no one, slaying even the mothers with their children.

The Rashbam is in substantial agreement with Ibn Ezra, his contemporary, as indicated by his comments concerning the prohibition of seething a kid in its mother's milk:

> It is a crude and gluttonous act to consume the milk of the mother along with her offspring. This resembles the other prohibitions of slaughtering a mother and its offspring on the same day, as well as the command to send away the mother bird before taking the young. The Torah desires to inculcate civilized behavior through these enactments. (commentary to *Shemot* 23:19)

On our passage, the Rashbam amplifies his earlier comments: "It is an act of cruelty and gluttony to take away, slaughter and cook a mother with its offspring" (commentary to *Devarim* 22:6).

In his brief words, the Rashbam shows that a careful reader of the text can detect the Torah's desire to broaden these narrow ritual observances into character-shaping experiences. Thus, we have one law that speaks of lambs or kids and sheep or goats (seething a kid in its mother's milk), a second law that mentions cattle (slaughtering a cow and its offspring on the same day), and a third that addresses birds (sending away the mother bird). The implication is clear: the Torah wants us to have sensitivity to all other creatures, especially those with whom we tend to have the most interaction. At the same time, the Rashbam suggests that there is deliberateness in the Torah's discussion of *taking* the chicks or eggs away from the mother bird, *slaughtering* a cow and its offspring on the same day and *cooking* a kid in its mother's milk. These three acts describe three distinct stages in the process of exercising control over other creatures: we take them from nature, we kill them, and we prepare them for consumption. The Torah therefore is suggesting that humane and compassionate behavior is required at every juncture of our interaction, even during the final act of cooking by which time the link between the mother and the offspring has already long been severed!

In sum, Ibn Ezra and Rashbam both demonstrate that the specific ritual of sending away the mother bird has comprehensive application. This they do by linking our context of the bird with the others concerning the cow and the kid. We should note that each one of these prohibitions occurs in a different book of the Torah (*Devarim*, *VaYikra* and *Shemot* respectively), supporting their thesis that we are dealing with a pervasive foundation principle. The prohibition of taking the life of the mother with its young, in all of its variations, therefore addresses a much broader concern – the Torah demands that we recognize the sanctity of all life.

Exegetically, Ibn Ezra adds one important point concerning the reward:

> "You shall merit length of days" – because you did not destroy the whole nest and left behind its main element. (*Devarim* 22:7)

The Torah's unusual description of a reward associated with this ritual – length of days – parallels the rationale behind the act. By not taking the mother together with the young we not only have avoided an act of gratuitous cruelty. We have also allowed for the possibility of the species to regenerate, for if the mother bird remains behind then she can still lay more eggs and raise more chicks to maturity. By ensuring "length of days" for the birds, one merits "length of days" for oneself as well. To respect life is to merit life.

Maimonides and Concern with Emotional Anguish

In his philosophical Guide to the Perplexed, Maimonides addresses the mitzvah of שילוח הקן or sending away the mother bird.

> The command concerning correct slaughter is essential, for proper nutrition depends upon vegetation as well as upon meat. The healthiest meats come from those animals that the Torah has permitted us to consume, as any physician knows. Since our nutritional needs depend upon the consumption of other creatures, the Torah has mandated for us the most painless and humane method of killing them. Thus, one is forbidden to cause unnecessary pain to those animals by using methods of slaughter that are slow or less effective, or by cutting off a limb from a living creature.
>
> The prohibition of slaughtering the mother and her offspring on the same day is a safeguard, lest one come to kill the offspring in front of its mother. The anguish that the mother would suffer under those circumstances is very great, for there is no difference between the pain of a human being and the pain of an animal in that situation. After all, the love and concern of a creature for its young is not a function of enhanced cognitive ability, but rather of emotional states that are common to most higher life forms. The Torah has limited this law to the cow, sheep and goat, for these domesticated creatures are the ones that we typically consume, and in these cases the mother of the offspring can generally be identified.

> This is also the reason for the command to send away the mother bird. By doing so, her anguish is minimized when the eggs and chicks are taken away. Additionally, the eggs that she has already roosted upon as well as the young chicks are generally unfit for human consumption. It is therefore likely that the person will, in the end, decide to leave the nest untouched. If the Torah shows concern for the emotional wellbeing of animals and birds, all the more so should this be true of our concern for human beings in general. I maintain that the *mitzvot* have a rationale and are not simply divine imperatives . . . (Guide to the Perplexed 3:48)

In the above passage, Maimonides teaches us that the Torah is concerned not only with the physical pain but also with the emotional feelings of lower creatures. Although we are permitted to consume other animals, we must be especially careful not to cause undue distress and suffering in the process. The method of killing must therefore be quick and immediate and we must avoid causing any emotional torment, by not dispatching the offspring in the presence of its mother. Although humanity is separated from other creatures by an unbridgeable chasm – we possess reason, moral choice, and awareness of God – with respect to innate emotion and feeling, we are the same. Every mother feels compassion for its young and experiences intense pain when the natural bond of parenthood is unexpectedly and cruelly severed. However, explains Maimonides, the aim of the Torah's legislation is not to create a kinder, gentler world for animals, but rather to fashion a more compassionate world for people!

Maimonides concludes his remarks with what might be mistakenly regarded as an afterthought, but it is actually pivotal: "I maintain that the *mitzvot* have a rationale and are not simply divine imperatives . . ." Some of us believe that the *mitzvot* of the Torah are nothing more and nothing less than divine decrees that have no rational basis, and that from our point of reference are arbitrary. According to such a conceptual model, the attempt to comprehend God's commands according to logical or moral principles is unproductive and misguided. We perform God's commands because that is His will and not because we understand His will. To take our example, the mitzvah to send away the mother bird has nothing to do with inculcating compassion and kindness but is simply a divine directive. As the Talmudic view advocating this approach states: "God's attributes are not expressions of compassion and mercy, but rather definitive decrees" (Mishna *Berachot* 5:3).

Maimonides vehemently disagrees with this approach. According to his view, the *mitzvot* can be comprehended rationally because they have a rational basis. Maimonides concurs (and here he parts ways with some modern exponents of his view) that performance of the *mitzvot* does not *hinge* on understanding them; rather, we must perform them because we are subject to God's sovereignty and not because we feel that they are reasonable. For Maimonides, just because we don a rationalist mantle does not grant us the license to jettison *mitzvot* that we do not comprehend or those that strike us as anachronistic. At the same time, however, the *mitzvot* are not to be construed as unfathomable acts that are to be performed solely as expressions of our allegiance to the supreme being. Rather, they are inherently meaningful activities that human logic and analysis can grasp and appreciate and that our divinely-inspired moral will can recognize as good.

Comparisons and Contrasts

Although Maimonides' approach of shunning savagery agrees with the views of Ibn Ezra and Rashbam, there are nevertheless a number of subtle but significant differences between them. According to Maimonides, the passages can be understood in the most direct and straightforward way. Send away the mother bird so that she does not suffer the pain of seeing her young taken from her. Do not slaughter the mother and its offspring on the same day so that you will not come to slaughter the offspring in its mother's presence.

For Ibn Ezra and Rashbam, on the other hand, there is a more nuanced message that must be extrapolated from the specific injunctions. Their thesis of the sanctity of life is an abstract inference that naturally arises from the three cases. The Torah mandates the sending away of the mother bird so that one does not come to kill the mother and the chicks. The injunctions concerning seething the kid in its mother's milk or killing the animal and its offspring on the same day are understood as protests against a savage worldview that would sanction ruthless and indiscriminate killing. To kill a mother and its young is to extirpate man's ethical sense; it is the abnegation of any noble higher purpose to which man must aspire. It is not a concern with the pain of a *specific* mother or offspring that lies at the core of the Torah's legislation, but rather with the more inclusive (and elusive!) aim of indelibly imprinting upon the human psyche the ideal of life's inestimable worth.

Significantly, unlike Ibn Ezra and Rashbam, Maimonides does not link these two injunctions with the third, namely the prohibition of seething the kid in its mother's milk. Maimonides prefers to associate the latter with idolatrous practices that the Torah repudiates, rather than with ideals of sympathy and compassion. This omission is readily intelligible for Maimonides, since the case of seething the kid in its mother's milk is the only one of the three that involves an offspring that has already been killed. By the stage of food preparation the mother is not likely to be present nor is the meat of the kid readily identifiable as her offspring and therefore compassion for her feelings cannot be involved. For Maimonides who focuses upon the actual animal, this prohibition must therefore be explained in some other way. But for Ibn Ezra and Rashbam who develop a more formal principle about life's inviolability, the injunction of seething a kid in its mother's milk is very much part of the discussion. It is an act that shows insensitivity not towards a specific mother and her kid but rather towards the precious life-affirming relationship that exists between them.

The Ramban's Contribution

Like his predecessors, the Ramban sees in this mitzvah a condemnation of cruelty and brutality. Like the others, he connects it to the prohibition of slaughtering a mother and its offspring on the same day. Like Maimonides, he embraces the principle of a rational basis for the *mitzvot*, for "each one of them is beneficial for the improvement of the human character, in addition to carrying a reward from God who commanded them" (commentary to *Devarim* 22:6). Ramban also emphasizes that when we say that the *mitzvot* have a rational basis that is comprehensible and meaningful for man, that does not imply that they are rational from God's perspective. That is to say that the utility of the *mitzvot* is exclusively one-sided. God, as an absolute and transcendent being, derives no efficacy whatsoever from our performance of the commandments:

> Rather, their benefit is for humanity, to save us from harm, to preserve us from false beliefs, to eliminate loathsome character traits, to remind us of God's miracles and wonders so that we may come to know Him . . . (commentary to 22:6)

Towards the end of his remarks, Ramban offers an insightful comment that highlights the difference in approach between himself, the Ibn Ezra and Rashbam on the one hand, and Maimonides on the other. The Talmudic source that Maimonides found troubling, namely that "God's attributes are not expressions of compassion and mercy, but rather definitive decrees," is not a rejection of the attempt to apply human reason to comprehend the *mitzvot*. Rather, the Ramban explains, it is an emphatic statement that

> these commandments concerning animals and birds are not acts of compassion towards them but rather decrees *that are meant to teach us proper conduct*.

Like Ibn Ezra and Rashbam, the Ramban is suggesting that the command to send away the mother bird or to not slaughter the cow and its offspring on the same day is not motivated by the Torah's compassion for these hapless creatures specifically, but rather by its desire to see us nurture proper character traits. Of course, this appears paradoxical. How are we to achieve this "proper conduct" that is the goal, except by demonstrating kindness and compassion towards these very cattle and birds?! Is Maimonides incorrect in proffering that "there is no difference between the pain of a human being and the pain of an animal in that situation. After all, the love and concern of a creature for its young is not a function of enhanced cognitive ability, but rather of emotional states that are common to most higher life forms?"

But considering the matter from the perspective of Ibn Ezra or Rashbam, Maimonides' explanation may be limiting precisely because it is so reasonable! It may indeed be the case that animals suffer great pain when their offspring is wrenched from them. It may indeed be the case that to do so is cruel and brutal. In fact, it is so obviously insensitive that it is difficult to conceive of any reasonable person behaving so crudely. What human heart could see the suffering of that mother and not be moved to compassion? That, says the Ramban, is precisely the drawback of Maimonides' thesis. The Torah does not only ask of us to be compassionate towards cow "x" or sheep "y" or bird "z," to exercise sympathy when confronted with the specific situation of slaughter or the particular episode of the bird's nest. These are rather local occurrences that will no doubt elicit an instinctive stirring of concern from every human heart, excepting perhaps one made out of stone. But very few of us will ever engage in slaughter, and almost none of us will have occasion to come across the bird's nest. And besides, the aim of the Torah, as Maimonides readily acknowledges, is not that we should be compassionate under only such circumstances, but under all circumstances, not only towards these animals, but also towards all animals and all people. How then will we succeed in inculcating the compassion that the Torah demands, so that it affects every aspect of our lives and becomes part and parcel of our very disposition? We may never have occasion to perform this mitzvah or others like it, for the unique set of circumstances that are necessary for its fulfillment may not occur during the course of our rather routine lives. Conversely, we may merit the opportunity to come across the mother bird and send it away as the Torah requires, but how shall we incorporate that singular event into the very fiber of our being so that its impact doesn't quickly dissipate and become inconsequential?

The answer, says the Ramban, is to regard these *mitzvot* as *object lessons*. True, they may have specific applications that are to be realized in this coarse world of ours; they are not simply metaphors for good living. But at the same time there is a truth to these acts that surpasses their narrow context of fulfillment to address the broader problem of the human condition and the recalcitrant human heart that still delights in causing pain. Having mercy on a specific animal and bird may not be enough to develop a more refined character. The instinctual sort of identification that occurs when a human parent witnesses the pain of an animal parent will not, in and of itself, be translated into moral development. The Ramban alerts us to the fact that moral development comes from constant effort, from deliberate and prolonged contemplation of the good, from the persistent and unceasing exercise of the moral will. Only by considering the sending away of the mother bird as more than a specific act, as greater than a local episode, as a grand and comprehensive charge to develop a benevolent and thoughtful character, can we do justice to its deceptively simple rationale.

FOR FURTHER STUDY:

(1) Whether or not the *mitzvot* have a meaningful rationale and how central this might be to our relationship with God is an ancient and unresolved discussion. Maimonides' comments in his Guide to the Perplexed (3:48) should be compared and contrasted to what he says in his commentary to the Mishna, *Berachot* 5:3 as well as in his codification of the laws of prayer:

> One who says in supplications: "May the One who had mercy upon the bird's nest not to take the chicks in the presence of the mother and not to kill the cow and its calf on the same day, may He also have mercy upon us!" or similar things of this nature is to be silenced. This is because these *mitzvot* are divine decrees of the scriptures and not expressions of mercy. If the matter was really about mercy, then God would not have permitted us to slaughter at all . . . (*Mishneh Torah*, Laws of Prayer 9:7)

KI TAVO

The Bringing of the First Fruits

Deuteronomy 26:1-29:8

When you enter the land that God your Lord gives to you as an inheritance and you shall possess it and dwell in it. Then you shall take from the first of all the fruits of the earth that you shall bring from the land that God your Lord gives you and you shall place them in a basket. You shall go to the place that God will choose to cause His name to dwell there. You shall approach the Kohen who shall be there at that time, and shall say to him: "I declare this day before God your Lord that I have come into the land that God swore unto our ancestors to give us." The Kohen shall take the basket from your hands and place it down before the altar of God your Lord.

You shall proclaim before God your Lord: "A wandering Aramean was my father. He went down to Egypt and sojourned there few in number, and there became a great, powerful and populous nation. The Egyptians dealt harshly with us and afflicted us, and put upon us difficult labor. We cried out to God the Lord of our ancestors, and God heard our voice, saw our affliction, our burden and our distress. God took us out of Egypt with a strong hand, an outstretched arm, awesome acts and signs and wonders. He brought us to this place, and gave us this land, a land flowing with milk and honey. And now I have brought the first fruits of the earth that You have given me God," and you shall put them down before God your Lord and prostrate yourself before God your Lord.

You shall rejoice in all the good that God your Lord has given to you and to your household, you and the Levite, and the convert that dwells in your midst. (*Devarim* 26:1–11)

PARASHAT KI Tavo begins with a description of one of the most poignant and dramatic ceremonies of Temple times, namely the presentation of the ביכורים or "first fruits." First profiled in Sefer Shemot in terse and non-descriptive terms (*Shemot* 23:19, 34:26), the ritual is here elaborated upon and spelled out at some length. As we consider some of the laws associated with the bringing of the first fruits, we shall discover that the Torah here presents us with an exceptional opportunity to study how a fundamental, underlying theme can color every aspect of a mitzvah's fulfillment.

Some Preliminary Questions

The outline of the rite is straightforward enough, and can be conveniently broken down into three discrete elements, as indicated by the above quotation: (1) a description of the bringing of the first fruits to God's house and their presentation to the Kohen; (2) an emotional proclamation recalling the enslavement in Egypt; (3) an injunction to afterwards celebrate with the less fortunate. We should take note of the fact that while the account of our Parasha is presented from the perspective of the individual, the verbal declaration is phrased in the plural. In it, the supplicant provides a very concise outline of Jewish national history and places particular emphasis on the experience of the enslavement in Egypt, the Exodus and the entry into the Land. The themes of the declaration pivot around contrasts: few ancestors becoming a multitude, oppressed slaves achieving freedom, and homeless people acquiring a land "flowing with milk and honey."

Although the text speaks of "first fruits of the earth" it does not delineate which specific species of fruits are to be brought. Are first fruits to be presented from all species of the farmer's crops, or only from a select few? Also, the passage is ambiguous concerning the placing of the fruits in a basket. Is this a purely utilitarian means of conveying them to the Temple, a short lesson in biblical realia, or does it perhaps represent an intrinsic part of the rite? Significantly, the biblical word employed for "basket," טנא, is an unusual usage that occurs only four times in the entire scriptures, all of them in our Parasha: (1) ". . . you shall place them in a basket (טנא) (*Devarim* 26:2); (2) "The Kohen shall take the basket (טנא) from your hands" (26:4); (3) "Blessed be your basket (טנאך) and your kneading trough" (28:6); (4) "Cursed be your basket (טנאך) and your kneading trough" (28:17). In contrast, the much more common word for basket, סל, occurs fifteen times in Tanakh.

This much is clear: the emotional thrust of the account in the Torah is to foster gratitude on the part of the individual who offers the first fruits. He is to express thankfulness to God for having merited enjoying the fruits of his labor, and this he does by presenting the choicest of them before Him at His abode.

The Account of the Mishna

One of the tractates of the Mishna, the final section devoted to the agricultural laws, is *Masechet Bikurim*. It is in the main devoted to the laws concerning the ceremony of the first fruits. Compiled in the aftermath of the Second Temple's destruction, it provides a rare glimpse of how the people observed this commandment while the Temple still stood at Jerusalem. We shall quote from some of the relevant *mishnayot*, especially those of chapter 3, and shall then compare and contrast them to the text from the Parasha of Ki Tavo.

> **Mishna 1**: How are the first fruits designated? A person goes down to his field and when he notices that a fig or grape cluster has started to appear, he marks it with a band and says "these shall be for first fruits . . ."
>
> **Mishna 2**: How were the first fruits brought? All of the people dwelling in the villages of the *ma'amad* would gather in the town of the *ma'amad* and sleep in the streets rather than in the houses. Early the next morning, the appointed leader would exclaim: "Arise and let us go up to Zion, to the house of God our Lord"!
>
> **Mishna 3**: The nearby villagers would bring fresh figs and grapes, and the outlying ones would bring dried figs and raisins. An ox with gilded horns and a wreath of olive leaves would go before them. The flute would play until the procession neared Jerusalem. When they came close to Jerusalem, they would beautify and ornament their first fruits. The governors, officials and treasurers of the city would

> go out to greet them, in accordance with the importance of the arrivals. All of the craftsmen of Jerusalem would stop their work and stand to greet them, saying: "Our people of such and such a place, enter in peace"!
>
> **Mishna 4**: The flute would play before the procession until they reached the Temple Mount. When they reached the Temple Mount, even Agrippa the king would take the basket upon his shoulder, and proceed until he entered the forecourt. When he entered the forecourt, the Levites would burst into song: "I praise You, God, for You have raised me up and have not allowed my enemies to rejoice over me"!
>
> **Mishna 6**: While the basket was still upon his shoulder he would recite from "I declare this day," until he finished the entire passage. Rabbi Yehuda says: until he reached "A wandering Aramean was my father." When he reached that passage, he would remove the basket from his shoulder and hold it by its rim. The Kohen would place his hand under the basket and ceremoniously wave it. The presenter would then recite "A wandering Aramean was my father" and complete the passage. The basket would be placed down beside the altar, and the presenter would prostrate and exit.

Before analyzing the specific matters enumerated in the Mishna, a number of general observations are in order. First of all, we note that the structure of each of the *mishnayot* is the same: there is a description of a particular action, and this is followed by some sort of pertinent affirmation. Thus, the first fruits are set apart by being marked with a band, and then they are *vocally designated* as such by the field owner. The villagers would sleep in the streets, and next morning the procession leader would exclaim: "*Arise*!" The people would arrive in Jerusalem, and the inhabitants would *greet* them. The presenter would enter the forecourt, and the Levites would *sing*. Evidently, the Mishna models all of these preliminaries on the Torah text itself, which, as we have seen, combines the offering of the first fruits with an associated verbal declaration. By adopting this textual structure, the Mishna obliquely indicates to us that the binary aspects of ceremonial act and formal declaration are inextricably bound up with the essence of the first fruits. Deed and verbalization are therefore felt at every stage of the ceremony's fulfillment.

Secondly, we notice that in contrast to the description of Ki Tavo, the portrayal of the Mishna is decidedly collective. We experience the ceremony from the perspective of the people. They gather and go up to Jerusalem not as individuals but as an aggregate. The officials and people of Jerusalem greet them in accordance with their number. The king, in a seeming act of democratic identification, joins the masses and offers his own basket like them. The forecourt of the Temple would no doubt be filled with a joyous throng as the Levites would sing. All of this suggests that the ceremony of the first fruits constituted an important vehicle for fostering unity among the people. Individuals would come together as would whole villages, Jerusalem the capital would greet the people of outlying towns and even the king would circulate among his subjects.

Thirdly, in contrast to the solemn and serious tone of the Torah text, the Mishna's narrative is preoccupied with joy and exaltation. The passage in Ki Tavo mentioned happiness in generic terms, as the climactic consequence of the entire ceremony – "You shall rejoice in all the good that God your Lord has given to you and to your household . . ."

– but it contained no description of music, singing, or celebration as part of the rite. In the Torah, the critical declaration is not exuberant but somber, and it is this section that constitutes the main part of the biblical account of the mitzvah. In the Mishna, on the other hand, we read of a parade led by "floats" (the crowned ox with the gilded horns), musical accompaniment of the flute, and the gaiety of joyous song. The pensive declaration is mentioned in outline and is not the focus of the Mishna's account.

Specifics of the Mishna's Account

The Mishna's description raises a number of issues that require elaboration. In Mishna 2, the villagers would gather in town but would sleep in the streets rather than entering the houses. Was this a function of large crowds and inadequate lodgings or were there perhaps other considerations at work? Also, it is important to note that the leader's exclamation the next morning is actually a quote from *Yirmiyahu* 31:5, which in its larger context describes the bright future of the redeemed and restored people of Israel:

> Thus says God: "The nation that was a remnant from the sword has found grace in the wilderness, and Israel has sought rest." God has appeared to me from afar, saying: "I have loved My people with an everlasting love and have therefore drawn you to Me in compassion. I will again build you and you shall be built, virgin of Israel; you shall again be adorned with your timbrels and go out to joyously dance. You shall again plant vineyards on the hills of Shomron – the planters shall plant and enjoy the fruit. For there shall come a day when the watchmen on Mount Efraim shall exclaim: 'Arise and let us go up to Zion, to the House of God our Lord!'" (31:1–5)

Although the expanded passage from Yirmiyahu presents us with an obvious connection to our Parasha's theme of enjoying the fruit of one's labor, we must ponder if there are other grounds for the inclusion of this specific verse in the rite of the first fruits.

In Mishna 3, we were treated to a description of the festive parade that the villagers staged enroute to Jerusalem. The inclusion of the ox is, in all probability, a concrete expression of its centrality to the agrarian economy of antiquity, for the ox was the most important beast of burden and especially critical for plowing. The closest modern-day parallel might be the role of the adorned tractor in kibbutz celebrations of the bringing in of the harvest!

Mishna 4 described the arrival at the Temple Mount. Here, we are told, "even Agrippa the king would take the basket upon his shoulder, and proceed until he entered the forecourt." Agrippa, the grandson of Herod, is known to us as the final king of the Second Temple period, and his brief reign is recalled in Jewish sources as one of stability and peace. Caligula, with whom he had been brought up at the Roman court, first appointed him as king, and Caligula's successor, the Emperor Claudius, gave him dominion over all of the Roman province of Palestine. Agrippa combined political acumen with sensitivity to Jewish tradition, but his three-year reign ended suddenly in 44 CE when he died at Caesarea. We can therefore date the Mishna's description of the ceremony of the first fruits to the final decades of the Jewish state, for the Temple was destroyed by the Romans in 70 CE.

Curiously, the selection sung by the Levites as the first fruits were brought into the forecourt of the Temple is not one of joyous celebration or praise, as one might have expected given the other features of the procession. Rather, it is one of perseverance: "I praise You, God, for You have raised me up and have not allowed my enemies to rejoice over me!" Taken from the thirtieth chapter of Sefer Tehillim, the hymn was composed by David on the occasion of the "Dedication of the House." Its imagery is that of being rescued from certain death, of preservation by God from "descending to the pit" and from "everlasting doom." In it, David praises God who has saved him from the clutches of his foes, and has turned his mourning into jubilation. It is not immediately clear why this Psalm was chosen to be chanted during the rite – the mood that it evokes seems jarringly out of place.

Finally, Mishna 6 describes the actual conferral of the first fruits. The basket would be removed from the shoulder and ritually waved, indicating the presentation of an offering, and the declaration would then be made. Soon afterward, the basket would be put down next to the altar and the supplicant would prostrate and take his leave. Once again, we are left to wonder about the significance of the basket and its special role in the entire affair.

The Description of Maimonides – More Pieces of the Puzzle

Maimonides, in his Laws of First Fruits, organizes and codifies the statutes of the Torah, Mishna, Talmud and associated texts concerning the first fruits, and we shall only make mention of elements that we have not already seen:

> **Chapter 2:1** – It is a positive command to bring first fruits to the Temple, and they are only brought as long as the Temple stands and within the land of Israel, as the verse states "the first fruits of your land you shall bring to the house of God your Lord . . ." (*Shemot* 23:19; 34:26).
>
> **Chapter 2:2** – One does not bring first fruits except from the seven species enumerated in the "praise of the land." These are wheat, barley, grapes, figs, pomegranates, olives and dates. If one presents first fruits from other species, they are not sanctified.
>
> **Chapter 3:10** – It is a positive commandment to offer an affirmation at the time that the first fruits are presented at the Temple . . . and it can only be recited in the holy language of Hebrew . . .
>
> **Chapter 3:11** – One who brings first fruits may give them to his servant or relative to convey enroute, until they reach the Temple Mount. When they reach the Temple Mount, however, he himself must take them upon his shoulder, even if he is an exalted king in Israel . . . He recites the passage of "a wandering Aramean" and puts down the fruits on the southwestern corner of the altar . . .
>
> **Chapter 3:14** – First fruits require overnight stay. How so? One who has presented his first fruits at the Temple, recited the proclamation and offered his sacrifices, may not leave Jerusalem on that day to return home, but rather must remain overnight and return home to his own town only on the morrow . . . Thus, first fruits require seven things: bringing to the place, a vessel, the declaration, sacrifice, song, ceremonial waving and overnight stay.

Maimonides includes a number of new and important details. The first fruits can only be brought from the land of Israel, and only from the so-called seven species that he cryptically refers to as "the praise of the land," and only as long as the Temple stands. This "praise," in fact, is based upon another context that sees these particular fruits as manifest expressions of the land's beauty and blessing:

> God your Lord is bringing you to a good land, a land of water streams, of springs and deep pools, issuing forth in the valleys and from the hills. It is land of wheat and of barley, of grapes, figs and pomegranates; it is a land of olive oil and (date) honey. It is a land in which you shall eat bread without deficiency, you shall lack nothing in it; it is a land whose stones shall yield iron and from whose mountains you shall extract copper. You shall eat and be satisfied, and you shall bless God your Lord concerning the good land that He has given you. (*Devarim* 8:7–10)

We might reasonably assume that in our own times the seven species have been usurped by the ubiquitous Jaffa orange or else the seasonal strawberry, both modern-day symbols for once-barren tracts now blossoming with bounty, but the traditional sources provide for no such modification. Why not?

Maimonides relates that the first fruits can be conveyed in any manner, but upon reaching the Temple Mount, the presenter must himself carry the basket on his shoulder. He understands the example of Agrippa as not simply a touching expression of monarchy mingling with the masses, but rather as a normative Halachic requirement. Thus, the basket and the manner of its conveyance both turn out to be necessary features, although their significance is still unclear.

Maimonides also indicates that the declaration must be recited in Hebrew. In other words, it is not sufficient to make mention of the themes of the passage such as the descent to Egypt, the enslavement, or the Exodus. Rather, the passage is a *formula* that must be recited verbatim in its original language. In contrast, we might consider other *mitzvot* of the Torah that require some sort of verbalization or statement, such as grace after meals (8:10), prayer (11:13), recitation of the Shema (6:4), or even the confession concerning tithes (26:12–15) that immediately succeeds our section. In all of these cases, as well as in the vast majority of other *mitzvot* requiring recitation, there is no requirement at all that the text be recited word for word in Hebrew.

Finally, Maimonides makes mention of an overnight stay. Why must the presenter not return home immediately? Is there any deeper significance to this provision other then its positive impact on the local hotel industry?

The Fundamental Axiom

Thus far, we have seen a wealth of texts pertaining to *bikurim* and have raised a large number of perplexing queries. Now, considering the meaning of a single, central feature will shed a brilliant light on the entire matter. Recall that the Torah spoke of a טנא or basket. We wondered about the almost singular usage of the term and if or how it differed from a סל. We later discovered that the carrying of the basket on one's shoulder was a critical rite that even the king was expected to perform, and also learned that at the conclusion of the declaration, the basket was to be placed down at the side of the altar.

When we reflect upon the action of "carrying upon the shoulder" from a broader perspective, a number of other biblical examples instantly come to mind. Recall that Rivka, ascending from the well with "her pitcher upon her shoulder" (*Breisheet* 24:15) graciously offered water to Eliezer and the camels. When the Israelite camp broke up and moved to a new location, the Levites of the clan of Kehat conveyed the holy vessels "upon their shoulders" (*BeMidbar* 7:9). Most striking of all, at the time of the Exodus, the people left in such great haste that they "took their dough before it was leavened, their kneading troughs bound up in their garments upon their shoulders" (*Shemot* 12:34). In all of these cases, the expression to "carry upon one's shoulder" indicates the action of conveying an object from point A to point B, while in the interim it *cannot be put down*. In other words, when the Torah describes the act of carrying upon the shoulder, it invariably associates it with a situation in which the object in question must be borne aloft until a suitable resting place is found.

In the context of the first fruits, then, the significance of carrying the basket is not simply to convey it from one's field to the Temple, but to actually relive *the existential journey from homelessness to settlement*! We must carry the *bikurim* because we are symbolically re-experiencing the dispossession of our ancestors who had no land. We bear the basket on our shoulder because we are recalling their condition of anxious destitution, of having meager possessions and nowhere to rest them. Etymologically, the word טנא is connected to its cognate Aramaic term טונא meaning "a burden" or "load," and the טנא therefore differs from the basket in that it is used not as an ornamental receptacle but rather as a container for conveyance of goods and possessions. One may still see it in use in the land of Israel among the Arab peasants of the Judean and Samarian hills, who carry their produce in baskets borne upon their heads or shoulders.

Reevaluating the Text of the Torah

Returning to the biblical text, the focus of the declaration recalls the descent to Egypt, the enslavement, the Exodus, and the entry into the land, for this national experience more than any other commemorates the dynamic movement from rootlessness to possession. It is precisely because we were homeless sojourners in the land of Egypt that we were vulnerable to the whims of our hosts. The Pharaoh who welcomed the family of Joseph with open arms could so easily be succeeded by the cruel Pharaoh of the oppression, and how quickly were our fortunes transformed!

It is therefore not surprising that the biblical ceremony concludes with the basket being gently put down. After reliving the desperation of exile by laboriously transferring that basket from place to place, we can sincerely appreciate God's gift of the land. Having recognized His bounty, we then put down the basket next to the altar. This is to suggest the state of national "rest" that is the antithesis of exile and wandering, as if to say "now I have a home in which I can place down my possessions, and that home is God's precious gift of a land."

The connection with the Temple is now obvious, for the nation state of the Jews that the *bikurim* come to celebrate is incomplete without it. If the first fruits are about the people of Israel achieving a settled and secure status, then the Temple must be standing at Jerusalem. If it lies in ruins, then one cannot rightly perform a ceremony that celebrates national permanence and tranquility, for the Temple edifice is the concrete expression of this sublime achievement.

Reevaluating the Text of the Mishna

The account of the Mishna began with the villagers sleeping in the streets. Rather than being an expression of insufficient housing or a mechanism for fostering camaraderie, we can now see that it is the most appropriate means of beginning the procession. If the first fruits are evocative of nomadic and unsettled wandering, then let their consignment commence with a physical act of sleeping in the unsheltered open.

The rousing words of the procession leader, in actuality a quote from Yirmiyahu, the prophet of the destruction, remind the people that separation from homeland is not only a historical event from the dim and distant past, but also a theme of urgent currency. The enslavement in Egypt was followed by the Babylonian exile and later still by the domination of Rome, and the ideals of political stability and national reconciliation with God still remain distant hopes. The first fruits, then, call our attention to this ancient dynamic even while anticipating better days:

> I will again build you and you shall be built, virgin of Israel; you shall again be adorned with your timbrels and go out to joyously dance. You shall again plant vineyards on the hills of Shomron; the planters shall plant and enjoy the fruit. For there shall come a day when the watchmen on Mount Efraim shall exclaim: "Arise and let us go up to Zion, to the House of God our Lord"! (*Yirmiyahu* 31:3–5)

The song of the Levites, passionate and pained, speaks not of joyous celebration and unmitigated happiness, but rather of struggle and eventual triumph. The quoted verse – "I praise You, God, for You have raised me up and have not allowed my enemies to rejoice over me"! – does not describe sentiments of complacency and comfort, but rather those of endeavor and exertion. Settling the land is no easy task; remaining cognizant of both the human efforts invested in achieving national rest as well as of the divine support that makes it at all possible are the critical keys to maintaining our hold.

Reevaluating Maimonides

Maimonides records the tradition that the first fruits are to be brought only from the seven species. These particular fruits are referred to as the "praise of the land" and undoubtedly are expressions of its bounty and beauty. In light of the above analysis, however, a more startling fact emerges: these seven fruits, to the exclusion of the proverbial Jaffa orange and its ilk, are *indigenous* to this land. In other words, if the ritual of the *bikurim* addresses the themes of taking root in the land and becoming integrally connected to it, then the choice of fruits should highlight especially those species that from time immemorial have been regarded as native to its shores. But it is not exclusivity that the Torah seeks, for some of these seven may thrive in other locales as well. Rather, it is the idea of organic connection to a place and deep attachment to its soil that these seven species so eloquently symbolize.

Maimonides' curious assertion that the declaration be recited in Hebrew is now comprehensible. What could be more appropriate than the national language of the Jewish people for conveying our profound emotional bond to the land as well as our gratitude to God for His precious gift? Although we might succeed in capturing the essence of those themes in other tongues, the subtlety and sublimity of the matter would be lost in the translation.

As for the overnight stay, it forms the perfect conclusion to the rite. The ceremony began with sleeping outdoors in the open countryside, as if bereft of home and hearth. The ritual concludes by staying overnight in the national capital of Jerusalem, to emphatically proclaim that now the people of Israel have "somewhere" to rest their weary heads, namely the "place that God shall choose to cause His name to dwell there."

Summing Up

We began our lesson with a quotation from the Parasha delineating a particular mitzvah that at first glance appeared to be straightforward. We quickly saw, however, that the secondary sources were actually quite lengthy and complex. Once we deciphered the fundamental theme of the mitzvah, however, the seemingly unrelated and arbitrary details began to fall into place, ultimately revealing an intricate ceremony with many layers of meaning. Let us conclude by returning to the structure of the main biblical text, this time singling out the recurring Hebrew words that together constitute the "equation" for which we have been searching:

> When you enter (תבוא) the land that God your Lord gives (נתן) to you as an inheritance and you shall possess it and dwell in it. Then you shall take from the first of all the fruits of the earth that you shall bring (תביא) from the land that God your Lord gives (נתן) you, and you shall place them in a basket. You shall go to the place that God will choose to cause His name to dwell there. You shall approach (ובאת) the Kohen who shall be there at that time, and shall say to him: "I declare this day before God your Lord that I have come (באתי) into the land, that God swore unto our ancestors to give (לתת) us." The Kohen shall take the basket from your hands and place it down (והניחו) before the altar of God your Lord.
>
> You shall proclaim before God your Lord: "A wandering Aramean was my father. He went down to Egypt and sojourned there few in number, and there became a great, powerful and populous nation. The Egyptians dealt harshly with us and afflicted us, and put upon us (ויתנו) difficult labor. We cried out to God the Lord of our ancestors, and God heard our voice, saw our affliction, our burden, and our distress. God took us out of Egypt with a strong hand, an outstretched arm, awesome acts, signs and wonders. He brought us (ויבאנו) to this place, and gave us (ויתן) this land, a land flowing with milk and honey. And now I have brought (הבאתי) the first fruits of the earth that You have given (נתתה) me God," and you shall put them down (והנחתו) before God your Lord and prostrate yourself before God your Lord.
>
> You shall rejoice in all the good that God your Lord has given (נתן) to you and to your household, you and the Levite, and the convert that dwells in your midst. (*Devarim* 26:1–11)

It is clear that the passage pivots around three recurring verbs: בוא (six occurrences), נתן (seven occurrences), and נוח (two occurrences). They mean respectively "to enter," "to give" and "to be at rest." The equation is thus clear: to enter the land and to recognize it as God's gift, with all of the responsibilities that are implied by that recognition, is to be able to achieve the state of national rest for which we yearn. Failure to fulfill one of the conditions is to forfeit that rest and to experience a "gift" of another sort. As Nechama Leibowitz (20th century, Israel) points out, the pivotal occurrence of the verb "to give," the seventh usage that seems to upset the perfect balance that would otherwise exist with the six occurrences of entry, is credited to the Egyptians who "put upon us hard labor."

In other words, the Egyptians also bestowed a "gift" upon us, but it was not the precious bounty of a fruitful land. It was the backbreaking labor of the brick pits.

FOR FURTHER STUDY:

(1) Consider that the declaration of the first fruits constitutes the central passage of the Maggid section of the Haggadah (see Maimonides, Laws of Chametz and Matzah, 7:4). The critical phrase "ארמי אבד אבי" is variously translated as "a wandering Aramean was my father" or else "an indigent dweller in Aram was my father." Rashbam understood it as a reference to Abraham who hailed from Aram and wandered far from home to the land of Canaan, while Ibn Ezra saw it as a reference to Jacob who fled empty-handed from his brother's wrath to Aram. The Mishnaic authors of the Haggadah, however, explain it as a reference to Lavan the Aramean "who sought to destroy my father (Jacob)." This reading is both impossible grammatically, as well as difficult contextually (see the commentary of Ibn Ezra). For the sake of what more important lesson did our Sages choose to overlook grammatical precision and thematic consistency, and how is this lesson directly related to our discussion of *bikurim* above?

NITZAVIM

Return and Restoration

Deuteronomy 29:9-30:20

> All of you stand before God your Lord this day, your tribal leaders, elders and officers, all of the men of Israel. Your children and wives, the convert who dwells in your camp, from the hewer of your wood until the drawer of your water. In order that you might enter into God your Lord's covenant and His oath, that God your Lord seals with you this day. In order that He might establish you this day to be His people and He will be your God as He spoke to you, and just as He pledged to your ancestors, to Avraham, Yitzchak and Ya'acov . . . (*Devarim* 29:9–12)

THE REVIEW of the commandments now completed, Moshe prepares to extend his final message to the people of Israel before his demise. Though the people stand before God at Canaan's gates ready to enter into a covenant with Him, committed to uphold the terms of the Torah and keen to champion His presence in the world, Moshe knows that darker days lie ahead. Israel will encounter many challenges on the other side of the Yarden, chief among them intimate contact with value systems that are at direct odds with their own, and many in their ranks will falter and fall. In the end, exile will overtake them and, with it, the wretched vulnerability that statelessness confers. But Israel will survive, sustained by a silent God who patiently awaits their return. Moshe extends to his people the promise of their eventual *teshuva*, of their sincere reconciliation with the destiny that had always been theirs. And God will respond in kind.

The Passage of Return

> When all of these things concerning you shall come to pass, the blessing and the curse that I have placed before you, then you shall take matters (והשבות) to heart among all of the nations into which God your Lord has driven you. You shall return (ושבת) to God and hearken to His voice, according to all that I command you this day, both you and your children with all of your heart and with all of your soul.
>
> God shall return (ושב) your captivity (שבותך) and have compassion upon you. He will once again (ושב) gather you from among all of the nations into which He scattered you. Though your expulsion may be at the ends of the heavens, from there God shall gather you and from there He shall take you. God your Lord will bring you into the land that your ancestors once possessed, and you shall possess

> it, and you shall enjoy more goodness and increase than those ancestors. God your Lord will circumcise your heart and the heart of your descendents, so that you love God your Lord with all of your heart and with all of your soul, so that you may live.
>
> God your Lord will place all of these curses upon your enemies and foes that pursued you. You will return (תשוב) and hearken to God's voice, to fulfill all of His commandments that I command you this day. God your Lord will grant you increase in all of your endeavors – your children, animals and harvests – all for the good. God will again (ישוב) rejoice over you for the good just as He rejoiced over your ancestors. When you hearken to the voice of God your Lord, to observe His commandments and decrees that are written in this book of the Torah, when you return (תשוב) to God your Lord with all of your heart and with all of your soul. (30:1–10)

This powerful passage of restoration is directed towards the entire people of Israel. Its stirring verses do not speak to the individual nor address his existential plight. The man who is estranged from God is free to return to Him and will find Him receptive, but his story is not to be found in our passage. It is the *nation* that is the subject of these charged phrases, a nation exiled from its land and scattered to the four corners of the globe like so much chaff. The Torah indicates that the interminably long exile will one day come to an end, the people will return to their land, and God will return to them.

There is a single word that echoes throughout this section and across the generations that it foresees, and that word is "*teshuva*" or "*return.*" During the course of ten verses, it occurs eight times in various forms of the verb שוב. The restoration of fortunes after the long night of exile, the return to the land of an indestructible remnant, represent the physical manifestation of this process, but at the core of the matter is the spirit. During the course of our analysis we will use the Hebrew word "*teshuva*" to describe this progression, rather than the more common translation of "repentance." This latter word is from an old French or Latin root signifying "remorse" "contrition" or "regret." Although these elements are indeed included in "*teshuva*," the Hebrew term is much more comprehensive. *Teshuva* describes an all-encompassing and transformative state in which one is restored to God and to the deepest truth of his innermost being and after which life cannot be the same.

An Ancient Dispute

> Rav said: All of the appointed times [for redemption] have already passed, for the matter depends entirely upon *teshuva* and good deeds. Shemuel demurred, saying: the mourner is sufficiently sustained by his mourning (the suffering endured by Israel in exile has provided sufficient merit for them to be restored, even in the absence of their *teshuva* – Rashi, ad loc.). This disagreement is similar to the following dispute among authorities of the Mishna. Rabbi Eliezer says: If the people of Israel return then they will be redeemed, but if not, then they will not be redeemed. Rabbi Yehoshua says: Will they not be redeemed if they fail to do *teshuva*? Rather, God will establish a king whose decrees will be as harsh as those of Haman, and then Israel will return and be restored to the good… [does not the verse state

that] ". . . when the time has passed and the holy nation suffers utter degradation, then all these things will be realized" (*Daniel* 12:7)? Rabbi Eliezer fell silent. (TB *Sanhedrin* 97b–98a)

In this famous quarrel, Rabbi Yehoshua and Rabbi Eliezer disagree concerning the role of sincere *teshuva* in the redemptive process. According to the view of Rabbi Eliezer, unless the Jewish people genuinely return to God and embrace the observance of His Torah, then redemption will remain a distant chimera. The event of redemption is entirely a function of free choice and the intense longing for God's word. As long as the people of Israel remain deaf to the siren call of *teshuva*, then their tragic exile will be prolonged endlessly. Rabbi Yehoshua, however, disagrees. Redemption will follow the bitterness of exile, as surely as the aurora follows the night's darkest gloom. In the opinion of Rabbi Yehoshua, if the people of Israel do not return of their own volition, then God will assist the process with the appointment of a tyrannical king who will "encourage" them through his dictates.

Ultimately, both authorities agree that *teshuva* is central to the redemptive process. They part ways, however, concerning the necessity for *sincere* repentance, the type of return that can only be the consequence of an autonomous choice. For Rabbi Eliezer, in its absence, redemption is impossible. Rabbi Yehoshua, on the other hand, argues that there is another form of return, one that is precipitated not by genuine and heartfelt feelings of longing, but rather by cruel necessity. Even if the people abjure God's overtures, refusing to embrace the holy destiny that has set them apart from every other nation since the dawn of human history, redemption can still be theirs. But in this less meaningful variation, it will unfold as the only remaining option after every other attempt to overcome oppression and adversity has been exhausted. In this model, *teshuva* is a last resort, a mechanistic reaction to trials too difficult to bear. But as surely as Rabbi Eliezer falls silent in the end and cannot refute Rabbi Yehoshua's proof text, in its wake redemption still dawns!

Considering the Process of Return

Our passage from Parashat Nitzavim sheds much light on the discussion. It describes the process of national return, and intimates that Israel's restoration is a direct consequence of their *teshuva*. Does it not explicitly support the view of Rabbi Eliezer, who demands sincere return as a prerequisite for restoration? Nevertheless, the verses are puzzlingly repetitive, for they seem to describe the same event no less than three times! On three occasions, we are told that the people will return with "all of their heart and with all of their soul." On two occasions, we are told that God will restore them to their land and rejoice over them, bringing them increase and success. It would seem that from Rabbi Eliezer's perspective, the story could have been told in its entirety utilizing half of the verses!

A closer reading of the passage reveals a different possibility. There is actually a reciprocal dynamic at work between Israel and God, signified by the recurring usage of the verb שוב. We may illustrate it by presenting the passage as a series of progressive steps:

(1) *The people return* to God – "When all of these things concerning you shall come to pass, the blessing and the curse that I have placed before you, then you shall take matters to heart among all of the nations into which God your Lord has driven you. You shall return to God and hearken to His voice, according to all that I command you this day,

both you and your children with all of your heart and with all of your soul." (*Devarim* 30:1–2)

(2) *God responds* by returning their captivity – "God in turn shall return your captivity and have compassion upon you. He will once again gather you from among all of the nations into which He scattered you. Though your expulsion may be at the ends of the heavens, from there God shall gather you and from there He shall take you. God your Lord will bring you into the land that your ancestors once possessed, and you shall possess it, and you shall enjoy more goodness and increase than those ancestors." (30:3–5)

(3) *The people return* to Him again – "God your Lord will circumcise your heart and the heart of your descendents, so that you love God your Lord with all of your heart and with all of your soul, so that you may live. God your Lord will place all of these curses upon your enemies and foes that pursued you. You will return and hearken to God's voice, to fulfill all of His commandments that I command you this day." (30:6–7)

(4) *God responds* by rejoicing over them – "God your Lord will grant you increase in all of your endeavors – your children, animals and harvests – all for the good. God will again rejoice over you for the good just as He rejoiced over your ancestors." (30:8–9)

(5) *Finally, they return* to Him again – "When you hearken to the voice of God your Lord, to observe His commandments and decrees that are written in this book of the Torah, when you return to God your Lord with all of your heart and with all of your soul." (30:10)

It emerges that the *event* of national return so eloquently recounted in our passage is actually a lengthy *process* over time that is set into motion when the people of Israel take their first halting step. They will then be encouraged by God's magnanimous response. He will detect in their hesitant move a glimmer of *teshuva* and respond by initiating the *physical* ingathering of their exiles. But this ingathering is not at all the culmination of the process. Israel will need to overcome many more challenges in order to secure their sovereignty; they will need to achieve not only physical security but spiritual sensitivity as well. They will therefore return "again" to God, not as a repetitive act but rather as a progressive one, for this second return will incorporate a fragment of that essential spiritual component that was initially lacking. God will again respond, showering them with His bounty and illuminating them with His radiance. Finally, the people of Israel will be ready to initiate the final act of their return, the comprehensive, transformative, transcendent *teshuva* that must follow.

In this reading, *teshuva* is exactly what we know it to be intuitively: a gradual awakening of the mind and soul to God's call, a measured but steady process of self-evaluation and reflection, a plodding and sometimes faltering series of steps that includes dead ends, blind alleys, and even devastating retreats. But once unleashed, the momentum of the process cannot be stayed. This paradigm accords with the view of Rabbi Yehoshua, who proclaims a *teshuva* of necessity, a return motivated by insincere motives and imposed from above. But in the end, the opposing views of Rabbi Yehoshua and Rabbi Eliezer converge, as long as we are discussing the totality of the *teshuva* process and not simply its starting point! There is, therefore, a spectrum of *teshuva*. On one extreme is an extrinsic *teshuva* that is precipitated by cruel external forces; on the other, an intrinsic *teshuva* that is self-inspired and sincere. The *teshuva* of Parashat Nitzavim, unfolding as a lengthy process and not as an event, incorporates both aspects into a single continuum. This is also the conclusion of Maimonides who codifies the matter in his Laws of Teshuva 7:5:

> All of the prophets commanded concerning *teshuva* and Israel will not be redeemed except by doing *teshuva*. The Torah has already promised that finally Israel will do *teshuva* at the end of their exile and they will be redeemed immediately. As the verses state: "When all of these things concerning you shall come to pass, the blessing and the curse that I have placed before you, then you shall take matters to heart . . . You shall return to God and hearken to His voice, according to all that I command you this day . . . God in turn shall return your captivity and have compassion upon you . . ."

Returning to the Text

A number of textual anomalies are resolved by this approach. The first mention of return, the blessed *teshuva* that should have heralded a glorious and final reconciliation, is here curiously described as a "taking to heart" rather than as a return to God: "When all of these things concerning you shall come to pass, the blessing and the curse that I have placed before you, then you shall *take matters to heart among all of the nations* into which God your Lord has driven you . . ." Does this not indicate that the first, halting step need not even involve a conscious recognition of God and a desire to embrace His word? Here, the national return of the people of Israel is simply a "taking to heart," a questioning of the meaning of their bitter exile and an attempt to finally solve the riddle of Jewish suffering.

The next stage of this initial return is directed towards God but nevertheless deficient: "You shall return *to God* and hearken to His voice, according to all that I command you this day." In the original Hebrew, the verse states that "you shall return עד God," which is here translated as "to God" but is more accurately rendered as "until God." The preposition עד implies a distance that remains to be bridged between the deity and the people of Israel. Israel returns, but having reached the threshold, they can advance no further. The reconciliation at this point is incomplete.

The divine response to Israel's hesitant overtures is the initiation of that ingathering of which our ancestors dreamt, but correspondingly devoid of any spiritual content. It is a physical restoration of Israel to its ancient land, the perfect analog to a *teshuva* that lacked earnestness and depth. At this stage in the process, though the people of Israel are committed to the endeavor of nation building with "heart and soul," they are still painfully unaware that they remain shorn of their spiritual patrimony. Only with the next stage is this dimension awakened: "God your Lord will circumcise your heart and the heart of your descendents, so that you love God your Lord with all of your heart and with all of your soul, so that you may live." This circumcision of the heart is understood by the commentaries to refer to some sort of stirring of the spirit, in which the insensitivity and callousness of the heart is shed, to be replaced by a more profound awareness of the divine and a more pronounced commitment to the Torah. Thus, "you will return and hearken to God's voice, to fulfill all of His commandments that I command you this day."

Israel's more profound *teshuva* is again reciprocated by God with still greater impact: "God your Lord will grant you increase in all of your endeavors – your children, animals and harvests – all for the good. God will again rejoice over you for the good just as He rejoiced over your ancestors." The divine rejoicing, coupled with a fond reminisce of the people's ancestors, the devoted and steadfast patriarchs and matriarchs, signals the people's return to their former status of favor in God's eyes, to their unblemished past. That ideal state had existed but briefly during the thousand years of the biblical period. It had been characterized by a harmony between God and man, between man and man and between man and himself. Now it will be reconstituted under the unfurled banner of God's love.

A final act of *teshuva* will complete the people's transformation: "When you hearken to the voice of God your Lord, to observe His commandments and decrees that are written in this book of the Torah, when you return to God your Lord with all of your heart and with all of your soul." In contrast to their initial return, Israel's *teshuva* is here described in the original Hebrew as a "return אל God," with the use of a preposition that means "to" rather than "until." This *teshuva* is the complete return to God's waiting embrace as all distance evaporates.

Lessons for Our Time

We live in confusing times, especially as regards the Jewish people and the Jewish state. Our world is in a constant state of flux and upheaval, and to predict the next day's events seems the height of recklessness. Some of us look at the Jewish state and can see nothing remarkable, as if the foretold return of the Jews is an event like any other, as if the resurrection of a people and their language all but given up for dead is as mundane and meaningless as the weather. Others look at the Jewish state with studied alarm, as if their cherished vision of a flawless and complete redemption has been monstrously twisted out of shape by godless men.

In order to truly appreciate the magnitude of our times, one must maintain as broad a perspective as possible, one that embraces the totality of Jewish history and experience. And from that perspective, a fundamental principle emerges: the *teshuva* of the nation is an arduous process over time. As a process, it must begin with the preliminary stage of physically restoring the Jews to their ancient homeland and to national autonomy. As a process, it must address the material aspects of the Jews' national life in their land, some of which have not been seriously considered for two millennia: sovereignty and good government, economic development and trade, environmental responsibility and self-defense, to name but a few. As a process, *teshuva* must restore Israel to God and to the Torah, overcoming the estrangement and apathy that has plagued our people for almost three centuries. As a process, *teshuva* can be incremental, static and sometimes even run in reverse. It can frustrate us with its snail's pace and with its maddening detours. But as human history marches on, the Jewish people slowly advance forward and God patiently waits for our next move.

As we anxiously embark on yet another chapter of our history that has always been colored with uncertainty and often underscored with dread, let us tightly clasp Moshe's portentous words: "You will return and hearken to God's voice, to fulfill all of His commandments that I command you this day. God your Lord will grant you increase in all of your endeavors, your children, animals and harvests, all for the good. God will again rejoice over you for the good just as He rejoiced over your ancestors . . ." (*Devarim* 30:1–10).

FOR FURTHER STUDY:

(1) The above quote from Maimonides highlights the ultimate agreement between Rabbi Eliezer and Rabbi Yehoshua concerning *teshuva*. Recall his conclusion:

> All of the prophets commanded concerning *teshuva* and Israel will not be redeemed except by doing *teshuva*. The Torah has already promised that finally Israel will do *teshuva* at the end of their exile and they will be redeemed immediately. As the verses state: "When all of these things concerning you shall come to pass, the blessing and the curse that I have placed before you, then you shall take matters to heart . . ." (Laws of Teshuva 7:5)

The statement that "Israel will not be redeemed except by doing *teshuva*" is, strictly speaking, the opinion quoted in the name of Rabbi Eliezer (TB *Sanhedrin* 97b–98a). But the conclusion of the Talmud as well as the generally accepted convention elsewhere is that when Rabbi Eliezer and Rabbi Yehoshua disagree, the Halakha follows Rabbi Yehoshua (see TB *Bava Batra* 133b and Rashbam ad loc.)! It must therefore be the case that fundamentally Rabbi Eliezer and Rabbi Yehoshua agree about the *necessity* of *teshuva*. They disagree, however, concerning what sort of *teshuva* is needed in order for the redemptive process to be unleashed. Maimonides is therefore quoting what amounts to a consensus view. His cryptic remark that "Israel will do teshuva at the end of their exile" is an allusion to Rabbi Yehoshua's comment concerning *teshuva*'s painful trigger: "Rabbi Yehoshua says: . . . 'God will establish a king whose decrees will be as harsh as those of Haman, and then Israel will return and be restored to the good . . .'"

VAYELECH

The Commandment to Write a Torah Scroll

Deuteronomy 31:1-30

PARASHAT VAYELECH brings us to the verge of the conclusion of Sefer Devarim and the entire Torah. Moshe has completed his review and explication of the *mitzvot*, he has assembled the whole people of Israel in order to initiate them into the covenant, and he has anxiously enjoined them to faithfully observe the tenets of the Torah. Now he is ready to die, and the leadership of Israel is formally transferred to his faithful and steadfast student, Yehoshua. Preparing to take his leave for the last time and cognizant of the awesome challenges that loom ahead, Moshe heartens both the people as well as Yehoshua with the same stirring charge: "Be strong and courageous, do not be fearful or afraid" (*Devarim* 31:6–7).

With the completion of the Torah text, Moshe now entrusts the precious scroll to the hands of the Kohanim and the elders. That remarkable moment is marked by the introduction of the commandment of *Hakhel* or "Assembly." Once in seven years, as the agricultural cycle begins anew and the people prepare to celebrate the festival of Succot, the entire nation is to gather as one in order to hear a public reading of Sefer Devarim at the "place that God will choose" (31:11). The event of *Hakhel*, incorporating public reading, study and exhortation, embracing the men, women, and children, perpetuates the overwhelming experience of the Revelation at Sinai. There too, the entire people of Israel came together at the foot of the mountain to witness the awesome spectacle of God's teachings being proclaimed and to hear the thunderous pronouncement of His Decalogue (*Shemot* 19:16–19). In order to remember the sublimity of that moment and to communicate to future generations an inkling of its grandeur, the command of "Assembly" is now introduced. There are events and ideas, the extraordinary ones, which outlast the individual and live on in the memory of a people not as remote and timeworn things, but rather as living truths.

At last, God informs Moshe that his end has come. By His command, Yehoshua is summoned to the Tent of Meeting and there, in Moshe's presence, he is invested with the onerous responsibility of leadership. As the two listen attentively, God ominously spells out the future infidelity of the people, their descent into idolatry, their abrogation of the covenant, and the consequence of divine indifference that must follow: "I will surely hide My face on that day because of the wickedness that they have done, for they have turned to other gods . . ." (*Devarim* 31:18). These terrible certainties , as well as the assurance that the people will one day return, are to be recorded for posterity:

> Now therefore write for yourselves this song, and teach it to the people of Israel so that they know it by heart, in order that this song shall serve as My witness against them. For when I bring them to the land that I swore to their ancestors, a land flowing with milk and honey, and they shall eat, drink and wax fat, then they shall turn to other gods and worship them, thus abrogating My covenant to anger Me. When many great tribulations and troubles befall them, then this song shall serve as witness, for it will never be forgotten from among their descendents . . . (31:19–21)

With vivid terseness, Israel's future is thus described. Moshe will die and Yehoshua will successfully bring them into the land. They will settle it and enjoy its bounty to excess but many will be the dangers that lurk in its verdant valleys and on its terraced hilltops. Israel will fall prey to the widespread idolatry of the Canaanites, their alluring and licentious rites bereft of any higher meaning, the relativism that numbs and soothes but makes no ethical demands, and many will succumb to its spells. The holy covenant struck with God, Israel's singular destiny to be His treasured nation and to serve as an exemplar to all of humanity, will be discarded and forgotten. God will withdraw His providential care and their fate will be no different than that of the inhabitants of any other small and insignificant country: certain extinction.

God, however, provides His people with a glimmer of hope: Israel will maintain a fragile foothold in human history, just enough to survive so that they might one day fulfill their mission, as long as a remnant remembers the song and is able to transmit it down the generations.

The Song Refers to Shirat Ha'azinu

There is much discussion among the commentaries concerning the identity of this song, and most see it as a reference to *Shirat Ha'azinu* or "Hearken," Moshe's eloquent outline of Jewish history. This elegy, that immediately follows our Parasha in chapter 32 of Sefer Devarim, is a charged depiction of the history and destiny of the people of Israel. It begins with a description of God's perfect justice, and goes on to outline His providential care of the Jewish people, notwithstanding their unfaithfulness. Mirroring themes of our section, the song of Ha'azinu lyrically traces the tragic consequences of abrogating God's covenant, but concludes with a promise of redemption and national renewal.

Among the classical commentaries, the Ramban adopted this identification, remarking that:

> "Write for *yourselves*" in the plural refers to Moshe and Yehoshua, for both of them were commanded to write it. This is because God wanted Yehoshua to already function as His prophet while Moshe was yet alive. Moshe wrote the song while Yehoshua stood by his side and read it . . . The expression "this song" refers to the song that I (God) will now tell you, namely *Ha'azinu*. The verse refers to it as a song for the people of Israel shall always recite it as a musical composition. Also, it is composed with the structure of a song, for the textual divisions parallel the musical breaks. (commentary to 31:19)

The key to Israel's survival, then, lies in the preservation of this song and its message. It is not difficult to imagine how the safekeeping of such a startling vision as *Shirat Ha'azinu*, its predictions borne out exactly by the unfolding events of Israel's history, might sustain a people, even when every other meaningful connection to its identity has been surrendered.

In contrast to this reading, the Talmud offers an interpretation that appears to be at odds with the plain sense of the text, for it maintains that "this song" refers not to the song of *Ha'azinu*, but rather to the entire Torah:

> Rabba said: even though a person may have inherited a scroll of the Torah from his ancestors, it is nevertheless a commandment for one to write his own, as the verse states: "Now write for yourselves this song." (TB *Sanhedrin* 21b)

This opinion is further amplified by another Talmudic passage that relates:

> Rav Yehoshua bar Abba said in the name of Rav Giddel, who reported in the name of Rav: a person who purchases a Sefer Torah in the marketplace has snared a mitzvah for himself, but one who writes his own scroll, it is as if he has received the Torah from Mount Sinai. Rav Sheshet added: one who corrects even a single letter in a defective scroll, is likened to one who has written the entire scroll. (TB *Menachot* 30a)

These Talmudic excerpts are not mere homilies, for according to Jewish tradition, they actually serve as the source for the final positive commandment recorded in the Torah, the commandment to write a Torah scroll. Maimonides, in his Book of the Commandments, where he painstakingly records the six hundred and thirteen commandments of the Torah, says:

> The Torah commanded that each person should write a Sefer Torah for himself. If he writes it by his own hand, it is if he has received it from Mount Sinai. But if he is unable to write his own, he may purchase one or hire a scribe to compose it for him. This mitzvah is derived from the verse "now write for yourselves this song." Since one is not permitted to write a scroll of the Torah that is composed of only some sections, the term "song" must therefore refer to "the entire Torah that *contains this song*." (Book of Commandments, Positive Commandment #18)

In his Laws of Sefer Torah codified in his *Mishneh Torah*, Maimonides records the remainder of the Talmudic ruling:

> . . . although one may have inherited a Torah from his ancestors, it is nonetheless a mitzvah to write one's own . . . If one writes it by his own hand, it is as if he has received it from Mount Sinai. If he is not able to write it, others may write it for him. One who corrects even a single letter of a scroll, it is if he has written the entire scroll. (Laws of Sefer Torah 7:1)

For Maimonides, there are therefore three possible fulfillments of this mitzvah that emerge out of the consolidation of the Talmudic sources, in descending order: (1) Where possible, one should write the Torah scroll by his own hand. This is equivalent to "receiving it from Mount Sinai." (2) If one is not capable of writing a Torah scroll himself, due to ignorance of the scribal laws or lack of technical skill, then one may fulfill the mitzvah by purchasing a scroll or else hiring a scribe to write it. (3) The correction of even a single letter of a defective scroll is equivalent to having written it. Insofar as our discussion is concerned, Maimonides was confronted with the difficulty of reconciling the verse that spoke of writing "the song" with the Talmudic tradition maintaining that "the song" meant "the entire Torah." He offered a harmonizing solution predicated upon another Halachic principle: Since we know from elsewhere that it is forbidden to write a scroll composed of an anthology of Torah passages (see TB *Gittin* 60a), it is inconceivable that the Torah would command us to write a scroll containing *only* the song of *Ha'azinu*. The meaning of the text must therefore be to "write an entire scroll of the Torah that will of necessity include this song as well."

On the one hand, Maimonides succeeds in preserving the plain meaning of "song" as a reference to *Ha'azinu*, for that Parasha is certainly poetic, rhythmic, and lyrical. On the other hand, his interpretation forces us to incorporate Halakhic assumptions that are not at all grounded in our passage.

The View of the Rosh

Other medieval authorities also discussed the practical ramifications of this commandment, and arrived at some novel conclusions. The 14th century German scholar, Rabbenu Asher ben Yechiel (known as the "Rosh"), who wrote a useful compendium of Talmudic law that is still regarded as a standard text, said the following:

> The mitzvah to write a Torah scroll was applicable in earlier generations when people studied the text from the actual scroll. Nowadays, however, when the Torah scroll is written and then deposited in the synagogue ark for the liturgical purpose of public readings, it is a positive mitzvah upon every Jew who has the means to write the text of the Pentateuch, the Mishna, the Talmud and their commentaries in order to study from them, as well as their children. The purpose of the command to write a Torah scroll was to facilitate the study of Torah, as the verse states: "Teach it to the people of Israel until they know it by heart." It is through the study of the Talmud and its commentaries that one comes to know the explanation of the *mitzvot* and the laws. These then are the books that one is commanded to write . . ." (commentary to TB *Menachot* 30a)

For Rabbenu Asher, the command to write a Torah scroll is not only or even primarily an injunction to formally copy out the text of the Torah after the manner of the scribe. Rather, it is to provide the necessary structure for the direct study of Torah to be accomplished. Since in earlier times the Torah scroll was itself the primary text that was studied, the Torah therefore spoke of "writing the song." Later, however, the oral traditions that had been associated with or generated through the direct study of the text of the scroll developed into written sources such as the Mishna and the Talmud. In the end, the Torah scroll itself was no longer needed for immediate study and instead became redefined as a purely liturgical object that was publicly read at set times.

Therefore, argues Rabbenu Asher, since the commandment to write the Torah is really a command to provide texts to facilitate study, the mitzvah of writing a scroll is no longer to be understood as a scribal exercise with its precise requirements concerning parchment, ink, quill and highly specialized lettering. Rather, it is the mitzvah to write or to secure all manner of appropriate texts for Torah study, be they Pentateuchal or Mishnaic, in scroll form or as folios, handwritten or printed. Of course, Rabbenu Asher was active before the invention of the printing press, when all texts were precious commodities because they were hand written. But his emphasis is not on the writing of the text *per se*, but rather on making it available *for the purposes of study*.

The position of Rabbenu Asher is eminently reasonable. It has the added advantage of absolving people from undertaking the onerous task of studying the scribal arts and transcribing a Torah scroll, a process that takes even accomplished scribes up to a year to complete. But insofar as the term "song" is concerned, the Rosh proposes no solution to bridge the Torah text with the Talmudic tradition.

Contrasting Rosh and Maimonides

To adopt Rabbenu Asher's position is to single out Torah study as a highly unusual and precious mitzvah, for where else does the Torah regard the provision of the necessary foundations of a mitzvah as a separate mitzvah act? Thinking for a moment of other "scribal" commands, the Torah enjoins the placing of a *mezuzah* upon one's doorposts (see *Devarim* 6:9). It is obviously understood that in order to place a *mezuzah*, one must first write one, but the Torah does not consider the inscribing of the *mezuzah* to be a separate mitzvah act in its own rite. Or consider the mitzvah of sounding the *shofar* on Rosh Ha-Shanah. Here again, although it is the case that one cannot possibly sound a *shofar* unless one first prepares the animal horn in an appropriate manner, the Torah does not regard those preparations as a separate mitzvah but simply as a prerequisite. The mitzvah consists in the utilization of the finished product and not in its preparation. It must therefore be the case that the mitzvah of Torah study is so paramount, that even the steps necessary to provide the required texts are enjoined by the Torah as freestanding mitzvah acts.

In contrast to Rabbenu Asher, recall that Maimonides ruled that the mitzvah is to write a scroll as does a scribe, just as the straightforward reading of the Talmudic sources indicates. Maimonides made no provision for the fulfillment of this mitzvah through the acquisition or commissioning of other Torah texts. In fact, it seemed as if Maimonides, in keeping with the tone of Talmudic sources, regarded the act of writing the Torah scroll as the essence of the mitzvah: "It is a positive command for each Jew to write a Torah scroll for themselves . . . *if he actually writes it, it is like he received it from Mount Sinai* . . ." To write a scroll by one's own hand is to engage in an act of transmission of the Torah that ties the writer to the events of Mount Sinai when God gave the Torah to Moshe and he in turn passed it on to Yehoshua and the people. To write a scroll, avers Maimonides, is therefore to *relive* the events of Mount Sinai, to stand there once again in order to receive the word of God and to pass it on to others. It is just like the mitzvah of *Hakhel* that follows Moshe's transfer of the scroll to the hands of his successors – a consciously evoked memory of the transcendent moment of Revelation.

For Rabbenu Asher, on the other hand, whose inventive opinion was adopted by subsequent codes of law as the Halakha, it is the *study* of Torah that is at the core of our experience of Revelation. Recall that the earlier episodes in the Parasha included the formal transfer of leadership to Yehoshua, the completion of the Torah text, the commandment of Assembly, and the injunction of writing "the song" as the key to ensuring the survival of a remnant. The thrust of all of these things is the perpetuation of the Torah's teachings as living laws that are transmitted to subsequent generations, with all of the exhilaration of the experience at Sinai. Really, says Rabbenu Asher, the study of Torah is qualitatively different, for it alone can guarantee the continued existence of the Jewish people. Only through the study of its laws and instructions can the people of Israel survive to achieve their destiny. The Torah's continuity can be guaranteed only by ensuring that the texts needed for its study are always available.

The existence of the Torah scrolls that fill many a synagogue ark will not ensure the survival of the Jewish people, says Rabbenu Asher. One scroll more or one scroll less, when those scrolls themselves cannot serve as study texts, will not generate more Torah learning, the lifeblood of Israel. Only the ongoing devotion to the study of the text, an activity that has always been regarded as defining in Jewish tradition, can ensure our eternity, and for that study to take place, appropriate texts must be available. The provision of those texts therefore becomes the independent mitzvah act of facilitating study, for the future of Israel as a faith community and a nation depends upon it. In effect, since the broader context of our Parasha speaks of survival and the transmission of legacy, the difficulty of bridging the Talmudic tradition with the Torah's "song" is obviated. For the Rosh, how can the song of our Parasha – whose transcription preserves the remnant of Israel – be referring to anything but the entire Torah, just as the Talmud asserts? Therefore, "write this song, and teach it to the people of Israel so that they know it by heart, in order that this song shall serve as My witness against them."

FOR FURTHER STUDY:

(1) In more recent times, the Netziv (Naftali Zvi Yehuda Berlin, 19th century, Lithuania) addressed the same textual issue as Maimonides and the Rosh, but offered a different explanation that is compelling as well as profound. The problematic word, as we have seen, is "song." In the third section of the introduction to his commentary to the Torah, the Netziv considers the meaning of song and contrasts it with prose. Typically, he suggests, we distinguish the two forms according to strict linguistic criteria, by describing prose as factual narrative, and poetry as metrical verse. While this is true, there is an interpretive distinction as well.

The Netziv avers that prose relates events in straightforward terms that in and of themselves contain no allegorical or hidden explications. Prose writing attempts to convey facts or observations without embellishment. Poetry, on the other hand, is more allusive, for its rendition of events is couched in emotive language that consciously conveys multiple meanings, often with an economy of words. Also, poetry has structural constraints that paradoxically result in a larger number of possible interpretations. By employing rhyme, rhythm, alliteration, acrostic and other literary devices, clarity of expression is often sacrificed for the sake of artifice, and shades of ambiguity are thereby introduced. The result is that a poetic rendition conveys subtleties of thought and layers of meaning that a prose rendition is not able to communicate. However, only one who is well-versed in poetry can be truly appreciative of these effects. The uninitiated, in contrast, failing to grasp the power and profundity of the poetic expression, take the words at their face value and unwittingly misconstrue and misinterpret them.

In a similar vein, says the Netziv, the entire Torah is really a form of poetry. Even the narrative passages that appear to be prose in terms of their structural form are actually poetry in disguise! They therefore contain in their conciseness multiple meanings and penetrating insights. To return to our text, the command of "write for yourselves this song" really *is* a reference to the entire Torah, just as the Talmud maintains. For the Netziv, *all* of the Torah, from beginning to end, is actually composed as a "song." It is our precious mission to unravel those deeper dimensions of the text.

HA'AZINU

The Eternity of the Jewish People

Deuteronomy 32:1-52

IN A DEPARTURE from the rest of Sefer Devarim, Parashat Ha'azinu is composed as a poem. It is Moshe's last exhortation to the people of Israel, and with it he concludes his review and explanation of the *mitzvot*. But the song of *Ha'azinu* contains no mention of commandments, no clarification of God's laws, no expressions of warning or promises of reward. It is instead a testimonial document, describing in moving verse the broad sweep of Jewish history. The dominant theme of the song is the singular relationship between God and the people of Israel, and Moshe traces the triumphs and tribulations of that unique bond from the beginning of human history until its eschatological conclusion.

In terse and measured words, Moshe details the pivotal events in the life of the nation of Israel. He describes their election as God's special people, His providential care of them in the wilderness after the Exodus, and their entry and successful settlement of the land. Moshe goes on to spell out the people's subsequent downfall, as they succumb to a lethal combination of the new land's material plenty and the Canaanites' moral and spiritual decay. It is estrangement from God that is the inevitable result. Setback follows, in the form of enemy domination, conquest, exile and near extermination. God stands aloof and remote, as His once-cherished people call out to their false gods for salvation, but to no avail. Finally, He intervenes, crushing their enemies in order to vindicate the ideals for which Israel once stood. At the end, the land, for so long desolate and deserted, achieves "atonement" as the people of Israel are restored to it.

Without a doubt, in this song Moshe invokes the "prophetic" tense of time. Although the people have yet to cross the Yarden when he sings it to them, in his mind's eye Moshe can already see far into their future. Their triumphant settlement of the land and their eventual infidelity are writ large before him. His dire predictions, so often intimated during the course of Sefer Devarim, are here spelled out as Israel's inevitable destiny. In the song of *Ha'azinu*, the distinctions between past, present and future blur and then fade away, as the story of Israel's history is presented as a seamless continuum informed by one immutable truth: the people of Israel can never cast off the onerous mantle of responsibility with which God has cloaked them. They are His special people and, while that distinction places them in a unique position to enjoy the rewards of their election, they must also embrace its demands.

Idolatry and Exile

Let us consider the matter as it is revealed in the eloquent words of the Ramban. .The context of his comments is the critical passage that describes the dire aftermath of Israel's forgetfulness of the God who "gave birth to them":

> God saw and was enraged by the infuriating conduct of his sons and daughters. He said: "I will hide My face from them and see their end, for they are a rebellious generation, children of no faith. They have angered Me with false gods and have enraged Me with their vanities; I will discomfit them at the hands of an infamous nation and a barbaric people. For a fire burns in My nostrils and engulfs even the netherworld, it consumes the land and its produce, igniting the foundations of the mountains" . . . I said: "I will scatter them far and wide, and cause their memory to cease from among humanity." But for My fear of the enemy, lest their tormentors turn to their false gods, lest they say that "our hand is raised upright, and God has not done all of these deeds . . ." (*Devarim* 32:19–27)

These ominous verses, like much of the rest of the song, contain phrases whose exact meaning is doubtful, thus allowing for multiple interpretations among the commentaries. Nevertheless, the broad outline of the passage is clear: Israel will forget God and turn instead to idol worship and to the corrupt values that inform it. God, "enraged," will remove His providential care and Israel will be attacked by a foreign power that will show neither compassion nor kindness. God will set into motion His vengeful plan, to scatter Israel to every corner of the globe and to bring about their demise. But paradoxically, that plan will be foiled, by the "unwilling" exercise of His self-restraint. As Rabbi Avraham Ibn Ezra provocatively understands it, God will be, so to speak, "afraid" to completely destroy the Jewish people, for to do so would only reinforce the enemy nations' mistaken beliefs, who would ascribe victory over Israel to their own strength and to the triumph of their gods.

A Nation vs. a Religion

The Ramban elaborates on these ideas at length:

> God's expression that "I will cause their memory to cease from among humanity" refers to our current state of exile. We, the remnants of the tribes of Binyamin and Yehuda, have no renown among the realms, and are not considered to be a people or a nation at all. The verses here declare that according to the strict attribute of justice, we ought to remain in exile forever, were it not for the "anger" of the enemy. This indicates that in our present exile, the merit of our ancestors has been exhausted. Our only hope of preservation and salvation from the hands of the nations is for God to act on behalf of His great name. So too says the Prophet Yechezkel, when God proclaims that "I will gather you from the lands into which you have been scattered, and I will be sanctified through you in the eyes of the nations . . . and you shall know that I am God when I act with you for the sake of My name, and not in accordance with your evil ways and corrupt deeds, O House of Israel!" (commentary to *Devarim* 32:26, quoting *Yechezkel* 20:41–44)

As the Ramban sees it, the verses of the song that spell out widespread exile and its torments are a description of the state of the Jews after the destruction of the Second Temple up until the contemporary period. Few in number and scattered far and wide, the people of Judea, already only a remnant of the former tribes, utterly lost their status as a nation as a consequence of being forcibly removed from their land. No nation or populace exists without a land, and so the Jews became instead a religion, settled as small and powerless faith communities in often-hostile surroundings. The respect (and self-respect) associated with nationhood was denied to the Jewish people, and henceforth they were subject entirely to the caprices of their hosts.

And so it should remain forever, for as the Ramban describes, the merit of our ancestors, the accrued reward of their trust and steadfastness in God, is insufficient to effect the redemption of their children from exile. The people of Israel do not deserve restoration based upon their own virtues, while the recompense for their ancestors' good deeds has already been spent.

For the Ramban, the verses in Sefer Yechezkel are instructive. In context, the prophet addresses his harsh words to the people of Israel who were exiled to Babylon only to settle down comfortably and then completely forget their eternal mission. Instead, these expatriates forcefully voiced their desire to "be like the other nations, the families of other lands, to embrace their gods of wood and stone!" (*Yechezkel* 20:32). The Torah, the words of the living God, the mission of the Jews to be a "kingdom of priests and a holy nation" was rejected, as the people of Israel speedily overcame the trauma of exile and embraced their new status as a landless ethnic community. For the Ramban, Yechezkel's thundering words address not only the Jews of Babylon in the 6th century BCE but also the 13th century Jews of Spain, and every other exilic community since, who severed their ties to the hope of one day being re-established as an independent nation in the land of Israel. Under such circumstances, there can be only one prospect for redemption: God will act not for the sake of His people Israel, but rather for the sake of His great name.

The Ramban continues:

> Omnipotent God could care less about showing His power to the nations, who are regarded as frail and feeble in His sight. Rather, God had created humanity with the hope that man would recognize his creator and acknowledge Him. He gave man the exclusive ability to choose good or evil. When all of them willfully transgressed and denied Him, only one nation remained associated with His name. Through them, God indicated by signs and wonders that He was indeed the supreme God and the ultimate sovereign, and so He became known to all of the nations. If God now acts to destroy the people of Israel, then the nations will forget His signs and deeds and will never recount them, and any historical success of the Jews will be regarded as passing fortune. Thus, the purpose of creation and of man will be negated, for none will remain to acknowledge their creator, but only to anger Him!
>
> Therefore, it becomes necessary for God to preserve the people of Israel forever, for they are the closest people to Him, who acknowledge Him more than any other nation. This is the meaning of the concluding verses: "God will judge His people and reconsider His conduct to His loyal servants . . ." (*Devarim* 32:36), for then He will compassionately remember that they have been His people from time immemorial. He will remember their loyalty, for during the course of their exile, they suffered much oppression and torment on His behalf, as the verse says "they are My people and loyal children . . ." (*Yeshayahu* 63:8)

God's Name and the Jewish People

What is the nature of God's name, a concept that seems to so preoccupy the prophet Yechezkel and the Ramban alike? At the most basic level, a human personal name is an expression of one's essence, the identity that one projects during the course of one's life. Similarly for God, the name evokes the sum set of acts by which He is known, the attributes that describe His involvement in human history and the affairs of men. God's name is associated with a particular people, those who first introduced it to a non-receptive world some thirty-three centuries ago. Before the advent of the people of Israel, there was no concept of a single, incorporeal God, of a united humanity descended from a set of parents who bore the imprimatur of His image, of an absolute moral code that obligated and held liable tyrant and serf alike while seeking to elevate them both, of a world that could be the product of free, autonomous human will and loving, divine concern rather than the impersonal and indifferent playground of mercurial fates, and of the exalted notion that human life is invested with inestimable worth and infinite meaning. These were new and revolutionary ideas that are still little appreciated in many corners of the globe.

Our ancestors, the patriarchs and matriarchs, overcame many obstacles and maintained steadfast trust in this God. For themselves, they achieved great spiritual progress and for their descendents, concomitant reward. Avraham and Sarah, Yitzchak and Rivka, Ya'acov, Leah and Rachel all embraced these new ideas with enthusiasm and accepted the responsibilities that they entailed. So God's name became associated first with a family, then with a tribe and finally with a nation. And as the rest of humanity ardently embraced polytheism and idolatry, continuing on the destructive path of warfare, slavery and moral relativism, Israel went down to Egypt. In Egypt, Israel was born as a nation and the Exodus was its pivotal moment in history. It was God's pivotal moment as well, for it revealed Him to the world as an omnipotent, omniscient and omnipresent being with a particular interest in human spiritual development and moral progress. Henceforward His name or perceived involvement in the affairs of men was to be associated with the people of Israel.

The Jewish People and Their Association with the Name

According to the Torah, man has a mission. That mission is to acknowledge God and to utilize his free choice to build a better world, a world founded upon the twin pillars of ethical conduct and a recognition of higher meaning, if it is to survive. The Jewish people, as the bearers of those truths, are therefore instrumental in this unfolding of human history. And curiously enough, the Jewish people remain bound up with the revolutionary and noble ideas of their origins even when they forget or willfully reject them. Having become early on coupled with the concept of God, they cannot cast off their essential identity to instead embrace the false gods that litter the path torturously tracing human history. Even when the people of Israel stray mightily from their course, inviting divine indifference to their plight and the scourge of exile, God cannot abandon them completely or allow them to be destroyed for their infidelity. To do so would spell not only the end of Israel, but also the end of the "God idea" in the world.

Of course, other concepts of this God might survive the destruction of the Jewish people, since Judaism has since given rise to other "great monotheistic faiths." No one was more aware of this than the Ramban who lived in medieval Spain torn asunder by religious wars between Christianity and Islam. But the *unique* conception of God as creator and liberator, supremely transcendent and incorporeal but nevertheless near and immediate, who insists upon an exalted trust while demanding attentiveness to a comprehensive code of behavior, who nowhere requires the conversion of the uninitiated or else their slaughter as infidels, who wins over the obstinate human heart by reason and kindness and not by the tip of the sword, such a conception of God, the God of Israel, would perish with the demise of the Jews.

Thus, God, so to speak, has no choice but to preserve us, until such a day as He glorifies His name by redeeming His people, returning them to their land, and inspiring them anew to follow His commands. In the meantime, as long as Jews survive in the world, so will God. As long as Jews suffer for their connection to God's name, though some of them have rejected their identity and therefore suffer by association, God's Torah will not be forgotten.

FOR FURTHER STUDY:

(1) The Ramban's perceptive words go a long way towards explaining the eternally vexing issue of anti-Semitism. The widespread phenomenon of Jew-hatred, repackaged for modern sensibilities as anti-Zionism, is as old as the Jews themselves. This is because, as Jewish tradition realized early on, hatred of the Jews has little to do with their wealth or poverty, power or weakness, influence or helplessness, education or ignorance, or any of the other myriad often mutually exclusive causes frequently advanced to explain it. Hatred of the Jews is a function of something much more sinister yet also more elusive. As our Sages concisely put it: ". . . whosoever arises against Israel, it is as if they arise against the Holy One blessed be He . . ." (Mechilta 6).

The oft-stated goal of the dictator, the tyrant, or the despot, to dispense with the Jews forever, is by any other name the subconscious desire to finally extinguish the Jewish idea of God so that His incessant demands for universal freedom, fairness, justice, goodness, and accountability can be buried and forgotten for evermore. In a region rid of Jews, repressive, undemocratic and totalitarian regimes can all sleep easier, utterly unperturbed by their masses' stifled stirrings for liberty, equality, integrity and decency. Those of us who have studied the song of *Ha'azinu*, however, know better. Israel will survive because it must, not only for our sake but for God's sake as well. Redemption will be completed and Israel will be fully restored to its land, to at last complete its remarkable task.

VEZOT HABERACHA

Following God's Ways

Deuteronomy 33:1–34:12

WITH MOSHE'S farewell blessing to the people of Israel finished, he reluctantly takes his leave from them and ascends Mount Nevo. Standing at its craggy summit, he looks with longing westwards, towards the Promised Land. Surveying the land from afar, he breathes deeply, contemplating his long life of devotion and loyalty to his people's needs and to his God's expectations. Moshe's intense contentment of having lived his life well is also tinged with sadness, for the objective of the journey, the entry and settlement of the new land, is to remain beyond his grasp forever.

> God showed him the whole land, from the Gil'ad to Dan. He showed him the land of Naftali, the land of Efraim and Menashe, and the whole land of Yehuda, until the western sea. He showed him also the dry, southern land, the plain of the valley of Yericho, from the city of palms until Tsoar.
>
> God said to him: "This is the land that I swore unto Avraham, Yitzchak, and Ya'acov saying 'to your descendents shall I give it.' I have shown it to you with your own eyes, but over to there you shall not go." (*Devarim* 34:1–4)

Moshe's Death

Having scanned the regions where the tribes will soon settle, from the fertile northern boundaries of Naftali to the parched southern reaches of Yehuda, and from the sandy shores of the Mediterranean Sea in the west to the plains of the winding Yarden River in the east, Moshe is now ready to die.

> Moshe the servant of God died there in the land of Moav, by God's word. He buried him in the valley in the land of Moav opposite Bet Pe'or, but no man knows the place of his grave until this very day. Moshe was one hundred and twenty years old at the time of his death, but his eye was not dimmed nor was his natural vigor abated . . . (34:5–6)

Moshe, God's loyal servant, secures that most sought-after of deaths, a death unheralded by debilitating illness, unaccompanied by discomfort and suffering, and unburdened by regret or misgivings. He dies by experiencing the so-called "divine kiss," by which the soul is gently and effortlessly drawn out of the body as "a hair is drawn out of a bowl of milk" (TB *Berachot* 7b). Then, the bestower of life buries him in a secret place, for no prying eyes are to intrude on that breathless moment and no trespassers are to later cheapen it, by turning his grave into a garish shrine.

Burial as a Moral Act

Thus, the final events of the Torah describe the end that awaits all mortals, for no man can escape the eventuality of death. No other experience among all of life's other myriad events is as fearfully assured or as frustratingly unknown. Even Moshe the law giver, the loyal servant of God, the only man to have spoken with the deity "face to face" must die and return to the dust. Remarkably, the account of Moshe's mysterious demise and cryptic burial serve the rabbis of the Talmud not as grist for mystical meditations on the enigmatic matters of dying, internment and the afterlife, but rather as a rational and life-affirming lesson in ethical and moral behavior:

> Said Rabbi Chama ben Chanina: What is meant by the verse commanding us to "walk after God your Lord" (*Devarim* 13:5)? Is it then possible to walk after God's presence? Behold, the verse states that God is "a consuming fire" (4:24)! Rather, it means to follow the attributes of the Holy One blessed be He. Just as He clothes the naked, as the verse states: "God the Lord made garments of hides for the man and for his wife and He clothed them" (*Breisheet* 3:21), so you too must therefore clothe the naked. God visited the sick, as the verse states: "God appeared to Avraham in Elonei Mamre, as he was sitting at the opening of the tent in the heat of the day" (18:1), so you too must therefore visit the sick. God comforted mourners as the verse states: "After Avraham's death, God blessed his son Yitzchak" (25:11), so you too must therefore comfort mourners. The Holy One blessed be He buried the dead, as the verse states: "He buried him in the valley in the land of Moav opposite Bet Pe'or" (*Devarim* 34:5), so you too must therefore bury the dead. (TB *Sotah* 14a)

This celebrated Talmudic passage serves as the central source for one of Judaism's most important ideas. It opens, predictably, with a question. The Torah in a number of places asks of us to walk after God and to follow Him, "follow after God your Lord and revere Him; observe His commandments, hearken to His voice, serve Him and hold fast to Him" (*Devarim* 13:5). But how does one follow in the ways of an absolute being, the fashioner of the vast and impenetrable cosmos, a supreme entity too transcendent to be comprehended by our mortal minds or even to be described by our finite and inadequate terms? How indeed does one follow in the path of "a Consuming Fire?"

The Talmud overcomes this unsettling theological conundrum by translating it into a concrete and comprehensible guiding principle: it is only possible to "follow" God by following the example that He Himself has set. Just as God clothed the naked, visited the sick, comforted the mourner, and buried the dead, so must we do likewise. By expressing the idea of *imitatio Dei* (imitating God), the Torah indicates to us that God's remoteness and otherworldliness need not be a barrier to our experience of His presence. We are not in need of abstruse specialized knowledge in order to fulfill His word. It is true that in abstract and conceptual terms, God's essence may remain forever beyond our ken; but within the concrete reality of human existence, His immediacy can be found in acts of loving kindness.

The Four Examples

The Talmudic passage above is quite selective in its examples, for only four episodes are singled out for the construction of the principle. The first concerns Adam and Eve, who abrogated God's command and ate from the tree of knowledge. Having thus secured self-awareness of their physical nakedness, they attempted to conceal their vulnerability with fig leaves, but God instead fashioned for them more substantial garments.

The second example concerns father Avraham, who had just fulfilled the commandment to be circumcised, as a sign of the covenant between his descendents and God. God appeared to the aged patient as he uncomfortably sat at the entrance to his tent, attempting to escape the heat and lethargy of the midday sun. Avraham was invigorated by the visit and gladdened by the tidings of offspring that God at that time bestowed.

The death of Yitzchak's mother left a void in his life that remained unfilled until he took compassionate Rivka as his wife. After the demise of his father some four decades later, Yitzchak mourned once again, and God then blessed him with words of comfort and strength.

Finally, in our example, Moshe's lifeless body was laid to rest by God Himself, who lovingly interred him in his hidden tomb. Here, the recipient of the act of kindness was not physically conscious or capable of any response whatsoever.

Universality, Life's Contingencies and Vulnerability

Why did the Talmud choose to emphasize these four expressions of divine kindness as being archetypical of the ones that we should follow in our quest to emulate God? First of all, these four things are *universal*. All of us can relate to the experience of nakedness, all of us have felt the enfeebling effects of illness at some point during our lives, all of us have sought shelter and solace from the buffeting winds of tragedy, and everyone experiences death. In other words, one of the foundations underlying moral behavior is the recognition that to be an effective moral agent we must be able to identify with the plight of the injured or the aggrieved. This empathy is possible precisely because we all partake of the human condition, and can therefore understand the needs of others if we so choose.

Secondly, the four examples under discussion constitute a broad sample of a lifetime's *typical* experiences, and the dependence upon others thus engendered. We enter the world naked and cold, in immediate need of clothing to alleviate our discomfort. During the course of our transient lives, we feel the debilitating effects of sicknesses great and small. We then require the loving care of friends and family, the medical advice of experts, and the miracle of medications to restore our health and spirits. As we nurture more relationships and acquire more things, we begin to experience the distress of loss with greater frequency – of possessions destroyed, of precious people wrenched from us, and of dreams and hopes that took flight with the wind. And finally, we stand before the menacing specter of death that will engulf our declining physicality and grind it into the dust. In the end, we are powerless before its ruthless grasp, and like all those that came before us, we must submit.

But, suggests the Talmud, the very experiences that seem to overwhelm our finitude provide the keys to our salvation. These four things (and others like them) provide the potential for moral living that can connect us not only with others but also with God, a

God who is caring and compassionate, a God who holds the promise of our eternity in His hands.

Finally, we note that not only are these four experiences universal as well as typical nodes along the span of a human life, but also that without exception they involve some sort of *real vulnerability*. The one who is naked is at a disadvantage because he has no clothes to cover his body or his shame. The one who is ailing cannot provide for all of his own physical and emotional needs and may in fact be incapable of taking care of any of them. The mourner who is bowed by sadness or by tragedy needs a caring and sympathetic heart to share the burden of his sorrow and his pain. The dead human being is, in a manner of speaking, the most "needy" of all, for there is nothing whatsoever that he can do to take care of himself or to alleviate his plight.

By singling out these four, the Talmud therefore traces the contours of the Torah's vision of morality. Ethical and moral conduct ought to be practiced at all times and under all circumstances. Nevertheless, the truest test of a person's moral mettle is not gauged by how he treats his friends, loved ones, equals or superiors, but rather by how he treats those who are clearly weaker than he is. And frequently, those who cannot fight back and represent no counter threat are either indifferently ignored or else brazenly exploited. To behave morally and ethically in these kinds of situations, then, is to truly follow in God's ways. Accordingly, the Torah repeatedly demands of us to show special deference to the "convert, orphan and widow" for these represent elements of society that are often downtrodden, marginal, economically depressed or friendless. And after all, standing before an absolute being, are we not all at a disadvantage? When God therefore extends His kindness and His love to us, we must be not only grateful but also patently aware that we must respond in like manner to all of those that need our compassion as surely as we require God's.

FOR FURTHER STUDY:

(1) The Talmudic passage adds a postscript to the above passage:

> Rabbi Simlai explains: the Torah begins and concludes with acts of loving-kindness. It begins with God clothing Adam and Chava in their nakedness, and concludes with God interring Moshe at the plains of Moav.

In a manner of speaking, the thrust of the Torah's message is bracketed by these two events, for they are the story of God's interaction with humanity. Adam and Chava are the first humans to be given life by Him, and God cares for Moshe at his death; in between these two narratives the drama of the Torah's guiding illumination unfolds. Surely it is more than serendipity that this Rabbi Simlai, who so eloquently describes the theme of *imitatio Dei* by highlighting the Torah's preoccupation with acts of loving kindness, is the same Rabbi Simlai who elsewhere transmits what is undoubtedly one of the Talmud's most celebrated traditions:

> Rabbi Simlai expounded: Six hundred and thirteen commands were given to Moshe at Sinai. Three hundred and sixty five (prohibitions) like the days of the solar year, and two hundred and forty eight (positive commands) like the number of organs in the human body. (TB *Makkot* 23b)

Taken together, these two dicta of Rabbi Simlai are complementary – the six hundred and thirteen *mitzvot* of the Torah that comprehensively address every part of the body and every day of the year, are inextricably bound up with the objective of fostering care and concern for others. It is as if the entirety of the Torah's laws could be reduced to the precious ideal of practicing loving kindness. Standing to complete the Torah and to immediately begin its study anew, the whole enterprise is informed by this precious lesson of גמילות חסדים, the acts of thoughtful benevolence that make life meaningful and human existence heroic.

תם ונשלם שבח לא-ל בורא עולם

The *Rishonim*: 11th – 16th Centuries

- **Shelomo ben Yitzchak or Rashi** (1040–1105), France – Rashi is the most important explicator of both the Bible as well as the Talmud. In his commentary he searches for the plain meaning of the text but also includes Midrashic readings. Along with Ibn Ezra and Ramban, he is regarded as one of the pillars of medieval biblical commentary on the Torah.
- **Shemuel ben Meir or Rashbam** (1080–1160), France – Rashbam was a Talmudist and one of Rashi's grandsons. Along with his brothers Rabbi Yitzchak and Rabbi Ya'acov (Tam), he is responsible for the founding of the school of the *Tosafot*. His concise commentary on the Torah is characterized by a zealous allegiance to the *peshat*, sometimes leading him to controversial conclusions.
- **Ibn Ezra, Avraham** (1089–1164), Spain – Ibn Ezra was a poet, grammarian, astronomer, physician, philosopher and exegete. His terse and direct comments are usually grounded in the immediate context and he has little patience for Midrashic flights of fancy. Ibn Ezra wandered extensively, visiting Italy, France and England.
- **Maimon, Moses ben** (1135–1204), Spain, Egypt – Maimonides or Rambam was the most influential Jewish scholar in the post-Talmudic era. His *Mishneh Torah* or code of Jewish law was a watershed in the development of the Halakha and his philosophical "Guide to the Perplexed" exerted tremendous influence. He was also a gifted physician.
- **Kimchi, David** (1160–1235), Provence – Known by the acronym "Radak," Kimchi was the most distinguished member of a famous family of commentators. His interpretations combine the straightforward and the homiletic, but he never blurs the boundaries between the two. His careful work on Biblical Hebrew laid the groundwork for the systemization of Hebrew grammar.
- **Chezkiah ben Manoach** (13th century), France – The *Chizkuni* is a commentary written in the 13th century. Rashi's interpretations often form the backdrop for *Chizkuni*'s comments.
- **Nachman, Moses ben** (1194–1274), Spain – Nachmanides or Ramban was active in Christian Spain during a trying time for the Jewish community. He was an exceptional Talmudist as well as a Bible commentator. His commentary on the Torah is

quite comprehensive, incorporating *peshat*, *derash*, philosophy, Jewish law and mystical insights. He often disagrees with Rashi, Ibn Ezra and Maimonides.

- **Arama, Isaac** (1420–1494), Spain – Isaac Arama was a Talmudist and philosopher. Arama's commentary, known as the "Akedat Yitzchak" is a philosophic treatment of the text that is homiletic in style. After the expulsion from Spain, he settled in Naples where he died.
- **Abarbanel, Isaac** (1437–1508), Spain – Don Isaac Abarbanel was a commentator and philosopher as well as a statesman and advisor to kings. He was expelled from Spain with the Jewish community in 1492. His commentary is lengthy, incisive and highly informed by his political experiences.
- **Seforno, Ovadiah** (1470–1550), Italy – Seforno was a Talmudist, philosopher and physician. His commentary tends towards the *peshat* and to readings that have an ethical import.